# DISCARD

# ANTHEMS AND MINSTREL SHOWS

# ANTHEMS
## *AND*
# MINSTREL
# SHOWS

*The Life and Times of Calixa Lavallée*
*1842–1891*

Brian Christopher Thompson

McGill-Queen's University Press
Montreal & Kingston | London | Ithaca

© McGill-Queen's University Press 2015

ISBN 978-0-7735-4555-7 (cloth)
ISBN 978-0-7735-8415-0 (ePDF)
ISBN 978-0-7735-8416-7 (ePUB)

Legal deposit second quarter 2015
Bibliothèque nationale du Québec

Printed in Canada on acid-free paper that is 100% ancient forest free (100% post-consumer recycled), processed chlorine free

This book has been published with the help of a grant from the Canadian Federation for the Humanities and Social Sciences, through the Awards to Scholarly Publications Program, using funds provided by the Social Sciences and Humanities Research Council of Canada.

McGill-Queen's University Press acknowledges the support of the Canada Council for the Arts for our publishing program. We also acknowledge the financial support of the Government of Canada through the Canada Book Fund for our publishing activities.

Library and Archives Canada Cataloguing in Publication

Thompson, Brian, 1962–, author
Anthems and minstrel shows : the life and times of Calixa Lavallée, 1842–1891 / Brian Christopher Thompson.

Includes bibliographical references and index.
Issued in print and electronic formats.
ISBN 978-0-7735-4555-7 (bound).–ISBN 978-0-7735-8415-0 (ePDF).–ISBN 978-0-7735-8416-7 (ePUB)

1. Lavallée, Calixa, 1842–1891. 2. Composers – Canada – Biography. I. Title.

ML410.L32T46 2015          780.92          C2015-900792-
                                           C2015-900793-3

To Gabi

# Contents

# Figures and Tables

## FIGURES

## TABLES

# *Preface*

I discovered Calixa Lavallée in the summer of 1993 while employed at the Canadian Broadcasting Corporation (CBC) music library in Toronto. While I had by that time earned two music degrees in Canada, my knowledge of Canadian music extended back no further than Claude Vivier, Oscar Peterson, and The Guess Who. At the CBC, I found copies of Helmut Kallmann's *Catalogue of Canadian Composers* and *History of Music in Canada, 1534–1918*, as well as the numerous photocopies of scores Kallmann had collected while he had been employed at the CBC in the 1950s and 1960s. There were also a handful of recordings. These all led me to the then recently released 2nd edition of the *Encyclopedia of Music in Canada* (now available online as part of *The Canadian Encyclopedia* through Historica Canada), to the ongoing publications of the Canadian Musical Heritage Society, and to a few other books, among them Eugène Lapierre's *Calixa Lavallée: Musicien National du Canada*.

It was Lavallée and his music that intrigued me most. I knew nothing of the musician who had composed "O Canada" and who had lived an intense and eventful life, but I sensed that there was much missing from Lapierre's account. Despite positioning Lavallée as the "national musician," his biography seemed to raise as many questions as it answered, and so I began the research that now results in this book. To the usual challenges associated with a research project of this sort, I complicated things further in the fall of 1995 by moving to Hong Kong. Bringing my growing collection of material with me, I continued to work on Lavallée in what became my new home, returning to North America occasionally for research trips and presenting some of my findings at conferences in many parts of the world and in journals.

This book provides answers to many of the questions I had back in the 1990s about Lavallée's life and music. It will also, I hope, raise new questions about politics and culture in our own time.

# Prologue:
## Music and the Nation

In a scene that was in equal measure solemn and carnivalesque, citizens of Montreal gathered on Lafontaine Street in the early evening heat of 13 July 1933. The crowd had swelled into the thousands when, just after 7:30, a hearse appeared on the upper span of the city's new Harbour Bridge and gradually descended to the waiting spectators. As it slowed to a stop, the seventy-nine-year-old bandleader Edmond Hardy signalled to his men, beginning a sombre rendition of "O Canada" to mark the return to Canada of the remains of the anthem's composer, Calixa Lavallée.[1]

The media was ready and photographers captured the band in action. (See figure 0.1) And as the crowd watched from sidewalks and balconies, Lavallée family members and dignitaries alighted from their vehicles to pose for pictures against the drab background of a blank wall and brick tenements. (See figure 0.2) They then boarded their cars once again to complete the journey to Notre-Dame Church (now Notre-Dame Basilica). From the bridge, the procession had both the character and the ultimate destination of a *Fête nationale* parade. It was led by the police, mounted and on foot. Firemen came next, then Hardy's 195-piece band, flag-bearers carrying the Canadian Red Ensign and the banners of national and patriotic societies, the hearse, repatriation organizers and other dignitaries dressed in top hats and tails, cars carrying Lavallée's relatives, and marching members of national associations and labour unions. After the official members of the parade had passed, spectators joined the almost-celebratory cortège as it travelled along the four-kilometre parade route to Place d'Armes.

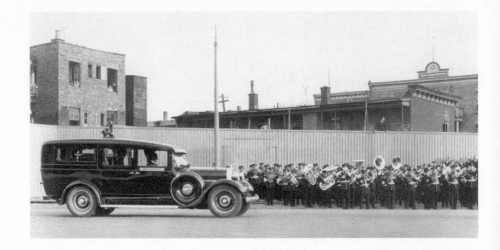

Figure 0.1  A band led by Edmond Hardy performs at the arrival in Montreal
of Lavallée's remains in July 1933.

Figure 0.2  Surviving members of Lavallée's extended family assemble
for a photograph as his remains are repatriated.

By the time the hearse had reached its destination, spectators had packed the square. The band took its place and played Lavallée's anthem once again, this time accompanying members of the Association des chanteurs de Montréal. Pallbearers then carried the casket up the steps, past a guard of honour, and into the church where they rested it upon a large catafalque and draped over it the Union Jack. From his position at the great organ, high above, Benoît Poirier played "O Canada" followed by the funeral march Lavallée had composed for Pope Pius IX. The brief ceremony concluded with six buglers, each representing one of Montreal's six regiments, playing the "Last Post."

The same evening, as the remains lay in state, the Grenadier Guards Band, led by Lieutenant J.-J. Gagnier, played a free concert of Lavallée's music at Parc La Fontaine. During the intermission, Eugène Lapierre, publicist for the repatriation committee, gave a speech on the importance of patriotism to Lavallée, who had died in Boston forty-two years earlier.[2] At 9 a.m., the next morning, Abbé Émile Lambert presided over a Requiem Mass that concluded with the simultaneous playing of "O Canada" by Notre Dame's organist Poirier and the Grenadier Guards Band, positioned outside the church. Once again, spectators lined the street and followed the procession uptown from the church. After proceeding on foot to Sherbrooke Street, family members and others boarded cars to ascend the slope of Mount Royal to Côte-des-Neiges cemetery, where the remains were interred with further pomp, ceremony, and speeches. More concerts featuring Lavallée's music were given in the city's parks on the following nights. On 19 July the repatriation celebrations ended with a mass gathering of national societies and religious organizations.[3]

For the media, Lavallée was a popular topic. In the lead-up to the repatriation week, general interest periodicals printed stories about Lavallée, and in August the music magazine *Le Passe-temps* printed a special issue devoted to him.[4] Several of the repatriation events were broadcast over the recently established Canadian Radio Broadcasting Commission (CRBC) network.[5] The daily newspapers published detailed reports on each event. Picking up on the nationalist fervour that motivated the repatriation, some of these published accounts went beyond simply reporting. *Le Devoir*, the city's most nationalistic newspaper, linked Lavallée's achievements to those of the patriot leaders of the rebellions of 1837 and 1838 and to the political figures George-Étienne Cartier and Honoré Mercier.[6] In another, it proposed that the city and province provide money for a mausoleum or pantheon for Lavallée, for the poets Octave Crémazie and Louis-Honoré Fréchette, and for other artists.[7] The English-language press used a similar tone in reporting on repatriation events and in their descriptions of Lavallée's life and achievements. It was, in sum, an exercise in nation building that was without precedent in Canada.

❖❖❖

Despite all of the attention, a misleadingly narrow interpretation of Lavallée's life emerged in 1933. Writers such as Eugène Lapierre portrayed Lavallée as a humble French Canadian forced into exile by the ignorance and injustice of his time.[8] In speeches and articles, they focused on "O Canada," using it as a symbol of its composer's patriotism, and carefully avoided discussion of Lavallée's personal ambition, restlessness, and love of adventure. These elements of his personality shaped the direction of his life and were apparent in the 1840s and early 1850s, when he was still a child. He had studied first with his father, an amateur musician and instrument maker in the small town of Saint-Hyacinthe. Then, from about the age of thirteen, he furthered his musical training with two French immigrants in Montreal. In the colony's metropolis, then divided nearly equally between French and English speakers, he found a hybrid culture where touring companies from the US frequently occupied the theatres. As he developed as a musician, he grew intimately familiar with Anglo-American popular culture. In 1859, at the age of sixteen, he set off for the United States to pursue his career.

For the next four years, Lavallée resided in the US. Recruited by a Providence-based minstrel show company, he travelled the continent as an itinerant musician, passing through nearly every town and city east of the Rocky Mountains. Blackening his face each night, he played the piano, violin, and cornet, and was soon leading the band. After the Civil War began, he published several pro-Union compositions and then put the theatre behind him to become a bandsman with the Fourth Rhode Island Regiment. For a year, he played the cornet as his regiment slogged its way along the east coast, through hurricanes and bloody skirmishes. After the catastrophic battle at Sharpsburg, Maryland, in the fall of

1862, he left the military and returned to his minstrel troupe. With the war still raging, life on the road was often hazardous and the profits frequently meagre. Late in 1863, four years after departing from Canada, Lavallée put his career on hold and returned to Montreal.

Much had changed in Canada during his absence and further developments were at hand. Under threat of a US invasion of Canada, Britain was now prepared to divest itself of its colonies. Confederation was the topic of the day and Lavallée threw himself into the debate with the same fervour he applied to everything he did. He aligned himself with the most radical element of the "no" side, a group of young lawyers and journalists led by Médéric Lanctôt, L.-O. David, and Wilfrid Laurier, who advocated either annexation to the US or outright independence for Lower Canada. He contributed to the cause by staging charity concerts to raise funds for the poor, for education, and for monuments to defeated martyrs. He also began to write music criticism, publishing pieces influenced by the political spirit of the times. His opposition to Confederation left him with a difficult decision after it was approved by a vote in the legislature in March 1865. Six months later, he returned to the US, where he lived a largely nomadic existence for the next seven years.

With the Civil War over and the entertainment business once again roaring, Lavallée's talents were in demand. Through the rest of the decade and into the 1870s, he criss-crossed the continent, living in hotel rooms, travelling by coach, by train, or by steamer, and residing briefly in Philadelphia, New York, and Boston. In 1867, on a tour stop in Lowell, Massachusetts, he married a young Franco-American woman, Joséphine Gentilly, but was back on the road the next day with his wife now travelling with the company. He wrote songs and an operetta, played the piano when he could, but mostly he served as a minstrel show music director, leading the band and orchestra. His world was one of clog dancers, dwarf entertainers, female impersonators, and banjo-playing comedians. Maudlin one moment and boorish the next, the minstrel show prized its satire, sentimental songs, and coarse humour equally. Performers blackened their white faces with burnt cork even when feigning an Irish brogue. Hugely competitive, minstrelsy was to the 1860s what television would be a century later. It was a culture of the moment, continuously adapting to the changing political landscape and economic environment, and rarely associated with grand ideas or with "serious" musicians. And then, in the spring of 1873, everything changed for Lavallée.

Seemingly frustrated with the direction of his career and tired of constantly touring, the thirty-year-old musician had returned to Montreal and was preparing to give a grand concert. In an effort to help promote the event, Lavallée's former colleague of a decade earlier, L.-O. David, published a short biographical article referring to him as the "national musician."[9] Soon after, a group of supporters provided the funds that would enable him to live and study in Paris for nearly two years. It would be a turning point in Lavallée's career and life. He studied composition with Bazin and Boïeldieu, completing the orchestral overture *Patrie*, and publishing several other pieces, including what would be his most successful piano composition. He studied piano with the celebrated teacher Antoine-François Marmontel, whose students then included a very young Claude Debussy. As his studies helped to refine his skills as a musician, the heated political climate in Paris intensified his linking of national identity and culture. He returned to Montreal in the summer of 1875 determined to transform his compatriots' views of the arts, cultivate the public's tastes, and provide training for a new generation of musicians.

For the next five years Lavallée performed, taught, and lobbied the government on behalf of the arts. Teaming up with the Belgian violinist, Frantz Jehin-Prume, he introduced audiences to the music of romantic composers such as Schumann and Weber. He transformed a church choir into an opera company and staged successful productions of Gounod's *Jeanne d'Arc* and Boïeldieu's *La Dame Blanche*. The Quebec government recognized his achievements by commissioning from him a grand cantata of welcome for the new governor general, the Marquis of Lorne, and his wife, Princess Louise. In the area of education, he set up a teaching studio in his home in Montreal; he joined and contributed to the work of the Académie de Musique de Québec, an examination board; and he attempted to get a subvention from the provincial government for a music conservatory. When the government proved resistant to this initiative, he moved to Quebec City and doubled his efforts. By the summer of 1880, he was in debt, exhausted, and exasperated. One of his final accomplishments was the composition of a national hymn, "O Canada," to be sung that summer at the congress organized by the Société Saint-

Jean-Baptiste. Not long after this event, he once again left for the United States, this time with no intention of returning.

Settling in Boston, Lavallée found employment as a piano teacher and, with it, achieved financial stability. He formed a lasting relationship with the Henry F. Miller piano firm, whose instruments he endorsed. He contributed music criticism to Boston newspapers and music periodicals, and he directed the choir at the Cathedral of the Holy Cross. Through published songs, piano pieces, orchestra and band music, operettas, and sacred works, his reputation extended well beyond New England. Among fellow musicians, Lavallée gained fame through the Music Teachers' National Association (MTNA). Joining in the summer of 1883, by 1887 he was the association's president, and in 1888 he travelled to London as the organization's first delegate to the annual conference of British musicians. Mainly, he used the MTNA to draw attention to the concert music of US composers. Through his writings, his performances, and his organizing of numerous concerts, he became known as a leading advocate for American music. As throughout his life, he eventually overextended himself financially and physically. Overworked and impoverished, Lavallée began to suffer from the effects of tuberculosis in the late 1880s, and died in 1891 at the age of forty-eight.

❖❖❖

Given the more than one hundred and twenty years since his death, Lavallée's life and achievements are long overdue for detailed study. The serious biography must explore the interconnected facets of his professional life – as a composer, instrumentalist, conductor, administrator, educator, and critic – and situate his life and work in the time in which he lived. Although a minor composer when compared with such contemporaries as Dvořák or Gounod, in the context of North America, Lavallée was a major figure. At a time when opportunities to compose grand operas and symphonies were non-existent, he composed comic operas, overtures for band and orchestra, songs, and piano music. Much of his music survives largely because it was composed for the marketplace, and for a time it was widely popular. Reviews of the published works and of their performances give us some indication of their success. The same types of sources also reveal something of the works he composed that were lost, in part because of the limited market for serious music – music that included a secular cantata for soloists, chorus, and orchestra; sacred and chamber music; and virtuosic pieces intended for his own performance.

Lavallée's place as an instrumentalist and conductor is arguably of greater importance than his legacy as a composer. His first instrument was the piano, and he found audiences for his performances while in Montreal and Quebec City, then later in the US. His repertoire reflected the tastes of the time and then his pushing forward of these boundaries, building audiences first for the more intellectually challenging music of European composers and then for new music by his contemporaries in the US. After many years of honing his skills as a music director and bandleader, he was a formidable conductor. He found outlets for these talents directing church choirs in Montreal, Quebec City, and at Boston's Cathedral. He organized and conducted at large-scale opera productions, major concerts, and numerous community events. Lavallée's career was remarkable for many things, but especially in the many ways in which he was able to shift between the often-opposing worlds of classical and popular music. Opera emerges as a common territory, especially in the 1850s and 1860s. Building audiences and training young performers dominated Lavallée's life in the 1870s and 1880s.

The three-part organization of the book follows the major patterns in Lavallée's life: part one exploring his childhood and the early years of his career; part two tracing the events of the eight-year period beginning in 1873; and part three picking up his story in 1880, after he returns to the United States. The opening chapter covers the first twenty-one years of Lavallée's life. It introduces the social and political context of Canada in the 1840s and 1850s, his early experiences in music, and his education. The Lavallée family is central to Calixa's pursuit of music. His father, Augustin Lavallée, an instrument maker and bandleader from the Richelieu River Valley, was his first teacher. The chapter follows Calixa's move to Montreal to continue his studies, in about 1855, and the cultural opportunities he found there. It then traces his early years in the United States, as a minstrel show performer and military band musician in the Union Army. Lavallée left nothing in his own words about his life as a minstrel show performer or band musician. His travels with the New Orleans Minstrels, from Montreal to Louisiana, are documented in the daily newspapers of the time, in minstrel show songsters (lyric books), and in published music. The events of his life in the Army of the Potomac are culled from regimental histories and the memoirs of other soldiers. With each event of his life, each decision or unexpected turn, his character emerges and the theme of rebellion comes to unify the chapter, as it stretches from the aftermath of the rebellions of 1837 and 1838 in Lower Canada through the early years of the Civil War in the United States.

Lavallée's return to Montreal, late in 1863, marked the beginning of the two-year period in Canada that is the subject of chapter 2. Montreal newspapers are the main sources for Lavallée's activities in 1864 and 1865, and illustrate how four years of professional experience had transformed him from an unknown teenager to a leading figure in the city's musical community. His participation in both the US Civil War and the debate over Confederation allow for some fascinating insights into these two closely connected events. Scholarship on the origins of Confederation and the politics of the 1860s, pioneered by Monet and Bernard in the late 1960s and early 1970s, has had little to say about the place of the arts in the debate.[10] The chapter illustrates how, during these years, Lavallée was at the centre of a circle of musicians who were deeply engaged in the politics of their time. The social activism that propelled him through these years reveals a part of his character that was behind much of what he did right up to the time of his death.

Chapter 3 traces Lavallée's activities between 1866 and 1873. During these years he travelled continuously throughout North America, first with Charles Duprez's New Orleans Minstrels, and later with the San Francisco Minstrels and Morris Brothers' Minstrels. Minstrelsy remained popular in the post–Civil War era by evolving to meet the needs of the changing society and changing tastes. The programs, filled with satires of current events, reveal much about the issues that concerned and amused the public during these years. Lavallée adapted to change, constantly arranging music and writing songs. His experience in minstrelsy provides an extraordinary window into what was the most popular form of entertainment in the 1850s and 1860s. Few detailed studies of individual minstrel show performers have been published and none have been written about the musicians who made their careers in blackface. This account of Lavallée's travels provides a vivid history of an important part of musical life in an increasingly urban society, connected by an ever more elaborate network of roads, rails, and waterways. Lavallée's association with the same touring company in the years preceding, during, and after the US Civil War provides insights into how these companies evolved and prospered despite political pressure and economic turmoil. Nationalism slipped into the background during these years, but never disappeared. Politics emerges in Lavallée's connections to the struggles of Irish nationalists in North America, and during his brief return visits to the new Dominion of Canada in 1867 and 1868.

Part two explores Lavallée's efforts to develop musical life in Canada in the 1870s, after finally abandoning his career in minstrelsy. Chapter 4 opens with Lavallée's sojourn in Paris immediately following the Franco-Prussian War, providing an account of musical life in the French capital and Lavallée's activities there, including his studies and publications. It then follows his career in Montreal, from 1875 to 1878, when he devoted his time to cultivating audiences and educating musicians, giving concerts with Frantz Jehin-Prume, and staging opera. Chapter 5 traces his life in Quebec City, from the fall of 1878, where he organized numerous events, many of them within the Irish community. The chapter documents the events surrounding the composition and performance of the cantata of welcome for the Marquis of Lorne, and "O Canada."

Lavallée's life in Boston in the 1880s is the subject of part three. Chapter 6 examines the first three years, when he was focused on establishing his career in the US. His connections to the Miller piano firm and the Petersilea Academy provide the context for a larger study of the importance of piano manufacturing and education in the US in the 1880s. Discussion of Lavallée's comic operas, *The Widow* and *TIQ*, is placed within the context of the rise of English-language opera in the US. Nationalism returns on several levels in chapter 7, which follows the final six years of Lavallée's life. Most prominent is his work with the Music Teachers' National Association in promoting the music of contemporary composers in the US. At the same time, he remains active within the French-Canadian community in New England, composing occasional pieces and organizing concerts to raise funds for Catholic charities, for pro-annexation organizations, and for the family of Louis Riel.

Finally, the epilogue traces Lavallée's shifting posthumous status. In the early decades of the twentieth century, performances of his music in the US declined as tastes changed, while in Canada, "O Canada" emerged as the favoured national song. The epilogue traces the song's rise and, with it, Lavallée's re-emergence as the "national musician," and a symbol of French-Canadian/Quebec identity. The epilogue considers the popularity of "O Canada" with both French- and English-Canadians, its evocation of music's classical era, and the impact of Lavallée's involvement in popular culture on his ability to compose a national song. Bringing the subject into the present, it looks at the more recent politics of the song: the timing of its official designation as the country's national anthem, in 1980, and its current status within and outside of Quebec.[11] Just as the anthem was the main reason for French Canadians recognizing Lavallée's achievements in 1933, since 1980 it has been responsible for the publication of occasional pieces about Lavallée in the English-language press.[12] Far more tenuous is the song's place in Quebec, where, despite its having been composed for the 1880 *Fête nationale* celebrations, many nationalists consider it tainted by its place as the anthem of Canada, and with some frequency call for the creation of a new anthem for Quebec.

Through a careful examination of Lavallée's life and times, this book explores the importance of music in culture and the meaning of "O Canada." As its title suggests, *Anthems and Minstrel Shows* is a book about seemingly unconnected places in the world of music. "Anthems," of course, makes direct reference to "O Canada." It also refers to the many other national songs that Lavallée heard, composed, and performed. Indeed, the place of nationalism in music, or the effect of nationalism *on* music, provides the context in which this book views much of Lavallée's life and work. As such, it provides new perspectives on a subject that scholars have been writing about for well over a century. In that time, most have focused on Europe, the creation of nationalist music, and especially the orchestral music of the nineteenth century.[13] Their neglect of musical life in North America during this era is understandable. There was no tradition of orchestral or operatic composition and, thus, no body of orchestral or operatic works.[14] Nevertheless, music making could still be infused with nationalism, and it often was. As the ethnomusicologist Philip Bohlman has written, nationalism not only "enters music from the top, that is, from state institutions and ideologies, but may build its path into music from just about any angle, as long as there are musicians and audiences willing to mobilize cultural movement from those angles."[15]

But this is also a book about minstrels, or more generally, about popular culture. It was through the minstrel show and popular music that Lavallée found opportunities to see the world and attain a degree of fame, if not fortune. It is through the minstrel show paper trail – advertisements, reviews, and published songs – that we track his movements as a travelling music director. Details about the performances he led reveal much of the changing social landscape of the 1860s and 1870s. Lavallée's reasons for abandoning the world of popular culture in the 1870s raise interesting questions about him and about societal attitudes toward 'high' and 'low' culture. Ultimately, his experience offers an opportunity to reflect on questions of culture and identity in our own time.

# PART ONE

# On the Road

## 1842–1873

In the misty night we crossed Toledo and went onward across
old Ohio. I realized I was beginning to cross and recross towns
in America as though I were a travelling salesman.

Jack Kerouac, *On the Road*

# 1

## *Rebellion*

### *1842–1863*

The first Lavallées to arrive in New France came as soldiers. In 1665, to counter the ongoing threat from the Iroquois, Louis XIV despatched the Carignan-Salières regiment to the New World. After the signing of the 1667 peace treaty, the soldiers were offered land should they want to remain in the colony, and a good number did just that. The former soldiers became settlers, or *habitants*.[1] Many of them settled in the Richelieu Valley, southeast of Montreal, where the officers became seigneurs – the landholding nobility – and the settlements and seigneuries took their names (Varennes, Verchères, Sorel, and others). Many of the former soldiers married young women sent to New France in the 1660s and early 1670s – the so-called *filles du roi*. Calixa Lavallée's ancestry has been traced back to the soldier Isaac Pasquier dit Lavallée, a native of Poitou, in west-central France.[2] On 1 February 1670, he married Elisabeth Meunier at Château-Richer, near Quebec City, settled on the nearby Ile d'Orléans, and started a family.

Nearly a century passed before New France fell to the British in 1759. In 1763, the Treaty of Paris marked the end of the Seven Years' War, and in many ways life continued as before. Gradually, as the decades passed, French-speaking inhabitants began to see themselves as a nation – united in language, religion, history, and geography, but also in their conflict with the colonial administration.[3] An economic crisis in the Saint Lawrence River valley fuelled dissent.[4] The Parti Canadien became the political choice of many French Canadians, and its newspaper, *Le Canadien*, articulated their views.[5] The Parti Canadien steadily increased its influence under the leadership of Louis-Joseph Papineau. Renamed the Parti Patriote in 1826, by the 1830s it held more than a third of the Assembly's seats. Still, they could do little more than hold up approval of government spending, and on several occasions such tactics caused the governor of Canada to simply dissolve the Assembly (as Governor Craig did on two occasions). In the pages of *Le Canadien* and elsewhere, moderates sought constitutional reforms that would see an end to abuses of power and the creation of responsible government. More radical members of the Assembly dreamt of a new republic, free of colonial rule. To this end, a group that became known as the Fils de la liberté (Sons of Liberty), modelled on the American revolutionaries, began organizing what would be an armed revolt. In 1834 the Assembly issued ninety-two resolutions, calling on Britain to reform the constitution. Three years later, on 2 March 1837, John Russell, British colonial secretary, finally responded by issuing his own resolutions to Parliament, in which all of the Canadian demands were dismissed. By fall, many Canadians had decided to fight.

It was in the Richelieu Valley, where the Lavallées had eventually settled, that many of the key events of the rebellions took place. The brief but violent insurrection pitted the poorly armed farmers and tradesmen, or self-styled *patriotes*, against the British army. In the first major encounter, on 23 November at the village of Saint-Denis, the rebels stunned the British, forcing them to retreat. But two days later, at Saint-Charles-sur-Richelieu, British troops routed the rebels, and within a month had put down the uprising. Many of the fighters fled across the border into the United States, from which in 1838 they launched a second rebellion that ended more quickly than the first. The two failed uprisings left much of Lower Canada, and the Richelieu region in particular, in worse condition than before. The British inflicted retribution on those communities that had challenged their authority by allowing troops to pillage and burn. Authorities executed twelve of the *patriote* leaders, exiled fifty-eight to the penal colony in Australia, and jailed hundreds of the insurgents. The immediate result for the Richelieu region was further economic hardship, and deeper resentment toward the colonial administration. London sent Governor General John Lambton (Lord Durham) to investigate the causes of the rebellion. In his report, issued in 1839, Durham downplayed the economic and political factors, attributing the insurrection primarily to a conflict between French- and English-speaking inhabitants, or, as he put it, "two nations warring in the bosom of a single state."[6] The solution proposed, and subsequently carried out with the Act of Union (1841), was to merge Upper and Lower Canada (present day Ontario and Quebec, respectively) into a single province, with the ultimate goal of assimilating French Canadians through immigration from Great Britain.[7] It was in this environment that Calixa Lavallée came into the world in the final days of 1842.

Little more than anecdotal information on the early lives of Lavallée's parents has survived. His mother, Charlotte-Caroline Valentine, was of Scottish and French heritage, her surname descending from James Valentine, a Scottish soldier who had arrived in Canada in 1780.[8] Lavallée's father, Jean-Baptiste Augustin Lavallée, was born in 1816 and apprenticed with his father to become a blacksmith. The twenty-one-year-old Augustin Lavallée and his father were said to have set out quickly to join their compatriots at Saint-Charles, only to find the battle had already been lost.[9] Around the time of the first rebellion, Lavallée began to discover his true vocation while enrolled at a newly opened classical college at Sainte-Thérèse, north of Montreal. There, he met Joseph Casavant, a like-minded student and former blacksmith whose family later established the famous organ-building firm.[10] The college's founder, Charles-Joseph Ducharme, was also the music teacher, and Lavallée excelled in his studies with him. Casavant's biographer, Mathieu-Robert Sauvé, has written that when Ducharme had Casavant assemble an organ that he had imported from Europe, Lavallée performed at its inauguration that December and continued on as chapel organist.[11] The organ attracted considerable attention, and Casavant was soon receiving orders for instruments, many of them coming from Upper Canada (now Ontario). Lavallée worked with him for some time, Sauvé writes, but eventually chose to return home to the Richelieu Valley, where on 5 April 1842 he married Charlotte-Caroline Valentine.[12] Nine months later, on 28 December 1842, Calixa Lavallée was born.

The day of his birth, Lavallée was taken to the parish church, Saint-François-Xavier de Verchères, and baptized Calixte, a name he would later modify to Calixa.[13] The reason for his parents' somewhat curious choice of name is not known. In its Latin form, Callistus, it had been chosen by three medieval popes. The family may have hoped their first-born would be destined for the priesthood, or perhaps simply thought that the name might offer some protection from life's hazards. Being born in the dead of winter was itself perilous at a time when hardly more than fifty per cent of children survived infancy. He would spend his first years in a small, stone house alongside a country road called the Rang de la Beauce, in the parish of Saint-François-Xavier de Verchères. The house was destroyed by fire, but the village has otherwise remained much as it was in the mid-nineteenth century, hardly more than a cluster of build-ings surrounded by rolling farmland.[14] It became the parish of Saint-Théodosie de Verchères in 1878, and in 1974 took the name of its most famous son.

After the birth of his sister Cordélia, in 1846, Lavallée's family left the rural parish of Saint-François-Xavier for the town of Saint-Hyacinthe, where Augustin renewed his association with Casavant. Saint-Hyacinthe, on the banks of the Yamaska River, was then a growing community of about 3,000 inhabitants, of which nearly all were French-speaking Catholics.[15] During these years the town grew as a result of new rail links to Montreal via the Grand Trunk Railway and to Boston (as the western terminus of the St Lawrence and Atlantic Railroad).[16] In 1852, the town became a re-gional administrative centre with the creation of the Diocese of Saint-Hyacinthe.[17]

The Lavallées' move to Saint-Hyacinthe allowed Calixa the opportu-nity to get a formal education, albeit briefly.[18] The records of the Collège de Saint-Hyacinthe indicate only that he was among the students regis-tered during the 1852–53 academic year.[19] At a time when education was accessible to only a minority of Quebec children, the privileged students of the Collège followed a classical curriculum of languages, arts, and sci-ences.[20] The school's reputation helped to draw students from through-out Quebec, Ontario, and the northeastern United States.[21] However, this education was for those intended for the civil service or the priest-hood, professions for which Lavallée had little aptitude, and was prob-ably beyond the means of the Lavallées.

The new opportunities available in Saint-Hyacinthe also enabled Au-gustin Lavallée to gradually give up the blacksmith trade and make a liv-ing repairing and building musical instruments. Advertisements from as late as 1862 show him to be building organs and pianos. He would go on to become the first important Canadian violin maker.[22] With the debut of the town's first regular newspaper, the *Courrier de Saint-Hyacinthe*, in 1853, we find some of the earliest documentation of Augustin Lavallée's activities. The *Courrier* contains a number of advertisements for Lavallée's music shop, first on Saint-Hyacinthe Street and later on Cascade Street, where he taught piano, sold sheet music and books, and repaired "organs, pianos, harmoniums, accordions, violins, clarinets, wind instruments etc."[23]

Little information about Calixa Lavallée's childhood has survived. Perhaps as compensation for this lack of evidence, in 1873 L.-O. David provided a colourful description of Lavallée as a child: "small, thin, the hair black like ebony, the eyes as bright as gems, quick, light as a butterfly, he had the appearance of an imp, or a gremlin as described in histories of witchcraft."[24] The description might not have been entirely fanciful. Lavallée never grew much past five feet in height. As a child with small hands, his ability to perform difficult piano music must have increased the public's awe of him. While in Saint-Hyacinthe, he had access to the Casavant organ workshop, and he was reported to have been playing at services at Notre-Dame du Rosaire church by the age of ten.[25] In another apocryphal story, an obituary writer claimed that as a small child he accompanied the choir of Montreal's Notre-Dame Church at a performance in Saint-Hyacinthe, compelling the choir's director, Lazare Arsène Barbarin, to predict that Lavallée would "one day become a great artist."[26] Similarly, Lavallée's younger cousin, Mcgill Valentine, recalled the young Lavallée's ability to notate music he heard performed by a band at the Verchères quay, and believed he had begun composing by the age of nine.[27] The family business was his classroom, and he soon learned to play the many other instruments sold and repaired in his father's shop. Early biographical articles credit Augustin Lavallée as Calixa's first music teacher.[28] He went on to teach the rest of his children, with Cordélia becoming a skilful singer and pianist and all three sons making careers in music. Calixa learned to play keyboard, wind, and string instruments, eventually focusing on the piano, violin, and cornet.

The *Courrier de Saint-Hyacinthe* shows Augustin Lavallée to have been leading the town band at civic events. One such event took place at the Hôtel Pageau on 25 June 1854, when his band played at the inauguration

of Saint-Hyacinthe's branch of the Institut canadien, an institution established in Montreal, in 1844, in the wake of the rebellions of 1837 and
1838.[29] The Institut aimed to develop intellectual life in Lower Canada by
providing members with access to lectures and a well-stocked library. In
doing so, the Institut soon found itself in conflict with the Roman Catholic
Church, but continued to open branches in several towns and cities. In
Saint-Hyacinthe, the Institut's president was the town's mayor, the seigneur
and journalist Louis-Antoine Dessaulles, an opponent of the Church and
advocate of annexation to the United States. A decade later, Calixa would
join that debate. But in 1854, the eleven-year-old was more likely interested in music than politics, and already a band member. In an article
published in 1909, Gustave Comte, the husband of one of Lavallée's nieces,
wrote that Calixa began taking part in these performances at the age of
three, playing a cymbal at the rear of the marching band.[30] By the mid-
1850s, he was able to play a much larger role.

Among the small number of anglophone residents of Saint-Hyacinthe
at this time was the Unsworth family. James Stanley Unsworth had brought
his family to Canada from Liverpool, England, in about 1850 and, in
1854, was employed as a clerk in Saint-Hyacinthe. His wife was likely a
frequent visitor to the Lavallées' music shop. Mary Unsworth was the sister of the well-known pianist and composer John Liptrot Hatton. The
Unsworth's eldest son, James Jr, later became one of the leading minstrel
show entertainers of his time. By the mid-1850s he was already a promising musician and evidently an important influence on the young Calixa
Lavallée. He would seem to have been behind the creation of a local
group called the Plantation Minstrels, who gave a benefit performance
for the Saint-Hyacinthe branch of the Institut canadien on Saturday, 1 July
1854, a week after Augustin Lavallée's had performed for the same institution. The precocious Calixa Lavallée was quite likely a member of
the group. Only a few weeks later, however, James Unsworth Sr died, and
his wife and children settled in Montreal. Perhaps by coincidence, a year
later Lavallée also left for Montreal.

By about 1855, news of Lavallée's talent had reached Léon Derome,
a thirty-year-old Montreal businessman with a passion for the arts.[31] He
was a member of the Institut canadien, and it may have been through the
opening of the Saint-Hyacinthe branch, in 1854, that Derome heard of

Lavallée. Derome was not an obvious intellectual or patron of the arts. He ran a butcher shop in the Bonsecours Market, on Saint-Paul Street, and lived on Beaudry, a new and relatively spacious street, in what was then the city's east end.[32] In 1855, Derome and his twenty-nine-year-old wife, Rose-de-Lima, already had six young children and also provided lodgings for staff from the shop.[33] One more person must not have seemed like much of a burden, since they took in Lavallée. Seemingly out of his love of music and a desire to assist with a talented boy's education, Derome became Lavallée's benefactor.[34] For Lavallée, the move provided the next stage in his musical training and his introduction to a much larger world.

❖❖❖

Compared with Saint-Hyacinthe, mid-nineteenth-century Montreal was a culturally and economically diverse city. The population of about 60,000 was almost equally divided between English- and French-speaking residents, with the large Irish population helping to make Catholics the majority.[35] (See table 1.1) Many of its contrasts were evident to visitors from the US, such as Henry David Thoreau, who travelled through Quebec in 1850 and described Montreal as making "the impression of a larger city than you had expected to find ... In the newer parts it appeared to be growing fast like a small New York, and to be considerably Americanized."[36] Elsewhere it appeared to him much more European: "The names of the squares reminded you of Paris, the Champ de Mars, the Place d'Armes, and others, and you felt as if a French revolution

*Table 1.1 Population of Montreal, 1852*

| Canadian-born | | Immigrants | | Total |
|---|---|---|---|---|
| French-Canadians | Anglophones | British (including Irish) | Others | |
| 26,020 | 12,494 | 17,744 | 1,457 | 57,715 |
| 45% | 22% | 30% | 3% | 100% |

Source: *Census of 1852* published in the *Montreal Directory 1856–57* (Lovell, 1856), 383.

might break out any moment. Glimpses of Mount Royal rising behind the town, and the names of some streets in that direction, make one think of Edinburgh."[37]

While revolution was unlikely in the 1840s and 1850s, ethnic, linguistic, and religious tensions were often close to the surface. Cracks had appeared in the Union as early as the mid-1840s. Britain's abolition of the Canada Corn Act in 1846 had worsened what was already a dismal economy.[38] In the Saint Lawrence Valley, the economic downturn accelerated French-Canadian emigration to United States.[39] Tensions were greatest in Montreal, which had served as home to the legislature from 1843. In the 3rd Parliament, following the elections of January 1848, the Baldwin-LaFontaine coalition formed the government and subsequently introduced the Rebellion Losses Bill, which would require the government to compensate individuals whose property had been destroyed by British troops during the rebellions of 1837 and 1838. Opposition to the legislation was most vehement among Montreal Tories. On 25 April 1849, when Governor General James Bruce, Earl of Elgin, upheld its passage, they pelted his carriage with paving stones and burned the Parliament building. Sporadic rioting continued for several days, and as a relative calm returned, many anglophones in Montreal began to agitate for annexation to the United States, a solution also favoured by some French-Canadian nationalists, albeit for different reasons.[40] Ethnic-linguistic tensions continued to surface periodically. Riots broke out in both Montreal and Quebec City at the lectures given by the apostate monk and Italian nationalist Alessandro Gavazzi. In Montreal, a detachment of the Twenty-sixth Regiment fired on the mob, resulting in at least forty casualties.[41] Orange Day parades frequently resulted in violence. As in most of the Empire, wealth was concentrated among the few. For many of its citizens, Montreal was a city of Dickensian poverty. The economy had stagnated through much of the 1840s, causing a steady stream of emigrants.[42] In July 1852, an accidental fire devastated much of the east-end Faubourg Québec district, and as far north as Sainte-Catherine Street, destroying the cathedral and bishop's palace. Over 9,000 inhabitants were left homeless. In the cramped and squalid conditions of the aftermath, periodic outbreaks of cholera restricted city life for nearly three years.

Lavallée arrived in the city just as the situation was turning around. Although no longer the capital of the Province of Canada, Montreal remained the financial centre and largest city of British North America, and by the end of 1854, the quality of life in the city was improving.[43] The economy was spurred in part by the passage of the Canadian–American Reciprocity Treaty (1855–66) and expansion of the railroad network.[44] Health conditions also improved, bringing renewed immigration and a general awakening of public activity.[45] The events of the Crimean War provided Montreal's British and French-Canadian communities with a rare common cause. Responding to news reports of the Siege of Sevastopol, in January 1855 they demonstrated their unity by organizing a 'grand patriotic concert,' an event that drew a full house to the 3,000-seat City Concert Hall, specially draped in French and British flags.[46] Later the same year, cultural activity received further impetus through the re-establishment of formal relations with France after nearly a century, an event marked by the arrival in port of the French naval vessel *La Capricieuse*.

Performance venues built in the early part of the decade began returning to life. The City Concert Hall, mentioned above, was the largest venue. Known in French as the Salle de Concert de l'Hôtel de Ville, and located on the second floor of the Bonsecours Market, it had opened in January 1852. There were also several smaller venues. On Craig Street (now Saint-Antoine), there was the 1,200-seat Bonaventure Hall. And by the end of the decade there were three venues on Great Saint James Street (now Saint-Jacques): the Odd Fellows' Hall, Mechanics' Hall, and Nordheimer's Hall. Most popular was the 800-seat hall of the Mechanics' Institute, which was located on the third floor of their building, above the library and classrooms. (See figure 1.1) Nordheimer's Hall, the showroom and concert facility of the Toronto piano maker A. & S. Nordheimer Co., was inaugurated in the summer of 1859 with three performances by an opera company brought in from New York.[47]

The main centre of entertainment in the 1850s was the 1,500-seat Theatre Royal. (See figure 1.2) Centrally located on Côté Street, just north of Place d'Armes, it was the city's fourth theatre with this name. The house was built by local businessman Jesse Joseph and designed by architect John Wells. The drop curtain from the third Theatre Royal,

Figure 1.1 The Mechanics' Institute on Great St James Street (now Saint-Jacques Street), a popular venue for concerts in the 1860s.

Figure 1.2 Interior of the Theatre Royal on Côté Street, the site of Lavallée's first appearance as a soloist and of many subsequent performances.

featuring an illustration of Windsor Castle, was incorporated into the new theatre.[48] It was intended that the famous Irish singer Catherine Hayes inaugurate the hall, but when her arrival was delayed, a French vaudeville troupe gave the first performances. Hayes arrived later that summer and was followed by the violinist Ole Bull, Wood's Minstrels, and a mix of other performers, since the theatre's size and agreeable acoustics made it suitable for theatre, concerts, and variety shows.[49] From its opening until 1872, John Buckland managed the theatre and frequently featured his wife, the Irish-American actress Kate Horn, in many productions. Lavallée made his début here in 1859.

With its place on the edge of the continent's touring circuit, Montreal enjoyed a wide variety of entertainment. "Curiosity shows" were highly popular, allowing spectators to view strange or deformed creatures – often human – for a small fee. A pair of African Siamese twins, for instance, attracted large crowds to the Mechanics' Hall in June 1855.[50] Although less sensational, dioramas and panoramas of historic events, such as Napoléon's funeral and the Battle of Waterloo, were popular, and circuses were even more so. Most circuses came from the United States but at least one claimed to be from China and boasted of the decapitation of "a different member of the troupe every night."[51] Even more popular than circuses were the travelling minstrel shows that frequently appeared at the Theatre Royal and the Mechanics' Hall through the 1850s. Even a decade later, one American periodical noted that Cuba and Costa Rica would be fertile ground for summer tours of opera companies while Canada was still "overrun by Negro minstrels and wild ballade singers, and other 'artists' of the seventh or eighth order."[52] The minstrel show's popularity in the 1850s and '60s inspired the creation of local troupes, and from these amateur ensembles, professional companies recruited performers.

The high cost of travelling made tours by orchestras and opera companies comparatively rare. Still, the Seguin Opera Troupe, Boston's Germania Orchestra, and other companies toured Canada during the period.[53] More common were visits by soloists, and during his years as a student in Montreal, Lavallée had opportunities to hear several of the leading virtuosos of the day. Successful concert tours by pianists Leopold de Meyer and Henri Herz in 1845 and 1846, respectively, had inspired

Figure 1.3
The violinist Camilla Urso,
who was the same age as
Lavallée, first performed in
Montreal as a child star in
1855 and returned for an extended visit in the fall of 1863.

many other European soloists to travel to North America.[54] Several child
prodigies visited in 1855: the eleven-year-old vocalist Adelina Patti, and
two violinists, Camilla Urso and Paul Julien. Urso had made history at
the age of seven by becoming the first girl admitted to the Paris Conservatoire. (See figure 1.3) Now twelve, she performed across North America that year to great acclaim.[55] She played in Montreal in May and then
returned in July, when the captain and officers from *La Capricieuse* attended her final performance at the City Concert Hall. She and the other
young performers Lavallée had the opportunity to hear would have fired
his competitive spirit. He likely also heard more seasoned performers. The
Norwegian violinist Ole Bull also made a stop in Montreal in 1855.[56]
Among the celebrated pianists to visit, the great Austrian pianist Sigis-
mund Thalberg, Franz Liszt's rival, was the most famous. He gave three
performances at the Mechanics' Hall in 1857, performing his virtuosic
fantasies on popular opera melodies.[57]

❖❖❖

Lavallée's education reflected opportunities available to young musicians at the time. The city had no conservatory, either private or public. Its classical colleges, seminaries, and convent schools provided only limited musical training, and its university offered no music courses at all.[58] The choices were limited to going abroad or studying with a private teacher. Journalist L.-O. David reported in 1873 that soon after bringing Lavallée to Montreal, Léon Derome arranged for him to audition for the German-trained organist Jean-Crysostome Brauneis II. After Lavallée had played for about twenty minutes, Brauneis acknowledged that the child had talent but expressed doubt that he was the genius that Derome claimed, so they moved on to the studio of Paul Letondal.[59] We have no first-hand account of either meeting, only Lapierre's report that of the two teachers, Letondal was sufficiently impressed to have agreed to take Lavallée on as a student and to offer him lessons free of charge.[60]

Letondal was born in the French town of Montbenoît, near the Swiss border. Blind from birth, he had been educated at l'Institut des jeunes aveugles in Paris, where he studied the piano under a disciple of the renowned virtuoso Friedrich Kalkbrenner, who had developed a teaching method using 'hand guides.' Letondal had travelled to Canada in 1852, at the age of twenty-one, to teach at the Jesuits' Collège Sainte-Marie, on Bleury Street, and to play the organ at the adjoining Gesù Church.[61] Like Kalkbrenner, Letondal proved to be an astute businessman. Soon after his arrival in Montreal, he was involved in many aspects of the city's musical life. By the mid-1850s he was importing sheet music and instruments from France, including Pleyel pianos.[62] He wrote concert reviews and performed on both piano and cello.[63] His contributions to the city's musical life were acknowledged as early as 1856, when he was appointed head of music in the newly created Institut philotechnique, an academy of arts and sciences.[64]

In addition to giving lessons at the Collège Sainte-Marie, Letondal maintained a teaching studio at his home on Saint Lawrence Street (now known as boulevard Saint-Laurent), and it was there that Lavallée and others would take their lessons.[65] The pianist Gustave Smith, who had himself arrived from France in 1856, later discussed Letondal's significance, recalling that he often saw Letondal being guided by a child and, on eventually meeting him, was greatly impressed: "I admit that I immediately felt great esteem for this person. Spiritual, eloquent, with clarity in his ideas, one recognized the distinction of this artist." Smith noted the success Letondal's students had achieved. He credited the teacher with bringing the French school of piano playing to Canada and, more specifically, with introducing the teaching methods of Kalkbrenner.[66] The point was underscored by the New Orleans pianist and composer Louis Moreau Gottschalk, who, during his visit to Montreal in the early 1860s, noted in his diary that the blind pianist Letondal had been "very polite" to him, and also that Kalkbrenner's *l'Ange déchu* was "the object of attraction" in the city.[67] Lavallée does not seem to have had any pieces by Kalkbrenner in his repertoire, but he did comment on his former teacher's talents. In a review of a performance by the pianist Marie Regnaud, Lavallée congratulated the "excellent professor, for having trained such a fine student," and mentioned several others with whom Letondal had had success. The inability to see, he concluded, had in no way limited Letondal's skill as a teacher.[68]

Paul Letondal's son Arthur was perhaps the first to mention in print that Lavallée also studied with Charles Wugk Sabatier.[69] A true romantic, Sabatier remains one of the most enigmatic cultural figures of nineteenth-century Canada. He was born at Tourcoing, in northern France, to a French mother and a German father, who was also a pianist.[70] The Canadian music historian Helmut Kallmann wrote that the pianist may have called himself Sabatier to fit more easily into French society.[71] After studies at the Paris Conservatoire from 1838 to 1840, he pursued a career in France, publishing compositions with the Paris firms of E. Challiot and S. Lévy, and claiming the title of "pianist to the Duchess of Montpensier."[72] Neither the date of his arrival in Canada nor his reasons for leaving Europe have been determined with certainty. The political turmoil of 1848 would seem to have been a factor in his decision to leave France.[73] Finding a bust of Napoléon III in Quebec City's Hôtel Blanchard, the enraged Sabatier was said to have heaved it out of a window onto Place Nôtre-Dame-des-Victoires.[74] The French periodical *Le Ménestrel* mentioned in June 1848 that Sabatier had travelled to Guernsey, the British-administered island off the Norman coast, where Victor Hugo would later live in exile.[75] Sabatier later composed a piece for piano that he titled *Souvenir de Guernsey*. From there, he travelled to Britain, and some time after 1852, made his way to Quebec City. He held various positions as a church musician and teacher in and around Quebec City and then Montreal, but seems to have been either unable or uninterested in keeping a job for long. His contemporaries hailed his musicianship while lamenting his lifestyle. Nazaire Le Vasseur, a Quebec City writer and amateur musician, described Sabatier as "a man of good size, with an ancient Gaulish head, but a Bohemian in all senses of the word, who loved good wine and was never without it."[76]

In 1855 and through the early months of 1856, Sabatier lived in Newark and New York, where he gave concerts with the young violinist Paul Julien, among others, and taught piano. Back in Canada late in 1856, he settled in musically, composing "La Montréalaise," a pro-Union song, on words by another French immigrant, Félix Vogeli, that urged French Canadians to "wake up" and work together with the British for the common good – a song that may have been helpful to his career as well as reflecting his admiration for the British.[77] Presumably, Lavallée was present on 24 October 1856 when Sabatier performed a two-hour program of his own music at the City Concert Hall. It was still very unusual to give solo concerts and unheard of that one should play a whole program of his own music, so it was not out of place for the critic of *La Patrie* to describe Sabatier's efforts as "Herculean."[78] Sabatier's piano music mostly took the form of popular dances, fantasies, and marches that served primarily as vehicles for his prowess as a performer, and Lavallée later had Sabatier's *Marche au Flambeaux* (Torchlight Procession), op. 153 in his repertoire.[79] In November 1856, Sabatier collaborated with the French painter Clément-Auguste Andrieux in an event at the Mechanics' Institute, performing the *Panorama des habitations à Sucre et à Coton*, the *Panorama des Grand Lacs, Detroit, Cleveland, Pittsburgh, avec Sa Grand Cathédrale, Messe de Minuit*, and other pieces that would have fuelled the imagination of the young Lavallée.[80] Two years later, Sabatier composed his most enduring work, a solemn setting of Octave Crémazie's new poem "Le Drapeau de Carillon," telling of the French victory over the British at Fort Carillon in 1758. Lavallée would have been present for its premiere by the baritone François Lavoie at a Saint-Jean-Baptiste promenade concert that year, a performance that helped to establish Crémazie as the "national poet" and cement Sabatier's place as the colony's leading musician.[81]

❖❖❖

The move to Montreal also brought Lavallée back into the Unsworths' circle. Both Mary and James Jr were now teaching music at their home on Saint-Antoine Street. Mary Unsworth organized concerts for her students and sometimes for herself. On at least one occasion in 1856, she gave a concert with Paul Letondal at the Mechanics' Institute. James was then beginning to make a career as a banjo player. He had organized a minstrel troupe soon after arriving in Montreal, and in 1857 he departed for the US to pursue his career. Given Lavallée's Saint-Hyacinthe link to the Unsworths, and his later activities, it seems quite likely that he was briefly a part of Unsworth's Montreal minstrel troupe.

The Unsworths were like many of the city's musicians in the 1850s, dividing their time between teaching and performing. The number of musicians in the city fluctuated widely during these years, given the transient character of the population as a whole, and of musicians in particular. City directories provide listings of music teachers, instrument makers, and retailers. Concerts provided few paying opportunities. Orchestras rarely stayed together long enough to earn a profit. In the summer months, military bands frequently performed on Champ de Mars and at Place d'Armes. Local musicians held concerts throughout the year, but usually to raise money for charities. Typically, they featured both vocalists and instrumentalists performing a mix of popular songs, arias, and light instrumental pieces, often based on themes from operas. Social events provided regular jobs for musicians. Instrumentalists could make a good part of their earnings by playing in bands and orchestras that hired themselves out for dancing and to provide incidental music in the theatre.[82] The quadrille was the popular social dance of the time, and balls took place most often in hotels, such as Donegana's, Rasco's (later known as Clifton's), and the famous St Lawrence Hall.[83] Visiting performers would hire a local band. Even the troupe of "Famous Chinese actors, jugglers and magicians," mentioned above, employed William Hardy's band.

Lavallée may also have been performing in pit orchestras while still in his teens and likely attended English-language productions. In nineteenth-century Montreal, the British middle class and military were keen supporters of the theatre, while the Roman Catholic Church viewed it as a threat to morality.[84] Nevertheless, its efforts to discourage attendance may have had limited success. Discussion in the French-language press suggests that a significant part of the Theatre Royal's audience was French-speaking and enthusiastic.[85] There were several efforts to create permanent French-language theatres during this period. In 1856 a French actor named Gimié created the Théâtre des Variétés in the Faubourg Québec neighbourhood. The first revue opened on 21 July, and for 30 sous (15 for the cheap seats) the audience enjoyed a program made up of *Capitaine François*, a one-act vaudeville, 'Romances nouvelles,' and some 'chansons comiques.' An evening's entertainment usually began with a two- or three-act comedy or drama and concluded with a one-act comedy. Occasionally, soloists would perform during the intermissions. Lavallée made his début as a soloist at such an event.[86]

In the late 1850s, Les Amateurs Canadiens, a theatre ensemble headed by the singer Alexandre Trottier, staged a series of successful productions. They performed their first *soirée dramatique* at the Theatre Royal on 31 December 1858 and followed it with a second in January 1859. In mid-February they advertised their third performance, a program of Claude Lévesque's three-act drama *Vildac* and Jean-Toussaint Merle's one-act comedy *La Carte à payer*, to be held on 28 February under the patronage of His Excellency the Lieutenant-General Sir William Eyre, K.C.B., the commander of the British forces in Canada. The advertisement also mentioned that during the intermission, Henri Gauthier, the conductor of the orchestra, was to play a flute solo and Lavallée was to play one on the piano.[87] The inauspicious debut turned out to be a minor triumph for sixteen-year-old Lavallée. In its review, *Le Pays* did not mention the intermission performance but called the evening an even greater success than the previous performances, noting the presence of Eyre and his *état-major* among the large and enthusiastic audience.[88] *La Minerve* offered equally spirited praise of the actors, but devoted half of its brief review to the entr'acte: "We must not conclude without mentioning the first appearance on a Montreal stage of a young Canadian pianist, Mr Lavallée, of St Hyacinthe; a well-deserved reputation preceded this artist to Montreal, and the different pieces that he played were greeted with thunderous applause; and, to please the avid audience, he was obliged to return to the stage many times. These successes assure him of one of the most distinguished positions among the small number of artists we possess in Canada."[89] It was a bold prediction from this anonymous critic.

Other newspapers made only passing references to the event, and none of the advertisements or reviews mentioned what Lavallée performed that night. Nevertheless, he had his first press clipping in his hand and his career had officially begun.

One can only wonder if members of Lavallée's family were present for his debut. No evidence seems to have survived indicating how often Lavallée returned to Saint-Hyacinthe between 1855 and 1859. During that time, Augustin Lavallée had relocated his business to Cascades Street.[90] His mother had given birth to two sons, Augustin Antoine Joseph Lavallée in 1857, who seems not to have survived, and a year later, Joseph Magloire, who would be known simply as Joseph. Busy with small children and the family business, it seems unlikely that Lavallée's parents visited Montreal often, but perhaps did so when he performed.

Four months after his debut, Lavallée made a much higher profile appearance. The event was the 24 June Saint-Jean-Baptiste Day celebrations. Each year, Montreal's *Fête nationale* festivities would begin at 8 a.m. with music and banners, as members of patriotic and educational organizations marched along a short route leading to Notre-Dame Church, where

Figure 1.4 An advertisement for the 1859 Fête Nationale Concert in Montreal at which 16-year-old Lavallée played the piano.

a Mass would be celebrated. After a day of picnics and family gatherings, the highlight of the evening was a promenade concert and dancing at the City Concert Hall. Advertisements for the 1859 concert listed the performers as comprising amateur vocalists, a quadrille band, an orchestra (under the direction of Henry Prince), and Lavallée – presiding at the piano.[91] (See figure 1.4) And in this case, the promenade concert was not only a celebration of the French-Canadian national day but also a benefit to raise funds for a monument to those who had died in the rebellions of 1837 and 1838. The event may have caused a rift within the membership of the Saint-Jean-Baptiste Society. The Catholic Church had been opposed to the rebellions, and in a letter published in *Le Pays*, a correspondent criticized the concert's organizing committee for politicizing what he felt was a sacred day.[92] Few details emerged of the event's success in raising funds, but it may have been limited, since Lavallée would revive the cause several years later.

Lavallée's activities in the weeks that followed are unknown. He may have been spending some of his time with James Unsworth, who had returned to Montreal to recuperate from an illness. In less than two years, he had risen to the top of the profession, performing in New York with Bryants' Minstrels, the company that had that year given the premiere of "Dixie." Unsworth had carved a niche for himself as a "stump orator," giving satirical commentaries on the political and social events of the day. Given the timing of his return to Montreal, it is possible that he was present at Lavallée's debut at the Theatre Royal. In any event, he returned to New York later that summer, and in the fall both he and Lavallée were in New England: Unsworth in Boston, while Lavallée joined the troupe that Charles Duprez was assembling in Providence, Rhode Island, the New Orleans Minstrels.[93] From there, he set off on what would be an extraordinary adventure to the Deep South.

❖❖❖

Historians usually cite 1843 as the year in which the minstrel show was born. A hastily assembled quartet calling themselves the Virginia Minstrels presented a show at New York's Bowery Theater comprising a collection of satirical skits and songs.[94] Their impersonation of blacks through costumes, dialect, and music was not new to the theatre, but presenting an entire show based on this idea was novel. Throughout its development, the impersonation of blacks remained a defining element.[95] Impersonation was, as historians have claimed, a form of mask that freed the performers to say and do things that would not otherwise be accepted, and their success generated a score of imitators and the rapid standardizing of the genre's features.[96] In recent years, scholars such as Dale Cockrell and William Mahar have revealed some of the complex social layers beneath the racist surface of minstrelsy. It was much more than it seemed, as audiences responded to it in the North and South, on both sides of the Atlantic, and as far away as Australia.

By the 1850s, the minstrel show had become North America's leading form of entertainment and evolved into a highly formalized performance genre. Performers, "blacked up" with burnt cork and dressed in extravagant costumes, formed a line or semi-circle across the stage with an interlocutor in the middle engaging in comic dialogue with the "endmen," "tambo and bones."[97] The show was originally divided into two parts: the first focusing on the urban dandy, the second on the Southern slave. By the late 1850s, this had evolved to a three-part format. The first part was a concert of instrumental and vocal music. The next part was devoted to a variety of comic skits and dances. And the closing section featured a big production, often a satire of a popular opera or other stage work, and usually culminated in a noisy "extravaganza" or "walkabout" bringing all the performers onstage and sometimes through the theatre. Troupes had grown in size, with most having between ten and twenty performers. Filling out the cast were comedians such as the female impersonator, or "wench dancer," clog dancers, musicians, and vocalists. A strong tenor was essential to a troupe's success, and many ballads featured a male vocal quartet (with soprano and alto sung falsetto) at the chorus. Apart from the tambourine, bones, and banjo, the most common instruments were the violin and cornet, both of which Lavallée played.[98]

Lavallée's ability to play a number of instruments made him a valuable asset. He had probably taken part in amateur minstrel performances in Montreal, or even in Saint-Hyacinthe, and was undoubtedly well acquainted with the standard routines and musical styles. He would have learned much about the United States through visitors and acquaintances who lived there. But war was looming as he set out from Canada in

22

1859, and whatever knowledge he had was little preparation for the four-year odyssey of music and mayhem he was embarking upon.

## THE NEW ORLEANS MINSTRELS

We're the boys for pleasure as you shall plainly see,
We always give good measure so happy, light and free.
And when the work is over the senses we will please,
Just like the scented clover that floats among the breeze.
Opening Chorus[99]
Duprez and Green's Minstrels

Despite its name, the New Orleans and Metropolitan Burlesque Opera Troupe and Brass Band (hereafter the New Orleans Minstrels) were based in Providence, Rhode Island. The company formed in the late 1850s, with members drawn mostly from the northeastern United States.[100] Like many travelling troupes, the New Orleans Minstrels toured an average of ten months each year, playing in towns and cities across the continent. During the summer months, the company often performed in the resort town of Rocky Point, Rhode Island. Charles Duprez managed the troupe throughout its twenty-five-year existence. Most sources claim that Duprez was born in Paris and came to North America as a child.[101] They report that the family went first to Canada, where Duprez's father worked in grain shipping and river navigation between Montreal and Quebec City, and then to the United States, where Charles Duprez apprenticed as a tailor before entering show business. Given that most show business biographies involved at least an element of invention, an obituary claiming that Duprez had been born and raised in Lowell, Massachusetts, was likely closer to the truth.[102]

Like other minstrels companies from the northern states, Duprez's troupe had a name that evoked images of the South. If the Virginia Minstrels suggested cotton fields, the New Orleans Minstrels brought to mind the urban South, and Duprez made a point of hiring francophones like Lavallée to help bolster the apparent connection to French-speaking Louisiana. The company's other co-owners were the comedian and stage manager J.G.H. Shorey, the banjo player John Carle, and the tenor Joseph E. Green, a widely known performer whose signature piece was a mockingbird song. The rest of the company's cast of singers, comedians, and instrumentalists changed constantly. Principal attractions in the fall of 1859 included the comic singer Charley Reynolds; John Carle's daughters, Estelle and Celestine (a dance team billed as the "Star Sisters"); and a young clog dancer known as Master Tommy.

Duprez may have taken a little time to decide how best to use Lavallée's talents. Early on, the New Orleans Minstrels advertisements occasionally listed Lavallée as a pianist, and while in upstate New York, he published his first composition, a lively 'polka de salon' titled *La Fleur de mai*.[103] Lavallée dedicated the piece to Martha Ann Laithe (née Squires), a contralto from Troy, New York, whose connection to him remains unknown. The choice of publisher was probably the result of convenience. On 23–24 November, the New Orleans Minstrels performed in Troy, where the music publisher Cluett & Sons had an office. A 26 November notice in the *Troy Daily Times* referred to the piece as "a charming Polka, brilliant, but not too difficult."[104] It achieved sufficient popularity for the publisher to issue a second edition in March.[105] Other compositions would follow, but with *La Fleur de mai* he marked not only the milestone of his first published composition but also his *re*-baptism, from Calixte to Calixa Lavallée.

The teenage musician was now really off on an adventure, travelling by wagon, train, and, occasionally, steamship. Passing through the towns and cities of upstate New York, the troupe crossed into the Midwest as autumn changed into winter.[106] Duprez would often follow a circuitous and seemingly erratic route, sometimes venturing great distances to avoid direct competition with other troupes. (See figure 1.5) But as was normal, the general movement at this time of year was southward. After passing through Kentucky and Tennessee, they boarded a steamer at Memphis to complete the journey down the Mississippi River, arriving in Louisiana in February.

With its tumultuous history, exotic mix of European and African cultures, and reputed decadence, New Orleans was unlike any other city in antebellum America. With a population divided among Anglo-Americans, Europeans, free blacks, and slaves, it was among the most cosmopolitan

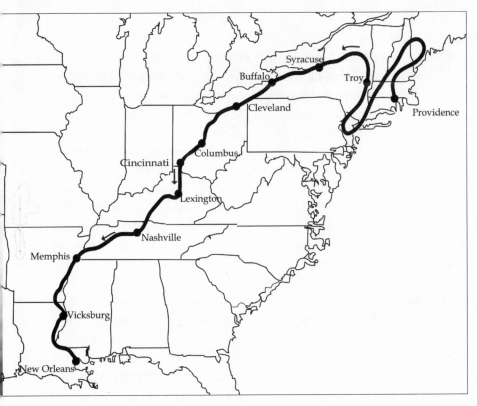

Figure 1.5 The southward route of the New Orleans Minstrels in 1859–60, as Lavallée travelled through the US for the first time.

cities anywhere.[107] It was also known as one of the liveliest. Much of the nightlife was concentrated in the city's many prostitution and gaming houses, or "concert saloons," such as the Napoléon and the Royal Palace Beer Saloon and Concert Hall.[108] But there was also opera. New Orleans was the first North American city with a permanent opera company (established ca. 1793), and by the mid-nineteenth century, productions in French, English, German, and Italian were all common. The city boasted several of the continent's most famous theatres of the nineteenth century: Le Spectacle de la rue Saint-Pierre (ca. 1790), the St Philippe Theatre (1810), the Théâtre d'Orléans (1825), and the St Charles Theater (1835). The last of these venues was a 4,100-seat home for Italian and English opera, built at a cost of $325,000 at a time when the city's population numbered only 20,000.[109] The last great theatre, the opulent New

Opera House (soon known as the French Opera House) was completed in 1859, just prior to Lavallée's arrival. Indeed, the city was flush with cash and entertainment, as resident and itinerant opera troupes, minstrels, actors, and comedians kept the city's halls and theatres crowded through all but the hottest summer months.[110]

With the theatrical season in high gear, Duprez and Green faced considerable competition. On 26 February 1860, the *Times-Picayune* notified its readers of the troupe's arrival: "Their programme is very inviting and promises a rich treat to the lovers of fun, if we may judge from the list of the songs, burlesques, operas, etc. J.G.H. Shorey is the stage manager, and Mons. C. Lavallée musical director."[111] The next night, the company gave its debut performance. It is difficult to know how well the performance was received. On 28 February, the *Picayune* simply noted that they had performed to a "very good audience," and that there was "a good deal of talent among these sixteen minstrels."[112] The *New Orleans Courier* claimed that the troupe had drawn "a very good house" and was "decidedly among the best Ethiopian performers we have seen here."[113] A "good house" in New Orleans was in fact quite lucrative. Whereas Duprez charged an admission price of twenty-five cents for adults almost everywhere else in the country, in New Orleans he doubled it, while admitting children and servants for twenty-five cents. But the venues were booked up and the company was limited to four performances divided between two venues. After two nights at the Odd Fellows' Hall, they had to make way for the child pianist Blind Tom, and move over to Union Hall.[114] After the final show, on 3 March, the troupe began the trek northward along the eastern seaboard. (See figure 1.6)

From Alabama the company made stops in Savannah, Atlanta, Macon, and Augusta, Georgia, before spending a week in Charleston, South Carolina, where the *New York Clipper* reported them to be "averaging $400 per night" at the 2,000-seat Institute Hall – which, if true, would have required nearly sold-out performances.[115] During May they performed in fifteen cities in five states, including a week-long engagement at Philadelphia's Concert Hall. After performances in Williamsburgh, New York (now part of Brooklyn), they closed the tour in Connecticut and returned to their summer base at Rocky Point, Rhode Island. We have no records of whether or not Lavallée returned home for a holiday after this long

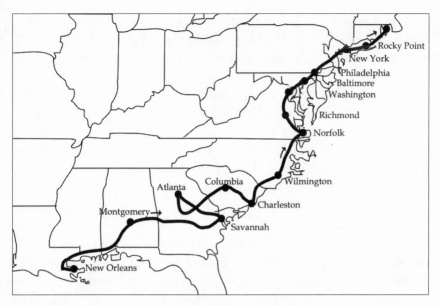

Figure 1.6 The New Orleans Minstrels return route in the spring of 1860 from New Orleans to the summer resort town of Rocky Point, Rhode Island.

tour. It was common for members to do so, and he would certainly have had stories to tell, but there are no references to him in the Montreal newspapers that summer; he may simply have chosen to continue working during the lucrative summer season.

Late in the summer of 1860, Duprez began advertising the forthcoming tour of what he termed the "Most Complete and Largest Minstrel Troupe in the World."[116] The 1860–61 tour was to be more extensive than that of the previous year: this time the troupe was to be "on the move for the West, South, and the Island of Cuba."[117] Duprez elevated Lavallée's position, listing him as "1st violinist, 1st alto horn player, and musical director of the troupe," and referring to him as "a modern Thalberg, whose difficult execution on the pianoforte surpasses all belief."[118] He also hired George Lavallée, quite possibly a cousin of Calixa, to play violin in the orchestra and baritone horn in the ten-piece brass band that was then being led by John Pratt. The most notable change in personnel was the departure of John Carle. Quite possibly sensing the trouble that lay ahead, he quietly sold his share in the troupe to Duprez and returned with his daughters to their native Pittsburgh.[119] Nevertheless, the troupe was expanded, with J.G.H. Shorey taking over as tambo, Charles Bovée as 'brudder bones,' E.N. Slocum as interlocutor, and L.J. Donnelly as the wench dancer.

Lavallée's second tour with the Duprez troupe followed a route similar to that of the previous year and initially achieved much the same success. The newly abbreviated Shorey, Duprez, and Green company travelled first through the cities of New England, in September, before moving into New York State, again along the northern route, then down into western Pennsylvania. During their engagement at Pittsburgh's Masonic Hall, the *New York Clipper*'s correspondent wrote that they were playing to large audiences. He described the troupe as being among the best then touring "and with a few desirable changes in the company, will rank as one of the very best in the business."[120] He did not indicate precisely where changes should be made, although subsequent events point to Shorey as a liability. Otherwise, the programs featured burlesques of operas, such as Verdi's *Un ballo in maschera* (*The Masked Ball*), and a parody of the popular Italian soprano Maria Piccolomini. Other acts focused on current events. The recent opening up of Japan to the West and the arrival in the US of Japanese diplomats were hot topics for minstrel shows, and their most extravagant skit that fall was titled "Japanese Embassy."[121] In an age when ethnic humour was the norm, it seems that nothing could be funnier than white men with blackened faces impersonating Asians.

Politics and internal disputes began to threaten the troupe's success as it travelled southwest. They were in Indiana on 6 November when Abraham Lincoln was elected president. From there, they continued southward into the developing maelstrom that saw South Carolina break from the Union on 20 December. Just a few days later, the troupe experienced its own upheavals when Shorey made an acrimonious departure while at Baton Rouge. Without discussing the nature of the dispute, Duprez announced the split six weeks later in the 16 February 1861 issue of the *New York Clipper*, stating that it had been "brewing for some time." In the same issue, Shorey alleged that Duprez forced troupe members to go unpaid, and had "swindled him" by not giving him the full amount of his share in the troupe. A week later, Lavallée and twelve other cast members published a "Card to the Public," claiming to have agreed to work for their board as a *ruse* by which to force Shorey out of the company, "on account of his incapability as a performer or manager."[122] Given Duprez's reputed parsimony, Shorey may have had a case, but other members remained with the troupe and the re-formed Duprez & Green's New Orleans and Metropolitan Burlesque Opera Troupe continued the tour. From his home in Great Falls, New Hampshire, Shorey issued a notice calling Duprez "a scoundrel and a swindler, and," perhaps with no irony intended, "one of the lowest specimens of a pretended white man that ever travelled."[123] He and Duprez continued to debate the issue publicly with each threatening legal action as the country itself fell into chaos.[124]

Following South Carolina's lead, between 10 and 12 January, Mississippi, Florida, and Alabama had all seceded from the Union. The company was performing in Atlanta when Georgia seceded on 19 January.[125] Although one might expect attendance at theatrical performances to have plummeted as a result of the political upheaval, the troupe's shows were more popular than ever. The *Atlanta Confederacy* reported the Athenaeum to have been "crowded to its utmost capacity." The newspaper claimed these performances to be a timely distraction for the citizens, without which they "would have shortly been in a state of stark madness from political super-excitement," and urged the public to attend the final performance "and prolong life by the full and wholesome exercise of all your laughing powers."[126] The company enjoyed continued success with other stops in the South. A six-night engagement in Savannah, Georgia, was followed with another in Charleston, South Carolina. At the latter, Duprez reported his first night's receipts to be $600.[127] Even if the actual gate was only half of that reported, it was a substantial sum given the circumstances under which the troupe was performing.

On 4 February 1861, the *Charleston Daily Courier* reported that Duprez had extended his engagement at Secession Hall (previously known as Institute Hall) by three days to meet the demand. It noted that, "at this period, when so much engrosses and absorbs attention, no common entertainment could commend even partial success here."[128] The same column also noted that that evening's performance would include the premiere of a new state song, titled "Our Flag." It was not clear if this was the song composed by the popular singer Harry Macarthy or another of the same title.[129] The 6 February *Courier* reported that the troupe performed "this stirring and patriotic song to a large and delighted auditory."[130] From the "rapturous applause with which it was greeted," the reporter predicted that the song would become very popular and urged readers to go and hear it that evening. For Lavallée, the event undoubtedly had much resonance. The political intensity of the moment, and its expression in song, was a recurring theme in his life.

From South Carolina, the company had continued northward as news arrived that Jefferson Davis had been elected the provisional president of the Confederacy and inaugurated at Montgomery, Alabama, on 18 February. They closed a five-day engagement at Washington, DC's Odd Fellows' Hall on 2 March, just two days before Abraham Lincoln's inauguration, and were in New York State on 12 April when news arrived that federal troops guarding Fort Sumter, in Charleston Harbor, had been fired on and that the war had begun. None of these events seem to have caused Duprez much concern. Public perception at the time was that the conflict could not last very long, and the troupe had been enormously successful while in the South. Rather than returning to their summer home of Rocky Point, the company continued through upstate New York and back down into Ohio with plans to return to the South.

The excitement building up over several months had a powerful effect on music publishing, as patriotic songs and piano pieces flooded the market. Many of these still evoke strong images of the conflict. Some of the most enduring patriotic songs, such "Battle Hymn of the Republic," "Bonny Blue Flag," and "Maryland, My Maryland," relied on existing music. More often than being sung, these and other songs of the era were performed by bands in instrumental arrangements. Louis Moreau Gottschalk – a Unionist despite his New Orleans origins – toured the northern states and Canada through much of the war years and frequently closed his concerts with *L'Union, paraphrase de concert*, op. 48, in which he quotes several patriotic songs and at the finale combines "Yankee Doodle" in the right hand with "Hail, Columbia" in the left.[131] Some instrumental works, such as Blind Tom's *The Battle of Manassas*, depicted the events of the war.[132]

In May, Lavallée composed and published the first of several war-related compositions. His *Col. Ellsworth Gallopade* was one of many musical tributes to the Union's first martyr, the twenty-four-year-old Colonel

Elmer Ephraim Ellsworth. After he was shot while pulling down a Confederate flag from a lodging house in Alexandria, Virginia, his death sparked a flurry of songs and poems.[133] The New Orleans Minstrels were in the Union state of Ohio at the time, and E.P. Danks of Cleveland published Lavallée's homage, its cover featuring an engraving of the soldier holding the US flag. (See figure 1.7) It was the first of several pieces that Lavallée composed in the popular galop, or gallopade, form: a quick dance in 2/4 time, with the right hand providing the melody and the left hand supporting with an "oom-pah" or stride bass accompaniment. It is a surprisingly cheerful piece of music, given that it is a piece memorializing a hero killed in battle. Later that year, the S.T. Gordon firm, of New York, published two more of Lavallée's piano compositions. Although in a popular style, Lavallée's *The First Welcome*, a 'polka characteristique,' is technically demanding, as are many of his piano compositions. Unlike other pieces, it is programmatic, with the various sections labelled with puzzling descriptive titles, such as "Among the Rocks" and "Au Revair" [*sic*].[134] The other piece, *The War Fever*, is unambiguous. It is a raucous galop, in which Lavallée evokes the intensity of the times through performance indications such as *attacca subito*, *furioso* and *con tutta forza* and by utilizing the full pitch and dynamic ranges of the instrument.[135] (See figure 1.8)

If the war was providing inspiration for composers and songwriters, it was also beginning to make life difficult for performers. The armies increasingly used theatres for recruiting, and the war dampened the public's interest in entertainment. On 27 April 1861, the *New York Clipper*'s city column began: "We are in the midst of a war excitement, and the week closed heavily in the entertainment world. Every place of amusement felt the depressing effects of the fearful news daily received from the seat of hostilities; in some of the theatres the falling off in the attendance being very large. The war, the mustering of soldiers, and the leave takings of relatives and friends, swallowed up everything else, and the people had enough to engage their time and attention without going to the theatres."[136] For a travelling troupe the situation was worse still, as troops filled the trains and military convoys clogged the roads. In June, the *New York Clipper* reported that John Shorey's new troupe had disbanded, having "succumbed to the pressure of the times."[137] The solution for some

Figure 1.7  The cover of Lavallée's first Civil War–era published composition, dedicated to the Union martyr Colonel Elmer Ephraim Ellsworth.

Figure 1.8 The introductory measures of Lavallée's *The War Fever*, with allusions to the conflict then taking place in the US.

performers was to go to Europe; many others went north. The *New York Clipper* noted that there was "an exodus of showmen from the US to Canada and the Provinces" taking place, with at least twenty-seven recently in Saint John, New Brunswick.[138] Duprez and Green decided to conclude their tour while in Ohio. The *Clipper* reported that "owing to the pressure of the times," Duprez had decided not to go to Hannibal, Missouri, as planned. It gave no further details, but travelling in so-called border states was increasingly dangerous.[139] They turned back to the northeast, closing the tour patriotically, with a 4 July performance in Providence. There, they announced plans to "rusticate" on Rhode Island over the summer and begin a tour of the east coast of Canada and the West Indies in September. Over the previous few months, the *New York Clipper* had listed the arrival of several letters for Lavallée at its New York office, a service they provided for touring performers. We might expect that they came from his family, naturally concerned about his safety. If they were hoping he would return to Canada, they would be disappointed. He remained on Rhode Island through the summer, but only days before the tour was to begin, he quit the troupe for a new adventure, this time in a regimental band.

❖❖❖

## THE BAND OF THE FOURTH RHODE ISLAND REGIMENT

Beat! beat! drums! – blow! bugles! blow!
Through the windows – through doors – burst like a ruthless force,
Into the solemn church, and scatter the congregation,

Into the school where the scholar is studying;
Leave not the bridegroom quiet – no happiness must he have now with his bride,
Nor the peaceful farmer any peace, ploughing his field or gathering his grain,
So fierce you whirr and pound you drums – so shrill you bugles blow.

*Leaves of Grass*
Walt Whitman

On 17 September 1861, just three months shy of his nineteenth birthday, Lavallée entered Providence's High Street recruiting office and enlisted for three years of service in the band of the Fourth Rhode Island Regiment.[140] We do not know why Lavallée chose to take part in a conflict in a country where he had lived for only two years. Many Canadians joined the thousands of other foreigners on both sides of the conflict – most in the better-financed Union Army.[141] The clergy in Quebec did their best to discourage French Canadians from enlisting, fearing it would lead to emigration and assimilation in what many thought to be an immoral society.[142] As Lavallée was already residing in the US, he was free to make his own decisions. At a time when professional prospects were dwindling, an advertisement appeared in local newspapers that caught Lavallée's eye. Two twenty-four-piece bands were being recruited. Six of the musicians would be paid $34 per month, six would be paid $20, and twelve would be paid $17, presumably based on skill.[143] Financially, it looked a much better prospect than Duprez's planned tour of Newfoundland outports, and for someone of Lavallée's temperament, it undoubtedly looked like much more of an adventure. Among the few surviving primary sources of this time in his life are his war records and a photograph of him in uniform. (See figure 1.9) In this, the first known photograph of Lavallée, taken when he was about eighteen years old, he appears very much the proud Union bandsman, if still somewhat uncertain, as he looks into the camera.

In his history of American song, the musicologist Charles Hamm wrote, "in no other war in American history has music played such an important role among the men involved in the campaigns and battles."[144] He might well have extended the assertion to any conflict. Lincoln's second call for troops, in April 1861, inspired George Frederick Root's "Battle Cry of Freedom," and marching bands helped to build the sense

Figure 1.9
A photograph of Lavallée
in a Union Army uniform,
probably dating from
soon after he enrolled
in the band of the 4th
Rhode Island Regiment
in the fall of 1861.

of urgency and patriotism needed to attract 75,000 fresh volunteers. Having a band parade through town playing spirited renditions of "The Star-Spangled Banner" proved an effective means of gaining the public's attention and stirring enthusiasm for the cause. In fact, it proved so successful that a regiment without its own band would have to hire one to help with recruitment. The Forty-fourth Massachusetts paid $3,000 for the temporary services of the famous Flagg's Band. Others gained the services of well-known bands or musicians on a longer term basis. The Thirteenth Massachusetts had several members of the Germania Band, while the Twenty-fourth Massachusetts recruited Patrick Gilmore's celebrated ensemble.[145]

In Rhode Island, the American Brass Band (ABB) was considered the state's finest ensemble. Led by the bugler Joseph C. Greene, the ABB had travelled to Washington, DC, in April 1861, accompanying the First Rhode

Island Regiment. Greene had led the band since 1838 and served for three months with this regiment.[146] On his return to Providence, later that summer, he agreed to recruit musicians for the Third and Fourth Rhode Island regiments and to lead the band of the Fourth. At forty-one, Greene was the eldest of the Fourth's twenty-one band members. Others ranged in age from eighteen to forty, with most being in their early twenties.[147] George Lavallée joined the same regiment the day before Calixa. (As it was common to anglicize foreign names, both were enlisted as Levalley.) Given Greene's reputation, aside from the Lavallées, some of these young men were probably also professional musicians. Military records contain no details of what the individual members played. Standard instrumentation of regimental bands consisted of bugles (E-flat and B-flat) and over-the-shoulder-style horns (alto, tenor, and bass) and tubas, with drums and perhaps trombones or a clarinet.[148]

From the High Street recruitment office, the new enlistees reported to Camp Greene, just outside of Providence. In his eloquent history of the regiment, George H. Allen described the heady and naive atmosphere at the camp, filled with visiting families: "Indeed, each day seemed a holiday, and as we young soldiers were the centre of observation, in our bran [sic] new suits of blue, and on duty with our muskets and new equipments [sic], we thought there was nothing so nice as the life of a soldier."[149] The "holiday" lasted only until the beginning of October when the regiment, under the command of Col. Justus I. McCarty, was reported full. On 5 October, led by their regimental band, the 1,200 new recruits marched into Providence and boarded the *Commodore* at Fox Point Wharf.[150] The steamer transported them to New York where they transferred to trains to complete their journey to Washington, DC.

The condition of the capital took some members by surprise. "We were soon greeted with the first view of the huge, half-finished dome of the Capitol building, looming high in the air not far away," Allen reported.[151] Lavallée was familiar with Washington after stops there with Duprez's troupe. Other members of the Fourth were unimpressed with their first view of the capital: "Fancy our surprise at seeing so few large buildings, no parks or fountains, very few of what might be called handsome blocks, plenty of low, flat, or shed-roofed houses, of all sizes, shapes, and conditions, plenty of filthy mud and pond holes, with plenty of ducks, geese, hogs, and dirty juveniles wallowing therein."[152] From the train depot they marched to Camp Sprague, and the next day continued on to Camp Casey, on the outskirts of the capital, to begin two months of basic training. There, while soldiers drilled, the musicians rehearsed and played for reviews. They had their first important performances on 18 October, when the Fourth and Second Rhode Island regiments and a Pennsylvania Battery were reviewed first by Governor Sprague of Rhode Island, and later that day by President Lincoln. They were mustered into service on 30 October at Upper Marlboro, Maryland, having marched there the previous day, and where their first assignment was to help preserve order during the 6 November election that would see Jefferson Davis elected to a six-year term as president of the Confederacy.[153]

Real action came at the end of November when General Ambrose E. Burnside selected the Fourth Rhode Island Regiment to participate in his North Carolina Campaign. Lavallée's regiment joined with the Fifth Rhode Island and the Eighth and Eleventh Connecticut regiments to form the third brigade of the Coast Division. Allen described the mood as jubilant on the morning of 9 January 1862 as they steamed out of Annapolis, Maryland, on board the *Eastern Queen*, bound for the North Carolina coast. As the ship weighed anchor, "we broke out into cheers and shouts," he wrote, "while our musicians of the band blared to the extent of their lungs, and our steamer proudly swept on down the bay with all colors flying."[154] At Fortress Monroe, on the Virginia coast, the barely seaworthy vessel merged with the rest of the makeshift fleet. It was soon pounded by violent winter storms along the North Carolina coast, but on its way to victories at Roanoke Island and New Bern in February and March. The adjutant general described the latter as an intense battle during which the Fourth established itself "by an impetuous bayonet charge [that] decided the fate of the day."[155] Disease was also taking many lives and the band lost at least one member to typhoid in April.[156] In May, the regiment took part in the bombardment and surrender of Fort Macon, and for a time remained encamped there in what was considered a healthier environment, before moving on to capture towns and cities in North Carolina through the summer months. Henry J. Spooner, a young lieutenant sent to the regiment late in the summer of

1862, later described the Fourth as already "a veteran regiment," having "earned a high reputation" in its campaign along the coast.[157]

Throughout these battles Lavallée and the other musicians rarely played direct roles in combat. When a battle was expected, they helped to set up the field hospital and served as an ambulance corps.[158] While encamped or on the march, bands took part in many aspects of the regiment's activities. They would often lead the regiment out of bivouac, play serenades for officers, and perform on the parade ground and at other ceremonies. Beginning with *reveille*, they played a series of daily calls, announcing duties and meals, *tattoo*, or evening roll call, and *taps* at 'lights out.' They were also responsible for 'drumming out' deserters and for performing at funerals and executions, after which they would play some uplifting tunes to lighten the mood. None of this would have been entirely new to Lavallée, who had been around marching bands all his life, and who had had frequent opportunities to hear British military bands in Montreal.

In several anecdotes, Allen reveals something of the band's role in the life of the regiment. On the morning of 3 July 1862, while at Beaufort, North Carolina, the regiment was misinformed that Richmond, the Confederate capital, had fallen. "In a few minutes the streets and wharves were filled with soldiers and citizens, cheering, shaking hands, and congratulating each other on the joyful event," wrote Allen. "The band came out in force, and the inspiring notes of 'Hail Columbia,' and the 'Star Spangled Banner,' floated joyfully through the morning air, and were echoed by a rousing salute of forty-four guns from across the harbour."[159] The next day they learned that the report had been a mistake, and to bolster morale they marched to the city's main street where they listened to a reading of the Declaration of Independence. Allen reports: "After the reading was over, we formed into a column of companies and marched through the principal streets of the town to the inspiring music of our band. In the evening the band closed the exercises of the day by turning out in antique costume, and marching through the town, playing all sorts of – anything but music – to the great amusement of soldiers and citizens, and the uproarious delight of the colored population: and thus ended the day."[160] Allen did not elaborate on what he considered "antique" costumes and was at a loss for words to describe the music. His recounting of these events suggests the band was performing something like a minstrel show walkabout, a routine that he might not have been familiar with but which Lavallée would have been well prepared to organize.

By the summer of 1862, bugles and horns had become nearly as ubiquitous as muskets and cannons. Vigorous recruiting during the early months of the war had attracted many of country's professional and amateur musicians. One source estimated that in July 1862 there were 618 bands in the Union Army, comprising nearly 15,000 bandsmen.[161] When whole divisions were encamped together during 1861 and 1862 the number of regimental bands located in the same physical space could produce an impressive volume of sound. This was especially true of the Army of the Potomac. Recounting his experiences as bandleader for the 114th Pennsylvania Regiment (also known as P.V. Collis's Zouaves), Frank Rauscher described the situation in the early years of the war, when there were between thirty-six and forty bands in each army corps: "When a division was encamped in a small space, which was frequently the case when on the march, and the band of each regiment performing at the same time at Regimental Headquarters, the effect of the confusion of sounds produced can hardly be imagined."[162] The numbers of musicians and their effect may have inspired Patrick Gilmore's massive festivals of 1869 and 1872 and the post-war experiments of George Ives (father of the composer Charles Ives), then the very young leader of a Connecticut regimental band.

The federal government had realized that the large number of musicians was causing a financial burden quite early in the war.[163] In August 1861, the War Department began to slowly trim the number of regimental bands and on 2 October, only two weeks after Lavallée enlisted, the adjutant general's office banned further enlistment of bands for volunteer regiments. This still left a lot of musicians in the military. By 1862, with expenses running out of control, the paymaster called for the abolition of the regimental bands, citing a potential saving of $5,000,000 per year.[164] Following passage of a bill by Congress on 17 July 1862, the War Department issued General Order 91, on 29 July.[165] Each volunteer brigade – three regiments and one artillery unit, in most cases – was allowed only sixteen musicians, and within a month of the decree, many band members were on their way home. In early July, Greene returned to Providence to recruit new musicians for the brigade band, and raise funds for new instruments. In his absence, George Lavallée was among those discharged from the Fourth Rhode Island and was mustered out of service along with several other band members on 16 August 1862. With Greene still in Rhode Island, Calixa, however, remained for what would be the bloodiest single day of the war.[166]

Antietam has figured prominently in many histories of the Civil War, and in most writings about Lavallée.[167] His march towards that catastrophic event began in July 1862, when the Fourth Rhode Island Regiment joined General George McClellan's Army of the Potomac. By mid August, Lavallée was among the 90,000 Union troops in and around Washington, DC, waiting for what many considered the inevitable assault from General Robert E. Lee's Confederate forces. Henry Spooner later recalled that it "was almost universally feared that the capital would fall into the hands of the enemy and the war would be transferred to Northern soil. Local newspapers and citizens echoed the general apprehensions that the most serious crisis of the war had arrived and that the Union cause was in imminent peril."[168] Spooner arrived in Washington on 4 September and later described the city as then resembling "a great military camp, full of bustle and activity." He located the Fourth Rhode Island Regiment in bivouac on a suburban hillside, three days before orders arrived to break camp. On 7 September, the regiment joined the long column of infantry, artillery, cavalry, and supply wagons that rolled out of Washington in slow pursuit of the Confederate army.

The battle took place from dawn till dusk at Sharpsburg, Maryland, on 17 September. Three days earlier, on 14 September, after several days of scattered fighting, Lee had stopped and positioned his army to engage McClellan's forces on rolling farmland between the Potomac River and Antietam Creek, about fifty kilometres from Washington.[169] McClellan waited until the morning of 17 September before launching a series of piecemeal attacks during which combatants slaughtered each other in greater numbers than at any other time in the war, with Union casualties estimated at 12,000, while 10,000 Confederates were killed, wounded, or captured.[170] In the end, the rebels did not attempt to push further. Facing far larger numbers of Union forces still waiting in reserve, Lee's troops rested and helped their wounded back across the Potomac into Virginia before withdrawing during the night of 18 September.

Several writers have claimed that Lavallée was among the wounded on 17 September.[171] The story may have originated with Lavallée himself, as

40

we will see a little later. Although his war records provide no evidence, it may have been true. Officially, the regiment's casualties that day numbered 102, with seven more taken prisoner. Spooner, however, wrote that there was "scarcely one of our officers or men engaged who did not bear the mark of at least one bullet upon some part of his clothing or equipments [sic]."[172] According to Wise and Lord, some of the Federal bands had accompanied troops into battle at Antietam.[173] If musicians of the Fourth crossed Antietam Creek, into the heart of the raging battle, it would likely have been to retrieve the injured. If Lavallée was himself wounded, the injury did not prevent him from soon being discharged.

Over the next two weeks, the Fourth Rhode Island Regiment remained at Sharpsburg, tending to the wounded, burying the dead, and waiting for Lincoln. The president arrived from Washington on 1 October to spend four days inspecting troops. He visited Burnside's corps on Friday, 3 October, and later that day the remaining members of the Fourth Rhode Island Regiment Volunteer Band were mustered out of service.[174] For Lavallée, the war had reached a horrific climax, exactly a year to the day after he had enlisted back in Providence, and ended with the close of Lee's Maryland campaign.

❖❖❖

DUPREZ AND GREEN'S MINSTRELS

The minstrel's returned from the war,
With spirits as buoyant as air;
And thus on his tuneful guitar,
He sings in the bower of his fair.
"The Minstrel's Returned from the War"
John Hewitt

Over the previous year, Duprez had kept his troupe together under what must have been very difficult conditions. They had not gone to the West Indies in the fall of 1861, as planned, possibly due to the complexity of travelling along the east coast in the early months of the war. Instead, they went north, travelling by steamer from Boston to Newfoundland, and spending the next six months there, in Nova Scotia, and in New

Brunswick. The *New York Clipper* reported their return to the United States in April 1862, noting vaguely that "although a tedious trip, [it] seems to have remunerated them."[175] They remained in the northeast throughout the summer months. Despite advertising a cast of "25 star performers," Duprez continued to recruit cast members.[176] Over the course of the summer he may have somehow been in contact with Lavallée. Only two days after Lavallée's discharge from his regiment at Sharpsburg, Duprez advertised him as the New Orleans Minstrels' bandleader at the tour's opening date at Providence.[177]

Lavallée joined a large and still-changing cast. Top billing went to the contortionist known as "Signor Monteverde, The Great Spanish India Rubber Man." Comedians Harry Slate and Billy West played as tambo and bones, respectively. John Kelk had taken over as musical director in Lavallée's absence. The thirty-two-year-old French baritone Gustave Bidaux, had joined Duprez in the summer of 1862 and served as stage manager.[178] He had arrived in the US in the late 1850s, hoping to make a career in opera. Among his big numbers was "Largo al Factotum," Figaro's entrance piece from Rossini's *The Barber of Seville*. With the war breaking out, he made a speciality of national anthems, singing "La Marseillaise," "God Save the Queen," and "The Star-Spangled Banner," with fellow minstrels as chorus. He and Lavallée were likely quite close and collaborated on a number of pieces. They posed together for a photograph, both wearing medals that they may have just been awarded.[179] (See figure 1.10) It is the only known photograph of Lavallée holding a violin, the instrument he would have played most often at this time.

The company remained in the Northeast through the fall as Duprez completed arrangements for a tour that was to take the company to the West Indies and South America.[180] For reasons that remain unknown, this trip fell through. In its place, Duprez opted for a winter engagement at New Orleans's Academy of Music, and on 25 November the company sailed from New York's Pier 13 on the merchant steamship *Bio Bio*, bound for Louisiana.[181] After a stop in Key West, Florida, they landed in New Orleans on 5 December and announced their arrival and impending engagement by giving an impromptu concert at the office of each newspaper between the pier and the Academy of Music.[182]

Since their previous visit to New Orleans, nearly two years earlier, the formerly thriving city had been devastated by the war.[183] Through 1861,

Figure 1.10 Lavallée and the French vocalist Gustave Bidaux, who joined the New Orleans Minstrels in 1862.

it had been depopulated as thousands of the city's men enlisted. At the same time, the economy had collapsed under the Federal blockade. And then, in the spring of 1862, Union forces captured the city. General Benjamin Franklin Butler – known to many as "the beast" – governed the city for seven months, before being replaced by the more conciliatory

General Nathaniel P. Banks. Gradually, the citizens of New Orleans had begun to adjust to the occupation. Some of the theatres reopened, and in November Christy's Minstrels played an engagement at the Varieties Theater, closing only a week before Duprez's company arrived.

At first the New Orleans Minstrels were well received. The *New Orleans Bee* reported large audiences at the Academy, noting the popularity of Bidaux, Green, Slate, and Campbell.[184] In a lengthy review, the *Daily True Delta* reported a full house for opening night and called the entire troupe "first class," praising the company's musicianship and singing, and singling out a number of performers, among them, Green ("a very sweet, sympathetic tenor for ballads, and manages it with marked and judicious control"), Harry Slate ("a favorite at once"), and Fred Florence, who was said to dance "with almost bewitching grace" the Spanish burlesque "La Madrilena." It also noted, however, that "twenty-two days at sea, the hurry and bustle of getting up the river, the want of time to rest or prepare before giving their first performance, &c., had told heavily on some of them – especially Mr Bidaux."[185]

The *New York Clipper* reported on Duprez's initial success in New Orleans, while observing that "business generally is quite dull."[186] Duprez's only competition was Lewis Baker's dramatic company, which was then performing at the Varieties Theater and appeared not to have been doing very well. Christy's Minstrels had suffered a similar fate in November, and had cut their ticket prices to help fill the hall. Duprez soon did the same as business began to decline. He had set ticket prices at the pre-war ticket level of fifty cents (or twenty-five cents in the "colored gallery"), which few could now afford. Worse still, several cast members had fallen ill en route. Bidaux had not recovered quickly, and soon Lavallée too fell ill.[187] By January they both seem to have not only recovered but also written a burlesque called "Don Giovanni of Portugal," a piece that gave Bidaux a new opportunity to exploit his abilities in Italian comic opera.[188] The *New York Clipper* reported that the company was doing only "a trifle better."[189] A little later that month, Duprez faced additional competition when Commodore Foote's Troupe opened at Spalding and Rogers's Museum, adjoining the Academy.

"Commodore Foote" (Charles Nestel) and "Colonel Small" (Joseph Huntler) were diminutive entertainers cast from the same mould as P.T.

Barnum's Tom Thumb. The impresario "Colonel William K. Ellinger" managed the pair, having acquired them to exhibit at his Baltimore variety hall, Ellinger's Continental Opera House.[190] He produced a promotional booklet that described his altruistic devotion to the education and cultivation of the two unfortunate young men, and demonstrated it on stage.[191] Ellinger blended the banter of the little comedians with music. His sixteen-year-old daughter, Mary Ellinger, played the piano and sang, sometimes performing novelty acts such as simultaneously playing different tunes with each hand, or playing the piano with one hand and castanets with the other.[192] These attractions might have gone over well in 1860, but times were hard. On 12 January, the *Bee* reported: "We perceive that an arrangement has been entered into by which the visitors of the minstrels may also enjoy a night of the two Lilliputian wonders."[193] That Ellinger and Duprez decided to pool their resources rather than compete gives an indication of how well – or poorly – they were doing. The company retained the name the New Orleans Minstrels while advertisements featured Foote and Small, Ellinger became Duprez's ticket seller and treasurer, and the newly combined company continued on at the Academy for another two weeks.

The *New York Clipper* later concluded that business in New Orleans never really improved "with the exception of the holidays," but put a positive spin on the outcome, claiming that the company had turned a small profit on the trip and could be "perfectly satisfied, taking the times into consideration."[194] There could be truth in the latter part of the statement, if in fact they did make a profit. There is little doubt that they were playing mostly to very small audiences in a city where many were still struggling to survive. For their final Saturday evening performance, on 24 January 1863, they gave a benefit for Green and Lavallée. A few days later, they sailed for the Northeast, performing a brief engagement at Havana's Villanueva Theatre, before continuing on to New York.[195]

Before the war, Duprez had avoided travelling through the Northeast in the winter months. Now forced to change their practice, the company enjoyed a profitable winter season in the North. Opening in Newark, New Jersey, they performed several engagements around metropolitan New York before travelling up the Hudson River, through Vermont, and into Canada. (See figure 1.11) Minstrelsy remained as popular as ever in Canada,

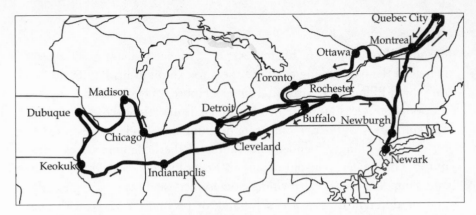

Figure 1.11 A map showing the route of the tour that brought the
New Orleans Minstrels back to Canada in the winter of 1863, as they
avoided the Civil War in the US.

and in Montreal Duprez was able to extend the engagement by three
nights.[196] Reports of his successes sometimes took on a comic tone. The
*New York Clipper* of 21 March claimed that the company's engagement
at Quebec City's Music Hall (where they were "surrounded by mountains of snow and ice") produced "the best [business] they have done
since their organization," and two weeks later reported the troupe to
have amassed such an amount of money that "they hired a sleigh to convey it to the depot."[197] During the company's visit to Quebec City the
previous spring, *L'Écho du Cabinet de lecture paroissial* had reported
that "all these companies succeed here," and among the audience members on opening night were many people one might expect to have more
refined tastes.[198] Rather than lamenting this situation, as one might expect, he not only noted that it was justified by the generally high standard
of performance, but also suggested that members of the city's oratorio
society might benefit from hearing them. In the early months of 1863, the
minstrel business was more competitive than ever, leading many performers to jump to better paying companies. Kellogg and West left
Duprez's troupe while in Quebec City and were replaced with two Montreal musicians, Alphonse Bergeron and J. Camille.[199] In upstate New
York, the company lost Harry Slate but recruited 'star' comedians Lew
Benedict and Charley Reynolds. When John Kelk left, Lavallée returned
to the post of musical director while remaining leader of the brass band
as the troupe passed through the Midwest.

Duprez seems to have taken a highly pragmatic position on the American Civil War, depending on where the troupe was performing. At the start of the war, the company was performing pro-Confederacy songs while in the South. Their 1862 programs eschewed references to the war, especially while in occupied New Orleans. Their 1863 and 1864 programs, performed in the North, contained numerous war-related numbers. Mixed in with the purely comic elements of the 1863 program were numerous references to the conflict, beginning with the opening overture, the "Downfall of Fort Sumter." (See figure 1.12) The 1863 songster includes the texts of several war ballads, such as "Kiss Me, Mother, e're I'm Dead" ("Mother oh, we bravely battled / Battled till the day was done / While the leaden hail storm rattled / Man to man, and gun to gun"), and comic songs as well.[200] A program reproduced in the company's 1864 songster lists two of the wartime pieces: Charley Reynolds's comic song "How Are You, Conscript?" and Green's "Bugle Song." The program shows the troupe performing two war-related scenes: "The Returned Contrabands!" – a comic reference to General Benjamin Butler's recently coined term for slaves, and "The Dying Young Hero!" a miniature melodrama intended for Union audiences. Its three parts touched a range of emotions: from the sentimental ballad "Oh, Mother, I've Come Home to Die" to the upbeat "The Young Hero" and concluding with the exuberant "Fight for Uncle Abe." They closed the evening's performance with burlesques that appear to have been unrelated to the events of the war, allowing the audience to leave in a lighthearted mood.[201]

We do not know how much music Lavallée composed during this time. The songsters that were sold at performances usually provided only the words of the songs and the dialogue of skits. They rarely indicated who had composed the music that was being sung. Lavallée achieved some success in 1863 with the song "Do I Love You?" in which he collaborated with Finley Johnson, a lyricist who in 1862 had authored a Union version of "Maryland, My Maryland."[202] "Do I Love You?" was published by the New York firm of Wm A. Pond & Company, and it has many of the characteristics of the era's sentimental ballads: extravagant lyrics ("Do I love you? / Madly, wildly, dearer than I love my soul"), a simple melody with four-part harmonies (SATB) at the chorus, and a dedication to a young woman on the cover of the sheet music (in this case,

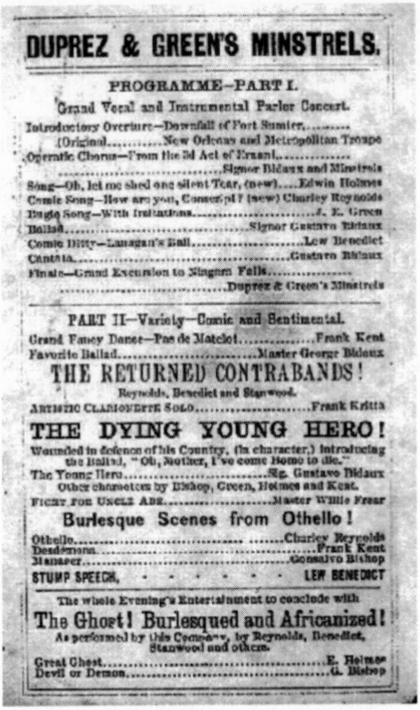

Figure 1.12 *Left and opposite* A New Orleans Minstrels' wartime program, listing some of the Union-oriented numbers the company performed while in the northern states.

to "Miss Jennie King, of Washington, DC"). The cover of the Pond edition also announced that it was sung "with great success" by the popular vocalist Sherwood Campbell.[203] The lyrics were published in Duprez & Green's 1863 songster and Bidaux performed the song as the troupe travelled through the Midwest.[204] The same year, Lavallée also collaborated with Bidaux on "A Hero's Death," although this song seems to have remained unpublished.

The war itself was never far from anyone's thoughts. Duprez now made a conscious effort to avoid it. Rather than continue down the Mississippi, this time the New Orleans Minstrels followed an unfamiliar route further west than they had previously travelled. In late April they performed in Chicago for the first time.[205] If this four-night engagement was a success, many others in the small towns of the Midwest ran no more than a night or two, where they were in competition with other travelling companies. And although the route was chosen to minimize direct contact with the war, such could not be completely avoided. Even far

# DUPREZ & GREEN'S MINSTRELS

PROGRAMME - Part I
Grand Vocal and Instrumental Parlor Concert
Introductory Overture - Downfall of Fort Sumter ...............................
      (Original..................................New Orleans and Metropolitan Troupe
Operatic Chorus - From the 3d act of [Erna].......................................................
.............................................................................Signor Bidaux and Minstrels
Song - Oh, let me shed one silent Tear, (new)............................Edwin Holmes
Comic Song - How are you, Conscript [new] Charley Reynolds
Bugle Song - With imitations............................................................. J.E. Green
Ballad.__................................................................................Signor Gustavo Bidaux
Comic Ditty- Lanagan's Ball ...........................................................Lew Benedict
Cantata..................................................................................Gustavo Bidaux
Finale - Grand Excursion to Niagara Falls .....................................
.......................................................................Duprez & Green's Minstrels

PART II - Variety - Comic and Sentimental.

Grand Fancy Dance-Pas de Matelot..............................................Frank Kent
Favorite Ballad..........................................................Master George Bidaux
## THE RETURNED CONTRABAND !
Reynolds, Benedict and Stanwood.
ARTISTIC CLARIONETTE SOLO ......................................Frank Kritta
## THE DYING YOUNG HERO !
Wounded in defense of his Country. (In character,) introducing
the ballad, "Oh, Mother I've come home to die."
The Young Hero.........................................................Sig. Gustavo Bidaux
      Other characters by Bishop, Greens, Holmes and Kent.
Fight for Uncle Abe ...........................................Master Willie Frear
## Burlesque Scenes from Othello !
Othello.......................................................................Charleys Reynolds
Desdemana....................................................................Frank Kent
Manaver........................................................................Gonsalvo Bishop
STUMP SPEECH, - - - - - - - - - - - - - - - - - - - - - - - LEW BENEDICT
The whole Evening's Entertainment to conclude with
## The Ghost! Burlesqued and Africanized!
As performed by this (company), by Reynolds, Benedict,
Stanwood and others.
Great Ghost.....................................................................E. Holmes
Devil of Demon.................................................................G. Bishop

from the battlefields of the Southeast, tensions occasionally arose that compelled touring companies to clarify their allegiances. In Keokuk, Iowa, for instance, Duprez was twice obliged to take out advertisements to dispel rumours that the troupe sided with the South.[206] The return route brought the company to Cleveland, Detroit, and many of the same cities they had visited on the outbound journey, before they closed the tour with three benefits in the Hudson River valley. The last of these, in Newburgh on 8 July, was for Lavallée, and earned him $145.[207] From there, the troupe arrived in New York City and disbanded for the summer, with many performers seeking work in summer resorts.[208] Duprez and Ellinger decided to part company. The "Colonel" formed a new variety show troupe, Ellinger and Newcomb's Great Moral Exhibition, and persuaded Lavallée to be its musical director.[209]

❖❖❖

## ELLINGER AND NEWCOMB'S MORAL EXHIBITION

Lavallée likely had several reasons for switching to the new company. Ellinger may have offered him a higher salary than notoriously tight-fisted Duprez.[210] More important to an adventurous young man not yet twenty-one years old was the chance to take part in the European tour that Ellinger announced they would soon embark upon. It was also to be an opportunity to present opera, rather than cover his face in burnt cork and perform minstrel show numbers. In the company's advertisements, Lavallée was billed as a pianist and as director of the 'parlor opera' portion of the show – a format recently popularized in New York by the baritone Henri Drayton.[211] But Lavallée may also have developed something more than a professional relationship with Mary Ellinger, who was just a little younger than he. Around this time, he published the *Ellinger polka de salon*, a piece "Composed and dedicated to" Mary Ellinger.[212] Like most of the piano music he published before joining the military, it is a highly marketable piece with conventional harmonies and bright tunes. As it is only of moderate difficulty, he probably would not have performed it on stage.

In addition to Lavallée and Mary Ellinger, the Colonel had assembled an eclectic cast. There was Mr Booth, "the blind pianist"; John (J.H.)

Murphy, a tenor from New London, Connecticut; and W.B. Harrison, the "popular impromptu poet and comic vocalist." Harrison's primary duty was to "display" the trio of miniature comedians who was the troupe's main attraction. Commodore Foote, Colonel Small, and Foote's sister, Eliza Nestel, began their act as they arrived in each town, travelling from the train depot to the hotel in an ornate, miniature carriage drawn by four goats.[213] Ellinger's self-proclaimed acts of charity toward Foote and Small provided the pretext for the troupe's name, although at least one critic mused "did anyone suppose [Ellinger's troupe] was immoral?"[214]

Ellinger opened the tour at the Maryland Institute, in his home town of Baltimore. The city's close proximity to the war had not forced theatres to close. Nor did the city's divided allegiances prevent pro-Union artists from visiting. Even Gottschalk performed there in early November 1862, noting in his journal his love for Baltimore and its people: "I am assured that they are Secessionists, but I do not wish to know anything about it ... at Baltimore they love the arts."[215] The city was clearly receptive to the Ellinger show, which opened on 7 September for a scheduled two weeks of evening and matinee performances. The *Baltimore Sun* reported Lavallée's opera troupe to have comprised "a rare combination and display of talent," but provided few details.[216] Throughout the troupe's engagement, the newspaper's reports focused on the comedians, claiming on 12 September that the performances were "of a superior class and style, in vocal and instrumental music; and this 'show' by the diminutive department has in it enough of the comic and marvelous to amuse and astonish the young and old."[217] The engagement proved successful enough for Ellinger to extend it by three days.

From Baltimore, extravagant advertising and favourable reviews attracted large audiences to the troupe's performances. The *New York Clipper* reported "crowded houses" during the troupe's stay in Frederick, Maryland, and wrote of their success: "The three little people – Com. Foote and his sister, Eliza Nestel, and Col. Small – are immense favorites. Mr W.B. Harrison, the extemporaneous poet, is a good feature with the show. Mr J.H. Murphy is said to be one of the sweetest ballad singers ever heard in this country. Miss Mary Ellinger is a pleasing singer, possessing an excellent voice, and also a good pianist. Mons. Lavallee is pronounced to be a pianist of rare ability. In fact taken altogether, this is one of the best shows that will be on the road this season."[218]

Dates followed in Washington, DC, and Wilmington, Delaware, as the company proceeded northward. In Philadelphia, it seems that only the last evening's performance, on 10 October 1863, was poorly attended, due perhaps to a massive "Union torchlight procession" that was held that night. From there, they continued through Pennsylvania, New Jersey, and New England. En route, Ellinger's advertisements grew increasingly extravagant. On 4 December the opera section of the show was advertised under Lavallée's name: "Mons. C. Lavallée's Parlour Opera Troupe, Sentimental, Musical, and Comical," and Lavallée himself as "the eminent Pianist, Cornetist, Violinist, and composer, pupil of the Conservatories of Paris, who stands Unrivaled as a Musician."[219] We do not know if this claim of having studied in Paris came from Ellinger and his agent. Lavallée would later pad his curriculum vitae with the same false information.

Foote and Small, however, remained the main attractions, and were no doubt largely responsible for steady ticket sales. More often than not, they were the only part of the show that the critics mentioned. Several days into their engagement in Springfield, Massachusetts, and after devoting considerable space to Foote and Small, the critic of the *Daily Republican* added, as an afterthought, that there was also "both vocal and instrumental music in abundance."[220] Continued emphasis on Foote and Small might have begun to diminish Lavallée's interest in the company. There was also reason to doubt that a European tour would ever take place. His name appears in the company's advertisements in Lowell, Massachusetts, but some time after he quit the tour and returned to Montreal in time for Christmas and his twenty-first birthday.[221]

After all that had taken place over the past four years, Lavallée's return seems to have been a rare sign of contrition from a young man whose life up to this time had been marked by defiance. Born in the region hit hardest by the effects of the rebellions of 1837 and 1838, its after-effects had formed him. His willingness to leave his family at the age of thirteen was itself an early sign of his independence. His unwillingness to make easy choices or to conform to the limitations of the time seems to have been established within his personality early on. If his family was hoping he would continue his studies in Europe, or perhaps get a secure job playing organ in a church, they were surely disappointed by his first career moves. He was a young man with the confidence to make his own career choices. At a time when the Catholic Church vehemently opposed the theatre, emigration to the US, or participation in the Civil War, Lavallée made his debut at Montreal's Theatre Royal, left for the US to work as a minstrel show musician, and joined the Union Army. And even within Duprez's company, Lavallée had the confidence in his abilities to resign twice.

No direct comments from Lavallée on his experience during the Civil War or his decision to enlist in the Fourth Rhode Island Regiment have survived. Lapierre speculated that Lavallée was motivated by the injustice he had witnessed in the American South. He may have been correct. But while Lavallée had seen much of the South while touring with the New Orleans Minstrels, in the fall of 1861 the main Federal argument for war was not slavery but preserving the Union. For Lavallée, financial gain was likely a greater factor. Still, a better explanation may be that he simply got caught up in the spirit of the times, as could certainly happen to any twenty-year-old, and especially a young man from a family with a tradition of soldiering.[222] The best evidence of this is his music and especially *The War Fever*. In retrospect, though, joining was also consistent with Lavallée's adventurous personality and his often ambivalent sense of nationality. His decision not to return home after being mustered out of service was perhaps a greater act of defiance. In returning to Duprez's troupe and returning to the South, he asserted his independence – in his way, telling his family that he would be back on his own schedule. His return, late in 1863, saw him being welcomed back into the community but entering into yet a new period of unrest.

# L'Union Nationale: Montreal

## 1863–1865

Lavallée returned to Canada transformed by four years in the US. Having left as a talented novice, he was now an experienced musician. Already, he had seen and done more than many of his contemporaries ever would. A photograph dating from about this time captures the intensity of the young musician in the early 1860s. (See figure 2.1) The photograph was taken in the studio of David B. Spooner, in Springfield, Massachusetts, quite likely during Lavallée's stop there late in November 1863.[1] In it, he sports the facial-hair style made famous by the Union Army's General Ambrose Burnside. But what is most striking about the photo is the highly unconventional pose. Whereas photographers almost always angled their subjects' heads slightly, having them gaze thoughtfully into the distance, Lavallée looks straight into the camera, as if challenging the viewer. He looks like a young man ready for a fight.

As it turned out, a battle was brewing over the future of Canada, and Lavallée would join the fray. The Civil War in the United States weighed heavily on the mood north of the border. As in Britain, when the Civil War began, Canadian public opinion favoured the Confederacy.[2] For some French Canadians, historical links to the South and to Louisiana in particular were a factor. For some, their aversion to slavery was increasingly tempered by their fear of "Northern aggression." On 8 November 1861, the US navy intercepted the British mail ship *Trent*, arresting two Confederate diplomats, John Slidell and James M. Mason, who were on board, en route to Europe. The subsequent diplomatic standoff, known as the Trent Affair, threatened to bring Britain into the Civil War, and

Figure 2.1 A photograph of Lavallée likely dating from November 1863, about a month before his return to Montreal.

with it, its North American colonies. Even if that did not happen, Britain's tense relations with the US led many to fear economic reprisals for British colonies if not an actual invasion by the Federal army.[3] A political solution was needed most urgently in the Province of Canada, where the temporary stability achieved in the 1850s was quickly slipping away. In Upper Canada, the Reformers competed with Conservatives. In Lower Canada, the Rouges fought the Bleus. The Rouges, forerunner of the Liberal Party, had formed in the 1840s, and gradually assumed the place of the Parti Canadien.[4] Many of its members supported the annexation of Canada to the United States. Although considered radical, it elected four members to the legislature in 1851, and eleven in 1854. Advocating the principles of liberal democracy, including universal suffrage and the separation of church and state, party members debated their ideas at the Institut canadien and expressed them in the pages of *L'Avenir* and *Le Pays*.[5] The Bleus articulated a conservative vision through their newspapers, *La Minerve* and the *Journal de Québec*.[6] Maintaining closer ties to business and to the powerful Catholic Church, they proved more successful at the polls. After holding power for five years, the Conservative–Bleus alliance, led by John A. Macdonald and George-Étienne Cartier, had lost its majority in May 1862.[7] The Reformers and Rouges then held office for a year, but the session ended in May 1863 with a no-confidence motion. For some, independence from Britain seemed a practicable solution. By the spring of 1864, the Reformers had made peace with the rival Conservatives and Bleus. United as the 'great coalition,' the three parties put forward a plan for the creation of a Confederation of Britain's North American colonies into an independent country. Lavallée would engage in the debate through political and musical connections.

Lavallée's reasons for returning home after four years are not known. Having performed in Montreal with Duprez in 1862, he would have been aware of the opportunities the city offered. The opening of the Victoria Bridge, just after his departure in 1859, had stimulated an economic expansion that had brought many changes.[8] Railroad construction and new industries brought an influx of rural French Canadians and a wave of migrants from Upper Canada, the United States, Great Britain, and Europe. The population rose from 58,000 in 1858 to 100,000 in the early 1860s, consolidating Montreal's place as Canada's metropolis and making it the ninth largest city in North America (See tables 2.1 and 2.2).

Table 2.1 *Population of Montreal, 1861*

| Residents born in Lower Canada | | | Immigrants British Isles | Other | Total |
|---|---|---|---|---|---|
| French origin | British origin | Other | England (4,394), Scotland (3,235), Ireland (14,469) | Upper Canada (1,208), France (184), Germany (363), USA. (1,706), other countries (793) | |
| 42,886 | 21,647 | 121 | 22,098 | 4,254 | 91,006 |
| 47.1% | 23.8% | 0.1% | 24.3% | 4.7% | |
| | 64,654 | | | 26,352 | |
| | 71% | | | 29% | 100% |
| | | | Suburban population | | 10,433 |
| | | | Total | | 101,439 |

Source: *Census of 1861* published in the *Montreal Directory 1863–64* (Lovell, 1863), 368.

Table 2.2 *Population of the twelve largest cities in North America, ca. 1858–62*

| City | Population |
|---|---|
| 1. New York City | 1,474,779 |
| 2. Philadelphia | 565,529 |
| 3. Baltimore | 212,418 |
| 4. Mexico City | 200,000 |
| 5. Boston | 177,840 |
| 6. New Orleans | 168,675 |
| 7. Cincinnati | 161,044 |
| 8. Chicago | 112,172 |
| 9. Montreal | 91,006 |
| 10. Buffalo | 81,128 |
| 11. Washington | 51,122 |
| 12. San Francisco | 56,802 |

Sources: Canadian census figures (1861) are taken from the *Montreal Directory 1863–64*. Figures for US cities are from Anderton, Barrett, and Bogue, *Population of the United States*. The population of Mexico City (1857) is taken from Keith Davies, "Tendencias demográficas urbanas durante el siglo XIX en México," *Historia Mexicana 83* (January–March, 1973): 482–3, 501, cited in Arrom, *The Women of Mexico City*, 285.

The overall population increase and economic vitality had a direct impact on opportunities for musicians. Several new performance venues catered specifically to the interests of the growing middle class. In the summer of 1863, the Terrapin Restaurant, on Notre-Dame Street, advertised "a soirée musicale every night," with Charles Sedgwick conducting a band that played opera selections and quadrilles.[9] On nearby Place d'Armes, an ensemble of seven to ten musicians and singers performed nightly at Gianelli's Cosmopolitan Hotel, catering largely to the tastes of the financial district.[10] The Theatre Royal was still the city's most vibrant performance venue and regularly required a pit orchestra. The City Concert Hall and the new Crystal Palace, on Sainte-Catherine Street, hosted promenade concerts and other large-scale performances. Local concerts took place most often at Nordheimer's Hall or at the Mechanics' Institute, which had been renovated and enlarged in 1863.

Most of the musicians arriving in the city earned their livelihoods through teaching and through the manufacture and repair of instruments. This included the Lavallées. Not long before Lavallée returned to Montreal, Augustin Lavallée had moved his business and family there from Saint-Hyacinthe. With twenty-one-year-old Calixa's return, it was now a family of nine: Augustin, forty-six, Charlotte-Caroline, forty-three, Cordélia, seventeen, Charles, thirteen, Marie Anne, eleven, Catherine, nine, Joseph, five, and Ida, three.[11] The 1864–65 Montreal Directory shows the family residing at 90 German Street, near the corner of Dorchester Street (these streets are now known as avenue de l'Hôtel de Ville and boulevard René-Lévesque, respectively). The family's home also served as Augustin's workshop, where he built organs and repaired instruments of all sorts, before specializing in violin making.[12] When Calixa arrived, he took another room in the family home as a teaching studio, advertising in the city directory as "Mr C. Lavallée, Professor of Music, 90 German Street, Montreal."[13] He may also have given lessons in the homes of young women, as most potential students were from the bourgeoisie.[14] We have little information on his success in attracting students, but he faced considerable competition. The Montreal Directory of 1863–64 alone lists nineteen entries under "Music Professors."[15]

Paul Letondal, now in his early thirties, remained the city's most highly regarded music teacher. In the summer of 1860, he had married Élizabeth

Gagnon, a younger sister of the influential Quebec City musicians Ernest and Gustave Gagnon. He and Élizabeth had settled in a new home on de la Gauchetière Street where Letondal taught. He was also teaching nearby at the Collège Sainte-Marie, and at the Institut Nazareth, a school for the blind that he had helped to found in 1861.

Lavallée's other teacher, Sabatier, had reached the height of his career in the summer of 1860, when the Canadian government commissioned him to compose a cantata for the inauguration of the Victoria Bridge. Civic and business leaders used the 1860 visit of the Prince of Wales (and the future King Edward VII) to publicize the completion of what was at the time the world's longest bridge. Sabatier conducted his grand *Cantate en l'honneur de Son Altesse royale le Prince de Galles* in an 8,000-seat temporary pavilion constructed for the event.[16] The triumph was short-lived for Sabatier. He was back in New York City later that year, where he gave a concert at Chickering Hall, but soon returned to Montreal, where he checked into Hôtel-Dieu Hospital to cure himself of alcoholism. Two years later, he suffered a stroke and died at the age of forty-two.[17] His life and fate reads like a story by Balzac. Like Vivaldi and Mozart, Sabatier was buried in a pauper's grave at a ceremony witnessed only by groundskeepers.[18] Funds from the publication of a late composition, *Sancta Maria succurre miseris!*, by the firm of Boucher et Manseau were used to help pay off Sabatier's debts. Gustave Smith published three excerpts from the grand cantata in *Les Beaux-arts*.[19]

Since Lavallée's departure, Smith, now thirty-seven, had emerged as a leading figure in the musical community. He was born in London but was raised in Paris by his English father and Swiss mother. He studied both painting and music. At the Paris Conservatoire, he had studied the piano with Joseph Zimmermann and the organ with Charles-Alexandre Fessy. He was about twenty-one years old when the revolution of 1848 began, and chose to serve on the republican side. He subsequently pursued his career as musician and visual artist, and travelled as far as India.[20] In Montreal, he married Louise Émilie Hermine Leprohon, daughter of the woodcarver Louis-Xavier Leprohon, converted to Catholicism, and earned his living by teaching piano and directing the choir at St Patrick's Church (since 1989, St Patrick's Basilica) and teaching music at Sacré-Coeur Convent School at Sault-aux-Recollet, on the north side of the

Island of Montreal, where Emma Lajeunesse (later, better known as Emma Albani) was a student.[21] He was part of a literary circle and contributed articles to *Le Pays* and *L'Écho du Cabinet de lecture paroissial*, and in 1863 began publishing *Les Beaux-arts*.[22] He would become something of a mentor to Lavallée, and together they would lead a group of musicians in organizing numerous concerts.

This loose association of musicians included the twenty-six-member Montagnards Canadiens. Created in 1861, this ensemble had been inspired by a popular French vocal troupe, Les Chanteurs Montagnards Français.[23] Like their French counterparts, the Canadian troupe dressed in "national costume" (red breeches, black and purple mantle trimmed with gold, and fez cap), and performed a repertoire dominated by choruses from French and Italian opera.[24] Many of the other performers that took part in concerts with Lavallée and Smith were still in their late teens or early twenties. Several were piano students of Paul Letondal. These included Moïse Saucier, Dominique Ducharme, Marie Regnaud, and Rose-de-Lima Derome, Léon Derome's eldest daughter.[25] The young soprano and pianist, Marie Regnaud, may have been the most talented of the group. After graduating from Convent School in 1860, she studied with Letondal, and was confident with demanding repertoire for both voice and piano.[26] Other vocalists included François Lavoie, Frédéric Lefebvre, Napoléon Legendre, Joseph Boucher, and Alexandre Trottier, who in the late 1850s had been an organizer of Les Amateurs Canadiens. Instrumentalists included another familiar figure from the late 1850s, Henri Gauthier, the flutist who had performed at Lavallée's debut in 1859.[27] Led by Lavallée and Smith, these performers would function much like a concert company, dramatically raising the number of concerts offered.

In addition to French Canadians, the Lavallée–Smith circle included several Italian and English musicians. Most notable among them was the oboe player known as Signor Baricelli, and the sisters Elena and Eugenia de Angelis. The de Angelis family had arrived in Montreal around the same time as Lavallée, and he may have known them in Providence. Sicilian-born Gaetano de Angelis had served as bandmaster with the Ninety-third Highlanders. He and his wife, Veneranda, had produced children in each of their many postings.[28] Their third daughter, Emilia, had married in 1863

60

and moved to Boston. Lavallée developed a particularly close relationship with twenty-year-old Elena, who was teaching singing at the family home on Union Avenue.[29] Two British musicians also performed a number of times with Lavallée. In addition to Charles Sedgwick, mentioned above, Lavallée frequently collaborated with the talented violinist Frederick Torrington, organist at the Great St James Street Wesleyan Methodist Church and a colleague of Paul Letondal at the Collège Sainte-Marie. Lavallée's interaction with these and other anglophone musicians would draw criticism from more conservative quarters. As in New Orleans, Montreal's cultural life was split largely along linguistic lines – or as they were likely to describe it in the 1860s, by nationality – and in 1864, all aspects of culture became politicized to a new level.

❖❖❖

Lavallée made at least four concert appearances in January 1864. The first took place on 4 January at the Mechanics' Hall. The occasion was a concert held by local musicians to raise money for the widow and children of one of their colleagues, P.H. Carpentier. Organizers had the program printed in *La Minerve* on 31 December, concluding with: "Mr C. Lavallée, the distinguished young Canadian artist, has agreed to lend his much appreciated support."[30] The wording acknowledges the high regard local musicians had for him. At this concert, he performed just one piece, a composition of his own simply referred to as a *Grande fantaisie de concert*, but was welcomed back enthusiastically. *La Presse* reported: "Everyone was delighted with our young pianist Mr Lavallee. According to connoisseurs, he is a truly remarkable force and promises to become one of the glories of the profession."[31] It was to be just the beginning of his re-engagement with all aspects of life in Montreal.

The Carpentier concert was the first of many. Several times that winter, Lavallée joined colleagues in a convoy of sleds that crossed the frozen Saint Lawrence River for concerts in South Shore communities. The first such, on 16 January in the village of Longueuil, raised funds for the Société Saint-Vincent de Paul.[32] The second took place on 24 January in the nearby village of La Prairie. On 26 January, Lavallée gave a "grand concert" under his own name and for his own benefit at the Mechanics'

Hall. Here, as at the concert two days earlier, he performed on violin, cornet, and piano. He played two of his cornet compositions, simply listed as an "Obbligato" and a Fantaisie, as well as Charles de Bériot's *Grande fantaisie, ou scène de ballet* for violin. But the piano was his main instrument, and the one for which he composed most frequently. At both concerts, he performed a *Grande fantaisie* of his own (identified on 26 January as being based on two themes from Bellini's *Norma*). To this, he added two other pieces on the 26th. He and F.X. Valade opened that evening with Gottschalk's *Ojos Créolos caprice brillant* for piano duet and Lavallée closed with his rousing galop *The War Fever*.[33]

Reviewers refrained from commenting on the size of the audience at the concert, which suggests it may not have been very large. They did comment on Lavallée's playing and reception. *La Minerve*'s critic described the performance as a "stunning success," noting "the public's eagerness to hear [Lavallée] perform" again. "Our young Canadian artist has a truly remarkable talent," he wrote, saying that it was "difficult to say which instrument he plays the best."[34] In its review, *La Presse* also responded to Lavallée's multiple talents, noting that "it would be difficult to find in this country an artist who was equally strong on these three instruments." Acknowledging his "extraordinary talent," the writer claimed that with "encouragement and study" Lavallée could become among the most distinguished artists.[35] The critic may have been Gustave Smith, who was contributing to *La Presse*, and whose style of writing the short review resembles.

*La Presse* was the creation of Lavallée's former schoolmate, Médéric Lanctôt. The similarities between the two were numerous. Both were physically small men, of considerable intensity and determination. Their roots, in both the Richelieu Valley and Montreal, connected them directly to the politics of the late 1830s. A true child of the rebellions of 1837 and 1838, Lanctôt was still in his mother's womb when his father, Hippolyte Lanctôt, a twenty-two-year-old notary, was arrested for his participation in 1838, convicted of high treason, and exiled to Australia. Historian Jean Hamelin has written that on his return to Canada, five years later, Hippolyte remained committed to the principles of democracy, republicanism, and nationalism, and instilled these values in his children.[36] Médéric turned out to be as combative as his father. He had attended the Collège Saint-Hyacinthe, but left before completing his studies. There is a legend that he was one of four students expelled after threatening to burn down the school, but he may simply have refused to repeat a year after failing Latin. His father then found him a position apprenticing with the firm of the financier Augustin Cuvillier in Montreal, where he became an active member of the Institut canadien.[37] In the mid-1850s, Lanctôt returned to Saint-Hyacinthe to write for *Le Courrier de Saint-Hyacinthe*. After two years in that post, he relocated to Montreal to study law, taking a clerk position with the firm of Rouges lawyers Joseph Doutre and Charles Daoust on Saint-Gabriel Street.[38] His anticlerical stance quickly landed him in trouble when he was arrested for breaking the windows of the Jesuit library, as a protest against their conservative collecting policies. After being convicted and fined, he channelled his energy into journalism, contributing polemic articles to *Le Pays*. Since 1861, that newspaper had been edited by the former Saint-Hyacinthe mayor Louis-Antoine Dessaulles, who was now also president of the Institut canadien in Montreal. But even Dessaulles was too moderate for Lanctôt, and in October 1863, with partners Toussaint Thompson and C.C.E. Bouthillier, he launched *La Presse* and installed himself as editor.[39] At a time when most of Montreal's newspapers were affiliated with political parties, *La Presse* would be fiercely independent. It would also differentiate itself from the city's other newspapers by the amount of space it devoted to cultural issues and especially to music.

At a concert on 19 February 1864, at Nordheimer's Hall, Lavallée performed for the first time his most ambitious piano composition to date: *Une Couronne de lauriers, caprice de genre*, op. 10. It is the first piece in which Lavallée begins to diverge from a standard sectional formal construction, offering the pianist a good number of challenges while remaining tuneful. When the printed version appeared in the summer, with a dedication to Marie Regnaud, Gustave Smith reviewed it in *La Presse*, drawing attention to features of its form and harmony, and praising the publisher Laurent, Laforce & Cie, for their "entrepreneurial spirit" and their encouragement of young musicians. He concludes by calling the *Caprice* not only "very well written and in fine taste" but also "the first major piece that has been issued by a Montreal music publisher."[40] It was a fair assessment of the piece and of the publishing environment. Although by 1864 there were ten city firms publishing music, it was mostly as a sideline to importing and selling sheet music and instruments from Europe and the United States.[41] The music they published was what they knew might sell: light vocal pieces (usually referred to as romances), patriotic songs, and short character pieces for piano. The *Caprice* was unlikely to turn a profit, simply because it was beyond the level of most amateurs. With its quick tempo and rapid 32nd-note figures it challenged the skilled pianist, as in the middle section (mm. 61–92), where the accompaniment (still in 32nd notes) shifts to the right hand while the left picks out the melody in the upper range of the piano (see appendix 2). Lavallée performed it on at least one other occasion, 5 October 1864, when he paired it with his *Le Souvenir-Méditation*.[42]

Lavallée's reputation in the wider community was evident in March when he was asked to organize the annual St Patrick's Day promenade concert at the City Concert Hall. At this event, he led the ensemble, until recently under the baton of Henry Prince and now renamed the Montreal Brass Band (although sometimes referred to as the Montreal City Band). The band opened with the overture from Henry Bishop's opera *Guy Mannering*. It later returned to the stage to play Prince's *The Star of Erin* quadrille, a medley from *La Traviata* that Lavallée had arranged, and Dodworth's *Emerald Isle* medley, which closed the concert. Between these selections, Lavallée performed Thalberg's piano variations on "Home, Sweet Home," and he had a number of his now familiar colleagues play and sing, among them, Regnaud, Dupré, Ducharme, and the Montagnards Canadiens. The only anglophone soloist was Mr Muir, who sang some Scottish songs. In its review, the *True Witness and Catholic Chronicle* noted some of the selections and singled out the contributions of Regnaud and Dupré.[43]

While the St Patrick's Day program seems to have been well received, when Lavallée conducted the same band two nights later, at a concert held to raise money for orphans (through the Union Saint-Joseph), he was criticized for not leading a francophone band.[44] Reviewing the concert in *La Presse* was Frédéric Ossaye, a professor of agricultural economics at the École normale Jacques Cartier, who took exception to Lavallée's choice of ensembles, writing: "The concert began with a piece performed under the direction of Mr Lavallée by an English orchestra.

This piece, well rendered, would have impressed us more, under the circumstances, if it had been played by a French Canadian band ... Hopefully our passionate and clever Mr Lavallée will be fortunate enough to organize an orchestra with our artists, who are in no way inferior to those of other origins."[45] Ossaye did not specify how French-Canadian musicians might have given a more impressive performance. Lavallée had opened the concert with the overture to Verdi's *La Traviata*. Later in the program, he also conducted a piece of his own, listed only as a *Quadrille Canadien*. Ossaye failed to note this, but was most interested in politics. He devoted half of the review to a speech given during the intermission. The speaker was to have been the lawyer Francis Cassidy, a founding member and former president of the Institut canadien. When he was unable to attend, his place was taken by Pierre-Joseph-Olivier Chauveau, the superintendant of public instruction, and a close ally of George-Étienne Cartier. Ossaye then used the review as a vehicle to criticize Chauveau's "empty rhetoric," writing that "we love to hear talk of patriotism and nationality, but would like something more useful than expressions of love." In the larger context of the review, Ossaye's denunciation of Lavallée was a minor point but one that revealed that no one was above criticism in the increasingly heated environment. While Lavallée's connections to Smith and Lanctôt already linked him to the "no" camp on the issue of Confederation, more radical nationalists could still question his commitment.

April was quiet in many ways. With little to report nationally, newspapers looked elsewhere. The Civil War in the US continued, seemingly without end in sight. In Europe, the Danish–Prussian war was being played out. In France, Louis Napoléon placed Archduke Ferdinand Maximilian, of the House of Hapsburg, at the head of the Second Mexican Empire, his North American puppet state. Maximilian's wife, the Empress Carlotta (Charlotte of Belgium), would set about making the Mexican court an essential port of call for European musicians. In Montreal, Louis Moreau Gottschalk returned for two concerts. He was then touring the US northeast with Adelina Patti's brother, violinist Carlo Patti. In their support for opposing sides of the Civil War, they were odd travelling companions. The Spanish-born Patti had given the New Orleans premiere of "Dixie" and soon after joined a Tennessee regiment. The

New Orleans–born Gottschalk was an ardent supporter of the Union. Soon after checking into St Lawrence Hall, widely known as a meeting place for Confederate spies, Gottschalk noted in his diary that Patti had quickly made new friends.[46] Their performances were the most noteworthy musical events that month. Lavallée seems to have appeared at only one concert, a benefit for the vocalist François Lavoie, on 7 April, when he performed on both the violin and piano. He also played a violin solo at Easter services at Notre-Dame. How he was surviving financially is unknown. Smith printed a brief article of support for him in *Les Beaux-arts*, reminding readers of his musical talent and community work: "We know this name too well, and he is altogether too kind to the Montreal public for us not to seize an excellent opportunity to talk about this young artist."[47] Smith went on to congratulate Lavallée on his work thus far, and to wish him a bright future.

After yet more charity concerts in May, on 7 June 1864, Lavallée took part in what was billed as a Grand Opera Concert at Mechanics' Hall. For this concert, he and Elena de Angelis were joined by two guests, billed as Sig. G. Martini, tenor, and Sig. C. de Lamar, baritone. William G. Vogt, a local pianist, served as accompanist.[48] It was the sort of event that enabled Lavallée to exploit his own operatic repertoire for piano. As we see at many of these events, Italian opera was most popular, and especially the works of Donizetti and Bellini, with those of Verdi gaining popularity in the 1860s. French composers Thomas and Adam were also popular. Visiting virtuosos, such as Thalberg and Vieuxtemps, had done much to popularize these genres. Lavallée's advantage was that he could perform this difficult music on three instruments. His piano fantasies and transcriptions for the piano were probably similar to those of Kalkbrenner, Herz, Gottschalk, and others that he would have heard many times, a series of variations or elaborations on prominent melodies.[49] None are known to have survived. He may have performed these works from memory without ever having taken the time to write them down, as publishers were interested only in music for amateurs.

During the month of June, a French touring ensemble based at New York City's Niblo's Garden, and led by actor and manager Ernest Gravier, arrived in Montreal for an extended season at the Theatre Royal. The company's specialty was the music of Offenbach, then little known in

North America, and they presented *Orphée aux enfers* and *Tromb-al-ca-zar*. To appease the Church, they also presented less daring pieces, such as Adolphe d'Ennery's "moral drama" *Grace de Dieu!*, and it seems to have been a successful combination. The company also played at Quebec City's Music Hall and possibly in other towns and cities that summer. Montreal benefited additionally from the visit, when the company's conductor, the Belgian violinist Jules Hone, decided to settle there.

On 24 June, Lavallée led the *Fête nationale* concert at the Mechanics' Hall, through which he aimed to raise funds and public interest in completing the monument to the "victims of 1837–38," begun years earlier. The event was not without controversy, as it competed directly with the official promenade concert at the Bonsecours Market. Conservative newspapers neither advertised nor commented on Lavallée's concert, while *La Presse* published a communiqué arguing for the need to support the construction of a monument and *Le Pays* printed the concert program, a mix of opera excerpts and patriotic pieces, and later reported a full house for the event.[50] (See figure 2.2) He conducted the City Band in Verdi's overture to *La Traviata* and also in his own arrangement of national airs, billed as *Les Quadrilles Canadiens*. His direction of the event was also evident in the number of his own works on the program. In addition to his *Quadrilles Canadiens*, his recently published arrangement of M.F.E. Valois's "La Mansarde" (The Attic) was sung by Napoléon Legendre.[51] And Lavallée performed his transcription, the *Grand Marche Solennelle* from Gounod's *Faust*. François Lavoie sang both Sabatier's "Drapeau de Carillon" and Lavallée's "Hommage aux Victimes de 1837–38," the latter composed for the occasion on a text by L.-O. David.

Lavallée's association with the Montreal City Band provided further opportunities for composition and performance. For a Grand Promenade Concert at the City Concert Hall on 25 July 1864, he composed *Quickstep sur les airs nationaux canadien* for the band, a portion of which may have been published in 1912.[52] There may have been other works, but for many of their performances no record survives of what they played. This is true of a pair of concerts at which he led the City Band on 14 and 15 September that featured the veteran British soprano Anna Bishop.[53] The venue for these events was the Jardins Guilbault, Joseph-Édouard Guilbault's pleasure gardens at Sherbrooke and Saint

Urbain streets. Since their opening in 1852, they had become Montreal's answer to London's Vauxhall Gardens, displaying exotic plants and animals, hosting circuses, and staging alfresco concerts during the summer months.[54] Repertoire in such an environment was typically light and lively. Two days later, on 17 September, Lavallée led the Band in the music competition at Victoria Skating Rink. The contest was the closing event

---

1. Overture to *La Traviata*, Verdi
Montreal City Band, conducted by Lavallée
2. Cavatina from *Norma*, Bellini
Louis-Ludger Maillet, tenor
3. "Ah, vous dirai-je maman" (with variations taken from the opera
*Le Toréador*), Adam
Mme. Saint-Louis, soprano
4. *Grand Marche Triomphale*, for two pianos (from *Aida*), Verdi
Smith and Lavallée
5. *Hommage aux Victimes de 1837–38*, L.O. David-Lavallée
François A. Lavois, baritone
6. "Casta Diva," selection and fantasy, for solo flute (from *Norma*) Bellini
[performer not stated]
7. *Les Quadrilles Canadiens* (Adapted from a selection of national airs), Lavallée
Montreal City Band, conducted by Lavallée
8. Bayard, scène et air, Concone
M. Ducharme, baritone
9. "Di piacer mi balza il cor" (from *The Thieving Magpie*), Rossini
Mme. Saint-Louis, soprano
10. Grand Marche Solennelle de "Faust," Gounod-Lavallée
Lavallée, piano
11. "Le Drapeau de Carillon," Crémazie-Sabatier
François A. Lavois, baritone
12. "La Mansarde," romance, M.F.E. Valois-Lavallée
Napoléon Legendre, tenor
13. Solo de basse, Lefebvre
[Performer not specified]
"Vive la Canadienne"
"God Save the Queen"

---

Figure 2.2   Program of the 1864 Fête Nationale Concert at the Mechanics' Institute, held to raise funds for a monument to the "victims of 1837–38."

of the annual Exhibition of the Horticultural and Agricultural Society, and typically drew a good crowd. Lavallée's band took first prize in the brass band section. After all the prizes had been awarded, the City Band closed the event with "God Save the Queen," and then, with the Prince of Wales Band, proceeded to the Dorchester Street residence of the Society's president, George Desbarats, for a late-night serenade – after which Desbarats invited Lavallée and members of his band inside where they played a few more pieces. They then played another outdoor serenade at the Saint-Antoine Street residence of John Torrence, another Society official. Newspapers reported no complaints from neighbours about brass bands playing in the street well past midnight.

Lavallée may have been busy teaching that fall. In July, *La Presse* reported that he was to begin teaching at the Collège Saint-Laurent, noting, "we are certain that all the distinguished families who honour this institution with their trust, will learn this news with pleasure."[55] Located in the northwest part of the Island of Montreal, the school had been established in 1847 by the Pères de Sainte-Croix. No evidence has yet emerged that Lavallée actually took up teaching duties. If he did not, it seems possible that the job simply fell through or that he decided against committing himself to teaching.

❖❖❖

Politically, things were coming to a head in the autumn of 1864. Since the start of the Civil War, and especially during the past year, discussions had intensified over the future of the British colonies. The pieces had started to fall into place in June 1864, when Conservatives from Upper and Lower Canada (led by Macdonald and Cartier) joined the Reformer George Brown to form a Grand Coalition aimed at achieving a federal union of the British colonies. On 1 September delegates from the Province of Canada and the east-coast colonies met at Charlottetown, Prince Edward Island, to begin negotiations. After a break, they resumed negotiations on 9 October in Quebec City. The second conference ended on 27 October with delegates from Canada having reached an agreement with their counterparts from New Brunswick and Nova Scotia. With this agreement in hand, they travelled to Montreal to celebrate with a banquet at St Lawrence Hall on Saturday, 29 October. The band of the Sixtieth Regiment supplied the music, opening perhaps symbolically with the overture to *La Dame Blanche*, a popular French opera based on a Scottish story, as 260 delegates drank and dined throughout the afternoon, cheering speeches by Galt, Cartier, McGee, and many others, praising their own efforts and the outcome of their deliberations. On Monday, Lanctôt printed the names of the French Canadians present at the banquet as a way of holding them accountable for what he considered their treason, and emphasizing their minority status.[56] Among the names was that of Lavallée's former patron, Léon Derome, whose status had risen steadily over the past decade. In the early 1860s, he moved his family into a new home on Sainte-Catherine Street and accepted an appointment as a justice of the peace. His support of the pro-Confederation side was not surprising for a member of the petit bourgeoisie. If this resulted in a rift with Lavallée at the time, they seem to have resolved it in later years.

Economic development and fear of a US invasion drove the argument of many advocates of Confederation. The security issue came to the fore even during the Quebec Conference, when news arrived that Confederate soldiers had entered the US from Canada, robbed three banks in the town of St Albans, Vermont, and escaped back into Canada. The raiders, as they became known, were arrested but not turned over to US authorities.[57] The legal standoff increased fear of US retaliation and added a sense of urgency to the negotiations taking place in Quebec City. Otherwise, representation by population, or gaining greater power within the federal legislature, drove the argument in Upper Canada.[58] Details of where power would lie – what control the federal government would have – proved to be the main points of contention.[59] But in Lower Canada, Cartier's Conservatives downplayed the powers that the federal government would hold, instead emphasizing the creation of an independent, provincial legislature where French would be the language of the majority and arguing that Confederation would bring about independence, as French-speaking Canada would have a province of its own. As *La Minerve* would claim on 1 July 1867, "as a distinct and separate nationality," French Canadians form "a state within a state."[60]

There was also considerable opposition to Confederation, especially in the colonies of the east coast. In Lower Canada, the Rouges, led by Antoine-Aimé Dorion, advocated democratic reforms but preferred annexation to the US or independence for Lower Canada, rather than a union with the other British colonies, and they would challenge the Bleus's contention that Confederation would provide security for French Canada. Their ties to the Institut canadien and their advocacy of the separation of church and state, however, made the Rouges the enemy of the Catholic Church and of Montreal's Bishop Ignace Bourget, who labelled them as extremists.

Compared with Lanctôt, most Rouge politicians were moderates. Lanctôt and many others were convinced that Confederation would be the end of French-Canadian identity, and time was short. He had responded quickly to the coalition's initiative by launching, on 3 September 1864, *L'Union nationale*, a newspaper aimed directly at thwarting the plan for Confederation.[61] The fiery Lanctôt attracted a dedicated group of young writers, fiercely committed to maintaining French-Canadian identity. Among them was Ludger Labelle, a disenchanted former supporter of the Liberal–Conservative alliance, who also agitated against Confederation through the Club Saint-Jean-Baptiste, a secret society based in Montreal that gave refuge to one of the St Albans Raiders.[62] The twenty-four-year-old conservative L.-O. David served as editor. A little later, they were joined by twenty-three-year-old Wilfrid Laurier, then just out of law school and penniless. Like Lanctôt, Laurier was a member of the Rouge party and the Institut canadien, and although he would later enter federal politics (and serve fifteen years as prime minister), in 1864 he was vehemently opposed to Confederation. In the spring of 1865, he and Lanctôt formed a law firm, located at 24 Saint-Gabriel Street. L.-O. David would later write of the "serious and melancholy" young lawyer whose "office was next door to that of us writers whose articles railed against Confederation."[63]

Lavallée showed his support for *L'Union nationale* from the start, placing an advertisement in the first and subsequent issues, and later contributing reviews. Like *La Presse*, *L'Union nationale* regularly devoted space to cultural issues and many of its writers had a special interest in music. Laurier was at the time engaged to Zoé Lafontaine, a music teacher.[64] Labelle expressed his appreciation of music by organizing a benefit concert to help fund the young soprano Emma Lajeunesse's studies in 1862.[65] While *L'Union nationale*'s articles and concert reviews were sometimes unsigned, many were attributed to Lanctôt, Thompson, Smith, and Lavallée.

Just as arguments against Confederation filled most of *L'Union nationale*'s columns in the winter of 1864–65, discussion of music took on stronger political overtones. In the first of a short series of articles, Smith discussed the place of music in various European countries and the importance of exchanging ideas.[66] His emphasis on 'progress' in music was both typical of the time and specific to his hopes for music in Canada. Related to the latter point, his second article focused on the need for critical writing about the arts in Canada.[67] On 15 November, Smith followed up these pieces with a 1,500-word article exploring the problems created within the Montreal musical community by linguistic – or national – divisions. Toward the end of the article he mentioned that the struggling French-Canadian orchestra, the Société Philharmonique Canadienne (SPC), had decided to recruit English musicians as a means of surviving, a strategy he predicted would soon end in failure.[68] The seemingly offhand example sparked an angry response from the SPC's secretary, Napoléon Legendre, who accused Smith of jealousy since he had not been asked to lead the orchestra.[69] This was followed by replies from both Smith and Lavallée, who likened adding English musicians to spoiling the soup with too much pepper, further noting that it might go well for a concert or two but that it was unlikely to last.[70] The same day that *L'Union nationale* published Lavallée's letter, *Le Pays* published Legendre's detailed description of the SPC's plans, comfirming the constitutional changes that Smith had argued against, noting that the organization had decided to "apply to their organization a little *Confederation*" by inviting English musicians to join.[71] Two days later *L'Union nationale* published a letter from Legendre in which he made peace with Smith, but referred to Lavallée as "overzealous"; it would be several months before they resolved their differences.[72] Legendre's reference to Confederation suggests that differing political views may have been a factor in the dispute. This would be supported by subsequent events, including J.B. Labelle's composition in 1868 of the cantata *Confédération*, which he dedicated to George-Étienne Cartier.[73] Nevertheless, a decade later, Lavallée and Legendre would work together on a new project.

Another issue raised in Smith's 15 November 1864 article was audience etiquette. This was even a problem at times for Louis Moreau Gottschalk, who noted in his diary after an April 1864 concert at the Theatre Royal that "the parterre is generally occupied by those who care less for being seen than for listening to the music. They applauded with enthusiasm, and listened with an attention which singularly contrasted with the noise made by some in the boxes."[74] Smith was especially concerned with what he considered the lack of appreciation shown by audiences toward the artists who gave their time and talent for charity concerts. Henri Gauthier, he wrote, had recently decided to perform less often. He continued: "Another artist whom the Creator endowed with extraordinary talent, our sincere friend Mr Lavallée, is no better treated at the moment. Instead of listening closely to this excellent pianist, one pleases oneself to giggle and chat during the performance. Mr Lavallée has decided that he will no longer appear in public."[75] While Lavallée seems to have left no statement on this problem, his absence from a number of concerts through the fall and early winter months suggests he had tired of performing. Instead, he devoted more of his time to writing, and his spirit was cheered in November by the arrival of the young French-born violinist Camilla Urso.

After her highly successful North American tours in the mid-1850s, Urso had returned to her studies. She resumed her career late in 1863, with concerts in New York, Boston, and other major US cities. In the fall of 1864, she toured with the young pianist billed simply Mlle de la Grange, but who was the adopted daughter of the soprano Anna de la Grange. They arrived in Montreal at the beginning of November 1864 for a series of concerts at the Theatre Royal. The two musicians were engaged by the actor-manager Ernest Gravier, whose French theatrical company had been in residence at the theatre since September and who was looking for new novelties. The plan succeeded – perhaps beyond Gravier's expectations. The Urso–de la Grange concerts took place in the second part of the program over six nights, between 3 and 12 November and attracted the attention of all the city's newspapers, despite the intense political discussion then underway. Even before the first performance, *Le Pays* published a lengthy article that reminded readers of Urso's life story.[76] During the engagement, the *L'Union nationale*'s printer, J.A. Plinguet, published J.O. Turgeon's *Biographie de Camille Urso*, providing the violinist's admirers with a memento of her short stay in Canada.

The enthusiastic reception persuaded Urso to return to Montreal later that month for a full-length concert with local performers. She engaged Smith as accompanist, several other local artists as soloists, and the band of the Chasseurs Canadiens. Lavallée may have still been refusing to perform, but he reviewed the event for *L'Union nationale*. In the review, he highlighted the achievements of both Urso and the local artists. Describing the "exquisite delicacy" of Urso's technique, he concluded that she was "the equal of the great artists that we have already heard in Montreal."[77] He then singled out several of the local performers who had taken part, describing Marie Regnaud as "a credit to our young country." After paying tribute to the abilities of Baricelli and Smith, he turned his praise of baritone François Lavoie into a lament on the lack of adequate training available in Montreal. He noted that this was the first concert appearance of the band of the Chasseurs Canadiens, a French-Canadian militia regiment created soon after the Trent Affair, advising band members to "pay closer attention to their tuning and to the nuances of the music," and urging them to "bring honour not only to the ensemble ... but also to our beautiful city of Montreal."[78] It was a style of writing seen often in *L'Union nationale*, linking national (or civic) glory and artistic achievement, in a mix of didactic and nationalistic rhetoric.

Although Urso left Montreal to perform in other cities, she later returned. On 19 December 1864, Smith, Letondal, Regnaud, Lavallée, and Torrington wrote to Urso, urging her to remain a little longer in Canada. *L'Union nationale* published their letter and her positive reply a few days later.[79] On 21 December, Lavallée published a report of Urso's planned return to Montreal, writing vividly of her concert tours and her admirers, among them Emperor Maximilian, and promising that her return to Montreal would be marked by a grand musical celebration befitting her talent.[80]

A week later, Lavallée published another review, this time a scathing critique of the quality of touring opera companies that visited Montreal.[81] He aimed his comments at the Campbell and Castle Opera Company, which had been performing at the Theatre Royal (after Gravier's company closed), and disdained the public's willingness to attend their performances: "Poor Montreal, when will you stop being overwhelmed by such itinerant opera troupes? Are you so poor in artists that you must receive with open arms the mediocrities other countries send you?"[82] This might seem ironic coming from a writer who himself had been directing an itinerant opera troupe only a year earlier, but he knew from experience that troupes such as this one were often slapped together with few rehearsals and sent out on the road, performing a hodgepodge of arias in costume, but turning a profit just the same. Lavallée's criticism was uncommon. Critics rarely wrote critically. Their job was to fill columns and sell advertising. A withering attack from the pen of a twenty-two-year-old neophyte critic was rare, and in Montreal it was only possible in *L'Union nationale*.

❖❖❖

The first of Urso's return performances took place on 2 January 1865, with Gustave Smith serving as musical director, and featured a program of opera excerpts. The concert included appearances by the band of the Sixty-third British Regiment, led by cornetist George John Miller. The regiment had been deployed from its base in Halifax to Upper Canada in 1861 to defend the colony in the event of an invasion by Union troops. As the likelihood of an invasion decreased, the regiment returned eastward and arrived in Montreal in September 1864.[83] The band opened the concert with the overture to Auber's *Fra diavolo*. Urso performed a fantasy from Bellini's *La Sonnambula* and Paganini's ever-popular *Carnival of Venice*. She even sang an aria from Charles Gounod's *Faust*. Lavallée was persuaded to return to the stage, and played his own transcription of *La Prière de Moïse* ("Moses' Prayer") from Rossini's opera *Moses in Egypt*, and *Ojos Créolos* for four hands with Smith.[84]

Perhaps moved by the adulation, Urso remained in the city for another week and for several more concerts. On Thursday, 5 January, she and Marie Regnaud took part in an Irish community concert at the City Concert Hall, at which Urso performed Bishop's sentimental favourite "Home, Sweet Home" and *Carnival of Venice*. After three nights off, during which time Gottschalk performed, on Monday evening Urso was the featured performer at a concert given in honour of Ernest Gravier and his wife, the soprano Madame Gravier-Maillet. Lavallée also took part, performing the Prudent *Fantasy* and the Herz duet, with Smith. On Tuesday, 10 January, Urso also took part in the annual concert of the

Montagnards Canadiens, now directed by twenty-two-year-old Charles Christin. She performed three violin solos at this event. Lavallée played two piano solos, both his own compositions, *Rêverie du soir* and his *The War Fever*. Aside from these pieces, the event was primarily a vocal concert, and the songs performed by the chorus and soloists included Laurent de Rillé's "Les enfants de Lutèce," Ambroise Thomas's "France! France!," and Alfred Hector Roland's "Tout pour la patrie," giving the event a decidedly patriotic feel.

Within days of Urso's departure, Lavallée announced plans for a concert for his own benefit, again to be held on 26 January. For this event, he recruited Madame Gravier-Maillet, Smith, Gauthier, Frédéric Lefebvre, D.G. Maillioux, Joseph Boucher, the Montagnards Canadiens, and the Band of the Royal Light Infantry of Montreal, which he conducted. The band opened the concert with the overture to *La Traviata*, and later performed Louis-Antoine Jullien's *Les Charmes, Valse élégante*, and a "Sélection Canadienne." Lavallée joined Smith in Herz's *Grand duo brillant*, and played three pieces of his own: *Rêverie du soir*, a *Grand fantaisie de concert*, and the new *L'Oiseau mouche* (The Hummingbird), *Bluette de salon*, op. 11, drawing attention in the concert advertisement to its publication and availability through Laurent, Laforce & Cie.[85] Overall, it was a very full program and an impressive demonstration of his abilities as a soloist, conductor, and organizer. Despite this, there is no evidence that it turned a profit for him.

In the weeks leading up to the concert, *L'Union nationale* provided support through two preview notices. On 13 January, Lanctôt's partner Toussaint Thompson published an article praising Lavallée. His "large and noble soul has helped to fill the hands of the poor, and one may say that there has not been a charity concert in Montreal for which [Lavallée] has not played a part," Thompson wrote.[86] He urged readers to show the same generosity, and predicted the turnout would be "worthy of the fine reputation of our leading Canadian artist."[87] Twelve days later, on 25 January, Smith published a short piece urging readers to "loosen their purse strings" in order to help "keep among us an artist who brings honour to Canada."[88] The plea suggests that advance ticket sales had been slow, and that Lavallée was growing weary of his life in Canada. Later, he was likely cheered by reviews of the concert, such as the one in

*La Minerve*, which referred to him as "unquestionably the greatest glorification of Canadian talent."[89] Still, that none mentioned the size of the audience suggests that it was not a good turnout. There may simply have been concert fatigue by the end of that busy month.

Just four days later, many in the musical community were surprised to read that Urso, now in New York, had engaged Smith for a concert tour.[90] They were to embark for Havana on 8 February, and give performances in New Orleans and at the court of Emperor Maximilian in Mexico City. The newspaper reported with some pride that in selecting Smith, Urso had shown "high regard and a serious appreciation" for his talent, "when there are so many artists in New York who would have been extremely happy to make this trip." The brief news item went on to praise Smith's humility and his desire to "make himself useful to Canada." It noted that the trip should be good for his health, which had suffered "due to constant work," and wished him "a happy voyage and speedy return among us."[91] A week later, the same newspaper reported that the tour would be delayed until the following November due to difficulties in booking venues in Cuba.[92] Urso remained in the US through the spring and summer, but eventually abandoned the tour plans and returned to Europe.[93] The real reason for the postponement and eventual cancellation may have been political instability in Mexico. Smith's disappointment extended beyond his career, as by spring there was also bad news on the political front.

In February 1865, debate over Confederation intensified in the press and in the Lower House of the legislature, which was at this time in Quebec City. Ultimately, the electorate was not consulted. A vote took place in the Legislative Assembly on 10 March 1865, at which the plan for Confederation was approved by a margin of 91 votes to 33. We have no clear evidence of Lavallée's reaction to the news. On *L'Union nationale*'s front page a devastated Lanctôt printed in bold the names of the 'traitors' who voted in favour. The fight against Confederation was not yet over, but opponents of the plan in Lower Canada faced the well organized Bleus, the powerful Catholic Church, and public indifference.[94]

For Confederation's opponents, a humorous and musical response may have been the best approach to the seemingly hopeless situation, and later that spring one came in the form of a piano piece titled the

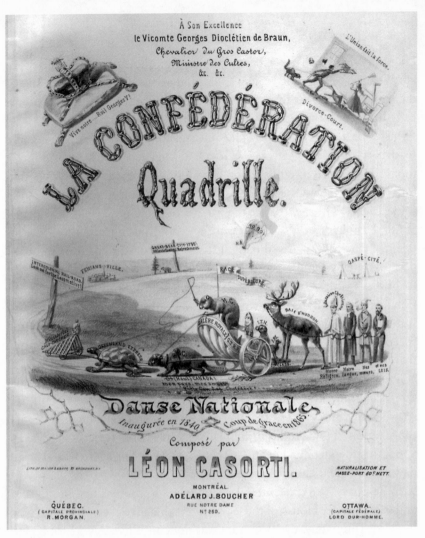

Figure 2.3 The cover of *Confédération Quadrille*, which may have been created by Gustave Smith. The music is credited to a Léon Casorti, an otherwise unknown musician, which suggests this may have been a pseudonym – perhaps of Lavallée

*Confédération Quadrille: Danse nationale*, published by A.J. Boucher. In reviewing the publication, *L'Union nationale* provided readers with a detailed description of the cover, which is an elaborate parody of many aspects of Confederation. (See figure 2.3) The anonymously written review is itself something of an enigma: "This poor confederation … has found a refuge in the lyre of Terpsichore: of all the festivities in which she has taken part, there will remain one fine memory, in the form of a lively and cheerful quadrille, a piece that is both limber and nimble, by a composer of substance who evades public ovations behind the pseudonym Léon Casorti." Close inspection of the music may one day help to determine the identity of the composer, but the next sentence of *L'Union nationale*'s review may provide a hint, as the writer draws an analogy to the form of dance itself, writing, "But one cannot really know whom to give credit to, because at the musician's side is a cartoonist, and if that one gathers the laurels (*'lauriers'*) in the 'chain of ladies,' it certainly puts us on notice to weave crowns (*'couronnes'*) of his talent and originality."[95] The 'chain of ladies,' or *'chaîne des dames*,' is a configuration formed by couples dancing a quadrille. This cryptic phrase may point to Lavallée as the composer, as his *Couronne de lauriers* was published a year earlier and reviewed in the same newspaper by Gustave Smith – who would be the obvious designer of the cover as he had been trained in the visual arts and was an experienced lithographer.[96]

April brought little good news. In the US, the Confederate Army surrendered on 9 April, but just five days later John Wilkes Booth assassinated Abraham Lincoln. At least briefly, the killing raised new concerns of US retribution since Booth had been in Montreal in October, meeting with Confederate agents.[97] The murder also elicited a genuine expression of grief among many in Montreal. On 19 April, as a sign of respect on the day of the murdered president's funeral, most businesses closed at noon. Mayor Beaudry led a vigil at the Mechanics' Hall, at which the local MP D'Arcy McGee proposed that a resolution be drafted on behalf of the citizens of Montreal that the murder was "not only a crime against the laws of the United States but a crime against humanity and Christianity."[98] At the same time, spring flooding was causing havoc, first in Montreal, and then with devastating consequences to a large region east of the city. Lavallée himself appealed to the community to help provide financial assistance, presenting it as "a cause of both patriotism and of charity," and proposing to hold a concert if the public would support the initiative.[99] He and Smith subsequently formed a committee and scheduled a concert for Saturday, 29 April, with Smith as musical director and himself as violinist in the chamber orchestra. The program was to open with the overture to Auber's *La Muette* and feature Lavallée conducting his orchestration of Offenbach's one-act operetta *La Leçon de chant électromagnétique,* with vocalists Boucher and Trottier.[100] On Thursday evening, Lavallée took part in a benefit concert at Nordheimer's Hall for the Saint-Vincent de Paul Society. At this concert, he made what was becoming an increasingly rare appearance as a violinist, playing Charles de Bériot's *Rondo Russe.* The proceeds of this concert appear to have been lost the next evening, when Lavallée was assaulted in the street.

The circumstances of this attack remain sketchy, with details coming mostly from the *Union nationale.* It appears that Lavallée and the two singers had spent the evening of Friday, 28 April, rehearsing at Smith's home on de la Gauchetière Street. Around 11 p.m., the three left to return home, walking together for several blocks before going in separate directions. Earlier that year, the Lavallées had moved to Saint-André Street, near Mignon (now de Maisonneuve). According to the report, Lavallée had set off in that direction, proceeding up Saint-Denis Street and around the back of Saint-Jacques Church, where he was attacked by two men.[101] One grabbed him, while the other attempted to stab him with a dagger. He raised his right hand and blocked the knife, but was then hit in the stomach. The muggers then made off with his chain, and a gold cross "given to him by the ladies of New Orleans," which he was said to have often worn when on stage. Presumably this is the medal he is pictured wearing in the photograph with Bidaux. They also took from him $140 in proceeds from the concert given the night before.[102] Lavallée made it the rest of the way home, and Augustin took him to Dr Venne, who was said to have reported the events to *L'Union nationale.* Later in the day, after going to the police, Lavallée himself visited the *Union nationale* offices, where he related the events.[103]

News items about street crime had appeared with greater frequency over the past year, perhaps due to a general influx of migrant workers. The *Union nationale* article did not explain why Lavallée was carrying the money from the previous night. It closed by noting that Lavallée's injury would prevent him from performing as planned that night, but that he would none the less play some role.[104] In a separate column on the same page, Smith published a plea to the public to attend the concert that evening. He concluded by saying that two members of the organizing committee would deliver the funds raised to the Saint-Vincent de Paul Society on Sunday, after vespers, no doubt to allay concerns of another robbery.[105] Evidently, the concert took place, but newspapers carried no reports of its outcome or of Lavallée's contribution to it. In the weeks that followed, he remained out of the public eye, but was back on stage at the beginning of June.

Musically, the high point of the summer of 1865 was the arrival of another francophone violinist, Frantz Jehin-Prume. Like Lavallée, the twenty-six-year-old violinist, best known as Frantz Prume, came from a family of musicians, the most famous being his uncle, the celebrated violinist and composer François Prume, with whom he made his debut at the age of nine. After studies in Liège and Brussels, in 1855 Frantz Prume began performing throughout Europe. In 1864 he accepted an invitation from the Empress of Mexico (previously Princess Charlotte of Belgium) and travelled to Mexico City. After a number of performances for the court, he travelled north by way of Havana. While in New York he arranged concerts for the fall and winter, and then travelled to Montreal to visit his childhood friend and fellow violinist Jules Hone.[106] Together, they organized several performances that attracted the attention of both French- and English-speaking communities. Prume performed a repertoire that contained familiar pieces, including Vieuxtemps concertos and the ever-popular *Carnival of Venice*, and also pieces rarely if ever heard in public concerts in Canada, including the works of J.S. Bach. Billing himself as "Violinist to the King of the Belgians," Prume himself received royal treatment. On 23 May, Hone and Prume took part in a soirée at the Collège Sainte-Marie. He then organized a full concert with Lavallée, Smith, Regnaud, and others, at Nordheimer's Hall on 1 June 1865. In its preview, *L'Ordre* advised readers not to miss the opportunity to hear "perhaps the most famous violinist ever to visit the continent."[107] In his first public appearance since being assaulted in April, Lavallée performed just one piece, his piano transcription of *La Prière de Moïse*. In its review, *L'Ordre* called the concert "the best of the season, artistically perfect."[108] In *L'Union nationale*, Smith began his review by calling Prume "the equal of Vieuxtemps."[109] He noted that the violinist had come to Montreal just for a rest but expressed the hope that he would give another performance. As it turned out, there would be several more. The next took place a week later, on 8 June, this time at the Mechanics' Hall with a string orchestra provided by the Twenty-fifth Regiment. Soloists included a Mr Mayerhoffer and Marie Regnaud, who played a piece by Chopin.[110] Although billed as a "farewell concert," it would not be Prume's last performance. A few days later, he set off for Quebec City and other destinations, but over the next few months he used Montreal as his base.

Politics continued to dominate the news throughout the summer, even though delegates had set off for London to work out the final arrangements for the implementation of Confederation. In Montreal, conservatives and liberals continued to trade barbs in the press. They were even divided on the *Fête nationale* arrangements, in part due to the exclusion of the Institut canadien from the procession. With 24 June falling on a Saturday, Lavallée and Smith held a long-anticipated Fête Nationale Concert to raise funds for the monument to those who had died in the rebellions of 1837 and 1838. (See figure 2.4) The traditional celebrations were shifted to Monday, 26 June, so that the promenade concert and dancing could take place. After this, Lavallée remained in the city through the fall, but appeared at only a few events. On 3 July Prume returned for what was billed as a "farewell concert," but wasn't. Lavallée took part in a concert in Longueuil later that month, but little other evidence appears on how Lavallée was spending his time until Prume's return in September. After this, things grew even quieter. Lavallée seems to have made his final public appearance at a benefit concert for J.B. Labelle on 9 November. Several of Lavallée's colleagues had already departed.

❖❖❖

After a decade in Canada, Smith had quietly been making plans to relocate since soon after the tour with Urso had fallen through. On 10 February, he wrote to the archbishop of New Orleans, Jean-Marie Odin, enquiring about a position as organist, claiming that he planned to move to New Orleans and establish himself there as an organist and professor of piano. At the beginning of his letter he states that he, like Odin, was French, despite his name, and that he hoped to find students among the city's French-speaking population. He attached a copy of a letter from the Conservatoire's director Daniel Auber, attesting to his training, and two letters of introduction, one from Father Dowd, of St Patrick's Church, and another written on behalf of Montreal's Bishop Bourget.[111]

Figure 2.4
With 24 June falling on
a Saturday, Lavallée and Smith
held a long-anticipated Fête
Nationale Concert to raise funds
for the monument to those who
died in the Rebellions of 1837
and 1838.

While waiting for a response, he remained active. To counter rumours that he planned to leave, he published an advertisement asserting that he was remaining definitively in Montreal and giving lessons at his home.[112] It is difficult to know if the claim was sincere. The mood had changed in Montreal after the 10 March vote in the legislature, and before the year was out, he and several others had departed.

Prume returned to New York in the fall, where audiences received him with enthusiasm. He made his debut at Irving Hall on 18 November at a concert with the pianist S.B. Mills and the young contralto Zelda Harrison.

Concerts with New York Philharmonic followed, and at a testimonial concert given for him at the Brooklyn Academy of Music on 13 December, Marie Regnaud made her US debut. She was well received and chose to stay on in New York to study with Mills.[113]

With the political course determined, Frantz Prume's arrival in Montreal that summer had probably only postponed the departures of Lavallée and Smith. Other opponents of Confederation were also leaving. The twenty-seven-year-old poet Louis-Honoré Fréchette left for Chicago in 1866, where he agitated for the annexation of Canada to the US. Lanctôt fought on until 1868.[114] Wilfrid Laurier, suffering from chronic bronchitis, left Montreal for his health in 1866. He settled in the town of Victoriaville, where he edited the Liberal newspaper *Le Défricheur*. He continued to oppose Confederation until it was proclaimed, and then he too made his entry into politics.

For Lavallée, the events of the mid-1860s had deepened the connections between music and politics. The charismatic Lanctôt had no doubt influenced Lavallée's thinking, but his direction was already evident. And with Smith, his bond was both musical and political. They were the most gifted performers in the city and shared a similar world view. Cosmopolitan and yet patriotic, they both favoured a republican form of government, Smith having demonstrated his leanings in choosing the republican side in the Revolution of 1848, Lavallée having opted for a life in the US and a year in the Union Army. In Montreal of the mid-1860s, their grassroots effort to keep Lower Canada out of Confederation had failed. Smith found a position in New Orleans. Lavallée returned to the world he had abandoned in 1863, that of the travelling minstrel.

# The Journeyman Musician

## 1866–1873

On 3 February 1866, the *New York Clipper* reported that Charles Duprez had "secured the services of Mons. Lavallee, the well known musician from Montreal, C.E., as first violinist, thus adding to the attractions of this troupe." Lavallée was on the road again, and would be for most of the next seven years. His tours with Duprez brought him south again, and then back and forth between New England and the Midwest, with periods of stability in Chicago and Philadelphia, before he left for a competing company from New York, and then for another from Boston. He shared the stage with the leading entertainers of the era. He married, had a child, played the violin and cornet, published songs, arranged music for stage productions, composed an operetta, and reinvented himself.

It had been nearly three years since Lavallée had left the New Orleans Minstrels, first to tour with Ellinger and then to return to Montreal. For Duprez, it had been business as usual. Each fall, he set out on a tour that brought him through northern US and Canada. Each tour brought new cast members. Following Lavallée's departure in 1863, Duprez had recruited a number of new musicians, among them John Kelk, as first violinist and musical director, and the band leader Alphonse Bergeron, whom he billed as the "Royal Cornettist of Canada." As the 1865–66 tour began, there were three musicians with the name Koehl – Charles, Jacob, and James (presumably brothers) – and Edward Parmelee was leading the band. Other leading cast members that fall included the vocalist Bidaux, the wench dancer Frank Kent, and the comedians Billy West, Gonsalvo Bishop, and Lew Benedict. When, in November 1865, Green withdrew to form his own company, Benedict took his place in the renamed Duprez & Benedict troupe. Lavallée took over as musical director while the troupe was in New England, in January 1866. Duprez had advertised for a "first class, thorough violinist" and musical director. The advertisement reveals some of the requirements of a minstrel musical director, a position that would not be easily filled today. Like the other musicians, he would have to be a multi-instrumentalist, playing both violin and a brass instrument. And in this instance, he was expected to be sober ("steady") and "perfectly competent to arrange vocal and orchestra music brilliantly." The job demanded a thorough understanding of many musical styles, especially in producing the parodies that were central to the minstrel show. Resuming his old post with Duprez, Lavallée was on the road again, beginning what would be four years of criss-crossing North America as the company's bandleader and musical director.

Without changing the format of the New Orleans Minstrels' show, as musical director, Lavallée increased the number of operatic numbers in the company's programs. Many of these excerpts were overtures and choruses frequently heard in Montreal, such as Adam's "Les Enfants de Paris." Also in their repertoire was a burlesque on Meyerbeer's L'Africaine, but the more obvious racial humour was becoming a thing of the past.[1] Frank Dumont, one of Lavallée's colleagues, later described the period up to 1864 as "the golden days of minstrelsy as a picture of Negro life in the South. With the end of the war or emancipation of the slaves, the Negro lost his pathetic or attractive position as an object of interest. The draft riots in New York were levelled at the Negro." Minstrelsy, he said, had to be "renovated on different lines." War songs and sentimental ballads, "superseded the slave songs. We saw the Negro in a new light and important innovations were made in the way of special acts or more attention paid to the singing and instrumentations."[2] At a time when all social classes were well acquainted with the works of Donizetti and Bellini, opera was a viable substitute for plantation songs. And as the company began to dispense with the patriotic numbers required during war and perform essentially the same program everywhere, a new popular culture began to emerge.

While in Rochester, New York, in March 1866, Lavallée published perhaps his only piano piece of this four-year period. It is also among the most curious pieces that he composed. The title, *Shake Again Galop, an Answer to "Slap Bang" or Here We Are Again*, op. 27, refers to the comic song by Harry Copeland, published earlier the same year.[3] Either Lavallée or his publisher, Alexander Barnes, appears to have used this song as the basis of a musical satire of the burgeoning evangelical Christian movement.[4] The dedication page of Lavallée's galop reads: "To the Holy Rollers of Rochester, NY"; and on the title page is inscribed the motto: "We neither laugh nor sing, but we shake and dance. H.R's." Musically, Lavallée's galop is related to the song only in that both pieces are in 2/4 meter and have lively tempos. But the galop also contains a musical pun, beginning and ending with four measures of quarter notes, above which is noted "shake," which could be interpreted as a trill. From this and its title, it appears that Lavallée or his publisher may not have distinguished between the Holy Rollers (a disparaging term used to describe followers of Pentecostalism) and the Shakers, a sect whose form of worship, like that of the Pentecostals, was highly physical.[5]

Still more interesting was a song also published in Rochester that year, "Flag of Green." This was not one of the traditional melodies known by this title but a newly composed political song, published by Cook & Martin. On its cover, above a pair of flags, each bearing the image of a golden harp, was a dedication to the "Fenian Brotherhood throughout the world."[6] (See figure 3.1) Compared with the hackneyed Irish ballads that publishers churned out in the hundreds each year, this was musical nationalism at its most direct.[7] The simplicity and directness of Gustave Bidaux's tune and J.B. Murphy's lyrics may have helped to make it a crowd-pleaser among partisans. Lavallée produced a rousing arrangement for solo voice and three-part chorus. The thirty-five measure introduction, marked "Martial and con bravura," builds tension with rising figures, dotted rhythms, and dissonant chords, all leading to the opening statement (see appendix 2). Designed to inflame passions, this war song gained some popularity in the US, where it was sung at St Patrick's Day concerts and other Irish community events. At minstrel show performances, it contrasted sharply with the sentimental Irish ballads usually sung in the middle section of the show, and illustrates that politics was prominent on the minds of some members of the audience. Although it was published and performed in the US, "Flag of Green"

Figure 3.1
Cover image of Lavallée's arrangement of "Flag of Green," a song forcefully advocating Irish independence. ·

would not have been performed on stage while the company was in Canada, where militia regiments were organized specifically to guard the border against Fenian attacks.

With transportation returning to normal, the New Orleans Minstrels were able to travel further than ever before and return to the South. After bringing the troupe for the first time up the Missouri River in the New Territories (now Nebraska), Duprez decided against taking the usual summer break in New England. Instead, the troupe remained in the Midwest through July and August, and then made their way south. The trip itself was unusually rapid. From Louisville, Kentucky, they travelled by train to Tennessee for four-night engagements in Nashville and Memphis. From there, they travelled by river, playing brief engagements at Vicksburg, Mississippi, and Baton Rouge, Louisiana, before making what would be a calamitous return to New Orleans.[8]

Although the war had ended, the occupation was over, and many veterans had returned, the economy of New Orleans had yet to recover.[9] The social and economic changes brought about by the outcome of the war left many whites angry, displaced, and fearful of the future – a situation that often escalated into violence. Only a month before the New Orleans Minstrels' arrival, a riot had left at least forty blacks dead.[10] The dire mood of the city put many musicians and entertainers in an especially desperate financial position. Neither opera nor other forms of entertainment succeeded as they had before the war. To attract clients, the Academy of Music announced that it had been "renovated, redecorated and enlarged, to meet the wants and comfort" of the citizens.[11] Others could ill afford renovations. In what should have been high season, the St Charles Theater was available for rent by the night or week, and previously busy musicians scrambled for work.[12]

Given the circumstances, Duprez & Benedict opened to what must have seemed to be a good house at the St Charles Theater on 5 September 1866. Attendance then began a precipitous fall, even though in this case the only competition was a circus. The *New York Clipper*'s correspondent noted that the decline might "be attributed to the inclemency of the weather," but added that minstrelsy was "becoming rather obsolete in this city, and that unless sandwiched between some other kind of performances it cannot flourish for any length of time."[13] Economics undoubtedly played a role in the declining popularity of the minstrel show in the South. A review published in the 10 September 1865 *Times-Picayune* summed up the troupe's situation in the city: "the entertainment offered seems to have been selected with a view to attract a good share of the amusement seekers who have remained in the city, despite the warm weather, cholera and the dull season."[14] To what extent white southern audiences may have been repelled by 'black' images on stage is unclear. For some in the South, the minstrel show was a painful reminder of a way of life that had been forever changed.

A deposit on the theatre may have been the only reason for the troupe remained in the city, and the mood grew increasingly grim. On 19 September, Duprez sacked Gustave Bidaux after the entertainer made "some uncalled for remarks" about the St Charles Theater's management.[15] Considering his experience in 1862 and the return of cholera in 1866,

Bidaux may have been looking for a way out. As other members of the troupe began falling ill, Duprez finally decided to cut his losses. The *Times-Picayune* reported on 21 September that the comedian Charley Reynolds, who had rejoined the company in April, was seriously ill and that the troupe would be leaving town without him the next day.[16] On 22 September they boarded the *Mary Forsyth*, of the Atlantic and Mississippi Steamship Company, bound for the Midwest. All are believed to have survived with the exception of Sam Pond, the company's agent, who was said to have died of "congestive swamp chills" near Cairo, Illinois.[17] Duprez appears never to have returned to New Orleans with the troupe nor to have visited other parts of the South, where his company had for years been an audience favourite.

The rest of 1866 passed uneventfully. By December, the company was in Canada and from there it travelled into New England, celebrated the New Year with performances in Providence, and continued the tour without a break for a further six months, coming to an end in Ontario in July 1867, just weeks after Confederation had come into effect.[18] Lavallée then returned to Montreal for a brief holiday, during which time he gave concerts around the province with Henri Gauthier, A.J. Boucher, and Salomon Mazurette, a student of Letondal. Interestingly, Lavallée's repertoire included a transcription of the Austrian national anthem (as of 1867, the anthem of Austria-Hungary), Joseph Haydn's "Gott erhalte Franz den Kaiser" (God Save Emperor Franz), with which he was on one occasion said to have "surprised the connoisseurs with the flexibility and strength of his performance."[19] One might wonder if Lavallée had added it to his repertoire earlier in the year in reference to the imperilled – and, by June, dead – Emperor Maximilian, or if he was perhaps already musing over possible anthems for the new country. Like "O Canada," Haydn's anthem is in the form of a slow march and in the key of G major. Haydn, too, had been inspired by Britain's "God Save the King" and had set out to create something comparable for the Austrian Empire.[20] The idea may have stayed with Lavallée, but it would have to wait. By September 1867, he was back at work in New England.

Duprez was again advertising for new members at the start of his ten-month 1867–68 tour. Despite his usual reminder that "salaries must be moderate," he hired four musicians and three singers within two weeks

---

### Singers, Dancers, Comedians

Gonsalvo Bishop, 'basso,' 'interrogator'; Lewis Benedict, 'tambo'; Billy West, 'bones'; Edwin Holmes, tenor balladist; James W. Dearborn, alto balladist; L.E. Hicks, balladist; C. Slocum, comedian, 'general performer'; Frank Kent, 'burlesque prima donna'; Lew Collins, vocalist, clog dancer; Frank Parkhurst, vocalist, clog dancer

### Musicians

Calixa Lavallée, 1st violinist, musical director; Kilian Jordon, 2nd violinist, tenor horn; Edward White, clarinet, 2nd alto horn; Tom Woodbury, flute, piccolo, snare drum; Fleming Adams, bass viol, tuba; Ferdinand Heinrich, cello, E flat cornet; L.E. Hicks, 1st alto horn; Warren Richards, B flat cornet

Charles H. Duprez, general manager; Alfred Hurn, treasurer; George Hall, baggage handler

---

Figure 3.2   The New Orleans Minstrels' cast and crew at the start of the 1867–68 tour.

and published the new and very versatile lineup in mid-September. (See figure 3.2) The cast list shows Lavallée as first violinist, musical director, and leader of an eight-member brass band. Several of the vocalists were also band members: L.E. Hicks played 1st alto horn and Warren Richards played B-flat cornet.[21] Most of the comedians from the previous season returned. Lew Benedict, Billy West, and Gonsalvo Bishop formed the centre, as tambo, bones, and interlocutor, respectively. Frank Kent resumed his role as the wench dancer, and Duprez added a new duo of clog dancers, Frank Parkhurst and Lew Collins. Part way into the tour, they were joined by Frank Dumont, a twenty-year-old Franco-American comedian and musician.

The tour saw Duprez attempting to draw a more mixed audience to the company's performances. As the American musicologist Dale Cockrell has written, working-class men from the towns and cities filled most of the seats.[22] As early as 1860, Duprez had attempted to attract more women to his performances. Admission cards noted that "front and center seats [were] for ladies and gentlemen accompanying them."[23] Men presumably occupied other parts of the hall, and minstrelsy's reputation for profanity and sexual innuendo dissuaded more women from attending performances.[24] To remedy the situation, Duprez pledged to present a more chaste program on the 1867–68 tour. He noted that some members of the public had refrained from attending minstrel shows "by the dread of having their sensibilities wounded by the utterances of low remarks, or the demonstration of gross and unbecoming action."[25] He claimed that his company's performances would "be conducted in a high toned and dignified manner. Nothing shall be said or done that in the slightest degree could offend."[26] Duprez made these statements frequently in advertisements, and his advance agent, Charles Slocum, persuaded reviewers to remind readers that he provided "family" entertainment. A correspondent from Troy, New York, reported the troupe's jokes to be fresh but "thoroughly refined, and nothing is said to offend the most fastidious."[27] Later, the *Daily Pioneer* of St Paul, Minnesota, reported that "the reputation of this unsurpassed troupe is so well established, and the fact so well understood, that everything they say or do is entirely free from every species of vulgarity, that the best and leading citizens of the city were present last evening, and all went away delighted."[28]

The troupe's Minnesota performances may have attracted the society's elite, but Duprez's continuing efforts to draw women and the middle class illustrate that the minstrel show still required careful marketing. The 1867–68 programs contained very little political satire. Duprez & Benedict was one of several troupes to present a burlesque on the Ku Klux Klan, but overall, Duprez avoided current events.[29] Extant programs reveal no references to the impeachment proceedings against President Andrew Johnson that coincided with the Duprez & Benedict 1867–68 tour. The failure of Reconstruction policies may have been simply too sensitive an issue to bring to the stage. Instead, Duprez & Benedict presented entertainment that brought distractions from everyday concerns with Parkhurst and Collins's comic song-and-dance numbers, and tenor Warren Richards's sentimental ballads, many of them supplied by Frank Dumont.

Midway through the tour, on 21 December 1867, Lavallée was married in Lowell, Massachusetts.[30] He was then just a week shy of his

Figure 3.3 Photograph of Joséphine Gentilly dating from about 1867, the year she and Lavallée married.

twenty-fifth birthday, and his bride was Joséphine Gentilly, a nineteen-year-old native of the town. A photograph of her dating from about this time shows a sweet looking young woman with dark hair. (See figure 3.3) Although the marriage lasted twenty-three years, surprisingly little is known of Joséphine. The marriage records list her as a resident of the nearby town of Lawrence, Massachusetts.[31] Given that Lawrence was known almost exclusively for its mills, it seems likely that she had gone there to find work. Both her father and brother were reported to have died while fighting on the side of the Union during the Civil War, which helps to explain Joséphine's need for employment.[32] It is unclear where she was residing in the fall and winter of 1867. Her mother, Elizabeth Gentilly, was still alive and Joséphine may have been visiting her when she and Lavallée met. The New Orleans Minstrels had visited Lowell in the early months of 1866 and had stopped in twice in 1867 to perform at Huntington Hall, first on 28 October and then on 14 December. And then they returned a week later, "for one night only."[33] The wedding took place during the day at St Anne's Episcopal Church, and in the evening Lavallée took part in the troupe's performance.[34] The *New York Clipper*'s minstrelsy column of 4 January 1868 notified readers of the marriage, stating simply "Calixa Lavallée, the violinist and Musical Director of Duprez and Benedict's Minstrels, is said to have married at Lowell, Mass., December 21 to Miss Josephine Gentilly of that place."[35]

Marriage did not seem to slow or change Lavallée in any noticeable way. After their wedding night, he was back on the road for the remainder of the tour and presumably Joséphine was with him until it closed in New Haven, Connecticut, on 4 July 1868. As with the wives of Duprez, Shorey, and others who travelled with the company, she would likely have assisted with costumes and meals. She was certainly known to the members of the company, as Dumont and Hicks dedicated a song to her.[36] Nine months after the wedding, she was back in Lawrence, where she gave birth to Calixa Jr on 20 September 1868.[37] Lavallée would often be an absent parent, and was at this time 400 kilometres away in Montreal.

❖❖❖

It had been more than a year since Confederation had been realized. Led by John A. Macdonald, the Conservatives were in power in Ottawa, governing a semi-autonomous country with four provinces: New Brunswick, Nova Scotia, Ontario, and Quebec. The Conservatives were also in power in Quebec City, where Pierre-Joseph-Olivier Chauveau was premier.[38] *L'Union nationale* had closed down the previous year, and Lanctôt had just recently left for the US. Laurier had married Zoë Lafontaine and established a law practice in Arthabaska (now Victoriaville). Gustave Smith and Marie Regnaud were still in the US. But many of Lavallée's colleagues of the mid-decade were still in Montreal. L.-O. David was practising law. Thompson had married in 1866 and left journalism for the insurance business. The industrious A.J. Boucher, whom Lavallée had toured with the previous summer, was conducting the choir at Gesù Church and running a successful music publishing business. Augustin Lavallée's business had prospered, and he had moved his music shop and *lutherie* to 43 Côte Saint-Lambert (St Lambert Hill), which is now the lower end of boulevard Saint-Laurent. Located on the east side of the street, where the courthouse now stands, the shop would remain in this location for several decades and become something of a local institution. The Lavallée family was now residing just down the hill, at 85 Saint Lawrence Street, two blocks north of Augustin's shop.[39]

Lavallée took part in two major concerts in September. The first, on 3 September, was the inauguration of St Patrick's Hall, a four-storey limestone structure erected on Victoria Square, just a short distance from St Patrick's Church. (See figure 3.4) Its main feature was a concert hall on the second floor with a seating capacity of 2,000. For the inaugural concert, the St Patrick's Society hired Lavallée and Frederick Torrington to lead the orchestra, and gathered a large number of soloists, among them François Lavoie, Jules Hone, and Madame Petipas, a French vocalist who had recently arrived from South America, by way of New Orleans.[40] The program opened with a performance of a piece simply called "St Patrick's

Figure 3.4 St Patrick's Hall, Victoria Square, Montreal, was inaugurated on 3 September 1868 with a concert featuring Lavallée. Later that month he gave a concert there under his own name. The building was destroyed four years later when the roof collapsed.

Day," and speech from Dr William Hingston. After this, it was Handel, Haydn, Mendelssohn, and Bellini, along with a number of national songs.[41] Despite there being several competing events, including the great Lucille Tostée performing Offenbach with H.L. Bateman's company at the Theatre Royal, the concert appears to have drawn a full house, and a follow-up concert was quickly arranged.

Lavallée did not take part in the second concert, a week later. He was by then preparing for his own concert at the same venue on 16 September. It was an auspicious time, with scores of visitors in the city to attend the Industrial Exhibition, which was being held at the Crystal Palace, and the annual Agricultural Exhibition, then taking place at Victoria Skating Rink. As with the inaugural concert, he had Frederick Torrington conduct the orchestra, which was likely the same ensemble put together for the concert on 3 September. Among the other soloists, he gave second billing to Madame Petipas (as *"Prima Donna des principaux Théâtres d'Europe, premier prix du Conservatoire, etc., etc."*).[42] Also on the program was the pianist Salomon Mazurette, whom Lavallée had performed with the previous summer, and Oscar Martel, a talented young violinist from nearby L'Assomption, who had come to Montreal to study with Jules Hone. Both Liberal and Conservative newspapers promoted the event. *La Minerve*'s unnamed critic claimed "everyone is talking [about] the grand concert [to be] given by our Canadian artist, Mr C. Lavallée."[43] In a small notice published on 15 September, *Le Pays* reminded readers of the participants and location, noting that it would be unnecessary to encourage readers to attend, and simply referring them "to the program which cannot fail to attract a considerable crowd."[44]

Part of the anticipation resulted from the knowledge that Narcisse-Fortunat Belleau had agreed to act as the official patron. Belleau had organized the events of the Prince of Wales's 1860 visit, and been knighted by the prince in part for that work. In 1865, during the transition to Confederation, he served as the final premier of the United Province of Canada, and in 1867 he became Quebec's first lieutenant-governor, the Queen's representative. Although a long-time Conservative, Belleau was admired by Liberals as well, and perhaps also by Lavallée, who composed a song for the occasion, "Salut à la noble bannière," and dedicated it to Belleau.[45] The words of the song were written by Benjamin Sulte, a translator and journalist originally from the town of Trois-Rivières.[46] Although Sulte would later earn a reputation as something of a liberal, and the two were about the same age, in 1868 he and Lavallée seemed unlikely collaborators. In 1861, when Lavallée had joined the Fourth Rhode Island Regiment, Sulte had enlisted in the Canadian militia to defend against a possible invasion of US troops. In 1866, he was editing the Conservative Ottawa newspaper *Le Canada* and from there became a translator at the House of Commons. The song itself seems not to have been published, leaving one to wonder which "banner" the title referred to. It was sung on this occasion by the tenor Ludger Maillet. A self-taught vocalist, Maillet had performed with Lavallée in 1865 when he was studying law with Joseph Doutre.[47] Now twenty-three, and a member of the Bar, Maillet remained active as an amateur performer and was no doubt quite capable since Lavallée had him perform the song.[48]

Belleau arrived from Quebec City by steamer on 15 September, attracting considerable attention. With some lingering ill-feelings toward the institution, if not the man himself, *Le Pays* noted that from the pier the lieutenant-governor's entourage consisted of seven carriages accompanied by a cavalry detachment, that his suite of rooms at St Lawrence Hall was paid for by the city, and that in the evening he dined with Mayor William Workman – presumably also at the taxpayers' expense.[49] The military protection may have been prudent. In April, the Montreal MP D'Arcy McGee had been assassinated, and the trial of his alleged killer, Patrick Whalen, was coming to a conclusion that same day. Given the timing, Fenian attacks on British institutions were a possibility. On this occasion, nothing unexpected happened. On their arrival at St Patrick's Hall that evening, Belleau and his retinue were greeted by a performance of "Vive la Canadienne." Aside from Petipas's withdrawing at the last moment, the concert seemed to go well. *La Minerve* claimed that Lavallée could be proud of his success in organizing the event.[50] On 18 September, *Le Nouveau Monde* noted that the concert attracted the "*beau et grand monde*" of the time, among them cabinet ministers and military leaders. Belleau was said to have complimented Lavallée and Sulte on the song they had created in his honour. No doubt they thanked him for his patronage. There were musicians to pay and presumably a rental fee for the hall, and Belleau's presence had helped to fill it. Lavallée may have been reminded of his debut, nearly a decade earlier, at a performance patronized by Lieutenant-General Sir William Eyre. He had learned early the value of political connections. He may also have been looking for an opportunity that would allow him to abandon the life of a minstrel show musician.

❖❖❖

Lavallée seems to have left the New Orleans Minstrels in July with no fixed plan to return. Late in August, Charles Duprez was advertising for a new musical director-violinist-trumpeter.[51] Lavallée evidently responded and this time Duprez came to Montreal in September to put the company together and opened the 1868–69 tour at the Mechanics' Institute on the night of Lavallée's concert. In *Le Pays*, the advertisement for Lavallée's concert was placed immediately above that for Duprez's engagement at the Mechanics' Institute. As usual, newspapers said nothing of Lavallée's presence in the minstrel show performances. Presumably, he took part in rehearsals and in the company's performances on 17–19 September. On 20 September he said farewell once again and was on the road, travelling that fall through Ontario into the US Midwest, and then back through New York State and into New England where, in December, he would have an opportunity to see his three-month-old son, Calixa Jr. Perhaps at that point Joséphine and the baby joined the company. If not, it was likely a year before he saw them again, as the tour zigzagged southward to Tennessee, and from there back into the Midwest.

During the 1868–69 tour, Duprez's company featured two large opera burlesques. One was a parody of the massive National Peace Jubilee that Patrick Gilmore staged in Boston in the summer of 1869. Duprez & Benedict were in the Midwest when the jubilee took place, which gives some indication of how much attention it had attracted. In the parody, Gonsalvo Bishop played Gilmore and the entire company took part in the famous "Anvil Chorus" (the Gypsy chorus "Coro di Zingari," from Giuseppi Verdi's *Il trovatore*), which had for years been a staple for parody by minstrel troupes. The popularity of the original music and the high standard of musicianship among Duprez's performers helped to make the parody such a hit that they kept it in their repertoire for more than a year, and performed it as far west as San Francisco in 1870. Performances of the Gilmore/Verdi burlesque alternated with one of *La Belle Hélène*. Offenbach's works had suddenly taken New York and the rest of the Northeast by storm. Their spirited music and racy productions provided abundant opportunities for satire by an all-male cast experienced in the art of female impersonation and equipped with an extensive costume wardrobe.

Sentimentality also remained a core element in the minstrel show of the late 1860s, and talented songwriters were in demand. During his time with Duprez & Benedict, Lavallée published several of his songs with the Whittemore firm, of Detroit. Like many minstrel show songs of the era, they were written for solo voice with chorus. The best known of these was "The Beautiful Girl of Kildare." (See figure 3.5) Irish subjects were popular, particularly with recent immigrants, and sentimentality sold well, helping to make the song a hit.[52] In this ballad, the singer laments having left a young woman "far o're the sea," and dreams of seeing her again one

Figure 3.5
The cover of Lavallée's "The Beautiful Girl of Kildare," which capitalized on the popularity of Irish themes in music.

day. Warren Richards wrote the lyrics and performed the song. And although there is nothing obviously Irish from the piano-vocal score, Lavallée's arrangement for performance in the minstrel hall likely featured a plaintive solo fiddle, or flute, and Richards would likely have sung it in costume and with an Irish brogue. The song remained popular for several years. It was reissued in London in 1874, and in the early 1880s at least one US writer remembered Lavallée as "the author of the well-known minstrel ballad 'Beautiful Girl of Kildare.'"[53]

From the fall of 1868, the New Orleans Minstrels remained continuously on the road for nearly a year. From Montreal, they travelled through Ontario, Michigan, upstate New York, Connecticut, Rhode Island, and, by December, were in Massachusetts. From the start of the New Year, they performed in New Jersey, New York State, Maryland, Pennsylvania, Ohio, Indiana, Kentucky, and Tennessee, then returned northward, stopping in Indiana, Illinois, and Minnesota, before making another loop around the Midwest before arriving, in August, at Philadelphia's Arch Street Theatre. And here Duprez decided he would stop. In the spring of 1868, he had attempted to establish a permanent base at Chicago's 1,200-seat Library Hall. The venture failed, due perhaps to the theatre's location or to strong competition from Arlington's Minstrels.[54] A successful run at the Arch Street Theatre in early August 1869 presented another opportunity. During that engagement, Duprez leased the Seventh Street Theater.[55] Over the weeks that followed, as the company continued to travel, alterations were made to the theatre, and on 25 October it reopened as Duprez & Benedict's Opera House.

Unlike the arrangement in Chicago, this time the permanent base worked well. On 6 November, the *New York Clipper* attributed Duprez's success in part to the appearance of the 1,100-seat theatre, claiming it to have been "greatly improved by numerous gas lights and jets and tasteful decorations."[56] Strong attendance soon enabled Duprez to expand the company and to draw back some of his star talent. In November, Frank Kent returned to the troupe after ten weeks with the San Francisco Minstrels. He joined two other wench dancers, Justine Robinson and George Wilkes. Frank Dumont had become the troupe's main writer and a part-time comedian. Charley Reynolds, who had long since recovered from the ailment that had nearly taken his life in New Orleans, returned from his engagement with Arlington's Minstrels in Chicago.[57] He, Benedict, and Bishop formed the trio of bones, tambo, and interlocutor, respectively. They were all overshadowed to some extent when the veteran comedian Frank Brower joined them in December. The *New York Clipper*'s minstrel show reporter devoted a column to Brower's arrival in the company, writing that his "Ginger Blue" characterization "would meet the test of criticism upon the legitimate stage, as in every test of word and action he exhibits the true artist."[58] The attention helped to keep the hall busy six nights a week throughout the winter.

The permanent base would seem to have been preferable to life on the road. Although they were still residing in hotels, it would have certainly been easier, with a young child, to have a normal family life. Lavallée, however, may have been growing restless. In January 1870, now twenty-seven, he left Duprez's troupe to take a new position with the San Francisco Minstrels in New York. His exact reasons for leaving the New Orleans Minstrels are unknown. Duprez had given him top billing (as "Prof. C. Lavallée") in a company of stars, and the troupe had a long-term engagement and appeared to be thriving.[59] He had been with Duprez longer than anyone else. Together, they had travelled many thousands of miles and witnessed enormous social upheavals, but change was the norm for itinerant musicians, and for Lavallée as much as any. New York now offered him steady employment and new opportunities found only in the continent's cultural metropolis.

❖❖❖

In the five years since they settled in New York, the San Francisco Minstrels had become one of the country's best-known troupes. George C.D. Odell, chronicler of New York arts and entertainment, described the company as "that organization which seems to me to have been the most dignified, the most settled at that time in the city ... [They] had attained a strong hold on the affections of lovers of blackface art, and the San Francisco Minstrels were to be for many years, now, a regular institution of the metropolis, their name extending as far as to the city whose name they bore."[60] The troupe's founding members were all entertainment veterans from the Northeast. The thirty-nine-year-old comedian William Birch had been an endman with George Christy in the early 1850s. The

Figure 3.6 Promotional material for the New Orleans Minstrels shows the standard stage arrangement of the performers, with the musicians on the left.

tenor David Wambold had toured North America and Europe and was, in 1870, considered one of the great ballad singers of the time. Comedians William Bernard and Charley Backus had both performed for audiences in places as distant as Asia and Australia. They came together as a quartet in San Francisco in 1864 and were an immediate hit. When the war ended they sailed for New York, making their debut there on 8 May 1865. They acquired the former French Theatre, at 585 Broadway, and filled out their ranks with itinerant performers. (See figure 3.6) The company's 1869–70 season opened with a strong cast that featured the tenor Bobby Newcomb, the vocal quartet of Shattuck, Oberist, Templeton, and Wambold, and the former New Orleans Minstrels comedians Billy

West and Frank Kent. Illnesses, however, quickly sidelined several of the star performers. On 5 March, the *New York Clipper* announced that the post of the company's ailing musical director, Ira Paine, would be taken up by Lavallée.[61]

The San Francisco Minstrels' performances followed the standard three-part format. They opened with a selection of songs that featured Wambold's ballads, continued with a variety of skits and dances, and closed with a large-scale burlesque. In this final section of the show they usually satirized the operas and plays staged elsewhere on and around Broadway: from Charles M. Barras's immensely popular *Black Crook*, in 1867, to Offenbach's *Barbe Bleue*, a year later (which they offered as *Barber Brown*). To Odell, "every new sensational hit in the regular theatres was manna and spice for the minstrel humorists."[62] Many of the 1869–70 season's burlesques targeted the impresario and railway 'robber-baron' James Fisk Jr.[63] (See figure 3.7) Still in his thirties, Fisk was one of New York's most flamboyant public figures and the *enfant terrible* of finance. With funds from the Erie Railroad, which he managed, he had entered the entertainment business early in 1869, first acquiring

Figure 3.7
James Fisk Jr, proprietor and manager of the Grand Opera House, NY, proprietor of the Fifth Avenue Theatre, comptroller of the Erie Railroad, president of the Narragansett Steamship Company, and colonel of the Ninth Regiment.

Figure 3.8 The Grand Opera House, opened in 1868 and leased by James Fisk Jr soon after; its upper floors served as offices for the Erie Railroad. (Collection of the New-York Historical Society)

Pike's Opera House, on Eighth Avenue and West Twenty-Third Street, renaming it the Grand Opera House, and Bateman's operetta company, which he renamed Fisk's Opera Bouffe (See figure 3.8). He then gained control of Brougham's Theatre (which he renamed the Fifth Avenue Theatre), and the Brooklyn Academy of Music.[64] He tried his hand at all sorts of theatrical ventures but operetta became his mainstay, and the theatres helped Fisk to gain even wider coverage in the media. On 18 June, he treated President and Mrs Grant to a much-publicized evening of *La Périchole*, before travelling with them to Boston to attend Gilmore's music festival, where he upstaged the president and acquired the nickname "Jubilee Jim."[65] Only a few months later, he and his business partner Jay Gould caused a run on the gold market that became known as Black Friday.[66] The subsequent cash flow crisis forced Fisk to give up all but the Grand Opera House and Fisk's Opera Bouffe.[67] By that time he had completed some $250,000 in renovations to the Grand and moved the Erie Rail offices into the three upper floors of the building, making it the base of all of his operations. In the early months of 1870, Fisk produced a lavish spectacle by Joseph E. Foster and John E. McDonough entitled *The Twelve Temptations*. After months of pre-publicity and several delays, the $75,000 production opened on 7 February 1870 to mixed reviews but full houses. The show played continuously into the summer, attracting a largely male clientele with a cast that included one hundred cancan dancers.

The San Francisco Minstrels responded to Fisk and his activities with a number of burlesques that nearly all failed to deliver the usual critical and financial dividends. Two weeks after Lavallée's arrival as musical director, and just three days after the premiere of Fisk's *Twelve Temptations*, the San Francisco Minstrels opened a burlesque, suggestively titled *Thirteen Temptations, or Fisk Raised One*. The *Thirteen Temptations* was an immediate failure, probably because New Yorkers were far more interested in seeing the original. After two weeks the troupe withdrew it in favour of another sketch based on Fisk. In "The Female Brokers of Wall Street, Good Haul," Bernard played Jim Fisk and John Mulligan caricatured another 'robber baron,' Cornelius Vanderbilt ('C. Wanderbilt'). This too failed to pull in an audience. On 26 March, the *New York Clipper* reported the show to be doing only "fairly" at the box office, as it was "not calculated to create a *furore*. The wit and humor of the piece [being] limited" and failing to capitalize on the easy foibles of the "leading operators of the street ... Mulligan does Vanderbilt well, but Fisk is not as well burlesqued as he might have been. To 'hit folly as it flies' requires skilful handling of a strong bow supplied with a quiver of arrows pointed with sharp wit and keen sarcasm. This we have a right to expect from a troupe like the San Francisco Minstrels."[68] Whereas travelling troupes might be able to rely on a limited repertoire, a New York–based company was expected to continuously offer new entertainment, and a high standard was expected of the San Francisco Minstrels.

The city's critics offered no explanations as to why the troupe was unable to meet its usual standards. In March 1870, the *New York Clipper* reported "the San Francisco Minstrels possess all the elements of success, but their business has not been so good of late as it was at the opening of the present season, and this cannot be attributed to the absence of

Mr Wambold, for this decline was apparent before he retired. Messrs Norman and Lavallee have been added to the troupe since Wambold abdicated."[69] Ticket sales declined from $8,050 in November 1869 to $5,020 in April 1870, while receipts at the Grand Opera House during the same period rose from $17,385 to $33,839.[70] The troupe continued to limp along. At the beginning of May, they added the vocalist William Dwyer, whom the New York Clipper reported to be "a desirable acquisition to the company, though incapable of filling the void created by Wambold's temporary withdrawal."[71] A week later, they acquired Rollin Howard, the comic singer who had gained fame as the originator of "Shew Fly, Don't Bother Me."[72] He should have had strong drawing power, but his presence did little to change the situation. The company struggled on for another month before the "rather abrupt termination" of the season, when members began departing for summer engagements with other troupes.[73] Thus ended what must have been a disappointing first season in New York for Lavallée.

Lavallée's whereabouts during the summer of 1870 remain unknown, but by the fall he had completed his first operetta, Peacocks in Difficulties. An announcement in the New York Clipper on 1 October 1870 characterized the music of Peacocks as being "full of charming melodies, funny features and novelties in the accompaniment. Among the gems of the operette are mentioned a drum song, a "lager bier" song, a charming Bolero, one duett [sic], a trio and the drinking song 'Vive le Champagne.'"[74] The librettist, P. Arnold de Thier, appears to have only just arrived in New York, and perhaps had little experience in the theatre.[75] The absence of biographical information about him may suggest that the name was a pseudonym. Lavallée later mentioned that de Thier was Belgian, and true enough among his first publications was an homage to Princess Charlotte of Belgium, the former empress of Mexico, in the form of a "polka mazurka" titled Emperatrice Charlotte (New York: C.H. Ditson, 1870).[76]

Peacocks was to be produced in New York by Lina Edwin's company, a troupe that specialized in comedy and burlesque. Their 1869–70 season took place at Hooley's Theater, in Brooklyn, where Edwin supplemented her acts with French wrestlers and gymnasts. During July 1870, the company performed in Brooklyn while Edwin renovated Hope

Chapel (a popular venue located at 720 Broadway), which she renamed Lina Edwin's Theatre. Her 1870–71 cast included some fifteen actors, an "efficient chorus of male and female voices," and a brass band and orchestra led by John B. Donniker.[77] The season opened on 12 September with a production of Frederick Phillips' play *A Bird in the Hand Is Worth Two in the Bush*, and a burlesque of *Black-Eyed Susan*, with Edwin heading the cast.[78] This ran until October, when Edwin staged an adaptation of Charles Dickens's *Barnaby Rudge* and burlesques of *Cinderella* and *La Somnambula*. Ticket sales languished throughout this time, and early in November the *New York Clipper* reported, "ominous rumors fill the air with regard to Lina Edwin's Theatre. A reduction in the prices of admission was made some time since, and now a reduction in salaries has taken place."[79] The company continued through the spring, appearing before dwindling audiences in a collection of now-obscure pieces, but did not stage Lavallée's *opéra bouffe*.[80] When the regular season closed, Edwin went on a brief tour of the Northeast before putting her theatre up for rent, departing for Europe, and leaving *Peacocks* unperformed. A year later, her theatre burned to the ground.[81]

Lavallée appears never to have been a member of Edwin's company. He had resumed his post as the San Francisco Minstrels' musical director for the 1870–71 season. (See figure 3.9) His band and the entire cast was essentially the same as that of the previous season. Wambold had rejoined partners Birch, Backus, and Bernard; Rollin Howard and most of the other leading performers returned; and on 1 September 1870, the *New York Times* devoted a column to the troupe's opening, noting that "The quartet of artists whose united names have been before the public for years, is still in the foremost rank of the company."[82] Acknowledging Wambold's popularity, in 1870 music publisher Wm. A Pond issued a four-song collection titled *Songs and Ballads Sung by D.S. Wambold*, featuring the performer on the cover and a contribution from Lavallée titled "Pretty Little Dark Eyes." Still, the *New York Times*'s columnist complained that Wambold had not been supplied with a truly fine new ballad, although his efforts were still deserving of the "nightly encore" he received.[83] The writer praised the company's acting, imitations, and dancing, and predicted – accurately, as it turned out – a successful 1870–71 season.

| | |
|---|---|
| Tambo, Bones, Interlocutor | Billy Birch (bones), Charley Backus (tambo), Billy Bernard (Interlocutor) |
| Singers, Dancers, Comedians | Wambold, Dave (tenor), Rollin Howard (comedian, vocalist), Johnny Queen (comedian), Billy West (comedian), Billy Emmett (banjo, comedian), John Mulligan (comedian), Templeton, Oberist, Dwyer, Rockefeller, Shattuck (vocalists) |
| Musicians | Calixa Lavallée (musical director), Schmidt, Marshall, Adams, Buchner, Juch |

Figure 3.9  Cast of the San Francisco Minstrels, 1870–71 Broadway season.

Through the fall of 1870, each of the show's three parts received favourable reviews. The opening third, devoted to comic and sentimental songs, began with Lavallée's orchestral overture and concluded with the ever-popular "Railroad Overture," in which performers imitated the sounds of a steam engine.[84] In the comedy of the second part, they mixed old chestnuts with the new (and newsworthy). "Laughing Gas," long a stock minstrel skit topic, was added to the program early in 1871 and performed by an ensemble of six. Bernard played Dr Colton, one of the early experimenters in the use of nitrous oxide as an anaesthetic.[85] In "Dr Livingstone's African Cabinet," they satirized the exploits of the Scottish missionary-explorer David Livingstone who had gone missing in Africa (and who would in November 1871 be rediscovered by the *New York Herald* correspondent Henry Morton Stanley, who was famously said to have quipped "Dr Livingstone, I presume?").[86]

The exploits of James Fisk Jr again provided the San Francisco Minstrels with enough material for the season. "He's a Private in the 9th," made reference to "Colonel" James Fisk Jr, who was then bankrolling the Ninth New York Regiment and using it as his personal security force.[87]

The company's greatest success that season began in December with the burlesque of Offenbach's *Les Brigands*. Fisk's production, the US premiere, had opened at the Grand Opera House on 14 November and been an immediate hit – aided in part by a growing number of top French performers fleeing from besieged Paris. The San Francisco Minstrels' advertisements quipped that its show had been "Produced at an Expense of $46,000. A Triffle [*sic*] More than the Crook." (See figure 3.10) The reference, while referring specifically to *The Black Crook*, parodied the extravagance and extravagant claims of the theatre world.[88] It also alluded to the "crooks" of *Les Brigands*, and no doubt to the questionable reputation of Fisk himself. Lavallée's adaptation of Offenbach's score played on Fisk's reputation as a robber baron, with the Ninth Regiment as his private army. The names of the characters made conspicuous reference to Fisk's well-known love of food ("Carbineer de Beans," "Princess Ham," etc.), as did the note in the advertisement: "Refreshments furnished by Jim Jubilee."

On 31 March 1871, the San Francisco Minstrels gave their final performance of the season and began a tour of the Northeast and Midwest. The vocal portions of the show remained popular, as in Connecticut, where the *Hartford Courant*'s critic claimed, "a finer quartette [had] never sung with a minstrel company in Hartford."[89] They continued to feature the burlesque of *Les Brigands*, as Fisk's reputation extended well beyond New York. The *New York Clipper* reported the company to have opened to "a packed house" in Cincinnati on 12 May and continued to draw large audiences.[90] After a week at De Bar's Opera House in St Louis, the San Francisco Minstrels concluded the tour by making their Chicago debut, opening their engagement at Crosby's Opera House on 29 May.[91] Despite the company's apparent success, and his own contribution to it, Lavallée left his position later that summer to join the Morris Brothers' Minstrels.

❖❖❖

Lavallée's reasons for joining the Morris Brothers are unknown. The move to a less famous troupe was inconsistent with Lavallée's ambitious nature, but may simply reflect his restless character, and perhaps even a desire to remain on the road, or to spend more time in Massachusetts. It

NEW YORK, TUESDAY, FEBRUARY 21 1871.

# San Francisco Minstrels.

**585 Broadway, opposite Metropolitan Hotel.**

## IMMENSE SUCCESS
### OF THE
## FAMOUS LEADERS OF MINSTRELSY,
## BIRCH, WAMBOLD, BERNARD & BACKUS'
## SAN FRANCISCO MINSTRELS.
## 22 ARTISTS,

Who have for several years nightly appeared before the most SELECT ASSEMBLAGES which the Great Metropolis affords

## ORGANIZED in 1854.

IMMENSE HIT OF THE SCREAMING BURLESQUE OPERA ENTITLED

# LES BRIGANDS!

Produced at an Expense of $46,000. A Trifle More than the Creek.

Music ............................. arranged by ......................... C. Lavalle

---

THE TROUBLE COMMENCES AT 8

## TUESDAY EVENING, FEB. 21, 1871,
### Entertainment a la Salon, Part Premier.

Overture—(Arranged by C. Lavallee) ............................... Orchestra
Ballad—"Merry Land of Childhood," ...................... C. Templeton
Tyrolean Song, ............................................. J. F. Oberist
Comic Song—"Carry de News to Mary" ................... Charley Backus
Ballad—"God Bless the Little Church Around the Corner" .. D. S. Wambold
Comic Refrain—"Old Grimes' Cellar Door," ............... Billy Birch
Ballad—"When You and I were Young, Maggie" .......... Wm. Dwyer
FINALE—"Mary had a Little Lamb"

SAN FRANCISCO MINSTRELS

---

### PART 2d.—Diamond Fields of Africa.
## LET ME BE!
Written by Rollin Howard for ......... Johnny Queen and Billy West.

## OH! AIN'T HE SWEET ON ME?
### ROLLIN HOWARD.

# LAUGHING GAS.

Dr. Colton ...................... W. Bernard | German Gas ............ D. S. Wambold
Heavy Gas ................... Charley Backus | Mrs. Shingle .............. Billy Emmett
Light Gas ......................... Billy West | Solomon Shingle .............. Billy Birch

## FAVORITE BALLAD .......... WM. DWYER.

## THE FARMER'S SONS,
Messrs. Birch, Backus, Emmett and Templeton.

## THE BROADWAY DANCING MASTER,
### JOHNNY QUEEN.

---

To Conclude with the Burlesque Opera, entitled

# LES BRIGANDS.

With the Laughing and Whispering Choruses and the March of the Carbineers to Hash. Refreshments furnished by Jim Jubilee.

Fiorella Montelana de Billy ........................................ Rollin Howard
Princess Ham .................................................. Johnny Queen
Foolscappa, Big Chief No. 6 ................................... D. S. Wambold
Pie Eater, his Lieutenant ...................................... J. F. Oberist
Duke of Harlem ..................................................... Wm. Dwyer
Count de Gould ................................................... C. Templeton
Baron de Bay Rum ............................................... C. F. Shattuck
Fragoletto, a Farm Hand, holds four ........................ G. W. Rockefeller
Carbineer de Beans, Captain General ........................... W. Bernard
Carbineer de Terripin, Aid de Camp ............................. Billy Birch
Carbineer de Brown Bread, his Staff ......................... Charley Backus
Carbineer de Buchu, Surgeon ................................... Billy Emmett
Carbineer de Mutton Pie, Major ................................. Billy West
Carbineer de Crab, S-cout ..................................... Charley Sturgis

The Whole Terminating
## With the Duel on Horseback on two Mexican Mustangs!

Figure 3.10  San Francisco Minstrels playbill,
24 February 1871, featuring the company's
burlesque of Offenbach's *Les Brigands*,
with music arranged by Lavallée.

is difficult to imagine that Joséphine and Calixa Jr, not yet two years old, were following him around. More likely, they were with Joséphine's mother, either in Lowell or Lawrence. Led by the singer Billy Morris, the Morris Brothers' Minstrels were something of a New England institution. The ensemble had evolved from the Morris Brothers, Pell & Trowbridge's troupe of the 1850s and 1860s, and continued to operate its own theatre in Boston.[92] Reviews and reports published in the fall of 1871 provide little information on the instrumental music performed or the musicians in Lavallée's band. As usual, the comedians and singers received most of the attention. They included the comedians Billy Emmett and Charles Sutton, both former members of the San Francisco Minstrels; the ballad singers Frank Campbell and Edwin Holmes; and Thomas Dilverd, the diminutive African-American comedian who was known by the stage name of Japanese Tommy and who played the role of wench dancer.[93]

Despite the talented cast, few critics found anything compelling in either the company or its show that season. It toured continuously for more than a year, from New England to the Midwest and then throughout the Northeast again, despite often mediocre reviews. At the end of March 1872, the critic of the Lawrence, Massachusetts, *Sentinel* described the previous night's entertainment as one that "might have been considered a fair performance for an amateur company."[94] Reviews provide no real explanation as to why such experienced performers would give such a lacklustre show. Audiences may simply have been tiring of minstrelsy. Whether Lavallée, as musical director, was seen to be the problem and was asked to leave or he simply tired of the road and the entertainment business remains unknown. Whatever his reason, he did not remain with the Morris Brothers for long. His name was listed in the advertisement for the company's performances in Portland, Maine, on 15–16 March 1872, but not when they reached Providence, Rhode Island, a month later.[95]

Rather than returning to New York, Lavallée settled briefly in Boston, where he took a room at 23 Blossom Street, near Almont Place.[96] Again, we have no evidence of Joséphine and Calixa Jr's presence, but we do know something of Lavallée's professional activities. His move to Boston had brought him into contact with David C. Hall, the famous bandleader and entrepreneur from Lyme, New Hampshire. Hall manufactured musical instruments and kept several bands performing under his name, all using and promoting his products. Lavallée would very likely have heard Hall's bands while in his teens. They toured Canada in 1858, performing three very successful concerts in Montreal, with Hall and his famous gold bugle accompanied by his "Brass Band, Reed Band, and Orchestra."[97] After each concert, the floor was cleared and Hall's Quadrille Band provided dancing music. By the late 1860s, Hall's Band was a veritable institution, much like Gilmore's Band or the Germania Orchestra. It was a mainstay of the Boston concert season and of the summer season in the resort town of Saratoga Springs, New York. In the summer of 1872, the Hall's Band was one of dozens of ensembles that took part in Patrick Gilmore's massive, eighteen-day World Peace Jubilee and International Music Festival. Staged in a specially constructed coliseum in Boston's Back Bay, the event was ostensibly held to commemorate the end of the Franco-Prussian War.[98]

One of Hall's regular summer jobs was performing on board the steamships of the Fall River Line. The company had been given that name in 1869 by none other than James Fisk Jr. That year, he had bought a controlling interest in the Narragansett Steamship Company, and made himself president and "commodore." The company acquired the Bristol Line's steamers *Bristol* and *Providence*, which sailed between New York and Fall River, Massachusetts, where passengers boarded trains to complete the journey into Boston's Old Colony Railroad Depot on Kneeland Street.[99] Fisk had renamed the company the Fall River Line, lavishly refurbished the ships, and hired bands to entertain passengers through the summer months. Dodworth's Orchestra performed on the steamers during the first part of the 1869 season, but from September, D.C. Hall's "Celebrated Gold Bugle, Brass, String and Reed Bands" gave the promenade concerts each evening.[100] A news item in the *Orpheus*, a popular music journal of the day, referred to the steamers as "veritable floating palaces" on which a voyage was "made doubly satisfactory by the fine music of Hall's Band."[101]

Lavallée stayed on in Boston after the 1872 summer season ended, perhaps determined to make his career as a pianist. He made his debut there on Saturday, 21 December 1872, with Hall's Band and Orchestra, performing Mendelssohn's Concerto in G minor, op. 25, a Chopin mazurka, and several works of his own. The concert was a benefit for "working-women" who had lost their sewing machines and other property in Boston's Great Fire of 9 November 1872.[102] The concert took place in the grand Tremont Temple but received little attention in the local newspapers; the *New York Clipper* reported a "small audience."[103] The *Boston Evening Journal* claimed that Lavallée "made a very pleasant impression and was well received."[104] Whatever the level of success of the concert, Lavallée had determined to take a new direction. Soon after his Boston debut, he returned to Montreal, leaving behind once and for all his life as a minstrel show musician.

❖❖❖

In Montreal, Lavallée set about preparing a concert that was to take place at the Mechanics' Hall on 13 March 1873. As part of the pre-concert publicity, L.-O. David published an engraving of the musician along with an article that was to that time the most substantial piece published about Lavallée. (See figure 3.11) Since his days fighting against Confederation, David had become a Liberal and in 1870 the founder of the well-respected newspaper *L'Opinion publique*.[105] Over the years, he had lost none of his passion and his writing style was nothing if not colourful. In this March 1873 article, he portrays the "naturally undisciplined" Lavallée as "trained in the school of nature as well as that of art." He elaborates on this theme by describing Lavallée's performances at the keyboard, noting the pianist understanding:

> Above all, the goal of the artist is to go straight to the soul of the audience, to strike at their senses; he has the boldness and swiftness that astonishes, rapid movements like lightning, shocking bursts like thunder. He does not cease to be classical, however, he is stunning as he shifts easily from stern to gentle, from turbulent to graceful. It is the murmur of the brook next to the roar of our waterfalls streaming tumultuously from our great lakes; it is the calm of our beautiful nights, the serenity of our starry sky after stormy days; it is the image of our nature like that of our character, with its striking contrasts, and thus can we say that the talent of Mr Lavallée is essentially national.[106]

CALIXA LAVALLÉE.

Figure 3.11 Engraving of Calixa Lavallée published just ahead of his March 1873 concert in Montreal.

The Romantic notion of the artist embodying the spirit of the natural landscape was aimed directly at David's readers' nationalist sentiments. The biographical elements of the article developed this theme while using historical fact as only a starting point.

Although David says nothing about Joséphine or Calixa Jr, he does mention that Lavallée was staying at his parents' home. He likely interviewed the pianist, whom he had known from their time as contributors to the *Union nationale* in the mid-1860s. Since David's main source of information was likely Lavallée himself, much of the article's content can be attributed to him. It is the first summary of Lavallée's career to this point printed in a reputable newspaper. One hundred and forty years after publication, the errors, omissions, and exaggerations contained in it continue to be repeated and deserve careful consideration. Some of the claims made were just the sort of exaggeration that was common in promotional material. Lavallée claimed to have been an officer in the Union Army. The much-reproduced photograph of him in uniform (see figure 1.8) seems to have supported the claim, as he appears with a sabre and at least part of the uniform of a cavalry officer.[107] He also asserted, "to obey his parents' wishes he had quit the army and returned to Montreal."[108] He may have been a dutiful son, but he had of course been mustered out along with most other musicians in 1862, and rather than return to Montreal, he immediately embarked on a tour with Duprez that brought him back to Louisiana. After that, he had set off with Ellinger, before finally returning to his family toward the end of 1863. Similarly, he claimed to have made his concert debut at the Theatre Royal at the age of eleven, when he had in fact been sixteen at the time. He accurately noted that he had left Montreal in 1859, but stretched the truth on what he was doing.

Overall, the article gives the impression that Lavallée had been primarily a pianist during his early travels. It was true that during his first weeks with the New Orleans Minstrels, Duprez promoted the young musician as a piano soloist. This was unusual for a minstrel troupe and it did not last long. Nevertheless, it was the only thing David drew attention to when he wrote that Lavallée had "made a brilliant debut in New Orleans, and then joined the famous Spanish violinist Olivera [sic] for a concert tour of Brazil and the West Indies."[109] No evidence of such a concert tour has yet emerged. Jacques Oliveira was, in fact, a young Dutch violinist who arrived in the United States in December 1859.[110] He had been brought to the United States by the impresario Phineas T. Barnum who billed him as a "Spanish violinist" and sometimes even as "principal violinist to the Queen of Spain."[111] Oliveira performed in and around New York in 1860 and 1861 before settling in New Orleans in 1862, where he died in June 1867. Duprez's troupe was touring the Midwest when Oliveira made his New York debut, but Lavallée may have later met the violinist in 1862 and early 1863 – at the time when the New Orleans Minstrels were performing at the Academy of Music, Oliveira was performing during intermissions at the Varieties Theater.

Oliveira was also active in the city during Lavallée's visit there in 1866. Lavallée's chronology through these years, however, leaves no room for an unaccounted-for tour with the violinist.[112]

From 1866, the New Orleans Minstrels' advertisements list Lavallée only as musical director or bandleader, and he appears to have for a time abandoned his career as a pianist and composer of piano music almost entirely. After publishing a number of piano pieces in the first five years of his career, the *Shake Again Galop* is the only piano composition Lavallée is known to have published between 1866 and 1873. In discussing Lavallée's post-war travels in the United States, David makes no mention of Duprez, even though he was well known in Montreal. He reports simply that when Lavallée left Montreal he toured the United States and Mexico "gathering honours all the way to California."[113] Lavallée appears to have been taking pains not to be connected to the minstrel show. He performed in Montreal several times with Duprez, but was never announced in the advertisements. This might not be unusual except that his presence would have helped to sell tickets. On at least one occasion the opposite seems to have taken place. During the troupe's four-night stay at the Mechanics' Institute in November 1866, the *Montreal Herald* reported them to have again "taken the town by storm."[114] At the time, a notice appeared in the November issue of *Le Canada musical* stating that Lavallée had decided to reside in New Orleans, while remaining vague on Lavallée's actual activities, noting that "after having travelled through the western and southern states on a tour, our Canadian musical prodigy, Mr Calixa Lavallée, has recently elected to settle in New Orleans."[115] It did not mention that he had been in the city with the New Orleans Minstrels, but went on to predict that he would have "a brilliant future and a distinguished position in the artistic capital of the South." In linking himself to New Orleans, Lavallée seems to have hoped to exploit the city's cachet as a cultural centre. By March 1873, he seems to have been borrowing from the actual events of Gustave Smith's life. Smith had arrived in New Orleans late in 1866 and pursued his career there for about two years, performing on several occasions with Oliveira.[116]

Lavallée may have tried several times to leave minstrelsy behind. He parted from Duprez to join the Union Army in 1861, and to tour with

Ellinger in 1863. He may have tried to leave again in 1868. In September, Duprez was attempting to recruit a new musical director, suggesting that Lavallée may have hoped his concert in Montreal would lead to something more substantial and that the "something" had failed to materialize.[117] Duprez arrived in Montreal at the same time and Lavallée set off with him once again. If he was a reluctant minstrel, he was not alone. Bidaux had hoped to make his name in Italian opera. There were likely many others. The vocalist Sherwood C. Campbell was one of the few to make the transition to the more reputable stage.[118]

David's reporting of Lavallée's activities in New York again strays far from the reality. Rather than writing that Lavallée had become musical director for the San Francisco Minstrels, David claims that James Fisk Jr had appointed him as "superintendent of the Grand Opera."[119] The Grand Opera House was, of course, home to Offenbach rather than Meyerbeer and Wagner, but few of David's readers would have been aware of that. Nor apparently was Lapierre, who repeated this information. If Lavallée was the source of this invention, it was undoubtedly because it sounded far more impressive than having been performing burlesques of Fisk and his productions. David also discusses Lavallée's operetta. He refers to it as *Lou-Lou*, possibly to avoid drawing attention to the English-language title. He provides a bit more factual information about it, writing that Lavallée and Arnold de Thier, "a well known Belgian writer," had completed it in three months. However, he also claims that its premiere was scheduled for the Grand Opera House, where, "as Mr Lavallée himself has written, his work created great enthusiasm among the actors."[120] The premiere, he writes, was cancelled when "a tragic event that created a sensation around the world closed the doors of the Grand Opera: Fisk fell murdered by an assassin's bullet."[121] The dramatic story at least had an element of truth.

Fisk's murder on 6 January 1872 had indeed been a sensation. Legal battles with his former lover Josie Mansfield had drawn headlines throughout 1871 and reached a climax when Ned Stokes, Mansfield's current lover and Fisk's former business partner, opened fire on the unguarded Fisk with a pistol in a stairway of the Grand Central Hotel. The murder and subsequent trial were front-page news across the continent and on both sides of the Atlantic. It would seem that for Lavallée, the

Fisk story provided an opportunity to inflate his career in the eyes of the Canadian public. Few would have known that Fisk had ceded control of his theatre and left show business several months prior to his death.[122] If Fisk had expressed an interest in *Peacocks in Difficulties* (or *Lou-Lou*) his death appears not to have been a factor in its cancellation. The reasons behind Lavallée's failure to have *Peacocks in Difficulties* staged were probably much more mundane, but the story shows the extent to which he had learned the art of promotion. High expectations back home would also have added pressure for him to achieve more than he had.

Given the wide popularity of the minstrel show in Canada, the United States, and Europe, Lavallée's distancing himself from it demands explanation. His rejection of minstrelsy was probably not of an ethical or moral nature. Few commentators of the time raised objections to its disparaging characterizations of blacks and other minorities. It is equally doubtful that Lavallée was concerned about the Catholic Church's condemnation of the theatre. If so, he would not have claimed to have been employed by James Fisk Jr, whose Opera Bouffe company had frequently been labelled immoral by the conservative press. Minstrelsy's enormous popularity attracted many of the most talented entertainers, and there was keen competition between troupes. From a professional standpoint, it demanded a very high standard of performance. In an account of his travels in the Americas in 1869, the French pianist and composer Henri Kowalski wrote of his admiration for the unique character of this *spécialité*, and of his being "struck by the perfection with which the performers of these troupes performed their pieces."[123] As Lavallée's activities have shown, the best troupes required highly trained musicians and, in particular, a versatile musical director.

Quite likely, Lavallée was loath to be associated with minstrelsy because it placed music subordinate to comedy. After an 1863 performance, the *Detroit Daily Advertiser and Tribune* offered some surprising observations on this issue, and on the musical side of the New Orleans Minstrels: "In Duprez & Green's company, judging from some of the pieces that were executed last evening, there are musicians that would do credit to almost any orchestra or chorus. The burnt cork, unique costumes, and fantastic contortions, were not necessarily to interest those who can appreciate real musical merit. Indeed, there were some present last evening who regretted that talents of such a high order should be thus prostituted, in pandering to what, after all, view it in the best light you can, is a vitiated and depraved taste."[124] The writer of the column concluded that, "for good music, and a diversity of low comedy, the performance last night excelled any similar entertainment that has thus been given in Detroit in a long time."[125]

For at least a small minority, music and the concert performer rested atop a cultural order. This evidence of a clear hierarchy in the 1860s contradicts the position held by cultural historians who have pointed to the wide popularity of opera and the works of Shakespeare as evidence of an egalitarian culture.[126] While there is no doubt that opera in its many forms reached a wide cross-section of the public in the 1850s and 1860s, beneath the outward appearance of universality, there were strong lines of division between popular and 'high' culture by mid-century.[127] The *New York Musical World*'s criticism of the violinist Oliveira, in 1860, was such an example. Finding his interpretations tasteful only within the restricted confines of a variety show hall, the critic wrote that: "His style would be condemned by the classical musician, but Senor Oliviera [*sic*] will always please a general audience, as he has tone, sentiment and dexterity."[128] The implication appears to be that a "general audience" wished to be entertained, but was perhaps little interested in the finer points of a musical performance. This idea of a class division between styles of music would become central to Lavallée's later career, when he would take a position quite similar to that of the *Musical World*'s critic. In 1873, concerned with how he appeared back home, the image of the "national musician" simply did not mesh with a man blackening his face with burnt cork.

The concert at the Mechanics' Hall on 13 March 1873 was Lavallée's first Montreal appearance since 1868. Since that time, Torrington had moved to Boston, so Lavallée hired the conductor A.J. Boucher, whose orchestra opened the concert with Conradin Kreutzer's *Das Nachtlager in Granada* and returned in the second part with Johann Strauss Jr's *An der schönen blauen Donau (On the Beautiful Blue Danube)*. The other soloists were Madame Leduc, soprano, and Ludger Maillet, tenor, with Patrick Curran as accompanist.[129] Lavallée had performed frequently with Maillet a decade earlier, and at this performance he had him sing a cavatina from *Peacocks in Difficulties*. The unnamed critic from *L'Opinion publique*, who may have been David, reported the piece to have been "applauded with enthusiasm," and to have been "as pretty, and as inspired as the pieces of like character drawn from the best operas."[130] But he added that "it is truly unfortunate that *Lou-Lou* has not yet been performed in a theatre; it would be a great success for Mr Lavallée and an honour, we believe, for Canadian art."[131] Lavallée billed himself in the concert advertisements as the "great pianist of Canada, whose success on the American continent, and recently in California, has been unparalleled."[132] Reviews mention only two of the compositions that he played. The *Montreal Herald* reported that he performed his *Fantasia on themes from 'Il Trovatore'* "in a masterly style, and was loudly encored," and that he closed with the "Wedding March" from Mendelssohn's incidental music to *A Midsummer Night's Dream*.[133]

Around this time, Lavallée made two important contacts, Frantz Prume and Guillaume Couture. Lavallée had crossed paths with Prume several times since they had met in the summer of 1865. After travelling through the southern States, the Belgian violinist had returned to Canada in the spring of 1866 to marry Rosita del Vecchio, a young woman he had met the previous summer when she sang at a soirée hosted by Mayor Jean-Louis Beaudry.[134] They were married at Notre-Dame Church on 17 July 1866, and after a honeymoon trip to Niagara Falls, Prume returned to the road with a concert company organized by Max Strakosch for a tour of the United States and Central and South America.[135] Both Prume and Lavallée were in Montreal in the summer of 1868 and likely met. They may have met again in 1869, when Prume's concert tour visited Philadelphia, where Lavallée was directing Duprez & Benedict performances.[136] Prume and del Vecchio travelled to Europe in 1871, but were back in Montreal in the spring of 1873. When Lavallée gave a concert under his own name at the Mechanics' Hall in March, Prume was beginning a concert series at Queen's Hall. Two months later, on 26 May, Lavallée joined the violinist at the final Queen's Hall concert, and the next night he skipped a scheduled performance as soloist with the recently founded Montreal Philharmonic Society to take part in a lecture-recital with Prume and the writer Arthur Buies, who was promoting his book *Chroniques: Humeurs et caprices*.[137]

Lavallée found a new colleague in Guillaume Couture, a musician who would eventually become the leading figure in Montreal's musical life. Although he was just twenty-four years old at this time, already Couture surpassed almost all local musicians in talent and determination. He had learned music while attending a school run by the Christian Brothers. By his early teens he was teaching solfège at the École normale Jacques-Cartier and conducting church choirs, first at his home parish of Sainte-Brigide and three years later at the much larger Saint-Jacques Church.

In May 1873, Lavallée brought Couture with him as accompanist when he made his Quebec City debut as a soloist, at the Salle de Lecture. The concert also featured several local musicians, among them, Arthur Lavigne, violin; Mr Brun, clarinet; Frédéric Lefebvre, basso profundo; and Mlle Dessane, soprano. Lavallée appeared third on the program with his '*Il Trovatore*' fantasy. He returned to the stage in the second part to play Schumann's *Warum?* (no. 3 of the *Phantasiestück*, op. 12), several pieces of his own (which reviews failed to identify), and Mendelssohn's "Wedding March." The performance drew enthusiastic reviews from both the English- and French-language press. The *Quebec Daily Mercury* wrote that he played the Schumann piece "with a delicacy of sentiment and expression which few artists possess."[138] The unnamed reviewer continued: "Of M. Lavallée's playing we had heard much and had read the praises literally showered on him by the New York and Boston press, but we must admit that he anticipated our most sanguine expectations. His playing is neat and correct, showing conscientious study and careful training, and devoid of that exaggeration of expression into which so many pianists are apt to fall. His rendering of the fantasia on *Trovatore* last evening took the small but select audience by surprise and thunders of applause thanked the artist for the pleasure he had given."[139] The critic at the *Courrier du Canada* painted a more animated portrait of Lavallée: "The reputation of M. Lavallée preceded him to Quebec City, and indeed the audience at Friday night's concert was not disappointed in its hope to hear a great pianist."[140] He called Lavallée's playing "lively, forceful, and energetic: He impresses, he moves, he captivates. The musician knows how to communicate with the audience something of the feelings that inspire his soul."[141]

The strong critical success of this performance provided some compensation for a concert that drew a very small audience. The performance had been well publicized: Lavallée had placed advertisements in the daily newspapers and David published a revised version of his biographical article in the *Courrier du Canada* two days before the concert.[142] Despite this, the turnout was so poor that Lavallée cancelled a planned second performance and returned to Montreal. Newspapers attributed the lack of interest to the heavy rain and a high ticket price (fifty cents), but Lavallée's limited credentials could not have helped.[143] He had advertised himself as the "great pianist of Canada" for this and the Montreal concert, and claimed to have recently completed concert tours of the United States and South America.[144] Missing from his CV, however, was the cachet of having studied in Europe. For his generation, study in Paris was the only way to convince the Canadian public of one's talent. Many musicians went to Europe intending to make their names as pianists and composers. Ernest Gagnon had studied in Paris in the late 1850s. In the 1860s, Dominique Ducharme, Moïse Saucier, and Salomon Mazurette had studied in Paris with Marmontel, Stamaty, and Herz, respectively. Charles-Marie Panneton was then in Paris, studying with Marmontel. Marie Regnaud, one of the few young Canadian women of that generation to pursue a career in music, had continued her studies in New York with S.B. Mills. With the financial help of Léon-Alfred Sentenne, the young parish priest of Saint-Jacques Church, Guillaume Couture departed for the Paris Conservatoire in the spring of 1873, studying voice with Romain Bussine and composition with Théodore Dubois. Lavallée might have preceded them all had he not leapt straight into professional life. However, it was not too late.

In the early months of 1873, Léon Derome and other supporters made arrangements to provide funds that would allow Lavallée to go to Paris for study.[145] With the organization of fundraising in Derome's hands, the thirty-two-year-old war veteran – a professional musician for fourteen years – was finally to complete his formal studies. A decade later, Lavallée would reflect that the successful musician remains a student: "I would say to all alike that the terms 'student' and 'master' are applicable to the same person at the same time. No one is so willing to learn as he who is acknowledged to be a great man."[146] In 1873, there was also the recognition that a "national musician" could not be a minstrel show musician and that a French-Canadian "national musician" could not be a musician whose career was based largely in Anglo-American popular culture.

To what extent Lavallée considered his family when deciding to travel to Europe is not known. Joséphine and Calixa Jr would be left behind again, this time in Montreal. Rather than depart directly for Europe, Lavallée returned to the United States for the 1873 summer season, conducting Hall's Band on the Fall River Line and at other engagements. Two of these engagements illustrate his strong ties in the burgeoning French-Canadian community of Fall River, Massachusetts. On 16 July he conducted Hall's Band on board the steamer *Canonicus* when the town's Saint-Jean-Baptiste Association organized an excursion to Rocky Point, Rhode Island. Later that summer, one of his final performances before leaving for Europe took place once again in Fall River, when on 5 September he participated in a concert celebrating the final withdrawal of Prussian troops as France paid off its war indemnity. With confident speeches and the singing of "Vive la Canadienne" and "La Marseillaise," the 5 September event was a celebration, and Lavallée gave an inspired performance, playing his fantasy on *Il Trovatore*, his transcription of themes from Gounod's *Faust*, and pieces by Chopin and Schumann – the latter suggesting a note of reconciliation.[147] The event was organized by Honoré Beaugrand, then editor and publisher of Fall River's French-language newspaper *L'Écho du Canada*. The twenty-five-year-old Beaugrand was a liberal, a republican, and a strong advocate of strengthening the ties between French Canadians and Irish immigrants. He and Lavallée had much in common and clearly hit it off. Later that month, Beaugrand held a farewell gathering for Lavallée in the offices of *L'Écho*, presenting him with an engraved conductor's baton and persuading him to write letters for the newspaper. And soon after, Lavallée was off for Paris, leaving minstrelsy and the first stage of his career behind.

# PART TWO

*The National Musician*

*1873–1880*

$$\overline{\underline{4}}$$

# Paris and Montreal
## 1873–1878

Life in Paris had resumed a level of normalcy with remarkable speed. But in the fall of 1873, there were still numerous ruins to remind citizens and visitors that only two years earlier the city had been besieged by the Prussian army. Starvation had been widespread. Even Victor Hugo, who had returned from exile after the fall of Louis-Napoléon and declaration of the Third Republic, was forced to eat zoo animals and then, infamously, "the unknown."[1] After the elections of February 1871, the Royalists under Adolphe Thiers made peace with the Prussians and then slaughtered upwards of 20,000 of their own citizens in putting down the Commune. They then jostled with republicans for power and the right to determine what form of government the country would have. By the early months of 1873, Thiers was gone, replaced by the monarchists' choice of Marshal de MacMahon, who remained in power until the end of the decade. Unified by little else, monarchists and republicans found common ground in the humiliation of their defeat to the Prussians, in the loss of Alsace-Lorraine, and in the destruction that still surrounded them. The nationalism that rose in the aftermath of the war found expression in the arts, and in music most of all.

Charles Gounod had gone to England in 1870. From that safe vantage point, he demonstrated his patriotism through the cantata *Gallia*, which was performed in Paris and London. The London performance took place at the recently opened Royal Albert Hall, where the soprano Georgina Weldon was a featured soloist. Gounod later ended up living with Weldon and her husband in Tavistock House, a former home of Charles Dickens, in Bloomsbury. While there, he composed the incidental music for an-other patriotic work: Jules Barbier's five-act drama *Jeanne d'Arc* (which he dedicated to the Weldons). The first production opened at the Théâtre de la Gaîté in Paris on 8 November 1873, around the time of Lavallée's arrival in Paris, and caused a scandal when both Gounod's wife and Georgina Weldon, with whom he was assumed to be having an affair, attended the premiere. That distraction from the music did no harm, as few considered it to be among Gounod's best. If Lavallée did not attend that first performance, he certainly heard about it, and later mounted an enormously successful production of *Jeanne d'Arc* in Canada.

Nationalist music took many forms in post-war Paris. Patriotic songs grew in popularity, as did the music of earlier French composers, from Rameau to Berlioz.[2] A prominent forum for musical nationalism in Paris at this time was the Société National. Directed by Camille Saint-Saëns and Romain Bussine, it held its first concert on 25 November 1871 and provided an outlet for young composers. Chamber music and orchestral associations multiplied in the 1870s as instrumental music gained pop-ularity.[3] French music was the focus at most of the other venues in the city. Notable among them was the *Concerts populaire (de musique clas-sique)*, a series of moderately priced concerts conducted by J.E. Pasde-loup, that took place at the Cirque d'hiver, on rue Amelot, in the 11th arrondissement. At the same time, Adolphe Maton conducted concerts three times a week at the more up-market Frascati café-garden, where people went to eat, drink, and gamble.

In general, it was a stimulating time to be in Paris, and there were once again many foreign students and visitors. Having studied in Paris in the 1850s, the Quebec City organist Ernest Gagnon returned for a visit in 1873. He sent back letters describing his travels that were published in *Le Courrier du Canada* and subsequently collected as *Lettres de Voyages*. In one, Gagnon mentions attending a Pasdeloup concert at which eight Canadians were present, including Guillaume Couture.[4] And toward the end of his stay, he notes, Lavallée visited him at his hotel in the Latin Quarter.[5]

Lavallée had accepted an offer from Honoré Beaugrand to write for Fall River's *L'Écho du Canada*. On 22 November 1873, the newspaper published a letter from Lavallée, dated 31 October, in which he reported on his early impressions of Paris, a city he had expected to find "in ashes and ruins." He begins with a lengthy discussion of the political situation, noting that the French were facing big decisions on the form of government they would choose. He mentions being asked the opinion in Canada on France's political future and having avoided a direct answer to the "delicate question." Turning to opera, he refers to the burning of the Salle Le Peletier (two days earlier), lamenting the loss of the site where "the masterpieces of Rossini, Auber, Mayerbeer and of other illustrious talents were created." He mentions that the administration of the Théâtre du Châtelet had made that venue available until the completion of Opéra's new venue (the Salle Garnier). The Paris Opéra eventually shared space at the Salle Ventadour through 1874 with the Théâtre-Italien, a company Lavallée also refers to, noting that it was then fashionable and that the singer Maria Gabriele Krauss was "all the rage right now."[6] He said nothing of his own activities.

On 26 December, Lavallée wrote again to Beaugrand. He begins this letter with an apology, claiming that he is a musician and not a writer, and finds the process of writing to the public difficult, which helps to explain his silence over two months. In the first half of this missive, he describes Christmas in Paris, using the residents of a presumably fictional apartment building to illustrate how different families celebrated the holiday. Turning to opera, he describes a recent production of Gounod's *Roméo et Juliette* at the Opéra-Comique, with "the queen of French singers," the great soprano Caroline Carvalho. He waxes eloquent in his description of her performance, focusing on the balcony scene of the second act, which he describes as the counterpart of the garden scene in *Faust*, in which "this inseparable trinity of the actress, the singer, and Ms Carvalho disappears, leaving in their place, leaning on the terrace of the house of old Capulet, Juliet in person, Juliet of the Italian legends, of Shakespeare and of Gounod, whose white form cuts the darkness by moonlight, and whose severe and passionate mouth, exchange with Romeo serious promises of love and marriage."[7] Turning to more worldly concerns, he complains about the rain but says there are still plenty of distractions, among them Pasdeloup's Sunday concerts, and the many little theatres, with music for all tastes. Aside from his implied presence in the theatres and concert halls, the only mention of his own activity is that he reads *L'Écho* regularly. He promises to write again soon – and again, provides no details of his studies.

❖❖❖

## MARMONTEL

Paris had for decades been the centre of the piano world and home to Chopin, Liszt, Thalberg, Kalkbrenner, and most of the great Romantic pianists. Lavallée's main reason for travelling there was to study with the famous piano pedagogue Antoine François Marmontel. (See figure 4.1) In the mid-1870s, Marmontel was at the height of an illustrious teaching career. He had studied at the Conservatoire under Joseph Zimmermann, earning a *Premièr Prix* in piano in 1832. He took over his teacher's class in 1848 and was, by the 1870s, a senior faculty member and a leading figure in the Parisian musical establishment. Over the course of his career, Marmontel produced dozens of publications. His biographical *Les pianists célèbres* remains a frequently cited source on nineteenth-century pianists. His students helped to disseminate his many compositions and études, as well as his editions of other composers' works. His class at the Paris Conservatoire attracted many of the most talented students of Europe and the Americas.[8] Vincent d'Indy, Isaac Albéniz, and a twelve-year old Claude Debussy were all members of Marmontel's class during this period. Roger Nichols has written that Marmontel's class, with its emphasis on Chopin and Schumann, was largely responsible for shaping Debussy's musical tastes.[9]

Georges Bizet had studied with Marmontel in the 1850s and later wrote that in his class "one learns something besides the piano; one becomes a musician."[10] The music critic Camille Bellaigue began studies with Marmontel in 1875 and later wrote a colourful description of his teacher and of student life at the Conservatoire. He described Marmontel thus:

A bald-headed little man with a long, grey, pointed beard, with grey fingers too, stunted as if they had been worn down in the practice of his art ... Perhaps he had at one time been a virtuoso; he was

Figure 4.1
Portrait of Lavallée's
piano teacher, Antoine-
François Marmontel,
dating from the 1850s.

now not even a pianist. At any rate none of us had ever heard him play. The most he would sometimes do, and even this was difficult for him, was to play a run, illustrate a fingering, or the value or accent of a note, but it was done so clumsily that he himself was the first to smile. But how he made up for this shortcoming in his lessons! In everything he did he showed impeccable style. He had the purest and steadiest taste; a passionate love of his art, but at the same time an even greater sense of reason that tempered the passion; the mix or rather the perfect equilibrium between intelligence and sensitivity, these two halves of music and all musical performance, that was the nature of the incomparable professor Marmontel; in this consisted the base, or rather the soul and the life of his teaching.[11]

This devotion to his students, and the admiration he earned from them, made Marmontel's class different from those of other piano teachers. Perhaps the closest parallels we might draw would be to the cult-like following attracted by Franz Liszt, in Leipzig a decade later, and the analysis class of Olivier Messiaen, at the Paris Conservatoire in the twentieth century.

Marmontel tailored his teaching methods to the needs of each student. He taught on the second floor of the old Conservatoire building on rue Bergère, in the 9th arrondissement. The room was furnished with only a few benches and a large Érard grand piano, at which each student would take his or her turn seated next to the master. Each student worked on different repertoire. Among Marmontel's pedagogical techniques was the practice of sending his best students for lessons in phrasing with the singing teacher Cécile Eugènie Mayer, wife of the Spanish baritone Manuel García. Marmontel discusses this at some length in *L'Art classique et moderne de piano*, a book he was completing at the time that Lavallée was his student.[12] In the first of the two volumes, Marmontel discusses many aspects of teaching and playing piano: from solutions to playing chromatic scales and trills to more advanced issues, such as expression and legato playing. Throughout the text, he recommends published studies that would address each problem. The second volume lists these and other publications. The book shows Marmontel to be introducing his students to a wide range of keyboard music, both old and new. Still, it is difficult to judge from this book what effect he may have had on Lavallée's playing. Marmontel's greatest contribution to his students may have been the camaraderie and love of learning that he shared with them.

Marmontel's students recognized their teacher's devotion to them. Teaching music was his life, wrote Bellaigue: "He loved music, and he loved us too for what we meant in music for him, this old master surrounded by his apprentices."[13] Students would often take additional lessons at Marmontel's home when competitions were approaching. The old house was nearby on rue Saint-Lazare. Bellaigue describes how, on entering, one would pass through several antechambers before reaching the music room. There, "the light shining through stained-glass windowpanes cast a mottled effect all over the pictures on the walls. Bronze and marble figures, brass and china covered the tables or stood on brackets.

Music was scattered over the piano and over the carpet. In the midst of this disorder, something of a museum or curiosity shop, the figure of Marmontel, in his dressing-gown, seemed stranger than ever – a character from a tale of Hoffmann or a novel of Balzac."[14] It was an endearing image to many of his students. When Marmontel retired, Bellaigue described him as "much more than a teacher; he was a master, in the most noble sense of the word."[15]

❖❖❖

## COMPOSITION TEACHERS AND COMPOSITIONS

Lavallée also took lessons with two of France's leading composition teachers, François Bazin and Louis-Victor Boïeldieu.[16] After winning the Prix de Rome in 1840, Bazin pursued a career as a teacher, theatre composer, and as conductor of the Orphéon de Paris. He taught harmony and singing at the Conservatoire, published a successful harmony textbook, and, when Ambroise Thomas became director of the school in 1871, Bazin assumed his post as professor of composition.[17] His greatest artistic success as a composer of comic operas came in 1865 with *Le voyage en Chine*.[18] Boïeldieu was the illegimate son of the opera singer Thérèse Regnault and François-Adrien Boïeldieu, the composer of *La Dame blanche*. The younger Boïeldieu did well but never quite emerged from his father's shadow. He enjoyed success at the age of twenty-three, when his opera *Marguerite* (1838) was staged at the Opéra-Comique. *La Fille invisible* (1854) was also popular. In the spring of 1874, *La Minerve* published a letter from Boïeldieu, who wrote that Lavallée had a piece from an opera performed at a Pasdeloup concert, and that he would benefit from spending more time in Paris.[19]

Little is known of what Lavallée learned from Bazin and Boïeldieu. One might expect that composing vocal music would have occupied most of his time. However, all of the extant works composed in Paris are instrumental: one overture for orchestra and three piano pieces. All date from 1874. The Paris firm of Éveillard & Jacquot published two of the piano compositions: the *Grande marche de concert*, op. 14, and the *Souvenir de Tolède, mazurka de salon*, op. 17. Louis-Marin Éveillard had

## SOUVENIR DE TOLEDE

C. LAVALLEE

Figure 4.2 The opening measures of *Le Souvenir de Tolède*, one of Lavallée's three piano compositions published in Paris in 1874.

just gone into business and was building his catalogue. He sometimes worked in partnership with the older Jacquot firm, which also specialized in dances and opera arrangements for piano.[20] These two pieces by Lavallée are both technically demanding, and show Lavallée moving beyond the sectional forms popular in North America and giving greater independence to right and left hands. The *Grande Marche* might be better described as a salon piece rather than concert work. It has panache, but at nearly five minutes in length, it is probably a bit longer than is justified by the material. The *Souvenir de Tolède* begins without introduction, opening with a rhythmic figure and wide chords that provide most of the material of the piece. (See figure 4.2) The *Music Trade Review* described the piece as "very well written" but also "very difficult," with chords that were "too full and the stretches too big altogether."[21] The wide stretches may say something of Lavallée's technical abilities, but it was true that the physical demands of the piece would limit sales and per-formances. There is something unfortunate in this, as the piece has an el-egance and pathos that is rarely found in Lavallée's music. We may never know if this was an imagined image of Toledo or his real experience.

In contrast, the third of the piano pieces from this time, the short, ebullient *Le Papillon, étude de concert*, op. 18, was one of Lavallée's greatest successes. Éveillard issued it without Jacquot, perhaps recog-nizing its commercial potential. While the first two pieces are not strik-ingly different from Lavallée's earlier works, *Le Papillon*, a lively study for the right hand, and of moderate difficulty, was unlike anything he had previously published. Beginning with a simple, fluttering figure, Lavallée varies the idea, passes it to the left hand, works it up and down the key-board, and creates a piece that is effectively structured and entirely sat-isfying to listen to, while serving the purpose of developing technique (see appendix 2). In a review of these pieces, *Le Canada musical* de-scribed *Le Papillon* as "the most natural and the least elaborate of the three," and the "most successful.²² The *Music Trade Review* called *Le Papillon* "an excellent study in every respect; useful, original, practical, well written with great purity, and well conducted."²³ It proved to be Lavallée's most popular piece during his lifetime and remained in print through most of the twentieth century, published in anthologies with similar short pieces by Chopin, Beethoven, and other leading figures of the nineteenth century. In addition to the numerous printed editions of the sheet music, early piano rolls produced by Beryl Rubinstein, Felix Gerdts, Mettler Davis, and Herman Avery Wade attest to the *Étude*'s popularity.²⁴ Numerous interpretations can now be found on YouTube.

Lavallée dedicated *Le Papillon* to his piano teacher Antoine François Marmontel. Dedications on the other two pieces tell us something of Lavallée's social circle while in Paris. He dedicated the *Grande marche* to Madame Marie Annie Bossange (née Coindreau), the Cambridge, Massachussets–born wife of Gustave Bossange. This may have been sim-ply out of respect for the influential family. That the Bossanges' business was a meeting place for French Canadians was sufficient reason, but the bookseller may also have provided pecuniary assistance in some way for the financially strapped musician. Bossange would have met many in sim-ilar circumstances. French Canadians residing in and passing through

Paris in the early 1870s would meet at his bookshop in the 2nd arrondissement.[25] From this location, at 16 rue du 4 septembre, and from an office at Le Havre, Bossange served as the European agent for Canada's Department of Immigration, as well as for the Allan Shipping Line, the Grand Trunk Railway, and the Banque de Québec.[26] Octave Crémazie, living in exile after fleeing Canada and arrest for fraud, lived through the Franco-Prussian War and the siege of Paris, and eked out a living with Bossange. Others simply dropped by to meet compatriots and catch up on the news. In one of his letters, Ernest Gagnon mentions that in his daily visits to Bossange's shop to read the Canadian newspapers he would meet Guillaume Couture.[27] Given the dedication of the *Grande marche de concert* and Lavallée's social nature, it seems that he also got to know the Bossanges well.

More intriguing is Lavallée's dedication of the *Souvenir de Tolède* to Ida Astruc. She was the wife of Zacharie Astruc, the critic and artist who was closely connected to the impressionist movement and a participant in the 1874 exhibition that gave them their collective name. The Astrucs were close friends of Édouard Manet, who produced several portraits of them. In Henri Fantin-Latour's famous painting *Un atelier aux Batignolles* (A Studio at Les Batignolles), of 1870, Manet is depicted painting Zacharie Astruc, while looking on are the painters Otto Scholderer, Pierre-Auguste Renoir, Frédéric Bazille, and Claude Monet; the writer Émile Zola; and the musician Edmond Maitre. In Manet's famous *La leçon de musique (The Music Lesson)*, also of 1870, Zacharie Astruc is pictured playing guitar. The woman in that painting was likely Ida Astruc.[28] Both husband and wife had long had a strong interest in Spanish culture. Zacharie Astruc had helped Manet prepare for his 1865 journey to Spain, and in 1877, Manet completed a bust of Ida Astruc in Spanish costume.[29] While this may help to explain Lavallée's choice of title, and why their circle contained many musicians, how he became acquainted with the Astrucs is still unknown.

❖❖❖

In the early months of 1874, Lavallée had opportunities to observe musical events that would have a profound influence on his activities in North America. That spring, two national concerts presented in Paris were devoted entirely to contemporary French music. Among the works performed were some by leading figures of French music, including excerpts from Charles-Marie Widor's Symphony in A minor and Saint-Saëns's Variations on a Theme of Beethoven (performed by husband and wife pianists Alfred Jaëll and Marie Trautmann-Jaëll). Marcello, *La Chronique musicale*'s critic, wrote favourably about Jules Massenet's *Scènes pittoresques*, describing it at "one of the greatest successes of the National Concerts," but was critical of composers who imitated the style of French music from earlier times.[30] US critics would raise similar questions a decade later about some of the works on the programs of Lavallée's American concerts. Nevertheless, the inspiration for those concerts of the 1880s (discussed in chapter 7) is found in what was happening in Paris of the mid-1870s. Similarly, Lavallée was also in Paris to study French educational methods with a specific aim of establishing a conservatory in Canada.[31] As an auditing student, he did not need to go through examinations, but he would have taken a keen interest in the process and the outcome for his classmates. For piano students, in 1874, both males and females were required to play an étude, while male students were assigned Chopin's Piano Concerto No. 2 in F minor, op. 21, and female students played Alkan's Concerto-Étude in G-sharp minor. Among the men, the *premier prix* in piano was won by Paul Chabeaux, from the class of Georges Mathias (who had been a pupil of Chopin and Kalkbrenner). Debussy was awarded a certificate of merit for his playing of Chopin's Concerto.[32] Three women won firsts in piano: Mesdemoiselles Poitevin, Manotte, and de Pressensé.[33] Among the composition students, the Prix de Rome that year went to twenty-year-old Léon Ehrhart, a student of Henri Reber.[34] Observing the examination process in Paris shaped Lavallée's later work with the Academie de musique de Québec and the American College of Musicians.

Summer months should have provided Lavallée time to travel. Couture travelled to Belgium, the Netherlands, and Italy.[35] If they travelled together, no record of it seems to have survived. Lavallée devoted part of his time to composition. A gap in opus numbers of the published pieces may indicate that he composed at least two other significant works in Paris. Several articles have stated that two orchestral works were performed during his sojourn in Europe. In an 1888 article that he likely provided information for, the *Musical Courier* reported that a "'Suite d'Orchestre,' an overture, and 'Marche Triomphale,' [were] all produced in Paris."[36] Another article in the same journal reported that an orchestra of eighty musicians conducted by the "celebrated *chef d'orchestre*" Adolphe Maton performed at least one work.[37] This composition may have been the one discovered in 1990. That year, researchers located a manuscript bearing Lavallée's signature and the handwritten title "Patrie, ouverture," (Fatherland, overture), in a collection acquired by the Bibliothèque et archives nationales du Québec. Lavallée's re-discovered score was performed – perhaps for the first time – by the Orchestre symphonique de la Montérégie on 14 October 1993 in Longueuil, Quebec, and was included in an anthology of orchestral music published by the Canadian Musical Heritage Society (CMHS).[38] As Elaine Keillor, editor of the CMHS anthology, has pointed out, the sectional form of the overture is reminiscent of a suite and terms such as "suite" and "symphony" were used inconsistently in Lavallée's time.[39] The manuscript had been in the possession of the Montreal violinist and bandleader J.-J. Goulet. He had likely received it from Ernest Lavigne, a bandleader and publisher who had published and performed a number of Lavallée's compositions.[40] Although it was in poor condition, "12 août, 1874" is clearly legible at the top of the first page. Perhaps coincidentally, Georges Bizet composed an overture with the same title. It was first performed in the Concerts Populaire series, conducted by Pasdeloup, on 15 February 1874.[41] In their common title, both works reflect the nationalist mood in Paris in the early 1870s.

Given the date on Lavallée's *Patrie* manuscript, he may have also intended the work for performance in Montreal that fall. On 8 October 1874, A.J. Boucher, Derome, and others staged a benefit concert at the City Concert Hall to enable Lavallée to continue his studies.[42] The concert opened with Rossini's *William Tell Overture*, and the program consisted mostly of opera choruses and overtures, performed by Boucher's orchestra and a chorus of 150 singers drawn from various church choirs. Lavallée's younger brother, Charles, now twenty-three and starting to make a name for himself, played a cornet solo. Given the date on the front page of Lavallée's manuscript, he may have sent it back to Canada for this performance. He wrote on the front page: "If you find some errors, please correct them, as the score was prepared very quickly."[43] If the overture was intended for this event, it may also explain the patriotic title. Nevertheless, the overture was not mentioned in the advertisements and likely arrived too late to be performed.[44]

The program of the 8 October concert did contain at least one new composition by Lavallée. The penultimate work on the program was a cantata he had recently composed, and it was sung by the tenor François Lavoie with chorus.[45] Lapierre reported the "naïve" text to have been the work of priest Flavien Martineau, and quoted the choral refrain that alternates between the second and third person:

| | |
|---|---|
| Loin du pays, mais pour sa gloire | Far from home, but for his glory |
| Aimable ami, chante toujours | Good friend, sing always |
| et pour assurer ta victoire | and to assure his victory |
| Nous te jurons constant secours.[46] | We vow constant assistance. |

This poem was titled "l'Exilé: chant canadien" and included in the posthumously published collection of Martineau's poetry, *Une voix d'outre-tombe: poésies de M. Martineau, P.S.S.*[47] Neither Lavallée nor contemporary critics provided a date of composition for the cantata. Presumably he was sent the text, completed the work, and mailed the score back to Canada. On 7 October, *La Minerve* published an engraving of Lavallée as well as the concert program. Even so, it provided few details two days later, reporting only that "the immense hall of the Bonsecours Market was almost full."[48] Lavallée may have felt obliged to set the words, but given the weakness of the text, he may have turned out the cantata as quickly as possible – and just as quickly forgotten about it, as it is not mentioned in any subsequent biographical articles.[49]

Funds from the October concert helped Lavallée to remain in Paris through the winter. During this period, politics and culture were more intertwined than ever. The spirit of the times was evident in the city's opera houses. In general, operetta and vaudeville houses such as the Théâtre du Châtelet and the Folie Dramatique prospered. For a time, Parisians shunned the German-born Jacques Offenbach, whose operettas had so successfully mocked the values of the Second Empire. After the Franco-Prussian War, authorities banned performances of his satire of militarism, *La Grande-Duchesse de Gérolstein*, which had been a great success in

Figure 4.3 Engraving of the Palais Garnier, Paris, which was inaugurated in January 1875.

1867. By the middle of 1873, Offenbach gambled on a new venture at the Théâtre de la Gaîté, on the rue Papin, in the 3rd arrondissement. He enjoyed some success, with new productions of *Orphée aux enfers* and *Geneviève de Brabant*, but in 1875 had lost the theatre. In the 9th arrondissement, and at the other end of the social spectrum, Napoléon III's monumental opera house, his Academie Imperiale de Musique, was finally completed.[50] In 1870, after the emperor's fall, it had been named the Théâtre National de l'Opéra by the Third Republic's government, but the name on the building was the Academie Nationale de Musique when MacMahon inaugurated it on 5 January 1875. (See figure 4.3) Given its grandeur, it became known as Palais Garnier, in honour of its architect, Charles Garnier. At this most conspicuous of French cultural institutions, Italian opera continued to be heard most often, along with works of Halévy, Meyerbeer, Auber, and other composers of the war-horses of the French repertoire.[51] Less heavily subsidized by the state, the Opéra-Comique, under its director Camille du Locle, had since the end of the war begun to add to its standard fare of Boïeldieu, Auber, and Adam.[52] The 3 March 1875 premiere of Bizet's *Carmen*, at the Salle Favart, was easily the most surprising of a mostly cautious expansion of the repertoire. In the summer of 1874, a delegation from the Society of French Composers appeared at the National Assembly to lobby for greater representation of French music in the city's subsidized theatres.[53] Neither the hefty subventions nor the increasing preference given to French composers would be lost on Lavallée.[54]

The spring and early summer months brought the Conservatoire's competitions. Guillaume Couture, who had had his *Rêverie*, for orchestra, performed at the Société Nationale concert on 15 May, won a 1st Certificate of Merit in harmony.[55] No *premier prix* for piano was awarded to a male student that year, but two female students took that honour: Mlles Taravant and Poltier (both students of Félix Le Couppey).[56] The winner of the Prix de Rome was André Wormser, a fellow student of Lavallée's in the classes of both Bazin and Marmontel.[57] Lavallée appears to have had a congenial relationship with Marmontel. He would have stood out from most of his classmates in age and experience. He could not claim a *premier prix,* but when he left Paris, he took with him a letter of strong support from Marmontel:

My Dear Lavallée,
As you return to your country, I bid you a cordial farewell, and wish you all the success that you merit by your constant and courageous work. I am certain that your friends, so kind and devoted, shall find your talent transformed both in terms of style and restrained daring.

I count on you to transmit to your compatriots the advice that I have given to you, and which you have well appreciated. Continue to love and understand beautiful music, esteem art and artists, and prove to the envious and the detractors that you have a talent beyond all reproach. I count on you and do not doubt for an instant your honour or your refinement. Follow well the plan outlined of your studies, exercises, etc. Farewell, and may God guide you, and give you all the joys of family, and all the success you desire, and consideration you deserve.

Your professor and friend, Marmontel.[58]

Later that year Marmontel dedicated to Lavallée one of the études in his *L'Art moderne du Piano-50 études de salon*, and in 1876 he listed all three of the piano compositions Lavallée published in Paris among the recommended works in *Art classique et moderne du piano*.[59]

The exact date of Lavallée's departure from France remains unknown. He returned to Canada in July 1875, but appears to have travelled through parts of Europe before beginning the voyage home. In an 1883 article, he mentions the "different countries of Europe in which I have travelled," and a year later, he wrote of "having travelled a great deal throughout [Europe's] extent, as well as having followed my profession there."[60] Although these comments might have been calculated to inflate his reputation in North America, they contained some truth. Given his propensity for travel, it seems unlikely that he would have just stayed put, despite the attractions Paris offered. In addition to France, he may have visited Belgium, where future collaborator Frantz Prume and his wife Rosita del Vecchio were then living, and Spain, if the *Souvenir de Tolède* is to be accepted as evidence.[61] He saw at least some of Great Britain as he sailed back to Canada from Liverpool on 9 July on board the steamer SS *Nova Scotian*.

After nearly two years in Europe, Lavallée must have felt satisfied with what he had achieved. Among his credentials he could now claim to have travelled in Europe and had compositions published and performed in Paris, and he had a letter of support from a leading piano teacher. He also left France having experienced the nationalist fervour of the times. The link between the arts and national identity had never been made so strongly, even though Lavallée had had two French teachers in Canada in the 1850s. Unlike in North America, opera and concert music were not simply *divertissements*, but expressions of identity.[62] Returning to Canada, he eschewed popular music and devoted the rest of his career to classical music. Over the next five years, he directed his efforts toward developing musical life in Canada, both through concerts and large-scale productions, and through education. This was perhaps partly a means of repaying his sponsors, but he appears to have accepted the role of Canada's *"musicien national."*

❖❖❖

After an eleven-day journey from Liverpool, the SS *Nova Scotian* arrived in Quebec City's harbour on the morning of 20 July 1875 with its cargo of mail and immigrants. The *Journal de Québec* reported Lavallée's return to Canada, and the events of the next five years are among the best documented in Lavallée's life.[63] Not only do newspapers provide an abundance of information but also, beginning in May 1875, Montreal's music community had a new voice when A.J. Boucher launched *Le Canada musical*, a periodical that provided news on musical events in Canada and abroad.[64] With a wife and child to support, Lavallée found work as a church musician and, for the first time in his life, devoted much of his time to teaching. Much of his energy went into performing at chamber concerts he organized and conducting large-scale stage and concert productions. Determined to make his mark, he was driven by a desire to improve music education in Quebec and enrich cultural life.

The day after landing at Quebec City, Lavallée returned to Montreal and his family, joining Joséphine and Calixa Jr at his parents' home. Calixa Jr was now nearly seven years old, and presumably attending school nearby. We have no record of Joséphine's activities. For the first few months, she, Lavallée, and their son lived with his parents and siblings. From 1871 the Lavallées had resided at 339 de la Gauchetière Street, near Saint-Denis Street, but a few months before Lavallée's return the family had settled into a new home at 158 German Street, just below Sainte-Catherine Street. The house may have been too small for the extended family of ten or eleven people, and later that year they moved to a larger house at 170 German Street. It was the same street they had lived on a decade earlier, but a little further north, in an area that was working class and predominantly francophone. Many of the neighbours were artisans like Augustin Lavallée. Over the previous decade he had begun to specialize in violin making. His shop on Côte Saint-Lambert had prospered, and he brought his second son, Charles, into the business as a partner.[65] (See figures 4.4 and 4.5) Charles, now twenty-five, had become one of the city's leading cornet players and bandleaders. The

Figure 4.4 Photograph of the 1894 *Fête nationale* parade, showing the Lavallée et fils music shop on Saint-Lambert Hill in Montreal. By the time the photograph was taken. the workshop-store had been in existence for nearly thirty years.

Figure 4.5
Interior view of Lavallée et fils (ca. 1890) showing Calixa Lavallée's father, Augustin, at work on a violin.

third son, seventeen-year-old Joseph, had left school by the age of thirteen and worked as a trombonist and cellist. The eldest daughter, Cordélia, now in her late twenties, was an amateur vocalist and likely worked in the family shop.

The 1870s were a time of change and adjustment. By that time, Montreal's population had surpassed 160,000, with many feeling the effects of the economic downturn that had begun in 1873.[66] Socially, French-Canadian society had grown increasingly conservative. In 1870, Bishop Bourget began work on a new cathedral on Dorchester Street, in what was then the west end.[67] Modelled on Rome's St Peter's Basilica, the new cathedral was to be a visual affirmation of ultramontanism. In 1876, before a scandal could force him from office, the bishop transferred power to his protege, Édouard-Charles Fabre. In these early years of Confederation, debate in French-speaking Canada turned largely to the conflict between conservatism and liberalism.[68] Politically, Confederation had experienced a few bumps. The Pacific Scandal had brought down the government in 1873, after Macdonald's Conservatives were found to have accepted bribes from tycoon Sir Hugh Allan's Canada Pacific Railway Company. On 7 November 1873, the governor general, Lord Dufferin, transferred power to Liberal leader Alexander Mackenzie, who subsequently won a majority in the 22 January 1874 election – an election that saw the arrival of Wilfrid Laurier on the federal scene. In Quebec City, the Conservatives, under Chauveau, had held power after the election of 1871 and, under the leadership of Charles-Eugène Boucher de Boucherville, again after the election of 7 July 1875. Both levels of government struggled to combat the economic fallout of the Panic of 1873 – the effects of which would have a direct impact on Lavallée's achievements. Throughout these years, Lavallée walked a careful path in his attempt to build musical institutions and further the cause of culture.

Montreal gained several new performance venues in the early 1870s. On the Champ de Mars, in the old quarter of the city, the Gosford Street Church was converted into the Palais Musical.[69] At the same time, developers were transforming the uptown area, where Sainte-Catherine Street attracted many shopping and entertainment establishments. The 1,100-seat Queen's Hall, at the corner of Sainte-Catherine and University streets, had opened in time to host Anton Rubinstein during his

1872–73 concert tour. The Crystal Palace also occupied a location close by, on Sainte-Catherine Street at Victoria Street. It would soon be relocated to Fletcher's Field (now known as Jeanne-Mance Park). Still bullish, despite the stock market crash of 1873, businessmen and civic leaders opened several new concert halls and theatres. A consortium led by Sir Hugh Allan commissioned the construction of the Academy of Music, just a little further up Victoria Street from the Crystal Palace.[70] Opening in November 1875, and managed by the actor Eugene Addison McDowell, it was a theatre that reflected the aspirations of the bourgeoisie. To the middle class, the Theatre Royal looked increasing rough, with its adjacent casino and surrounded by saloons and stables. In its uptown location, the Academy aimed to cater to a more upscale clientele. Designed by architect Andrew B. Taft, the 2,100-seat theatre was constructed of brick with a stone facade. Inside, it offered four orchestra sections, four boxes, and two balconies. It had several advantages over the Theatre Royal: it was heated, electrically lit, and its stage was slightly larger.[71] (See figure 4.6)

The city's concert life, however, had not changed substantially since Lavallée had lived there in the mid-1860s. Touring troupes of all types continued to visit. Among the companies appearing in Montreal during the mid-1870s were the Holman Comic Opera Troupe, a Strakosch ensemble, Tom Thumb's company, Barnum's Circus, Haverly's Minstrels, and many others. Several large local ensembles had also formed. Of these, only Joseph Gould and his Montreal Mendelssohn Choir performed regularly.[72] Most local concerts were still charity events, where audiences continued to hear a repertoire of songs, opera arias, fantasies, marches, and overtures. This began to change with the return of Lavallée and several of his contemporaries. Guillaume Couture returned soon after Lavallée, resuming his posts at Saint-Jacques Church and the École normale Jacques Cartier, and becoming *La Minerve*'s music critic. He was followed by Frantz Prume and Rosita del Vecchio, who returned from a two-year stay in Europe.[73] As a group, these four musicians attempted to cultivate the public's appreciation of classical music and what, in Montreal, was a new repertoire of romantic works.

Mendelssohn's *Capriccio brillant* in B minor, op. 22, Carl Maria von Weber's *Konzertstück* in F minor, op. 79, and Beethoven's Sonata No.

Figure 4.6
Interior view of the Academy of Music, Victoria Street, Montreal, soon after its opening in 1875.

14 in C-sharp minor ("Moonlight"), op. 27, no. 2 figured prominently in Lavallée's repertoire. Along with these works were many shorter pieces by Chopin, Schumann, Théodore Ritter, and Mendelssohn. As encores, he frequently performed Émile Prudent's *La danse des fées, caprice*, op. 41, and his own *Le Papillon*.[74] Prume performed Mendelssohn's Violin Concerto in E minor, op. 64, and several sonatas by Beethoven, but his repertoire still contained many pieces derived from operas, including his own *Fantasy on Themes from 'Faust.'* Not surprisingly, del Vecchio sang mostly operatic selections, notably those from Gounod's *La Reine de Saba* and *Mireille*.

Lavallée waited until the Prumes had returned to Montreal before giving the first of several performances. This was a free concert for those who sponsored his studies. The venue he chose for the concert was the

Sulpicians' Notre-Dame Street reading room, the Cabinet de lecture. Some four hundred invited guests packed into the hall for the event on 9 September 1875. A feature of the two-hour program was Weber's *Konzert-stück*, with the orchestral part taken up by a quintet that included Augustin Lavallée making a rare concert appearance.[75] Prume performed *La Mélancolie*, the most famous of his uncle François Prume's compositions, with Lavallée accompanying. This event was followed later that month by a concert in Ottawa, during that city's annual exhibition.[76] On 5 November Lavallée travelled to Quebec City with Prume and del Vecchio for two concerts at Music Hall. After rehearsals with the Septuor Haydn, Quebec City's main chamber ensemble, the first performance took place on 8 November. They then took part in a fundraising concert for the band of the Faubourg Saint-Jean at the Salle Jacques Cartier on 11 November. A week later, on 18 November, they gave a second concert at Music Hall that seems to have been well attended, then stayed for another night to play at a fundraising event for the Septuor Haydn, before returning home. Finally, Lavallée, Prume, and del Vecchio gave a public concert in Montreal at the Mechanics' Hall on 9 December. A string quintet again took the place of an orchestra in both the *Capriccio brillante* and the Violin Concerto. This ensemble was expanded to a double string quartet for Beethoven's *Prometheus* overture, op. 43, and Conradin Kreutzer's overture to *Das Nachtlager in Granada*.[77]

A number of the concert reviews commented on how Lavallée's playing had changed. In a review that was reprinted in Paris's *Le Ménestrel*, L.-O. David's *L'Opinion publique* reported that Lavallée's playing had been "completely transformed, and that the methodical performance removed none of the spirit and feeling of the personal style of our artist."[78] The anonymous critic of *Le Canada musical* (probably A.J. Boucher) wrote that "Lavallée's execution today is characterized by a remarkable precision – by a sure technique, served by a brilliant and energetic style of playing, restrained of all excess – and by an interpretation respectful of the composer's intentions."[79] David's correspondent in Quebec City was Joseph Marmette, a journalist and writer of historical novels. (See Figure 4.7) If his picturesque commentaries give little evidence of musical training, they do convey his enthusiasm: "Listening to Lavallée revive the great passionate soul of Chopin, I find myself suddenly at Majorca."[80]

Figure 4.7 Photograph of Lavallee's confidant,
the writer Joseph Marmette.

Guillaume Couture, writing in *La Minerve*, provided the most thorough account. He devoted more than two columns of the newspaper to the 9 December performance, writing:

I was very happy to note that Mr Lavallée has not only the bravura style we had heard. This manner of playing is quite trivial and demands only technique.

He has other things more precious. Technique speaks to the man; style speaks to the artist. Technique represents the body; style represents the soul. Technique may be acquired easily; style can live only with those whose heart is of extreme sensitivity and with those who are able to understand the beautiful ideal that one can only see with the eyes of the soul.

However, Mr Lavallée is an artist, he has feeling, expression, and refinement. Moreover, a tireless worker, he searches continuously to perfect his art and succeeds so well that he has all that it requires.[81]

The unnamed critic of Le National, the new Liberal newspaper, was the least complimentary in his coverage of Lavallée's early events, citing what he considered to be an excessive use of the damper pedal at times and a lack of nuance in Lavallée's interpretations of certain movements. On his method of playing, the critic conceded that Lavallée played with "enthusiasm and gusto" and that he possessed "superior fingering," but claimed that he floated between the reflective (réfléchi) style of Rubinstein and Ritter and the "fiery" style of Liszt, and would do well to stay with the former.[82] In Quebec City, Le Canadien noted Lavallée's "immense progress" under Marmontel, and commented more specifically on how Lavallée's style of playing had changed over the past two years: "[Lavallée] has lost none of the brilliance and the passion that distinguished [his playing], but he has acquired in his fingering more perfect equality and great delicacy, with a quickness of which only he seems to know the secret of." The performance of Mendelssohn's Capriccio gave "an idea of the amazing power of our Canadian pianist." Oddly, the critic then compares the playing of Lavallée, "a true artist," to that of the "mediocre" Salomon Mazurette.[83] Where the reviewers agreed was that his interpretations were more refined or measured while still robust, and these points would be echoed in subsequent reviews.

What these early performances also revealed was that Lavallée's repertoire itself had changed radically. During the 1860s, he had relied to a great extent on his own compositions and on his transcriptions and fantasies based on opera themes. He continued to perform his own music from time to time, but much less often than previously. From this point, Lavallée and Prume occasionally performed the works of Baroque and Classical composers but focused mostly on those of the Romantics. They did not purge their concert programs entirely of display pieces, but turned from a largely Franco-Italian repertoire to Austrian and German music. Instrumental forms of Weber, Mendelssohn, and Beethoven replaced the fantasies drawn from the operas of Bellini and Donizetti. Weber's *Konzertstück* became Lavallée's signature piece. Completed just before the premiere of the composer's most famous work, *Der Freischütz*, the *Konzertstück* is arguably the definitive Romantic piano concerto. No doubt Lavallée felt a personal connection to its program and musical depiction of separation, grief, reunification, and triumph. The availability of various arrangements of the orchestra part made it possible to perform the work under different circumstances.

Opinion was divided on the change in Lavallée's repertoire. The critic of Quebec City's *Le Canadien* noted how Lavallée had especially captured the "poetic sadness" of Chopin, the composer whose music he would be most noted for performing.[84] The music of Chopin and of the other Romantics still had an element of novelty. After the 9 December performance, the unnamed critic of *Le Canada musical* wrote that: "never … has a more interesting program been presented to our musical public."[85] Couture described the event as inaugurating a "new musical era" in Canada.[86] He noted the public's resistance to some Romantic composers and congratulated Lavallée, "particularly on his Chopin étude," and advised him to "continue to perform his great works, although the public receives them coldly; it is only a question of time."[87] Couture's supportive comments hint at what must have been the public's incomprehension of a repertoire that, although increasingly performed in New York and Boston, was still largely unfamiliar to most Montreal concert-goers. It signalled a change that we today might not fully appreciate: the operatic excerpts widely performed up to this time were what we would now consider a form of popular music, admired for their emphasis on melody. The music of Schumann and Weber required a greater level of concentration from listeners. For Lavallée and Couture, the cultivation of this music was a form of national development. Interestingly, whereas the nationalist mood in post-war Paris had given rise to an increase in the performance of French music, Lavallée had turned increasingly to the music of Chopin and of German composers – music emphasized in Marmontel's classes. It was one of the contradictions one finds in the narrow definition of nationalism projected by Lavallée's posthumous supporters and also, more generally, in the limited understanding of how music may be used for nationalist purposes.

On 28 December 1875, Prume, del Vecchio, and Lavallée took part in a concert at the Mechanics' Hall showcasing Guillaume Couture's talents as conductor and composer.[88] Couture conducted an orchestra and the choir of Saint-Jacques Church in a long program that was a curious mix of the secular and the sacred. Opening with the overture from Handel's *Messiah*, the program featured works by Meyerbeer, Mendelssohn, and Berlioz, as well as three of Couture's compositions: *Memorare*, *Ave Maria*, and a *Hymne Nationale*. *Le Canada musical* reported the concert to have been a "brilliant success" and expressed hope that the full hall produced "abundant receipts."[89] The Protestant *Daily Witness* was one of the few newspapers to mention the concert, doing so unusually with a review in English and another in its regular French-language column, each of which took a different jab at Couture. In English, after favourable passing reference to the soloists, the anonymous critic wrote that, with the exception of the opening overture, the orchestral pieces "showed a want of training on the part of the members of the orchestra scarcely pardonable in so able a musician as Mr Couture." The choir was said to have given a good performance of a chorus from Gounod's *Philémon et Baucis*, but "manifested, like the orchestra, a lack of training in their other pieces." Finally, he described Couture's "French Canadian National Hymn," as "rather tame, and not sufficiently stirring to make its adoption likely by our French-Canadian countrymen."[90] In the French-language review, the writer conceded that Couture had talent as a conductor but ridiculed his abilities as a composer. He praised the epic scale of the concert and Lavallée's and Prume's contributions to it. "Without Mr Couture and without his cemetery music," he wrote, "it would have been a musical feast. Unfortunately the 'Memorare,' Ave Maria Solo and 'Hymne National' threw a pall on the enthusiasm generated by the wonders born under the magic touch of Mr Prume and Mr Lavallée." Later, he added, the *Hymne Nationale* was applauded quietly "to be polite and because it was the last of the three."[91] It was the sort of harsh criticism that Couture himself was known for dealing out, but it must have stung the young musician, who had only been back for six months.

Around this time, Lavallée, Joséphine, and their son found a home of their own at 82 Cathcart Street, closer to potential students. A few months earlier, Lavallée and the Prumes had established a joint teaching studio on Beaver Hall Square. The area would be associated with the visual arts in the early decades of the twentieth century but was then among the most prestigious addresses in the city. The teaching studios were located at 41 Beaver Hall Hill, a block predominated by the medical profession. The arrangement lasted only a few months, perhaps due to the high rent.[92] Lavallée's Cathcart Street address was less glamorous but only two blocks north of Beaver Hall Square, and it was still a good location for a teaching studio. On this short street, running parallel to Sainte-Catherine, just a block south, his middle-class neighbours were professionals and office workers. They were also almost entirely anglophone, with the notable exception of the violinist Jules Hone, who lived with his family just a few doors down at number 90.[93]

Whatever the reason for the failure of the Beaver Hall venture, it had no effect on Lavallée and Prume's working relationship. During their visit to Quebec City in the fall of 1875, they accepted an invitation to join the Académie de musique de Québec (AMQ).[94] The AMQ was essentially an examination board that held annual exams in performance and music theory. Quebec City musicians had founded the Académie in the late 1860s in the hope of standardizing music education and improving the state of music in the province. The first meeting of the organization had taken place on 2 May 1868 at the home of Ernest Gagnon, on Saint-François Street, where several resolutions were passed and Gagnon was elected as president.[95] At a second meeting, a week later, members selected the pianist F.W. Mills as assistant director and passed a resolution to issue diplomas in harmony, composition, and in performance.[96] The AMQ made modest progress, adding Paul Letondal, Gustave Smith, and other members from outside of Quebec City in 1869.[97] The following year it extended honorary membership to Marmontel and three others in France. It later established links with two teachers' colleges, the École normale Jacques Cartier and the École normale Laval. In November 1871, the AMQ requested official recognition from the lieutenant-governor, and by the mid-1870s the Québec government provided the Académie with funding of $100 per year. This appears to have been the AMQ's only significant source of revenue, and it helped to defray printing and advertising expenses. Both Lavallée and Prume took their work with the AMQ quite seriously. In February 1876, they submitted lists of piano and violin pieces to be added to required repertoire, and later took up administrative positions.

By the spring of 1876, Lavallée's activities as an educator were occupying much of his time. In April, he participated in discussions with musicians who had proposed the creation of a local conservatory of music. It would have been a rare collaboration between the city's anglophone and francophone musicians, headed by Paul Letondal and the English organist Charles F. Davies.[98] Local newspapers appear never to have explained the reasons for the project's collapse, but it might have been seen as an omen for future efforts. Nevertheless, Lavallée's move to the expanding and predominantly anglophone uptown area of the city appears to have been a shrewd decision. In April 1876, the editor of the news column in *Le Canada musical* reported being "pleased to learn that the size of Mr Calixa Lavallée's musical clientele continues to *crescendo*. In addition to the numerous French Canadians, many of the leading English families have demanded his professional services."[99] The note had obvious promotional value for Lavallée and may have contained more than an element of truth. The Lavallées had need of financial stability in the early months of 1876 as Joséphine was by this time several months along in a pregnancy.

Through the spring and into the summer of 1876, Lavallée, Prume, and del Vecchio performed several times a month, appearing at everything from soirees to orchestral and choral concerts. On 12 January 1876, they performed at a soiree at Rosebank, the Longueuil home of the celebrated photographer William Notman. Prume and del Vecchio had sat for portraits with Notman in 1871. (See figures 4.8 and 4.9) After the soiree, Lavallée had his photo taken, as did the Prumes' young son Jules.[100] (See figure 4.10) During April and May, they staged their first series of chamber concerts in the third floor lecture hall of the YMCA's new building on Victoria Square.[101] The popular venue in the busy area offered the potential of bringing in a younger, and predominantly anglophone, audience. It is difficult to know just how successful this venture was. The unnamed critic at the *Montreal Star*, who was likely to have been Couture, noted that the room was "nearly filled with admirers of high class music" for

Figures 4.8 and 4.9  Portraits of Frantz Jehin-Prume and Rosita del Vecchio, taken in 1871 by William Notman.

the first concert, and that "Prume and Lavallée deserve the highest praise for raising the public's taste up to their own standard, instead of lowering art by pandering to what we might term popular support, and giving music which has only the effect of vitiating the taste of those who listen to it."[102] Such encouragement for their project was rare and undoubtedly appreciated.

Lavallée and Prume visited Quebec City often in 1876. In the spring and early summer months, they gave a series of concerts in Victoria Hall, in the Upper Town. This Sainte-Anne Street venue, built in 1816 as a Wesleyan Methodist church, had from about 1848 until 1873 served primarily as a lecture hall. It had reopened in January 1874 with a performance of "Le Forgeron de Chateaudun," a drama about the Franco-Prussian War, and had become a popular location for both theatrical performances and concerts.[103] Soon after, it was leased to the Literary

Figure 4.10
Photograph of
Lavallée, taken soon
after his January
1876 performance
at a soiree at the
home of the noted
photographer
William Notman.

and Historical Society, which managed it. The room was smaller in size than the 1,500-seat Music Hall, making it a pragmatic choice for Lavallée and Prume.[104] The first of three planned concerts, held under the patronage of the governor general and his wife, Lord and Lady Dufferin, took place on 22 May, with both del Vecchio and Couture as vocalists and the Quebec City musician Gustave Gagnon as accompanist. In its review, the *Daily Evening Mercury* noted Lavallée's interpretations of Chopin, but also drew attention to the fact that he played everything from memory, something that seems not to have been the norm.[105] US writers noted the same thing about Lavallée's playing a decade later, when his repertoire consisted mostly of new music. At the concert a week later, on 29 May, Couture was replaced by Napoléon Legendre, and a chamber ensemble was added, performing selections from Gounod's

*Faust* ballet suite.[106] The next day, 30 May, a fire engulfed the Faubourg Saint-Louis district of the city, destroying dozens of buildings. It is not clear whether Lavallée and Prume were still in Quebec City at the time, but a decision was made not to stage the third of the planned concerts.

On Thursday, 2 June, they were back in Montreal for what turned out to be Couture's "concert d'adieu." He had returned from Europe with expectations that exceeded what could be achieved in the short term, and while circuses and popular dramas drew large audiences, concerts of serious music were sparsely attended.[107] Attributing the problem in part to a lack of serious criticism, he wrote, "Always, the following day, one reads an account such as: 'The concert of Mr___ was given last night to a crowded hall.' – Or better: 'Despite the bad weather last night, a select audience went to the concert of Mr___, wishing to show the high esteem they have for him.'"[108] While this is an accurate assessment of most reporting on concerts, his own tough critiques had led to public feuds with both the singing teacher Madame Petipas and the organist Peter MacLagan, and won him few friends.[109] Even at this concert, the *Daily Witness* wrote favourably of Couture's conducting skills while disparaging his abilities as a singer and as a composer. As in the earlier review, the writer raised the issue of popular tastes. After acknowledging his respect for Beethoven, Mendelssohn, and Wagner, he concluded that "nevertheless, one would shamelessly give all the concertos in G minor and all the *Tannhäusers* of the world for the 'chorus of the conspirators' of [Charles Lecoq's operetta] *La fille de Madame Angot*. This is outrageous, but it's how we are made. If Mr Couture doubts it he should once try playing *Madame Angot*."[110] While the writer was projecting his own view, the programs of popular concerts of the time show his tastes to be those of the majority, and it gives some indication of the difficulties faced by Lavallée and Prume as well as by Couture.[111]

June was shaping up to be a hectic month. Just four days after Couture's concert on 5 June 1876, Lavallée took part in another farewell event. This one was for the young violinist François Boucher, who was to leave for studies in Belgium later in the summer. He was the son of Lavallée's friend Adélard J. Boucher and a student of both Prume and Oscar Martel. Lavallée performed Field's 5th Nocturne and a piece of his own composed for the occasion, a galop entitled *Bon Voyage*.[112] Reviewing the concert for *La Minerve*, Couture described the work as "full of verve and spirit," and also noted that Lavallée "hadn't taken the pain to write it out."[113] There is no evidence that he ever did. If Lavallée was too busy at this time to write out a composition, it was partly due to his teaching load and later to his duties at Saint-Jacques Church. But his home life was also in transition. On 10 June, Joséphine gave birth to her second child. The baby boy was named Joseph François Augustin Lavallée for his grandfather and possibly Marmontel.[114] The baptism took place at Notre-Dame on 11 June with Léon and Rose Derome as godparents.[115]

On 19 June, Lavallée took part in the AMQ's assembly and examinations at the Académie commercial catholique de Montréal, on Sainte-Catherine Street. He served on the piano jury, along with Ernest Gagnon, J.A. Defoy, Letondal, J.B. Labelle, and Moïse Saucier. The meeting resulted in a number of changes, as members voted to divide the AMQ into Montreal and Quebec City sections, with boards for each city but a single president. Letondal declined the first nomination for the post of president and suggested Lavallée take his place. Members ratified the choice and ended the gathering with a banquet at the Hôtel de France.[116] A few days later, the Académie commercial hosted the main dramatic-musical event of the *Fête nationale*. As usual, the day began with the morning procession leading to Viger Square for speeches and songs, and then on to Mass at Notre Dame. In the evening, A.J. Boucher led the orchestra, opening the event with *"Vive la Canadienne"* and closing with Couture's *Hymne National*.[117]

Through the final days of June, Lavallée was busy preparing a farewell concert for Prume, who also planned to return to Europe. Beyond touring Europe for financial reasons, he was also considering del Vecchio's career – she was now thirty and still looking to make her name. However, del Vecchio herself may have had reservations about leaving Montreal. Lavallée gave her top billing among a full slate of artists that included the French tenor Paul Wiallard, Alfred De Sève, and François Boucher. A.J. Boucher led the orchestra, Rose de Lima Derome (billed as Madam Béliveau) was accompanist, and Augustin Lavallée played in the chamber ensemble and orchestra. The concert drew a full house at the Mechanics' Institute, and influenced Prume's plans. The next day, the *Montreal Star* reported that Prume "had abandoned the idea of deserting Montreal and will return in the fall." He and Lavallée then returned to Quebec City for the long-delayed third chamber concert. They played well, but attendance was poor, perhaps due in part to the economic impact of the fire.[118]

At least briefly, Lavallée had the benefit of a church job when he took over the direction of the Saint-Jacques choir following Couture's departure for Paris that summer.[119] Rebuilt as a parish church after the fire of 1852, Saint-Jacques remained geographically at the heart of francophone Montreal, and its spire, newly completed in 1876, soared eighty-five metres above Saint-Denis Street. The position provided Lavallée with some much-needed income and offered him an opportunity to work with one of the city's best choirs.

Later that summer, Lavallée suffered a serious blow when his young son died. Joseph was not quite two months old. A funeral was held in the family's home on Cathcart Street on 4 August.[120] The death of an infant was a common occurrence in the nineteenth century, but left parents devastated just the same. No record of Joséphine's reaction has survived. Lavallée seems to have stayed out of the public eye until late in the month when he performed at the funeral of Nazaire Dupuis, the Acadian entrepreneur and founder of the Sainte-Catherine Street department store Dupuis Frères. At thirty-two, Dupuis was a year younger than Lavallée, and the two deaths, coming weeks apart, would have given him cause to reflect on the unpredictability of life and what he was achieving.

Despite his commitment to developing musical life in Canada, Lavallée had not entirely abandoned his career in the US. He still had many contacts there, among them Matthew Arbuckle, a leading cornettist and fellow Union Army veteran. In September 1875, Arbuckle was a soloist at Gilmore's Garden in New York, performing with Patrick Gilmore's 100-piece band. Lavallée composed a *Grande fantaisie de concert* for Arbuckle that was given its premiere on 10 September and was later published by Carl Fischer.[121] Late in the summer of 1876, Lavallée had been planning to restart music lessons at his home when he received an invitation to perform in New York. The event was the unveiling of a bronze statue of Lafayette by Frédéric Auguste Bartholdi, the sculptor who would achieve his widest fame a decade later with the Statue of Liberty. On 4 September, Lavallée and members of the newly reformed Bande de

Figure 4.11 An engraving of the scene at the unveiling of the statue of Lafayette on Union Square in New York City on 6 September 1876.

la Cité departed from Bonaventure Station. In New York, they joined up with other regiments brought in for the occasion, many of them comprising Franco-Americans, and some of them aged veterans of the War of 1812. The statue itself was a gift to the City of New York for aiding Paris during the Franco-Prussian War, and the ceremony was very much a celebration of US-French solidarity. The event took place on the afternoon of Wednesday, 6 September, and began with a military parade, where Lavallée and the Bande joined some fourteen other regiments in a column that formed opposite Hotel Brunswick and proceeded down Fifth Avenue to Waverley Place and up Broadway to Union Square. Crowds lined the route and filled the square where, the *Daily Tribune* reported, "almost every tree and lamppost held its clinging occupant."[122] (See figure 4.11) At Union Square, the large US flag that covered the statue was raised by the sculptor himself, and Mayor William H. Wickham officially accepted the gift from the French consul general. Speeches were interspersed with music. The choral society L'Espérance sang

Laurent de Rillé's "France," and cannons provided counterpoint during what must have been a raucous performance of "La Marseillaise" by the massed bands. For francophone veterans like Lavallée, it was an emotional occasion, while in Quebec the conservative *La Minerve* reported the events cautiously, clearly opposed in principle to republicanism and the revolutions that the event was celebrating.[123]

It was the middle of September by the time Lavallée resumed lessons at his home. Teaching and administrative duties occupied much of his time in the autumn and winter of 1876. On 25 November, he had some of his students give a semi-public performance at his home on Cathcart Street. The evening's program shows him to have been teaching a wide repertoire, from opera arrangements to works by Beethoven and Marmontel. Four female students were mentioned in the program: Mlle Gauthier, Mlle Désautels, Mlle Dorais, and Léon Derome's daughter, Caroline, then about sixteen. Two male students took part, V.L. Couturier and Alexis Contant. The eighteen-year-old Contant would go on to become a leading musician of his generation in Canada. That evening he performed a Tarantelle by a composer identified only as Cunio, and Joseph Raff's *Caprice espagnol*.[124] At a concert in early January, Lavallée provided an opportunity for Contant and Couturier to perform in public when they gave the Montreal premiere of Gottschalk's *Pasquinade*, op. 59, at the Mechanics' Hall.[125]

That fall, Lavallée and Prume found a new performing partner in Gustave Jacquard, a French cellist, quite possibly related to the more famous cellist of the time, Léon Jacquard. Gustave had lived in Montreal at the beginning of the decade, teaching in a rooming house on Saint-Antoine Street.[126] During that time he sat for a photo with Notman, which shows an elegant-looking man posing with his cello. (See figure 4.12) After his first appearance with Lavallée and Prume, at the Mechanics' Hall on 5 December, he was welcomed back by the local critics. *Le Canada musical* wrote that "Mr Jacquard returned to us, manoeuvring his bow with all the charm of the past. With the brio and skill with which we are accustomed from him, this distinguished cellist now adds the assurance of maturity to his talent."[127] At this performance, Jacquard was said to have "literally elevated his listeners" with his interpretation of Adrien-François Servais's *Fantaisie de concert*.[128] He performed with Lavallée

Figure 4.12 An 1870 portrait of the French cellist Gustave Jacquard by Notman. Jacquard played frequently with Lavallée and Prume in the early winter of 1876–77.

and Prume several times in the winter of 1876–77, playing Schumann's Quintet for Piano and Strings in E-flat major, op. 44, piano trios by Beethoven and Mendelssohn, and other chamber works.

❖❖❖

The early months of 1877 brought a new opportunity for Lavallée to make use of his conducting experience. He had worked hard with the Saint-Jacques choir since Couture's departure and had a good relationship with the parish priest Sentenne. The Church hierarchy, on the other hand, may have complicated things. Édouard-Charles Fabre had become Bishop of Montreal in May 1876, continuing ultramontane authority, and plans were afoot to ban the use of mixed choruses in diocesan churches. Even before the decree was passed, Lavallée resigned.[129] Taking the choir with him, he set about staging Charles Gounod and Jules Barbier's lyric drama, *Jeanne d'Arc*.

The details of how Lavallée came to choose *Jeanne d'Arc* remain uncertain. Eugène Lapierre wrote that it was *curé* Sentenne who proposed staging an opera as a means of maintaining the choir, and recommended *Jeanne d'Arc*, but this may have been Lapierre's way of claiming that no rift existed between Lavallée and the Church.[130] Both Prume and Lavallée would have been well acquainted with *Jeanne d'Arc*. Frantz Prume and del Vecchio were in Spa when Charles Gounod visited there with Georgina Weldon, causing a scandal, not long before the premiere of *Jeanne d'Arc*. Lavallée was in Paris at the time of its premiere, and although the work was not very well received in Paris, it was in some ways a natural choice for Quebec.[131] Readers of *L'Opinion publique* had learned of it in 1873.[132] The subject would appeal to francophone nationalists and the Catholic Church could hardly label it immoral. Gounod's music was mostly for chorus rather than soloists, making it possible to rely on Lavallée's singers. It might only have been considered an unusual choice for one important reason: it was stage play, and the performers were not actors. A cantata or oratorio would have seemed a more logical choice for a church choir. In addition to the justifications already mentioned, then, from the start it must also have been intended as a vehicle for Rosita del Vecchio.

On 15 December 1876, Rosita del Vecchio had turned thirty. It was late to be making her stage debut, and no doubt she and Prume were thinking that it was now or never. Her reputation in Canada had grown slowly, due in part to her travels. She had made her professional debut at St Patrick's Hall in November 1868, but performed infrequently. In November 1875, Joseph Marmette hailed her Quebec City debut a triumph, writing that "the soft, pure and pleasing voice of Madame Prume captivates, moves and ravishes by the extreme charm of her diction and phrasing."[133] She had garnered similar praise in Montreal, and expanded her repertoire to include such demanding arias as that of the Queen of Night, from Mozart's *The Magic Flute*. Her reputation and repertoire were growing in the winter of 1876–77. At the concert at the Mechanics' Hall on 5 December 1876, she gave the first public performance of Lavallée's "Valse de Concert," which may have become the aria "Smiling Hope" in his operetta *The Widow* (discussed in chapter 6), and performed it again on 16 January 1877. As an actress, her abilities were as yet untried. For the lead role, Barbier's five-act drama has a good deal more acting than singing.

To raise funds for a production, Lavallée and the Prumes held their final concert of the season, at the Mechanics' Hall on 2 March 1877, as a benefit. It should have been an attractive event. They presented the Canadian premiere of Schumann's Quintet, op. 44, as well as Boccherini's Minuet and opera selections from Gounod, Bellini, and Félicien David. Prume performed his fantasy on themes from *Faust* and Max Bruch's Violin Concerto No. 1 in G minor, op. 26, and Lavallée played the Weber *Konzertstück* and several shorter pieces.[134] The event may not have raised a large amount, judging from a review published in *Le Nouveau Monde* of 3 March. It called the event a "brilliant success," but also mentioned it had been performed for the community's "elite," and noted the "unfavourable weather," which likely implied that the public stayed home and out of the snow.[135]

Even with a work that would interest a large segment of the public, Lavallée and Prume faced several obstacles. In early April, the *Canadian Illustrated News* reported that "the outlay for costumes, scenery, and other accessories [amounted] to more than $2,000."[136] The benefit concert on

2 March appears not to have produced more than half that amount and Lavallée may have turned to Léon Derome for support. Even then, to succeed financially, *Jeanne d'Arc* needed to attract an audience from both of Montreal's linguistic communities. Lavallée and Prume could expect the support of the French-speaking population no matter where the work was performed. Given the subject, anglophones might have viewed the production with some suspicion, and perhaps at least partly for this reason Lavallée and Prume chose to stage it at the Academy of Music, in the largely anglophone business district of the city, a distance some still considered too far from most residential neighbourhoods.

Casting the production presented a serious challenge. Travelling opera troupes had been visiting Canada since the 1840s, but local productions were extremely rare, due as much to the absence of a conservatory as to the objections of the Church.[137] Lavallée was starting with a well-rehearsed chorus of eighty voices. He knew who were the capable singers, but none were trained actors. Much of the direction fell to stage manager Achille Génot. The French-born Génot had travelled to New York in 1868. He visited Montreal in 1874 with the Achille Fay-Génot Société dramatique française and chose to settle there despite the hostility of Bishop Bourget.[138] Lavallée and Prume had the challenge of putting together the orchestra. Finding capable string players was also difficult. Nevertheless, on 7 April, the *Canadian Illustrated News* reported that 239 persons were involved in the production in some way and that Lavallée and Prume had organized an orchestra of "80 instruments," and a cast comprising "34 active parts, 10 silent parts and 40 figurants."[139] Three of Lavallée's sisters, Cordélia, Catherine, and Ida (ages thirty, twenty-three, and fifteen) had minor roles. Clorinde Gauthier, one of Lavallée's students, played Saint-Catherine. The role of King Charles VII was played by Charles Labelle, a twenty-seven-year-old lawyer who had studied singing with Mdm Petipas and who was the husband of Marie-Louise Derome, one of Léon Derome's daughters.[140]

After three months of preparation, *Jeanne d'Arc* opened on Monday, 14 May, for a six-night run. Evidence suggests that the audiences were both large and receptive. Coverage of the performances in the English-language press indicates that the production drew an audience from both linguistic communities.[141] Most of the reviews were very favourable.[142] The *Canadian Illustrated News* published some of the more judicious observations:

> Barring a few reservations, which we will not be so ungracious as to enumerate, it may be said generally that the representation was equal to that of many theatrical companies which we have had here, and superior to several others. The consequence was a brilliant artistic as well as financial success, upon which we congratulate the enterprising managers, Messrs Prume and Lavallée.
>
> With such a conductor as M. Lavallée at the head of a large and well-balanced orchestra, and such an artist as M. Prume as chef d'attaque, it was to be presumed that something like a genuine interpretation would be secured. And it was secured.[143]

Del Vecchio received much of the credit for the production's success. The critic of the *Canadian Illustrated News* advised that Lavallée and Prume, "with their efficient stage manager, M. Genot, should form a regular company, ... [as] the soprano is *toute trouvé* in Madame Prume."[144]

A little over a week after *Jeanne d'Arc* closed, Lavallée and Prume assisted the young Scottish organist and conductor Peter R. MacLagan in a three-day music festival modelled on the triennial festivals of Boston's Handel and Haydn Society, and Cincinnati's May festivals. MacLagan had arrived in Montreal about three years earlier to take up the position of organist at Christ Church Cathedral. Soon after arriving he had married a seventeen-year-old local girl, Louisa Führer, and he seems to have been the inspiration for Grandison, the lusty organist in his mother-in-law Charlotte Führer's novel, *The Mysteries of Montreal*.[145] Like Grandison, MacLagan was undoubtedly ambitious. He established the Philharmonic Society in the mid-1870s, and for the 1877 festival, he expanded its ranks with musicians from the United States.[146] He held the event at the Victoria Skating Rink, the city's main arena, where he had a pipe organ erected. The timing of the event may not have been propitious, as it coincided exactly with an engagement of P.T. Barnum's circus, which had set up its big top at the Montreal Lacrosse Club grounds, making it a kind of showdown between high and popular culture. Even though newspapers said little about attendance at either event, based on previous experience, one might assume that Barnum's elephants and famous hippopotamus attracted more devotees than did Frederick Handel.[147]

As president of the AMQ, Lavallée convened the organization's 1877 sessions on 6 June at the Mechanics' Institute. *Le National* described the examinations as among the best yet, noting that the results were achieved with only a very modest subsidy from the government. Among those awarded prizes were five of Lavallée's piano students: Mlle Dorais (1st, with distinction), Alexis Contant (1st), Caroline Derome (2nd, with distinction), Mlle Désautels (2nd, with distinction), and Ernest Favreau (honourable mention). In his report, the anonymous writer from *Le National* went on to make a pitch for a music school that sounded very much like it came from Lavallée himself: "Yesterday's results have clearly shown us that there could be a music school just as there is one for the fine arts and that this school should be funded in a manner that best encourages the continuation of work and the spread of this the most noble and beautiful art, the one that best raises the soul toward its creator."[148] In describing the AMQ's general assembly, which followed the examinations and explored ways in which the Academy should move forward, *Le National* again went beyond reporting: "Several important issues were discussed that should be used to improve this institution, of which the country must today be proud. Hopefully these valiant artists, who are usually paid only in glory, will at least have the satisfaction of laying the first stone of an edifice that sooner rather than later will be the glory of our country."[149] The congress closed following elections for the coming year's executive, which resulted in Prume being elected president, with Ernest Gagnon as vice president. Lavallée became a Montreal board member, along with Peter MacLagan, Jean-Baptiste Labelle, and Paul Letondal.

After this, Lavallée may have taken some time off before he and Prume began preparing for the Fête Nationale Concert on 25 June. (See figure 4.13) They chose to return to Victoria Skating Rink for this event celebrating Saint-Jean Baptiste. As usual, the concert attracted numerous provincial politicians and Mayor Beaudry.[150] The venue provided considerably more space for the public than did the City Concert Hall. The

Figure 4.13 An advertisement for the 25 June 1877 Fête Nationale Concert at Montreal's Victoria Skating Rink that featured Charles Gounod's music from *Jeanne d'Arc* sung by Rosita del Vecchio and chorus.

program included a performance by Prume of a Fantasie by Vieuxtemps, but it was mainly a vocal event with Lavallée's chorus and soloists del Vecchio, Cécile Hone, Clorinde Gauthier, and Charles Labelle. The main feature was Gounod's music from *Jeanne d'Arc*. Perhaps purely by coincidence, in the days leading up to the *Fête nationale*, just a few blocks away, at the Academy of Music, Max Strakosch's company enjoyed the greatest success of its engagement with the actor George Rignold in Shakespeare's *Henry V*.

July brought further commemorations. On Dominion Day, Canadians marked the tenth anniversary of Confederation with more reflection than fanfare. Three days later, hardy annexationists celebrated the Fourth of July, as did the Bande de la Cité, which travelled to Ogdensburg, New York, for the occasion. Protestant celebrations of the Battle of the Boyne heightened the usual religious tensions in Montreal in the 1870s. In the summer of 1877, the annual commemoration known as The Twelfth brought a riot and threat of even greater violence.[151] At the end of the month came news of the death of Lavallée's old friend Mérédic Lanctôt, at the age of thirty-eight. His funeral took place at Saint-Jacques Church on 2 August, and later that month, L.-O. David published a lengthy article remembering Lanctôt's eventful life.

In September, Lavallée resumed teaching at his home and planning autumn events. Prume and del Vecchio had travelled to Belgium on hearing that his mother was gravely ill. Their absence had left Lavallée without his performing partner, and threw into question his plan to re-stage *Jeanne d'Arc* that fall.[152] By mid-autumn he had a solution in Theresa Newcomb, then a member of the stock company at the Academy of Music. On 18 October, a notice appeared in *Le National* in which he called on all the performers to meet at the Theatre Royal at 8 p.m. on Saturday, 20 October. A month later, on 19 November, the production once again opened for a six-night run. While French-Canadian critics may have regretted the absence of del Vecchio, they received Newcomb warmly. *La Minerve* wrote that the public was curious to see how Newcomb would perform in a role that she accepted at the last minute and that was in her second language. After the opening night, the newspaper concluded that she could not make one forget Madame Prume entirely but "filled one with admiration": "Her diction is perfect, her intonation rich and varied, her poise and taste artistic; she is, in a word, an enchanting actress."[153] *Le National* called the first performance an artistic and popular success, and predicted Newcomb would become a star of the French-language stage.[154] The *Montreal Star* noted simply that "too much praise cannot be given her."[155] The public appears to have agreed, as Lavallée added six performances. He announced the extension to the public after the second act of the Saturday, 24 November, performance, when the cast presented him with a bouquet. In his brief speech, he informed the audience that the additional performances would include benefits for the cast and crew, and close on 1 December with a fundraiser for the poor.[156]

In December, Lavallée welcomed back to Montreal Guillaume Couture, who appears to have returned for financial reasons.[157] At twenty-six, Couture now seemed resolved to make his career in Canada, and he resumed teaching, performing, and writing for various newspapers, mostly without incident. He continued to be supportive of Lavallée, who celebrated his thirty-fifth birthday in the final days of 1877. During the early weeks of 1878 Lavallée's time was occupied with plans for coming events, including an opera production in the spring and a band competition in June.

The death of the much-revered Pope Pius IX on 7 February 1878 signalled a period of mourning in the Catholic world. French Canadians were especially fond of the conservative pontiff. We have no clear evidence of Lavallée's feelings, but he promptly composed the *Marche funèbre*, perhaps on commission from Ernest Lavigne, who published it and had it in the shops before the end of the month at forty cents a copy.[158] From its opening measures, with the left hand imitating a roll on a snare drum, the piece is unquestionably the work of a seasoned band musician, and is perhaps best heard in the open air. *La Minerve* published a favourable review, possibly written by Couture. The writer describes the work as evoking a "true and religious sentiment that obviously inspired it" and makes specific reference to, "among other passages, the modulation to A flat and the transition to B natural [which] produces a magical effect on a good instrument," and which takes place from measures eleven to fourteen.[159] (See figure 4.14) The review noted that the piece was suited to both piano and organ and could be played at funerals. As noted earlier, it was played on the organ at Notre-Dame Church and in an arrangement for band when Lavallée's remains were repatriated in 1933.

At about the same time, news came of del Vecchio's European debut. Montreal newspapers reported on her success, quoting from a review in *L'Union*, of Verviers, Belgium: "It was Wednesday in fact that Madame Jehin appeared for the first time on the European continent, and we feel, having heard her under these conditions, able to tell our fellow citizens the intimate and delicate satisfaction of the astronomer when his eye falls upon a newly discovered diamond in the Celestial River."[160] The news built on existing French-Canadian pride in del Vecchio and the hope that she might rise to the level of Emma Albani. It would be another year before they would see her again. While in Europe, she took lessons with Charles-Marie Wicart, a tenor at the Opéra de Bruxelles, and with Théophile Vercken at the Conservatoire de Liège. During this time, Prume continued to perform in Belgium and France before beginning a tour of Germany, Switzerland, Italy, and the south of France.[161] Del Vecchio's continuing absence forced Lavallée again to find an alternative star for his planned spring opera season.

Figure 4.14  An excerpt from Lavallée's *Marche funèbre* (mm 11–14). A review in *La Minerve* noted the "magical effect" at this passage, where Lavallée modulates from C minor to E-flat major.

As it turned out, casting would be less of a problem than events beyond his control. In the early months of 1878, a new political controversy took place that would play out over the next three years and become known as the 'Letellier affair.' Briefly, on 1 March 1878, Quebec's premier Charles-Eugène Boucher de Boucherville was forced to resign by Liberal-appointed Lieutenant-governor Luc Letellier de Saint-Just, who then asked the Liberal opposition leader, Henri-Gustave Joly de Lotbinière, to form a government. Letellier's actions were widely considered to be unconstitutional, and were even opposed by the Mackenzie government. While federal politicians considered what to do with Letellier, a provincial election was soon called in Quebec and campaigning began.[162]

❖❖❖

By March, plans were well underway for a new stage production. Some of the choices were not difficult to make. Of the three basic categories of French musical theatre, grand opera was too costly to produce and required a whole cast of professionally trained singers. While opéra bouffe was manageable on a budget, feasible in its vocal demands, and popular with audiences, it did not project the serious image usually associated with a national opera. It was also especially open to criticism from the Church. So it really had to be *opéra comique*: serious but not too serious, with a mix of sung and spoken text, it could be produced without elaborate staging or foreign singers. The genre was well known through performances by visiting troupes and through innumerable concert performances of selections and overtures. From this repertoire Lavallée made an obvious choice for the fledgling opera company: François-Adrien Boïeldieu's *La*

*Dame blanche.*[163] As part of his larger scheme of winning support for a conservatory, it was an opera with something for everyone.

Like most of the popular opéra comiques of the Romantic era, *La Dame blanche* dropped out of the standard repertoire in the early years of the twentieth century. In 1879, it was still much admired and often performed. It had notched its 1,000th performance at the Opéra-Comique in Paris in 1862 and was the most successful French opera to that time (later surpassed by *Carmen*). It had been performed in London, throughout continental Europe, and in New York and New Orleans. It was especially popular in Germany, where it was usually sung in German. Boiëldieu's score spawned numerous instrumental fantasies and even some satires. The first act had been staged in Quebec City in the 1850s by the French immigrant Antoine Dessane.[164] In his 1871 memoire, Adolphe Adam, a student of Boiëldieu, devoted a chapter to *La Dame blanche* and his own role in its creation; this was reprinted by *Le Canada musical* in 1875.[165]

The opera is one of many based on the stories of Sir Walter Scott.[166] Here, librettist Eugène Scribe adapted elements from two of Scott's novels: *Guy Mannering* (1815), which tells the story of Harry Bertram, the son of the Laird of Ellangowan, who, having been kidnapped as a child, makes his way home to Scotland and fights to reclaim his inheritance; and *The Monastery* (1820), which is set in southeast Scotland in about 1550 and tells of the fate of the Avenel family and the threat to Kennaquhair monastery. Scribe retained the eighteenth-century setting of *Guy Mannering*, aspects of its general conflict, and some of its main characters. From *The Monastery* he took the mysterious White Lady, the protector of the Avenel family. The more serious elements of Scott's novels, such as the depictions of criminality in the eighteenth century and the more violent aspects of the Scottish Reformation, are omitted from Scribe's adaptation.[167] The libretto is a model of opéra comique aesthetics: dramatic and entertaining, with much mistaken identity, and a clear sense of good and evil.

The main roles are George Brown (tenor), a young officer in the English army who, unknown even to himself, is Julian Avenel; Anna (soprano), a young woman who as an orphan was raised by the now-deceased Count and Countess of Avenel and who recently nursed the wounded

Brown back to health in Germany; Dickson (tenor) and Jenny (soprano), tenant farmers on the Avenel estate; Marguerite (contralto), the Avenels's elderly servant; Gaveston (bass), the scheming former steward of the Avenels's estate; Gabriel (bass), employed on the Dickson and Jenny's farm; and MacIrton (bass), a justice of the peace. The opera opens with a boisterous chorus ("Sonnez!") as the highland peasants arrive for a christening at the home of Dickson and Jenny. Just as they learn that the baptism will be cancelled because the intended godfather is ill, a pleasant stranger arrives on the scene. George Brown, a young soldier on a walking tour, befriends the parents, is invited to stand in as godfather, and happily consents. He then reveals that he has only a few memories of his boyhood, having been kidnapped and taken abroad as a child. During dinner, conversation leads to the intended sale of the castle and to the White Lady, protector of the Avenels. When Dickson is summoned to Avenel castle by the mysterious White Lady, Brown is intrigued and agrees to take his place. Act II opens at the castle, where the faithful elderly servant, Marguerite, sings of her sad fate and that of the Avenels, and Gaveston reveals to Anna his plan to purchase the estate and its title. George arrives and requests that he be allowed to spend the night. Anna appears disguised as the White Lady to give Dickson instructions for the following day and discovers George Brown has taken his place. She then persuades him to do as she instructs the next day. In the morning MacIrton arrives to conduct the auction of the estate, and following the White Lady's instructions, Brown outbids Gaveston. Act III opens in the old castle, which MacIrton has now unlocked. The long-forgotten surroundings and the songs of the peasants are strangely familiar to George Brown. While searching for the Avenels' lost family treasure, Anna overhears MacIrton privately tell Gaveston that he has just learned that George Brown is Julian of Avenel, and the two decide not to tell the others until after Brown defaults. Just as George is about to be taken away by MacIrton for defaulting, Anna, dressed as the White Lady, arrives with the treasure and tells all that Brown is Julian of Avenel. Gaveston angrily exposes Anna as the White Lady, but this only brings further joy to everyone else as Julian recognizes her as his childhood sweetheart.

In Montreal of the 1870s, *La Dame blanche* was a story that offered something for everyone. For French Canadians, it worked on a number of levels. Most importantly, there was nothing in the story that the Church could easily object to. With its rustic setting and focus on the ritual of baptism, it recalled the quasi-feudal society of New France and the only recently abolished seigneuries. Politically, much might have been read into the story and the popular defeat of the scheming Gaveston. Montreal anglophones already had much to admire in *La Dame blanche*. In a country that seemed dominated by Scottish industrialists and politicians, it must have been only natural to produce an opera based on Walter Scott's novels and Lavallée marketed it that way.[168] Whereas the advertisements in the French-language press emphasized Boïeldieu's name, those in English drew attention not only to Scott but also to his most widely read work of the time, *The Lady of the Lake*. (See figure 4.15) On 17 April, *The Gazette* published an article about the forthcoming production, discussing the origins of the libretto and providing a good synopsis of the plot, emphasizing the popularity of *The Lady of the Lake*, while noting "nessessarily a flavoring of the 'Guy Mannering' stamp."[169] The writer describes the music as being "suitable to the words and scene," mentions the costumes ("the garb of old Scotland"), and the "irrisistable charm of the legend," all likely leading to a successful production.[170]

Boïeldieu made several references to Scotland in his music. The first comes just twelve measures into the overture in the form of a quotation from the tune, "The Bush Aboon Traquair," a melody that does not appear later in the opera.[171] A second appears at the Allegro, in the form of a march tune.[172] He makes very sparing use of the "scotch snap," most notably in the final section of "Chantez, joyeux ménestrel," sung by George and the chorus near the end of Act III.[173] Among the more popular numbers in the opera are Jenny's ballad of the White Lady and George's number "Quelle plaisir d'être soldat," both from Act I, and George and Anna's duet "Ce domaine," from Act II.[174]

Once again, Lavallée cast soloists from his choir in the main roles.[175] George Brown was played by Tancrède Trudel, a thirty-year-old physician. Charles Labelle, who had appeared in *Jeanne d'Arc*, took on the role of Dickson. The three remaining leads – Gaveston, MacIrton, and Gabriel – were played by three relatively inexperienced members of Lavallée's choir, Frédéric Lefebvre, Félix Chartrand, and Auguste Charest.[176]

# THEATRE ROYAL.

Director.........................C. LAVALLEE.
Manager...................... DESIRE.

### For one week, commencing on

# MONDAY, the 22nd instant.

### For the first time in Canada,

# LA DAME BLANCHE,
## OR
## The Lady of the Lake.
### (Scott.)

Opera in Three Acts. Music by Boieldieu. Represented at Paris, London, Vienna, &c., with
the greatest success.

Special engagement of MLLE. MARIETTA
HASSANI, of the Grand Opera of Vienna, to
perform the principal character, assisted by
Mme. Filiatrault, Mlle. Lavallee, Messrs. Trudel, Lefebvre, Labelle, Chartrand, Charest,&c.

Chorus of Scotch Highlanders, composed of
50 chosen voices. Orchestra of 30 of our best
musicians.

Will commence with **Le Cheveu Blanc,
or The White Hair.** Comedy in One Act,
by Octave Feuillet, member of the French
Academy. Special engagement of MADAME
GRANGER and of MR DESIRE.

Admission—Orchestra, Parquet and 1st Gal-
ley, with coupon $1. Seats not reserved in
Parquet and 1st Gallery, 75 cents; Gallery, 50
cents; Boxes, $6 and $8. Tickets for reserved
seats for sale at the Music Store of H. Prince,
Notre Dame street.

Doors open at 7.30. Performance commences at 8 o'clock.                          89

Figure 4.15 Advertisement for *La Dame blanche* in the
English-language press in Montreal in 1878, emphasizing Sir Walter Scott
and his best-known work at the time, *The Lady of the Lake*, even though it
was based on different works by the Scottish writer.

Lavallée's sister, Cordélia, now thirty, played the part of the elderly Marguerite, which gives us an indication of her voice type as well as her acting ability. Finally, the role of Jenny was taken by Octavie Desmarais-Filiatreault, a young woman originally from Verchères, whose family had long been close to the Lavallées. Her participation, as well as that of Lavallée's family members, gives some indication of how close the musical community was. Her connection to Lavallée is important to note in part because of her husband. The previous November, she had married Aristide Filiatreault, a liberal writer and publisher who had become a good friend of Lavallée. The twenty-four-year-old Filiatreault had returned to Montreal in 1875, after residing in the US, and was working at a typesetter. Years later, he described to L.-O. David his first meeting with Lavallée at Mass at Saint-Jacques, when he was still choir director there, after which Lavallée told him he sang like a savage, a comment that seems not to have seriously offended Filiatreault.[177] They became close friends a decade later. There is no surviving membership list of the fifty-voice chorus, now dubbed the "Montagnards Ecossais" (Scottish Highlanders), but Filiatreault appears to have been among them.

Lavallée also recognized the need to have an international performer in the cast. He kept the identity of the star attraction a secret until March, when he announced that he had signed Marietta Hassani for the role of Anna.[178] Local newspapers reported Hassani to be a regular member of the Vienna Grand Opera – presumably the Vienna Court Opera (Wiener Hofoper) – but published no biography to support the claim, no doubt because Lavallée chose not to provide one. She had in fact arrived in Montreal by way of South America, having been with a French company in Brazil in 1876 and 1877 performing at Rio de Janeiro's Alcazar Lyrique. Her roles there were more eclectic than Lavallée might have wanted the public to know. They included Leonora in Verdi's *Il Trovatore*, Euridice in Offenbach's *Orphée aux Enfers*, and Jeanne, in Paul Lacôme's new opéra comique, *Jeanne, Jeannette, et Jeanneton*.[179] The reasons for promoting Hassani in Montreal as Lavallée did are obvious: while she may have been adept at serious roles, she was performing mostly in opéra bouffe with this company, which was inconsistent with the serious tone he wished to set for the company.

Nevertheless, as an opener, Lavallée added to the program Octave Feuillet's one-act comedy from 1860, *Le Cheveu blanc!* (*The White Hair!*).

It was a clever thematic tie-in with *La Dame blanche* that must have made for a long evening. For this piece, Lavallée hired Anna Granger Dow, a French-trained actress and soprano whose company had played an engagement at the Academy of Music a few months earlier.[180] She starred alongside actor and stage manager Monsieur Désiré in this short piece.

A bilingual libretto of *La Dame blanche* that Lavallée had produced for sale at performances provides many of the surviving details about the 1878 production.[181] It indicates that Lavallée devoted greater attention and more money to the visual aspects of the production than he had with *Jeanne d'Arc*. To design and build the sets, he hired the painter R.J. Garand, who had worked on the *Jeanne d'Arc* production. The costumes were designed by tailor Joseph Chrétien and made by the Saint Lawrence Street tailor shop of Boisseau & Frère. Some of these costs were covered through advertisements placed in the published libretto.[182] The Lavigne libretto provided no credit for the rhyming English-language translation. It was an important element for attracting an anglophone audience, and faithfully followed the original text, which was itself unaltered. The only change from the original was a judicious omission of the setting: Scotland in 1759 (the year of the Conquest of New France) – a year that Lavallée would not want to draw attention to.

Full rehearsals began in early April. By this time, Lavallée had assembled a thirty-piece orchestra, whose members included his father and his brother Charles. On 10 April, Marietta Hassani arrived in Montreal and took a room at the Richelieu Hotel, on Saint-Vincent Street, a few blocks from the Theatre Royal.[183] This left only a little over a week to complete preparations. With Sunday, 21 April, being Easter, the final full rehearsal was held on Saturday. On Friday, *The Gazette* announced that the rehearsal would be open to the public, and the following Monday noted that it had been well attended. The same Monday notice reminded its English-speaking readers that as an opéra comique, *La Dame blanche* was "the antipodes of opera bouffe."[184]

The production then opened on Monday, 22 April, for a six-night run. Tuesday's morning newspapers noted that the opening performance had ended too late for them to publish a review that day. On 24 April, *Le National* published a full review, drawing attention to most of the leading performers, placing some emphasis on the significance of the production: "So we finally have the right to say that we can appreciate the art of music in Canada, whereas until very recently so many people did not. But it was enough last night to see the large audience enthusiastically applauding our artists to convince us that French Canadians love music. If it has not been able to prove this fact before now it is because of a lack of opportunity. In the future, our ability to distinguish between entertainers and real musicians will be the proof of our good taste and progress in the arts."[185] They followed up each day with updates from the previous night and reminders to the public to show their support for the company. *The Gazette*'s review was unsigned but evidently written by a singer – possibly the soprano known simply as Madame Petipas – and its even-handedness lends it much credibility as an objective assessment of the performance. The writer begins with some harsh comments on the ensembles: "the want of finish in some of the duetts [*sic*] and arranged parts for three or more voices. This was especially noticeable in the auction scene in the second act, wherein the voices of Mlle Hassani and Messrs Trudel and Lefebvre, although equal, 'crowded' out the voices of Mlle Filiatreault, Delle C. Lavallée and M. Labelle, and were so loud that the chorus did not seem to be doing their duty. In fact it seemed a race with the first-named trio as to force of lung and throat." The love duet between George Brown and Anna ("Ce Domain") was described as "decidedly well rendered, except that M. Trudel's bad habit of singing falsetto marred the effect." The writer offered several more observations on Trudel's vocal production, and concluded by describing his acting as "capital throughout." Hassani "a voice of great power and although she exhibits a lack of warmth, or rather of unison of voice with sentiment, her admirable execution carries her with the audience," which was said to have responded enthusiastically. The writer continued: "she acts fairly, dresses admirably and is pleasing in form and feature." Lefebvre was said to have "sung his parts admirably," but was limited as an actor and would do better in oratorio. Filiatreault was said to have "made good use of a very sweet and well-trained voice, while her acting was natural and easy." Labelle's role was said to have required a buffo with more "life and vim." The chorus was described as "strong," "very well together, and in much better form than the orchestra, which was very often harsh with the soloists. To look back at the whole performance, it must be said that to have produced such an effect from among our amateurs with the aid of one professional prima donna is creditable to all concerned, and we trust that the efforts of Mr Lavallée will be encouraged." The writer concluded by reminding readers of the Scottish setting and that the opera would be "very interesting to many who have read Sir Walter Scott's manner of dealing with the legend of the white lady of Avenel."[186]

Much of the critical reception in *Le National* and elsewhere focused on Hassani. Couture had resumed work as music critic at *La Minerve* and offered serious discussion of the soprano's abilities and contribution to the production. He described her performance as "very intelligent and very competent," but added that "her movements and gestures are too solemn for opéra-comique." He attributed these "shortcomings" to what he believed to be her singing "nothing but grand opera."[187] Clearly, Lavallée had not even let his friend in on Hassani's actual vocation. Couture also discussed the other performers. Without mentioning them by name, he dismissed the contribution of Trudel and Labelle: "What is missing in the performance that would make *La Dame blanche* really good? A first-class tenor. A rare bird; not always found even on first-rate stages."[188] More generally, Couture was pleased by the progress made during his absence. He praised the quality of Lavallée's chorus and orchestra, noting the unusually fine playing of the cello section. With one caveat, he attributed much of the success to Lavallée's direction and conducting: "He conducts his personnel with great assurance. We can only reproach him for one thing: to have slowed almost all the movements, altering in this way the character of many pieces. Knowing the score thoroughly, he has his eyes on the singer or instrumentalist for every entry; all the nuances and accents are marked by his bow. His gestures connote an artist of the most discrete style, the error he rarely commits. He is a genuine conductor. The first we have possessed."[189] Coming from Couture, this was high praise, and the type of recognition Lavallée had long been seeking, after so many years as a theatre conductor and musical director.

Following a short break, on 7 May the cast travelled by steamer to Quebec City for three performances at Music Hall.[190] The company settled into two hotels, the Saint Louis and Russell House, and it seems that Lavallée brought Joséphine with him. The *Daily Telegraph* published a column about the production on 6 May, emphasizing the point that this was the full opera and not excerpts as the public had come to expect from travelling troupes. It was also said to be a "chaste and delicate entertainment," unlike the still-popular minstrel shows.[191] Reviews were enthusiastic and attributed much of the success of the performances to Lavallée.[192] *L'Événement* described the orchestra's performance as "a bit too loud sometimes," but reported that "a foreigner attending yesterday's performance would never have believed that the orchestra comprised mostly amateurs."[193]

Returning to Montreal, the opera reopened for a week at the Academy of Music. Again it attracted regular and generally positive reviews throughout this second run. On the eve of the opening, *The Gazette* again noted *La Dame blanche*'s Scottish connections, referring to the opera as "one of the best of Sir Walter Scott's creations," and saying nothing about the music or its composer.[194] In all, *La Dame blanche* was performed sixteen times. Given the scale of the production, it is difficult to determine how Lavallée funded it or how he earned a living during these months. It seems unlikely that he could have received much financial compensation for several months of work and one might wonder how he and his family were getting by. The local singers and the chorus might have sung for free, but Hassani's salary and the musicians of the orchestra would have to be paid. The final Friday performance was a benefit for Hassani, during which she was to sing three additional pieces. The next day the company gave both a matinee and an evening performance, with the final one being a benefit for Octavie Filiatreault, who added an aria from Bellini's *I Puritani*. Newspapers were typically inconsistent on reporting how full the halls were. For the final two performances of the opening run, Lavallée reduced ticket prices for the parterre seats from fifty to twenty-five cents. In Quebec City, newspapers reported large audiences each evening, but it is less clear how well attended the Montreal performances were. The day after the production reopened in Montreal, *The Gazette* noted that "the theatre was not as well filled last night as the quality of the piece merited."[195] For many members of the public, opera might have seemed a luxury during the economic difficulties that had begun five years earlier. In a summary of the events of 1878 published in *La Revue de Montréal*, Couture described the public as "recalcitrant," either due to apathy or to the state of the economy, and noted that it was difficult to draw an audience to the concert hall, even for "patriotic enterprise such as the performances of *La Dame blanche*."[196]

❖❖❖

Apparently absent from performances of *La Dame Blanche* was the political elite that Lavallée was hoping to attract. Newspapers seem to have published no references to politicians visiting the theatre either in Montreal or Quebec City. If this is true, the reasons may not have been a lack of interest but rather that they were preoccupied with the election campaign that was underway in the lead-up to the production, and that took place on 1 May. The vote itself did not end the distraction, as it was inconclusive, and only after some manoeuvring were the Liberals under Joly able to form a minority government.[197] More political and social distractions that summer would complicate life for many, and frustrate Lavallée's plans to develop music education.

Lavallée's primary goal as an educator in the 1870s was the creation of a 'national' music conservatory for Quebec. Little had changed since Lavallée was student. North America still had no public conservatories, and in Canada, there were not even private music schools that offered professional training.[198] The staging of *La Dame blanche* in 1878 had been part of his plan to win the provincial government's support for the project. A number of journalists were already sympathetic to the idea before the opera opened. In an article discussing the roles that local singers would play, an unnamed writer at *La Minerve* reported, "we have the talent that requires only a school."[199] Following the opera's performance in Quebec City, Lavallée's close friend and supporter Joseph Marmette wrote a review of the opera that amounted to an open letter to the government: "If the material needs of the people are the first concerns that governments must consider, the State must not neglect to see to the intellectual and moral progress of its subjects as well. In contributing seriously to the cultivating of musical art in a country as gifted as ours, however, not only do we create new opportunities for our virtuosos, but also steer the population away from the degrading shows offered too often by the American minstrels."[200] Marmette's comments clearly articulated Lavallée's musical goals and, by presenting the project as morally elevating, anticipated possible objections of the Church.

*L'Événement* reported that Lavallée planned to follow *La Dame blanche* with a production of *Fra Diavolo* in Montreal, but this did not happen.[201] On 15 June, Lavallée submitted a letter to the Legislative Assembly petitioning the government to fund a conservatory of music and dramatic arts. It advised the government to provide a suitable site, hire a director and instructors, and provide free tuition to ten students each year, with others required to pay annual fees of $40.[202] The three other signatories of the letter were Faucher de Saint-Maurice, Octave Chavigny de la Chevrotière, and Napoléon Legendre. Of the four, only Lavallée was a professional musician. Faucher de Saint-Maurice was a politician and writer. Chavingny, a notary by profession, was an amateur flutist and occasional member of Quebec City's Septuor Haydn. Since 1865, Legendre had pursued a career in law and journalism but had remained connected to the world of music. In 1867, he married Marie-Louise Dupré, Lavallée's former student. He occasionally wrote concert reviews, and in 1874, he published a biography of Emma Albani.[203]

In the meantime, Lavallée had been asked to adjudicate at a band competition that was organized by business leaders, in part to bring in tourists to help fill the new and very large Windsor Hotel, on Dominion Square. The "Jubilee" attracted nineteen ensembles and more controversy than anyone could have imagined. The bands came from throughout Quebec and Ontario and competed in either the military or civilian category. Lavallée headed the panel of judges that included Ernest Gagnon, from Quebec City; Dr Crozier, from Belleville, Ontario; the instrument manufacturer Charles G. Conn, from Elkhart, Indiana; and Lavallée's former employer, D.C. Hall, from Boston. Performances were held in the Victoria Skating Rink. Located on Drummond Street, just west of Dominion Square and about three blocks from the Academy of Music, the Rink had opened in 1862 and in 1875 hosted the first organized hockey game.[204] With a sixteen-metre high ceiling and natural and gas lighting, it was a popular indoor venue for summer events both day and night. On this occasion, it was fitted out with a stage at one end, with seating for the 600 bandsmen and up to 9,000 spectators. Preliminary rounds, starting at 2:30 p.m. and 8 p.m., took place on Friday and Saturday, 21 and 22 June. The first two days went smoothly. In addition to selections chosen by each band, all were required to play an unfamiliar piece to test their sight-reading. For this purpose, Lavallée composed a quickstep he called *Harmonie*, a title that proved to be at odds with the mood at the final event, on 24 June.[205]

For the French-Canadian bands participating, the day began early with the Saint-Jean-Baptiste procession, Mass, and performances at the picnic on Saint Helen's Island. Patriotic fervour of the national holiday may have inspired their performances. In the afternoon, the bands paraded from Champ de Mars to the Windsor Hotel, led by organizers and judges riding in carriages. The first concert of the final round started at 3 p.m. and the second at 8 p.m. For the evening concert, Victoria Skating Rink was nearly filled to capacity. Each band was given an opportunity to play a selection of its choice, and the audience listened to such popular compositions as *The Siege of Paris* and the overtures to *Zampa* and *Maritana*. It was nearly midnight when Lavallée stepped forward to announce the winners: Bande de Beauport, second-class independent; Bande de la Cité, first-class independent; and Victoria Rifles, first-class military, as well as the awarding of secondary prizes in each section. The audience and participants greeted each with a mix of cheers and hisses, but the victory of Ernest Lavigne's ensemble in the military category outraged its competitors, who claimed the competition had been rigged.[206] Second- and third-prize trophies as well as cash prizes were returned to the stage, and some members of the Battery "B" Band were reported to have threatened to throw Lavallée into the river.[207]

Bloodshed and drownings were somehow averted, and the event was brought to a close with "God Save the Queen," but neither the losers nor the public were ready to let it drop so quickly. Later that night, the *Post* reported, a crowd gathered in front of Mayor Beaudry's home and sang "'we'll hang Mayor Beaudry to a sour apple tree,' and other kindred airs."[208] In their coverage of the competition, *The Witness* and *The Herald* happily fanned the flames of anger along religious and linguistic lines, while *La Minerve* fought back with a lengthy editorial, noting that the "explosion of English animosity toward French Canadians [was] not new," but that it was exceptional, as the issue in this case was "not complicated by politics."[209] On both sides, the public seemed hungry for a fight. A concert was organized for the Hamilton Orange Band at the Mechanics' Institute on Tuesday, 26 June. After it ended, the Orange Young Britons Fife and Drum Band, from Point-Saint-Charles, escorted their Ontario colleagues along Notre-Dame Street back to their hotel, followed by a menacing crowd and some stone throwing. This event, and the band competition as a whole, would in retrospect seem a prelude, and perhaps to some extent a stimulus, to the sectarian riots that would follow in July. The organizing committee of the Jubilee, headed by Judge

Charles-Joseph Coursol, held a public meeting at St Lawrence Hall on 27 June to explain the procedures and rules, and this seems to have satisfied at least some of the critics.[210]

Lavallée appears not to have attended the meeting, perhaps for his own safety. Quite likely he had already departed for Quebec City, to be greeted there by more bad news. His petition to the government worked its way through the system. It had been read in the Legislative Assembly on 19 June, and read in the Council chambers a week later. It was then sent to the Committee on Standing Orders and Private Bills for study, and there it was rejected, along with a number of other petitions, on procedural grounds.[211] Timing was certainly a factor, with a slate of proposals to address in a session that would last only until 20 July. In the background was not only the ongoing Letellier de Saint-Just affair but also a dispute over labour conditions that resulted in Quebec City being rocked by the dock workers riot. With people going hungry and troops guarding the streets, the government was preoccupied. Still, the rejection of the proposal cast a shadow over that year's AMQ meeting, held at the beginning of July. In its report on AMQ events, *L'Événement* rebuked the government for its decision: "Analyzing the public feeling regarding serious musical institutions, one soon discovers a profound ignorance of the importance of music, of the necessity of institutions organized appropriately in its interest, and of its potential as the co-efficient of a superior civilization. This ignorance is found to some extent everywhere, among the governed and the governors, but is most serious among the governors."[212] The unnamed writer (possibly Napoléon Legendre) argued that a conservatory would eventually be established and that the AMQ had made the "first serious step" in its creation.

As bad as things may have seemed, there were bright moments that summer. On 26 June, Lavallée attended his sister Cordélia's wedding at Notre-Dame, where she married the US-born violinist John-Alfred Duquet. He performed at several events, including a memorial service in Quebec City for the Queen of Spain. The big news, however, came from the Quebec government. Soon after it rejected his conservatory proposal, it offered Lavallée a commission that would at least temporarily counter his disappointment. Together with Napoléon Legendre as librettist, he was asked to compose a cantata of welcome for the incoming governor general. The work was to be the centrepiece of celebrations marking the first visit to the provincial capital of the newly appointed governor general. Lavallée must have been stunned by the offer of the commission. Until this time, he had been known primarily as a pianist and conductor. His reputation as a composer rested largely on the piano music he had composed for his own performances, and during the 1870s, he composed comparatively few works for piano, having focused instead on performing works of European Romantic composers. Given the prestigious nature of the commission he set to work immediately, at first anticipating that the composition would be performed that autumn. With this performance in mind, as well as plans to continue his efforts to establish a conservatory, in early September he took a room in Quebec City, leaving Joséphine behind once again. He may have intended the move to be temporary, but it marked the end of his time in Montreal and the beginning of another stage in his career.

# Quebec City
## 1878–1880

On 13 September 1878, the *Journal de Québec* reported: "We recently learned with great pleasure that Mr Lavallée has taken up residence in Quebec City. We wish him all the greatest success merited by the fine talent and long studies that have enabled him to achieve such powerful performances, and we expect the musicians and students of this city, who wish to further pursue their study of the piano, will wish to do so under Canada's most brilliant pianist."[1] Lavallée must have been grateful for the support. After having established himself in Montreal over a three-year period, he had given up a lot: not only the teaching practice that was his livelihood but also the opera company to which he had devoted so much time. It was consistent with his restless character that once seemingly settled, he would find a reason to move on. But for Joséphine, who stayed behind in Montreal with Calixa Jr, the future must have looked uncertain.

Quebec City was for French Canadians the 'national capital,' and in 1867 it became the home of the provincial legislature. But with the federal capital established at Ottawa, Quebec City saw the departure of its garrison and many civil servants.[2] The city's population had grown by 42 per cent through the 1860s, but slowed dramatically over the next decade, first with the shift of political power and then as a result of the 1873 stock market crash.[3] The riots in the summer of 1878 give some indication of the mood. But Lavallée had an important commission, he was on a quest to win government funding for a provincial conservatory, and he had the support of the city's intellectual community, which greeted his arrival with enthusiasm. While things did not go as he hoped, it was to be among the most important and productive periods of his life.

Ernest Gagnon no doubt played a role in Lavallée's decision to move to Quebec City. The forty-one-year-old organist had made important contributions to musical life in Canada. Influenced by Johann Gottfried von Herder's publications of German folksong in the 1770s, Gagnon had composed pieces based on the music of First Nations peoples, and published a collection of French-Canadian folksong.[4] In 1875, two years after meeting Lavallée in Paris, he had accepted a job as a public servant with the provincial government. He was Lavallée's entrée into the world of politicians. He also set Lavallée up in the boarding house he owned at 22 Couillard Street. (See figure 5.1) Still standing and converted into condominiums, the building bears a plaque marking its significance to Lavallée and Canadian music. A year before Lavallée moved in, the building had served as the French consulate and as the home of Consul Albert Lefaivre. When Lavallée moved in, the only other occupants listed in the city directories were Antoine Verrault, an insurance agent, and his wife, Emma, who ran the house.[5] Quiet and centrally located, it was ideal for

Figure 5.1
Rooming house at 22 Couillard Street, where Lavallée resided and taught piano on moving to Quebec City in the fall of 1878.

teaching, and Lavallée set about finding students, advertising through Arthur Lavigne's music store on Saint-Jean Street. He was soon teaching some gifted students, among them the bandleader Joseph Vézina, who was already thirty years old and a professional musician, and Antonia and Nancy Dessane, daughters of the recently deceased Quebec City musician Antoine Dessane.[6] He supplemented his income by composing and performing.

Lavallée made an auspicious debut on 12 September 1878, at Music Hall, as director of the Septuor Haydn, a chamber group that had been founded by Arthur Lavigne and other local musicians in 1871.[7] The Société Saint-Jean Baptiste organized the concert for Lord Dufferin, departing from Canada at the close of a six-year term as governor general.[8] Dufferin had been widely admired and most of the city's diplomatic, political, religious, military, and business elite were present to pay tribute to him. *The Daily Telegraph* reported Dufferin to have arrived with his guard of honour at 8 p.m. sharp, accompanied by the archbishop, the lieutenant-governor, military officers, and clergymen. After the singing of "God Save the Queen," Lavallée led the Septuor in the overture to *Zampa* by Ferdinand Hérold. He then took the first violin chair in a quartet from Weber's opera *Oberon* and in a selection arranged for sextet from Gounod's *Ballet de Faust*. He performed three works for piano: G. Délisle's *Rêve charmant*, Emile Prudent's *La Danse des fées*, op. 41, and Mendelssohn's *Piano Concerto no. 1*, in G minor, op. 25.[9] His efforts were acknowledged in reviews, with one critic describing his performance of the Mendelssohn concerto as the "the highlight of the evening."[10] Among the other performers on the program were his students Antonia and Nancy Dessane. After singing a duet in the first half, Antonia returned after the intermission to sing a selection from Ambroise Thomas's opéra comique *Mignon*, and Nancy gave a performance of Lavallée's *Grande Marche de Concert*, which was said to have been "most deservedly encored."[11]

Later that month, Lavallée wrote the introduction for the publication of a collection of songs by his friend, thirty-nine-year-old José Antonio de Lavalle Romero-Montezuma, generally known as the Count of Premio-Réal. (See figure 5.2) A multilingual polymath, the count served as the Spanish consul. He had arrived in Quebec in 1874 after holding

Figure 5.2
The Spanish consul in
Canada and president
of the Club des 21, the
Count of Premio-Réal
was a talented amateur
musician and a central
figure in Lavallée's social
circle in Quebec City.

diplomatic postings in Cardiff, Malta, Naples, and Hong Kong.[12] While
in Malta, he married Giulia Sant Fournier. It is unclear how long they remained together, but in Quebec City, the count led the life of a happy
bachelor. Music ranked very high among his many interests. During performances of *La Dame blanche* in Quebec City, Marietta Hassani interpreted one of the songs in the 1878 collection, "Seul," at the beginning
of Act Three, a practice that was not unusual at the time. *The Daily Telegraph* reported that Hassani sang the mélodie with "exquisite grace."[13]
Lavallée had orchestrated the song, perhaps in thanks for the count's
financial assistance with the Quebec City performances. The count later
noted that he could say much about "maestro Calixa Lavallée, the distinguished pianist and composer," but did not want it to appear that he
was simply repaying a debt to him.[14] In his introduction to the count's

collection, Lavallée discusses the state of French art song, noting that the romance, long popular among the middle class, had "definitely had its time" and had given way to the more sophisticated mélodie, due to "its harmonic richness and the skilful transitions with which the masters of the modern school embellish it."[15] The mélodie had actually been emerging since the 1830s, as Schubert's lieder began to influence French song, and Berlioz borrowed the term from Thomas Moore when he published his *Neuf mélodies imitées de L'anglais.*[16] Lavallée may have been referring primarily to the songs of Gounod, or to his experience in Paris. Public performances of newer European art songs were still rare in Canada. Lavallée's published mélodies, with their simple piano accompaniments and vocal ranges of a little over an octave, were easily performed by amateurs.

Lavallée's main concerns that September, however, were more with the cantata form and the commission. Transplanted and once again living as a bachelor, Lavallée was extraordinarily busy through September and early October as he set Legendre's text. The work gained special urgency due to the high-profile appointment. The newly appointed governor general was the Marquis of Lorne (John Douglas Campbell), the husband of Queen Victoria's fourth daughter, Princess Louise. The connection to the throne undoubtedly influenced the choice of British Prime Minister Benjamin Disraeli.[17] Given the ongoing economic difficulties, it was an opportunity for Britain to show a commitment to the young country in difficult economic times – and diminish the likelihood of a resurgence of the annexation movement. Disraeli was also playing to the various constituencies. Following the tenure of the Irish Lord Dufferin, the selection of Campbell was aimed to please both English and Scottish elements of the population. Campbell was London-born and Eton- and Cambridge-educated, but his family hailed from the west of Scotland and his father was the 9th Duke of Argyll. Campbell was also well qualified. He spoke fluent French, had experience as an MP, and had gained first-hand knowledge of Canada at the age of twenty-three, when he travelled extensively through North America.[18]

With the marquis and princess due to arrive in November, Lavallée and Legendre completed their *Cantate en l'honneur de Marquis de Lorne* with time to spare. Lavallée later claimed to have "composed and scored [the cantata] in one month."[19] On 24 October, he performed an extract of the work as the final selection at a concert at Victoria Hall. It was a regular concert of the Septuor Haydn, and that ensemble opened the concert with a Rossini overture, played Lavallée's arrangement of Boccherini's *Minuet,* and accompanied Lavallée in Weber's *Konzertstück*, op. 79. Lavallée also performed Schumann's *Warum?* (no. 3 of the *Phantasiestück*, op. 12), a piano transcription of Mendelssohn's "Wedding March," and his own *Le Papillon*, op. 18. Lavallée closed with the "First Chorus," a solo, and a duet from his cantata with vocalists Tancrède Trudel, Antonia Dessane, and Madame Le Vasseur, and with two church choirs. The next day he received his first critical feedback from the *Journal de Québec*, which noted that the chorus was "performed with a grand effect by the united choirs of Saint-Roch and Saint-Jean, and caused a delightful surprise. Madame Le Vasseur and M. Trudel sang the solos with great expression."[20]

Three weeks later, on 18 November, Lavallée presented the brilliant young violinist Alfred De Sève to a Quebec City audience for the first time. De Sève was a former student of Frantz Prume and of Oscar Martel. After two years of studies in Europe, De Sève returned to Canada in July with the title "Violinist to Her Majesty Queen Isabelle II of Spain" – the deposed monarch, then living in exile in Paris.[21] He began teaching at his home on Sainte-Elizabeth Street, in Montreal, and held a concert at the Academy of Music on 10 October 1878. For De Sève's Quebec City debut at Victoria Hall, Lavallée shared top billing, and also recruited the Septuor Haydn and a number of vocalists. Among critics, De Sève's performance made an especially strong impression on the *Journal de Québec*'s critic Gaston Labat, who described the violinist's interpretation of a *Fantasia* by Hubert Léonard as full of "a verve, a vigour, [and] a superb vitality," and called his playing of works by Vieuxtemps and Ernst "evidence of a delicate touch and exquisite feeling."[22] So impressed was Labat that he hailed De Sève as Canada's third great musician, after Albani and Lavallée, a trio he dubbed "la trinité artistique canadienne."[23] (See figure 5.3) It was both an auspicious debut for De Sève and the beginning of a long musical relationship with Lavallée.

For reasons that remain unknown, a decision had been made to delay the official welcome of the new governor general and the princess to

ALFRED DESÈVE

Figure 5.3
The violinist Alfred De Sève who, after studies in Paris, was one of Lavallée's frequent performing partners in both Montreal and Boston.

Quebec City. Scheduling conflicts were no doubt a factor, but there was also much work to be done in Ottawa. The Conservatives, having been returned to office after the federal election in September, were anxious to remove Letellier from office, but needed to consult with London's representative about the matter. By postponing the governor general's visit to Quebec City until the following summer, officials in the provincial capital gained time to complete public works that the marquis was open. The delay also gave Lavallée more time to prepare the performance, but he must have been disappointed, especially given the level of anticipation.

The marquis and princess landed at Halifax, Nova Scotia, on the SS *Sarmation* on 25 November 1878. After official greetings and some government business, the couple and their entourage left for Ottawa by train, making an official stop in Fredericton, New Brunswick, and drawing large crowds in each town and village en route. On their arrival in

Montreal they were met by an enormous crowd and feted with three days of fireworks, parades, and receptions. This was the first royal visit since Queen Victoria's third son, Prince Arthur, visited in 1869, and was especially embraced by the city's Scottish elite. The visit culminated in the annual St Andrew's Society ball, held at the Windsor Hotel. The governor general and princess finally departed from Bonaventure Station on 2 December, on the final leg of the journey to Ottawa and life in Rideau Hall. It would be another six months before they would make their official visit to Quebec City.

Life returned to normal for Lavallée, occupied again with teaching and performing. In December, the *Journal de Québec* announced the forthcoming publication of a piece titled *La Petite hermine* (The Little Weasle).[24] Arthur Lavigne was the publisher and Lavallée dedicated this publication to Nazaire Turcotte, the owner of a wholesale grocery store on Dalhousie Street in Quebec City, specializing in "wines, liqueurs, ales, etc."[25] One might speculate on the reasons behind the dedication, or the choice of title. As the *Journal de Québec* noted, it was lively and easy enough for amateurs – one of very few works for amateurs that Lavallée published. It is tuneful and technically undemanding, and proved sufficiently popular for *La Minerve* to reissue it a year later under the more attractive title *Vol au Vent* (Fly on the Wind).

The Christmas season brought elaborate musical celebrations in Quebec City's many churches. Lavallée took part in what must have been both the most ornate and the most politically advantageous of the midnight Masses, at the Seminary Chapel, which Premier Joly attended. The chapel was draped in British and Dominion flags for the occasion. Lavallée seems by this point to have resolved his differences with the members of Battery "B," who were there in force, and whose band performed a number of selections. Arthur Lavigne played the violin, and Madame Le Vasseur sang. Lavallée directed a number of singers, among them Napoléon Legendre, Alphonse d'Eschambault, and Tancrède Trudel, and as organist seems to have capped the event by improvising on Christmas carols, which the *Daily Telegraph* reported to be a "very rich treat."[26]

One might expect that Joséphine and Calixa Jr joined Lavallée in Quebec City in December. There were multiple causes for celebration: his wedding anniversary, Christmas, his own thirty-sixth birthday, and the

New Year. There is, nevertheless, no evidence that they had yet moved to Quebec City. Lavallée had been married for eleven years but bachelorhood suited him, judging by the frequency with which he was able to regain it. After so many years on the road, he was used to being in the company of other men. Socially, he was settling into life in the provincial capital, and an important part of his social life was the Club des 21, a society that he co-founded early in 1879. The name referred to the membership, which was restricted in number to twenty-one. Their first gathering took place at the Chien d'Or restaurant on 15 February 1879, after which they met at the Russell House Hotel.[27] Politically, the group appears to have been quite diverse. Members were writers, lawyers, and musicians, such as Joseph Marmette, Oscar Dunn, and Arthur Lavigne.[28] The group's central figure was the Count of Premio-Réal, who served as the group's first president. Victor Bazerque held the post of vice-president, while Lavallée and Le Vasseur served as secretaries.[29]

Figure 5.4
Photograph of the poet, playwright, and politician Louis-Honoré Fréchette, found in the Lavallée family album, and possibly dating from Fréchette's period of exile in the US.

194

Among the highest profile members of the club was the poet and politician Louis-Honoré Fréchette, who in 1871 had returned to Canada from self-imposed exile in Chicago. (See figure 5.4) A steadfast republican, Fréchette had been elected to federal parliament in 1874 as a Liberal MP for Lévis, opposite Quebec City on the south side of the Saint Lawrence, but lost the seat in the 1878 Conservative victory. He then turned his attention to writing, publishing a number of plays and collections of poems in the next few years. His *Fleurs boréales* contains a poem written for Lavallée:

À CALIXA LAVALLÉE[30]

Oui, berce-nous toujours dans des flots d'harmonie,
O pianiste! la foule acclame ; et pour ma part,
Même quand ta main court sur l'ivoire au hasard,
J'éprouve les frissons d'une ivresse infinie!

Yes, we still rock on waves of harmony,
O pianist! the crowd cheered, and for my part,
Even when your hand runs over the ivory randomly
I feel the thrill of infinite rapture!

Mais quand ton poing bondit sur un clavier d'Erard
En voyant tant de force à tant de grâce unie,
Chacun sent que la Muse alluma ton génie
A l'immortel flambeau des grands maîtres de l'Art.

But when your fist bounds over an Erard keyboard
One sees a unity of strength and elegance,
Everyone feels that the Muse lit your genius
In the immortal flame of the great masters of art.

Fanfares du clairon, doux cri des hirondelles,
Grondement du tonnerre ou bruissement d'ailes,
La nature à ton jeu prête ses mille voix.

Bugle fanfares, sweet cry of the swallows,
Rumble of thunder or rustle of wings,
Nature at your game lends her thousand voices.

| | |
|---|---|
| Comme Litz et Thalberg, ces nouveaux Prométhées, | Like Liszt and Thalberg, the new Prometheuses, |
| Tu sais donner une âme aux touches enchantées | You know how to give soul to the enchanted keys |
| Du royal instrument qui chante sous tes doigts! | Of the royal instrument that sings under your fingers! |

Given Fréchette's admiration for Lavallée, one might wonder what he thought of the musician's collaboration, the next year, with the Quebec City judge A.-B. Routhier on "O Canada." Lavallée would have known about the very public antipathy between the two men, but he still seemed able to maintain a relationship with each.[31] But before long Fréchette was gone again. Having married into the wealthy Beaudry family, Fréchette left for Montreal to devote his time to writing, leaving an opening in the Club des 21.

March brought the St Patrick's Day events, one of the Quebec City's most widely celebrated occasions. The city's large Irish community began the day with a parade through the snow-filled streets, the elite gathered for a "National" banquet, and the public filled Music Hall for a concert that became a four-hour marathon of speeches and songs that was not restricted to Irish performers. Lavallée had recently become director of the Quatuor vocale de Québec (QVQ), an ensemble that performed at soirees and concerts in the capital. At this concert he had the group sing a medley of Irish airs he had arranged, comprising "Come Back to Erin," "Believe Me If All These Endearing Young Charms," "The Minstrel Boy," and "The Harp that Once Thro' Tara's Halls" – music he would have learned while working in minstrelsy. L'Événement described the piece as "magnificent." The Daily Telegraph reported that the "composition and the manner in which it was sung roused the attention of all who understood and appreciated good music, and by connoisseurs who pronounced it to be the gem of the evening."[32]

The tenor Trudel was an occasional member of the QVQ and a frequent visitor to Quebec City. In the early months of 1879 he, too, became a resident of 22 Couillard Street. Thirty years old and a doctor by profession, he was spending a good deal of his time singing, with much encouragement from Lavallée, who himself benefited from having the singer available for rehearsals in the run-up to the cantata performance. When Lavallée received an invitation from the governor general and princess to attend a soiree to be held in his honour at Rideau Hall on 25 March, he brought Trudel, as well as the violinist Oscar Martel, with him. He also brought along a leather-bound copy of the cantata score, produced by the Quebec City bookbinder Georges Lafrance – a score that has since been lost.[33]

By late March, Parliament was in session and the federal capital was abuzz with what would be done with Quebec's lieutenant-governor Letellier, now that Macdonald's Conservatives were back in power. But politics seems not to have been the focus of the 25 March soiree at Government House, the governor general's residence better known as Rideau Hall. Lavallée appears to have arrived in Ottawa early and to have spoken to the press, who reported that he planned to present a copy of the cantata score to the princess.[34] He and Martel performed that evening and Trudel sang an excerpt from the cantata, the air "O brises parfumées!"[35] In a letter written the next day, Lavallée described the evening and the vice-regal couple in glowing terms. He characterized the Marquis of Lorne as "simply admirable," writing that the two spent the entire evening together – talking about fishing, among other things. "Despite his high position," Lavallée wrote, "the bohemian comes through, he is affable and puts one immediately at ease."[36] Lavallée described the princess as "more serious than [the marquis], but of a stunning simplicity," concluding: "We did not speak a word of English all night. Overall, I have had a wonderful trip."[37]

After the Rideau Hall event, Lavallée stayed on in Ottawa for several days, having received an invitation from Colonel Joseph-Goderic Blanchet, the Speaker of the House, who planned to hold a party in his honour that Saturday. The two might have seemed unlikely friends. Years earlier, while Lavallée had been a member of the Fourth Rhode Island Regiment, Blanchet had joined a militia regiment to defend the colony from a possible US invasion. Later, when Lavallée was performing music in support of the Fenians, Blanchet was guarding the border against them. In the fall of 1878, it had been Blanchet who defeated Louis-Honoré Fréchette in the constituency of Lévis. Still, an artist in search of government connections had to be pragmatic, and Blanchet held considerable clout in Quebec politics. As the local MP, he may have been present on 6 February when Lavallée had performed at a benefit concert for the poor in the town of Lévis. In any event, Blanchet knew Lavallée well enough to host a soiree in his honour. Lavallée reciprocated by performing at this Ottawa dinner party, as did Oscar Martel and his wife, soprano Hortense Martel.[38]

The month of April brought Easter, which Quebec City celebrated in grand style. Saint-Roch Church seems to have put on the most impressive display in 1879, with the help of the Société Sainte-Cécile (SSC), a sixty-member sacred music ensemble, founded in 1869 by Antoine Dessane and subsequently led by Célestin Lavigueur and Nazaire Le Vasseur.[39] Lavallée played and conducted, and many of the singers connected with him were present, among them, Trudel, Curran, d'Eschambault, and Laurent. In its account of the events at Saint-Roch, *L'Événement* noted the presence of the Count of Premio-Réal and also mentioned "Mad. Lavallée, Mad. Curran, etc.," providing evidence that Joséphine had given up the house on Cathcart Street in Montreal and joined her husband.[40] Later that year they moved temporarily to the town of Lévis, where in September, Calixa Jr started school at the Collège de Lévis.[41]

Later that week, Lavallée gave a concert of his own at Victoria Hall. He opened this 18 April event with a Duo concertant on themes from *Faust*, with himself at the piano and Adolphe Hamel playing organ. The rest of the program was divided nearly equally between solo piano music and vocal works. Lavallée played Beethoven's *Moonlight Sonata*, Duprato's *Saltarelle*, a nocture by John Field, a polonaise by Chopin, the "Presto" from Mendelssohn's Fantasia in F-sharp minor ("Sonate ecossaise"), op. 28, the "Melodie" from Schumann's *Album for the Young*, op. 68, and his own *Le Papillon*. The Quatuor vocale de Québec sang "Le Chant du Travailleur," a rare example of a worker's song performed at a concert of this kind, and a show of solidarity with the dock workers, who were still engaged in a fight for better pay. The audience seems to have been on side, and when called back for an encore, the singers responded with "Dieu Protège la France."[42] Trudel once again performed the solo "O brises parfumées!" and then closed the concert in a duet with Cora Wyse from Victor's Massé's 1876 opera *Paul et Virginie*.[43]

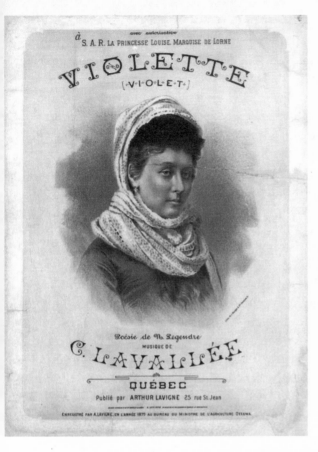

Figure 5.5
The cover of "Violette,"
featuring an engraving
of Princess Louise and
the dedication: "avec
autorisation à S.A.R.
La Princesse Louise,
Marquise de Lorne."
Lavallée composed
the song on words by
the cantata librettist
Napoléon Legendre.

Also on the program was "Violette," a new song that Lavallée had composed on words by the cantata librettist Napoléon Legendre. As with much of Legendre's poetry, "Violette" evokes images of nature. Lavallée's melody flows along gently, and largely in step motion with a range of just over an octave, making it accessible for amateurs. It seems likely that Trudel had sung it at Rideau Hall, as Arthur Lavigne published the song with an engraving of Princess Louise on the cover and the dedication: "avec autorisation à S.A.R. La Princesse Louise, Marquise de Lorne."[44] (See figure 5.5)

An English translation of Legendre's words was provided by another recent arrival from Montreal, twenty-eight-year-old Patrick Curran, an amateur musician who had performed with Lavallée in 1873. On taking up a post as translator at the provincial legislature, he threw himself into

Quebec City's social and musical life and, like Lavallée, became a popular figure in both English- and French-speaking communities. He became a member of the Literary and Historical Society of Quebec and the St Patrick's Church choir. On several occasions he performed as either vocalist or accompanist with Lavallée, who was likely the one who invited Curran to join the Club des 21 when Fréchette left town.

A few days after the concert at Victoria Hall, the *Journal de Québec* announced that Lavallée had accepted the post of organist at St Patrick's Church.[45] (See figure 5.6) The appointment changed his financial situation significantly.[46] Lavallée was a capable church musician, having briefly served as choir director at Montreal's Saint-Jacques Church and having often performed at special church events both in Montreal and in Quebec City. He had established connections with Curran and others in the Irish community. More importantly, he was the city's leading musician, and St Patrick's wanted to raise the standard of its music, and its prestige within the larger community. Located in the Upper Town, the church had been designed by the Quebec City architect Thomas Baillairgé and consecrated by Father McMahon on 7 July 1833. For nearly fifty years, the church had been a focal point for the city's large Irish community, which now numbered some 15,000, or nearly a quarter of the city's population.[47] Lavallée was introduced to the congregation on 27 April and began work a few days later. In a news item on his appointment, the *Daily Telegraph* reported that Lavallée's abilities were "acknowledged to be of the highest order" and "great things are expected of him."[48] His contract reveals that this was no part-time position. The church paid him a monthly salary of $50, and demanded a good deal for its money. Under the terms of his contract, he was to preside at the organ at "grand Mass and vespers on Sundays and Feast days … at Benediction on each Saturday evening … every evening during the month of May … at any other evening service when required … [and] at early grand Masses during the week at the ordinary hours and funerals during the day."[49] Ordinary hours for grand Masses during the week were from "half past five to half past seven o'clock in the morning in the summer and from half past five to eight o'clock in the morning during the winter."[50] The one-year contract also stipulated that he should "maintain in practice and keep up the choir and have regular rehearsals twice a

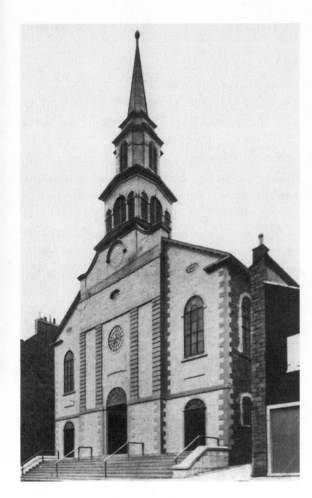

Figure 5.6
St Patrick's Church,
Quebec City, where
Lavallée served as
musical director in
1879 and 1880.

week during the said term except in the months of June, July and August, during which rehearsals shall be held once a week."[51] In addition to his regular salary, he would earn two dollars for funerals and for Masses "outside the ordinary hour," and sixty cents "for all chanters." As the church's musical director, his duties extended to other community events and especially to the St Patrick's Day celebrations – at which he performed that year. How he balanced his duties at St Patrick's with his increasing number of other activities is difficult to determine, especially as the date of the governor general's arrival approached.

❖❖❖

## THE *CANTATE EN L'HONNEUR DE MARQUIS DE LORNE*

At about the same time he started work at St Patrick's, Lavallée began intensive rehearsals for the cantata performance. He assembled a fifty- to sixty-piece orchestra of Quebec City and Montreal musicians, which included his brothers and François Boucher.[52] He recruited from all the local choirs to assemble a chorus of 150 voices. With many very capable singers to choose from, politics likely played a role in selecting soloists. Trudel was the only obvious pick, having been with Lavallée for much of the past year and having been specially prepared for his part. The bass was Pierre Laurent, an amateur singer who had appeared at a number of sacred and secular events, and who was then serving as president of the Société Sainte-Cécile.[53] For soprano and alto parts, he selected anglophone singers. The soprano, twenty-two-year-old Cora Eva Wyse, had been a piano student of Gustave Gagnon and appeared frequently in concerts. The alto, referred to only as Mlle Carbray, appears to have been nineteen-year-old Catherine Carbray, daughter of Felix Carbray, a businessman and president of the St Patrick's Catholic and Literary Institute.

The cantata itself was a sprawling work that might better have been described as a secular oratorio. No program for the event is known to have survived. Advertisements provide only basic information on the event and a single title: *Cantate*. Newspaper reports and surviving parts of Legendre's text provide some sense of the work's two-part structure. It opened with "Saluts enfants de Notre Reine" (Greetings to the Children of Our Queen), a number for chorus and orchestra. The first half included the now familiar "O brises parfumées!," for tenor solo, followed by a duet for tenor and soprano. In the second half, there was a number titled "As tu vu nos montagnes?" (Have You Seen Our Mountains), which involved all four soloists. The "Military Chorus" provided a close. At the climax of the final section, Lavallée was said to have superimposed "God Save the Queen," "Vive la canadienne," and the traditional tune associated with Robert Burns's "Comin' thro' the Rye."[54] If true, it would certainly have provided a pragmatic conclusion: acknowledging Britain's imperial authority and the Scottish culture of the governor general, while asserting French-Canadian sovereignty.

Much of the surviving text focused on French-speaking Canada. Legendre published "O brises parfumées!" in 1886 under the title "Stanzas." A glorification of nature, it makes specific reference to the Quebec landscape only in allusion to the Saint Lawrence River.

O brises parfumées![55]
Des grands bois odorants,
Chantez dans les ramées
Vos accords enivrants!

O perfumed breeze!
From the great fragrant woods,
Sing in the leaves
Your intoxicating harmonies!

Solitudes profondes,
Beaux lacs mystérieux
Dont les sonores ondes
Murmurent sous les cieux;

Deep solitude,
Beautiful, mysterious lakes
Of which the sonorous waves
Murmur beneath the skies;

Montagnes dont les cimes
Se baignent dans l'éther,
Mêlez vos voix sublimes
À l'immense concert!

Mountains, summits
Bathing in ether,
Mix your sublime voices
In an immense concert!

Chante, belle nature;
Et, toi fleuve géant,
Que ton profond murmure
Se mêle à notre chant!

Sing, beautiful nature;
And, you immense river,
That your deep murmur
Mixes with our song!

Au son de votre lyre,
Poètes, réveillez
La brise qui soupire
Dans les bois ensoleillés.

To the sound of your lyre,
Poets, awaken
The breeze that sighs
In sunlit woods.

Chantez avec l'aurore,
Chantez sous le ciel bleu,
Et que le soir encore
Porte vos voix vers Dieu!

Sing with the dawn,
Sing under the blue sky,
And in the evenings again
Let your voices carry towards God!

| | |
|---|---|
| Et, pendant la nuit sombre, | And, during the dark night, |
| Allez, mystérieux, | Go, mysterious, |
| Faire monter dans l'ombre | Let rise in darkness |
| Vos chants mélodieux. | Your melodious songs. |
| | |
| Le chant, c'est la prière, | Song, this is the prayer through which, |
| Le ciel vous entend | The sky hears you. |
| Et, pour bénir la terre, | And, to bless the earth, |
| Dieu vers vous descendra. | God will towards you descend. |

The military chorus was published in the same collection, with the title "Fragment from a cantata sung at the arrival of H.R.H. Princess Louise and the Marquis of Lorne." For the reception of the queen's new representative in Canada, it seems a particularly curious text, reminding listeners of glorious events of French history and victories over the English, very nearly urging French Canadians to rise in rebellion once again.

| | |
|---|---|
| *Premier soldat*[56] | *First soldier* |
| Le tambour bat, le clairon sonne, | The drum beats, the bugle rings, |
| Voici l'appel du régiment; | Here, the call of the regiment; |
| Sur les remparts le canon tonne | On the ramparts the cannon thunders |
| | |
| Allons, compagnons, en avant! | Let's go, companions, forward! |
| | |
| *Deuxième soldat* | *Second soldier* |
| Partons, déployons nos bannières, | Let us leave, let us show our banners, Oriflammes,[57] floats on the wind! |
| Oriflammes, flottez aux vents! | |
| | |
| Et toi, vieux drapeau de nos pères, | And you, old flag of our fathers, |
| Déroule tes plis triomphants. | Unfold your triumphant pleats. |
| | |
| *Choeur* | *Chorus* |
| I | I |
| Sonnez, clairons des batailles | Ring, battle bugles |
| Bronzes, tonnez vers les cieux! | Cannons, thunder towards the skies! |

| | |
|---|---|
| Éveillez de nos murailles | Awaken from our walls |
| Les échos si glorieux! | The glorious echoes of the past! |
| | |
| Et, vous guerriers magnanimes | And, you magnanimous warriors |
| Qui dormez sous les lauriers, | That sleep beneath laurels, |
| Levez-vous, héros sublimes, | Rise, sublime heroes, |
| Découvrez vos fronts altiers! | Show your proud foreheads! |
| | |
| Aux murs de la cathédrale, | To the walls of the cathedral, |
| Décrochez le drapeau blanc; | Unhook the white flag; |
| Dans la marche triomphale | In the triumphant march |
| Venez prendre votre rang! | Come to take your rank! |

| | |
|---|---|
| *Finale* | *Finale* |
| O jours de combats glorieux | O days of glorious combat |
| Où sonnait la trompe guerrière! | Where rang the warlike horn! |
| O vous tous, soldats valeureux | O all of you, brave soldiers |
| Qui dormez sous la même pierre! | That sleep under the same rock! |
| Soleil qui jadis éclairât | Sun that formerly illuminated |
| Tant de gigantesques batailles: | So many great battles: |
| Nuit discrète qui dérobât | Night discreetly reveals |
| Tant de sanglantes funérailles! | So many bloody funerals! |
| Le sang partout est effacé: | The blood everywhere is obliter- |
| | ated: |
| Mettons ensemble notre gloire, | Gather together our glory, |
| Des grands noms de notre passé | From the great names of our past |
| Chantons ensemble la mémoire! | Let us sing together our history! |

Closing with evocations of glorious French battles provided a dramatic close. As Lavallée had been a military musician and seen many battles over a relatively short period of time, one might see how he could find inspiration in the text. No doubt the opening sections of the cantata provided more opportunities to celebrate the arrival in Canada of the marquis and princess and to acknowledge their greatness. Nevertheless, the character of the text may have been the reason why organizers opted not to publish the words at the time of the performance.

The marquis and princess arrived in Quebec City to take up their summer residence at the citadel on 4 June 1879 and set about a series of public events. Their ceremonial duties included opening the Dufferin Terrace and laying the cornerstone of the new Kent Gate.[58] (See figure 5.7) They visited the Ursuline convent, inspected the harbour facilities, watched members of Battery "B" compete in a sporting event on the Plains of Abraham, and generally kept busy. On Saturday, 7 June, Lavallée attended a vice-royal reception at the legislature, where he joined a guest list dominated by the political, military, and business elite.[59] Rehearsals, however, occupied much of his time and continued up to the evening of 10 June. At this final rehearsal, on behalf of members of the orchestra and chorus, Arthur McCallum, a St Patrick's chorister, presented Lavallée with a new silver-handled baton.[60]

The cantata performance took place on 11 June before an audience estimated at between 1,000 and 1,500 people.[61] The venue was Quebec City's new Skating Rink. (See figure 5.8) Built in 1877 and home of the Bulldogs hockey team, it had been fitted with a stage for the performers and a "vice-royal box" for the guests of honour. Arriving at 8:15 p.m., the marquis and princess were received with the singing of "God Save the Queen." The program then began with Joseph Vézina conducting the band of Battery "B" in the overture to Adolphe Adam's comic opera *Le Brasseur de Preston*, which was followed by the first half of the cantata. At the intermission, Franz Prume, who had just returned to Canada, performed Heinrich Ernst's *Fantasy on Otello*. When called back for an encore, he responded with the familiar *La Mélancolie*. The second half of the cantata concluded the program.

Both the event and Lavallée's composition received enthusiastic reviews. *L'Événement* called the cantata "magisterial," and "unquestionably the most remarkable musical composition our country has yet produced."[62] *Le Canada musical* called the performance "the most remarkable musical event Quebec City had witnessed in a very long time," and "the most beautiful reception organized in the Old Capital."[63] The same critic was unequivocal in his admiration of the music, which he said placed Lavallée "among composers of distinction." The cantata "contains passages of great harmonic richness, and original character; among them, the military chorus, and especially the grand quartet with

Figure 5.7
Inauguration of the
Dufferin Terrace at
Quebec City by Marquis
of Lorne and Princess
Louise on 11 June 1879.

Figure 5.8 Quebec City's Skating Rink, site of the premieres of Lavallée's
*Cantate en l'honneur de Marquis de Lorne* on 11 June 1879, and "O Canada"
on 24 June 1880.

choral accompaniment, which concludes with a crescendo of extra-ordinary breadth, perfectly executed for ten to twelve measures."[64] Joseph Marmette, writing in the *Journal de Québec*, echoed many of these comments: "We particularly noted and applauded the entrance of the military chorus and final crescendo of the fourth part, which was of absolute beauty."[65] Marmette credited the performers with much of the success, writing that it "honours both our professional musicians and amateurs. The chorus and orchestra were irreproachable. Ensemble precision, correct and delicate observation of nuances, warmth of exe-cution, all was perfect ... As for the solos, they were rendered in a remarkable manner. M. Trudel beautifully interpreted the grand air "O brises parfumées!" in which there are ravishing orchestral effects, as well as the other solos that he performed."[66] In the first of two reviews, the *Daily Telegraph* reported on the soloists: "Miss Wyse's splendid soprano voice came in [in "Saluts enfant de Notre Reine"] with beautiful effect. Miss Carbray's silvery toned alto in 'A-Tu Vu Nos Montagnes,' was deliciously sweet. Both those young ladies have improved in power and compass wonderfully of late. Mr Trudel's powerful tenor was in most harmonious unison with the bird-like notes of the two fair soloists."[67] No first-hand account was recorded of the governor general's view of the events or of the princess's, although they were said to have applauded enthusiastically and at the end of the performance called Lavallée over to their box to congratulate him.[68]

❖❖❖

Lavallée had little time to bask in the glory of the moment. The next day he was back at St Patrick's, celebrating Corpus Christi with Mass and procession. Later that month he travelled to Trois-Rivières with Trudel and Prume for a concert at city hall. As the *Fête nationale* fell on a Tues-day, he had no duties at St Patrick's and likely participated in events at Saint-Roch. En route to that church in the morning, members of the pro-cession, led by the band of the 9th Battalion, stopped at the offices of lawyer and philanthropist L.-G. Baillargé to receive what some believed to have been the historic flag of Carillon, a ceremony that featured the playing of Sabatier's "Drapeau de Carillon."[69] At Saint-Roch Church it-self, newspapers noted, the embattled lieutenant-governor Letellier and his family took part in the proceedings. The Société Sainte-Cécile sang Haydn's Second Mass, directed by Le Vasseur, with Defoy at the organ and the band of Battery "B" providing the orchestra. Afterwards, the band of the Ninth Battalion provided music for an excursion by steamboat to Ile d'Orléans.

Early in July, Lavallée travelled to Montreal to attend the annual gathering of the AMQ, where he served on the piano jury.[70] Riding on his success in June, he was elected president of the organization for a second time. The selection did not sit well with Guillaume Couture, who had just served a term as secretary and may have been expecting to now lead the organization. Writing in *La Revue de Montréal*, Couture acknowledged that Lavallée was Quebec City's finest musician, but asserted that the position of president should alternate between the two cities, and that Lavallée now resided in Quebec City. More generally, he lamented the lack of progress made by the AMQ, claiming that the organization was like a private club.[71] He may have had a point, but his reputation for antagonism likely worked against him. Lavallée, now president, returned to Quebec City where he convened a meeting of the board on 10 July.

Through the rest of the month, newspapers devoted little space to anything but the ongoing political crisis. This finally resulted in Letellier's dismissal and, on the morning of Saturday, 26 July, a new lieutenant-governor, the Conservative Théodore Robitaille, was sworn into office. The following day, Sunday, 27 July 1879, Lavallée and Prume travelled with the SSC, the Septuor Haydn, and members of the public to the town of Sainte-Marie-de-la-Beauce (now simply known as Sainte-Marie), the birthplace of Archbishop Elzéar-Alexandre Taschereau, some forty kilometres south of Quebec City. Setting off by train from Lévis in a heavy summer downpour, the weather had cleared by the time they had arrived in the town. There they played in the first violin section, as the SSQ performed Haydn's Second Mass – presumably the same one that was performed at Saint-Roch on 24 June.[72] The event was a chance to please the archbishop by providing the community with a rare opportunity to hear a large-scale performance. Similarly, Lavallée and Prume returned to Trois-Rivières in August for a concert, bringing with them an orchestra comprising musicians from Montreal and Quebec City. Each of these larger performances required numerous rehearsals, and combined with administrative and teaching duties, they left Lavallée with little time to compose. He had been working on a Mass that was to be performed at that year's *Fête Sainte-Cécile*, but in September he notified the Union Musicale, organizers of the event, that it would not be ready in time. There is no evidence that he ever completed it.

On 22 September, Lavallée took part in a benefit concert for the Union Musicale, performing several piano pieces and conducting the Finale, or "Choeur militaire," from the cantata. By this time he himself was in need of fundraising. After their summer stay in Quebec, the marquis and princess had moved on to Toronto, where they were welcomed to the Ontario capital with music by Lavallée's old friend Frederick Torrington.[73] Back in Quebec City, Lavallée was still sorting out the bills from the June reception. According to an article published in the US six years later, Lavallée had run a deficit of several hundred dollars, and paid the amount himself.[74] This claim is impossible to verify. The government paid $3,386 to "sundry persons," for all the expenses related to the performance, but the records contain no detailed breakdown of the payments.[75] Admission to the reception cost $1.00, or $1.50 for a reserved seat, and the performance should have generated revenue of at least $1,000. If there was a larger-than-expected deficit, Lavallée may have been at fault for exceeding the government's budget. He conducted rehearsals through the fall and spring, and hired musicians from Montreal for the performance. His unwillingness to demand repayment from the government for these costs may have been because he did not wish to appear an incompetent manager. This financial burden ultimately became a factor in his decision to leave Canada.[76] In retrospect, *Le Canada musical*'s observation that Lavallée's cantata marked "a new phase in the artistic career of its author" proved ironic, though true.[77]

Concerts should have brought in some extra money in October. He and Prume planned a series of chamber concerts in Quebec City and Montreal. For the Quebec City performances, they received the official patronage of Lieutenant-Governor Robitaille and of a dozen society ladies, among them Madame Robitaille and Madame Routhier. The first was scheduled for Victoria Hall on 7 October, but was postponed to the 30th when del Vecchio became ill. On the evening of Tuesday, 28 October, Lavallée travelled by train to Montreal for a solo matinee recital planned for the next day at Nordheimer's Hall. The event was sponsored by the New York Piano Company, a firm that had just opened a showroom on Saint-Jacques Street and was promoting the newly arrived Weber grand piano.[78] It was the beginning of a marketing campaign by major piano makers and retailers that seems to have defied the still-difficult economic conditions. The heavy advertising likely helped to draw a good audience to the recital.[79] Lavallée then returned to Quebec City with Prume and del Vecchio for the Victoria Hall concert on Thursday, 30 October. After arriving, Rosita del Vecchio fell ill again and was unable to perform. To placate ticket holders, they issued coupons for a supplemental concert, with the date to be announced later, and added several selections to the program. They also brought in members of the Septuor Haydn, who joined them in playing "God Save the Queen" as the lieutenant-governor entered the hall, and Alphonse d'Eschambault, who sang two selections. Lavallée and Prume performed familiar works by Beethoven and Mendelssohn, as well as Saint-Saëns's programmatic *Dance Macabre*, for violin and two pianos, and Gottschalk's *Pastorella è cavaliere*. Quebec City audiences may have been less receptive to this unfamiliar repertoire than their Montreal counterparts, who by now had grown more accustomed to hearing a mix of unfamiliar and favourite works.[80] Marmette could be relied on for critical support. Here he refers to them as "two great artists, brothers of the heart and in talent," thanking them for their commitment to the cultural development of the young country.[81] He says nothing about the size of the audience, which presumably was not large.

Friday, 31 October, brought yet another change of government when five members of the Liberal party crossed over to the opposition and Premier Joly's government fell. As Lieutenant-Governor Robitaille handed power to the Conservatives, Lavallée might have thought it a promising sign, not because that party had shown an interest in culture but because he knew the new premier, Joseph-Adolphe Chapleau, who was but two years older than Lavallée and also a member of the Club des 21.

Lavallée had spent Friday at St Patrick's Church, making preparations for All Saints' Day. These events began with early morning Mass on Saturday. In this case, he conducted selections from two Mozart masses (the Kyrie, Gloria, Sanctus, and Agnus Dei from an unspecified Mass in C, with the Credo from the Missa Brevis in B-flat major, K275), with Charles Gounod's *Ave Maria* at the offertory. The *Daily Telegraph* reported that the music "under the able direction of Mr Lavallée was very effective," and drew particular attention to some of the soloists.[82] He seems to have found a new talent in the soprano known only as Mrs Caldwell (sometimes spelled Cauldwell). Her singing of the *Ave Maria* was said to have been "the best that has been heard in Quebec," while the Agnus Dei was "exquisitely sung and entranced the listeners." The other soloists were Miss Vézina, soprano; Arthur McCallum, bass; and three tenors: William Seaton, P. Whitty, and Joseph Marmette, who was mentioned as a first-time member of the choir. St Patrick's Church elders were evidently pleased with Lavallée's work and the attention it was receiving. Later that month, they announced plans to shrewdly invest $6,000 in a new organ – one with the keyboard positioned in such a way as to enable him to play and to conduct the choir at the same time.[83]

Much of the month was spent preparing for performances of Gounod's *Messe solennelle de Sainte Cécile*. The first took place at St Patrick's Church on St Cecilia Day, Saturday, 22 November. This was essentially a run-through for a musical extravaganza that he directed at Victoria Hall on the following Tuesday. The event involved most of the capital's musicians and vocalists. To a nucleus of Union Musicale musicians, Lavallée added the Septuor Haydn and the choirs of the Chapelle des Congrégationalistes and the Saint-Roch and St Patrick's churches. He selected soloists from different ensembles: Mrs Caldwell from St Patrick's, tenor Henri Bédard from the ssc, and baritone E. Belleau from the Union Musicale. Lavallée interspersed the different sections of Gounod's Mass with vocal and instrumental pieces by Kowalski, Flotow, Verdi, and others.[84] He ended the program with the military chorus from his cantata. The event, in the presence of the lieutenant-governor and many other politicians, was a musical triumph. Missing, however, was Premier Chapleau, whose new administration Lavallée needed to win over if he was to succeed in gaining funds for the conservatory.

Politics figured heavily in early-December concerts in Montreal. Even though the work involved in organizing the St Cecilia events had knocked Lavallée off his feet, he took part in a Montreal concert of the chamber music series on 2 December, performing Beethoven's "Appassionata" sonata, Mendelssohn's Concerto in G minor, and Rubinstein's *Melodie in F*. In addition to the selections performed by Prume, there were a number of chamber works on the program. The concert opened with a set of three works for a string ensemble that featured Prume, Martel, Reichling, François Boucher, and Alex Wills. The first selection was listed simply as a romanesca by Lully (this was grouped with two contemporary works: a minuet by Émile Pessard, and "Chanson d'Amour" by Wilhelm Taubert). Apart from a few novelty pieces on the program, the concert seemed unremarkable; however, it took on a political dimension in the press when the Conservative Party's Club Cartier scheduled their own event at the same time.[85] The date of the Conservative concert was eventually delayed until 4 December, but the press continued to discuss whether music had become politicized. The Cartier event had been heavily promoted and featured Alfred De Sève, along with several other instrumentalists, and vocalists Mr and Mrs Finn. A good portion of the evening was devoted to political speeches, with Premier Chapleau giving the closing address. In a brief article about the two concerts, the Conservative *Courrier de Montréal* commented that it was wrong to suggest that the Chapleau event had been planned to harm Prume's concert: "The arts know nothing of and should know nothing of politics. We do not know if Mr Prume and the artists who performed so brilliantly last night are Red or Blue. We do not want to know when it comes to enjoying them as artists."[86] Similarly, De Sève's participation in the Cartier concert may not indicate that was he was Blue. It does suggest, though, that the organizers saw the handsome twenty-year-old violinist as a good promotional vehicle for the party's youth vote.

While the lieutenant-governors may have been party members they were expected to remain above the fray; after the Letellier affair, Robitaille was especially careful with his image. Once again he was listed along with a group of society ladies as patron for Lavallée and Prume's 12 December concert at Victoria Hall. Since Rosita del Vecchio was still unwell – her place taken by Antonia Dessane – Robitaille's support was all the more important. Musicians clearly saw Robitaille as a potential boon, and on the afternoon of the same day a delegation of representatives from most of the city's musical organizations presented him with an official, if somewhat vague, petition.[87] Patrick Curran represented the

St Patrick's Church choir. Lavallée was not listed among the signatories of the petition, possibly because as president of the AMQ he was already receiving a subsidy. Perhaps there was something more.

As 1880 approached, Lavallée could look back on an eventful year. The artistic successes had come at a price, and there was still no guarantee of an eventual payoff. His twelfth wedding anniversary and Christmas, as well as his own thirty-seventh birthday, were all reminders of his precarious financial state, and Josephine was again about to give birth. Still, he brought in Christmas in style at St Patrick's with another performance of Gounod's *Messe solonnelle*, adding the musicians and singers of the Septuor Haydn and the Union Musicale to the church's choir. In its review of the Christmas events, the *Daily Telegraph* called it the "Mass of the season."[88]

The year 1880 started auspiciously for the Lavallées with the birth, on New Year's Day, of their third child. On 4 January 1880, the baby boy was christened Raoul Arthur at Notre Dame de Victoire Church, in Lévis, with the second name coming from the boy's godfather, Arthur McCallum, a member of the St Patrick's Church choir.[89] The surviving Lavallée family album has no images of Raoul, possibly confirming that it was left behind when the family relocated to Boston. It does contain two images of Calixa Jr, one as an infant and one taken at his first communion. (Figures 5.9 and 5.10)

The early weeks of January 1880 brought a variety of performances. Prume was in Quebec City for two concerts with Lavallée. The first, on 7 January, was held at Salle de l'Académie Commercial des Frères, and was advertised as a literary-musical soiree in honour of Reverend Auclair, the founder of the institution.[90] The second, the next evening, formed part of the festivities marking Charles-Félix Cazeau's fiftieth year as a priest.[91] This event was held at the University's Salle de pensionnat, which was decorated for the occasion with maple boughs and banners in green, white, and gold. Once again, Lieutenant-Governor Robitaille was among the audience of dignitaries. One of the pieces on the program was "Harmonie," Lavallée's simple, strophic setting of a poem by F.-A. Hubert La Rue, a well-known medical doctor, professor at the university, and member of the Club des 21. Lavigne published the song, advertising it as a "mélodie populaire."[92] On this occasion, it was sung by Alphonse

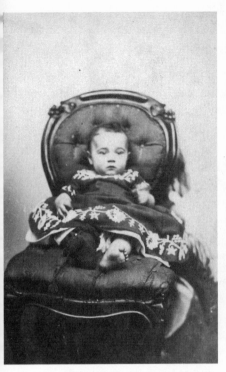

Figures 5.9 and 5.10 Photographs of Calixa Lavallée Jr. dating from about 1868 and 1880.

d'Eschambault. The rest of January and early February saw Lavallée busy with church music. He conducted a performance of Gounod's Mass at Chapelle des Congréganistes de la Haute-Ville in early February. Later that month, he directed the QVQ in the singing of a Mass by the Swiss composer Charles Alwens. On 1 March, Prume was back for a concert at Victoria Hall. There were familiar works by Weber, Vieuxtemps, and others. What the newspapers noted, however, was the performance of "Amaryllis," a piece of music credited to Louis XIII. To Marmette, this "curiously rhythmic" piece cast one back into historical memory.[93] Once again del Vecchio was unable to perform, and this time a Miss Hardman took her place. At about this time, Lavallée and Legendre dedicated a new song, "Nuit d'Été" (Summer Night), to Madame Robitaille. It was a gesture of thanks for her support of the concerts, but the two men were also still attempting to gather support – and financing – for the conservatory.

The English version of Legendre's text was one of Patrick Curran's final translations.[94] On Friday, 5 March, he died of what seems to have been pneumonia.[95] A funeral procession took place the next day from his home to St Patrick's Church, where Lavallée directed the choir in the singing of his setting of the responsory text "Libera me" (Deliver me).[96] Afterwards, some forty members of the St Patrick's Catholic and Literary Institute accompanied Curran's remains, by train, to Montreal for burial.[97] On Monday evening, Lavallée attended a meeting at St Patrick's, and the next day sent a letter of condolence to the *Morning Chronicle*, writing that "the members of St Patrick's choir take this means of publically [*sic*] testifying to the sincere regret which they feel at the demise of the late P.J. Curran, Esquire, in who the restless hand of death has deprived them of a fellow member whose brilliant talent and effective assistance will be long and faithfully remembered."[98] A popular figure, Curran was just thirty years old.

Lavallée's own health was a concern during what was turning into a hectic month. On the evening of Tuesday, 9 March, he attended a soiree at Spencer Wood, the lieutenant-governor's official residence. Ernest Gagnon was also there, and the two performed a four-hand version of the overture to Rossini's opera *Semiramide*.[99] The next day, he was back at work and busy with preparations for St Patrick's Day festivities. On the morning of 17 March, he conducted a Mass by Luigi Cherubini at St Patrick's, a service attended by Quebec's lieutentant-governor and premier. In the evening, he directed the musical portion of the St Patrick's Catholic and Literary Institute's event at Music Hall. He played the piano (Duprato's *Saltarelle* and Gottschalk's *Danse nègre*) and directed the St Patrick's Church choir. D'Eschambault sang Lavallée's "The Beautiful Girl of Kildare," with an additional verse relating to proposed changes to farm ownership laws in Ireland that was said to "have had the effect of bringing down the house."[100] Mrs Caldwell, Mlle Vézina, and several other singers also performed, and Lavallée closed the event with a specially arranged medley of Irish airs. Two days later, he played the organ at a morning service at the basilica, celebrating Taschereau's ninth anniversary as archbishop.

Frantz Prume arrived in Quebec City several days ahead of his 30 March Victoria Hall concert with Lavallée. A tragedy of a kind had befallen him in February: en route to a Montreal concert with the Mendelssohn Choir, his Guarnerius violin had fallen from the sled and been crushed under the horses' hooves. By way of explaining his inability to perform, the pieces of the instrument were shown to the audience in Mechanics' Hall.[101] While seemingly a lost cause, the violin was famously reconstructed by Augustin Lavallée. Easter Sunday, 28 March 1880, was a busy day for Lavallée. He conducted a Mozart Mass (listed as the composer's Twelfth Mass) at St Patrick's, with Ernest Gagnon making a guest appearance as organist. Soloists were Mrs Caldwell and Miss Loftus, sopranos; Miss Carbray, alto; White, Seaton, and La Rue, tenors; and McCallum and Duggan, basses.[102] From there, he and Prume went to Saint-Roch to take part in an especially grand celebration attended by Lieutenant-Governor Robitaille. They gave what may have been the first performance in Canada of Rossini's *Petite messe solennelle*. The Mass is small in the sense that Rossini scored it for a small number of voices, accompanied by only piano and harmonium. In this case, the performance seems not to have closely followed the composer's intentions, with performers drawn from the ssc, the Septuor Haydn, the Union Musicale, the Cercle Musical, and the Battery "B" Band. Soloists included Laurent and d'Eschambault.[103] Finally, on 30 March, Lavallée and Prume gave the last recital in the series at Victoria Hall.[104] At this event, Lavallée was forced to apologize to the audience for an injured finger.[105] Reviews no longer mentioned the absent Rosita del Vecchio. Vocal music was provided by Cora Wyse and by Frédéric Lefebvre, who came in from Montreal.

At about this time news emerged that organizers of the forthcoming Congrès Catholique Canadiens-Français had commissioned Lavallée to compose a national song.[106] The Congress was to open on 24 June 1880 and bring together francophone community leaders from across Canada and the United States for discussions on religious, social, and economic issues.[107] There was no shortage of patriotic songs at the time. To the required singing of "God Save the Queen," English-speaking Canadians frequently added Alexander Muir's "The Maple Leaf Forever," while French Canadians favoured the traditional "Vive la Canadienne." Still,

Figure 5.11
Judge A.B. Routhier,
author of the original
words of "O Canada."

organizers saw the event as an opportunity to create a dignified national song that would complement "God Save the Queen."

The poet selected was Judge Adolphe-Basile Routhier, president of the conference's program committee and one of the key speakers. (See figure 5.11) Routhier's qualifications as a poet were limited. He had won third prize for "La Découvert du Canada" in a poetry competition in 1867.[108] However, more important than his credentials as a poet were his connections to the Conservative Party and his commitment to conservativism. There was never any question of commissioning Quebec's best-known poet, the Liberal Fréchette.[109] The Congress was to be an affirmation of conservative values and Routhier was well qualified to express them in verse. He had been admitted to the bar in 1861 and made unsuccessful attempts to win the federal seat of Kamouraska for the Conservative Party in the 1869 and 1872 elections. He continued to fight liberals and liberalism through his writings and lectures. Given his friendship with Fréchette (whose photograph he kept in the family album), Lavallée's collaboration with Routhier seems somewhat out of character, but as in the past, he may have been demonstrating a degree of pragmatism. He still had hopes of establishing a conservatory and Routhier was an influential figure. Besides, compared with the effort required to compose and perform the cantata, all that was being asked of him now was the music for a song, albeit an important one. It seems likely that Lavallée and Routhier had agreed to collaborate on the song at the 9 March soiree at Spencer Wood, which they and Ernest Gagnon had attended.[110] Routhier later wrote that it was Gagnon, as president of the conference's music committee, who convinced him and Lavallée to write the song.[111] "Lavallée insisted on composing the music first and so he did," Routhier reported, after which "I made the verses, or the stanzas, with the metre and the rhyme that were suitable to the music."[112] A few weeks after that soiree, both music and text were ready.

In April, news came that Lavallée had composed a new national song, and that it would be published by Arthur Lavigne – "at last we have a veritable French-Canadian national song," the *Journal de Québec* proclaimed.[113] The notice stated that Lavigne would be printing 6,000 copies, with 5,000 to be distributed to the public.[114] L.-N. Dufresne designed the first edition, illustrating the cover with a portrait of the lieutenant-governor surrounded by such symbols of French-speaking Canada as the maple tree, the Saint Lawrence River, and the ubiquitous beaver. (See figure 5.12) As news of this piece of music spread, others tried their hand at creating a national song for the June 1880 fête. Célestin Lavigueur's national song, "Ô Canada, beau pays, ma patrie," was published by Bernard & Allaire.[115] Salomon Mazurette, now in Detroit, was reported to have contributed a march that he intended as a complement to Lavallée's *Chant national*.[116] Even the Marquis of Lorne had gotten involved. When Arthur Sullivan visited Canada in February, the governor general had the famous composer set a poem he had written. This "Canadian National Anthem" was placed at the top of the program of the Montreal Philharmonic Society's concert at the Victoria Skating Rink on 27 May, with the governor general, along with the

Figure 5.12 L.-N. Dufresne's cover of the "Chant national" ("O Canada"), published by Arthur Lavigne in 1880 and featuring iconic images of Quebec and the province's Lieutenant-Governor Robitaille.

princess and her brother Prince Leopold, in the audience; however, it was acknowledged as not being among the composer's best efforts. Even the humble correspondent of the *Montreal Daily Witness* reported that, although "it would not be a bad psalm tune," it would "scarcely find permanent favour with the people as a national anthem."[117]

In the lead-up to the Congress, Lavallée's schedule remained full and his life carried on as usual. In May, he moved his household back across the river into a house on Sainte-Ursule Street. The furniture and household effects of the previous resident of 12 Sainte-Ursule, a lawyer by the name of Charles Gethings, were auctioned on 1 May, and the Lavallées moved in soon after.[118] The attractive three-storey house, located just above Saint-Jean Street, still stands, and suggests that Lavallée was at least presenting himself as financially secure. Lavallée was in Montreal for a concert with Prume at the Mechanics' Hall on Thursday, 3 June. Martel was also on the program, and Rose de Lima Derome served as accompanist. Rosita del Vecchio had recovered her health and also took part, even though she was then in rehearsal for Fréchette's historical dramas *Papineau* and *L'Exilé*, which were about to open at the Academy of Music. Lavallée was unable to stay for the opening as he was directing the QVQ at a soiree at Spencer Wood on Saturday evening, at which the works they sang included his medley of Irish airs. At this event and again on 15 June, Lieutenant-Governor Théodore Robitaille and his wife hosted the governor general, Princess Louise, and Prince Leopold. The royal siblings left town later that month to tour the US, leaving the marquis behind to represent their mother at the Congress.

Delegates and other visitors began arriving in the thousands in the days leading up to the 24 June start of the Congress. They came from throughout Quebec, from the other provinces, and from the United States. Their actual number is difficult to determine. The hotels were fully booked long before, extra trains were scheduled, and newspaper reports suggest the city had never been so busy. The atmosphere seems to have been considerably lighter than the topic of the Congress might have suggested. Throughout the conference, the visitors were offered a variety of entertainment. Huron dancers performed on Place Jacques-Cartier, and brass bands from throughout Quebec and New England gave open-air concerts on the Dufferin Terrace and in the city's squares and parks.[119] Although not part of the official program, even Fréchette was there, giving performances of his dramas at the Music Hall. Laval-lée's *Chant national* was published just prior to the Congress, in time for visitors to buy a copy as a souvenir of the event.

❖❖❖

Those purchasing a copy of the new *Chant national* found a work of true poetic and musical eloquence. Routhier had risen to the occasion, producing a text that expressed the tenor of the times. The judge's text was both patriotic and religious. The first stanza gives a sense of its tone:

| | |
|---|---|
| O Canada, terre de nos aïeux, Ton front est ceint de fleurons glorieux! | O Canada, land of our ancestors, Your brow is encircled with glorious garlands! |
| Car ton bras sait porter l'épée, il sait porter la croix! | As your arm can carry the sword, it too can carry the cross! |
| Ton histoire est une épopée, des plus brillants exploits. | Your history is an epic, of the most brilliant exploits. |
| Et ta valeur, de foi trempée, | And your merit, steeped in faith, |
| Protègera nos foyers et nos droits.[120] | Will protect our homes and our rights.[121] |

The text emphasizes the primary characteristics of the French-Canadian conservative ideology of the era and of the conference: historical memory, a pastoral way of life, religious faith, patriotism, and status quo politics. It is a nostalgic text, evoking an image of the Canadian who grows with hope "under the eye of God, by the great river" and "guards the honour of his flag." Which flag was left open to the interpretation of the individual. Routhier's references to the British monarchy are sometimes oblique: a Canadian is "An enemy of tyranny / But full of loyalty, / He wants to keep harmony, / His proud freedom" but he concludes: "And [we] repeat, like our fathers, / The victor's cry: 'For Christ and the king.'" While Victoria had been on the British throne since 1841, Routhier may have been using poetic licence. He may also have been referring to the long line of French kings. The ambiguity of his text allowed it to be read as referring either to pre-republican France (Louis XV had been king at the time of the Treaty of Paris) or to then present-day Canada. Although arguably a lesser talent than his rival, L.-H. Fréchette, Routhier captured the mood in much of French Canada far better in his poem than did Fréchette in his dramas.

Lavallée's composition was the sort of stately piece that organizers hoped for, but it was not without controversy. On the surface, the music is simply a twenty-eight-measure march for chorus (SATB). It does, however, bear some resemblance to the opening measures of the instrumental "March of the Priests" from Act Two of Mozart's *The Magic Flute*. The two are similar in tempo, character, and overall form; they both begin with a three-note motif, which develops similarly. (See figure 5.13) Mozart's harmony is slightly richer than Lavallée's; both pieces move

Figure 5.13 A comparison of the opening measures of "O Canada" to W.A. Mozart's "March of the Priests" and to the Andante sostenuto theme from Franz Liszt's *Festklänge*.

first to the submediant and then to the dominant. Still, there is nothing unusual about these similarities. The Toronto composer and conductor Ernest MacMillan understated things somewhat when he dismissed the connection to Mozart's march as nothing more than "the first three notes," but the harmonic progressions, melodic patterns, tempo, and overall style could be described as standard elements in the genre.[122] The opening of the *Chant national*, for example, also bears a resemblance to the "andante sostenuto" theme from Franz Liszt's 1854 symphonic poem *Festklänge*. Whether or not Lavallée was familiar with *Festklänge* matters no more than whether or not Liszt knew of Mozart's march, which of course he did.[123] More interesting, however, was what has so far been overlooked: the intriguing relationship between the context in which "O Canada" was to be performed and the role that Mozart's march plays in *The Magic Flute*.

"O Canada" was to have had its first performance at the end of the conference's opening Mass on the historic Plains of Abraham. A crowd estimated to number 40,000 gathered in the meadow overlooking the Saint Lawrence River, where Archbishop Taschereau led the Mass, assisted by some 500 priests. The Mass selected was itself another reference to pre-republican France: the *Messe Royale* by Henri Du Mont, the Belgian-born maître of the Chapelle Royale at Versaille. The Basilica's organist, Gustave Gagnon, and choir director, Etienne Légaré, directed the performance, with a choir of several hundred voices singing the Ordinary, alternating with a choir of seventy-five singing plainchant. Instrumental ensembles accompanied both choirs.[124] In his published report on the Congress, Honoré Chouinard wrote that the Mass was to have been followed by a performance of "God Save the Queen," a speech by Bishop Racine, and finally "O Canada."[125] Similarly, the central characters in the Mozart's opera, or *Singspiel*, are the priests, led by Sarastro. At their meeting in Act Two, the orchestra plays the march while the priests circle the stage in a "festive procession." As they take their places, Sarastro appears and proclaims "that today's assembly is one of the most important of our time."[126] While the evidence is entirely circumstantial, it seems possible that Lavallée was referring to Mozart's Masonic Singspiel. He had spent the greatest part of his career as a minstrel show musician, where the central feature of each performance was a parody or burlesque of a well-known opera, play, or event. By the spring of 1880, he was growing disillusioned about Canada, and just *may* have intended to satirize the event and the community leaders who had little interest in the arts.[127]

Whether or not this was true, at the last minute "O Canada" was pulled from the program. It is plausible that organizers became aware of the similarity to Mozart's setting. They may also have been concerned about a breach of protocol. Adding "O Canada" at the end – after "God Save the Queen" – might have been seen as challenging British authority. Although Canada had been quasi independent for thirteen years, the British monarch was (and still is) the head of state, and the Catholic Church had no desire to question her authority. Whatever the reason, *Le Canada musical* later reported simply that "due to an unfortunate misunderstanding ["O Canada"] could not be performed after the Mass, as had been agreed," and a *Tantum ergo* was sung in its place.[128]

The actual premiere took place that evening, at the "national banquet." The location was the same as for the premiere of Lavallée's cantata: the Quebec Skating Rink, which this time organizers decorated with maple boughs and flowers, and draped with the flags and patriotic banners that had been carried there in a procession from the Dufferin Terrace. At this most important social event of the conference, catered by the kitchens of the Russell Hotel and the Hôtel Saint-Louis, some 500 to 800 individuals paid $2.50 each to dine in the presence of the elite of French-speaking Canada. At the head table was the president of Quebec City's Société Saint-Jean-Baptiste, P.J. Rhéaume; Archbishop Taschereau; Sir Narcisse Belleau (who had been knighted by the princess in a special ceremony in Montreal in May 1879); the bishops of Trois-Rivières and Sherbrooke; Judge Routhier and his wife; the Speaker of the House, J.-G. Blanchet; the governor general; Premier Chapleau; Lieutenant-Governor Robitaille and his wife; consuls; and mayors.[129] Among the other politicians present was Lavallée's former colleague from *L'Union nationale,* Wilfrid Laurier, now the Liberal Member of Parliament for the riding of Quebec-East. Speeches and toasts were interspersed with performances by the combined bands of Fall River, Beauport, and the 9th Battalion, all conducted by Joseph Vézina. In his published report on the Congress, Chouinard wrote that the band played "God Save the

Queen" after the first toast to Queen Victoria.[130] The playing of "O Canada" followed toasts to the lieutenant-governor and to the province of Quebec.[131] Most newspapers published extensive coverage of the speeches. Few said anything about the music. *L'Événement* and the *Courrier des États Unis* mentioned the performance of "O Canada," noting that "the *Chant national* had a great success and was loudly applauded."[132] If the actual premiere of "O Canada" was more modest than originally planned, it does seem fitting that it took place in a hockey rink.

The next day, "O Canada" was given another performance and this time received more attention. Vézina again conducted the *Chant national*, this time at an afternoon concert hosted by Lieutenant-Governor Robitaille at Spencer Wood. Organizers had bleachers constructed on the grounds, seating some 6,000 for the grand reception. For this performance, Vézina had an expanded ensemble of about 125 musicians drawn from the bands of Beauport, Charlesbourg, Maisonneuve, and the 9th Battalion, and the Union Musicale. He presented a program of popular works, with his own medley of national songs in the middle:

"March" from *Tannhauser*, Richard Wagner
*La Couronne d'Or*, overture, Alphonse Herman
"Waltz" (*Artist's Life*, op. 316), Johann Strauss Jr
Medley of French-Canadian Airs, Joseph Vézina
*Chemin de Fer*, gallop, Carl Arndt
Chant national, Lavallée
God Save the Queen

The *Montreal Star* reported that just as the band began to play Lavallée's anthem, "peals of thunder vibrated amongst the hills, giving the first indications of a storm, which finally drove the visitors to their homes."[133] The newspaper noted that "the anthem itself was sweet and impressive, and produced a fine effect."[134] At its conclusion, Lieutenant-Governor Robitaille addressed the audience, congratulating Lavallée on his composition and urging others to study music. In closing, he spoke of the benefits of "living beneath the British flag" and called for three cheers for the Queen, and for the playing of "God Save the Queen." By its conclusion, the storm had arrived, sending everyone running for cover.

The first public performance of Judge Routhier's words took place at a Mass held at Saint-Jean-Baptiste Church, on Sunday, 27 June. The lieutenant-governor and his wife were there, along with many other politicians. Gustave Gagnon conducted the choir, with Ernest Gagnon at the organ. Among the performers were Antonia Dessane, Pierre Laurent, and members of ssc. They performed Haydn's Third Mass, interspersed with works by Gounod, Beethoven, Cherubini, and Adam.[135] A program published the next day in the *Journal de Québec* shows the "Hymne national" sung as, or at, the "Elevation," positioned between the "Sanctus" and the "Agnus dei." *Le Canada musical* reported that the *Chant national* was sung "to great effect" after the "Dona nobis" (at or near the end of the service).[136] The unnamed critic – likely A.J. Boucher or Napoléon Legendre – ventured a prediction on the song's future: "This composition, in which we recognize the author of the *Cantata for the Princess Louise*, is a grand, patriotic song, and at the same time religious in character; it seems to combine the beauties that we like to find in the national hymn of a people, and as it circulates in our Canadian cities it will undoubtedly become the popular song of French Canadians."[137] *L'Événement* was more spirited after the anthem's performance at Quebec City's *Fête Sainte-Cécile*, on 22 November 1880: "We cannot express the feelings of patriotism aroused in us by the *Chant national*, this thoroughly Canadian work which is not inferior to the most beautiful inspirations of the masters of the art."[138] By this time, however, Lavallée was no longer present to appreciate the honour.

The rest of the summer proved uneventful. On 6 July. Lavallée presided over the AMQ sessions at which two of his piano students, Miss F. Lafrance and Miss F. Banks, were awarded second-class diplomas, and one, Miss Laure Paré, was awarded the first-class diploma and Laureate diploma.[139] At the business meeting, MacLagan became the president.[140] Lavallée was appointed to the board, as was Prume. In the weeks that followed, they gave some concerts in and around Quebec City. At the 7 September annual meeting of the Quatuor Vocale de Québec, Lavallée was appointed director.[141] The next day he was advertising for students, and on 12 September, he led the QVQ at Mass at St Patrick's.[142] Not long after this, he just slipped away.

❖❖❖

It seems that in the second half of September Lavallée had an opportunity to perform in the US, and he took it. By mid-October he was the house guest of a wealthy friend in Hartford, Connecticut, and making plans for an extensive concert tour with Prume. A letter that he wrote to Marmette on 22 October 1880 explains his mood at this time and shows that he had no immediate plans of returning to Canada: "I am here like a grand lord at the home of my friend Duclos, an intelligent man, and very rich. His home is princely, horses at my disposal, a grand piano for working, and magnificent company, in sum, all that is required to spoil a man of my temperament. The only thing that I regret is not having someone like old Marmette with me to enjoy my good fortune and exchange ideas."[143] Lavallée vaguely discusses his recent activities, writing that he had "travelled a great deal and been occupied with work in New York, Boston and elsewhere."[144] He provides more details on his current plans, describing a concert tour that was to see him depart from Baltimore on 25 November. He planned to visit Cuba and Mexico and then travel up the Mississippi and eastward, ending the tour at Hartford on 17 May 1881.

Lavallée reveals in his letter to Marmette something of the extent of his resentment over his life in Canada. Throughout the missive he alternates between his plans and the situation he left behind. After again describing the proposed tour, he returns to his feelings about leaving Canada, and discusses his reputation in Quebec: "Tachereau wrote to me and mentioned that there is much gossip about me ... Be certain about one thing, nevertheless, and this is that I have the sense to tolerate gossiping, as is being done about me. I have travelled too much to stop and listen to the pretentious counsels that I could receive there. When one returns here, one realizes the insignificance of the ideas of our poor country ... I have complete confidence in this trip as well as in others, and besides, an artist is not meant to rot in an obscure place and especially in an even more obscure country."[145] Once more he revisits his plans but closes by asking for news of his friends, and expressing hope that once touring again he will be in a better mood.[146]

A major reason for Lavallée's angry departure was his lack of success in establishing a conservatory. He had returned from France in 1875 determined to transform musical life in Quebec. Teaching and developing audiences for Romantic concert repertoire had been his main objectives. He had performed at more than sixty concerts, giving Canadian premieres of many works. Through his productions of *Jeanne d'Arc* and *La Dame blanche* he had helped to develop both audiences and performers. His work as a church musician went well beyond what was expected of him. He devoted his time to cultivating singers and presenting great works. When his efforts in Montreal were frustrated by the Church itself, he had turned to opera, and then, on relocating to Quebec City, had raised the level of music making at St Patrick's and within the larger community. Improvement of education and the creation of a conservatory had been his goals on moving to Quebec City in the summer of 1878. He had given up his Montreal teaching practice and started over in the provincial capital. His work with the AMQ gave the organization momentum and increased visibility. Of his Canadian students, the bandmaster Joseph Vézina was by this time himself a leading figure in Quebec City's musical life. Many of the others appeared regularly in concerts. His compositional output during this era gives an indication of his priorities. Between 1875 and 1880 he composed no piano works for his own performance, nor did he compose anything for Franz Prume. He composed the *Marche funèbre*, "Violette," "O Canada," the cantata, and other works for specific occasions. Each of these served a larger purpose, allowing him to gain favour from a particular constituency, be it the Church, the lieutenant-governor, or the governor general and Princess Louise. After five years his enthusiasm and patience were exhausted and he was in debt.

Financially, the cantata seems to have been the tipping point. As with the productions of *Jeanne d'Arc* and *La Dame blanche*, it had helped to raise awareness of the need for a school of music. But Lavallée had gambled on its success in helping to realize this goal, devoting much of his energy and resources to its creation and performance. His friend Joseph Marmette would have been well placed to see the impact this had on Lavallée's future and, in his review of the cantata performance, reflected a new urgency in writing an eloquent plea for the cause: "In the aftermath of Mr Lavallée's wonderful results, the government that has already generously assisted in the organization of this lovely musical event, must also help such a talent to develop and produce other works that will contribute to the artistic progress and glory of Canada. We only need to found a music conservatory where our talented young people – which we certainly do not lack – may take shape, and place at the head of that institution a man of unparalleled calibre such as Mr Lavallée."[147] In his frank appeal to the government, Marmette was likely expressing Lavallée's frustration. In an article written a decade later, Lavallée described how, having been "worn out from the lack of financial resources," he had to do like many others "and go into exile."[148] His decision to leave his family behind gives some indication of the severity of their financial troubles. St Patrick's had provided a stable income but not enough to achieve Lavallée's goals. Giving private lessons took much of his time without making much of an impact on his income. In that same review of the cantata performance, Marmette asked "what sign of sympathy and encouragement do we give [Lavallée]? We leave him to consume his talent and his life giving piano lessons!"[149]

In retrospect, the failure to win government support for a conservatory came down to bad timing and a lack of support from his fellow musicians.[150] The economy alone might have thwarted his efforts. His time in Canada coincided with the Panic of 1873, a financial crisis sparked in part by France's repayment of debt to Germany, which was only coming to an end in 1880. His efforts to influence the government were frustrated further by the Letellier affair and the related changes of administration. Even under the best conditions, however, the government had no cultural policy. As the historian Paul-André Linteau has written, the government's "activity was limited to acting as patron to a few artists and giving out the occasional subsidy," as was the case with the AMQ.[151] The government focused on building railways and had little money for basic education or health care – it provided full financing only for the province's insane asylums. In such difficult economic times, he was unable to persuade Quebec's leading musicians to join the cause. Years later, it was the musical community's lack of support that Lavallée recalled: "My experience in Montreal and Quebec City demonstrated to me that we are able to train professional musicians, and when, in 1879, I asked the local government for support in this goal, who gave me the greatest opposition? The musicians, if I may dignify these men with that title. We will never achieve any significant results as long as these self-proclaimed musicians are in positions of influence."[152] If local musicians chose not to support Lavallée's efforts, at least some had reason. Had a conservatory been established, those not hired as instructors would have likely seen their incomes decline. In that context, the AMQ may have been more concerned with teachers' interests than with the long-term development of musical life. This had certainly been the opinion of Couture, who in 1879 had likened the organization to a clique.[153] Even though he had played a leadership role within the AMQ, Lavallée had failed to win the support needed to achieve his goals. A decade after leaving Canada, when recalling the failure of the conservatory project, it was the negativity of Quebec's "so-called musicians" that he returned to.[154]

The 1880–81 plans for a tour with Prume, del Vecchio, and Trudel ultimately collapsed. On 3 December, they performed at Allyn Hall, in Hartford, where both Lavallée and Prume were well received. The *Hartford Courant* described Lavallée as having "considerable power of execution, and although his passages are not always faultlessly clean, he makes up for this shortcoming to a certain extent in force, and fire."[155] The same critic referred to Prume's performance as lacking the "breadth of tone and style of Wilhelmj," but described him as a "most finished and brilliant executant, [who] at once placed himself *en rapport* with his small but critical audience."[156] Del Vecchio, however, may have been unwell. The *Courant's* critic described her singing as having "a fair degree of cultivation and execution," but characterized her voice as "a light mezzo soprano, of ordinary range and quality."[157] Her fragile health had continued to decline. Concerts were scheduled for Baltimore on 8 and 9 December; it is unclear if the second took place. Only a few weeks later, on 11 February 1881, the thirty-four-year-old singer died at her family's home in Montreal. None of the newspaper reports explicitly stated the cause of death, but the evidence is that it resulted from complications from childbirth.[158] Just the day before, del Vecchio's mother, Elizabeth del Vecchio (née Olivier) died, and Rosita's death brought a great outpouring of public sympathy for the family. At the joint funeral, an immense crowd filled Saint-Jacques Church and the surrounding streets. Couture conducted the united choirs of Saint-Jacques, Notre-Dame, and the Gésu, accompanied by the band of the Sixty-fifth Regiment. From the church, the band followed the funeral cortège while playing the funeral march from Gounod's *Jeanne d'Arc*.[159]

Despite his close relationship with Prume, Lavallée did not return to Montreal for del Vecchio's funeral. Her death gave him another reason not to look back. Once more, he settled into a new life and bachelorhood. It would be three years before he and Joséphine would again be living together, and one can only wonder if he had made arrangements for her and his children. He had already set his mind to new challenges. His experiences in post-war France had inspired the conservatory project and shaped his career in the late 1870s, and they would continue to drive his efforts in the United States in the next decade.

# PART THREE

# "The Lafayette of American Music"
## 1880–1891

# *Boston*

## *1880–1883*

Late in 1880, Lavallée ended several months of wandering and settled in Boston, where opportunities were plentiful for an ambitious and talented musician. Over the next three years, he lived the life of a bachelor musician. He enjoyed a wide circle of friends and acquaintances, among them many members of New England's large French-Canadian community. He composed and published two comic operas and a number of minor works, and he performed constantly, earning an enviable reputation as a pianist. At the same time, his teaching practice grew steadily, providing sufficient income for himself and his family still back in Quebec.

In his letter to Joseph Marmette, written while still in Hartford, Lavallée writes, that "if it were not for some friends (artists) that I knew in New York and Boston, no one would ever have known of my existence in these two cities."[1] In New York, one of these musicians was the cornetist Matthew Arbuckle, for whom he had composed a fantasie in 1875. Arbuckle's reputation had continued to grow. In the fall of 1880, he was leading the late Jim Fisk Jr's Ninth Regiment Band at the American Institute Fair, and Lavallée composed another solo piece for him, *Méditation*, which he published with Carl Fischer. It is an unusually introspective piece for cornet, but Arbuckle was widely considered to be the most artistic cornetist of the time. Another important contact for Lavallée during this time was the bandleader D.C. Hall, who he had worked for in the early 1870s and who had been one of the judges at the 1878 band competition in Montreal. In the early 1880s, Lavallée again performed as a soloist with Hall's ensembles and also at concerts with Hall's daughters, who had recently returned to the US after studying in Europe. Marguerite ("Daisey") was a contralto (or mezzo-soprano), Gertrude ("Kittie") was a writer, and Grace ("Gigi") was a painter and writer.

Among Lavallée's other Boston contacts was the veteran cellist Wulf Fries. Born in Garbeck, Denmark, in 1825, Fries had immigrated to Boston in 1853. As a member of the city's Mendelssohn Quintet Club and Beethoven Quartet Club, Fries performed at hundreds of concerts throughout the United States and Canada, earning a reputation as "a kind of godfather to a generation of musicians."[2] Lavallée and Prume had met Fries in Montreal in the 1870s and planned a tour with him, although it seems not to have taken place. Lavallée also developed a close relationship with the German pianist and composer Louis Maas, who had only recently immigrated, abandoning a teaching position at the Leipzig Conservatorium to settle in Boston.[3] At about the same time, Alfred De Sève arrived in Boston. He made his Boston debut at Tremont Temple on 6 November 1880 in a concert given by the pianist William Sherwood, where *The Folio* reported that he was "received with marked approbation," and that his playing displayed "remarkable brilliancy and delicate strength."[4] He and Lavallée appeared together frequently, both at concerts in Boston and at events in the French-Canadian communities of the surrounding towns and cities. Yet another Canadian connection in Boston was the singer Emilia de Angelis. The daughter of Gaetano and Veneranda de Angelis, she had settled there in the 1860s with her husband Trefflé Garceau, a physician. It was with the Garceau family that Lavallée initially resided, moving into their home at 10 Highland Street, in Roxbury.[5]

In 1880, Bostonians were celebrating the 250th anniversary of their city's founding, and a time of great achievement. Although Boston was much smaller than New York City, Chicago, or Philadelphia, it had already gained a reputation as the intellectual centre of the United States.[6] Institutions such as the Massachusetts General Hospital, the Massachusetts Institute of Technology, and Harvard University brought many of the world's finest minds to the city, while the Lowell Institute, the Boston Public Library, and other organizations helped to cultivate the community's intellectual pursuits.[7] Through the 1860s, and especially after the fire of 1872, developers transformed the city's landscape. Economic expansion brought jobs, and immigrants to fill them. Like Lavallée, many of the newcomers were Catholics, who established their own institutions and reshaped the city's character.

For many musicians, Boston was North America's most desirable city. The French pianist Henri Kowalski visited North America in 1869 and concurred with Boston's reputation as the "Athens of the United States." He found the city "beautiful and, in certain places ... grandiose."[8] Louis Moreau Gottschalk visited often during the 1860s and called Boston "par excellence the aristocratic city."[9] Wishing the city farewell after performances in December 1864, he wrote: "Adieu Boston! You are stiff, pedantic, exclusive (Mr D. is its oracle)! Your enemies say that you are cold and morose. For myself, I say that you are intelligent, literary, polished; that your pedantry, if you have any, would be excusable, if it had produced only the grand organ of the Music Hall, that glorious monument." He goes on to praise the acoustics of Tremont Temple and Music Hall, finding them "superior to the best of this continent and of the old world."[10] The "Mr D" to whom he refers was John Sullivan Dwight, whose sober *Journal of Music* disdained the flamboyant pianist and his music in favour of German repertoire. In the sixteen years that had transpired since he jotted those words in his diary, the city had become less "stiff," while its musical culture had continued to flourish.

By the 1880s, numerous performance ensembles and societies contributed to Boston's diverse musical life. The Handel and Haydn Society held the chief position as the "largest and most noted musical association of the United States."[11] Since its creation in 1815, it had performed most of the major oratorios and other large vocal works many times.[12] Among the city's leading instrumental ensembles were the Germania Musical Society, the Harvard Musical Association, and the Philharmonic Society. From 1881, the new sixty-seven-member Boston Symphony Orchestra gradually surpassed these groups.[13] Chamber music performances had grown more frequent in the 1830s and '40s, especially through the Harvard Musical Association and, afterwards, through the Mendelssohn Quintet Club, the Beethoven Quartet Club, and others.[14] Even more widely known were Boston's bands; the Boston Brass Band, Flagg's Band, and Hall's Band were local institutions with national reputations. From its rich concert life, Boston developed a wide range of secondary

musical activities. Private music schools multiplied and helped to produce a knowledgeable public and a consumer base for musical products
and services. Boston produced almost half of the music journals published in the United States in the nineteenth century, and it was home to
a number of important publishers – such as Cundy-Bettoney; Schmidt;
White, Smith & Company; and Oliver Ditson – as well as important
instrument manufacturers, among them the Standard Brass Instrument
Company and the piano maker Mason & Hamlin.[15]

It was a contract with Boston's Henry F. Miller Piano Company that
had helped Lavallée to settle in the city. Since its creation in 1863, the
Miller firm had risen quickly to become a leading American piano maker.[16]
By 1869, the company was the eleventh largest in the United States.[17] In
addition to building square pianos, during the 1870s Miller began to
build upright and grand pianos, establishing a position as a maker of
quality instruments and winning four prizes at the 1876 Philadelphia
Exposition.[18] Competition was fierce in all areas of the piano trade, and
especially so in the high-end area of concert instruments. Like many other
manufacturers, Miller enlisted well-known pianists to promote its
instruments, just as Weber had Lavallée give a recital when it introduced
its new line of grand pianos in Montreal in 1879.[19] At performances,
agents ensured that the company's name was visible from the back rows,
and often colluded with music publications and newspapers to print a
few lines about the instrument in their concert reviews. Miller appears to
have accepted this aspect of doing business when he sponsored a concert
tour by the well-known pianist William Sherwood in 1881–82.[20] In the
latter part of the decade, Lavallée would become more aware of the
problems caused by this sort of conflict of interest (discussed in chapter
7). For now, the agreement required him to perform exclusively on Miller
pianos. In return, the company provided him with a teaching studio at
Miller's Washington Street headquarters in the heart of the shopping and
business district. (See figure 6.1) The arrangement was clearly beneficial
to Lavallée, as he maintained it for the rest of his life.

Lavallée's repertoire during the early 1880s was narrower than it
had been in the previous decade. The works of Beethoven, Schumann,
Mendelssohn, and Weber all but vanished from his performances. One
might assume that he felt that German composers were already well rep-

Figure 6.1 The Henry F. Miller Piano Company
building, 611 Washington Street, Boston, ca. 1881, where
Lavallée maintained a teaching studio.

resented in the concert programs of Dwight's city. In their place, he
played more pieces by Chopin and Gottschalk. He also frequently played
his own *Paraphrase de concert sur des motifs de 'Faust.'* As with his many
transcriptions and fantasias, this "paraphrase" on themes from Gounod's
*Faust* appears to have remained unpublished, and he may never have
written it out in full. Reviews provide few details about it. After a performance several years later, the *Boston Home Journal* called it "superbly

constructed" and "rendered with an enthusiasm which necessitated Mr Lavallée's response to several recalls."[21] The *Boston Herald* described it as being "well worthy" of Lavallée's high reputation as a composer of "scholarly musical taste and poetic nature."[22]

On 1 May 1881, Lavallée performed at a concert given at Music Hall by the now legendary singer Anna Bishop. In the seventeen years since Lavallée's 1864 appearance with her in Montreal, Bishop had travelled through much of the world. She toured Asia and Australia from 1865 to 1869, surviving a shipwreck off Wake Island and a 1,400-mile journey by lifeboat as well as other adventures. The *Boston Globe* critic noted that, despite the years, Bishop's voice and features had been "wonderfully preserved."[23] Among the others on the program in Boston were D.C. Hall's orchestra and military band, vocalist Daisy Hall, cornetist Henry Brooks, and Alfred De Sève. Organizers were required to advertise the performance as a sacred concert since it took place on Sunday, but this did not restrict the repertoire performed. Lavallée played his *Paraphrase de concert sur des motifs de 'Faust'* and an unnamed work by Chopin.

Later that month, Maurice Strakosch hired Lavallée to take part in a short tour by the Hungarian soprano Etelka Gerster. Although now nearly forgotten, Gerster was then a great rival of Adelina Patti and Christine Nilsson. She had just completed her second US tour with Henry Mapleson's opera company and had remained in the US to give a few final concert performances.[24] Billed as her "farewell tour," the series of concerts began in New England and ended with performances in Baltimore on 23 and 25 May, Washington on 24 May, and Philadelphia on 26 and 28 May. Gerster sang some of her favourite arias from operas by Verdi and Bellini. The music critic at the *Baltimore Sun* reported that audiences greeted her with even greater enthusiasm than they had expressed for Christine Nilsson or Jenny Lind, and that she sang with "utmost purity of style and brilliancy of execution."[25] As was the custom, Gerster was supported by a small company of soloists: Emily Winant, contralto; Signor A. Montegriffo, tenor; Adolphe Fischer, cello; and Lavallée; with George W. Colby as accompanist. Compared with the critical reception given Gerster, others rarely received more than passing mention. The *Baltimore Sun* noted that Lavallée's solos "were artistically rendered," while Philadelphia's *Sunday Item* reported only that he "played charmingly."[26] After the Lincoln Hall performance on 24 May, the *Washington Post* was more generous, claiming, "he played well, perhaps with too much tendency toward a robust idea of instrumental delivery, but with an evidence of high artistic ability, and his hearers were very much pleased." The same critic described the Miller piano as "hardly equal to the demands of the pianist, although in his later performance of Chopin's 'Berceuse' and 'Polonaise in A-flat,' some of its peculiarities of tone were forgotten in the brilliance of his execution."[27] After the final concert, Gerster sailed for Europe on board the *Britannia* and Lavallée returned to Boston by way of the Fall River Line.

At about the time of his return to Boston, Lavallée accepted a teaching post at the Petersilea Academy of Music.[28] The Academy was one of many music schools that had proliferated since the 1860s. It competed with the much larger New England Conservatory (NEC) by concentrating on piano instruction.[29] Its founders were Franz Petersilea and his son Carlyle. (See figure 6.2) Franz was born near Weimar in 1813 and studied with Hummel before immigrating to the United States in the 1830s, where he taught, performed, and published a number of compositions. After studies with his father, Carlyle enrolled at the Leipzig Conservatory, where his teachers were Plaidy, Wenzel, and Moscheles. He then studied briefly with Hans von Bülow and toured Germany before returning to the United States. Once back in Boston, he took up a teaching position at the NEC and resumed his performing career.[30] By the 1880s, many critics considered Carlyle Petersilea to be one of the finest pianists of his generation. The critic at the *New York Times* wrote that his playing "revealed intelligence, a thorough command of technique, and a firm and clean touch."[31] The New York–based *Musical Courier*, the leading US music periodical of the era, ranked him among the "best living" pianists.[32] He later tried his hand at writing novels as well as, in 1905, a collection of essays titled *Letters from the Spirit World*, which he claimed was "written through the mediumship of Carlyle Petersilea by his father, Franz Petersilea, and other celebrities."

Petersilea had left the security of the NEC in 1871 to start the Academy with his father, whose *System for the Piano-forte* provided the basis for instruction.[33] Located on Central Court, in the business district, it opened on 18 September and grew steadily over its first decade.[34] After

Figure 6.2
Carlyle Petersilea,
who in 1871 co-
founded the Petersilea
Academy of Music in
Boston with his father
Franz, and in 1881
hired Lavallée to
teach piano.

the first year, the school moved to more spacious quarters at 339 Washington Street, and four years later it reopened in a four-storey building
at 279–281 Columbus Avenue, near Berkeley Street. A large part of Petersilea's success came from flexible policies and fees that were affordable
for the middle class. Petersilea's aim was "to educate thorough musicians, fine soloists and teachers, upon the most reasonable terms."[35] For
a place in a class of four, tuition ranged from $10 to $15 per term. The
Academy offered instruction in piano, organ, violin, flute, harmony, and
composition, supplemented with classes in elocution, modern languages,
drawing, and painting. It issued its diplomas "according to the improvement of a scholar at the end of each year."[36] By the time Lavallée
arrived in Boston, the Academy's advertisements claimed an "alliance"
with London's Royal Academy of Music and with Petersilea's alma
mater, Leipzig's Royal Conservatory of Music.[37] This agreement allowed
some students to spend their final year studying in Europe.

During the summer break, Lavallée returned to a job that he had held almost a decade earlier: performing with and conducting Hall's Band and Orchestra on board the steamer *Bristol* of the Fall River Line. (See figure 6.3) The Gilded Age brought a sense of style that the wily Jim Fisk Jr had anticipated, and the ships of the Fall River Line had grown yet more luxurious in the decade since his death. While dining on crab and lobster, first-class passengers were entertained by an orchestra playing selections from the operas of Balfe, Audran, Offenbach, and other popular composers. Lavallée's *Bristol March* was the opening number at the promenade concerts in June. While the shooting of President Garfield, on 2 July, dampened the holiday mood that year, the crowds were still out on the Fourth of July, when concert programs announced the "special engagement for the season of M. Calixa Lavallée, the eminent Piano Virtuoso from the Conservatory of Paris."[38] As soloist, he performed the March and Presto from Weber's *Konzertstück*, op. 79, accompanied by the small orchestra, while the *Bristol* plied the waters of Narragansett Bay and Long Island Sound, and travellers sipped champagne.

Figure 6.3
The steamer *Bristol* of James Fisk Jr's Fall River Line, on which Lavallée conducted Hall's Band and Orchestra and played the piano.

In December 1881, Lavallée published the song "l'Absence" in Aristide Filiatreault's new *Album musical*. Earlier that year, Filiatreault had entered a partnership with the journalist Rémi Tremblay in the satirical publication *Le Canard*. The two were neighbours, living on opposite sides of Saint-Denis Street in Montreal, and it was Tremblay who wrote the words to "l'Absence," perhaps working with Lavallée on a suggestion from Filiatreault.[39] The song's strophic form, narrow vocal range, and easy piano accompaniment made it accessible to amateurs, following the goals of the periodical in which it was published. The lyrics begin: "Te souvient-il quand ta chère présence Troublait mes sens, exaltait mon amour? Seul, aujourd'hui, je pleure ton absence, jetant ma plainte aux échos d'alentour" (Do you remember when your sweet presence troubled my senses, and exalted my love? Alone today, I lament your absence, throwing my sorrow to the resounding echoes round about). At the time, Tremblay was editor of *Le Courrier de Montréal*, a newspaper that also served as the mouthpiece of La Fraternelle, a secret society he belonged to that advocated the repatriation of French-Canadian immigrants to the US.[40] The words of the song might be viewed in this light. What they meant to Lavallée, more than a year after leaving Canada and his family, are less clear, especially as he chose not to bring them to live with him.

❖❖❖

Around the same time, Lavallée found a producer for his opera *The Widow*. Opportunities had improved in the decade since he had completed the still-unperformed *Peacocks in Difficulties*. After a short-lived interst in French comic opera, US audiences were again enamoured of light opera in English, and opera companies were looking to expand their repertoire.[41] The 1880 premiere of Dudley Buck's comic opera *Deseret* at Haverly's Theater in New York received mixed reviews but showed U.S. composers that they had a chance of having their works produced; this may have revived Lavallée's interest in the theatre.[42] Little is known of how Lavallée came to compose *The Widow*, and questions remain about the identity of his collaborator. The Boston firm of J.M. Russell published the opera's libretto in 1881 and the vocal score early in 1882, crediting the "book" to an unknown writer named Frank

H. Nelson. The *New York Clipper* referred to Lavallée and Nelson as *The Widow*'s "Boston authors," and a newspaper article referred to Nelson as a US actor.[43] It seems likely that this was the same Frank Nelson who was then stage manager of the Boylston Museum, a Boston variety-show theatre.[44] Another report, however, suggested that the name might be a "mere pseudonym for some one of the other sex."[45] It may then have been that Nelson's role was that of translator or adaptor, as it was the only work that he published and the opera's bilingual title, *The Widow / La Veuve*, may indicate that the original was in French. Lavallée's dedication of the score to the Count of Premio-Réal and his completing it while in Canada lend further weight to that possibility. Yet another possibility is that *The Widow* is a reworking of *Peacocks in Difficulties / Lou-Lou*.

The story bears some similarities to Voltaire's *Nanine*, a three-act comedy from 1748, with a plot that revolves around the title character's right to marry whom she wishes. Voltaire had in turn adapted his play from Samuel Richardson's 1740 novel *Pamela*.[46] Whatever the source, *The Widow*'s libretto has many of the elements of opéra bouffe. Its three acts are divided into distinct numbers, separated by a minimum of dialogue. Events take place in the south of France, near the Spanish border, in the last decade of the eighteenth century, where the main characters, Doña Paquita (the widow) and the young Nanine, are both in search of husbands. The plot makes liberal use of misunderstanding and mistaken identity to create comic situations. In the end, all is resolved and each character has a mate.

In the fall of 1881, Charles D. Hess's newly formed Acme Opera Company secured the rights to stage *The Widow*.[47] (See figure 6.4) Hess had been an impresario since the 1860s. He had managed the Parepa-Rosa Opera Company, the Kellogg Opera Troupe, and Hess Grand Opera Company.[48] Early in 1881, he was co-manager of the Strakosch-Hess Opera Company, a troupe that presented a season at New York's Fifth Avenue Theater, performing works as diverse as *Aida* and *The Bohemian Girl*.[49] That spring, Hess divided this troupe to create the Acme Olivette Company, a touring troupe devoted to performing the English translation of Edmond Audran's *Les Noces d'Olivette*, the 1879 opéra comique that had been a huge hit in London, where it was performed in an English-

Figure 6.4  The Hess Acme Opera Company (en route to Mexico in 1883),
the company that gave the first performances of Lavallée's comic opera
*The Widow* in 1881.

language adaptation.[50] Hess's company opened at New York's Bijou
Opera House on 19 March 1881 with a cast headed by Selina Dolaro,
W.T. Carleton, and Henry Peakes.[51] He then expanded the troupe's reper-
toire and changed its name to the Hess Acme Opera Company (HAOC).
Lavallée likely approached Hess in July during his company's season in
Boston, and soon after Hess purchased exclusive rights to stage *The
Widow*. Music journals printed several false reports of the first perform-
ance of the opera in the fall of 1881. Hess may have planned the premiere
for New Orleans.[52] His troupe had a successful engagement at the city's
St Charles Theater in October, but performed only Audran's *Olivette* and
*The Mascot*.[53] In December, the first issue of *L'Album musical* incorrectly
noted that the premiere of *The Widow* had taken place in New Orleans
on 23 November.[54] In fact, by late November the company was working
its way northward and *The Widow* was as yet unperformed.

The premiere finally took place on 24 February 1882, during the company's two-week engagement at Chicago's Grand Opera House, with
Louise Searle as the widow and Adelaide Randall as Nanine.[55] Judging
from the critical reception the next day, the cast was not ready for opening night. While the *Chicago Tribune*'s critic found the staging attractive, he described the performance as unsteady, with the musicians and

the singers "constantly at variance, the fault being about equally divided."[56] The quality of the soloists' performances were uneven at best:

> Of the cast the chief honors belong to Miss Adelaide Randall (Nanine) and to Mr Mark Smith (Marquis) ... Miss Searle as Paquita was unfamiliar with her part and did not do herself justice. Miss Wadsworth can neither sing nor act, and ought to be promptly relegated to chorus work. The same might be said of Mr H.F. Fairweather. Mr Walter Allen has not the voice demanded for the part of Duc de Trop, and but little conception of the opportunities for comic acting it affords. Mr Henry Peakes should have had this place in the cast. Mr James G. Peakes was an excellent Passepoil, and Mr Wilkie sang fairly when he knew his music and was about as woodeny in action as tenors usually are.[57]

The chorus, on the other hand, the critic reported, was "strong and well-balanced and sang in tune" and with "considerable animation."[58] There was no mention of the stage direction or the playing of the orchestra.

Chicago's *Daily Inter-Ocean* noted "incongruities" in the libretto but described the opening-night audience as enthusiastic, and the music as "bright and breezy." It later published two selections in its *Musical Supplement*. With some caveats, the *Tribune* reported favourably of the opera itself. In his review of the first performance, the *Tribune*'s critic described the first act of the libretto as "the brightest and best, although the last contains the greater number of amusing situations." Overall, he expected it would be "improved and made more consistent" through repeated performance. He reported Lavallée's music to be "exceedingly bright and lively" and "the choruses are spirited and tuneful, while some of the principal melodies are equal to the best we have heard in comic opera. This is especially true of the waltz song in the first act, which is a little gem in the way of light music, and of Paquita's song, 'Free from all care are we.' Some of the concerted music also is admirable, and the impression made by the piece after a single hearing is a favorable one. There is no reason why it should not have a long and prosperous career."[59] The critic found a lack of originality in the score, but accepted that that was "more or less true of all light operatic work. M. Lavallée has sinned no

more than others, and is fortunate enough to be able to prove the possession of sound musical ideas of his own besides those he has 'assimi-
lated.'"[60] What *The Widow* needed was a more polished performance
and a cast that was determined to make it a success.

*The Widow*'s promising debut ended the HAOC's profitable engagement in Chicago. After sold-out performances on Friday evening and
Saturday afternoon, Hess replaced the scheduled *Olivette* with *The Widow*
on Sunday, the closing night of the season. Hess's company attracted
strong attendance and mostly favourable reviews throughout its engagement. Although negative criticism was the exception, the *Tribune*'s
critic took one more shot at the performers on the closing day, suggesting that by "eliminating at least three comparatively useless members
and adding another soprano to relieve Miss Randall from the amount of
work she is compelled to do, the company might take first rank as a
comic opera combination."[61] Hess may have taken such advice seriously,
as he made several cast changes in the weeks that followed.

From Chicago, Hess brought his troupe and Lavallée's opera through
the Midwest and eastward. The company had a repertoire of four works:
*The Widow*, *Olivette*, *The Mascot*, and *Chimes of Normandy*. Newspaper
reports indicate good audiences for *The Widow* and the other operas
through much of the tour. The *St Paul and Minneapolis Pioneer Press*
reported that "every seat was taken" for the premiere of *The Widow* in
Saint Paul and that "expectations were not disappointed."[62] In Baltimore, the *Sun* reported the opera "successfully rendered," with Randall
and Searle "much applauded in their respective roles."[63] Hess gave the
Washington premiere of *The Widow* at Ford's Theatre on 25 April 1882,
when it competed with Strakosch's production of Gounod's *Faust* at
the National Theatre, with Clara Louise Kellogg singing the role of
Marguerite.[64] The *Washington Star* reported that President Chester A.
Arthur (who had succeeded the assassinated Garfield) attended the opera
on 25 April but did not state which opera.[65] The *Washington Post* gave
Strakosch's company much more attention, but lauded Randall's performance and called *The Widow* "pretty, sparkling and catchy."[66]

On 1 May 1882, the company opened its season at New York's Standard Theatre, on West 33rd Street, with a week of *The Mascot*, while advertising that *The Widow* was "in active preparation."[67] It opened a

week later, on 8 May, to mixed reviews. The *New York Herald's* critic wrote favourably of the music. Admitting that at times the score suggested "portions of 'Olivette' and 'The Mascot,'" or "airs from some of the Italian operas," he noted that there were "several bright solos and some spirited choruses which are well written, original and effective. The orchestration throughout is quite good, and on the whole the music of 'The Widow' is very tuneful and much of it likely to become popular."[68] The *New York Clipper* reported that "the music, with the admirable way in which it was sung, will give the opera whatever success it may attain, as the story is improbable and poorly developed, and the words are lacking in wit and point."[69] Similarly, the *Herald* described the dialogue as being "of the trashiest nature, and what success the comic opera made last evening was due to the bright music and the liberal manner in which the piece was produced."[70] The *New York Times's* critic was more severe: "There is in the production an utter lack of probability or coherence, and when the performance was not dreary it was because the inherent absurdity struck the audience in a way very different from that intended."[71] The critical assault on the libretto gave the impression that the entire production was a disaster and obscured the more favourable points made in the reviews.

Most of the singers had by this time grown comfortable with their roles and were well received. Zelda Seguin had taken over the role of Doña Paquita, and was well known to New Yorkers (as Zelda Harrison). The *Times* reported that she "acted and sang well," and remained a local favourite.[72] The *New York Clipper* described her as a "great favorite" in the city, and reported that she "met with a very hearty reception. She acted the part [of Doña Paquita] with much of her old-time grace, and sang it in capital voice."[73] The *Herald* reported that Seguin "received a flattering welcome, as it was the occasion of her first appearance in years, [and] was very successful as the widow."[74] Others were equally well received. Randall, the *Herald* reported, sang "charmingly as Nanine and acted with grace," the chorus and orchestra performed "with great spirit," and "the piece was admirably mounted and the costumes were pretty and effective."[75]

The *Music Trade Review* responded by criticizing the critics: "A new opera, especially when composed by a musician living in this country, whose identity is familiar, is received here with a prejudice which foreign operas are not subjected to. Mr Calixa Lavallée, a Boston musician, has composed an opera called 'The Widow' which has more musical value than the majority of light operas produced in this city during the last two decades, and the only reason which prevents it from becoming a success is the fact that he does not reside three thousand miles away from here." After providing a synopsis of the plot, he noted that, "upon this slight fabric Mr Lavallée has built an excellent light opera, full of rich solos and delightful concerted numbers and effective choruses."[76] By the time these comments appeared in print, *The Widow* had been pulled. It had opened to a small audience on a Monday night during a heavy spring storm. When attendance did not improve on Tuesday night or at the Wednesday matinee, Hess replaced it with *The Mascot*. *The Chimes of Normandy* then began a week-long run, followed by *Olivette*, and then a new entry into the company's repertoire, Gilbert and Sullivan's *H.M.S. Pinafore*, which closed the season in New York.

*The Widow* remained in the HAOC's repertoire after New York but its popularity was short-lived. New performers assumed several of the leading roles with success. Emma Elsner (who had played Olivette) and a young singer referred to only as Miss St Quinten both performed the role of Doña Paquita, while Louise Eissing played Nanine. James Peakes and Mark Smith remained popular performers in their respective roles of Passepoil and Marquis Beausant. All five were well received during the HAOC's summer-long engagement at St Louis's "Indoor and Al fresco" Pickwick Theatre. The city's critics wrote extensively and quite flatteringly about *The Widow* during its week-long run.[77] Gradually, though, Hess staged *The Widow* less often, as he added more works to the company's repertoire. These were mostly older operas, such as Auber's *Fra Diavolo* (1830), Balfe's *The Bohemian Girl* (1843), and Flotow's *Martha* (1847). *The Widow* was still in the HAOC's repertoire when the company returned to New Orleans in December 1882, but it was not performed.[78] A year later, Hess did not include it in the company's list of works, and in the fall of 1884, he folded the company when he became the manager of Chicago's Grand Opera House.[79]

❖❖❖

Lavallée had continued to perform frequently in and around Boston. In the fall and winter of 1881, he organized a series of chamber music concerts with Daisey Hall, De Sève, Fries, and the accompanist Albert F. Conant. The venue was Union Hall, the 520-seat room in the Young Men's Christian Union building on Boylston (midway between Tremont and Washington).[80] The program was much the same as he had performed while in Quebec: Wolff's *Duo brillant*, for violin and piano, Mendelssohn's *Capriccio brilliant* in B minor, op. 22, Chopin's *Berceuse* in D-flat major, op. 57 and an unspecified Chopin étude, the final movment of Beethoven's Piano Sonata in F minor ("Appassionata"), Saint-Saëns's *Danse Macabre*, and Mendelssohn's Piano Trio No. 2 in C minor, op. 66. *The Folio* called a performance on 2 December "a fine success in every respect."[81] The *Boston Transcript*'s critic was terse, writing that Lavallée's playing was "clear, his phrasing intelligible and his general style refined."[82] The *Boston Evening Journal* provided thorough coverage of the concert, despite also publishing a lengthy review of Adelina Patti's concert, which took place the same night. It drew special attention to the chamber music on the program, claiming Lavallée played best in the Mendelssohn Trio.[83]

*The Widow* production required Lavallée to travel in the early months of 1882. Before leaving, he performed with Alfred De Sève, whose career had flourished in 1881.[84] Together, they appeared in Lowell at a fair organized by the Montreal-born cornetist E.N. Lafricain, a resident of Boston who also led Lowell's town French-Canadian band.[85] Some time after this, Lavallée set out to join Hess's troupe. He was present for some of the performances through the early months of 1882. Cleveland newspapers noted his presence at a press reception after the premiere of the opera in that city in early April. One of his reasons for joining the company seems to have been to help new cast members with their parts. An annotated copy of the vocal score, dedicated by him to Zelda Seguin, is contained in the Tams-Witmark Collection at the University of Wisconsin. During the summer of 1882, Lavallée made what appears to have been his final engagement on board the *Bristol*. He then took a short holiday at Saratoga, New York, after what had been a taxing few months.

On returning to Boston, Lavallée resumed his teaching schedule. In the early months of 1882, he had moved from Roxbury to a rooming house at 35 Essex Street, just a few blocks from the Miller piano company's building.[86] While there appears to be no evidence that Lavallée had a romantic relationship with Emilia de Angelis, at about the time he moved out of her home, she and her husband separated, and they later divorced. She took a suite in Tremont House, a hotel located near the Boston Common. There she lived and taught; on many occasions over the next eight years, she and Lavallée had their students give joint recitals.

Lavallée performed frequently in the 1882–83 season. On 1 October 1882, he took part in a benefit concert for Notre Dame Church in Worcester, Massachusetts. Frantz Prume was also on the program, along with his new wife, the young singer Hortense Leduc. This may have been Lavallée's final appearance with his old partner. Soon after, Prume travelled to Europe where he remained for the next two years, after which he rarely left Montreal. The event in Worcester was one of many for Lavallée that fall. He appeared with soprano Fanny Kellogg in the "Bay State Course" and the "Melrose Course," two concert series aimed at making classical music accessible to working-class audiences.[87] On 5 December, he took part in the Boston Philharmonic Orchestra's concert at Music Hall, performing Mendelssohn's Concerto in G minor, and "Venezia e Napoli – Tarantella," from Liszt's *Les Années de pèlerinages*.

As busy as Lavallée may have been with teaching and concerts, he was also hard at work on a new opera in 1881. In October of that year, the *New York Clipper* reported that he was composing the music for "an American satire."[88] The title of this work was *TIQ (The Indian Question), Settled at Last*, and its libretto was written by two little-known writers, Will F. Sage and Phillips Hawley.[89] In January 1882, the Kiralfy Brothers, who specialized in "spectacles" and were then performing *The Black Crook* in Boston, were reported to have purchased performance rights for *TIQ* and intended to produce it in New York. This plan eventually fell through, and in the summer of 1883, Edward H. Hastings, manager of Boston's Bijou Theatre, announced plans to produce it during the 1883–84 season.[90] Russell Brothers secured the copyright while Oliver Ditson published the score of this "melodramatic musical satire." The *Musical Courier* received an advance copy of the libretto in August 1883 and called the text "bright and witty, being a satire on the Indian question. Indians, commissioners, United States soldiers and missionaries are the principal personages who aid in settling that much-mixed question." The note concluded "Mr Lavallée is so excellent a musician that we have no doubt the opera is a meritorious work, and we hope it will be a success."[91] In November, the same journal mentioned that the score contained a number of copying errors, but described the faults as meaning "nothing in a work of the character of 'T.I.Q.' Melodies it has, and a good stage representation will no doubt make it a success."[92]

The subject was right out of the news of the day. Sitting Bull had returned to the US from Saskatchewan in the summer of 1881, surrendering himself to authorities six years after the Battle of Little Bighorn. By the summer of 1882, the fifty-one-year-old holy man was still in custody, with US authorities trying to determine what to do with him. It was in part the absurdity of the situation – where despite its resources, the US government was frustrated by the resolve of an individual – that Lavallée, Sage, and Hawley explored in a work that was influenced by the growing success of Gilbert and Sullivan. The story is a parody of the conflict between the Lakota Sioux Indians and the US government. The main characters are Sitting Bull, Colonel Carter, and Simeon Simon, the head of the commissioners. As Act One opens, the Indians are peacefully co-existing with nearby soldiers, who have failed to either corrupt or defeat them. Missionaries arrive from Boston to convert the "heathens," and commissioners arrive from Washington to destroy them through alcohol. The act ends in a finale with all of the braves drunk, Sitting Bull admonishing them, and the commissioners singing of their success. In Act Two, Sitting Bull asserts himself, capturing the whites and forcing them to either live peacefully with the Indians or leave his land. Some depart, others choose to live with the Lakota, and the opera ends in the grand finale "Joyful, Joyful" in which the chorus and soloists sing the praises of love and marriage, as "the Indian question" is settled.

While stylistically *TIQ* was firmly in the comic opera tradition, its subject was uniquely American, and chosen by Lavallée for that reason. The St Louis *Spectator* reported that he had "taken a native pride in referring to [*The Widow*] as an American opera."[93] The claim was somewhat overstated, given the absence of an American musical language, but justified in the choice of the Sitting Bull story. As cultural historian Susan Scheckel has written, "by claiming Indians, with their long history and mysterious origins, as part of their own national story, nineteenth-century Americans found a way to ground national identity in the distant, inaccessible, 'immemorial past.'"[94] This romanticized image of First Nations is projected in Henry Russell's "The Indian Hunter" (1837), in John W. Hutchinson's "The Indian's Lament" (1847), and in numerous other popular songs throughout the nineteenth century.[95] Pocahontas, in particular, was a fixture in nineteenth-century literature and theatre, and it was natural to bring an Indian subject into opera. In comedy, flawed characters offer the most opportunities for humour, and in *TIQ* Sitting Bull is the only heroic character. The score abounds with tuneful, rhythmic music, and a number of First Nations' music clichés that function in much the same way that Sullivan's *faux* Japanese music does in *The Mikado*, providing local colour. The opening number begins with falling perfect fifths, a common motif for "Indian music," as well as the use of duple meter and drone – in this case, the twenty measures of E-major chords that lead to the entry of a chorus of "maidens and braves," who sing the praises of Sitting Bull and dance. The most thorough-going attempt to create "Indian music" occurs in No. 22, "We Never Tell a Lie," in which the Lakota have captured Carter and Simon. The braves sing of the principles they live by while the maidens sing a wordless melody ("Ah!") above an accompaniment that simulates drums with alternating eighth-note figures in the bass, separated by a perfect fifth, then blow into 'fish horns' as they dance around their captives.[96] (See appendix 2)

Despite the advance acclaim, *TIQ* seems never to have been performed. The reason for this remains unknown. In his desire to create an "American opera," Lavallée may simply have chosen subject matter that was too potentially offensive for managers to risk financing. Sitting Bull and his followers are seen as peaceful and stoic; most of the whites are portrayed as malevolent and incompetent, or simply naive. Some members of the Bijou Theatre's audience might have taken particular offence to Theodosia and her fellow Boston missionaries (Fitzgigle, Fitznoodle, Fitzgerald, Fitzgibbon, etc.), who are most concerned with finding husbands. Others might have been uncomfortable with the scene in Act Two in which Simeon and Carter are tied up and forced to plead for their lives. Even though the scene is intended to be humorous, some would certainly be reminded of Little Bighorn, and that the "question" really had not yet been settled. After many years of working in the theatre, Lavallée should have known the line beyond which satire becomes objectionable. His treatment was comic, but the work's subject material was both serious and unresolved – and perhaps simply too hazardous for a theatre manager to experiment with. The North American subject may have proved *TIQ*'s undoing, but ironically, a year after Lavallée completed *TIQ*, entertainer Bill Cody established Buffalo Bill's Wild West, a travelling show that in 1885 featured none other than Sitting Bull himself.

At about the same time as Lavallée was hoping to get *TIQ* produced, he revealed his views on suitable subjects for US composers in a *Boston Home Journal* article. His topic was the opera *Pounce & Company, Or, Capital Vs. Labor* by the Boston composer Benjamin Woolf. He congratulated Woolf on his success but questioned the reason for the opera's English setting, writing that "the labor question is a universal one, and one that interests this country as well as others."[97] He continued, "I think that we have enough subjects now in this country that might suffice an author to write a genuine American plot."[98] Nevertheless, whether discouraged by the fate of *TIQ* or having simply lost interest in opera, Lavallée composed no more works for the theatre.

The article on *Pounce & Company* was one of several that Lavallée published at this time, relating his views on a number of musical issues. The *Home Journal*, one of Boston's more intellectual newspapers, with extensive coverage of the city's cultural life, provided a forum for his ideas. He was well qualified to write the first in this series. Its topic was Emma Albani, who was on a high-profile tour of North America. While in Boston, she sang Marguerite in *Faust*, Elsa in *Lohengrin*, and several other roles, and on 1 March, she held court for fellow French Canadians at her suite in Tremont House. Lavallée's article, published two days later, sketched out the early years of Albani's life for readers, who were largely unfamiliar with the singer's childhood in Canada. He made no mention of the fact that he had briefly been a part of her circle before her move to Albany.[99] Other articles also began essentially as reviews, but explored criticisms he had of the musical world. In one, he lampooned US critics who were attempting to emulate the style of Oscar Wilde, who was then visiting the country. In another, he criticized opera's star system, arguing that opera managers too often emphasized the star performer while disregarding the other elements of the production, and leaving little to sustain a performance when the star decides to take an "off night." In a review of a performance by William Sherwood, Lavallée turned his attention to the lack of opportunities for Boston's poor to study music.[100]

Lavallée's interest in education and critical issues led him, in the summer of 1883, to attend the seventh annual meeting of the Music Teachers' National Association (MTNA) in Providence, Rhode Island. This organization had been established in 1876 and held annual meetings at which music teachers discussed pedagogical and aesthetic issues, socialized, and attended and took part in recitals. Lavallée was part of a contingent from Boston that included Petersilea, Sherwood, and Maas. He read his paper, titled "Style and Expression," on 6 July, and it seems to have been well received.[101] The three-day gathering ended that afternoon with a clam bake at Rocky Point, a familiar spot for Lavallée, although he may not have mentioned to any of his new friends just how much time he had spent there in the 1860s. With the MTNA, he found a group of like-minded individuals aiming to raise the standards of music making in the US. His special interest was in expanding the opportunities for composers to have their music performed. He found a sympathetic ear in the organization's president, E.M. Bowman, when he suggested presenting a concert of music by US composers at the 1884 meeting in Cleveland, a simple recital that changed the course of his career.[102]

While Lavallée's career flourished in the early 1880s and was about to rise to a new level, his achievements came at the expense of his family. Joséphine had remained behind in Quebec City with her mother and their children. In the spring of 1881, at the time of the census, they were still residing on Sainte-Ursule Street. The expiry of the lease on that house in May likely prompted their move to more modest accommodations. One can only speculate on why, three years after his departure from Canada, Lavallée had not brought them to Boston. He appears to have been sending money, enabling Calixa Jr to continue his studies at the Collège de Lévis.[103] As his own studies in Saint-Hyacinthe had been cut short, providing his son with a good education in French may have been a priority. There is no evidence that Lavallée intended to return to Canada. He was putting all of his effort into making his name in Boston and, with *The Widow* and *TIQ*, throughout the US. Thus, it seems likely that they would have remained separated were it not for a tragedy in the summer of 1883. Joséphine, her mother, Calixa Jr, and Raoul were then in Saint-Jean-Port-Joli, a village on the south shore of the Saint Lawrence River, seventy-five kilometres northeast of Quebec City, where village historian Gérard Ouellet wrote that they lived in considerable poverty.[104] Calixa Jr was then still registered at the Collège de Lévis when he died of what may have been appendicitis.[105] He was buried in an unmarked grave in the village cemetery on 14 August, and soon after, Joséphine relocated to Boston with Raoul, then three years old.[106]

# 7

## American Concerts and the MTNA
### 1884–1891

To Mr Lavallee (a foreigner, too, be it said to the shame of some of our native artists) belongs the honor of inaugurating the present movement, on behalf of American composers and their works. The history of American art will accord to him [this] distinction.

Wilson G. Smith
Cleveland, Ohio, 15 March 1886[1]

The arrival in Boston of Joséphine and Raoul brought a sense of closure to Lavallée's life in Canada, as he focused all of his energy on professional and social activities in the US. He continued many of the pursuits begun during the preceding three years in the US. He contributed to the cultural life of the French-Canadian population of New England, especially through benefit performances. He continued to perform with familiar colleagues, to compose and find new outlets for his works, and to teach in the Miller building and at the Petersilea Academy. But in this final period of his life, his main project was to improve the place of composers in the US. His work with the Music Teachers' National Association and the American College of Musicians came to dominate his professional life and were remembered on his death as his greatest legacy.

By the time of Joséphine's move to Boston, Lavallée had achieved financial stability. During these busy and productive years, he had successfully established himself in a competitive city. He had sufficient income from teaching, performing, writing, and composing for the family to move into a new three-storey townhouse on Worthington Street, just south of Huntington Avenue in the middle-class Mission Hill district. Over the next seven years, they moved several times within the same area, and finally, as the family's fortunes declined, to nearby Dorchester.[2]

February 1884 brought the premiere of a new work, an offertory commissioned by the Boston archdiocese for performance at the dedication of St Peter's Church in the Dorchester district. Lavallée began setting the biblical text *Tu es Petrus* (Matthew 16–18) soon after completing TIQ. He composed the piece for soprano, chorus (SATB), orchestra, and organ. White, Smith & Company published a vocal score with a new English text by the music historian and translator Louis Elson, titled *Glory, Blessing, Praise and Honor*.[3] Lavallée's choral writing shifts between homophonic and contrapuntal textures; a brief bass recitative brings the first half of the work to a quiet close before the entrance of the soprano solo. Lavallée conducted a forty-piece orchestra and one-hundred-voice choir at the dedication on 18 February 1884. Joseph G. Lennon, Lavallée's colleague from the Petersilea Academy and the MTNA, played the organ. In a preview that was published the day before the premiere, the *Home Journal* described *Tu es Petrus* as "overflowing with rich and solid harmony." The same critic found Lavallée's work both "earnest and scholarly: One listens to the opening chorus of *Tu es Petrus* but to experience an animated impression of its religious and artistic value," and admonished Protestant churches for neglecting music, accusing them of having a "disreputable attitude in regard to music and art in general."[4] In a biographical article published a year later, the *Musical Courier* reported that the work was "considered to rank with the compositions of the great masters" and called its performance "a genuine success."[5]

The first half of 1884 was well filled with teaching and concerts. He took part in several events with the organist Joseph Lennon. Like Joséphine, the thirty-three-year-old Lennon had been born and raised in Lowell, and like Lavallée, he had studied in Paris and was committed to bringing good music to all classes of society. In April, Lavallée joined Lennon at the Easter performance of the Catholic Union, and on 29 May, he performed at the concert given by Lennon's Boston Oratorio Society. At several concerts that spring, Lavallée created opportunities for his more talented students. One of these was the pianist T. Reeves Jones, who, at a recital on 24 January, accompanied Lavallée in the Weber *Konzertstück*, op. 79 and played the second piano in Saint-Saëns's *Danse macabre*, op. 40. Both T. Reeves Jones and vocalist Maude Nichols performed at Lavallée's concert at Union Hall on 26 March. On 18 June, Lavallée staged a graduates' concert for his students at the Petersilea Academy.[6] He was also by then serving as temporary head of the school, since Carlyle Petersilea had left with a group of students for a year in Europe.[7] On top of all this, Lavallée was committing to memory the works he would be performing at his MTNA recital. Late in June, he set off for Cleveland.

Performances of American art music were rare in the early 1880s.[8] In the summer of 1882, an article in *The Folio* described encouraging American composers as "an uphill business," due to Theodore Thomas and "the storm of German music" then sweeping country.[9] It criticized Theodore Thomas in particular for not playing the music of US composers, but most concert-giving societies and soloists performed only European music.[10] Lavallée had himself been performing European music almost exclusively for ten years. His thinking on repertoire changed after he settled in the US. It seems that playing a program of music composed by one's U.S. contemporaries was something no one had ever considered doing. The novelty of Lavallée's planned recital for the 1884 MTNA meeting drew the attention of the *Musical Courier*, which reported that it had "never been done before, and the result of the recital will certainly be looked forward to with interest."[11] So two months before the event, he had already received some unexpected publicity from a major music publication.

With a recital of works by US musicians, Lavallée aimed to demonstrate the quality of music being written at the time. The concert took place on the morning of 3 July 1884 at Cleveland's Case Hall. It was paired with an essay by the Boston musician George Whiting titled "An American School of Composition." Lavallée opened the 'American concert' with pieces by Foote, Smith, and Emery, and short piano pieces made up the majority of the program. (See figure 7.1) Appearing with him was the New York soprano Nettie M. Dunlap, who sang Dudley Buck's "Sunset" and Louisa Cappiani's "Ave Maria," and Cleveland's Schubert Quartet, which performed works by Johann H. Beck, Silas G.

'American concert,' 3 July 1884

1. a) Gavotte                             Arthur Foote
 b) Mazurka                        Wilson G. Smith
 c) Sarabande and Scherzo        Stephen A. Emery
              Lavallée (piano)

2. a) Adagio from Quartet in C minor      J.H. Beck
 b) A Movement for Strings           S.G. Pratt
Schubert Quartet

3. a) Cradle Song                     John Orth
 b) Scherzo, Op. 41              William Mason
 c) Spring Idyl                      J.K. Paine
 d) Volktanz                       Louis Maas
              Lavallée (piano)

4. a) Sunset                      Dudley Buck
 b) Ave Maria                  Luisa Cappiani
    Nettie M. Dunlap (soprano) and Lavallée (piano)

5. a) Regrets b) Prelude       William H. Sherwood
 c) Vagabond Dance          Ferdinand Dewey
 d) Scherzino                G.W. Chadwick
              Lavallée (piano)

6. Trio in G min.                W.W. Gilchrist
   (Scherzo, Adagio, Finale-Vivace)
     Richard Zeckwer (piano), S.E. Jacobsohn (violin),
         Charles Heydler (cello)

7. a) Romance sans paroles – "The Tempest"   Carlyle Petersilea
    (transcription)
 b) Feu Follet                   Emile Liebling
 c) Gavotte                     C.L. Capen
Encore: Étude de concert, Le Papillon     Calixa Lavallée
              Lavallée (piano)

Figure 7.1  Program of Lavallée's 1884 'American concert' at the Music Teachers'
National Association meeting in Cleveland, 3 July 1884.

Pratt, and William W. Gilchrist.[12] Lavallée closed the concert with three piano solos and added his own étude *Le Papillon* as an encore.

In the afternoon, delegates formally discussed Whiting's paper, the concert, and the state of American composition. These discussions led to the drafting of a letter to members of the Senate and House of Representatives, pressing for the passage of copyright legislation for music.[13] The success of Lavallée's recital was immediately apparent, and MTNA members elected him as vice-president for the state of Massachusetts on the final day of the conference.[14] The novel idea of promoting the work of American musicians also caught the attention of journalists covering the event. The *Cleveland Herald* reported that George Whiting's essay "was followed by one of the most interesting of many musical treats thus enjoyed by the members of the association, namely, the recital of pianoforte compositions of native and resident composers, by Calixa Lavallée, of Boston, a most excellent pianist, by the way, who played the compositions of his brother-musicians."[15] *The Folio* praised Lavallée's "well-deserved success in Cleveland" and boldly predicted that his concert had inaugurated a "new departure in the musical history of this country."[16] It was a turning point for Lavallée. Having discovered a new way forward, he devoted himself entirely to the project of gaining acceptance of American music, and the MTNA would be central to his efforts as he quickly becoming the leading advocate of US composers.

The most controversial issue debated by the MTNA during the mid-1880s was the purpose of the proposed American College of Musicians (ACM). In 1883, the MTNA assigned a committee to study the feasibility of such an organization to examine and accredit qualified musicians and issue certificates, and the committee's work was to be reviewed at the 1884 Cleveland meeting. In the weeks leading up to that meeting, members engaged in a heated debate on the ACM's merits. The *Musical Courier* published pleas for calm from Petersilea, then in Berlin, and others. The quarrel may have reminded Lavallée of his efforts to create a conservatory in Quebec. Opposition again came from music teachers who were concerned that the creation of the College would have an adverse effect on their incomes. Lavallée wrote of his support for the College, adding that as "every true musician cannot help supporting every effort to elevate his art, as well as protect himself, it is bound to succeed."[17] Despite the strong opposition, the MTNA did approve the creation of the College. H.S. Perkins, president of the MTNA, concluded that the ACM was "inaugurated under most favorable auspices of the good cause of music and of the music-teachers of America," with the goal of examining "music-teachers, and certificating the proficient."[18] The founding committee established departments for piano, organ, voice, theory, and rudiments, and elected an eighteen-person examining board. The board was to hold examinations two days before the start of each MTNA convention.[19] The ACM would offer three grades or degrees: (1) Master of Musical Art; (2) Fellow of the College of Musicians; and (3) Certificate of Competency, and membership in the College of Musicians.[20]

Following his successful trip to Ohio, Lavallée suffered disappointment later that summer. Joséphine had become pregnant soon after arriving in Boston. On 16 August, she gave birth to a fourth son. The infant was baptized Jules, after Jules Hone, just as Prume and del Vecchio had named a child after that close mutual friend and colleague. The happy event was short-lived as the child refused to nurse, or Joséphine was unable to breastfeed, and he died two weeks later.[21] The cause of death was recorded as marasmus, a wasting away of the body. Joséphine is not known to have given birth to any other children.

Despite the loss, Lavallée threw himself into what was emerging as a time of change on many fronts. While in mourning, he busied himself with teaching, writing, and preparing for concerts. In November, he followed up his Cleveland recital with an article arguing in favour of studying music in the US. In a reference to Darwin's theory of evolution, he claimed that, musically, the United States was "walking, quite erect."[22] Political changes were also in the works that fall as Massachusetts's voters helped to elect Grover Cleveland as president, the first Democrat in office since 1861. A month later, Bostonians chose Hugh O'Brien as their first Irish-Catholic mayor.[23]

❖❖❖

Mayor O'Brien was the guest of honour on 21 January 1885 at a Meionaon Hall benefit concert for Boston's French-language church, Notre-Dame-des-Victoires, for which land had recently been purchased on Isabella Street. Referring to Boston as "the most Catholic city in the country," the new mayor drew cheers from the audience.[24] Lavallée led a cast of performers that evening that included Maude Nichols, harpist Florence Sherwood, and Alfred De Sève and his wife, Joséphine Bruneau. It was just one of several community events that occupied his time. In addition, he became president of La Prévoyance (known in English as "The French Language Society for Mutual Help"), an organization that assisted French-speaking immigrants. It was also a social organization and held an annual ball, for which Hall's Band provided the music in April 1885.

Lavallée followed the Cleveland concert with two 'American concerts' at Union Hall in the spring of 1885. The small advertisements he placed in local newspapers mentioned only his name, although the concerts themselves involved several of his students and colleagues. A piano trio comprising Ernst Jonas (cello), Alfred De Sève (violin), and Arthur Foote (piano) took part in the first concert; the pianist Milo Benedict played at the second; and the young soprano Maude Nichols, a student of Ellen D. Barrett at the Petersilea Academy, sang on both nights. Over the two evenings the performers played twenty-seven compositions: songs, solo piano pieces, and chamber works. Lavallée placed works by established New England composers – such as George Chadwick, John Knowles Paine, and Arthur Foote – alongside pieces by Wilson G. Smith, Ernst Jonas, and other lesser-known composers. He also performed five works of his own.

The *Boston Evening Journal* reported Union Hall to have been "packed with an enthusiastic audience" on 10 March.[25] The Union Hall performances attracted the attention of local newspapers and national music journals. The *Boston Herald* wrote that Nichols's "delightfully clear, true, fresh tones, her utter lack of affectation, and her native musical instinct [made] each of her songs alike enjoyable."[26] Lavallée came in for praise, in part because of his determination, performing despite being seriously ill. This may have been an early sign of the tuberculosis that would before long take his life. Despite this, the *Musical Courier* called his 10 March performance "extraordinarily fine," and performing in this condition may have endeared him to some of his listeners.[27] The *Boston Home Journal* acknowledged that Lavallée had performed "at a disadvantage which few could have undergone with so much pluck, and with a result so successful." Although "physically disabled and in constant suffering from pain, his piano playing was delightful and artistic to a degree that he has not yet manifested here."[28] The effects of Lavallée's illness conjured up a romantic image of the suffering, tubercular artist, enhancing Lavallée's reputation and bringing more attention to new American music.

Many, but not all, of the compositions performed received similar acclaim.[29] The unnamed critic at the *Boston Herald* derided works he felt to be inferior. The "'Scherzo' by William Mason, of New York," he wrote, was "a very unsatisfactory selection," and William Sherwood's piece "did not give evidence of his possession of anything more than the most commonplace attainments as a composer." The same critic praised the works of Jonas and Maas ("notably good evidence of the distinctive originality and ability of these composers") and the compositions of Smith, Buck, and Lavallée. He called Arthur Foote's Piano Trio "the most important work," and wrote that it "created a very distinct impression, and its merits as the work of a thoroughly trained musician, with a well-developed and melodious style, were quickly and thoroughly appreciated." The *Home Journal's* critic called the Trio an "elegant" work, created from "rich and original material." Benedict won acclaim for the maturity of his music, described as "pregnant with mature thought." It was the sort of critical evaluation Lavallée was hoping for: people were talking about American music. All of this publicity also helped to secure his own place in Boston's musical community, and nationally. Both *The Folio* and the *Musical Courier* printed cover stories about him that spring.[30] The *Boston Herald* reported that Lavallée had "fully demonstrated the wisdom of his action in bringing the resident composers thus prominently to the front."[31] Following the second concert, the *Home Journal* noted that Lavallée's recitals would "take rank among the praiseworthy events of the musical season."[32] In Boston, with its full schedule of concerts, getting noticed to this extent was already an achievement.

At some point late in 1884 or in the early months of 1885, Lavallée's youngest brother, Joseph, arrived in Boston with his wife, Isabella, and moved into Calixa and Joséphine's home on Delle Avenue. Up to this point there had been a number of references to Joseph at concerts in Quebec, where he usually played the cello or trombone. Little else is known of his life. The 1881 Canadian Census recorded him as being twenty-one and residing with his parents and siblings. Lavallée was in a position to help his younger brother find work, with Hall's Band or other ensembles. Joseph was in need of employment, as Isabella was then pregnant. He was listed as a music teacher, residing at 5 Delle Avenue, when the baby, which they named Calixa, was born. The infant died three months later, on 26 July, and as with Jules Lavallée, the cause of death was recorded as marasmus.[33]

❖❖❖

The ACM remained an extremely divisive issue. In the weeks leading up to the 1885 MTNA meeting and the first round of ACM exams, the *Musical Courier* and other journals again became a forum for the continuing dispute. While the possible failure to gain entry into the College was an understandable concern for some, others' motives for criticizing the organization are less clear. Following the 1884 meeting, some opponents of the ACM attempted to discredit the MTNA. An article in *Werner's Voice Magazine* warned that "the College has great obstacles to overcome, not the least being the antagonism of prominent musicians."[34] One particularly vocal opponent was Frederic Archer, an English organist who, like Lavallée, had settled in the United States in 1880.[35] When Archer claimed that the association was little more than an advertising vehicle for piano manufacturers, Lavallée published a bristling rebuttal, referring to Archer as having for several years made "himself conspicuous by criticizing everything that belongs to this country, and he has probably succeeded in gaining a certain notoriety in a restricted circle by trying to demonstrate to the circle that he is a great man. I admire Mr Archer's efforts in his own behalf, but when he attacks a body of musicians who represent almost every State in the Union, it is about time to say 'Halte la,' and to compare notes and see who are the persons that are working for a cause, and who is the one person that is simply trying to further his own selfish purposes."[36] Turning the argument from the issue of the piano companies, which may have been a legitimate criticism, Lavallée emphasizes the national scope of the MTNA and the wider good it served.[37] The personal nature of the dispute was a sign of the intensity of the disputes.

Much of the opposition came from the musical establishment, and especially from some of Boston's musical Brahmins. The small group of musicians that headed the city's top institutions wielded considerable influence and had no desire to weaken their place nationally. Outside of Boston, many resented this centralizing of music education. This conflict was apparent in an 1884 article in the *Chicago Indicator* deriding Boston's elite for disenfranchising many of the city's most talented musicians: "The conceit and impudent ignorance, gilded over with a superficial lacquer of musical slang, which characterizes the fashionable public of Boston, have prevented extensive recognition of talents the chief musical city of Europe delights to honor, and the whole professional life of an artist, no matter how talented, is, in that city, at the mercy of a heartless, well organized, and shrewd ring."[38] As a central figure in this "ring," Eben Tourjée, a co-founder of the MTNA and its first president, called for the abolition of both the ACM and the MTNA.[39] As director of the New England Conservatory, Tourjée feared that the ACM could undermine his business by allowing music teachers to gain accreditation without studying at institutions such as his. The forthcoming MTNA meeting was to be the biggest yet.

. With the financial support of the arts patron Jeannette Thurber, the MTNA raised its profile to a new level with its 1885 summer meeting in New York. Both the lectures and concerts took place in the Academy of Music, an impractical venue considering its size.[40] For the concerts, the association engaged an orchestra made up of musicians from Theodore Thomas's ensemble. This orchestra presented a program of seven orchestral works, three pieces for solo piano, and Paine's "Violin Sonata," op. 24. (See figure 7.2) The eclectic program reflected Anglo-American composers' continued preference for vocal genres, and their use of a wide range of modern and archaic forms. Maas's symphonic evocation of the American landscape was juxtaposed with Sternberg's gavotte and Paine's "Sonata."[41] The *New York Times* described the conference's proceedings each day, devoting a column to the concert and referring to it as "an imposing affair." The unnamed critic offered a frank discussion of the works. He referred to Gleason's *Montezuma* as "effective, although imitative of Wagner in its restlessness." Paine's "Violin Sonata" was "somewhat dry," but Maas' *American Symphony* he described as a "tone poem

'American Orchestral Concert,' 3 July 1885

Orchestra organised by Mr. Roebbelen

Part I

1. Introduction to Act 2                     Frederic Grant Gleason
   of "Montezuma"

2. Offertory, "Tu es Petrus" – soprano,          Calixa Lavallée
   bass, chorus

3. Sonata – violin and piano                     John K. Paine
   S.E. Jacobsohn, violin; William H. Sherwood, piano

4. Two movts from an "American Symphony"          Louis Maas
   a) Chorus "An Indian Legend (Adagio, Andante)
   b) "The Chase" (Scherzo)
                  Chorus and orchestra

5. Selections from opera "Zenobia"               Silas G. Pratt
   a) Chorus of Priests and Worshipers
   b) Closing ensemble
                  Solo voices, chorus and orchestra

Part II

6. a) Gavotte in C                          Constantin Sternberg
   b) Nocturne                              William Burr, Jr.
   c) Scherzo, Op. 41                       William Mason
                  William H. Sherwood, piano

7. Symphonic Overture to "Marmion"               Dudley Buck

8. Second Piano Concerto                     Robert Goldbeck
                  Robert Goldbeck, piano

9. Final chorus from the cantata,           Smith N. Penfield
   "the 18th Psalm"

Figure 7.2   The program of the 'American Orchestral Concert,' Music Teachers'
National Association meeting, New York, 2 July 1885.

of considerable richness of color, though not striking in respect of orig-inality."[42] The review provided rare exposure for American concert music and the MTNA in one of the country's most influential newspapers. Laval-lée's contribution was his offertory *Tu es Petrus*, which he conducted. The work and performance were well received, with the *New York Times* calling the offertory "a stirring specimen of semi-operatic music in the Italian style," and reported it to have been "loudly applauded."[43]

Lavallée's stature within the MTNA grew substantially as a result of the 'American concerts.' At the business meeting in New York he made two gestures that reflected his influence. The first was a speech in favour of Boston as the site of the 1886 MTNA conference. Many representa-tives from the Midwest had wanted to hold the next meeting in Ohio or Illinois, but were opposed by members from other parts of the country. New York's *Morning Journal* described the scene in detail:

Somebody shouted from the orchestra seats, "Where is Lavallée? Let us hear from Lavallée." All eyes were turned to a struggle going on between three men in the front row of the parquet circle, two of whom were trying to force a third and much smaller man on his feet, which was finally accomplished, when the little man, who proved to be Calixa Lavallée, extended both hands in the air, and commenced in a trembling voice, which grew firm and strong as he proceeded, a ringing speech in favor of Boston. "I offer you," said Lavallée, "on behalf of the people of Boston, the Tremont Temple, with its grand organ and seats for three thousand people. We offer you a grand orchestra for the production of original works, for our association is proving year after year that there are some composers in this country. We also offer a trained chorus of four hundred voices. And finally we offer you an American city of musical culture, where you will have the greatest reception you ever received."[44]

Charles L. Capen, correspondent for the *Musical Courier*, called it a "telling, forceful and decisive speech in favor of the metropolis of New England." He described being "somewhat awed that day by the praise-worthy audacity of our enthusiastic Frenchman." The effect of the speech, he reported, was an "ardent and unanimous decision in favor of

Boston as the next place of meeting."[45] After delegates approved the site of the 1886 meeting, they selected Lavallée to head the program committee for the Boston meeting.[46] He then attempted to pass a resolution influencing the nature of the concerts. As the *Musical Courier* noted, "after Boston had been chosen as the place of the next meeting, our energetic and radical friend, Mr Lavallée, tried to carry through a proposition to instruct the Program Committee to admit none but American compositions to the program of next year's recitals and concerts."[47] Lavallée had motioned to change the MTNA's name to the "American Society for the Promotion of Musical Art." Members rejected both proposals.[48] Nevertheless, Lavallée returned to Boston energized and with a busy fall and winter ahead.

❖❖❖

Lavallée was likely back in New York in early August for the funeral of Ulysses S. Grant. The Union general and former president died on 23 July. An estimated one and a half million people were reported to be on the streets and sidewalks on 8 August to witness the funeral procession. Civil War veterans from throughout the north and even from some Confederate states regrouped for the event.

Conflicts in both Canada and the US impinged on Lavallée's world in the summer and fall of 1885. In Canada, the Northwest Rebellion and the arrest of Louis Riel had divided the country along linguistic and religious lines.[49] For years, the charismatic and controversial leader of Manitoba's Métis had been a provocative symbol of the Catholic presence in the West. His interests, and those of First Nations peoples generally, were at odds with the expansionist goals of capitalists. At the conclusion of his five-day trial in Regina for treason, Judge Hugh Richardson sentenced Riel to death, with the execution to take place on 18 September. It was carried out on 16 November to the general satisfaction of the population of Ontario and outrage in Quebec and in the expatriate French-Canadian communities in the US. Lavallée immediately offered to stage benefit concerts for Riel's family, and at least one took place – on 28 December 1885 in Fall River, Massachusetts. (See figure 7.3)

While the Riel trial and subsequent execution ran its course, the French Canadians of Fall River were embroiled in what became known

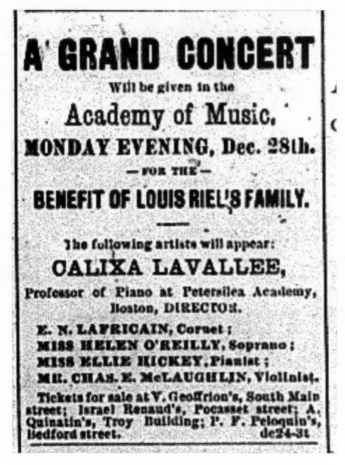

Figure 7.3 Advertisement for Lavallée's December 1885 benefit concert in Fall River, Massachusetts, for Louis Riel's family.

as the "Flint Affair." The conflict arose over the selection of a new priest in the parish of Flint Village, where the community demanded that a French-Canadian pastor succeed their late "patriot priest" Pierre Jean-Baptiste Bédard.[50] The Irish-born Bishop Thomas F. Hendricken, who advocated assimilation and who had been angered by Bédard's frequent circumvention of his authority, insisted on installing an Irish priest in the parish. For nearly eighteen months, francophone parishioners attempted to drive out each of the new appointees through boycotts and intimidation.[51] The dispute brought to the surface wider tensions between the two immigrant communities. In an oral history of French-Canadian life in New England's mill towns, Philippe Lamay describes the frequent conflicts between Irish-Americans and French-Canadians in New England in the nineteenth century: "Our troubles came mostly, not to say entirely, from Irish people who, it seems, were afraid that we had come here to take their jobs away from them in the mills and who tried hard to send us back to Canada by making life impossible for us in America."[52] For Lavallée, this conflict was quite the opposite of his experience in Quebec City, where he had become an integral part of the Irish community. Although his experience, as a professional and resident of Boston, was quite different from the workers in the mill towns, he understood and sympathized with their lot, as no doubt did Joséphine. The Flint Affair was only part of a wider Anglo-American discrimination against immigrants and, in particular, French Canadians. An article in the upmarket *New England Magazine* emphasized the "Old World" form of Catholicism practiced by French Canadians, describing them as "being almost Chinese in their exclusiveness."[53] Some of the opposition Lavallée faced in his work with the MTNA in the 1880s should be read in the context of his place as an outsider in old Protestant Boston.

In the wake of Riel's hanging and the Flint Affair, Fall River became a centre for protest, led by the city's French-language newspaper, *L'Indépendant*, and the base of the newly created Ligue des Patriotes. The Ligue adopted a militant stand on francophone rights: "First, to offer all French Canadians the opportunity to cultivate their intelligence and their physiques without being obliged to join foreign clubs. Second, to cultivate that military spirit and that national pride that makes a people strong. To prepare, with time, a generation that is courageous, strong, valiant, and virile."[54] Lavallée composed two patriotic songs at this time. "Restons Français," for solo voice, was the Ligue's song and first performed at its 7 February 1886 meeting. In contrast to the dignified "O Canada," "Restons Français" expressed the anger of 1885 through Lavallée's driving rhythms and a quick tempo, and through Rémi Tremblay's combative lyrics:

Le ciel est noir, l'orage s'amoncèle    The sky is black, the storm
                                         grows near

| | |
|---|---|
| Et la discorde allume ses brandons; | And the discord lights up its torch; |
| Pour étayer un pouvoir qui chancèle, | To shore up a tottering power, |
| Le fanatisme arme ses mirmidons. | Fanaticism arms its minions. |

The song's refrain urged members to "remain Frenchmen" (see appendix 2). Both in tone and style, it recalls Lavallée's "Flag of Green," of 1866. At about the same time, Lavallée appears to have completed a setting of Louis Fréchette's poem "Vive la France."[55] The words of this short piece for male chorus are no less emphatic:

| | |
|---|---|
| O Canadiens, rallions nous, | O Canadians, let us rally |
| Et près du vieux drapeau, | And by the old flag, |
| Symbole d'espérance | symbol of hope |
| Ensemble crions à genoux: | Together on our knees we cry: |
| Vive la France! | Vive la France! |

This song or other settings of these words may have found their way into oral culture, as there are a number of references to it in the early years of the twentieth century. The Canadian soldier, diplomat, and governor general Georges-Philéas Vanier cites a battlefield singing of Fréchette's words while in France during the First World War, after which, he writes, the soldiers marched to the tune of "O Carillon."[56]

Throughout 1885, Lavallée was busy composing. He was at work on an oratorio that was likely intended for performance by Lennon's Boston Oratorio Society. He was also busy with a number of popular works that were likely to bring in some money. Some of Lavallée's most popular works of the 1880s were pieces he had scored for band or band instruments. While Lavallée's *Bristol March* does not appear to have been published and is presumed lost, in 1885, W.H. Cundy published three overtures for band: *Golden Fleece*, *The King of Diamonds*, and *Bridal Rose*. Of these, the best known was *Bridal Rose*, a work that is still heard occasionally and has been recorded a number of times.[57] Lavallée also received a commission from the Boston City Council for music to be performed at the unveiling of a fountain dedicated to the former mayor Theodore Lyman, Jr. Coincidentally, the fountain was located in

Eaton Square, directly in front of St Peter's Church. Designed by M.D. Jones, the thirty-six-foot monument was made of bronzed iron and zinc, and ornamented with swans and dragons.[58] Organizers had Lavallée set James Russell Lowell's poem "The Fountain," and he composed a 'descriptive fantasy' on the words. Although strophic, it cannot quite be described as a song with band accompaniment. The conception may have been more instrumental than vocal and includes some awkward text setting. To allow the voice to be heard over the accompaniment, the band and vocalist exchange phrases through much of the piece. The phrases are not all in two- or four-bar units but, rather, are surprisingly irregular. At the 24 October 1885 unveiling, Lavallée conducted the Germania Band before a crowd of hundreds of spectators and dignitaries. Mayor O'Brien officiated. As at the unveiling of New York's Lafayette statue, speeches alternated with performances, in this case of works by Wagner, Meyerbeer, and Handel. Boston City Council's record of the unveiling contained a vocal score of Lavallée's work and a photograph of the ceremony. (See figure 7.4)

❖❖❖

New Year's Day 1886 brought Raoul's sixth birthday and the start of the most productive year of Lavallée's life. He announced details of the second part of his 'American concert' series early in January and held these performances in the early months of 1886.[59] No record of the first of these three concerts appears in music journals or in Boston newspapers. The other two, on 26 February and 28 April, were modestly advertised but widely reviewed. The venue was the former Chickering building at 156 Tremont Street, opposite the Boston Common and next door to the Boston Conservatory, on Piano Row.[60] The Henry F. Miller Piano Company had acquired the building in the fall of 1885 and renamed the intimate recital room Miller Hall.[61] Many of the performers from the previous year's concerts took part. They followed these performances with a final 'American concert' on 1 May, under Petersilea's name.

Lavallée selected mostly piano music for the February and April concerts and performed most of the pieces himself. On 26 February, he played works by Wilson G. Smith and Emil Liebling, and closed the concert with

Figure 7.4 Photograph of Lavallée conducting the Germania Band in a performance of his fantasia *The Fountain* at the unveiling of a fountain in Eaton Square, Boston, 24 October 1885.

four compositions by Gottschalk. Before this performance, he had only presented the music of living musicians in his 'American concerts.' By including these older works at the 26 February performance, he may have hoped to attract listeners familiar with Gottschalk's music, and to show that there were at least the beginnings of an American tradition. The pieces may have also enabled Lavallée to demonstrate his technique to better advantage. Critics reported favourably about both the music and his interpretations. Louis Maas wrote that Lavallée performed Gottschalk's *Tremolo, grand étude de concert*, op. 58 "with immense bravura," and by concluding with the Gottschalk pieces, "displayed a virtuosity that excited the admiration of all present."[62] Lavallée did not repeat the virtuoso pieces in the fifth concert on 28 April 1886, but performed from memory eleven pieces by ten composers.[63] (See figure 7.5) The *Boston Home Journal* reported that he "again displayed his rare technical ability as a pianist, as well as a wonderful memory, though the effect of his playing was frequently marred by an inconsiderate use of the pedal."[64] By "inconsiderate" the critic might have meant "inordinate" or "ill-considered,"

Fifth 'American concert' 28 April 1886, Miller Hall, Boston

1. a) Lullaby; Morceau a la Gavotte    Otto Floersheim
   b) Album Leaf; and Étude de Concert    F.W. Metcalf
   c) Scherzino    G.W. Chadwick
   d) Danse caractéristique    John Orth
   e) Polonaise    Edgar Sherwood
   　　　　　Lavallée, piano

2. Four songs: (a) "Thou Art So    G.W. Chadwick
   Like a Flower"
   (b) "In By-Gone Days"
   (c) "He Loves Me"
   (d) "The Miller's Daughter"
   　　　Maude Nichols, soprano; Lavallée, piano

3. Piano Concerto in E minor (first mov't)    Milo Benedict
   Benedict, piano; Petersilea, piano accompaniment

4. (a) "Far from Home"    Theodore Hurman
   (b) "My Heart is Like the Gloomy Night"    William Rhode
    (c) "The Young May Moon"    William Rhode
   　　　Maude Nichols, soprano; Lavallée, piano

5. (a) Allegro Patetico, Op. 12    William H Sherwood
   (b) Preludium – Rain Drops    Carl V. Lachmund
   (c) Berceuse; Scherzo    William Mason
   (d) Valse de Salon, Op. 39    Calixa Lavallée
   (e) Le Papillon, Op. 18    Calixa Lavallée
   　　　　　Lavallée, piano

6. Scherzo in E – for two pianos    Carl Walter
   　　　　Lavallée and Petersilea

Figure 7.5  The program of Lavallée's fifth 'American concert,' held at Miller Hall
on 28 April 1886. At this and the previous performance. he played most of the
compositions himself.

but one cannot be sure. Both Maude Nichols and Milo Benedict performed at the 1886 concerts. The *Boston Traveller* reported that Nichols's interpretations of songs by Lavallée and Arthur Foote "made a tasteful niche" in the 26 February program.[65] On 28 April, she performed songs by Chadwick, Hurman, and Rhode. At the first concert, Benedict performed three of his smaller compositions, and at the second he played the first movement of his Piano Concerto in E minor. The latter work, the *Home Journal* reported, "created a sensation of the best kind."[66] Petersilea played an orchestral reduction on a second piano in the Concerto, and together he and Benedict performed the entire work at Petersilea's 'American concert' on 1 May.

The most substantial of Lavallée's compositions heard at the 1886 concerts was his Suite for Piano and Cello, op. 40. It had been heard a year earlier, on 10 March 1885, when Lavallée performed it at Union Hall with cellist Ernst Jonas.[67] Among the other cellists to play it were Wulf Fries, who played it twice in the spring of 1886, and Cleveland cellist Charles Heydler, who played it at the 1890 MTNA meeting in Detroit. Despite the four-movement form (Allegro appassionata, Scherzo, Romanza, and Presto à la tarantelle), the work was sometimes referred to as a concerto. Lavallée is not known to have orchestrated it or even to have written out the piano part. It remained unpublished and is now presumed lost. What is known of the Suite comes from concert reviews. The *Boston Traveller* and the *Musical Courier* published substantial commentaries after the performance on 26 February 1886. The unnamed critic of the *Boston Traveller*, then in a dispute with Lavallée, called the Suite an interesting work that "will serve as a stepping stone to the enjoyment of the purest style of chamber music in the minds of those yet unlearned." He went on to write: "Yet only in the last movement does the composer give each instrument an individual freedom, or forget that good musicianship demands more than the stating of the harmonies, in arpeggios, or any pliant form of accompaniment in the one instrument, while the other has the theme. The writing for the piano forte is brilliant, though often at the expense of repose. Mr Lavallée writes tunefully for both instruments, but with an eagerness to do more than is compatible with a well-poised working out of ideas. The Scherzo is a clever dance, the Romance more sentimental than fraught with sentiment."[68] In his concert review for the *Musical Courier*, Louis Maas reveals more of the structure and character of the piece. He describes the first movement, in F-sharp minor, as having "a fine first motive, with a well contrasted second theme, and [being] well conceived and logically carried out and developed throughout. The scherzo is perhaps the most original, and quite delighted the audience with its quaint rhythms. The romanza is mainly sustained by the 'cello, while the tarantella is a dashing and brilliant piece of music, making a fine ending to a charming composition."[69] Since he knew Lavallée, Maas may have looked closely at the cello score and attended rehearsals of the piece. Comments on the performances on 1 May 1886 and in 1890 provided little additional information about the work. The critic at the *Detroit Free Press* described the *Suite* as "fresh, spontaneous and melodious, the workmanship revealing the thorough musician." It described Lavallée's compositional style as "rather Gallic, but none the less praiseworthy."[70]

Critics provided little information about the audiences that the 'American concerts' attracted. They frequently resort to commonplace formulae Couture had described a decade earlier. In the spring of 1885, Boston's *Evening Traveller* reported that Lavallée had drawn "a very large audience," and the *Transcript* that he had performed "before a large audience, which was very generous with applause."[71] The *Home Journal* did, however, report the 10 March 1885 performance to have been sold out.[72] Thomas Tapper, writing in *The Folio*, attributed the success of that concert to "the interest felt in the matter by 'musical Boston.'"[73] The *Globe* reported that the concert on 28 April 1886 was "enjoyed by [a] good-sized audience,"[74] while the *Herald* described the audience as having been "of limited proportion, but quite enthusiastic in its appreciation of the selections."[75] None of the reviews provided details on who the audience members were, or if the concerts attracted many individuals from outside of the musical community.

Lavallée's goal was to, in time, make serious music popular. Partly to that end, he published a number of accessible pieces in 1886. His main publisher was White, Smith & Company.[76] In 1886, it published Lavallée's edition of a collection of classical sonatas, as well as Stamaty's *Rythme des doigts* (Rhythm of the Fingers), a method that Marmontel described as "the most complete, sensible, and logical technical treatise that we

278

know."⁷⁷ Among Lavallée's original piano pieces, *Le Papillon* had become quite popular. It was republished in 1884 by Arthur P. Schmidt, along with the two other pieces that had been first published in Paris, and sold well enough for other publishers to begin picking it up. White, Smith & Company published it in 1886, then again in 1892, including it in the *Classical Collection for the Forte Piano*, thus making it more widely known to amateur pianists.⁷⁸ *Le Papillon* was one of three works for piano published by White, Smith & Company in 1886. The two others were the "Première Valse de Salon," op. 39 and the *Mouvement à la Pavane*, op. 41. Lavallée performed the graceful *Première Valse* at his concert on 28 April 1886. The Chicago pianist Nellie Stevens played the *Mouvement* at the Indiana Music Teachers' Association meeting in June 1888.⁷⁹ Both are of intermediate difficulty and intended for amateurs.

White, Smith & Company published two songs by Lavallée in 1886: "Andalouse," op. 38 and "Spring Flowers." The first of these, a bolero for soprano, is Lavallée's most ambitious art song and his only published song on a text by the French romantic poet Alfred de Musset. Musset wrote the poem in 1829 about his first lover, and called it "Madame La Marquise."⁸⁰ Lavallée's reason for changing the title lies at least partly in his treatment of the text. He omits stanzas ten and eleven, which contain direct references to "La Marquise." His setting of the remaining stanzas is the freest adaptation of any of the poems among his vocal works. (See figure 7.6) He sets eight of Musset's twelve verses, using the first as a refrain (which was freely adapted in the English version):

| | |
|---|---|
| Vous connaisez que j'ai pour mie | To all is known my heart is captured |
| Une Adalouse a l'œil lutin, | An Andalusian with eyes of night |
| Et sur mon cœur, tout endormie | Has with her glance, my soul enraptured, |
| Je la berce jusqu'au matin | By her side is my sole delight.⁸¹ |

Lavallée's setting for soprano is curious, given the male perspective of Musset's words. After his close collaboration with Tancrède Trudel, he worked mostly with female vocalists and dedicated this song to the

| Stanza | Text | Translation | Key area | mm | Indication |
|---|---|---|---|---|---|
| 1 | Vous connaissez que j'ai pour mie Une Andalouse a l'oeil lutin | To all is known my heart is captured an Andalusian with eyes of nigh | i | 1–10 | Tempo di bolero p |
| 3 | Gais chérubins veillez sur elle Planez, oiseaux sur votre nid | Bright cherubims hold vigil o'er her and peaceful birdlings round her sweep | i | 11–19 | P |
| vocalese | ah!... | | V | 19–25 | p cresc. F |
| 1 | Vous connaissez que j'ai pour mie Une Andalouse a l'oeil lutin | To all is known my heart is capture an Andalusian with eyes of night | i | 25–39 | p/ff |
| 4 | Car toute chose nous convie D'oublier tout pour notre amour | Each passing thought but flies onto her Each fancy unto her doth rove | VI | 40–49 | P |
| 7 | Oh! viens dans mon ame froissée | Oh come! they presence peace is sending | III | 50–57 | p poco cresc. |
| 6 (1st part) | Restons l'étoile vagabonde Dont les sages ont peur de loin | Oh star of love upon us beaming Some mortals fear thee from afar | flat IV | 58–61 | P |
| vocalese | ah!... | ah!... | | 62–66 | F |
| 6 (2nd part) | Peut être en emportant le monde peut être en emportant le monde | But peace in thy mild light is streaming Yes peace in thy calm light is streaming | VI | 66–72 | Pp |
| 9 (1st part) | Donne moi ma belle Maitresse Un beau baiser car je le veux | Give me love thy fond caresses For they belong by right to me | flat | 73–81 | P |
| piano | ---------- | ----------- | flat IV | 82–85 | F |
| 9 (2nd part) | Raconter ma longue détresse En carressant tes beaux cheveux | Oh let me fondle thus thy tresses Then I shall blest and happy be... | i | 86–93 | tranquillo/ |
| vocalese | ah!... | ah!... | V | 93–98 | cresc/sf |
| 1 | Vous connaissez que j'ai pour mie Une Andalouse a l'oeil lutin | To all 'tis known my heart is captured an Andalusian with eyes of night | i | 99–134 | pp/ff |

Figure 7.6 Formal structure of Lavallée's song "Andalouse." The table shows his adaptation of Alfred de Musset's text in the column on the left. It is unique among Lavallée's extant songs for its complex form and free adaptation of a poem.

young US soprano Emma Juch. Maude Nichols became the song's principal interpreter, performing it on several occasions. Its intricate rhythms and wide melodic range (stretching just over two octaves) made it a challenge. After an 1885 performance, the *Boston Home Journal* reported that Nichols "rendered it with charming effect, the intricate melismas in which the piece abounds being delivered with rare clearness and nicety."[82] Following another performance, a year later, a review in *The Folio* noted that she "sang the difficult *Bolero* with a brilliancy that fairly electrified the immense audience," and called her "one of the most promising vocal artists of the day."[83] Lavallée evidently saw more potential in the material and also produced a band arrangement. It was performed before a large audience in the Boston Common on 20 June 1886 by the Germania Band, directed by J.B. Claus, with the German-born clarinetist Eustach Strasser as soloist.

Unlike "Andalouse," Lavallée's other published song from 1886, "Spring Flowers," is a gentle, strophic song intended for the salon. The author of the words to this song was D.C. Hall's second daughter Gertrude ("Kittie") Hall.[84] Lavallée dedicated the song to Maude Nichols, in recognition of her interpretations and participation in the 'American concerts,' and she sang it at Petersilea's concert on 1 May 1886.

Despite the concerts, composing, and teaching, Lavallée devoted much of his time during the late months of 1885 and first half of 1886 to gathering public support for the Boston MTNA meeting and to ensuring that the event was a success. Charles Capen acknowledged the effectiveness of Lavallée's work in an article in the *Musical Courier*, writing that, "largely owing to Lavallée's personal efforts, a local interest of unusual import has been awakened here."[85] Lavallée had translated this interest into a "large contribution of money – nearly $2,000 thus far, I am told."[86] Capen added that an interview with Lavallée in the Sunday edition of the *Boston Herald* had helped to raise $100 in twenty-four hours.[87] The *Boston Home Journal* deemed Lavallée's work on behalf of US composers "statesmanlike," and "worthy of respect and admiration."[88] The advance publicity and funds appear to have been unprecedented in the MTNA's brief history and confirmed Lavallée's assertion that Bostonians would embrace the organization. But there were exceptions. The association's success had begun to concern some educators, including

Tourjée, whom Lavallée no doubt had in mind when, just ahead of the 1886 MTNA meeting, he wrote of "a certain class of so-called musicians, who, through bigotry, ignorance, or enviousness, will oppose all professional movements."[89] Again, it was a strong echo of his experience in Quebec City.

The meeting opened at Boston's Tremont Temple on 30 June and ran for three days.[90] Scholarly papers were interspersed with short recitals in sessions devoted to Church Music, the Pianoforte, the Voice, and Music in the Public Schools. All of the concerts featured works by US composers and two orchestral concerts comprised only works by US musicians. Among the seventeen works performed at these two concerts were compositions by members of the Second New England School, such as Chadwick, Whiting, and Paine, and by other leading musicians, such as Dudley Buck and Otto Floersheim. The *Evening Transcript* described the first program as "a fairly representative one, and one could gather from it a pretty adequate notion of the condition of the art of composition in America today."[91] There were overtures, pieces of incidental music, a piano concerto, selections from tone poems, and an oratorio. "Upon the whole," wrote the *Transcript*'s critic, "the showing made last evening was gratifyingly good, though ... let us not go off half-cocked and try to draw comparisons with contemporary French and German music."[92]

At the 1 July concert at Tremont Temple, Lavallée conducted extracts from an oratorio, *The Judgement of Solomon*, that he had begun sketching in the spring of 1885.[93] The two scenes performed were titled "The Judgement of Solomon" and "The March from the Throne." Fanny Kellogg, soprano, Gertrude Edmunds, contralto, and D.M. Babcock, bass, were the soloists. No information has emerged as to how he adapted the biblical text (1 Kings 3: 16-28) or why he chose this very familiar subject.[94] Given the knowledgeable public, presenting a new oratorio was an unpredictable venture in Boston. Lavallée increased the risk by selecting a subject already explored by Handel, and in this case the critic of Boston's *Evening Transcript* was unmoved by what he heard, writing that the two scenes performed "seemed rather cheap and commonplace, albeit not wanting in a certain physical effectiveness."[95] Lavallée seems not to have prepared a reduction with organ accompaniment for publication. No further performances are known to have taken place and the work is now presumed to be lost.

At the business meeting on the afternoon of 2 July 1886, members elected Lavallée president of the MTNA for 1886–87. The vote was between him and John C. Fillmore, of Milwaukee, but Lavallée had the support of the outgoing president, S.N. Penfield, who endorsed Lavallée as his successor:

> You may refer to last year, when American compositions were given in a very worthy manner at the Academy of Music in New York, with a large orchestra and chorus, under the auspices of the President and officers of that year. But what led up to that? One modest piano recital of the year before (applause) by a gentleman who staked his reputation upon it. That, in one sense, was the commencement of this policy of the Music Teachers' National Association, which has now grown to these dimensions. I have the honor to present, as your candidate for the Presidency in the ensuing year, the gentleman who gave that recital, Mr Calixa Lavallée, of Boston. (Prolonged applause.)[96]

After winning the vote, Lavallée promised to "put his heart and soul, and all his energy, into the service of American music," and expressed the hope that members would work together.[97] The result appears to have been viewed favourably. Johannes Wolfram of the Ohio Music Teachers' Association later published a letter congratulating Lavallée and calling the outcome of the election "very satisfactory to Ohio musicians."[98] With the conference over, Lavallée was able to enjoy a little relaxation and spend the Fourth of July holiday with his family, quite possibly joining the thousands of others on the Boston Common for J.B. Claus's concert.

Just as Lavallée's life seemed to be going very well, tragedy struck close to home, when a horseback-riding accident claimed the life of Joseph G. Lennon. The organist had taken an active part in the MTNA meeting and lived just opposite the Lavallées, at 4 Worthington. He had gone out for what the newspapers described as his regular morning ride on Friday, 9 July, and while on Blue Hill Avenue, his horse bolted. He was thrown to the ground and suffered a fractured skull. He was brought back to his home unconscious, and both a physician and a priest arrived soon after. He died the following Tuesday evening, 13 July. The

Lavallées' connections with Lennon were both personal and professional, and as he was single, his friends and colleagues made the funeral arrangements.[99] On Wednesday, Lavallée convened a meeting at Miller Hall to organize the performance of a Requiem Mass by Cherubini and rehearsed with the choir over the next two evenings. The funeral was held at St Peter's on Friday morning, after which Lennon's body was transported by train to Lowell for burial.

After a very quiet August, September began with a surprise announcement from Carlyle Petersilea, who had accepted a teaching position at the New England Conservatory. After fourteen years leading the school he had founded with his father, he announced that he was "disposing" of it.[100] The move may have originated with Tourjée as a means of reducing the competition. If so, it failed to quite achieve that goal. Published on the same page as Petersilea's announcement was another, stating that the name of the Petersilea Academy had been changed to the Massachusetts Academy of Music, Elocution, Languages and Art, and that the only other change was that Petersilea would no longer be teaching there.[101] The school remained in the Columbus Avenue building and classes, it said, would begin on schedule, on 13 September. It listed the members of the piano department as Lavallée, Milo Benedict, Albert Conant, and Carlyle Petersilea's wife ("all admirable exponents of the Petersilea system of pianoforte playing"). Later in the month, Lavallée informed the pubic that he would be teaching at the new Academy two days per week, and the rest of the week at Miller Hall.[102]

It was in the Miller building that Lavallée conducted much of the MTNA's business, and it was a busy time. In the fall, he initiated a dialogue with the British counterpart of the MTNA, the National Society of Professional Musicians (NSPM), and began to implement changes to the way the MTNA's program committee conducted business.[103] This work necessitated travelling to New York for meetings with the association's secretary, Theodore Presser, and program committee chairman, Smith Penfield, as well as travel to other cities. Lavallée also had to contend with the continuing debate about the ACM.[104]

Lavallée's administrative and teaching workload left little time for concerts or composition, but he still found time to play and to take part in activities within the French-Canadian community.[105] In October he performed at a soiree-concert at Fall River's Academy of Music for that city's French church. As an encore at this event, he played a selection of national songs reminiscent of the finale of his cantata of 1879. *L'Indé-pendant* reported that the medley of patriotic songs "enlivened the audience, the melancholy notes of 'Drapeau de Carillon' mixing harmoniously with the joyous sounds of 'Vive la Canadienne' and 'La Claire Fontaine' to move all hearts."[106]

Soon after this event, Lavallée was likely among the thousands of French-Canadian immigrants who travelled to New York for the unveiling of the Statue of Liberty. After numerous delays, Bartholdi's gargantuan symbol of French-US friendship had finally risen over New York's harbour and awaited official honours. Celebrations took place over several days. New York City welcomed the visiting French delegation with numerous dinners and receptions, and a concert of French music at the Academy of Music, conducted by Frank Van der Strucken, on 26 October. The big event took place two days later, beginning with a parade that may have surpassed Grant's funeral in the number of spectators and participants. Thousands of Civil War veterans took part, and dozens of bands were among those marching, as had been the case at the Lafayette unveiling and at Grant's funeral procession. President Cleveland led the procession to the Madison Square viewing stand, from which he watched the rest of the parade and heard each of the bands perform "La Marseillaise."

Back in Boston, Lavallée became more active in French-Canadian affairs and immigrant affairs. Working from his studio on Columbus Avenue, he organized and headed the French Mutual Benevolent Society, an organization that also assisted German-speaking immigrants. In early December, he travelled to Worcester, Massachusetts, for a concert at Mechanics' Hall with Alfred De Sève and his wife, Joséphine Bruneau, and an eleven-year-old boy violinist, Anatole Brazeau. The event was held to raise funds for the city's Naturalization Club and its reading room. So-called 'Naturalization Clubs' had sprung up in many New England towns and cities, in an effort to encourage French Canadians and other immigrants to begin the process of becoming US citizens. While Lavallée's participation in this event clearly suggests his support of naturalization, no evidence has yet emerged that he ever became a US citizen.

❖❖❖

The year's end brought Lavallée's forty-fourth birthday, his nineteenth wedding anniversary, and Raoul's seventh birthday on New Year's Day. Lavallée saw more of his family in 1887 than he had in 1886, but the early months of the new year brought considerable travel. He gave a concert in Washington, DC, on 7 January, stopping in New York for MTNA meetings, and then in the summer, attended the MTNA meeting in Indianapolis. He reviewed concerts for the *Musical Courier*, prepared for his own concerts, and organized several recitals for his students, including one on 30 April with Emilia de Angelis. His workload eventually took its toll on his health.

On 1 February 1887, Boston was visited by some three hundred members of Montreal's Le Trappeur snowshoe club, along with the Victoria Rifles Band, led by Edmond Hardy. Founded in 1883, the club was one of several in Montreal whose activities were centred around but not limited to sports. Its meeting place on Sainte-Elizabeth Street contained a library and rooms for billiards and dining. Outings normally concluded with dinner and music. Politically, Le Trappeur was Liberal. Its members included L.-O. David and Tancrède Trudel, as well as Honoré Beaugrand, Lavallée's old friend from Fall River, who was now the mayor of Montreal and who accompanied the club to Boston.[107] (See figure 7.7) Dressed in their blue costumes, they took part in excursions hosted by Boston's outdoor clubs and in a torchlight march. Boston's Mayor O'Brien hosted a reception for them at city hall and attended their concert at Music Hall. Lavallée did not appear on the program of this event but was likely present, as he had collaborated with Rémi Tremblay on the club's song, "Le Trappeur."[108] Tremblay's lyrics begin with, "Allons, gais trappeurs, chaussons la raquette" (Let's go, gay trappers, put on your snowshoes), before striking a more serious tone, evoking the hardy spirit of early settlers.[109] Lavallée's music may never have been published, but it was likely sung quite often, and it was on the program of the Boston concert along with "Vive la France."[110]

For Lavallée, the most significant aspect of Le Trappeur's 1887 visit to Boston was that it led to his return to Montreal. That return trip might have taken place in the spring of 1887, but it was already late to be planning concerts for the regular concert season. In Montreal, events surrounding Queen Victoria's golden jubilee were already expected to be a

Figure 7.7 Lavallée's friend from the early 1870s, Honoré Beaugrand, who in 1885 was elected mayor of Montreal.

major distraction, and in early May, the planned visit of the Irish nationalist William O'Brien was already causing havoc.[111] And Lavallée might simply have had too many things on his plate already. In addition to his regular teaching duties at both the Massachusetts Academy and at his studio in the Miller building, he was busy preparing for the upcoming MTNA meeting in Indiana.

Whether it was due to his busy schedule or the stress of dealing with constant disputes, Lavallée's fragile health began to decline again in the months leading up to the annual meeting. In May, the *Musical Courier* publicly advised him to reduce his workload, suggesting he "take a short vacation before the meeting in July, in order to be able to preside over the deliberations."[112] This was both an indication of Lavallée's declining health and intimation that debates would be vigorous at the forthcoming gathering in Indiana. By the time Lavallée reached Indianapolis, he could not conceal his exhaustion. On the eve of the conference, *The Folio* published engraved images of the MTNA executives, with President Lavallée in the middle. The eyes remained as sharply focused as ever, but intensely weary, the gaunt and haggard image revealing the extent of his illness.[113] After delivering the opening address on 5 July, Lavallée returned to his hotel room and remained there through much of the conference.[114]

The meeting proceeded with Indiana vice-president William F. Heath in Lavallée's place as chairman. Members discussed aesthetic, theoretical, and pedagogical issues in the formal sessions, and the program included a presentation by Edward Fisher of Toronto.[115] Among the ensembles at the meeting was the Frank Van der Stucken Orchestra. In the winter of 1884–85, Van der Stucken had conducted his professional orchestra in a four-concert series of "novelty concerts," featuring the music of several US-based composers.[116] The Van der Stucken Orchestra and Dannreuther Quartet, both of New York, and the Detroit Philharmonic Club took part in three large concerts. There was a tribute to the recently deceased Franz Liszt and performances of many works by US composers.[117]

The association's business meetings were again highly divisive, sparking debates that continued for months. The presence of piano manufacturers had been a contentious issue since 1885, when they first displayed their products at the New York meeting. As described in the previous chapter, they required pianists under contract to them to perform only on their instruments; as a representative of the Henry F. Miller Piano Company, Lavallée, like many others, had a potential conflict of interest. When the nomination committee, rather than holding a general vote, selected the Indianapolis choral director Max Leckner as president, some members alleged that Lavallée and his coterie had hijacked the association.[118] Without mentioning him by name, voice teacher Clara Brinkerhoff called Leckner a "dummy president" and argued that piano manufacturers were now controlling the organization.[119] The *Musical Courier* called this a "contemptible and vicious falsehood" perpetrated by "unscrupulous humbugs."[120] The issue inevitably reared again when Lavallée was named the MTNA's delegate to the 1888 NSPM congress in London.[121]

Exchanges between British and US professional associations had been a goal since 1885, and Lavallée became the first delegate from the US to visit the UK. In the months leading up to his departure, he continued to teach and to advertise for new students but he reduced his travels and performed very little. By mid-December, he seemed fit as he travelled from Boston to London with Henry Perkins.

The NSPM (now known as the Incorporated Society of Musicians) had been founded in Manchester in 1882 by the organist Dr Henry Hiles, with the goal of developing musical life in the provinces. The society's 1888 meeting, its third, took place in London from 4 to 6 January, with papers on pedagogical and aesthetic issues presented during the day and recitals in the evenings. The opening sessions were held at Drapers' Hall on Throgmorton Street, and the latter part of the meeting took place in the 'old room' of the Painters' Company on Little Trinity Lane. The evening concerts took place at the Prince's Hall, Piccadilly. An informal session was held at the Salisbury Hotel, just off Fleet Street on Wednesday, 3 January. On Thursday, London's Lord Mayor, Sir Polydore de Keyser, officially opened the conference. A controversial figure – Belgian-born and the first Catholic mayor since the Reformation – de Keyser had a keen interest in music education and was, in 1880, a founder of London's Guildhall School of Music. The rest of the morning was devoted to the organization's business.

In the afternoon, it was Lavallée who opened the first formal session with a paper titled "The Advancement of Music in the United States." In it, he outlined musical developments in the United States, concluding that there had been three periods of American music. Up to about 1850, he reported, music had been controlled largely by foreign musicians; from 1850 to 1870, it went through a period of "cheap sentimentality"; since that time it had been making rapid progress. He discussed the work of the MTNA, as well as the larger world of music in the US, citing the large number of musical organisations and institutions, and arguing that the United States had composers worthy of the epithet 'Classical.' The *Boston Herald* reported that he was "listened to with close interest and frequently applauded."[122] Many British and US newspapers reported on the events of the conference. The *London Standard* published Lavallée's paper the next day.[123] The *Musical Times* reported that "an additional charm was given to this year's conference by the attendance of a repre-sentative, and former President of the National Music Teachers' Associ-ation of America [*sic*] – Mr Calixa Lavallée, of Boston – who came to England to assure the members of the interest with which their move-ment was regarded in the United States."[124] The correspondent of one London newspaper, the *Globe*, wrote supportively of Lavallée's paper, acknowledging that the Americas were producing great performers, but questioned his contention that there were native-born composers worthy of being considered 'classical.'[125] It was a fair question at a time when lit-tle US concert music had yet been heard.

Lavallée's paper fit easily into the program. A few of the papers focused on performance issues but most fell somewhere between arts adminis-tration, education, and aesthetics. The chamber concerts consisted entirely of music by members of the organization, which likely pleased Lavallée, at least in intention. On Friday, the Lord Mayor hosted a luncheon for the musicians at the Mansion House. The conference closed with a ban-quet at the Salisbury Hotel in the evening, where Lavallée was the guest of honour. From London, Lavallée and Perkins returned to Liverpool and departed for New York on 8 January on board the *Umbria*.

After the warm reception in England, Lavallée arrived back in New York on 16 January to both acclaim and disapproval.[126] The *Boston Traveller*'s music critic, George Wilson, questioned the choice of Laval-lée as representative to the London conference and the value of the meet-ing itself. The day Lavallée returned, Wilson wrote: "we are very sorry Mr Lavallee went to London; with the kindest of feelings for him per-sonally, he must not be taken as a representative American musician, and we trust neither his music nor his address will get into type in the queen's countree [*sic*]."[127] The *Musical Courier* rebuked Wilson for his criticism, calling Lavallée "truly a representative American musician and composer, if there be any."[128] As proof, it listed Lavallée's achievements and com-positions, emphasizing those works produced or published in Paris.

In Canada, the first issue of *L'Écho musical* contained a biographical article about Lavallée and the second issue contained a story about his trip to London, along with a French translation of his address to the conference. The author of the article and editor of the journal was Charles Labelle. As Léon Derome's son-in-law, Labelle would likely have heard plenty about Lavallée as a boy. He had, of course, also known and worked with him in the 1870s. After performing in *La Dame blanche*, Labelle had gone to Paris to study. On returning to Montreal, he had conducted the choir of Saint-Jacques and then of Notre-Dame.

Just days after the second issue of *L'Écho* came out, Labelle was responsible for organizing the funeral of Lavallée's mother. Charlotte-Caroline Lavallée died on 5 February at the age of sixty-eight. She had raised eight children to adulthood, but was not a public figure and little more is known of her life. The scale of her funeral gives some indication of the Lavallée family's status among the city's musicians. Charles was now managing the family shop, which was by this time a local institution for musicians, and many of the city's choral societies and instrumental ensembles took part in the funeral.[129] Augustin survived his wife by another fifteen years. When he died, in 1903, at the age of eight-six, the funeral cortège was led by his surviving sons, Charles and Joseph, and a group of musicians playing on instruments he had made.[130] Calixa did not return for his mother's funeral in 1888. He had been away from Canada for more than seven years, and his absence likely surprised few.

Later that year, news came of another death in Canada. On 17 October, the Count of Premio-Réal killed himself with a pistol. The forty-five-year-old Count had fallen deeply in debt and chose what many Europeans considered the honourable solution. The Catholic Church took a dim view of suicide and denied him religious rites. Newspapers reported only the presence of many of the city's consuls in his funeral cortège; his body was interred in unconsecrated ground within Belmont Cemetery.[131] A catalogue of his library, produced later that year for the auction of his estate, showed it contained a copy of the Russell edition of *The Widow* that Lavallée had dedicated to him.[132]

Through the early months of 1888, Lavallée seems to have a made a point of taking better care of his health. He generally avoided travel and performed very little, taking part mostly in events in Boston. On 20 March, he and Wulf Fries assisted at Maude Nichols's concert at Bumstead Hall, the recital hall beneath Music Hall. He also hosted at least two social events at his home. *L'Indépendent* referred to the first as a French-Canadian soiree, with literary readings, music, and food. Laval-lée played Gottschalk's *Grande étude de concert*, op. 58 and served his guests oysters.[133] In April, he hosted a political soiree on the future of French Canadians in New England. Speakers included Judge Hugo A. Dubuque.[134]

By this time, Lavallée was completing plans for two concerts in Montreal, and he arrived in the city some time in the middle of May. His arrival coincided with that of Gabriel Dumont, Louis Riel's military com-mander in the Northwest Rebellion, who had been brought to Quebec on a speaking tour organized by L.-O. David.[135] On Thursday, 17 May, Lavallée and Dumont were given a reception at the Le Trappeur's Sainte-Elizabeth Street venue, where Lavallée played his *Paraphrase de concert sur des motifs de 'Faust.'*[136] The concerts took place at Queen's Hall on the next two evenings, 18 and 19 May, and received considerable attention in the press. On Friday, the *Daily Post* printed several single-line reminders of the concert, while *La Patrie* published a brief biography, reminding readers of Lavallée's years as a prodigy.[137] For these performances, he had brought with him Fries, Nichols, and the accompanist John Willis Co-nant. The program included many of the same pieces they were present-ing in Boston. Montreal audiences would have been familiar with Weber's *Konzertstück*, and pieces by Schumann, Beethoven, and Gottschalk, but not with the music of Chadwick or Sherwood, nor with Lavallée's *Valse Caprice* or "Suite for Piano and Cello."[138] According to *La Presse* and the *Gazette* on 19 May, neither Lavallée's name nor the program seems to have been sufficient to fill the hall. The reasons aren't clear, but they faced competition from Patrick Gilmore's recently announced 'grand mu-sical jubilee,' which was to take place a week later at Victoria Skating Rink and was being heavily advertised by Ernest Lavigne. On Sunday evening. Lavigne's Band de la Cité played an open-air concert at Viger Gardens that opened with a grand march by Gilmore billed as *The Mu-sical Jubilee*.[139] Earlier that evening, Lavallée performed on the organ at Vespers in Notre Dame Church, where he was joined by two old friends, Tancrède Trudel and Frantz Prume.[140] He likely remained in Montreal for Dumont's first lecture, which was held in the City Concert Hall, but was soon back in Boston.[141]

CALIXA LAVALLEE.

Figure 7.8
A sketch of Lavallée, at the Music Teachers' National Association's 1888 meeting at Chicago's Central Music Hall, reading a report about his recent trip to London as the MTNA's delegate to the conference of the National Society of Professional Musicians.

On the evening of 30 May, Lavallée directed a Memorial Day (then called Decoration Day) benefit concert for the House of Good Shepherd, conducting some five hundred performers at the Mechanics' Hall in works by Wagner, Rossini, Gounod, and many others.[142] As a raffle prize, he donated three years of tuition with himself. The concert was the concluding part of a day-long fundraiser for the convent, attended by both the governor and mayor. The next evening, members of New England's French-Canadian community held a banquet in Lavallée's honour at the Hotel Thorndike. A month later, he travelled to Nashua, New Hampshire, to take part in the *Fête nationale* celebrations, and then set off for the MTNA meeting in Chicago.

An engraving published in the *Chicago Tribune* depicts Lavallée, upon arrival, as looking fit but much older than his forty-six years. (See figure 7.8) At the business meeting on the opening day, 3 July, he read his report on the London conference, explaining how the U.K. society functioned and discussing British views on music in the US.[143] After a number of other reports were read, he was among some fifteen members appointed to a panel that would select committee members for the coming year. The sessions were held at Central Music Hall and the evening concerts at Exposition Hall. The orchestral concerts (by Theodore Thomas's orchestra, conducted by Frank Van der Stucken) were well attended and helped to produce a surplus of $1,000.[144] The Chicago press reported on the events of the conference in detail, including what must have been lively debates on the influence of Wagner and the future of music.[145] At the business meeting on 5 July, the committee appointments were announced. Among them, Lavallée had been selected as chair of the program committee for the next meeting. As the subject then turned to electing officers for the coming year, the *Daily Inter-Ocean* reported, "confusion reigned supreme."[146] Eventually, decisions were made, and Philadelphia's Academy of Music was selected as the site of the 1889 conference.

Debate over the Chicago appointments continued in the press in the days and weeks after the conference ended, and Lavallée's trip to London was again the subject of criticism. His report drew condemnation from Percy Betts (using the pseudonym "Cherubino") of London's *Figaro*. Betts wrote that he had never heard of the NSPM, and that Lavallée had naively attempted to have this society help him secure a performance at the triennial Birmingham Festival.[147] Lavallée responded through the *Musical Courier*, listing the names of some of the more prominent members of the NSPM, and writing that he had attempted to have Chadwick's *Symphony* performed at the Birmingham Festival but that the score had not arrived in time.[148] When his letter was reprinted in London's *Musical Standard* in August, Betts responded by restating that he had never heard of the NSPM, and suggesting that if Lavallée were to return "we should prefer him to make music rather than to make speeches."[149] To this, Lavallée responded with a stinging missive, denouncing Cherubino and the *Figaro* for their disregard of both British and US composers, concluding "when American music shall be accepted and appreciated in England, thanks will not be due to that journal, but to true and earnest musicians who do not inquire into the caste or nationality of its supporters, but to the real merits of the work presented."[150] In the US, George Wilson continued his attack, asserting that the conference had been little more than "a banquet and several inoffensive but ungrammatical speeches" for which the MTNA had paid Lavallée's fare.[151] The *Musical Courier* replied to this, calling it "an error that does great injustice," and asked why Wilson had "such animus against Lavallée?"[152]

For Wilson, who chose not to answer this directly, the issue was likely, at least in part, the growing influence of the MTNA, and especially the American College of Musicians, which Lavallée had vigorously supported. Lavallée was also a convenient target as an immigrant and a Catholic. The same could be argued of Betts's opposition to Lavallée, the NSPM, and to their sponsor, Lord Mayor de Keyser. As the chief patron of the Guildhall School of Music, in 1887 de Keyser assisted in the school's move to larger premises on John Carpenter Street, where it was in a better position to compete with the Royal Academy of Music (1822) and the Royal College of Music (1882).[153]

Back in Boston in the fall of 1888, administrative work and teaching left little time or energy for composition or performing. Lavallée took seriously allegations that the MTNA's procedures were not always above board. One of his first actions as chairman of the program committee was to require composers to submit works anonymously to adjudicators (Arthur Foote, chairman; William Foester; and August Hyllsted).[154] He also looked to reduce costs for the events in Philadelphia, after what was an expensive conference in Chicago.

Lavallée's one big event that season was participation in a day-long fundraiser at Mechanics' Hall for the Carney Hospital. The concert came at the end of a day of family entertainment and drew an estimated audience of 3,000.[155] Lavallée's reward for his work on behalf of Catholic charities and for his abilities in planning large events and directing large numbers of performers came later that fall when he was offered the position of music director at Boston's Cathedral of the Holy Cross. (See figure 7.9)

Aside from its remunerative benefits, the position at Holy Cross offered Lavallée new artistic opportunities with a carefully selected 100-voice choir. The cathedral had been a focal point for music making in the city since 1871, when services were first held there. As early as January 1872, one music journal noted that the new cathedral, the largest in New England, was becoming a popular venue for concerts.[156] A later item in the same journal mentioned that the new cathedral had "a space four and one-half times larger than that of Boston Music Hall," and that the Hook and Hastings organ was the largest ever built in the United States.[157] The *Musical Courier* noted that the position "would require

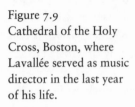

Figure 7.9
Cathedral of the Holy
Cross, Boston, where
Lavallée served as music
director in the last year
of his life.

considerable time and attention on the part of Mr Lavallée," and that it
was "probably the most important musical church appointment in New
England."[158] Perhaps to mark the occasion, Lavallée posed for a photograph, likely his final one. (See figure 7.10)

For the first time since arriving in Boston, Lavallée did not advertise
for students. Through the first half of 1889, much of his time was spent
either at the Cathedral or at Miller Hall. In addition to his duties at the
Cathedral, he was able to perform at several events and learn some new
pieces. In June, Lavallée travelled to Cleveland to give a recital at the
meeting of the Ohio Music Teachers' Association at Case Hall. He had
a special appreciation of that state, and of Cleveland in particular, where
he was regarded as something of a hero among the city's musicians. Arriving on stage that afternoon, he was received with a standing ovation,
before beginning a program that included piano music by Thomas Tapper, William Sherwood, George Chadwick, Frederick Brandeis, Wilson
G. Smith, Constantin Sternberg, and Hugo Kaun, as well as three of his
own pieces, and his Suite for Piano and Cello.[159]

Figure 7.10  Lavallée's last-known studio photograph,
taken in Boston early in 1889.

From Ohio, he made his way east to Philadelphia, where the 1889 MTNA meeting proved to be one of the organization's least controversial gatherings. In contrast to what had become annual rows over the MTNA's direction and purpose, there was a notable absence of open hostilities, even during the business meetings where, *Werner's Voice* reported, "undisturbed harmony" prevailed.[160] Among the achievements of the meeting was the presence of Edward Chadfield, head of the NSPM, as the first delegate from England to attend an MTNA annual meeting.[161] He gave the opening address on 3 July, entitled "National Associations and Their Duties." The same day, the *Musical Courier* marked the occasion with an engraving of both Chadfield and Lavallée on its cover. There were two orchestral concerts of American music and numerous short recitals. Only the quality of the orchestra and the absence of prominent soloists attracted criticism. *Werner's Voice* attributed the cause of the under-rehearsed orchestra to the usual difficulties of hiring an orchestra in the summer, when musicians were usually performing in resorts or on holiday.[162] In fact, Van der Stucken, who had performed at Indianapolis and Chicago, was at the Paris Exposition in 1889.[163] In any event, Lavallée appears not to have been faulted for any drop in the quality of the performers, and was re-elected as head of the program committee for the 1890 conference, which was to be held in Detroit.[164]

Cathedral duties and charity work figured high among Lavallée's priorities through 1889–90. He widened his choir's repertoire, performing Masses by Palestrina and Edouard Silas, in addition to the familiar ones by Beethoven, Mozart, and Gounod. Apart from the regular Masses and choir rehearsals, there were occasional events. On Washington's Birthday, in February 1889, he directed Cherubini's Requiem Mass at the Cathedral in memory of choir members who had died. He appeared at a big fundraiser at the new Grand Opera House, playing the piano duet arrangement of Beethoven's *Egmont* overture with the Cathedral's organist J. Frank Donahoe.[165] In May 1890, he directed a 200-voice choir drawn from the Cathedral and other churches in a concert by the Irish baritone William Ludwig at the Boston Music Hall. Events within the French-Canadian community included a concert in support of the Lafayette Club of Cambridge, and another for Lowell's Cercle Canadien, at that city's new Opera House.[166]

In the early months of 1890, despite being seriously ill, Lavallée was busy with articles and songs. In a 16 January letter to his friend Onésime Thibault, publisher of Fall River's *L'Indépendant*, he claimed that, although his health had improved, he was not yet well enough to travel.[167] In a 14 March letter to Filiatreault, in Montreal, he described working sixteen or seventeen hours a day, and being occupied with writing articles for US publications. The first of two articles for Filiatreault's *Canada Artistique* had appeared in February and Lavallée completed a second on 25 March. At about that time, he set three poems by Thibault's wife, poet Anna Marie Duval-Thibault.[168] She had moved with her family from Montreal to New York City at the age of three, where she was educated in English. She settled in Fall River in 1888, after marrying Thibault. The poet claimed to have met Lavallée only once, in 1890, when he came to Fall River to play for her the three settings, "Lost," "Love Come to Me," and "Sweet Violets."[169] Like many of Lavallée's works, the Duval-Thibault songs remained unpublished and are now presumed lost. Later that summer, Lavallée seems to have added one of the songs to the program of a recital at the MTNA meeting in Detroit.[170]

At that 1890 meeting, Lavallée addressed with a vengeance the criticism of the previous year's concerts. Recitals and sessions took place at the Opera House and orchestral concerts – three in all – took place at the Detroit Rink. More concerts were scheduled than at any previous meeting, and there were some excellent performers. Theodore Thomas's Orchestra performed at the evening concerts, with Fannie Bloomfield-Zeisler and Edward MacDowell among the soloists.[171] The young Chicago pianist Bloomfield-Zeisler had returned to the US in 1883, after studies in Vienna with Theodor Leschetizky. The New York–born MacDowell had only recently returned to the US after fourteen years in Europe, having travelled to Paris in 1876 to study with Marmontel. He was now quickly emerging as one of the most promising US composers. He performed his Second Piano Concerto on 2 July, in a program that featured Paine's *Island Fantasy* and Foote's Suite for Strings. Chadwick's Quintet for Piano and Strings was among the many works by American composers performed at the chamber concerts. The concerts appear to have attracted some of the largest audiences of any MTNA conference. The *Free Press* reported an "overflow audience" for the first concert, and claimed that the same venue was filled "to its utmost capacity" the next night.[172] The *Musical Courier* concluded that, "although suffering from bad health the past year Mr Calixa Lavallée has done magnificent work as chairman of the program committee," and congratulated him "heartily on the results of his labor."[173] He was again named chairman of the program committee for the next conference, to be held two years later (partly in order to raise sufficient funds) in Chicago, during the 1892 Columbian Exposition.

Lavallée's poor health prevented him from ever making progress on the 1892 program. He had been ill off and on since 1885, and was simply worn out.[174] Although he had recovered somewhat in the early months of 1890, by May of that year he had worsened again, and was unable to take part in a planned performance with Emilia de Angelis and members of the Boston Symphony Orchestra. Again, he pulled himself together to attend the conference in Detroit but was obviously in decline. The *Musical Courier*'s gossip columnist later remarked: "I thought Calixa Lavallée looked worn out. He needs a rest, so that he may buckle to for the big work" of chairing the 1892 MTNA program committee.[175] He seems to have heeded the advice, as he took a holiday in New Hampshire. By the beginning of October, he was back in Boston, but was forced to make frequent trips to his doctor, Pierre A.A. Collet, in Fall River, and perhaps to other physicians in Boston.[176] In November, the *Courier* warned: "Calixa Lavallée Must Seek Rest," and advised him to stop all work.[177] By December, his family and friends in Canada were alerted, and his brother Charles and Léon Derome arrived in Boston. They were at his home when he died on the night of 21 January 1891 at the age of forty-eight. His death certificate cites "phthisis" (tuberculosis) as the cause of death. Many American newspapers and journals reported his illness to be 'consumption,' as tuberculosis was commonly known in the nineteenth century. In Montreal, *La Minerve* referred to his ailment simply as "une terrible affliction de la gorge," while the *Star* wrote that he had been suffering from "cancer of the throat."[178]

Lavallée's funeral took place on the morning of Saturday, 24 January. The cortège left his home at 8 a.m. for the Cathedral of the Holy Cross, where Archbishop Williams presided. Placed among the bouquets and wreaths was a large banner emblazoned with the words "Lavallée: the friend of American composers of Music." The *Boston Herald* reported the cathedral "well filled with ... many of the leading musical directors of this city and the most aristocratic parishioners of the Cathedral."[179] Among the pallbearers were John J. McCloskey, bass soloist with the Cathedral choir, Henry F. Miller Jr, Alfred De Sève, Dr Pierre Collet, Judge Hugo A. Dubuque, and other members of the French-Canadian community: J.C. Lafrenière, J.W. Lespérance, and Adolphe A. Denis. No sermon or eulogy was delivered, but a choir of fifty sang Luigi Cherubini's Requiem Mass in C minor. From the Cathedral, the cortège passed out of the city to Mount Benedict Cemetery in West Roxbury, where a quartet sang the motet *De profundis* and Lavallée's body was interred.[180]

❖❖❖

The obituaries published in the days and weeks after Lavallée's death reveal the esteem with which he was regarded by his colleagues and by the public. The French periodical *Le Ménestrel* noted that "music in the United States is mourning the loss of one of its strongest supporters."[181] The *Musical Courier*, long supportive of his work, reported: "Another good man is gone, another friend of music and an ardent champion of the cause of the American composer has passed away. Calixa Lavallée is dead."[182] The writer added that MTNA members would recall Lavallée's "characteristic salutation, hearty, unaffected, with just a tinge of the Gallic in his pronunciation and no little of the Gallic impetuosity in his temperament."[183] Fall River's *L'Indépendant* described him as he was known in the French-Canadian community: "In effect, his individuality made a profound mark in our memories: Congenial companion, charming conversationalist, open heart, candid nature, an industrious artist with the highest ideals."[184] In Canada, *La Minerve* called his death "a loss for the country" as he had "brought honour to all Canadians through his work in the United States."[185] The *Daily Star* reported that many "could recall Mr Lavallée's brilliant performances in Montreal, and the pride with which the news of his successes abroad was received."[186]

Lavallée's move to Boston had in many ways been a great success. As a choral conductor, he was widely respected, especially toward the end of his life. With the help of the Miller firm, he established himself as a performer in a highly competitive city. In 1885, *The Folio* had reported that his "record as a pianist stands with the best in the country. His execution is brilliant and facile, he excels in grace and clearness, and possesses a wonderful technique."[187] He tailored his repertoire to create a niche for himself – as an interpreter of the music of Chopin, and of his own works, and then as performer of new music. In a sense, this final incarnation was the most demanding of his energy. To convince the public of the music's merit, he knew he had to give the best performance possible, and to do so, he committed this music to memory.

The names of some of Lavallée's students appeared in concert notices, but little is really known about his work as a teacher. Many of his students would have been young women from middle-class families who became piano teachers, or who were simply learning for their own pleasure. There were a number who achieved a level of recognition as performers, among them Mina Charland and Thomas Tapper. Among his Canadian students, Joseph Vézina, in Quebec City, became the first conductor of the Orchestre symphonique de Québec, in 1903. In Montreal, Alexis Contant established himself as a conductor and composer, but was also highly regarded as a pianist. After a concert at Montreal's Mechanics' Hall on 30 October 1882, Filiatreault's *Album musical* reported that Contant's interpretation of a Chopin polonaise "reminded us that he was shaped in the school of our great Canadian virtuoso, Calixa Lavallée – the same energy, the same spirit."[188] One of Lavallée's most important students was the pianist George Copeland, who studied with him as a child. After Lavallée's death, Copeland studied at the NEC with Carl Baermann and then in Europe, where he came in contact with Debussy. He went on to make his name as an early interpreter of the French composer's works, as well as the music of contemporary Spanish composers. He remembered his first teacher by adding *Le Papillon* to his repertoire.

In the second half of the 1880s, Lavallée had finally found the success for which he had long been searching. Through the MTNA he had been able to make the sort of contribution to music he had hoped to make, both as a performer and administrator. His efforts had been widely acknowledged during his lifetime and in the memorializing after his death. Whereas in 1884, it had been difficult for US composers to get their works performed, by 1891, they were no longer dependent on the MTNA. Performances were given at conservatories, and in 1889, musicians began forming 'manuscripts societies' to perform their works, first in New York and later in Philadelphia, Chicago, and other cities.[189] In a December 1890 concert review, the *Tribune*'s critic, Henry Krehbiel, wrote that the US composer, "after long suffering neglect, now seems to be in imminent danger of being coddled to death," but was generally pleased with New York's lively, composer-directed concerts.[190]

Musicians and critics began to acknowledge Lavallée's achievement in encouraging the performance of new music as early as 1886. The *Boston Home Journal* attributed the increased attention to Lavallée's 1884 concert. Since that time, it reported, "there has been a notable increase of interest in such compositions."[191] In an interview with the *Boston Herald* in May 1886, Lavallée deflected claims that he was responsible for the increased number of performances of American concert music, while expressing his enthusiasm for the changes that had taken place:

BOSTON HERALD: Do you think that the probabilities of an American school of music will be materially benefited by the influence which the M.T.N.A. is exerting upon the art?

CALIXA LAVALLÉE: Decidedly so. We can now extend to composers a hope for the realization of a long pent-up wish – that is, a chance for the presentation of their own works. For years the attitude of the public, and even professionals, was decidedly antagonistic to any work of an American composer; so, the desire to produce naturally waned, for you know that production of this kind is only fostered by recognition and encouragement when it deserves it.

BH: When and how was it proved that this prejudice was ill-founded?

CL: At Cleveland, at our meeting in July of 1884, when the first concert of American compositions was given.

BH: If I am not mistaken, were you not the one who gave that concert?

CL: Yes, to speak plainly. I was; but, then, that matter has ceased to be of enough importance to occupy our attention now that more serious matters are upon the *tapis*.

BH: Do you consider the fact that you are now able (if I am correctly informed) to present a programme of American orchestral works to be the outcome of your Cleveland piano recital?

CL: Well, I do think that it aided somewhat in giving the cause strength. I might say that it was the seed out of which our present tree has grown.[192]

Lavallée's wary statements came partly from modesty but were also an acknowledgement that others had supported him in Boston and elsewhere, and that other musicians had also begun presenting concert music by US composers, most notably the conductor Frank Van der Stucken, but also Petersilea and E.M. Bowman.

The MTNA acknowledged the impact of Lavallée's work at its meeting in the summer of 1892. The association had chosen that year to meet in Cleveland, after Chicago's Columbian Exposition was postponed. In his presidential address at the 1892 meeting, J.B. Hahn discussed the increased interest in American-cultivated music and attributed much of the change to Lavallée. This address – part eulogy, part history – remains an important source of information for the early development of the movement:

It was in this city – yes, in this very hall, eight years ago, that Calixa Lavallée sounded the key-note of a movement whose reverberations found a re-echoing and a responsive sentiment throughout the length and breadth of the land. Many here today will readily remember the occasion – a modest, unpretentious pianoforte recital, with the distinguishing characteristic that it was the first complete programme of American compositions ever presented.

Its marvelous import was but indistinctly understood.

The train of results which have sprung therefrom has been far-reaching beyond the wildest expectations.

The promotion of a more just and better appreciation of the works of our American composers by their own countrymen was a cause, although unpopular, yet dear to many of our musicians who had labored for its advancement.

No one would wish to detract from the great honor due these early workers, but in all fairness it must be said that this cause received its greatest impetus at the meeting of this Association held in this city in 1884.

For the first time, in a conspicuous manner, a programme was then made consisting entirely of the works of American composers, and for his patriotism, his courage, his judicious selection which led to victory and the leadership he then assumed, all honor to our late associate and ex-President, Calixa Lavallée, the Lafayette of our American musicians.

Lavallée's great strength with his brother musicians was the entire absence of jealousy; he worked for all, without favoritism, always persevering, and with great patriotism, sacrificing oftentimes his own interests for the sake of advancing the cause so dear to him.[193]

Hahn could also have given credit to Gottschalk and to the small number of other musicians who presented music of US composers before 1884, but there was a fundamental difference between their efforts and Lavallée's. While all, as composers, had a personal interest in having their music heard, Lavallée was the first to make a point of presenting the music of his US contemporaries, and his work had yielded results. Whereas major orchestras such as the New York Philharmonic and the Boston Symphony Orchestra had shown little interest in US works, in the spring of 1888 both cities heard the performances of MacDowell's Second Piano Concerto, followed by Arthur Whiting's Piano Concerto in D minor. In the 1890s, even Boston's venerable Handel and Haydn Society performed works by Chadwick, H.W. Parker, and J.C.D. Parker. In an 1894 review, a decade after Lavallée's Cleveland concert, the *Boston Herald*'s music critic reminded readers of the man's achievements by noting that if Lavallée's spirit had been hovering about Music Hall, it would be saying "I told you so."[194] Good-quality performances of American music were no longer a novelty, and audiences were accepting the idea that the US could produce composers of serious music.

As a composer of light music, Lavallée had been quite successful. Early in his career he was known mostly within professional circles, as a musical director and arranger, but the public also knew of him as a composer of exuberant piano pieces and of sentimental songs such as "The Beautiful Girl of Kildare." *Le Papillon* became popular in the late 1870s and grew even more successful in the 1880s, being published in numerous editions, often in collections with similar pieces by well-known European composers. *The Widow* had helped to make his name familiar to audiences around the US. The overtures he published in the mid-1880s, and *The Bridal Rose* in particular, were enormously popular. In 1888, Cundy-Bettoney published orchestral versions, enabling them to be heard even more widely.[195] In an obituary, Henry F. Miller Jr attributed this popular success to Lavallée's ability to "play almost every kind of instrument," something that had been the foundation of much of his career, and that made the band music attractive to both musicians and audiences.[196] A number of works would remain popular well into the twentieth century. Writing in 1913, the Canadian journalist John Daniel Logan drew attention to the "versatility of form and style" in Lavallée's music, as well as "melodic invention" and "expressive harmonies."[197] A half century later, the music historian Helmut Kallmann wrote of Lavallée's "inexhaustible gift for melody."[198]

As much as he tried, Lavallée was never able to leave the world of popular culture behind entirely. Henry F. Miller Jr reported that Lavallée played down his popular successes and shunned opportunities to further his career as a composer of band music. He claimed that the band publisher Cundy had said to him that, if Lavallée concentrated on composing band music, "he would make his fortune in a short time." When Miller questioned him about this, Lavallée's response was that he was "not seeking fame or advancement on that question [but] would rather devote [his] time to compositions which though less profitable, are more artistic," claiming that he "would rather be remembered for a few artistic compositions, than to grow rich in other lines of musical effort.'"[199] The obituary published in *L'Indépendant* went further, reporting that Lavallée "would have scorn for composing light music, because he had the moral strength and great idealism for his art."[200] Whether or not these comments were overstated, Lavallée had continued to distance himself from popular music, and from the early part of his career. Most biographical articles published in the 1880s repeated the same stories about his life and career. They never refer to his life as a 'blackface' minstrel or to any events of the 1860s, with the exception of his service in the war. The *Musical Courier's* April 1885 article, for instance, reports that after studies with his father and a debut at the Theatre Royal (at "about twelve years of age"), Lavallée continued his studies in Paris until he was "called from Paris to found a conservatory in his native country."[201] Although Lavallée contributed articles and letters to the *Musical Courier* and other journals, he never publicly refuted the content of this or any other biographical article. The polarization of popular and classical music was especially apparent in Boston, where John Sullivan Dwight's *Journal of Music* had left an indelible mark on the city's tastes and attitudes.[202] For Lavallée, fighting criticism from Wilson and others over his work with the MTNA, reputation was everything.

What had eluded Lavallée up to the mid-1880s was wide recognition as a serious composer. With the 1879 cantata, he had for the first time been considered something much more than a pianist and conductor. But such opportunities were rare. He went where there was opportunity: to comic opera, but abandoned that direction with the failure of *TIQ*. On a more modest scale, the offertory *Tu es Petrus* showed his potential as a composer of sacred music. It received several performances in his lifetime and, after his death, it became a popular piece for performance at Easter and on the Feast Day of St Peter and St Paul. At the time of his death, he was reported to have composed a Mass in D minor.[203] The Mass, like much of his serious music, remained unpublished and was lost. His administrative and teaching duties left him insufficient time to complete many of the compositions he had begun. With his many responsibilities by the mid-1880s, completing a Mass or oratorio was a nearly impossible task. He could not even find time to write out the piano part of the frequently performed Suite for Cello and Piano. Some works that had been written down remained unpublished, such as the Duval-Thibault songs, and were lost. Many others may have existed in a kind of shorthand he used before writing out the music in standard notation, but illness prevented him from completing them and they remained unintelligible to others after his death.[204]

Illness had also taken a heavy toll on Lavallée's teaching income in the final year of his life. Both illness and unpaid administrative work had often left the family in financial straits. In May 1887, the *Musical Courier* advised him to reduce his workload, writing that his efforts on behalf of the MTNA "have not only consisted of sacrifices of time and comfort, but also of pecuniary advantages, and there have been inroads upon his professional income on account of this."[205] The family's money problems in the final year had not gone unnoticed by friends. In a preview to a planned benefit for him in Montreal, the *Daily Star* noted that Lavallée's "brother musicians [in Boston], as well as the musical societies, have done much to help him in the time of need."[206] With his death on 21 January, the Montreal benefit concert became a 'Grand Testimonial Concert' to him and a benefit for his family. The event took place at Queen's Hall on 23 January and featured performances by the Mendelssohn Choir and Frantz Prume. Lavallée's friends and admirers organized several other benefits in Canada and the United States. After his death, the *Musical Courier* criticized the current executive of the MTNA for their financial management and for their treatment of the past president: "We understand that Calixa Lavallée died a poor man. He spent a greater part of his income on the Music Teachers' National Association. How much does the Association owe him and will that organization now pay his widow?"[207] If the allegations were true, it would seem that Lavallée had repeated the financial fiasco that followed the cantata performance in 1879, for the second time sacrificing his security to finance public projects. He seems never to have made providing for his family a high priority. In February 1891, the *Révue-Canada* began collecting money for Joséphine. Charles Labelle headed the committee, with Léon Derome as treasurer and Aristide Filiatreault as secretary. The MTNA started a fund at about the same time, and Fall River's French-Canadian community held a benefit in late May at that city's Academy of Music.[208] On 23 March 1891, the composer and pianist Amy Beach held a memorial concert at Union Hall, performing *Souvenir de Tolède*, *Le Papillon*, and pieces by Schumann and Chopin, as well as several songs of her own, in an effort to raise money for Lavallée's wife and son.

Many questions remain as to what became of Joséphine and Raoul. On 28 February 1891, an application was made on their behalf for Lavallée's Civil War pension.[209] Some time after this, they were likely forced to give up their home on Brookford Street, just as they had abandoned the house on Sainte-Ursule Street a decade earlier. The 1891 and 1892 editions of the *Boston City Directory* list Joséphine as residing at Miller Hall. After this, she and Raoul relocated to Montreal. They were living in a rooming house on Dorchester Street when, on 31 January

1895, with Raoul as a witness, Joséphine registered at Saint-Jacques Cathedral to marry a man named Adolphe Denis (presumably the same Adolphe Denis who had served as one of Lavallée's pallbearers).[210] Later that year, her Civil War pension record was updated to Joséphine Denis, but where she lived after this remains unknown.[211]

Raoul Lavallée returned to the United States, where he lived out his life. Like his father, he seems to have been something of a showman, (re)inventing his biography as needed and seeking adventure far from home. At the age of nineteen, during the Spanish–American War, he was reported to have been involved in the US invasion of Puerto Rico, where he was poisoned and left for dead.[212] However, about two years later, he was living in Morristown, New Jersey, styling himself either "Lord" or "Count" Raoul Arthur Phillips de Gentilly La Vallee, a descendent of the Marquis de Tracy of Paris. He made the news in 1900 when he challenged a rival for the affections of a young woman to a duel. In April 1902, the *New York Times* reported that he had gone missing, and that his relatives were "in a state of great alarm."[213] After this, there is no evidence to suggest he led anything but a quiet life. At the time of the 1910 US Census, he was living in a boarding house in Newark, New Jersey, and was employed as a bartender in a saloon.[214] A year later, and still residing in Newark, he renewed the copyright on *Le Papillon*.[215] Afterwards, little is known. Newspapers made no mention of his presence at the 1933 repatriation of his father's remains; he may not have been aware of it. By that time, he had married and had at least one son. They were living in Pittsburgh in 1942, the centenary year of Calixa Lavallée's birth.[216]

In the fighting spirit and quest for adventure shown in his early years, Raoul was much like his father. Calixa Lavallée lived his life with intensity and commitment. Over and over he sought adventure: moving to Montreal as a child, departing for the US as a teenager, enlisting in the Union Army, returning to life on the road as the Civil War continued and then again after it ended, travelling to Paris in 1873 to begin a new career, and then starting over again in 1880. He took community involvement as a given throughout his life, beginning with his benefit concerts in the 1860s and then his later efforts to develop Quebec's cultural life and establish a conservatory. In the 1880s, he transferred this energy to his work on behalf of US composers and to his volunteer work on behalf of immigrants, Catholic charities, and especially the French-Canadian organizations of New England. He was prepared to enter the fray on any issue he thought worthy – engaging in the political battles of the 1860s, and literally fighting to the death on behalf of the MTNA and the ACM. In an interview with the *Boston Herald* in the spring of 1890, nine months before his death, he was quoted as saying: "somebody must sacrifice themselves for the cause. When I read the dispatch from Washington two or three weeks ago about the successful concert of American composers given at that city I was delighted. I little dreamed six years ago that the incipient effort I made in that direction would find its reward so soon. No, American music has come to stay, and the sooner the American public realizes the fact the better for the cause and all parties concerned. Of course, we are working through a transition, which is the fate of every new country, and it may take some years yet before we acquire a national color to our music: but who knows how soon a genius may come to us to crown our labors."[217] His terms are those of the soldier he continued to be, always up for a battle and, in this case, fighting the good fight on behalf of music.

# Epilogue

In the years immediately after his death, several of Lavallée's compositions remained popular in the US, and some were performed as far away as Hawaii and Australia.[1] In Canada, few were heard with any regularity until after "O Canada" gained its place as the country's national song, by which time, in the US, the once-popular works had mostly fallen from the repertoire. Even more quickly forgotten after his death were his contributions to musical life in the US. In Canada, his reputation grew through the opening decades of the twentieth century as a result of the mythologizing that took place after "O Canada" became the country's national song. Built on mythmaking, Lavallée's posthumous rise as Canada's "national musician" has been vulnerable to political and social change.

The first myth was that "O Canada" was an immediate success. In reality, it took time to capture the public's attention. Three Montreal publishers are believed to have produced new editions of "O Canada" before the end of the nineteenth century, but there is little evidence that the anthem was heard often in public.[2] At the time of Lavallée's 1888 visit to Montreal, Ernest Lavigne closed his outdoor concert with the standard "Vive la Canadienne" and "God Save the Queen."[3] It would be several years before he added "O Canada" to a *Fête nationale* concert program. It was not included in either the 1890 or 1895 edition of the *Nouvelle lyre canadienne,* a collection of national songs. Arthur Letondal, the son of one of Lavallée's Montreal teachers, reported that "O Canada" began to be heard regularly alongside "God Save the Queen" only around 1900.[4] The event that changed the fate of the anthem took place in 1901, at the ceremonies welcoming the Duke and Duchess of Cornwall and York (later King George V and Queen Mary) to Quebec City, when Joseph Vézina included "O Canada" in the musical program.[5] Two years later, the melody and words of "O Canada" appeared in a collection of patriotic songs, and Charles Lavallée published an arrangement for band with solo cornet by the composer and bandmaster Louis-Philippe Laurendeau, issuing it along with arrangements of "Vive La Canadienne" and "God Save the King."[6] In 1904, *La Patrie* published an article recalling the 1901 singing of "O Canada" and arguing that it should be the official anthem.[7] In 1906, Thomas Bedford Richardson, a Toronto physician, produced an English version of Routhier's text titled *Our Father's Land of Old* (Toronto and Winnipeg: Wale, Royce & Company, 1908), and Toronto's Mendelssohn Choir added "O Canada" to their repertoire. Following their performance of the anthem at Massey Hall in February 1907, the *Toronto Globe* called it a "popular hit," describing the music as "simple, and yet broad and dignified," lending "itself well to massive choral rendering. The hymn stirred the patriotic feelings of the audience, and was tumultuously encored."[8] This performance was one of several that took place that winter in collaboration with the Pittsburgh Orchestra, among them two at Carnegie Hall later that month.[9] Motivated in part by these performances, the Collier's publishing firm held a competition for a new English-language version, which resulted in numerous adaptations and subsequent publications.[10] While none of these caught on, in 1908, Robert Stanley Weir, then recorder for the city of Montreal, produced an English version in time to be sung during the festivities marking the 300th anniversary of the founding of Quebec City. His words, though later modified, and still periodically the subject of criticism, gradually became the accepted English version of the anthem.[11] Competition among the different versions continued, though, as can be heard in the early sound recordings of "O Canada." These include Joseph Saucier singing in French (1907) and Harold Jarvis singing "Beloved Fatherland" (1908). Weir's words were recorded by the Columbia Mixed Quartet in 1913.[12]

Subsequent to this activity, in 1909, the critic and teacher Gustave Comte published the first of several articles about Lavallée and "O

Canada."[13] By the seventieth anniversary of Lavallée's birth, in 1912, "O Canada" was frequently sung in both French and English, and several articles had been published about Lavallée. The Canadian writer John Daniel Logan published an article examining Lavallée's music, and followed that up with a discussion of Lavallée and other Canadian composers. L.-O. David published a revised version of his 1873 article, adding a transcript of a letter to Lavallée from his teacher in Paris, Antoine François Marmontel, and a reproduction of the first page of the manuscript of Lavallée's *Pas redoublé sur des airs canadiens* for orchestra. Most of the writings about Lavallée published over the next two decades focused on "O Canada," to the near exclusion of anything else. Relying on little supporting evidence, most portrayed Lavallée as a patriot, and increasingly contributed to the impression that, in his time, he had been an obscure musician. Between 1915 and 1933, Arthur Letondal published four articles about Lavallée: one appeared in *Le Devoir*, one in the periodical *La Musique*, and two in the monthly magazine produced by the Ligue d'action canadienne-française, an organization founded in 1917 that borrowed its name – if not its goals – from the French fascist organization founded a decade earlier. In the lead-up to the sixtieth anniversary of Confederation, in 1927, and the fiftieth anniversary of "O Canada," in 1930, the historian Hormisdas Magnan published several pieces about Lavallée and his now famous anthem. And then in 1933, in the depths of the Great Depression, came the repatriation of Lavallée's remains.

The repatriation events of 1933 served to increase the number of Lavallée's compositions heard in Canada. Under conductor Rosario Bourdon, the ensemble that became the Orchestre symphonique de Montréal performed an orchestral arrangement of *Le Papillon* at its first concert on 14 January 1935, and again "à la demande général" at its concert on 17 December 1935.[14] But Lavallée's symbolic importance in Quebec soon outweighed his musical contribution. Eugène Lapierre sensed Lavallée's potential as a French-Canadian cultural icon.[15] In 1933, he had composed a three-act 'tragi-comédie' about Lavallée, *Le Traversier de Boston* (The Boston Ferry), which may have been intended for performance in July but appears not to have been staged. Three years later, he published the monograph *Calixa Lavallée: musicien national du Canada*. Given Lapierre's prominence in the 1930s, his book was enthusiastically received. It won the Quebec government's prize for non-fiction in 1937 and became the standard source of information on Lavallée.

Through the 1940s and '50s, Lapierre remained a champion of Lavallée. He expanded on some of the ideas contained in the biography in later publications. In *Un Style Canadien de Musique*, a pamphlet published in 1942, he attempted to illustrate the existence of a national style of music in Quebec based on the works of Lavallée and several other composers. The next year he discussed the unfulfilled promise of French-Canadian musicians in an article in *Le Devoir* awkwardly titled, "Seventy Years of Music, Confederation, O Canada, and the Current State of Calixa Lavallée." The sixtieth anniversary of "O Canada" in 1940 and the hundredth anniversary of Lavallée's birth in 1942 were part of the motivation behind these and other publications and events. At this time, another Lavallée champion was found in Félix Desrochers, a lawyer with strong ties to the Conservative Party, who was then the general librarian of Parliament.[16] Closely following Lapierre in tone and style, Desrochers gave a series of public lectures on Lavallée's life, including one on 22 September 1940 at the unveiling of a plaque in Sainte-Théodosie, on the house in which Lavallée was said to have been born. Other commemoration events included the naming of streets after Lavallée in many communities. In Montreal, such was the case for the street that enters Parc Lafontaine; as well, the cultural centre on that street was named in his honour. And in 1946, the village of Sainte-Théodosie itself became Calixa-Lavallée. Although less directly connected to Lavallée, the most significant of these activities was the creation in 1942 of the Conservatoire de musique du Québec, a state-funded school very much on the model Lavallée had advocated in the 1870s. The following spring, among the opening events of the new institution was a "Concert à la mémoire de Calixa Lavallée." Eugène Lapierre had been a member of the committee that had prepared a preliminary report for the government on the possibility of establishing a conservatory, but if he had expected to be appointed its director, he was to be disappointed. Conductor Wilfrid Pelletier was given that position. Nevertheless, Lapierre remained very much on the scene. In 1947, with writer Aimé Plamondon, he produced *Le Vagabond de la gloire*, a stage work based on Lavallée's life.[17] Two years later, he followed this with a biographical article about Lavallée, and in 1950 with a second edition of his book. The following year, L.-J.-N. Blanchet, who had chaired the Lavallée centennial celebration committee, published *Une vie illustrée de Calixa Lavallée*. Toward the end of the decade, Lavallée was once again evoked when the Société Saint-Jean-Baptiste (SSJB) established an annual prize for contributions to music in Quebec and named it the Prix Calixa-Lavallée.[18]

In the early 1960s, with the approach of Confederation's centennial year, the Pearson federal administration began a raft of nation-building projects. In 1964, it established a commission to study replacing the Canadian Red Ensign with a new flag. The following year, this resulted in the acceptance of the maple leaf flag – bearing a symbol borrowed from the Société Saint-Jean-Baptiste. Also in 1964, the government established a committee to explore the possibility of making "O Canada" the official national anthem. While this was being studied, the public had new opportunities to learn about Lavallée and his music. The CBC produced radio and television documentaries about him, and collaborated with RCA Victor on the release of an LP of excerpts from *The Widow*.[19] And in 1966, Lapierre published the third edition of his biography, an event that was celebrated with a reception at Montreal's city hall hosted by Mayor Jean Drapeau, a concert, and an exhibition of Lavallée artifacts presented by Les Publications de la Société historique de Montréal.

But times were changing. That same year, the SSJB awarded the Prix Calixa-Lavallée to the poet and songwriter Gilles Vigneault, a champion of Quebec independence. In 1967, Charles de Gaulle encouraged independence in his speech from the balcony of Montreal's city hall, and by the end of the decade, the movement had taken a violent turn. At the 1975 Saint-Jean-Baptiste concert in Montreal, Vigneault sang his "Gens du Pays," a song that would become for many an anthem for the new Quebec, and the next year, the Parti Québécois came to power under Premier René Lévesque. But even if the *"musicien national du Canada"* was a dated image for younger Quebec nationalists, federalists were still in need of symbols. Just four weeks after the 20 May 1980 referendum on Quebec sovereignty (which the "no" side had won by a margin of 59.56 per cent to 40.44 per cent), the Liberal administration of Pierre

Trudeau presented a new bill to Parliament: to make "O Canada" the official national anthem. Whereas the resolutions of the mid-1960s and early 1970s had stalled, this bill passed easily and quickly on 27 June 1980, the 100th anniversary of the first formal singing of "O Canada." On 1 July, a special ceremony was held on Parliament Hill in Ottawa, with descendants of Weir and Routhier in attendance, as Canada Post issued two seventeen-cent commemorative stamps, one bearing the images of Lavallée, Routhier, and Weir, and the other featuring the opening phrase of the music.

A wider knowledge of Lavallée's life came in the 1980s and after as the result of a general increase in scholarship on musical life in nineteenth-century North America. Universities in both the US and Canada began to embrace the study of musicians previously considered marginal and of music thought to have been unworthy of serious study. In the US, research was driven by the Sonneck Society (later the Society for American Music) and by academic publishers such as the University of Illinois Press. Digitization projects and the Internet facilitated this work and helped to bring it to the public. In Canada, the first edition of *Encyclopedia of Music in Canada* appeared in 1981, making a vast amount of information available to the public in both English and French. At about the same time, a group of music historians established the Canadian Musical Heritage Society and began publishing twenty-five volumes of Canadian music created prior to 1950. Many of Lavallée's scores were included in the series, including the overture *Patrie*, which was discovered and performed in the early 1990s.

Over the past three decades, several scholars have explored aspects of Lavallée's life, work, and music, among them Mireille Barrière, E. Douglas Bomberger, and Simon Couture. At the same time, Marie-Thérèse Lefebvre and Lucien Poirier, two of Quebec's leading music historians, examined the work of Eugène Lapierre and the history of music in Quebec in the early and middle decades of the twentieth century. Unsurprisingly, they found the research flawed and heavily influenced by the conservative ideology of the era. In an article on the history of the Conservatoire national de musique, Lefebvre describes Lapierre as having been "seduced by an article written in 1919 by his 'venerated master' [his journalism professor, Edouard Montpetit] in which [Montpetit] defined the artist as 'a producer of value, a producer of use, and a producer of action'; this idea of using art as a means of propagating an ideology of conservative values, as well as making art a commercially profitable activity, would become the principles on which Lapierre would rest throughout his career."[20] In a critique of Lapierre's 1942 pamphlet, *Un style canadien de musique*, Poirier writes that "Lapierre's opinions and the style with which he conveys them more closely resemble a rallying cry than critical or aesthetic reflection," with "the corpus of terms and ideas behind his discourse" is borrowed from the priest-historian Lionel Groulx and from "the official ideology of the Québec church."[21]

Neither Lefebvre nor Poirier wrote specifically about Lapierre's Lavallée biography. Had they, they would likely have come to similar conclusions. Writing in the 1930s, Lapierre sought to use Lavallée as a symbol of hope for French-Canadians suffering through the Depression. "O Canada" was Lapierre's most potent symbol of Lavallée's patriotism toward French-speaking Canada, so he used "the composer of O Canada" and "our hero" interchangeably and frequently when referring to Lavallée. Rarely concerned with historical accuracy, he freely exaggerated or embellished Lavallée's accomplishments.[22] What he left out was most revealing. By devoting the largest section of his book to Lavallée's activities in Canada, Lapierre created the false impression that Lavallée had been in the country for the greatest part of his career. The reality was that during his thirty-year career, Lavallée spent roughly two years in Europe, seven in Canada, and twenty-one in the United States. Of Lavallée's music, Lapierre omitted the minstrel-show songs and provided titles of other songs only in French, implying that they were on French-language texts. He referred to Lavallée's settings of songs by Anna Marie Duval-Thibault, for example, as "Trois Chansons," even though the poet reported to him in a letter that the titles were "Lost," "Love Come to Me," and "Sweet Violets."[23] Despite the limitations of Lapierre's book, journalists and scholars have relied heavily on it, often paraphrasing from it. Even the main dictionary articles on Lavallée – those published in the 1990s in the *Encyclopedia of Music in Canada*, the *New Grove Dictionary of Music*, and the *Dictionary of Canadian Biography*, are based primarily on Lapierre.

With the issue of Quebec sovereignty in the news through the early 1990s, the SSJB erected a new headstone at Lavallée's grave, commemorating the centenary of his death in 1991.[24] The society has continued to award the Prix Calixa-Lavallée, but in 1993 shifted it from an annual to a triennial prize (but then only awarded it in 1996, 2002, and 2012). In June 1994, the same organization attempted to halt a performance of "O Canada" before a Montreal Expos baseball game, stating that it would be inappropriate since the stadium grounds were to host events that evening marking the *Fête nationale* (Saint-Jean-Baptiste celebrations) – ironically, the same event for which "O Canada" had been created.[25] On Canada Day 1995, the federal government unveiled a plaque on the Couillard Street building in which Lavallée had lived when he moved to Quebec City.[26] The following October, the "no" side won a second sovereignty referendum, this time by a margin of only 50.58 per cent to 49.42 per cent. Although shaken by their narrow defeat, the Parti Québécois regrouped, and at its general meeting in September 1999, members discussed the creation of a new national anthem for Quebec. A decade later, the party's youth wing urged the PQ to revive debate about a Quebec anthem, constitution, and citizenship.[27] In 2011, the Société Saint-Jean-Baptiste commissioned poet and musician Raôul Duguay to create a new national song for Quebec. His song, "Ô Kébèk," with music co-written by Alain Sauvageau, emphasized the importance of the French language in defining and sustaining Quebec.

Throughout the past century, "O Canada" has had no serious rival as the Canadian anthem. The English words have been modified several times, and organizations and individuals have made appeals for further modifications. In 1990, the Toronto City Council voted in favour of lobbying the federal government to change the phrase "our home and native land" to "our home and cherished land," in recognition of the fact that a great many Canadians were born elsewhere. There have been similar initiatives to remove references to God, and especially to make the words gender-neutral, notably in 2002, 2010, and again in 2013.[28] On the other hand, perhaps due to simple familiarity or to some more profound connection, Canadians appear to have been content with the music of "O Canada," although it is doubtful that many know the anthem's origins, or could even name its composer.

❖❖❖

That "O Canada" had been accepted as an anthem by English-speaking Canadians reflects well on Lavallée's abilities as a composer, but it was also an accident of language – the opening words appeared to refer not solely to Quebec but to the dominion created in 1867. Eugène Lapierre exploited this coincidence by referring to Lavallée, in 1936, as the *"musicien national du Canada."* He was of course paraphrasing L.-O. David, who in the 1870s described Lavallée as the "cachet national" and likened Lavallée's performances to Canada's natural environment, and to Charles Labelle, who had in 1888 paraphrased David. They were both writing after 1867, but still referring to the narrower meaning – that of French Canada. To those singing Weir's words in the 1930s, it did not seem to matter where the music had been composed.

And yet, in an era when French Canadians were marginalized in many ways, Lavallée should have been a problematic figure for English Canadians on a number of levels. He was born and raised a French Canadian in British colonial North America. His identity was based largely on language, history, religion, and geography – the elements of an ethnic nation. Among his earliest recorded performances were those at *Fête nationale* concerts, and his actions and words throughout his life might now be termed those of a Quebec nationalist. His organization of and participation in benefit concerts, performances of chamber music, staging of operas, and efforts to establish a conservatory were all attempts to develop musical culture in Quebec and strengthen French-Canadian national identity. Once settled in the US, he naturally became a leading figure in the expatriate community, organizing events and raising funds for French-Canadian institutions, such as Boston's Notre-Dame-des-Victoires. And so, to his French-Canadian contemporaries on both sides of the border, he was "l'un de nôtres" (one of ours),[29] or "une de nos gloires nationales" (one of our national glories).[30]

By the time the first of these comments was published, in 1888, Lavallée was also very much an American. He had adapted easily to life in the US on arriving there in the late 1850s, and he maintained strong ties to that country, both culturally and politically, throughout his adult life. In the 1880s, as he transferred his zeal from the conservatory project in Quebec City to the development of music in the US, he focused on finding performance opportunities for serious composers. His move in 1880

to what he termed the "larger field" was not surprising: he was returning to the country in which he had spent half of his professional life.[31] In
doing so, he maintained a de facto dual nationality. A New York–based
music journal referred to him in 1889 as an "American in the less restricted sense of having been born on the great American continent."[32]
In an obituary, Henry F. Miller Jr, a close friend of ten years, was quoted
as describing Lavallée as "a thorough-going American, though he was
born in the Provinces and not in the United States." Miller claimed that
Lavallée had demonstrated his patriotism during the Civil War and also
through his work with the expatriate community in New England. "He
was in a sense their prophet, and his relations with all their leaders were
very intimate. He used all his influence with them to foster affection for
their adopted country. A few years ago I attended a banquet which was
given to him in Fall River. He made an address which was as much of a
success in its way as his musical triumphs. He urged the annexation of
Canada to the United States."[33] No transcript of Lavallée's speech is
known to have been published, but several obituaries make similar
claims. The *Musical Courier* reported that Lavallée "always advocated
the annexation of Canada to the United States and invariably urged
French Canadians in New England to be loyal to their adopted country."[34] Lavallée seems never to have actually made a statement in print
or to have been directly quoted on the issue of annexation, and yet he
may have held this view. The hanging of Louis Riel had galvanized opinion among many French Canadians on both sides of the border and
elicited new calls for annexation in the 1880s. The vibrant French-Canadian communities of New England were seen by some as proof that the
culture could withstand assimilation.[35] But regardless of his opinion on
the issue of annexation, Lavallée's ties to the US were deep, fostered by
years of travel throughout the country. In an interview conducted late in
his life, when asked about the future of music in the US, he said: "We are
a great people, and we need not feel astonished at any time what one of
America's sons may have in store for us."[36] At the time of the Indiana
MTNA meeting, the *Brooklyn Daily Eagle* reported: "Calixa Lavallee, the
Boston composer, says he was born near Montreal, Canada, lived in
Louisiana, as a boy, studied in France and is proud to be an American."[37]

And yet, much as the cosmopolitan Liszt or the émigré Chopin transcended nationality, so too did Lavallée. In Canada, he never limited his activities to his own ethnic community. Even at the time he was fighting against Confederation, he was still collaborating with British and Italian musicians. His connections to the Irish were even stronger. On several occasions they called on him to organize and perform at St Patrick's Day events. As a church musician, he was very much a member of the Irish communities of Quebec City and Boston. And in his arrangement of "Flag of Green," he conveyed the same force and emotion that one hears in his other national songs.

As an educator, Lavallée held a deep belief in the power of music to shape both the individual and the nation, and he had the talent and charisma to persuade others. Onésime Thibault, publisher of *L'Indépendant* and Lavallée's friend throughout the 1880s, wrote that Lavallée "possessed a pronounced personality ... which manifested itself as soon as he spoke of art, and especially when he filled the role of the artist."[38] He had little patience for those less committed. Ten years after leaving the country, he acknowledged that French Canadians in Canada had to fight to retain their language, customs, and religion, and he criticized those willing to "submit to the demands of the conqueror," but he was equally incensed by "another part of our population who, due to either negligence or ignorance, have no concern for the artistic future of our dear country."[39] He was no less critical of the United States, where "money is king, and ... dollars make the dividing line in society,"[40] and where "The government does nothing for art," and where the poor "cannot afford to pay for what is termed a *luxury*."[41] To Lavallée, music was a path to empowerment for the poor and the marginalized, and by raising the self-esteem of the individual, it served to help define the nation. As Philip Bohlman has written, music is "malleable in the service of the nation not because it is a product of national and nationalist ideologies, but rather because musics of all forms and genres can articulate the processes that shape the state."[42] To Lavallée, it was serious music that best served to shape the state as he envisioned it. But he knew the power of all types of music and spent his life bringing it to the public – as a performer, composer, teacher, and administrator.

Lapierre had acknowledged this when he dismissed the idea that Lavallée had become the "national musician" by composing "O Canada." "The opposite is true," he wrote. "A lifetime of similar effort enabled him to compose the national hymn."[43] Lavallée understood the common people because he had spent his youth and young adulthood performing for the masses – during the Civil War and after, leading brass bands and minstrel show orchestras. He understood the power of music to make one laugh, or cry, or to feel a deep sense of attachment to one's land and fellow citizens.

# Appendix One:
## Catalogue of Lavallée's Compositions

### INTRODUCTION

The information in this catalogue has been gathered from library collections of Lavallée's works and from secondary printed sources. The CBC's Toronto Music Library is an especially important repository of Canadian printed music. It contains copies of many published works that Helmut Kallmann collected while serving as head librarian in the 1950s and '60s.[1] Library and Archives Canada also holds a large collection of Lavallée's music. Its catalogue and many others are now searchable online, either independently or through databases such as WorldCat. In most cases, I have examined copies of the scores listed. Newspapers and music journals provide further information on the composition and performance history of many works. In several instances, periodicals are the only sources of information about works that are not known to have been published.

Works are listed by genre, and then chronologically by date of composition. Only the earliest publication of each work has been cited, unless copies of other early editions provide complementary information.[2] Titles, instrumentation, and dedications are based on the first publication, unless indicated otherwise. Plate numbers and keys are given when known. A work's genre follows its title. It is italicized or placed within quotation marks if it forms part of the title. The texts of vocal works can be assumed to be in the language of the title, unless indicated otherwise. Spurious or unconfirmed information is placed in square brackets and followed by a question mark. Locations of the scores are listed in parentheses after the publication information. Those works that have been reissued in the Canadian Musical Heritage Society's anthologies are listed using abbreviations that indicate the volume number. Those republished by the Canadian Institute of Historical Microreproductions are listed with the Institute's volume number. Selected information is provided on recordings. For early recordings, readers may wish to consult Library and Archives Canada's *The Virtual Gramophone* website (www.collectionscanada.gc.ca/gramophone/index-e.html) which provides access to recordings in the public domain. For more recent recordings, two good sources are iTunes and the Naxos Online Library.

## ABBREVIATIONS

| | |
|---|---|
| A. Lavigne | Arthur Lavigne, Quebec City |
| *L'Album musical* | Filiatreault: *L'Album Musical*, Montreal |
| Barnes | Alexander Barnes, Rochester, New York |
| Bernard & Allaire | Bernard & Allaire, Quebec City |
| Boucher | Les Éditions A.J. Boucher, Montreal |
| CIHM | Canadian Institute of Historical Microreproductions |
| Cluett | Wm Cluett & Sons, Troy, New York |
| CMHS 1 | Canadian Musical Heritage Society, *Vol. 1, Piano Music I*. Edited by Elaine Keillor (1981). |
| CMHS 7 | Canadian Musical Heritage Society, *Vol. 7, Songs II to French Texts*. Edited by Lucien Poirier (1987). |
| CMHS 10 | Canadian Musical Heritage Society, *Vol. 10, Opera and Operetta Excerpts I*. Edited by Dorith R. Cooper (1991). |
| CMHS 15 | Canadian Musical Heritage Society, *Vol. 15, Music for Orchestra II*. Edited by Elaine Keillor (1992). |
| CMHS 21 | Canadian Musical Heritage Society, *Vol. 21, Music for Winds I*. Edited by Timothy Mahoney (1998). |

| | |
|---|---|
| CMHS 22 | Canadian Musical Heritage Society, *Vol. 22, Piano Music III*. Edited by Helmut Kallmann (1998). |
| CMHS 23 | Canadian Musical Heritage Socity, *Vol. 23, Chamber Music III: Duos*. Edited by Robin Elliott (1998). |
| Cundy | W.H. Cundy, Boston |
| Cundy-Bettoney | Cundy-Bettoney, Boston |
| Danks | H.P. Danks, Cleveland |
| E. Lavigne | Ernest Lavigne, Montreal |
| Eveillard | Eveillard, Paris |
| Eveillard & Jacquot | Eveillard & Jacquot, Paris |
| Faulds | D.P. Faulds, Louisville, Kentucky |
| Fischer | Carl Fischer, New York |
| Gordon | S.T. Gordon, New York |
| Hiélard | J. Hiélard, Editeur-Commissionnaire, Paris |
| *Inter-Ocean* | *Musical Suppliment to the Inter-Ocean*, Chicago |
| Laurent-Laforce | Laurent & Laforce (or Laurent, Laforce et cie.), Montreal |
| *Minerve* | *L'Album de la Minerve*, Montreal |
| *Musical Bouquet* | *Musical Bouquet*, London |
| Oliver Ditson | Oliver Ditson & Company, Boston |
| *Passe-Temps* | *Le Passe-Temps*, Montreal |
| Pond | Wm A. Pond & Company, New York |
| Russell | J.M. Russell, Boston |
| Schmidt | Arthur P. Schmidt, Boston |
| White-Smith | White, Smith & Company, Boston & Chicago |
| Whittemore | J. Henry Whittemore & Company, Detroit |

COMPOSITIONS

Stage

*Peacocks in Difficulties / Lou-Lou, opéra-bouffe, in Three Acts,*
soloists, chorus, orchestra[3]
LIBRETTIST: P. Arnold de Thier. COMPOSED: New York, ca. 1870.
FIRST/EARLY PERFORMANCE: Only a cavatina from the operetta is
known to have been performed: 13 March 1873, Mechanics' Hall,
Montreal, Ludger Maillet (tenor).[4] PUBLISHED: No record of publication has been found. NOTES: The *New York Clipper* reported this
work to be in preparation for performance at Lina Edwin's Theatre
in New York.[5] No record of a performance by this or any other
company has been located.

*The Widow (La Veuve), Opera-Comique in Three Acts,* soloists, chorus
(SATB), orchestra
LIBRETTIST: Frank H. Nelson. COMPOSED: [Boston, ca. 1881?].
FIRST/EARLY PERFORMANCES: 24 February 1882, Grand Opera
House, Chicago, C.D. Hess Acme Opera Company, Louise Searle
(Doña Paquita, the widow), Adelaide Randall (Nanine), Mary
Wadsworth (Adele), and Walter Allen (Duc de Trop). Further per-
formances took place in New York, Saint Louis, and other Ameri-
can cities during the company's 1881–84 tour. In June 2001, *The
Widow* was staged at the Maison de la Cuture de Gatineau in a
French translation by Eugène Sauvé and new orchestration by Paul
McIntyre, and in February 2004 by the Toronto Operetta Theatre
with a new arrangement by Jose Hernandez of the original English-
language vocal score. PUBLISHED: Russell, ca. 1881, libretto
(Library of Congress); Russell, 1882, vocal score, 224 p. (Boston
Public Library; CBC Music Library, Toronto (microfilm, photocopy);
Library of Congress; Library and Archives Canada; New York
Public Library; CIHM no. 08876; CMHS 10 (5 excerpts)). Excerpts
published: "Happy and Free," Russell, 1882 (CBC Music Library,
Toronto (photocopy)); "I'm Too Delicate to Work" and "If Woman
is Curious, Then Nature is to Blame," *Inter-Ocean,* 1, no. 16

(22 March 1882), 5 p. (Library and Archives Canada); "The Rock and the Hills," Curwin, [1882?, 1885] (British Library); "With Pleasure in Each Glance," Curwin, [1882?, 1885] (British Library). DEDICATION: "To His Excellency the Count De Premio-Real. Superior Honorary Chief of Civil Administration in Spain. Grand Cross Isabella the Catholic. Grand Cross Nischan. Consul General of Spain for the Dominion of Canada and British and French possessions in North America, etc. Honorary President of Septuor Haydn, Quebec, etc." RECORDINGS: Arrangements by Ovid Avarmaa performed by CBC Winnipeg Orchestra and Chorus, conducted by Eric Wild (1966): RCA Victor; re-released in *"O Canada": The Life and Times of Calixa Lavallée* (1980): Radio Canada International (RCI 5113). Excerpts in: *Le Souvenir: Canadian Songs For Parlour And Stage* – Sally Dibblee, soprano, Russell Braun, baritone, Carolyn Maule, piano (1996): Centrediscs (CMCCD 5696); excerpts ("Waltz song: Smiling hope," "Duo: O trust my love") in *À la claire fontaine: Music in Kreighoff's Quebec* – Beckwith Ensemble (2000): Opening Day Records (ODR 9321).

*TIQ [The Indian Question], Settled at Last. A Melodramatic Musical Satire in Two Acts*, soloists, chorus (SATB), orchestra
LIBRETTISTS: Will F. Sage and Phillipes Hawley. COMPOSED: Boston, 1881–82. FIRST/EARLY PERFORMANCE: No record of a performance has been found.[6] PUBLISHED: Oliver Ditson, 1883, vocal score, 190 p. (Boston Public Library; CBC Music Library, Toronto (microfilm); CMHS 10 – 4 excerpts; Library of Congress). RECORDINGS: "Marche Indienne," arranged by John Beckwith: in *Music for Brass Bands* – Hannaford Street Silver Band (1991): CBC (SMCD 5103); "We Never Tell a Lie" in *À la claire fontaine: Music in Kreighoff's Quebec* – Beckwith Ensemble (2000): Opening Day Records (ODR 9321).

## Orchestra or Concert Band

*Quadrille Canadien*, brass band
COMPOSED: [Montreal, 1864?] FIRST/EARLY PERFORMANCE: Benefit

concert for the Union Saint-Joseph, 19 March 1864, Mechanics' Hall, Montreal, Lavallée conducting the Montreal Brass Band. PUBLISHED: No record of publication has been found.

*Quickstep sur les airs nationaux canadiens / Pas redoublé sur des airs canadiens*, concert band/orchestra
COMPOSED: [Montreal, 1864?]. FIRST/EARLY PERFORMANCE: 25 July 1864, City Concert Hall, Montreal, Lavallée conducting the Montreal City Band. PUBLISHED: No record of publication has been found. NOTES: In 1912 L.-O. David published an article about Lavallée that included the first page of an orchestral autograph bearing the title *Pas redoublé sur des airs canadiens* and the caption "composed 40 years ago."[7] If David's caption was correct, Lavallée may have orchestrated this piece for a performance by the D.C. Hall Orchestra, which he conducted in 1872 and 1873.

*Air Varié*, cornet solo and band
COMPOSED: [1873?]. FIRST/EARLY PERFORMANCE: Union Band, Oliver Bisson, cornet; Huntington Hall, Lowell, 13 November 1873. PUBLISHED: No record of publication has been found.

*Symphony* or *Suite*, orchestra
COMPOSED: [Paris, ca. 1874?]. FIRST/EARLY PERFORMANCE: [Paris Conservatoire, 1874?]. PUBLISHED: No record of publication has been found. NOTES: The White–Smith "Official Bulletin" lists a symphony among Lavallée's works.[8] An article in the *Musical Courier* reported that Lavallée had composed a "Suite d'Orchestre" that was performed in Paris in 1874.[9]

*Patrie, ouverture*, orchestra
COMPOSED: Paris, 1874.[10] FIRST/EARLY PERFORMANCE: [Paris Conservatoire, 1874?]; 14 October 1993, Longueuil, Quebec, l'Orchestre symphonique de la Montérégie. PUBLISHED: CMHS 15 (1992) is transcribed from the manuscript in the Fonds J.-J. Goulet at the Bibliothèque et Archives nationales du Québec. KEY: D major.

NOTES: This may be the "symphony" that Labelle reported to have been performed in Paris in 1874.[11]

*Grande fantaisie de concert*, op. 75, cornet and concert band
COMPOSED: [Montreal, 1875?]. FIRST/EARLY PERFORMANCE: Patrick S. Gilmore Concert Band, Matthew Arbuckle, cornet, Gilmore's Garden, New York, 10 September 1875. PUBLISHED: This may have been published by Carl Fischer in 1890.[12]

*Harmonie*, concert band
COMPOSED: Montreal, 1878. FIRST/EARLY PERFORMANCE: 21–24 June 1878, Victoria Skating Rink, Montreal. This was the imposed piece at a band competition. PUBLISHED: No record of publication has been found. NOTES: Lavallée organized the competition and headed the panel of judges.

*Bristol March* [concert band or orchestra]
COMPOSED: [Boston, ca. 1881?]. FIRST/EARLY PERFORMANCE: Summer of 1881, on board the steamer *Bristol* of the Fall River Line, Hall's Band and Orchestra. PUBLISHED: No record of publication has been found. NOTES: The *Fall River Line Journal* of June 1881 lists "March –*Bristol*" as the opening piece in the on-board promenade concerts by Hall's Band and Orchestra. It does not indicate the instrumentation of the work.

*Bridal Rose / La Rose nuptial, overture*, orchestra/concert band
COMPOSED: Boston, ca. 1885. FIRST/EARLY PERFORMANCE: No record of early performances has been found. PUBLISHED: Cundy, ca. 1885, reprint 1912, piano reduction, 4 p. (CBC Music Library, Toronto (photocopy); Library and Archives Canada); Cundy-Bettoney, 1888, reprint 1930, piano reduction, 4 p. and orchestral parts (Bibliothèque et Archives nationales du Québec). KEY: F major. NOTES: A.E. Harris arranged the work for publication in 1916 (Cundy-Bettoney, 1930). D. Silverstein re-arranged the work for orchestra in 1966 (2 full scores at the CBC Music Library,

Toronto). RECORDINGS: In *Light Canadian Orchestral Classics*, CBC Winnipeg Concert Orchestra; Eric Wild, conductor (1968?): Capitol (T 6261); In *"O Canada": The Life and Times of Calixa Lavallée* (1980): Radio Canada International (RCI 513). Brass quintet arrangement by Howard Cable: in *Musique Romantique* – Concert Arban (1988): Adés (20396); in *Northern Delights* – Hannaford Street Silver Band (1996): Opening Day Records (ODR 9308); in *True North Brass* – True North Brass (1998): Opening Day Records (ODR 9313).

*Golden Fleece, Companion to Poet and Peasant, overture*, orchestra
COMPOSED: Boston, ca. 1885. FIRST/EARLY PERFORMANCE: No record of performance has been found. PUBLISHED: Cundy, 1885; Cundy-Bettoney, 1888, full score and orchestral parts (CBC Music Library, Toronto (photocopy)); Cundy-Bettoney, 1914 (British Library).

*The King of Diamonds, overture*, orchestra / concert band
COMPOSED: Boston, ca. 1885. FIRST/EARLY PERFORMANCE: 3 May 1888, Paine Memorial Hall, Boston, D.L. White's Concert Orchestra (26 musicians). PUBLISHED: Cundy-Bettoney, 1885 and reprint 1888, piano reduction and orchestra parts (Library of Congress); Cundy-Bettoney, 1913, reprint 1941, piano reduction (Bibliothèque et archives Nationales du Québec). KEY: D major.

*Richmond March*, concert band
COMPOSED: [Boston, ca. 1886?]. FIRST/EARLY PERFORMANCE: 21 June 1886, Madison Park, Boston, Germania Band, conducted by J.B. Claus. PUBLISHED: No record of publication has been found KEY: Unknown.

*Marche Indienne*, solo cornet and orchestra
PUBLISHED: Oliver Ditson, 1891 (CMHS 21) NOTES: Extracted from *TIQ* RECORDINGS: Arrangement by John Beckwith for band: Hannaford Street Silver Band; Stephen Chenette, conductor in Brass in *The Hannaford Street Silver Band* (1991): CBC (SMCD-5103).

## Unaccompanied Chorus

*Libera me,* SATB
WORDS: Responsory text. COMPOSED: Quebec City, 5–6 March 1880.
FIRST/EARLY PERFORMANCES: 6 March 1880, St Patrick's Church,
Quebec City. PUBLISHED: No record of publication has been found.
KEY: Unknown. NOTES: Composed on the death of Patrick Curran
and sung at a service for him before his body was transported to
Montreal for burial.

*"O Canada," terre de nos aïeux: chant national,* SATB
WORDS: Adolphe B. Routhier. COMPOSED: Quebec City, 15 March–
17 April 1880. FIRST/EARLY PERFORMANCES: Instrumental ver-
sion: 24 June 1880, Skating Rink, Quebec City, combined bands of
Fall River, Beauport, and the Ninth Battalion conducted by Joseph
Vézina; 25 June 1880, Spencer Wood, the official residence of the
lieutenant-governor, Quebec City, 100-member band conducted by
Vézina; choral version: 27 June 1880, the Église Saint-Jean, Quebec
City, choir conducted by Gustave Gagnon. All three performances
took place during the 1880 national convention of the Société Saint-
Jean-Baptiste de Québec, for which the anthem was commissioned.
The premiere was given at a banquet, the second playing took place
at a public concert, and finally it was sung at the Mass that closed
the conference. PUBLISHED: A. Lavigne, [1880], SATB and rehearsal
piano, 3 p. (CMHS 7; Séminaire de Québec, Archives; Université de
Montréal, Bibliothèque de musique, Collection Villeneuve); Boucher
[ca. 1880] reprint of the Lavigne edition (Library and Archives
Canada). KEY: G major. NOTES: Numerous editions have been pub-
lished since 1900, many of them arranged for band. The officially
sanctioned English-language text was written by Robert Stanley
Weir in 1908. "O Canada" became the official national anthem of
Canada by an Act of Parliament in 1980. RECORDINGS: Joseph
Saucier, baritone; organ and brass quartet (1907): Columbia (E458);
Harold Jarvis, tenor, with orchestra (1908): Berliner/Victor (5517);
Victor Military Band (1915): Victor (17999); Columbia Mixed
Quartet (1918 or 1919)[13]: Columbia (A1369); RCA Victor Band

(1927): RCA Victor (216503); Edward Johnson, tenor (1928): RCA Victor (24005) – re-released on CD (Analekta AN 2 7802); in "O Canada": *The Life and Times of Calixa Lavallée* – 12 vocal or instrumental arrangements of "O Canada" (1980): Radio Canada International (RCI 513); multiple versions of "O Canada" (1908–2004) in "O Canada": *The National Anthem* (2004): Disques XXI-21 Records.

*Vive la France / Rallions-nous Canadiens*, TTBB
WORDS: Louis Fréchette. COMPOSED: [Boston, ca. 1885-86?]. FIRST/EARLY PERFORMANCE: No record of performance has been found. PUBLISHED: [Montreal, 1920?], 1 p. (Bibliothèque et Archives nationales du Québec). KEY: E-flat major. NOTES: The date of publication was taken from the original cataloguing of the piece, at the Bibliothèque et archives Nationales du Québec.

## Chorus and Orchestra (or Band)

*Cantate: Loin du pays,* soloists, chorus, and orchestra[14]
WORDS: Flavien Martineau (1830–1887). COMPOSED: [Paris, 1874?]. FIRST/EARLY PERFORMANCE: 8 October 1874, City Concert Hall, Montreal, A.J. Boucher's chamber orchestra, and a chorus (SATB) of singers from several churches conducted by Boucher. PUBLISHED: No record of publication has been found.

*Cantate en l'honneur du Marquis de Lorne,* soloists (SATB), chorus (SATB), and orchestra
WORDS: Napoléon Legendre. COMPOSED: Quebec City, September–October 1878–79. FIRST/EARLY PERFORMANCE: 11 June 1879, Skating Rink, Quebec City, 50-piece orchestra, a 150-voice chorus (SATB), and soloists Cora Wyse (soprano), Mlle Carbray (alto), Tancrède Trudel (tenor), and P. Laurent (bass), conducted by Lavallée; excerpts: 24 October 1878, 18 April 1879, 22 September 1879, and 25 November 1879, Victoria Hall, Quebec City; 25 March 1879, Rideau Hall, Ottawa. PUBLISHED: No record of publication has been found.

*Messe Sainte-Cécile* [soloists, chorus, orchestra?]
COMPOSED: Quebec City, August-September, 1879. FIRST/EARLY
PERFORMANCE: No record of performance has been found.
PUBLISHED: No record of publication has been found. NOTES:
The work was intended for performance by the Union Musicale de
Québec at the 1879 *Fête Sainte-Cécile*, Quebec City. Lavallée was
unable to complete it on time, and directed Gounod's *Messe Sainte-
Cécile* instead. He may never have completed the work. (See also
the Mass in D minor, listed among the spurious works.)

*Hymne à la Paix / Hymn of Peace*, soloists (SAT), chorus (SATB), and
orchestra
WORDS: The author of the text has not been determined. COMPOSED:
[Boston, 1872?]. FIRST/EARLY PERFORMANCE: The work was reconstructed and orchestrated by Eugène Lapierre, and performed
on 19 December 1954, City Hall, Montreal, Marcelle Langlois
(soprano), Denise Bernard (contralto), Armand Racicot (tenor),
Lapierre (piano), chorus and orchestra conducted by Pepin. PUB-
LISHED: No record of publication has been found. There are photocopies of Lapierre's 1954 manuscript at the CBC Music Library,
Toronto, and at Library and Archives Canada. DEDICATION:
"à tous les nations du monde." KEY: E-flat major (Lapierre's orchestration). NOTES: The work may have been composed for Patrick
Gilmore's 1872 World Peace Jubilee and International Music
Festival, at which Lavallée conducted Hall's Brass Band.

*Tu es Petrus, an offertorium*, soprano, chorus (SATB), orchestra, organ
WORDS: Biblical text, in Latin (Matt. 16–18); English version ("Glory,
Blessing, Praise and Honor") by Louis Charles Elson. COMPOSED:
Boston, 1883. FIRST/EARLY PERFORMANCE: 18 February 1884,
St Peter's Church, Boston, orchestra, chorus, and soloists conducted
by Lavallée; 2 July 1885, Academy of Music, New York, orchestra
and chorus conducted by Lavallée; 11 March 1886, Chickering
Hall, New York, New York Harmonic Society conducted by S.N.
Penfield. PUBLISHED: White-Smith, ca. 1883, vocal score, 20 p.,
plate no. 5221-20 (Boston Public Library; Brown University, John

Hay Library, Harris Collection; CBC Music Library, Toronto (photo-copy); CIHM no. 11921; Harvard University, Loeb Music Library; Library and Archives Canada; l'Université Laval (microfilm)). DEDICATION: "To the Rev. Fr Peter Ronan, Pastor of St Peter's Church, Dorchester District, Boston." KEY: B-flat major. NOTES: Commissioned for and performed at the dedication of St Peter's Church, Boston.

*The Fountain*, high voice, concert band
WORDS: James Russell Lowell. COMPOSED: Boston, 1885.
FIRST/EARLY PERFORMANCE: 24 October 1885, Eaton Square, Boston, Germania Band conducted by Lavallée. PUBLISHED: Vocal score published in *Proceedings of the Dedication of the Fountain on Eaton Square, Ward 24, October 24, 1885: In Memory of Theodore Lyman, Jr, Mayor of Boston in 1834–35*. [Boston]: City Council, 1886 (Boston Public Library; Brown University, John Hay Library, Harris Collection; New York Public Library; University of California, Berkeley, Music Library; Yale University, Music Library). DEDICATION: "Dedicated to the Hon. Nahum Capen." KEY: E-flat major.

*The Judgement of Solomon*, oratorio, soloists (SAB), chorus, and orchestra[15]
WORDS: The identity of the librettist has not been determined. Presum-ably the text was adapted from the Biblical story (1 Kings). COM-POSED: Boston, ca. 1885–86. FIRST/EARLY PERFORMANCE: Two scenes, "The Judgement of Solomon" and "The March from the Throne," 1 July 1886, Tremont Temple, Boston, chorus, orchestra, Fanny Kellogg (soprano), Gertrude Edmunds (contralto), and D.M. Babcock (bass) conducted by Lavallée. PUBLISHED: No record of publication has been found.

Chamber Ensemble or Solo Instrument (Other than Piano)

*Fantaisie*, solo cornet
COMPOSED: [1863?]. FIRST/EARLY PERFORMANCE: 26 January 1864, Mechanics' Hall, Montreal, Lavallée. PUBLISHED: No record

of publication has been found. The work may have been an improvisation.

*Grande fantaisie de concert sur deux themes de Norma*, violin, piano
COMPOSED: [1863?]. FIRST/EARLY PERFORMANCE: 26 January 1864, Mechanics' Hall, Montreal, Lavallée (violin), Mlle Derome (piano). PUBLISHED: No record of publication has been found.

*Méditation*, cornet, piano
COMPOSED: [1880?]. FIRST/EARLY PERFORMANCE: No record of performance has been found. PUBLISHED: Fischer, 1880, 5 p., plate no. 622 AC (CBC Music Library, Toronto (photocopy); SRC Musicothèque, Montreal; Yale University, Music Library (photocopy) CMHS 23). KEY: E-flat major. NOTES: Copyright of the Fischer edition is credited to the American cornetist Matthew Arbuckle. See Anderson, 1989.

Suite for Cello and Piano, op. 40, cello, piano
COMPOSED: Boston, ca. 1884. FIRST/EARLY PERFORMANCES: 1 March 1885, Union Hall, Boston, Ernst Jonas (cello), Lavallée (piano); 12 March 1886, Miller Hall, Boston, Wulf Fries (cello), Lavallée (piano); 1 May 1886, Union Hall, Boston, Fries (cello), Lavallée (piano); 1 July 1890, Detroit, Charles Heydler (cello), Lavallée (piano). PUBLISHED: No record of publication has been found. KEY: F-sharp minor. NOTES: The four movements were: allegro appassionata, scherzo, romance, presto à la tarantelle. The work was sometimes referred to as a concerto.

Sonata, op. 43, cello, piano
COMPOSED: Boston, ca. 1885. FIRST/EARLY PERFORMANCE: 20 March 1888, Boston.[16] PUBLISHED: No record of publication has been found.

Solo Piano

*La Fleur de mai (The May Flower), polka de salon*

335

COMPOSED: [Montreal, ca. 1859?]. FIRST/EARLY PERFORMANCE: No record of performance has been found. PUBLISHED: Cluett, 1859, 7 p. (Brown University, John Brown Library; Buffalo and Eire County Public Library; Newberry Library). DEDICATION: "To Mrs R.W. Laithe of Troy, NY"[17] KEY: D-flat major.

*Col. Ellsworth Gallopade*
COMPOSED: [Cleveland, May 1861(?)]. FIRST/EARLY PERFORMANCE: No record of performance has been found. PUBLISHED: Danks, 1861, 4 p., plate no. 6084 (Johns Hopkins University, Milton S. Eisenhower Library; Library of Congress, Music Division). DEDICATION: "To the memory of Col. E.E. Ellsworth." KEY: B-flat major.

*The War Fever, grand galop characteristique,* op. 4
COMPOSED: [Providence, Rhode Island?], ca. 1861. FIRST/EARLY PERFORMANCE: 26 January 1864, Mechanics' Hall, Montreal, Lavallée. PUBLISHED: Gordon, ca. 1861, 7 p. (CBC Music Library, Toronto (photocopy); Library of Congress; CMHS 1). DEDICATION: "To his Friend John E. Taber Esq." KEY: E-flat major.

*Grande valse de concert,* op. 6
COMPOSED: [While touring, ca. 1861?]. FIRST/EARLY PERFORMANCE: No record of performance has been found. PUBLISHED: Cluett, nd (SRC Musicothèque, Montreal (photocopy)). DEDICATION: "To Miss Alice Ingalls." NOTES: The SRC's copy of this piece was missing in 1998.[18] Information is taken from the Canadian Association of Music Libraries' 'data sheets.'

*The First Welcome, polka characteristique*
COMPOSED: [While touring, 1861?]. FIRST/EARLY PERFORMANCE: No record of performance has been found. PUBLISHED: Gordon, 1861, 7 p. (CBC Music Library, Toronto (photocopy); CMHS 1). DEDICATION: "To Miss Emma R. Bulkeley." KEY: E-flat major. RECORDINGS: Anna-Marie Globenski, piano, in *The Romantic Piano in Canada* (1999): SNE (648).

*Ellinger Polka de Salon,* op. 8

COMPOSED: [While touring, 1863?]. FIRST/EARLY PERFORMANCE: No record of performance has been found. PUBLISHED: Cluett, 1863, 7 p. (British Library; CBC Music Library, Toronto (photocopy); CMHS 1). DEDICATION: "Composed and Dedicated To Miss M. [Mary] C. Ellinger of Baltimore, Md." KEY: E-flat major. RECORDINGS: Linda Lee Thomas, piano, in *Early Music from Quebec* (1972): CBC (SM-204) and in *"O Canada": The Life and Times of Calixa Lavallée* (1980): Radio Canada International (RCI 513); Shelley Katz, piano, in *From Molt to McPhee* (1999): Carleton Sound (CD-1004).

*Grande fantaisie de concert*

COMPOSED: [While touring, 1863?]. FIRST/EARLY PERFORMANCE: 4 January 1864, Mechanics' Hall, Montreal, Lavallée. PUBLISHED: No record of publication has been found.

*Le Souvenir-Méditation*

COMPOSED: 1864? FIRST/EARLY PERFORMANCE: 5 October 1864, Mechanics' Hall, Montreal, Lavallée. PUBLISHED: No record of publication has been found.

*Une Couronne de lauriers, caprice de genre,* op. 10

COMPOSED: Montreal, ca. 1864. FIRST/EARLY PERFORMANCE: Possibly the *Grand caprice de concert* performed by Lavallée on 19 February 1864, Mechanics' Hall, Montreal. PUBLISHED: Laurent-Laforce [1864], 9 p. (Library and Archives Canada; CMHS 1). DEDICATION: "à Mademoiselle Marie C. Regnaud de Montréal." KEY: E-flat major.

*L'Oiseau mouche, bluette de salon,* op. 11

COMPOSED: Montreal, ca. 1864. FIRST/EARLY PERFORMANCE: 26 January 1865, Mechanics' Hall, Montreal, Lavallée. PUBLISHED: Laurent-Laforce, [1865], 7 p., plate no. 4902; Boucher, [1865],[19] 7 p. (BANQ; CBC Music Library, Toronto (photocopy); Free Library, Philadelphia; Library and Archives Canada; CMHS 1);

Hall, [1865] (Library of Congress). DEDICATION: "à Mademoiselle Rose de Lima Derome – de Montréal." KEY: F major. NOTES: The copyright stamp on Library of Congress's Hall edition reads: "South Dist. of NY, Wm Hall, 1865." RECORDINGS: Linda Lee Thomas, piano, in *Early Music from Quebec* (1972): CBC (SM-204), and in *"O Canada": The Life and Times of Calixa Lavallée* (1980): Radio Canada International (RCI 513); Anna-Marie Globenski, piano, in *The Romantic Piano in Canada* (1999): SNE (648); Shelley Katz, piano, in *From Molt to McPhee* (1999): Carleton Sound (CD-1004).

*Réverie du soir*
COMPOSED: [Montreal, 1864?]. FIRST/EARLY PERFORMANCE: 10 January 1865, Nordheimer's Hall, Montreal, Lavallée. PUB-LISHED: No record of publication has been found.

*Shake Again Galop, an Answer to "Slap Bang" or Here We Are Again,"* op. 27
COMPOSED: [Rochester, NY, 1866?]. FIRST/EARLY PERFORMANCE: No record of performance has been found. PUBLISHED: Barnes, 1866, 7 p. (CMHS 22; Eastman School of Music, Sibley Library). DEDICATION: "To the Holy Rollers of Rochester NY." KEY: F major. NOTES: The opus number may have been a publisher's error. RECORDINGS: John Beckwith, piano, in *À la claire fontaine: Music in Kreighoff's Quebec* (2000): Opening Day Records (ODR 9321); Elaine Keillor, piano, in *Sounds of North* (2012): Gala Records (GAL 108).

*Fantasia on themes from "Il Trovatore"*
COMPOSED: [Boston, ca. 1872?]. FIRST/EARLY PERFORMANCE: 13 March 1873, Mechanics' Hall, Montreal, Lavallée. PUBLISHED: No record of publication has been found. NOTES: Fantasy on *Il Trovatore*, by Giuseppe Verdi.

*Grande Marche de Concert*, op. 14
COMPOSED: Paris, 1874. FIRST/EARLY PERFORMANCE: 12 September 1878, Music Hall, Quebec City, Nancy Dessane. PUBLISHED:

Eveillard & Jacquot, nd, 9 p., plate no. 550 (CBC Music Library, Toronto (photocopy); British Library); Hiélard, 1875, 9 p. (same plates as Eveillard & Jacquot) (CMHS 1; Bibliothèque nationale de France). DEDICATION: "à Madame Marie Annie Bossange." KEY: E-flat major. RECORDINGS: Linda Lee Thomas, piano, in *Early Music from Quebec* (1972): CBC (SM-204) and in *"O Canada": The Life and Times of Calixa Lavallée* (1980): Radio Canada International (RCI 513); Anna-Marie Globenski, piano, in *The Romantic Piano in Canada* (1999): SNE (648).

*Souvenir de Tolède, mazurka de salon,* op. 17
COMPOSED: Paris, 1874. FIRST/EARLY PERFORMANCE: 23 March 1891, Union Hall, Boston, Amy Beach. PUBLISHED: Eveillard et Jacquot, nd, 9 p. (CBC Music Library, Toronto (photocopy); Bibliothèque nationale de France); Schmidt, 1884 (Saint Louis Pubic Library; Free Library, Philadelphia). DEDICATION: Eveillard edition: "à Madame Ida Astruc"; Schmidt edition: "A mon ami Carlyle Petersilea." KEY: E-flat major. NOTES: The back cover of Eveillard et Jacquot edition lists other works available from the publisher, including Lavallée's *Grande marche de Concert*; op. 14, *Souvenir de Tolède*, op. 17, *Le Papillon*, étude, op. 18 (3e édition). The revised Schmidt edition is subtitled "Remembrance of Toledo."

*Le Papillon, étude de concert,* op. 18
COMPOSED: Paris, 1874. FIRST/EARLY PERFORMANCE: 8 November 1875, Music Hall, Quebec City, Lavallée. PUBLISHED: Eveillard, ca. 1874, 9 p. (Metro Toronto Reference Library); Hiélard, 1875, plate no. L.E. 1906 (Bibliothèque nationale de France); Schmidt, 1884, 9 p., plate no. APS & Company 544.7) (CMHS 1; Library of Congress; Library and Archives Canada; University of California, Berkeley, Music Library); White-Smith, 1886, reprint 1892 (University of California, Berkeley, Music Library; University of Toronto, Music Library). DEDICATION: "à mon professeur et ami Monsieur A. Marmontel." KEY: E minor. NOTES: *Le Papillon* has rarely been out of print since the 1880s. In addition to the many individual publications of the music, it has been included in *Artists' repertoire: A*

*Collection of Classical and Standard Pianoforte Music by the Best Known Writers of the World* (White-Smith, 1885). RECORDINGS: Josephte Dufresne, piano (1969): CBC/Radio-Canada (RCI 252); Linda Lee Thomas, piano, in *Early Music from Quebec* (1972) CBC (SM-204) and in *"O Canada": The Life and Times of Calixa Lavallée* (1980): Radio Canada International (RCI 513); Robert Silverman, piano, in *The Parlour Grand* (1997): Marquis Classics (MAR 501); Anna-Marie Globenski, piano, in *The Romantic Piano in Canada* (1999): SNE (648); Elaine Keillor, piano, in *Canadians at the Keyboard* (2000): Carleton Sound (CD 1008).

*Bon Voyage, galop de concert*
COMPOSED: Montreal, 1876. FIRST/EARLY PERFORMANCE: 5 June 1876, Mechanics' Hall, Montreal, Lavallée. PUBLISHED: No record of publication has been found. DEDICATION: Composed for the farewell concert for François Boucher. NOTES: In his review of the 5 June concert, Guillaume Couture reported that Lavallée had not yet written the work down on paper.[20]

*Marche funèbre, hommage à Pie IX*
COMPOSED: Montreal, February 1878. FIRST/EARLY PERFORM-ANCES: Performed on a number of occasions as a solo organ piece and in an arrangement for band during the ceremonies marking the repatriation of Lavallée's remains in 1933. PUBLISHED: [E. Lavigne, 1878], 6 p. (CBC Music Library, Toronto (photocopy); CMHS 1; Library and Archives Canada; Université de Montréal, Bibliothèque de musique, Collection Villeneuve; Université Laval, Bibliothèque). DEDICATION: "Respectueusement dediée à Sa Grandeur, Monsei-gneur Charles-Edouard [*sic*] Fabre, Evêque de Montréal." KEY: C minor. NOTES: "Composé à l'occasion de la mort de N.S.P. Pie IX, décédé le 7 Février, 1878" is printed on the cover page. RECORDINGS: Linda Lee Thomas, piano, in *Early Music from Quebec* (1972): CBC (SM-204), and in *"O Canada": The Life and Times of Calixa Lavallée* (1980): Radio Canada International (RCI 513); Anna-Marie Globenski, piano, in *The Romantic Piano in Canada* (1999): SNE (648).

*Petite Hermine, galop brilliant et facile/Vol au vent, petit galop*
COMPOSED: Quebec City, 1878. FIRST/EARLY PERFORMANCE: No
record of performance has been found. PUBLISHED: A. Lavigne,
ca. 1878, 5 p. (Université de Montréal, Bibliothèque de musique,
Collection Villeneuve); also published as *Vol au vent, galop*, in
*Minerve*, ca. 1878, 4 p. (CMHS 1; Library and Archives Canada).
DEDICATION: "à Monsieur Nazaire Turcotte." KEY: F major.
RECORDINGS: Anna-Marie Globenski, piano, in *The Romantic
Piano in Canada* (1999): SNE (648); Shelley Katz, piano, in *From
Molt to McPhee* (1999): Carleton Sound (CD-1004).

*Paraphrase de concert, sur les motif de "Faust"*
COMPOSED: Boston, ca. 1881. FIRST/EARLY PERFORMANCE: 1 May
1881, Music Hall, Boston, Lavallée. PUBLISHED: No record of
publication has been found. NOTES: The piece was based on themes
from Charles Gounod's *Faust*.

*Première Valse de Salon*, op. 39
COMPOSED: Boston, ca. 1885. FIRST/EARLY PERFORMANCE:
28 April 1886, Miller Hall, Boston, Lavallée. PUBLISHED: White-
Smith, 1886, 11 p. (CBC Music Library, Toronto (photocopy);
Library of Congress; CMHS 1). DEDICATION: "à mon ami Louis
Maas." KEY: A-flat major. NOTES: The copyright date stamped on
the Library of Congress's copy is 4 February 1886. RECORDINGS:
Linda Lee Thomas, piano, in *Early Music from Quebec* (1972): CBC
(SM-204) and in *"O Canada": The Life and Times of Calixa Laval-
lée* (1980): Radio Canada International (RCI 513); Anna-Marie
Globenski, piano, in *The Romantic Piano in Canada* (1999): SNE
(648); Shelley Katz, piano, in *From Molt to McPhee* (1999):
Carleton Sound (CD-1004); Monique Rancourt, piano, in *La Belle
époque* – L'Ensemble Nouvelle France (2012); Espace Émergence.

*Mouvement à la pavane*, op. 41[21]
COMPOSED: Boston, ca. 1885. FIRST/EARLY PERFORMANCE: 25 June
1888, Indianapolis, Nelly Stevens. PUBLISHED: White-Smith,
[1886], 3 p. (CBC Music Library, Toronto (photocopy)). KEY:

G minor. NOTES: Timothy J. McGee included *Mouvement à la Pavane* in the anthology portion of his book *The Music of Canada*. RECORDINGS: Elaine Keillor, piano, in *Sounds of North* (2012): Gala Records (GAL 108).

*Chanson bachique*
COMPOSED: [Boston, ca. 1886?]. FIRST/EARLY PERFORMANCE: 11 October 1886, Academy of Music, Fall River, Lavallée. PUBLISHED: No record of publication has been found.

*Valse caprice*
COMPOSED: Boston, ca. 1886. FIRST/EARLY PERFORMANCE: 30 December 1886, Boston, Louis Maas. PUBLISHED: No record of publication has been found.

## Songs

"Do I Love You? ballad," voice, piano
WORDS: Finley Johnson. COMPOSED: [While touring, ca. 1860?]. FIRST/EARLY PERFORMANCE: New Orleans Minstrels' 1860–61 tour. PUBLISHED: Pond, 1863, 5 p., plate no. 5594 (CBC Music Library, Toronto (photocopy, microfilm); Library of Congress). DEDICATION: "To Miss Jennie King (of Washington, DC)." KEY: E-flat major. NOTES: Title page: "Sung by Mr S.C. Campbell with Great Success." The lyrics were printed in The New Orleans Minstrels' songster. See *The Peo[ple's] New Songster*.

"A Hero's Death," [voice, piano?][22]
WORDS: Gustave Bidaux. COMPOSED: [Summer, 1863?]. FIRST/EARLY PERFORMANCE: Duprez and Green's Minstrels, 1863–64 tour. PUBLISHED: No record of publication has been found.

"Hommage aux Victimes de 1837–38," voice and piano
WORDS: L.-O. David. COMPOSED: June, 1864. FIRST/EARLY PERFORMANCE: Fête Nationale Concert, 24 June 1864, City Concert Hall, Montreal, sung by François Lavoie. PUBLISHED: No record of publication has been found.

"Salut à la noble bannière," [voice, piano?][23]
WORDS: Benjamin Sulte. COMPOSED: Montreal, 1868. FIRST/EARLY
PERFORMANCE: 16 September 1868, St Patrick's Hall, Montreal,
Ludger Maillet (tenor). PUBLISHED: No record of publication has
been found.

"I'm So Happy Thou Art Near," solo voice, piano
WORDS: Unknown. COMPOSED: [While touring, ca. 1867-68?].
PUBLISHED: Whittemore, 1868. NOTES: Information is located in
Worldcat but no copy is listed.

"Beautiful Girl of Kildare," voice, chorus (SATB), piano
WORDS: R. [Richard] A. Warren. COMPOSED: [While touring, ca.
1869?]. FIRST/EARLY PERFORMANCE: New Orleans Minstrels,
ca. 1868–69. The caption "Sung by Mr Warren Richards of Duprez
& Benedict's Minstrels" appears on the cover of the Whittemore
publication. PUBLISHED: Whittemore, 1869, 7 p. (CBC Music
Library, Toronto (photocopy, microfilm); Library of Congress);
*Musical Bouquet* [1874], fol. no. 4683 (British Library). KEY:
F major.

"Leaving Home and Friends, song and chorus," voice, chorus (SATB),
piano
WORDS: Frank Dumont. COMPOSED: [While on tour, ca. 1869?].
FIRST/EARLY PERFORMANCE: New Orleans Minstrels, ca. 1868–
69. The caption "Sung by A. Vanderloeff of Duprez & Benedict's
Minstrels" appears on the cover of the Whittemore publication.
PUBLISHED: Whittemore, [1869], 5 p. (CBC Music Library, Toronto
(photocopy, microfilm); Library of Congress). DEDICATION: "To
my friend G.E. Hicks, Esq." KEY: D major. NOTES: The dedication
appears to contain a typographical error. L.E. Hicks was a member
of the New Orleans Minstrels in 1869.

"The Lost Love, melody" voice, piano
WORDS: Frank Dumont. COMPOSED: [While on tour, ca. 1869?].
FIRST/EARLY PERFORMANCE: No record of performance has
been found. PUBLISHED: Whittemore, ca. 1869, 9 p. (CBC Music

Library, Toronto (photocopy, microfilm); Library of Congress).
DEDICATION: "To Miss Clara Von Sicklen of Quincy, Ill." KEY:
E-flat major.

"Forget Thee My Darling, ballad," voice, piano
WORDS: No lyricist is indicated on the Faulds's publication. COM-
POSED: [New York, or while on tour, ca. 1871?]. FIRST/EARLY
PERFORMANCE: No record of performance has been found. PUB-
LISHED: Faulds, 1871, 4 p. (Library of Congress). DEDICATION:
"to my first love." KEY: F major. NOTES: Lavallée visited Louisville,
Kentucky, where Faulds was based, with Morris Brothers' Minstrels,
at the end of November 1871.

"Valse de concert," voice, piano
WORDS: Emmanuel Blain de Saint-Aubin.[24] COMPOSED: [Montreal,
ca. 1876?]. FIRST/EARLY PERFORMANCE: 5 December 1876 and
16 January 1877, Mechanics' Hall, Montreal, Rosita del Vecchio
(soprano). PUBLISHED: No record of publication has been found.

"Le Facteur," [voice, piano?][25]
WORDS: J.H. Malo. COMPOSED: Montreal or Quebec City,
1875–80(?). FIRST/EARLY PERFORMANCE: 9 February 1909,
Monument National, Montreal, A. Valeur. PUBLISHED: *Le Passe-
Temps*, XV, no. 361 (February 1909). KEY: F major.

"Violette (Violet), cantilène," voice, piano
WORDS: Napoléon Legendre (1841–1907); English version by Patrick
J. Curran. COMPOSED: Quebec City, January–April 1879.
FIRST/EARLY PERFORMANCE: 18 April 1879, Victoria Hall,
Quebec City, Tancrède Trudel (tenor). PUBLISHED: Lavigne, 1879
(Library and Archives Canada); CMHS 7; vocal line reprinted in
*Le Passe-Temps* (August 1933). DEDICATION: "avec autorisation
à S.A.R. La Princesse Louise, Marquise de Lorne." KEY: F major.
NOTES: The cover features a black and white engraving of
Princess Louise.

"Harmonie," voice, piano

WORDS: F.-A. Hubert La Rue. COMPOSED: Quebec City, ca. 1879.
FIRST/EARLY PERFORMANCE: 7 January 1880, Salle du Pensionnat,
l'Université Laval, Quebec City, Alphonse d'Eschambault (bass);
2 June 1880, Music Hall, Quebec City, C.L. Lefebvre. PUBLISHED:
A. Lavigne, [1879?], 3 p. (CBC Music Library, Toronto (photocopy);
CMHS 7). KEY: D major. NOTES: The words were also published in
*Souvenir du jubilé sacerdotal de Mgr. C. Cazeau, prélat domestique
de Sa Sainteté, vicaire-général de L'archidiocèse, célébré à Québec,
en janvier 1880.* Np: np, 1880.

"Nuit d'été (Summer Night), mélodie," voice, piano

WORDS: Napoléon Legendre; English version by P. [Patrick] J. Curran.
COMPOSED: Quebec City, ca. 1880. FIRST/EARLY PERFORMANCE:
No record of performance has been found. PUBLISHED: A. Lavigne,
1880, 7 p. (Library and Archives Canada; Université Laval, Division
des archives; Université Laval, Bibliothèque; Conservatoire de
musique de Québec, Bibliothèque; CMHS 7). DEDICATION: "Res-
pecteusement dediée à Madame Robitaille (Spencerwood)." KEY:
A-flat major. NOTES: The Collection Claude Champagne, at the
Bibliothèque et Archives nationales du Québec contains an unsigned
manuscript of this song. The CBC Music Library in Toronto holds a
photocopy of a manuscript in A-flat major (with French words only)
3 p. notated on Waley, Royce & Company, Ltd (Toronto) music
paper. RECORDINGS: Paul Dufault, tenor, with orchestra (1915):
Columbia Records (E2640); Paul Dufault, tenor, with orchestra
(1921): HMV (263093); In *"O Canada": The Life and Times of
Calixa Lavallée* (1980): Radio Canada International (RCI 513); in
*Musique: Canadian Songs for Parlour and Stage* – Gloria Jean Nagy,
soprano; Elaine Keillor, piano (2006): Carleton Sound (CD 1011).

"L'Absence," voice, piano

WORDS: Rémi Tremblay. COMPOSED: Boston, ca. 1881. FIRST/EARLY
PERFORMANCE: No record of performance has been found. PUB-
LISHED: *L'Album musical*, 1, Prospectus no. (Dec. 1881), 2 p.
(Conservatoire de musique de Québec, Bibliothèque; Bibliothèque

et Archives nationales du Québec, CMHS 7); Bernard & Allaire, [ca. 1885], (Library and Archives Canada); also published in: "Succés du salon, choix de romances, morceaux, etc., no. [1]. 3 p. (Library and Archives Canada; l'Université de Montréal, Bibliothèque de la musique); reprinted in *Le Passe-Temps* (August 1933). KEY: D major. NOTES: The Collection Claude Champagne of the Bibliothèque et Archives nationales du Québec contains an unsigned manuscript of this song. RECORDINGS: In *"O Canada": The Life and Times of Calixa Lavallée* (1980): Radio Canada International (RCI 513); in *Diana Gilchrist Sings Songs Of Canada* – Diana Gilchrist, soprano, Shelley Katz, piano (2000): Carleton Sound (CD 604); in *La Belle époque* – L'Ensemble Nouvelle France (2012); Espace Émergence.

"Le Trappeur," [voice, piano?][26]
WORDS: Rémi Tremblay. COMPOSED: Boston, ca. 1887. FIRST/EARLY PERFORMANCE: No record of performance has been found. PUBLISHED: No record of publication has been found. NOTES: This was the official song of the French-Canadian social club of the same name.

"Andalouse, Bolero for Soprano," op. 38, soprano, piano
WORDS: Alfred de Musset (1810–1857); English words by Louis C. Elson (1848–1920). COMPOSED: Boston, ca. 1883. FIRST/EARLY PERFORMANCE: 28 April 1886, Miller Hall, Boston, Maude Nichols (soprano), Lavallée (piano). PUBLISHED: White-Smith, 1886, 11 p., plate no. 6492-10 (Boston Public Library; CBC Music Library, Toronto (photocopy, microfilm); CMHS 7; Université Laval, Bibliothèque). DEDICATION: "To Miss Emma Juch." KEY: F-sharp minor. RECORDINGS: In: *Le Souvenir: Canadian Songs For Parlour And Stage* – Sally Dibblee, soprano, Carolyn Maule, piano (1996): Centrediscs (CMCCD 5696); in *Diana Gilchrist Sings Songs Of Canada* – Diana Gilchrist, soprano, Shelley Katz, piano (2000): Carleton Sound (CD 604).

"Restons Français, chant de La Ligue des Patriotes," voice, piano
WORDS: Rémi Tremblay. COMPOSED: [Fall River?], ca. January 1886.
FIRST/EARLY PERFORMANCE: 7 February 1886, Fall River, Massachusetts. PUBLISHED: *L'Indépendant* [Fall River, Massachusetts]
5 February 1886: 1. Reissued in *Supplément de L'Indépendant*
(28 Dec. 1888), 3 p. (CMHS 7; SRC Musicothèque, Montreal; Université Laval, Bibliothèque); reprinted in *Le Passe-Temps* (August
1933). DEDICATION: "Dedié à la 'Ligues des Patriotes.'" KEY:
D major. NOTES: This was the association song of the Ligue des
Patriotes. RECORDINGS: In *La Belle époque* – L'Ensemble Nouvelle
France (2012); Espace Émergence.

"Spring Flowers," voice, piano
WORDS: Miss Kitty [Gertrude] Hall. COMPOSED: Boston, ca. 1886.
FIRST/EARLY PERFORMANCE: 12 March 1886, Miller Hall, Boston,
Maude Nichols (soprano), Lavallée (piano). PUBLISHED: White-
Smith, ca. 1886, 5 p., plate no. 6225-4 (CBC Music Library, Toronto
(photocopy); Library and Archives Canada (photocopy); SRC Musi-
cothèque, Montreal). DEDICATION: "To Miss Maud [*sic*] Nichols."
KEY: D-flat major.

[Three Songs]: (1) "Lost," (2) "Love Come to Me," (3) "Sweet
Violets," voice, piano
WORDS: Anna Marie Duval-Thibault. COMPOSED: [Boston, ca. 1888].
FIRST/EARLY PERFORMANCE: 1888, Fall River, Massachusetts,
Lavallée (piano), unknown vocalist.[27] PUBLISHED: No record of
publication has been found.

"Love," voice, piano
WORDS: [Anna Marie Duval-Thibault?]. COMPOSED: [Boston,
ca. 1888]. FIRST/EARLY PERFORMANCE: 2 July 1890, Detroit,
Annie S. Wilson (soprano), James R. Rogers (piano). PUBLISHED:
No record of publication has been found. NOTES: A poem with this
title appears in a notebook in the author's collected papers at the
Houghton Library, Harvard University.

## ARRANGEMENTS

*Don Giovanni de Portugal* (Burlesque opera based on Mozart's *Don Giovanni*), voices, unknown instrumentation
COMPOSER/AUTHOR: W.A. Mozart / Lorenzo Da Ponte. ARRANGED: [New Orleans, 1863?] in collaboration with Gustave Bidaux. FIRST/EARLY PERFORMANCE: New Orleans Minstrels, Academy of Music, New Orleans, 23 January 1863. PUBLISHED: No record of publication has been found.

"La Mansarde, romance," voice, piano
COMPOSER/AUTHOR: M.F.E. Valois. ARRANGED: [Montreal, 1864?]. FIRST/EARLY PERFORMANCE: 29 June 1864, Mechanics' Hall, Montreal, Napoléon Legendre, tenor. PUBLISHED: Laurent & Laforce cie, [1864], 3 p. (Bibliothèque et archives Nationales du Québec; CBC Music Library, Toronto, (photocopy of 5th ed.); Library and Archives Canada (3rd and 5th eds); McGill University Libraries, Lande Collection). DEDICATION: "à Mademoiselle Marie Louise Dupré à Montréal." KEY: D major.

Transcription of *La Prière de Moïse*, piano
TRANSCRIBED: [Montreal, 1864?]. FIRST/EARLY PERFORMANCE: 7 April 1864, Mechanics' Hall, Montreal, Lavallée. PUBLISHED: No record of publication has been found. NOTES: From *Moses in Egypt*, by Gioachino Rossini.

*Les Quadrilles Canadiens*, band
FIRST/EARLY PERFORMANCE: 24 June 1864, Mechanics' Hall, Montreal, Lavallée conducting the Montreal City Band. PUBLISHED: No record of publication has been found. NOTES: a medley of unspecified national songs.

*La Leçon de chant électromagnétique*, tenor, bass, chamber orchestra
COMPOSER: Jacques Offenbach. ARRANGED: [Montreal, 1865?]. FIRST/EARLY PERFORMANCE: No record of performance has

been found. A performance was planned for 19 April 1865, at Nordheimer's Hall, Montreal. PUBLISHED: No record of publication has been found.

"Flag of Green, patriotic song," solo voice, SATB chorus, piano WORDS: J.B. Murphy; COMPOSER: Gustave Bidaux. ARRANGED: 1866. FIRST/EARLY PERFORMANCE: 15 March 1889, Tabernacle, Canton, Ohio.[28] PUBLISHED: Cook & Martin, Rochester, NY, 1866. DEDICATION: "Respectfully dedicated to the Fenian Brotherhood throughout the world." KEY: D major. NOTES: May have been composed for performance by members of the New Orleans Minstrels.

"Walking on the Beach," solo voice, piano WORDS AND MUSIC: Frank Dumont. ARRANGED: [Philadelphia, ca. 1869?]. FIRST/EARLY PERFORMANCE: "Great character song, sung by Frank Kent, the great burlesque artist of the San Francisco Minstrels, NY." PUBLISHED: Whittemore, ca. 1869, 5 p. (CBC Music Library, Toronto (photocopy); Library of Congress). NOTES: Frank Kent was a member of the San Francisco Minstrels in October and November 1869.

"Pretty Little Dark Eyes," voice, chorus, piano WORDS: Frank W Green. COMPOSER: Henry Parker. ARRANGED: [New York, ca. 1870?]. FIRST/EARLY PERFORMANCE: [1870, New York, San Francisco Minstrels?]. PUBLISHED: Pond, 1870, 3 p. (Indiana University, Bloomington, Lilly Library). KEY: E-flat major. NOTES: Originally published in London by C. Sheard in the 1860s.

*Les Brigands* (selections), vocalists, minstrel troupe orchestra WORDS: Henri Meilhac and Ludovic Halévy. COMPOSER: Jacques Offenbach. ARRANGED: [New York, ca. 1870?]. PERFORMANCE: February–April 1871, San Francisco Minstrels Hall, New York. PUBLISHED: No record of publication has been found.

Minuet (from String Quintet in E major, op. 13, no. 5), double string quartet
COMPOSER: Luigi Boccherini. ARRANGED: Montreal, 1876.
FIRST/EARLY PERFORMANCE: 9 May 1876, Association Hall, Montreal. PUBLISHED: E. Lavigne, 1878.

Medley of Irish Airs, chorus (SATB)
COMPOSER/AUTHOR: Traditional Irish. ARRANGED: Quebec City, March 1880. FIRST/EARLY PERFORMANCE: 17 May 1880, Music Hall, Quebec City, St Patrick's Church Choir, conducted by Lavallée. PUBLISHED: No record of publication has been found. NOTES: Lavallée created the work for performance at the St Patrick's Day concert on 17 May 1880.

"Andalouse," concert band with solo clarinet
COMPOSER: Calixa Lavallée. ARRANGED: [Boston, ca. 1886?].
FIRST/EARLY PERFORMANCE: 20 June 1886, Boston Common, Germania Band conducted by J.B. Claus, and E. Strasser, clarinet.
PUBLISHED: No record of publication has been found.

### SPURIOUS

All of the following titles are listed in the EMC (1993), unless otherwise indicated. I have, however, found no evidence that they were ever published or performed.

*Impromptu-Caprice*, piano

*Marche Americaine*, piano
FIRST/EARLY PERFORMANCE: [January 1888, London?]. PUBLISHED: No record of publication has been found. DEDICATION: "To the City of London."[29]

Mass in D minor, soloists, chorus, orchestra[30]
COMPOSED: [Boston, ca. 1890?].

Piano Trio, violin, cello, piano
NOTES: Listed in *L'Étude musicale* (April 1909).

Sonata, [violin, piano]

2 String Quartets
NOTES: Gustave Comte was the first to list string quartets among
   Lavallée works.[31]

Symphony, chorus, orchestra
COMPOSED: [Boston, ca. 1873 or ca. 1886?]. DEDICATION: "To the
   City of Boston."

Violin Concerto, [violin, orchestra]
NOTES: Arthur Letondal wrote that Alfred De Sève had told him that
   he had performed this work accompanied by Lavallée, since the
   composer had not written out the full score.[32]

# Appendix Two:
## Selected Compositions

Une Couronne de lauriers, caprice de genre, op. 10

"Flag of Green, patriotic song"

Le Papillon, étude de concert, op. 18

"We Never Tell a Lie," from *TIQ*

"Restons Français, chant de La Ligue des Patriotes"

# UNE COURONNE DE LAURIERS, CAPRICE DE GENRE, OP. 10

## Caprice

Calixa Lavallee

**Tempo primo**

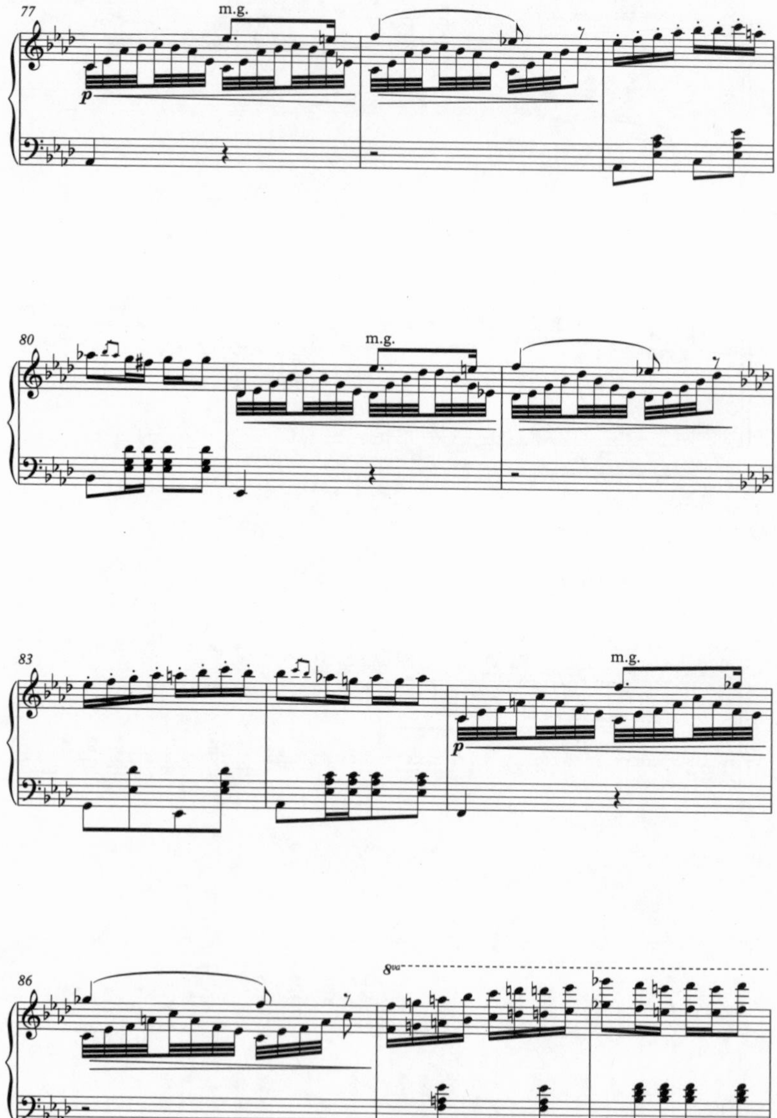
77
m.g.
p
80
m.g.
83
m.g.
p
86
8va

# FLAG OF GREEN!

CALIXA LAVALLEE.

Martial and con bravura.

53
sons__ will__ nev - er more be slaves!_____ Erin's sons__ will__
hopes to__ thee will ev - er burn._____ Erin's love__ for__
Harp_ for__ thee shall wake its lay;_____ Erin's God__ shall__

*pp*    *stacc.*

58
still no coward__ graves!_____ Swear ye all_____ this shall
thee will ev - er burn._____ Swear ye all_____ this shall
lead thy conquering way;_____ Swear ye all_____ this shall

*ff*

℘ed.    *

63
be;    Ire- land, Ire-land shall_____ be free!
be;    Ire- land_ Ire-land shall_____ be free!
be;    Ire- land_ Ire-land shall_____ be free!

*ff*    *f*    *mf*

℘ed.    *

By it swear to live and die!

sky swear to live and die!

sky swear to live and die!

A mon ami A. MARMONTEL.

# LE PAPILLON.
## (The Butterfly)

ETUDE de CONCERT

CALIXA LAVALLEE

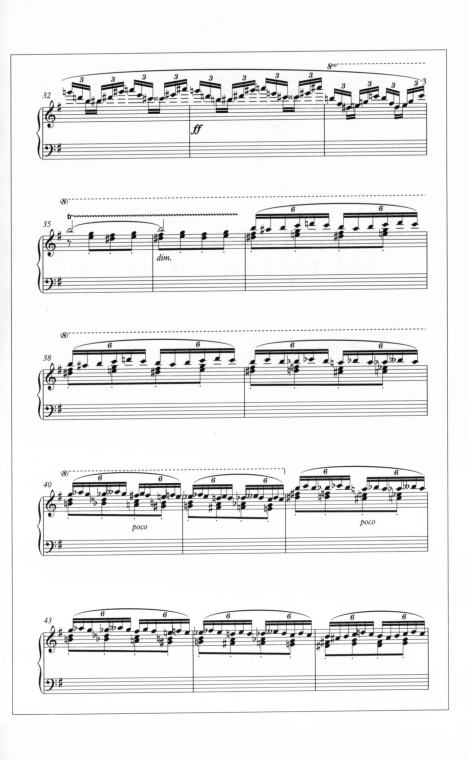

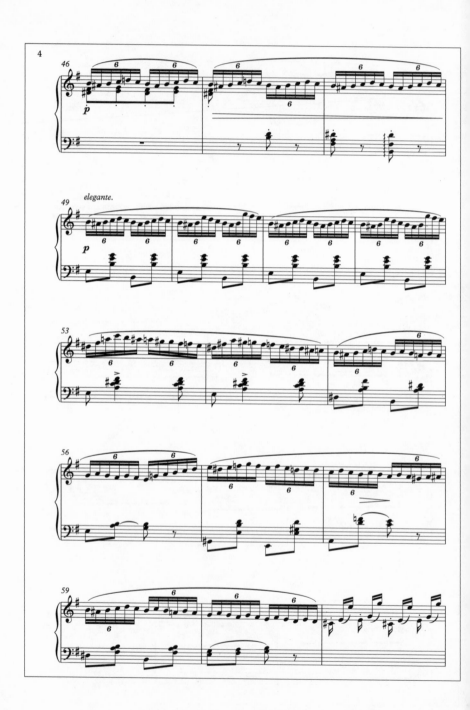

128

*Dance around captives and blow on fish Horns.*

# RESTONS FRANÇAIS

Paroles de REMI TREMBLAY

Musique de CALIXA LAVALLEE

1. Le ciel est noir, l'o-ra-ge s'a-mon-cèl-le    Et la dis-corde al-lu-me ses bran
2. Res-tons Fran çais! te nons tête à l'o-ra-ge;    Con-so-li-dons l'œu-vre de nos aï-
3. Grou-pés au-tour du dra-peau tri co-lo-re,    Francs Ca-na-diens, pré-pa rons l'a-ve-
4. Nous ta-cla mons, Li gue des pa-tri-o-trs,    Aux champs d'honneur nous suivrons nos ai

dons;    Pour é-tay-er un pou voir qui chan-cèl-le    Le fa-na-tisme ar-me ses mir mi
eux    En bu-ri-nant u-ne nou-vel-le pa-ge    Au li-vre d'or d'un pas sé glo-ri-
nir,    L'hor-rible af-front que notre or-gueil dé-vo-re    Grave en nos cœurs un cru el sou ve
nés;    Les Ca-na diens ne sont pas des i-lo-tes;    Nul ne sau-rait les te nir en-chaî-

2

dons;          As-sou-vis-sez     la  ra-ge des sec-tai-res      Frap-pez, frap-
eux.           Aux pré-ju-gés      op-po-sant u-ne-di-gue         No-tre jeu-
nir.           Ser rons nos rangs:  no-tre mé-re la Fran-ce       Pour la re-
nés,           Forts de nos droits,  lais-sant l'in-to-lé-ran-ce   S'em-poi-son-

pez! plats va-lets   des bour reaux;        Un peuple en-tier    mau-dit vos cau-da-
nesse, es-poir du    len-de-main,           De la dé-fense       or-ga-ni se la
vanche a-guer-rit    ses sol-dats:          Elle nous of-fre     un ray-on d'es-pé-
ner du suc de        ses fer-ments,         Nous res-te-rons     Français par la vail-

tai-res,     Et vos gi-gets font sur-gir des hé-ros.
Li-gue;      Mal-heur à qui sur nous por-te la main.
ran-ce       Et ses li-gneurs nous ont ou-vert leurs bras.
lan-ce.      Fran-çais de cœur, Fran-çais de sen-ti ments.

Quand l'op- pre - seur Quand l'op- pre - seur vent

nous for - ger des chai - nes, De son cour - roux Mé -

pri - sons les ac - cés, Et fiers du sang qui cou - le dans nos

veines___ Restons__ Fran - çais, Res - tons Fran - çais___ çais___

Au dernier couplet.

# Acknowledgments

The task of acknowledging all of the individuals who, in one way or another, have assisted me on this project is no simple matter, and I will inevitably overlook mentioning some. Nevertheless, working in chronological order, my thanks go first to Professor Peter F. McNally, of McGill University, who supervised my initial research project and continued to offer guidance. At the University of Hong Kong, my research supervisor, Michael Noone, provided frequent, thorough, and thoughtful critiques of my work, while my external examiner, Katherine Preston, of the College of William and Mary, gave generously of her time and expertise throughout my studies. Dr Preston's writings have been an inspiration as well as a source of information, illustrating how a scholar can make sense of the musical life of nineteenth-century North America in its many dimensions. And to John Beckwith and Carl Morey, both previous holders of the Jean A. Chalmers Chairs in Canadian Music and previous deans of the Faculty of Music at the University of Toronto, I express my thanks for their interest in my work and for their constant encouragement.

Among the many institutions that have helped to make this book a reality, I must first express my gratitude to the staff of the University of Hong Kong Libraries, who were of enormous help in obtaining the materials I needed between research trips to North America. Given the constraints of time and distance, I gathered vast amounts of information through correspondence, and must recognize the many individuals who took the time to respond to my queries, often going to considerable lengths to provide answers or information. Among those librarians and archivists whose assistance has been invaluable, I must thank: Paul Raspé, Bibliothèque du Conservatoire royal de Bruxelles; Bonnie Campbell, Library of Parliament, Ottawa; Richard Green, Roanne Mokhtar, Edwidge Munn, and Marlene Wehrle, Library and Archives Canada; Kathleen McMorrow, Faculty of Music Library, University of Toronto; Cheryl Martin, Metro Toronto Reference Library; the staff of the Bibliothèque et Archives nationales du Québec (Montreal and Quebec City); Nicole Boisclair, Conservatoire de musique de Montréal; Télesphore Gagnon, Grand Séminaire de Montréal; Jane Kingsland, McGill University Archives; the staff of McGill University Libraries; staff of the Bibliothèque de Musique and of the Archives of l'Université de Montréal; Françoise Ménard, Conservatoire de musique de Québec; Claude Beaudry, Bibliothèque de la Musique, l'Université Laval; James H. Lambert, Archives, l'Université Laval; Centre d'Archives du Séminaire de Saint-Hyacinthe; Bibliothèque Marie Bonenfant, Saint-Jean-Port-Joli; Laurence Benoist, Archives, Conservatoire national supérieur de musique et de danse de Paris; Florence Clavaud, Archives nationales de France; Catherine Massip, Département de la Musique, Bibliothèque nationale de France; Paul Machlis, Music Library, University of California, Santa Cruz; Susan Clermont, Charles Sens, and Wayne D. Shirley, Music Division, Library of Congress; Becky Cape, Lilly Library, Indiana University Bloomington; Louisiana Library Association; Laura Dankner, Loyola University, New Orleans; Isabella Athey, Maryland Historical Society; Edwin Quist, Friedheim Music Library, Peabody Institute, Johns Hopkins University, Baltimore; Joan Gratton, Milton S. Eisenhower Library, Johns Hopkins University; Aaron Schmidt, of the Prints Department, Boston Public Library, and the staff of the Music Department and Microfilms Collection, Boston Public Library; William Milhomme, Massachusetts Archives; Jean A. Morrow and Patrick H. Maxfield, Harriet M. Spaulding Library, New England Conservatory of Music; Mary Reynolds, Fall River Public Library; Peter S. Alexis, Pollard Memorial Library, Lowell, Massachusetts; Charles E. Brown, St Louis Mercantile Library, University of Missouri–St Louis; Nathan Eakin, Gaylord Music Library, Washington University, St Louis, Missouri; Buffalo and Erie County Public Library; Sion M. Honea and Mary Wallace, Sibley Music Library, Eastman

School of Music, University of Rochester; the staff of Music Division and the Microforms Room, New York Public Library; Timothy Cherubini, Assistant Director, Duke University Music Library; Suzanne Geisinger, Cleveland Public Library; Roland M. Baumann, College Archivist, Oberlin College Archives; Paula Mentusky, Free Library of Philadelphia; Rosemary L. Cullen, Peter Harrington, and Rita H. Warnock, John Hay Library, Brown University; Kenneth S. Carlson, Rhode Island State Archives; and Mrs C.A. Banks, The British Library.

Historical societies, museums, religious institutions, and other institutions have provided answers to many of my questions. In particular, I must express my thanks to: Douglas Cumming, Andrew Dunnett, and the late Helmut Kallmann, Canadian Musical Heritage Society, Ottawa; Paulette-Marie Sauvé, Musée Calixa-Lavallée; G.E. Proulx, Collège de Lévis; Luc Chaput, l'Orchestre symphonique de la Montérégie, Longueuil, Quebec; Caroline Sigouin, Concordia University Archives; Roxanne Léonard, Fabrique de la paroisse Notre-Dame de Montréal; Jane MacKinnon, Historic Theatres' Trust (Montreal); Nora Hague and staff of the Notman Photographic Archives, McCord Museum; Richard Coulombe, Archives de l'Archidiocèse de Québec; Martine Ménard, Archives de la Ville de Québec; Joseph Lonergan, Irish Heritage Québec; Simon Couture, Casavant Frères (Saint-Hyacinthe, Quebec); Kelly Nolin and Martha H. Smart, Connecticut Historical Society, Hartford, Connecticut; Gail R. Redmann, The Historical Society of Washington, DC; Jack Belsom, New Orleans Opera Association; Mark Cave and Pamela D. Arceneaux, The Historic New Orleans Collection; Sister Benedicta Burkart, Archivist, Hôtel-Dieu Hospital, New Orleans; Reverend John L. Doyle, Pastor of St Peter's Church, Boston; Leo Abbott, Cathedral of the Holy Cross, Boston; the staff of the Bostonian Society; Jamelle Tanous Lyons and Deborah L. Collins, Fall River Historical Society; D.R. Leggat, St Anne's Episcopal Church, Lowell, Massachusetts; Russell L. Martin III, American Antiquarian Society, Worchester, Massachusetts; Elizabeth Lessard, Manchester Historic Association, Manchester, New Hampshire; Buffalo and Erie County Historical Society; Carol Fede, Office of the City Historian, Rochester, New York; Starlyn D'Angelo, curator of the Shaker Museum and Library, Old Chatham, N.Y.; Robert N. Anderson, Rensselaer County Historical Society, Troy, New York; Joseph

Brye, Archivist, Music Teachers National Association (Cincinnati); Maureen Taylor, Rhode Island Historical Society; Karen A. Shaffer, Maud Powell Foundation, Arlington, Virginia; and Pamela Clark, The Royal Archives, Windsor Castle, Berkshire, United Kingdom.

Many individuals have assisted me in various aspects of my research. To John H. Baron, E. Douglas Bomberger, Robert Eliason, Sharon F. Flescher, John Gillespie, Reverend Pierre E Lachance, Peter Lee, Christina Magaldi, Andrew Mambo, Lynn Matheson, Patrick Meadows, Katherine Schulke, Sara Wong, the late Adrienne Fried Block, and the late Vera Brodsky Lawrence: I am most grateful.

A note of thanks also goes to my research assistants at the Chinese University of Hong Kong: Adriana Martínez Falcón, who created the maps, and Leung Chi-Hin, who prepared the scores. It has been a pleasure to work with the fine staff of the McGill-Queen's University Press and with my copy editor, Eleanor Gasparik, whose attention to detail and judicious advice have improved this book in many ways.

And finally, to my wife, Gabrielle, who over the years has located information for me, stored my stacks of microfilms, caught my typos, tolerated my mood swings, and much more, I express my greatest thanks. She has known of Calixa Lavallée nearly as long as she has known me, and I expect she considers us inseparable.

# Notes

## PROLOGUE

1 Hardy's ensemble comprised members of his own band and some from the Grenadier Guards, Victoria Rifles, Black Watch, Maisonneuve Regiment, the Royal Montreal Regiment, and the Fusilliers de Montréal. Hardy later reported the 13 July 1933 performance to have been his last. See Tracy S. Ludington, "Veteran Band Leader had 'Honor' of Introducing Saxophone Here," *Montreal Gazette*, 23 September 1938.

2 The text of Lapierre's speech was printed in "Lavallée est renter au pays et dans la gloire," *La Presse*, 14 July 1933.

3 Participants in the 19 July 1933 event included the Société Saint-Jean-Baptiste, the Knights of Columbus, and the St Patrick's Society.

4 "Numéro-Souvenir: Calixa Lavallée," *Le Passe-Temps*, 39, no. 864 (August 1933).

5 The CRBC, precursor to the Canadian Broadcasting Corporation, had been established in 1932 and began service in May 1933. On 14 July 1933, those tuning in listened to the organist Poirier perform as Lavallée's remains made their way to the gravesite. On arrival at the cemetery, the broadcaster switched to that location. The local radio station, CKAC, also took part, broadcasting some of the concerts, including Poirier's recital of Lavallée's music on 12 July.

6 "Les restes de Calixa Lavallée reposent maintenant en terre canadienne," *Le Devoir*, 14 July 1933.

7 "Projet de mausolée," *Le Devoir*, 19 July 1933.

8 I use the term "French Canadian" in preference to "Québécois," as it was used both in Lavallée's time and well into the twentieth century to describe the French-speaking inhabitants of what is now Quebec as well as other parts of Canada and the United States.

9 David, "Calixa Lavallée," 13 October 1873.

10 See Monet, *The Last Cannon Shot*, and Bernard, *Les Rouges, libéralisme, nationalisme et anticléricalisme*.

11 The Act of Parliament that made "O Canada" the official anthem of Canada received Royal Assent on Dominion Day (now Canada Day), 1 July 1980. See

"National Anthem: O Canada," www.pch.gc.ca/pgm/ceem-cced/symbl/anthem-eng.cfm.

12 General interest pieces on Lavallée appear with some regularity in the English-language Canadian press. See, for instance, Atherton, "'O Canada,'" and Abel, "'O Canada' Composer Fought for Union."

13 Recent publications, such as *Musical Constructions of Nationalism* (White and Murphy) and *Music Makes the Nation* (Curtis), follow in the tradition of such influential academics as Leon Plantinga and Roger Kamien in looking almost exclusively at the classical tradition. *Musical Constructions of Nationalism* examines the music of Scandinavia, France, Italy, and other parts of Europe. *Music Makes the Nation* focuses on three European composers: Grieg, Wagner, and Smetana. See also Plantinga, *Romantic Music*, 341–404; and Kamien, *Music: An Appreciation*, 367–89.

14 Although there was no national canon of orchestral or operatic works, Anthony Philip Heinrich, William Henry Fry, George F. Bristow, and a few other composers were active in the US before the Civil War. Few of their works would be given public performances. Similarly, the French musician Joseph Quesnel was active in Canada in the final years of the eighteenth century and early years of the nineteenth (see Beckwith).

15 Bohlman, *Music, Nationalism and the Making of the New Europe*, 5.

## CHAPTER ONE

1 See Greer, *Peasant, Lord and Merchant*, 3–15.

2 See Déragon, *Étude généalogique*, 81–2; Magnan (1927); and Potvin and Spier, "Calixa Lavallée." In his major study of French-Canadian genealogy, Cyprien Tanguay traces the earliest arrival of a Lavallée to another French soldier, Pierre Lavallée, who was born in France in 1645. The twenty-year-old Lavallée and his fourteen-year-old wife, Marie-Thérèse LeBlanc, landed in Quebec City on 12 January 1665 and later settled on the nearby Ile d'Orléans. See Tanguay, *Dictionnaire généalogique des familles canadiennes* (vol. 5), 199.

3 See Breton, "From Ethnic to Civic Nationalism," 93–4; Mann, *The Dream of Nation*, 48–66; and Cook, *Watching Quebec*, 68–72. The historian Gilles Chaussé has found that usage of the words "nationality" and "canadien-français" became common in Quebec around 1822, when Lower Canada (Quebec) was annexed to the anglophone province of Upper Canada (Ontario). See "Les Effets de la Revolution Française," 298.

4 Land could no longer be divided between offspring to create economically viable farms, nor could they acquire land nearby. Displaced young men could find work as day labourers or become artisans. Others sought employment in Montreal factories; in time, many more – both male and female, young and old – began to leave for the cotton mills of New England. See Greer, *Peasant, Lord and Merchant*, 217–31.

5 *Le Canadien*, a newspaper founded in Quebec City in 1806 by the Parti canadien (also known as the Parti patriote), played a leading role in shaping opinion and developing this nascent sense of national identity. See Reid, "L'Émergence du nationalisme Canadien-Français."

6 Lambton, *Lord Durham's Report*, 13.

7 See Bernard, *Les Rouges, libéralisme, nationalisme et anticléricalisme*, 22; Monet, *The Last Cannon Shot*, 24–5; and Mann, *The Dream of Nation*, 79–80. Upper Canada and Lower Canada became known as Canada West and Canada East, respectively, but the older names remained in common usage and are used here.

8 Valentine had arrived in 1780 and later settled in the Verchères region, where he married a French-Canadian woman named Leclerc. See Potvin and Spier, "Calixa Lavallée."

9 See "Mort de Monsieur Augustin Lavallée," *La Presse*, 16 February 1903; and "Talented Canadian Citizen Dead: Was Famous Maker of Violins," *Montreal Daily Star*, 15 February 1903.

10 Sauvé, *Joseph Casavant: Le Facteur d'orgues romantique*, 76. Abbé Ducharme had founded the Collège in 1825. A fire razed the main building in 1881, presumably destroying all of the early records. The school became part of Quebec's junior college system in 1967 and was renamed the Cégèp Lionel-Groulx.

11 Sauvé writes that Lavallée played works by Haydn and Handel, two fugues of his own, and improvised on a Kyrie. Sauvé, *Joseph Casavant*, 79. See also Auclair, *Un Éducateur d'il y a Cents Ans*, 18.

12 Marriage record, April 1842: Charlotte-Caroline Valentine and Augustin Paquet, Verchères. Quebec Vital and Church Records (Drouin Collection), 1621–1967.

13 The text of the birth certificate was published in Magnan, "Calixa Lavallée," 414; and reprinted in Magnan, *Cinquantenaire*, 23; and J.A.F. "Chronique d'Ottawa: Calixa Lavallée," *La Presse*, 10 July 1933. As the latter article points out, the certificate omits Augustin's full surname, Paquet dit Lavallée. Both articles provide the spelling that Lavallée later adopted: Calixa, rather than Calixte. "28 December 1842, by we the undersigned, priest, was baptized Calixa, born this day, of the legitimate marriage of Jean-Baptiste Paquet Jr, blacksmith of this parish, and Charlotte Caroline Valentine. The godfather was Jean-Baptiste Paquet Sr, and the godmother Charlotte Lalu, who could not sign. AD. Bruneau, Parish priest."

14 For a discussion of the architecture of the village, see *Calixa-Lavallée répertoire d'architecture traditionelle*.

15 See Gossage, *Families in Transition*, 6–7.

16 W. Williams, *The Traveller's and Tourist's Guide* (1851), 10–11.

17 See Louise Voyer, *Saint-Hyacinthe* (1980).

18 The Collège de Saint-Hyacinthe was incorporated as the Séminaire in 1833 but continued to use the name Collège. During the rebellions of 1837 and 1838, authorities viewed the Collège with suspicion. The old Collège building was destroyed in the 1854 fire. Since 1992, it has been a private secondary school, the Collège Antoine-Girouard.

19 *Catalogue des élèves du séminaire de Saint-Hyacinthe depuis 1818* (1875), 55.

20 Access to education had improved somewhat in the decade since 1842, when schools accommodated only 4,935 of the province's 111,244 children age five to fourteen. See Linteau, *Quebec: A History, 1867–1929*, 205.

21 Information on the Collège is taken primarily from Voyer, and from C.-P.

Choquette, *1811–1911 Histoire du Séminaire de Saint-Hyacinthe depuis sa formation*, Tome I (1911).

22 See "Mort de Monsieur Augustin Lavallée," *La Presse*, 16 February 1903, 1; "Talented Canadian Citizen Dead: Was Famous Maker of Violins," *Montreal Daily Star*, 15 February 1903, 6; and "Death of First Canadian Violin Maker," *Strad* 13 (1903): 368. In 2010, the Musée de la civilisation, in Quebec City, acquired what is thought to be the only surviving violin made by Lavallée. "Un violon signé Augustin Lavallée." Radio-Canada.ca, 30 June 2010.

23 "Augustin Lavallée," advertisement, *Courrier de Saint-Hyacinthe*, 27 May 1853.

24 David, L.-O. [Laurent-Olivier], "Calixa Lavallée," *L'Opinion publique*, 13 March 1873.

25 Gilles Potvin, "Music in Saint-Hyacinthe."

26 J.B. "Calixa Lavallée" (1891), 655. I have examined issues of the *Courrier de Saint-Hyacinthe* from 1853 to 1856 but have located no references to a performance by the choir. Barbarin (1812–75) served as maître de chappelle at the parish of Notre Dame de Montréal, 1854–61 and 1866–74. See Gauthier, *La Compagnie de Saint-Sulpice au Canada*, 25.

27 J.A.F., "Chronique d'Ottawa: Calixa Lavallée," *La Presse*, 10 July 1933.

28 David was perhaps the first to credit Augustin Lavallée with being his sons' first music teacher. David, L.-O. [Laurent-Olivier], "Calixa Lavallée," *L'Opinion publique*, 13 March 1873: 131.

29 See "Institut-Canadien," advertisement, *Courrier de Saint-Hyacinthe*, 23 June 1854; and "L'Institut Canadien," *Courrier de Saint-Hyacinthe*, 27 June 1854.

30 Comte, "Calixa Lavallée" (1909), 315.

31 See David, 13 March 1873.

32 The 1847 *Montreal Directory* (Lovell, 1847) lists "Derome, butcher," as residing on Visitation Street. After an absence from the 1848 edition, Léon is entered in the 1849, 1850, and 1852 editions (no publication in 1851) on Brock, near Dorchester Street. In 1853, he is listed as "Derome, Léon, butcher, Beaudry, near Dorchester" (p. 73) but does not appear again until 1857, as "Louis" (which is subsequently used interchangeably with Léon) at stall 72 of the Bonsecours Market. No residence is given in 1857, but in 1858, it is listed as 28 Beaudry (p. 111).

33 The 1861 Census recorded the family home to be a wood-frame house and possessions to have included one horse, one cow, two pigs, and two carriages, and the business to be worth $3,000. *Census of Canada for 1861: Montreal*. There were fifteen people residing in the house at the time of the 1861 census: Léon and Matilde, their nine children, and four others, at least two of whom appear to have been butcher-shop employees. The section of rue Beaudry on which the Deromes lived was cleared in the 1950s when Dorchester (now René Lévesque) Boulevard was widened and the Maison Radio-Canada built.

34 Lapierre wrote that, in 1855, having heard about Lavallée, Derome took the stagecoach to Verchères to hear him play, and that a week later the twelve-year-old Lavallée was living at Derome's house. Lapierre, "Calixa Lavallée:

Compositeur National" (1949), 37. Lapierre would seem to be mistaken on this point, since by 1855, the Lavallée family was living in Saint-Hyacinthe.

35 *Census of 1852* published in the *Montreal Directory 1856–57* (Lovell, 1856), 383. By 1861, Catholics made up just over 72 per cent of the city's population. *Census of 1861* published in the *Montreal Directory 1863–64* (Lovell, 1863), 368.

36 Thoreau, *A Yankee in Canada*, 27.

37 Ibid.

38 See Monet, *The Last Cannon Shot*, 272–3; and Mann, *The Dream of Nation*, 95–6. Under the Canada Corn Act of 1843, grain exporters from the colonies were given access to the British market at very low rates of duty. Britain repealed the Act in 1846 as it moved toward free trade (See Mccalla, "Canada Corn Act").

39 Linteau (*Quebec: A History*, 29) claims that during the 1840s, 35,000 francophones emigrated from Canada to the United States. This number rose to 70,000 in the 1850s, and continued to a high of 150,000 in the 1880s. By the time the Great Depression ended the exodus, some 900,000 had left. In *The French-Canadian Idea of Confederation* (p. 14), Silver cites more emigration, estimating that between 1844 and 1849, 20,000 French Canadians left for the US, and that over the subsequent five decades, as many as 500,000 may have departed.

40 See Monet, *The Last Cannon Shot*, 334–53.

41 The Gavazzi Riots took place in Quebec City and Montreal on 6 and 9 June 1853, respectively. In both instances, it was Irish Catholics that led the fight against Gavazzi. In Montreal, troops fired on the protestors. In the aftermath, Protestant newspapers accused the Catholic mayor, Charles Wilson, of ordering the troops to shoot. See Sylvain, "Charles Wilson."

42 See note 39.

43 After the events of 1849, the 1850s seemed relatively peaceful. Toronto served as capital for the remainder of the 3rd Parliament. Following the elections of October 1851, the legislature shifted between Toronto and Quebec City, as a symbol of power sharing. This situation continued up until 1865, even though in 1858, Queen Victoria had selected Ottawa as the future capital of the colony, and her son, Albert Edward, Prince of Wales, laid the cornerstone of the Pariament Buildings' Centre Block during his 1860 visit to North America.

44 Passed in 1854, the Canadian–American Reciprocity Treaty was in effect from January 1855 to March 1866. Officer and Smith (1968) challenge the widely accepted view that the Treaty itself was the reason for most of the economic growth in Canada. See also Cooper, "The Social Structure of Montreal in the 1850s," 63–6.

45 In October 1854, the society columnist of *La Patrie* announced that the first soiree of the season had taken place at the home of a Monsieur L___M.P.P., "one of our most pleasant citizens and most distinguished lawyers." The columnist expressed his hope that, with the epidemic finally over, this would be but the first of many such gatherings. "Chronique Montréal," *La Patrie*, 13 October 1854.

46 "Grand Concert Patriotique," *La Patrie*, 12 January 1855.

47 The Mechanics' Institute Hall remained a popular venue into the 1880s. The building was demolished at the end of that decade as the neighbourhood became the financial district and the residents moved to areas further north and west. The current Mechanics' Institute Hall is also known as the Atwater Library and is located on Atwater Avenue. See Mechanics' Institute of Montreal, *Mechanics' Institute* (1930). See also "Nordheimer Hall," *Montreal Pilot*, 30 June 1859. The A. & S. Nordheimer firm, established by Abraham and Samuel Nordheimer, was a major music retailer and publisher in nineteenth-century Canada.

48 The third Theatre Royal, known as the Royal-Hays, was located on Dalhousie Square. It was destroyed by the fire of 1852.

49 See Dufresne, "Le Theatre Royal de la rue Côté," 74–6.

50 See "Institut des artisans," advertisement, *La Patrie*, 19 June 1855.

51 The troupe of "Famous Chinese actors, jugglers and magicians" appeared at Odd Fellows Hall from 24 September 1855. See "Odd Fellows Hall," advertisement, *La Patrie*, 28 September 1855.

52 *Orpheus* I, no. 1 (July 1865): 6.

53 See Preston, *Opera on the Road*, 216–30.

54 Herz described his tours in *Mes voyages en Amérique*.

55 Perhaps as a way of illustrating Lavallée's musical prowess, Lapierre claimed he defeated Urso, among others, in a music competition in New Orleans. The story appears to have had no basis in fact. Lapierre, *Calixa Lavallée* (1966), 47–8.

56 Several newspapers noted the plans for a concert by the Belgian violinist Henri Vieuxtemps in the summer of 1858, but there is no conclusive evidence that he performed in the city until 1871.

57 Harold Schonberg has disparagingly referred to Thalberg as being "primarily interested in showing off his extensive bag of tricks," with "an introduction, a series of variations that includes one in a minor key, and a bang-up finale." Schonberg, "Keyboard Fantasies," 18.

58 From 1856 through the 1860s, Jean-Baptiste Benoît Larue taught music at Montreal's Grand Séminaire, which in 1857 moved into its new facilities on what is now Sherbrooke Street. See *Annuaire de Ville-Marie* (1863), 122–3, and the *Registre du Grand Séminaire de Montréal*, t. I, 1840–1900. At this time, the province had two universities, McGill and Laval, but they did not add music to their curriculums until early in the twentieth century. In 1857, two normal schools opened, one operated by McGill and the other being the École normale Jacques Cartier, both offering some music training for teachers. North American cities did not begin to develop European-style music conservatories until the late 1860s, and even then, they were in most instances private rather than public institutions.

59 See David, "Calixa Lavallée," 13 March 1873, 131.

60 Lapierre, *Calixa Lavallée* (1966), 43. Lapierre did not provide a source for this information.

61 See Potvin, "Paul Letondal," and Blanche Gagnon, "Paul Letondal."

62  See "Letondal & Cie.," advertisement, *La Minerve*, January 1855, 3.

63  In a review of a concert at which Letondal had performed on both instruments, the anonymous critic of *La Patrie* called Letondal's piano technique "serious and methodical," noting that "it is especially on the cello that he excels." "Revue Artistique," *La Patrie*, 30 December 1854.

64  See "Institut Philotechnique," *La Patrie*, 2 July 1856.

65  Letondal is first listed in the *Montreal Directory* in 1854 ("Letondal, Paul, musician") as living at 16 St Lawrence Street. From 1855 to 1860, he is listed at 105 St Lawrence. After being absent from the 1861 and 1862 editions, from 1863 to 1871 he is listed as residing at 223 de la Gauchetière Street.

66  See Smith, "Du mouvement musical en Canada." Smith refers to the organist Brauneis and the pianist and organist Leonard Eglau as representing the "German school" of piano playing in Montreal of the 1840s and '50s.

67  Gottschalk, *Notes of a Pianist* (2006), 157. Two of Letondal's students, Dominique Ducharme and Octave Pelletier, had both given performances of *L'Ange Déchu* in the early months of 1862.

68  Lavallée mentioned Dominique Ducharme, M. Saucier, and Miss Derôme. "This proves," he wrote, "that not only those who see clearly can teach piano well. The same cannot be said for all those who teach." Calixa Lavallée, "Le Concert de Camille Urso," *L'Union nationale*, 3 December 1864.

69  See Arthur Letondal, "Calixa Lavallée et l'Hymne National" (1915).

70  Both Sabatier and his father were teachers of César-Joseph Delespaul (b. 1841). See *Dictionnaire national des contemporains* [Tome cinquieme], 106.

71  See Kallmann, "Charles Sabatier."

72  Sabatier's claim to this title appears on the cover of his *Marche aux Flambeaux* (Philadelphia: G. André and Company, 1859), a composition that he dedicated to the pianist Ignaz Moscheles. The Duchess was the Infanta Maria Luisa Fernanda of Spain, who, in 1846, married Antoine d'Orléans, the youngest son of King Louis Philippe of France, and settled for a time in Paris.

73  Léo Roy wrote that his grandfather, Régis Roy, a tax collector for the Port of Quebec, was at the Hôtel Blanchard one day in 1848 when a French sailor came in for a drink. He soon found his way to the piano and astonished those present with his playing. Roy, apparently a connoisseur, asked Sabatier if he would be interested in remaining in Quebec to work as a professional musician. Sabatier agreed and Roy arranged to have him released from his commitments aboard ship. See "La verité sur Sabatier," *L'Action nationale*, 57, no. 8 (April 1968): 709. In his article, "Un Musicien oublié," (p. 132), Arthur Letondal claimed that Sabatier told the Quebec City musician Ernest Gagnon that he had left a wife and two daughters in France. If true, one of these daughters may have pursued a career in opera, as there are many references to a Mlle Wugk in Paris in the late 1860s.

74  See Le Vasseur, "Musique et musiciens à Québec," *La Musique*, 2, no. 22 (October 1920): 172.

75  The periodical reported that "the pianist C. Wugk Sabatier, formerly in Lille, has recently been heard in Guernsey, and the local newspaper has the highest praise for this young artist who must, they say, spend some time in this resi-

dence. This is a good acquisition for Guernsey." *Le Ménestrel* (Paris), 4 and 11 June 1848, np.

76 Le Vasseur, "Musique et Musiciens à Québec," *La Musique*, 2, no. 22 (October 1920): 172.

77 *La Montréalaise*, with words by Vogeli and music by Sabatier, was published by John Lovell in 1858. Vogeli was a veterinarian who was living in Montreal in 1857. See Fournier, *Les Français au Québec*, 286.

78 "Revue Artistique," *La Patrie*, 27 October 1856.

79 Sabatier performed the *March au Flambeaux* at a concert at Nordheimer's Concert Hall on 18 February 1860, after Lavallée's departure, but had published it in 1859. Lavallée performed it in Montreal on 27 October 1864.

80 "Le Sud et L'Ouest," advertisement, *L'Avenir*, 30 October 1856.

81 Alfrèd Paré had given the first public performance of "O Carillon" in Quebec City, with Sabatier at the piano, on 15 May 1858. The same year, J. & O. Crémazie published the song in Quebec City. The words of his song along with the lyrics of dozens of other national songs, including Vogeli's "La Montréalaise," were published in the *Recueil de Chansons Canadienne et Françaises* in 1859.

82 No records pertaining to Montreal theatre musicians have been found. In an 1848 discussion of the personnel requirements of a theatre, John Gaisford writes only that, "among the adjuncts to a Theatre, the Leader of the Band and the Musicians in the Orchestra must be included as expensive items." See Gaisford, *Theatrical Thoughts, and Conundrums, Sent to J. Gaisford, on the Occasion of His Benefit at the Theatre Royal*, 40.

83 Donegana's was located on Notre Dame Street, Rasco's on Saint-Paul Street, and St Lawrence Hall on Great St James Street.

84 For discussions of the Catholic Church's censure of theatre, see Barrière, "La Société Canadienne-française," 345–75; Barrière, "Le goupillon, le maillet et la censure du théâtre lyrique à Montréal (1840–1914)"; Jean Laflamme and Rémi Tourangeau, *L'Église et le théâtre au Québec*; and Hathorn, "Sarah Bernhardt and the Bishops of Montreal and Quebec."

85 When Oliver Goldsmith's comedy *She Stoops to Conquer* opened in June 1857 with a cast headed by an American named Belton, a heated debate ensued between the critics of two of the city's French-language newspapers over the appropriateness of his accent. No doubt there were political undertones in any debate between the Liberal-Conservative *La Patrie* and the Liberal *Le Pays*.

86 Most of what has been written about Lavallée's debut has been speculative and erroneous. The problem has resulted, in part, from confusion over his early appearance as an organist. David (13 March 1873) reported that Lavallée made his debut at the Theatre Royal at eleven years of age. US music journals published similar accounts in the 1880s, writing that he was twelve. "Calixa Lavallee," *Musical Courier*, X, no. 14 (8 April 1885): 212, *Brainard's Musical World*, 22, no. 5 (May 1885): 167. Later accounts varied little. Letondal, "Calixa Lavallée" (1919), for instance, wrote that Lavallée was eleven. I conducted a thorough review of Montreal newspapers of the 1850s but found no references to Lavallée until the early months of 1859.

87 "La Carte à payer," advertisement, *Le Pays*, 26 February 1859; "Canadian Amateurs," advertisement, *The Pilot*, 28 February 1859.

88 See "Théâtre-Royal," *Le Pays*, 3 March 1859.

89 "Théâtre-Royal," *La Minerve*, 3 March 1859.

90 "Augustin Lavallée," advertisement, *Courrier de Saint-Hyacinthe*, from November 1857 to February 1858. Much of Cascades Street had been rebuilt following the fire of May 1854. For a discussion of the effect of this and subsequent fires, see Voyer, *Saint-Hyacinthe: de la seigneurie à la ville québécoise*, 34–6.

91 "Un Grand Concert-Promenade," advertisement, *La Minerve*, 21 June 1859.

92 "Correspondances," *Le Pays*, 2 July 1859.

93 See "General Summary," *New York Clipper*, 1 October 1859, 190, and "General Summary," *New York Clipper*, 22 October 1859: 215.

94 The four members of the Virginia Minstrels were the circus performer Daniel Decatur Emmett, the dancer and singer Frank Brower, tambourinist Dick Pelham, and banjo player Billy Whitlock. In 1843, they travelled to England where Emmett's *Celebrated Negro Melodies* was first published. For two recent discussions of the early years of minstrelsy, see Cockrell, *Demons of Disorder* and Mahar, *Behind the Burnt Cork Mask*. The minstrel show impresario Charles White published a series of articles on the first history of minstrelsy in the *New York Clipper* in the 1850s and early 1860s. For a summary of his history, see Charles White, "Negro Minstrelsy" (1860): 15.

95 Theatrical representations of blacks by whites already had a long history. The use of black dialect in song, written and performed by white musicians, went back to at least 1815 and the publication of "Back Side of Albany Stands Lake Champlain." This piece was sung first in the city of its title, and soon after in New York, by Hopkins Robinson, a former circus clown turned comic actor, who appeared in blackface. See Cockrell, "Nineteenth-Century Popular Music," 165–75. Two stock characters of minstrelsy, the urban dandy or 'Zip Coon,' and the plantation slave, 'Jim Crow,' had been fixtures on the American stage since the late 1820s, and were central to the early minstrel show of the 1840s. The slave character Jim Crow is most closely associated with the New York actor Thomas Dartmouth Rice, and his Northern, free counterpart, Zip Coon, with the Virginia-born George Washington Dixon.

96 E.P. Christy's Original Band of Virginia Minstrels began an engagement at New York's Mechanics' Institute in 1846 that lasted for 2,792 performances. See Sanjek, *American Popular Music and Its Business*, 174.

97 In 1869, the *New York Clipper* published an article illustrating that the structure of the minstrel show had not changed significantly. It begins: "Ting a ling a ling. Curtain rises, discerning a row of gentlemen in broadcloth and patent leathers, with curly wigs and corked faces. A rather corpulent gent in the centre informs the audience that the evening's entertainment will begin with an overture; whereat they raise their instruments and attack the overture in a vigorous manner." "At the Minstrels" (1869).

98 See Winans, "Early Minstrel Show Music, 1843–1852." Illustrations of performances and advertisements for musicians are among the best sources of in-

formation on musicians, as reviews usually focused on the comedians and singers.

99 The "Opening Chorus" is quoted in the company's songsters without the printed music, which appears not to have been published.

100 The company published several songsters, each of which gives biographical material and a history of the troupe, though the dates are not consistent. See *The People's New Songster, Duprez & Benedict's New Songster*, and *Chas. H. Dupre's Famous Songster.*

101 See *Duprez & Benedict's New Songster* (ca. 1875), 3. The minstrel historian Daily Paskman stated that Duprez was "Parisian by birth" and had arrived in New Orleans with an unspecified touring French opera troupe. See "Charles H. Duprez," *New York Clipper*, 19 March 1864: 385; and Paskman, *Gentlemen, Be Seated*, 167.

102 "Charles H. Duprez Dead," *Boston Daily Globe*, 1 September 1902.

103 Lavallée is referred to as a pianist in "General Summary," *New York Clipper*, 14 January 1860: 310. The dedication on the sheet music reads: "To Mrs R.W. Laithe, of Troy, NY." Calixa Lavallée, *La Fleur de mai (The May Flower), polka de salon pour le piano* (Troy, NY: William Cluett and Son, 1859).

104 "New Music," *Troy Daily Times*, 26 November 1859. "We have received from Messrs Cluett & Son, *La Fleur de Mai (The May Flower) Polka de Salon*, composed by Calixa Lavallée and dedicated to our favorite songstress R. W. Laithe. This is a charming Polka, brilliant, but not too difficult. It is got up in the usual good style of Messrs C & Son's publications."

105 "Cluett & Son's New Music List," advertisement, *Albany Evening Journal*, 21 March 1860.

106 The *New York Clipper* reported that they did "a capital business" as they passed through Ohio, stopping in Cleveland, Mansfield, and elsewhere, in December and early January. "General Summary," *New York Clipper*, 24 December 1859: 310.

107 See Thompson, "Journeys of an Immigrant Violinist," 64–5.

108 The Napoléon, located on Saint-Louis Street, and the Royal Palace Beer Saloon and Concert Hall, on Royal Street, provided work for a large number of musicians, as did the Varieties and other major theatres.

109 See Kendall, *The Golden Age of New Orleans Theater*, 114. The Saint Charles was built by James H. Caldwell, a British actor, playwright, entrepreneur, and gambler.

110 The nineteenth century had brought an influx of immigrants and Anglo-American migrants, despite frequent floods and outbreaks of cholera and yellow fever. Citizens with the financial means would escape the city during the worst of times, but the majority survived as best they could, and often adapted remarkably well. Some of the first concerts of the newly created Philharmonic Society were organized as benefits for the widows and orphans of orchestra members.

111 "New Band of Minstrels," *New Orleans Times-Picayune*, 26 February 1860.

112 "Amusements," *Times-Picayune*, 28 February 1860. The troupe also advertised in the *New Orleans Daily Delta* and the *New Orleans Daily Crescent*, but neither of those newspapers reviewed their performances.

113 "Odd Fellows Hall," *New Orleans Courier*, 29 February 1860.

114 *Robert Le Diable* was playing at the New Opera House, a vaudeville at the Théâtre d'Orléans, pantomime and ballet at the St Charles Theater. Elsewhere, there were concerts, ballets, and panoramas.

115 "General Summary," *New York Clipper*, 5 May 1860: 23.

116 "Original New Orleans and Metropolitan Opera Troupe," advertisement, *New York Clipper*, 29 September 1860: 190.

117 Ibid.

118 Ibid.

119 See "General Summary," *New York Clipper*, 29 September 1860: 190. The *New York Clipper* of 9 March 1861 reported that Carle and his daughters had recently opened at Pittsburgh's Varieties Theater.

120 "General Summary," *New York Clipper*, 3 November 1860: 230. One critic described the hall on opening night as being "filled in every part." "The Minstrels," *Pittsburgh Post*, 24 October 1860.

121 The United States and Japan had signed the Harris Treaty on 29 July 1858, an agreement that secured commercial and diplomatic privileges for the United States.

122 See Duprez, "Card to the Public" (1861).

123 Shorey, "Card to the Public" (1861).

124 In his 'Card' of 23 February, Duprez offered to pay Shorey's way to Washington, where the troupe would be in the first week of March, in order to resolved the issue in court. Shorey appears not to have accepted the challenge.

125 Louisiana seceded on 26 January, followed by Texas on 1 February. Following the attack on Fort Sumter on 12 April 1861, the states of Virginia, Arkansas, Tennessee, and North Carolina joined the Confederacy.

126 *Atlanta Confederacy*, reprinted in "Minstrelsy To-Night," *Charleston Daily Courier*, 31 January 1861.

127 "General Summary," *New York Clipper*, 23 February 1861: 358.

128 "City Intelligence," *Charleston Daily Courier*, 4 February 1861.

129 Macarthy's "Our Flag and its Origin; Southern National Song" was published in New Orleans by A.E. Blackmar & Bro. (1862).

130 "City Intelligence," *Charleston Daily Courier*, 6 February 1861. The current state song of South Carolina is "Carolina."

131 Firth, Pond & Company published *L'Union* in 1862.

132 Blind Tom first performed *The Battle of Manassas* in 1861, but it was not published until 1866 (Chicago: Root & Cady). Geneva Handy Southall describes how Tom composed this work in *Blind Tom*, 3.

133 Among the tributes to Ellsworth were Benjamin Danforth's *A Patriotic Song* (Providence, 1861), Septimus Winner's *Col. Ellsworth's Funeral March* (Philadelphia, 1861), J.P. Webster's *Brave Men Behold Your Fallen Chief* (Chicago, 1862), and Warren G. William's *A Requiem in Memory of Ellsworth* (New York, 1861).

134 Spelling mistakes in the French titles suggest that the publisher may have added them. Being constantly on the move, it is doubtful that Lavallée would ever have been able to see proofs of pieces published while on tour.

135 The Cluett firm published both of Lavallée's other piano compositions of this

period: *Le Fleur de mai*, of 1859, and his *Grande valse de concert*, op. 6. No copies of *Grande valse* have been located. Data sheets compiled by a consortium of Canadian libraries provide the only source of information about the piece. At the time these sheets were prepared, the music library of the Canadian Broadcasting Corporation in Montreal held a photocopy of the piece that was subsequently lost. Neither Library and Archives Canada nor the Canadian Musical Heritage Society were able to locate other copies. The data sheet indicates that Lavallée dedicated it to a Miss Alice Ingalls. More than a decade later, the *Canada musical* reported that a work with the same title was to be performed in Montreal on 5 December 1876. *Le Canada musical*, 3, no. 8 (December 1876): 124.

136 "City Summary," *New York Clipper*, 27 April 1861: 14.
137 "General Summary," *New York Clipper*, 15 June 1861: 71.
138 "General Summary," *New York Clipper*, 25 May 1861: 47.
139 "General Summary," *New York Clipper*, 31 May 1861: 55.
140 Records of the Fourth Rhode Island Regiment supplied by the United States National Archives and the Rhode Island State Archives.
141 Neither army kept figures on foreign recruits, perhaps making the calculation of an accurate estimate of their numbers impossible. At a memorial service in Montreal in 1865, Abbé Hercule Beaudry asserted that 40,000 French Canadians had taken part in the war. This figure was reported in *L'Écho du Cabinet de lecture paroissial* on 15 February 1865 and subsequently repeated by many historians. See Winks, *The Civil War Years* (1998), 178–84. For a full discussion of other nationalities' participation in the war, see Lonn, *Foreigners in the Union Army* (1951).
142 See Jones, "Civil War" (2001), 62–3.
143 "Regimental Band," advertisement, *Providence Evening Post*, 24 August 1861.
144 Hamm, *Yesterdays*, 231. See also McWhirter, *Battle Hymns*.
145 Olson, *Music and Musket*, 63. The Boston-based Germania Band evolved out of the Germania Orchestra, an ensemble that had arrived in the United States from Germany in 1848. The Germania Band was still in existence in the late 1880s. See Jones, *A Handbook of Music and Musicians*, 62.
146 See *History of the American Brass Band and Orchestra 1837 to 1920* (1920); and American Brass Band Records, Rhode Island Historical Society.
147 Band members, with their ages, were listed as: Joseph C. Greene, leader, 41; Calixa Levalley, 21; George Levalley, 26; Oscar J. Douglas, 19; Chas F. Folger, 27; Jos. G. Jenison, 28; Wm H. Johnson, 32; William Nayder, 31; Daniel Jonge, 18; Isaac Barrows, 23; Jabez Butterfield, 22; Edward G. Bishop, 23; Charles G. Coggeshall, 31; Daniel P. Gladding, 18; John Guinness, 26; David Hudson, 23; John Leach, 23; Jas. McCormick, 40; William J. Nichols, 23; Orin G. Shaw, 27; Albert J. Smith, 18. Adjutant General, *Descriptive Book of the Fourth Rhode Island Regiment Band*.
148 See Garofalo, *A Pictorial History of Civil War Era Musical Instruments and Military Bands*.
149 Allen, *Forty-Six Months*, 13.
150 Ibid., 15.

151 Ibid., 18.
152 Ibid., 19.
153 Adjutant General, *Annual Report of the Adjutant General* (1893), 288. On 28 October, the regiment and ten others were reviewed by the 'Young Napoleon,' Major General George B. McClennan, commander of the Army of the Potomac, who revoked McCarty's commission and replaced him with Isaac P. Rodman.
154 Allen, *Forty-Six Months*, 45–6.
155 Adjutant General, *Annual Report of the Adjutant General* (1893), 119. The regiment sustained thirty casualties at New Bern, including eight deaths. Colonel Rodman was promoted to the rank of Brigadier-General as a result of his victory in the battle.
156 Bandsman Robert Williams was reported to have died of typhoind on 18 April. "Casualties Among the Newport Soldiers with Burnside," *Providence Evening Press*, 28 April 1862.
157 Spooner, *The Maryland Campaign*, 6.
158 Cavalry units usually had several buglers who charged into the fray with the rest of their mounted colleagues, but they were the exception. Those on foot were very rarely led into battle by either brass band or fife and drums. See Bernard, *Lincoln and the Music of the Civil War*; Lord, *Bands and Drummer Boys of the Civil War*, and Olson, *Music and Musket*.
159 Allen, *Forty-Six Months*, 120.
160 Ibid., 121.
161 Lonn, *Foreigners in the Union Army and Navy*, 332. Olson (*Music and Musket*, 72) writes that in December 1861 there were 7,836 band musicians in the Army of the Potomac alone. Similar figures are given by Newsom, "The American Brass Band Movement," 128.
162 Rauscher, *Music on the March*, 17.
163 The War Department acknowledged the problem early in 1861 and should have solved it through General Orders 15 of 4 May 1861. It prescribed a restructured military, with bandsmen amounting to no more than 2.5 per cent of all personnel.
164 Olson, *Music and Musket* (1981), 73.
165 Newsom, "The American Brass Band Movement" (1979), 128.
166 Military records seem to provide no explanation for some members remaining while others were discharged. George Lavallée, for instance, had enlisted only the day before Calixa.
167 See Sears, *Landscape Turned Red*.
168 Spooner, *The Maryland Campaign*, 6–7.
169 The most fierce fighting leading up to Antietam took place during the Battle of South Mountain on 14 September 1862, as Lee attempted to slow the Union Army.
170 See Boatner, *Civil War Dictionary* (1987), 17–21.
171 David (13 March 1873), Labelle (1888), Letondal (1915), Lapierre (1966, 81), and Denechaud (1966) were some of those claiming that Lavallée had been wounded at Antietam.

172  Spooner, *The Maryland Campaign* (1903), 26–7. Spooner wrote that two bullets had passed through his clothing, and a third had struck the swivel of his sabre.

173  Lord and Wise, *Bands and Drummer Boys of the Civil War*, 193.

174  *Annual Report of the Adjutant General ... 1865*, 288.

175  "General Summary," *New York Clipper*, 5 April 1862: 407.

176  In May, the company was in Montreal, where Duprez advertised for a new "'end man' able to dance and sing." "Duprez and Green," advertisement, *New York Clipper*, 3 May 1862: 22.

177  See "Duprez and Green," advertisement, *New York Clipper*, 11 October 1862: 206.

178  Bidaux's name is often spelled Bideaux. Minstrel show historian Edward Rice claimed that Bidaux was born near Paris on 12 March 1830 and that he "ranked with the great baritone singers of minstrelsy." See Rice, *Monarchs of Minstrelsy*, 76.

179  The photograph is in an album that forms the Fonds Calixa-Lavallée (P354), Division des archives de l'Université Laval. Evidence discussed later in the book suggests that the photograph may have been taken in New Orleans, or at least that the medals were awarded in New Orleans.

180  Advertisements in the newspapers of Portland, Hartford, and other New England cities emphasized that the troupe was soon to leave for the West Indies and South America.

181  "Duprez and Green," advertisement, *New York Clipper*, 15 November 1862: 246.

182  "Saturday Morning, December 6," *Daily Picayune*, 6 December 1862.

183  See Thompson, "Journeys of an Immigrant Violinist," 67–8.

184  "Academy of Music," *New Orleans Bee*, 8 December 1862.

185  "The Dramatic Season," *Daily True Delta*, 7 December 1862. "La Madrilena" was also a showpiece for Frank Kent, Florence's successor, perhaps because the company had a Spanish-style dress that fit him.

186  "Negro Minstrelsy," *New York Clipper*, 27 December 1862: 295.

187  On 10 January, the *New York Clipper* wrote that all the members were well, with the exception of Bidaux "who was quite ill, and unable to do anything for five days previous to the date of our correspondent's letter [21 December]. At one time it wasn't a sure thing that poor Gustave wouldn't peg out. He is getting better now, we hear." "Negro Minstrelsy," *New York Clipper*, 10 January 1863, 307. They later reported that "Lavallee and Bidaux had both been very sick for nearly two weeks, but were all right at last accounts, January 1st, and were on the bills again." "Negro Minstrelsy," *New York Clipper*, 17 January 1863: 318.

188  "Academy of Music," *Daily Delta*, 23 January 1863.

189  "Negro Minstrelsy," *New York Clipper*, 17 January 1863: 318.

190  In April 1862, the *New York Clipper* reported Ellinger's theatre to be "rising in public favor ... Mrs (Julia Hudson) Backus is among the vocalists ... [and] Miss Emma Ellinger is among the *danseurs*." "Music Halls," *New York Clipper*, 19 April 1862: 3.

191 In the booklet, Ellinger describes Foote as the son of Prussian immigrants and refers to himself as Foote's guardian. He claims to have brought Foote to Baltimore where he studied languages, dancing, and pantomime, before the young man made his first public appearance in April 1862 with Nixon's Equestrian Company at Palace Garden in New York. The same booklet reports that "Small" (Joseph Huntler) was born in Hamburg, Germany, and that on finding him selling newspapers in Baltimore, Ellinger "immediately formed the resolution of rescuing the poor little fellow from the life he was then pursuing." Some time later Ellinger adopted Huntler, and Mary Ellinger reportedly taught him languages and music. See *The History of Charles Nestel, Surnamed Commodore Foote; and Joseph Huntler, Surnamed Colonel Small, The Two Smallest Men Living* (New York: Torry Brothers, Printers, 1862), 8, 12.

192 The 1860 Census of Maryland lists William Ellinger as a forty-year-old Pennsylvania-born restaurateur living at 36 West Fayette Street in Baltimore. His daughter, Mary, was then sixteen years old. I am grateful to the Maryland Historical Society for examining this for me. Newcomb's background is not known. Mary Ellinger made her debut with the New Orleans Minstrels on 10 January and was said to have "met with a splendid reception … Her singing is greatly praised by the press of New Orleans." "Miscellaneous," *New York Clipper*, 7 February 1863: 342.

193 The report concluded optimistically that "this combination should nightly crowd the Academy." "Academy of Music," *New Orleans Bee*, 12 January 1863.

194 "Negro Minstrelsy," *New York Clipper*, 7 February 1863: 342.

195 The *New York Clipper* reported the troupe's engagement in Havana to have been "but momentary, the minstrel business having been killed in that place by a party called the 'Christy's,' hailing from New Orleans. The latter was an abortion, and the 'Habaneros' are now loathe to look upon a minstrel show. The difference between greenbacks and gold is also against performers from the States, in the matter of hall rent, etc." "Negro Minstrelsy," *New York Clipper*, 14 February 1863: 347.

196 The *New York Clipper* of 7 March reported Duprez to be "doing an immense business" during a ten-day engagement at the Theatre Royal in Montreal, "where gold and silver is plenty." The *Montreal Herald* claimed that given the demand for tickets, "those who secure seats will be fortunate." "Negro Minstrelsy," *New York Clipper*, 7 March 1863, 371. "Duprez & Green's Minstrels," *Montreal Herald*, 28 February 1863, 2.

197 "Negro Minstrelsy," *New York Clipper*, 21 March 1863: 390. "Negro Minstrelsy," *New York Clipper*, 4 April 1863: 406.

198 "Chronique musicale," *L'Écho du Cabinet de lecture paroissial*, IV, no. 16 (1 June 1862): 248. The writer concludes that it is the minstrels' simple desire to perform well that brings in audiences, and suggests that the city's amateurs ("and the disciples of Mr Carter especially") might learn from them. Henry Carter, organist at Quebec City's Anglican cathedral, had organized performances of oratorios.

199 While the troupe travelled through Ontario, Billy Sweatman, of Nashville, took the place of J.E. Campbell.

200 See *The Peo[ple's] New Songster Containing All the New Popular Songs of the Day as Sung by "Duprez & Green's Minstrels"* (np: Gustave Bideaux, 1863).

201 Shakespeare's *Othello* was a standard minstrel show subject. The identity of the other work, "The Ghost," is not known.

202 Finley Johnson's version of "Maryland, My Maryland" (Boston: Oliver Ditson, 1862) was written in response to James Rider Randall's 1861 song that was an appleal for Maryland to seceed from the Union. Randall's song was published first in the New Orleans *Sunday Delta*, in April 1861, and soon after in Baltimore by Miller and Beacham. Both Randall and Johnson set their words to the tune widely known as "O Tannenbaum."

203 Campbell was not a member of the New Orleans Minstrels, but as one of minstrelsy's most popular vocalists of the early 1860s, his name had advertising value. A few years later, Campbell would gain an equally wide reputation as an opera singer.

204 See *The Peo[ple's] New Songster* (1863).

205 The *New York Clipper* reported the New Orleans Minstrels to have filled the 2,500-seat Bryant's Hall "to suffocation" each night. "Negro Minstrelsy," *New York Clipper*, 16 May 1863: 38.

206 See "Negro Minstrelsy," *New York Clipper*, 6 June 1863: 59. The story did not provide details beyond stating that the rumour had begun after Duprez's advertising agent had visited the office of the *Gale City News*.

207 The 6 July performance in Troy was for the benefit of Gustave Bidaux; the following night, in Poughkeepsie, was for the interlocutor, Ainsley Scott. Lavallée did the least well of the three, as Bidaux earned $200, and Scott earned $150. See "Negro Minstrels," *New York Clipper*, 18 July 1863: 110.

208 The *New York Clipper* reported the troupe to have been "one of the best organizations that was out this past season" and claimed that it "returned to New York with any quantity of greenbacks." "Negro Minstrels," *New York Clipper*, 18 July 1863: 110.

209 Ellinger was the director of amusements and Newcomb was the business manager.

210 Duprez frequently claimed to pay "moderate but regular" salary. His advertisements for cast members invariably required applicants to state their lowest expected salary.

211 The Drayton Parlor Opera Company arrived from England in the fall of 1859 and presented brief, one-act operettas. See Thompson, "Henri Drayton: English Opera and Anglo-American Culture, 1850–1872."

212 Lavallée may have dropped the manuscript for the *Ellinger Polka* at the Cluett office on 6 July 1863 while in Troy, New York.

213 Ellinger appears to have gained the support of the *New York Clipper*, which described his troupe as far more extraordinary than that of P.T. Barnum's company and provided details on the troupe members' modest dimensions. "City Summary," *New York Clipper*, 8 August 1863: 131. The note continued: "Com. Foote is seven years older than Nutt, and weighs about 21 lbs., his sister is fourteen years old, 18 inches high, and weighs but 14 1/2 lbs., which is 7 inches shorter and 8 lbs. lighter than Minnie Warren. Col. Small is 29 inches high and 18 years old."

214 "City Items," *Daily Republican*, 19 November 1863.

215 Louis Moreau Gottschalk, *Notes of a Pianist* (2006), 169.

216 "Maryland Institute," *Baltimore Sun*, 12 September 1863.

217 Ibid.

218 "Miscellaneous," *New York Clipper*, 3 October 1863: 198.

219 "Ellinger & Newcomb's Moral Exhibition," advertisement, *New York Clipper*, 4 December 1863: 271.

220 "City Items," *Daily Republican*, 21 November 1863.

221 Ellinger's troupe was still touring the United States in the spring of 1864, "concertising on the Missouri River." See "Miscellaneous," *New York Clipper*, 30 April 1864: 23. Nestel and his sister were still working as entertainers in 1880, but promotional material from that time said nothing of his relationship to Ellinger. See E. Mack, *Commodore Foote and the Fairy Queen, Grand March* (np: W.F. Shaw, 1880).

222 While Lavallée chose the Union Army, many of his French-Canadian contemporaries were also searching for a cause. For some, it would be the defence of the French Empire in Mexico, for others the defence of the Roman Catholic Church from Italian nationalists. Two future writers, Narcisse-Henri-Edouard Faucher de Saint-Maurice and Honoré Beaugrand, both served with the French forces in Mexico in the 1860s. Another writer, Arthur Buies, joined the fight for Italian unification, serving in Garibaldi's army in 1860, while many other French Canadians fought on the side of the pope. In the late 1860s, Bishop Bourget raised funds and troops to defend the Vatican's control over the Papal States.

CHAPTER TWO

1 See Thompson, "Lavallée Portraits," 3–4.

2 See Adams, *When in the Course of Human Events*, 71–83; Ellison, *Support for Secession*; Vanauken, *The Glittering Illusion*; and Blackett's *Divided Hearts*.

3 See Winks, *The Civil War Years*, 206–43; and Foreman, *A World on Fire*, 170–2.

4 See Monet, *The Last Cannon Shot*, 285–7.

5 *L'Avenir* began in 1847 and continued until about 1858. *Le Pays* was published from 1852 to 1871.

6 There was also the moderate liberal Montreal newspaper *L'Ordre*, and at the same time five English-language newspapers: the *Gazette*, the *Herald*, the *Transcript*, the *Daily Witness*, and the *Evening Telegraph and Commercial Advertiser*, all of which would support Confederation.

7 The *Reformer-Rouge* coalition formed the government for just a few days in August 1858, with Upper Canada's George Brown as premier and the Rouge leader Antoine-Aimé Dorion as deputy.

8 The economic growth would continue for nearly a decade. See Linteau, *Quebec: A History*, 53.

9 "Terrapin Restaurant," advertisement, *Montreal Gazette*, 3 August 1863.

10 Admission to the Cosmopolitan restaurant-concert room was free for guests and diners. The management informed the public that "none but respectable

persons admitted. Boys not admitted." "Cosmopolitan Hotel," advertisement, *Montreal Gazette*, 5 December 1863. See also *Montreal Business Sketches*, 138–40.

11 *Census of Canada, 1861: District de recensement no. 2 de la cité de Saint-Hyacinthe*. The Lavallées' accommodations would have been less crowded than in Saint-Hyacinthe in 1861, when they shared a two-storey house with six members of the Birs family. The Census listed Augustin as a maker of musical instruments.

12 Augustin is listed on p. 263 of the *Montreal Directory* (1864–65).

13 "Mr C. Lavallée," advertisement, *Montreal Directory* (1864–65): 502.

14 It was much the same situation in Europe twenty to thirty years earlier. See Jeffrey Kallberg's Introduction to *"Parisian" Pianists*; and Loesser, *Men, Woman and Pianos*, 267–83.

15 *Montreal Directory* (1863–64): 345.

16 Promotional material claimed that among others, Sabatier directed the juvenile soloists Adelina Patti, fourteen, and Emma Albani, thirteen (then still known as Emma Lajeunesse). See *Relation du voyage de son altesse royale le Prince de Galles en Amerique*, 55. The *New York Clipper* called Sabatier's cantata "a masterly specimen of epic music." "General Summary," *New York Clipper*, 8 September 1860.

17 In an article published soon after Sabatier's death, the critic "Cœcilius" wrote of the pianist's attempts to quit drinking. "Despite the sad events, Sabatier had often fought vice – he had often embraced virtue – each new fall was evidence of the violence this unfortunate man inflicted on himself." "Chronique musicale," *L'Écho du Cabinet de lecture paroissial*, IX, no. 21 (November, 1862): 487. See also "Faits Divers," *Les Courrier des États-Unis*, 27 August 1862, which cites an obituary published in *L'Ordre*.

18 Letondal cited the records of Hôpital de L'Hôtel Dieu de Montréal, which gave the cause of death as apoplexy. He also mentioned that Sabatier was buried in a pauper's grave at a funeral witnessed by cemetery groundskeepers. See Letondal, "Un musicien oublié," 133. Coecilius "Chronique musicale," *L'Écho du Cabinet de lecture paroissial*, IV, no. 21 (1 November 1862): 487.

19 The arrangments were credited to Emma Albani (Emma Lajeunesse). Rosanna Mullins Leprohon, Smith's sister-in-law, had produced the English-language version of the cantata text. She was known simply as Mrs Leprohon. See MacMillan, McMullen, and Waterston, *Silenced Sextet*, 36.

20 Kallmann writes that in 1860 Smith was awarded the title of Chevalier of the Legion of Honour for heroism during the Revolution of 1848. See Kallmann, "Charles-Gustave Smith."

21 Smith's abilities as an educator are evident in the success of the pedagogical manual, *Nouvel Abécedaire Musical*, which he published in the fall of 1864, and which would remain in print well into the twentieth century. See, Alphonse Audet, "Instruction musicale," *L'Union nationale*, 3 October 1864.

22 In *L'Écho du Cabinet de lecture paroissial*, Smith published under the name Diérix. He published *Les Beaux-arts* at a press he established at Sault-aux-Recollet.

23 Founded in the Hautes-Pyrénées in the early decades of the nineteenth century by Alfred-Hector Roland, Les Chanteurs Montagnards Français had performed in Canada in the summer of 1856.

24 None of the advertisements or reviews appears to have explained the origins of the Montagnards Canadien's costumes. See "Opening and Inauguration of the Mechanics' Hall," *Montreal Gazette*, 16 December 1863.

25 The 1861 Census lists Rose de Lima Derome as a fifteen-year-old "musicienne." She advertised her services in *Les Beaux-arts*, I, no. 9 (December 1863): 70.

26 Regnaud received her diploma from the Congrégation de Notre-Dame de Montréal in 1860. "Les Examens à la Congrégation de N.-Dame," *L'Écho du Cabinet de lecture paroissial*, II (1860), 218–19.

27 Gauthier was at this time teaching violin at No. 72 Dorchester Street, just a few doors down from the Lavallées' home. "Henri Gauthier," advertisement, *Les Beaux-arts*, I, no. 4 (1 July 1863): 32.

28 Before settling in Canada in 1861, the family was recorded in the Scottish Census of 1851 and in the US Census of 1860 for Providence, Rhode Island. The children were: Elvira (b. Greece, ca. 1839), Elcusa (b. [Greece?], ca. 1840), Emilia (variously spelled Emelia and Amilia, b. England, ca. 1842), Elena (b. Edinburgh, Scotland, ca. 1843), Eugenia (b. Ireland, ca. 1844), Victoria (or Victorine; b. Spain, ca. 1849), Amalia (b. Corfu, ca. 1850), Frederick (b. Scotland, ca. 1853), Nestore (b. New Brunswick, ca. 1854), Theophalis (b. New Brunswick, ca. 1856), and Matilda (b. St John's, Newfoundland, ca. 1858).

29 The 1865 *City Directory* lists "Misses De Angelis" (Elena and Eugenia) as teachers of singing, along with Professor Sig. G. de Angelis, at 28 Union Avenue.

30 *La Minerve*, 31 December 1864.

31 *La Presse*, 11 January 1864.

32 On 25 January, *La Presse* reported the proceeds of the Longueuil concert to have been $42.72½. As admission was set at twenty-five cents per ticket, and assuming there were some expenses, it would seem that the concert had attracted an audience of close to 200.

33 The programs of the 24 and 26 January concerts were printed in *La Minerve* on 21 and 26 January, respectively. In 1864, François-Xavier Valade was the secretary of the Catholic Board of Examinations of School Teachers. He resided in Longueuil and was an organizer of events in South Shore communities.

34 "Le Concert," *La Minerve*, 28 January 1864.

35 "Concert de M. Lavallée," *La Presse*, 28 January 1864. "We do not hesitate to say that the talent of this young fellow who is barely eighteen [he had in fact just passed his twenty-first birthday], is wonderful and we believe it would be difficult to find in this country an artist who was equally strong on these three instruments: the piano, violin, and cornet. If encouragement and study can assist this extraordinary talent, we may long boast of having among us such a distinguished artist."

36 Hamelin, "Médéric Lanctôt."

37 Hamelin does not provide a date for Lanctôt's move to Montreal, but suggests it may have been in 1852. As Augustin Cuvillier died in 1849, it seems likely

that Lanctôt worked for Cuvillier's sons. Lanctôt's membership in the Institut canadien dates from 13 October 1853 to 15 July 1873. Dubinsky, Ira, Institut canadien Archives. http://collections.ic.gc.ca/icma/fr/index.html. (Accessed 10 April 2006)

38 In the summer of 1848, Joseph Doutre fought a duel with George-Étienne Cartier, who had been insulted by a farcical story published about him in *L'Avenir*. The story had, in fact, been written by Charles Daoust, who was later the editor of the more moderate *Le Pays*. See Monet, *The Last Cannon Shot*, 322-3.

39 Jean-Toussaint Thompson was born in Saint-Hyacinthe in 1838, the son of John Thompson, a tailor, and Marie Flavie Trudeau. Prior to joining Lanctôt, Thompson had worked on newspapers in the US and Toronto. He pioneered the use of stenography in Canada. See L.-S. C., "Le Premiere Stenographe Canadien-Français." Little is known of Bouthillier. Lanctôt's *La Presse* should not be confused with the Montreal newspaper of the same name, founded by William-Edmond Blumhart in 1884.

40 "Ce morceau est très-bien écrit et d'un gout parfait. Nous ferons remarquer que c'est le premier morceau d'importance qui ait paru chez un éditeur de musique de Montreal." Gustave Smith, "Musique," *La Presse*, 25 August 1864.

41 Several magazines and newspapers, such as *L'Écho de Cabinet de lecture paroissial*, *L'Artiste*, and *Les Beaux-arts*, made their appearances in 1860 and 1863; all contained printed music. See Maria Calderisi, *Music Publishing in the Canadas, 1800–1867* (1981), 110. Through the nineteenth century, music was published in books, newspapers, and journals, while several Montreal publishers issued music on its own from time to time. The *Montreal Literary Garland* (1839–40, and 1846–?) contained songs, waltzes, gallops, and quadrilles. Other publications included the newspaper *La Revue canadienne*, with its monthly *Album litteraire et musical* (from June 1846), the *Vocal Percepter* (published in 1811 by A. Stevenson), and the *Chansonnier canadien* (1825). Calderisi identified eighty-eight books published between 1800 and 1867 in Ontario and Quebec that contained or were primarily music, and fifteen newspapers and journals from the same place and period that included music.

42 The work was listed as a *Grand caprice de concert* in "Grand concert vocal et instrumental," advertisement, *La Minerve*, 18 February 1864. The *Souvenir-Méditation* appears not to have been published.

43 "St Patrick's Day Celebrations," *True Witness and Catholic Chronicle*, 25 March 1864.

44 Charitable and benevolent societies were organized to serve ethnic and religious communities, originating in the pre-1837 era and gaining a political dimension in the 1860s. See Cooper, "The Social Structure of Montreal in the 1850s," 68–70.

45 F.M.F. Ossaye, "Le Concert de l'Union St-Joseph," *La Presse*, 24 March 1864. Lavallée had also played de Bériot's 7th Violin Concerto. Marie Regnaud, François Lavoie and the Montagnards Canadiens were among the other performers taking part.

46 Gottschalk, *Notes of a Pianist*, 198–9.

47  "M. Lavallée," *Les Beaux-arts*, II no.1 (April 1864): 54. Lanctôt reprinted the article in *la Presse* on 9 May 1864.

48  The Vogt family had emigrated from Germany in the 1830s, establishing a piano-making company at Philadelphia before relocating to Montreal. See *Montreal Business Sketches*, 100–3.

49  For a detailed study of piano fantasies and transcriptions, see Suttoni, "Piano and Opera."

50  "Le concert au bénéfice du monument des victimes de 1837–38," *Le Pays*, 28 June 1864.

51  Lavallée dedicated "La Mansarde" (Montreal: Laurent, Laforce & Cie, 1864) to Marie Louise Dupré, one of his students at the time and the future wife of Napoléon Legendre.

52  Only the first page of the *Quickstep sur les airs nationaux canadien* survives as it was published in L.-O. David's "Galerie national: Calixa Lavallée," *La Presse*, 9 November 1912.

53  Bishop was still in reasonably good form despite a long and colourful career. She had gained a certain notoriety in 1839 by deserting her husband and three children for her accompanist Robert Nicholas Bochsa (whose wife lived in France). Together they toured Europe in the 1840s, then America, and Australia, where Bochsa died in 1856. Bishop later married the New York diamond merchant Martin Shultz but continued to tour. See "The Late Madame Anna Bishop."

54  See Montpetit, "Culture et exotisme."

55  "Faits Divers," *La Presse*, 28 July 1864. The Collège Saint-Laurent is now Cégèp Saint-Laurent, and continues to offer a program in music.

56  "Voilà la liste des Canadien-français qui ont souscrit au diner," *L'Union nationale*, 31 October 1864.

57  There is voluminous literature on the St Albans Raid and even a stage play and a movie. For a study dealing mostly with the political fallout of the Raid, see Stouffer, "Canadian-American Relations in the Shadow of the Civil War." See also Foreman, *A World on Fire*, 704–5.

58  See Silver, *The French-Canadian Idea of Confederation*, 33–50.

59  Ibid.

60  Ibid., 41.

61  Bernard, *Les Rouges, libéralisme, nationalisme et anticléricalisme*, 254–5.

62  See L.-O. David, *Mes contemporains*, 165–6; Massicotte, "Une société politique secrète à Montréal"; and Bernard, *Les Rouges, libéralisme, nationalisme et anticléricalisme*, 272 and 289. Labelle was also a lieutenant in the Chasseurs Canadien militia regiment.

63  David, *Laurier et son temps*, 20. David later wrote: "We were eleven contributors: M. Loranger, A.P. Letendre, H.F. Rainville, Chs de Lorimier, L.A. Jette, D. Girouard, A. Audet, Ludger Labelle, Médéric Lanctot, Chs Marcil, T. Thompson et L. O. David." Cited in Lemieux, *Wilfrid Laurier*, 8.

64  Lafontaine was teaching music at the Académie Française et Anglaise de Jeunes Madamoiselles. *Annuaire de Ville Marie: Origine, utilité et progrès des institutions catholique de Montréal* (1864), 165.

65 David, *Mes contemporains*, 170–1.
66 Gustave Smith, "Lettres sur la musique: De l'introduction des arts chez une nation," *L'Union nationale*, 17 October 1864.
67 Gustave Smith, "Lettres sur la musique: De l'opinion publique dans les grands centres artistique," *L'Union nationale*, 10 November 1864.
68 Gustave Smith, "Les Concerts," *L'Union nationale*, 15 November 1864. The *Montreal City Directory* (1864–65) lists the officers of the Society as J.B. Labelle, dir.; Comm: Hon. P.J.O. Chauveau, L.L. Beaudry, R. Trudeau, P.T. Delvecchio, N. Valois, and L. Beaudry.
69 Napoléon Legendre, "Correspondance," *L'Union nationale*, 17 November 1864.
70 Gustave Smith, "Correspondance," *L'Union nationale* 18 November 1864; and C. Lavallée, "M.M. Les Rédacteurs," *L'Union nationale*, 19 November 1864.
71 Napoléon Legendre, "La Société Philharmonique de Montréal," *Le Pays*, 19 November 1864. In his description of the orchestra's constitutional changes, Legendre mentioned, among other things, that the orchestra had also decided to accept women and that rehearsals would be open only to members. He also explained that J.B. Labelle had stepped down as music director and that Gaetano de Angelis had taken his place, but took pains to make clear that Labelle's departure was not a sign of a rift between him and the organizing committee. While the changes seem quite progressive, in his response, Smith raised specific questions about the safety of young women attending rehearsals on their own. See Gustave Smith, "La Société Philharmonique de Montréal, *L'Union nationale*, 25 November 1865.
72 Napoléon Legendre, "La Société Philharmonique de Montréal," *Le Pays*, 19 November 1864; Napoléon Legendre, "Correspondance," *L'Union nationale*, 21 November 1864. Perhaps in an effort to mend fences with Napoléon Legendre, on 23 February 1865, Lavallée published a review of Legendre's piano quadrille. C. Lavallée, "Platon Polichinelle," *L'Union Nationale*, 23 February 1865.
73 Achintre and Labelle, *Cantate, La Confédération*. Labelle had also set two of Cartier's poems to music: "Ô Canada! Mon Pays! Mes Amours!" and "Avant tout je suis Canadien."
74 Gottschalk, *Notes of a Pianist*, 201. Concerts by visiting performers were the exception, drawing both English- and French-speaking audience members. With Gottschalk's performance at the Theatre Royal on 26 April 1864, we have a rare glimpse of Montreal concert audiences through the performer's journal. In his diary he noted that, despite the heavy rain, the house was full and that "the ladies, elegantly dressed, produced a beautiful effect as seen from the stage." Gottschalk was vexed by a boisterous group of "elegant English officers, who were determined to attract attention to their blonde whiskers, their convex chests, and their white gloves, which they held at a foot's distance outside of the box ... Their conversation, which with noble condescension they made in a loud voice in order to permit the whole hall to enjoy their high-flown humour, was disagreeably interrupted from time to time by my piano." Two days later, after the second concert, Gottschalk was in better spirits when he wrote: "Thursday evening. Second concert. As much as I had played without pleasure

the other evening, so much I have excelled myself to-day. All my pieces have been encored." Gottschalk, *Notes of a Pianist*, 201

75  Gustave Smith, "Les Concerts," *L'Union nationale*, 15 November 1864.

76  "Mlle Camilla Urso et Mlle de la Grange," *Le Pays*, 2 November 1864.

77  Calixa Lavallée, "Le Concert de Camille Urso," *L'Union nationale*, 3 December 1864.

78  A regiment with the same name had taken part in the War of 1812, but had since been disbanded. Pierre-Joseph-Olivier Chauveau served as captain of the Chasseurs Canadiens and recruited students of the École normale Jacques Cartier into its ranks (see Hamelin and Poulin, "Chauveau, Pierre-Joseph-Olivier").

79  Gustave Smith et al., [Letter to Camille Urso], *L'Union nationale*, 19 December 1864. Camille Urso, [Letter to Gustave Smith], *L'Union nationale*, 21 December 1864.

80  Calixa Lavallée, "Le Retour de Camille Urso," *L'Union nationale*, 21 December 1864.

81  Calixa Lavallée, "L'Opéra Anglais," *L'Union nationale*, 30 December 1864.

82  Lavallée continued: "Mr. Campbell definitely has a very attractive voice, but we regret to report that he does not know how to sing." Campbell and Castle had recently completed an engagement at the Theatre Royal. Calixa Lavallée, "L'Opéra Anglais," *L'Union nationale*, 30 December 1864.

83  The Sixty-third Regiment would depart for England in August 1865. While in Montreal, many of the officers had their photographs taken in the Notman studio. See also World Military Bands, www.worldmilitarybands.com/influential-musicians-j-m/. (Accessed 25 October 2010)

84  In the next issue of *L'Union nationale*, Smith responded with what was not so much a review as a lengthy tribute to Urso. Gustave Smith, "Départ de Camille Urso," *L'Union nationale*, 5 January 1865. Rossini adapted his 1827, four-act opera *Moïse et Pharaon, ou Le passage de la Mer Rouge* (Moses and Pharaoh, or The Crossing of the Red Sea) from the earlier Italian work, *Mosè in Egitto* (1816). For the French-language opera of 1827, he used a new libretto, prepared by Luigi Balocchi and Etienne de Jouy. Jacques Offenbach had also created a fantasy on themes from this opera, which he first performed in 1853.

85  *La Minerve*, 26 January 1865. *L'Oiseau mouche*, a light piece intended for amateurs, was Lavallée's third publication with Laurent, Laforce & Cie. Later that year, this company sold its rights to *L'Oiseau mouche* and *Une Couronne de lauriers* to Boucher & Manseau.

86  T. Thompson, "M. Calixte Lavallée," *L'Union nationale*, 13 January 1865. Thompson writes: "Everyone has admired the zeal and boundless devotion of our young compatriot and artist Mr Lavallée; his fine talent has always been at the service of charitable work; the hands of the poor have been filled by this great and noble soul, and we can say that there has not been a charity concert in Montreal in which he has not played a part."

87  Ibid.

88  Gustave Smith, "Le Concert de M.C. Lavallée," *L'Union nationale*, 25 January 1865. Smith further wrote: "Every day we bemoan the emigration of our

young people, and for what reason do they leave? Simply because they lack encouragement."

89 "Le Concert de M. Lavallée," *La Minerve*, 28 January 1865.

90 See Thompson, "Gustave Smith's Louisiana Episode," 7–9.

91 "Depart de M. Gust. Smith pour la Havane," *L'Union nationale*, 30 January 1865.

92 [No title], *L'Union nationale*, 6 February 1865.

93 In its 11 February issue, *Wilkes' Spirit of the Times* noted that Urso had taken part in J.N. Pattison's first *soirée musicale* at Steinway Hall, where she played Vieuxtemps's "grande fantaisie de concert," accompanied by Mr G W. Morgan. On 22 April, the same publication reported Urso to have been "engaged for one year at twelve thousand dollars salary" to play the violin in concerts with the German pianist Ferdinand Hiller (1811–1885).

94 Lanctôt remained in Canada until Confederation in July 1867. He then closed *L'Union nationale* and left for Detroit, where in 1869 he began the weekly *Impartial*, followed by *The Anti-Roman Advocate*. He, too, returned to Canada to pursue political activity.

95 Barberousse. "La Confédération en Quadrille," *L'Union nationale*, 28 April 1865. At least one other piano composition was published under Casorti's name: *Loetitia, Caprice de Salon*, op. 17 (Montreal: Adélard J. Boucher, 1866). Its title page contains no illustration.

96 Although perhaps less likely, another possibility suggested by 'lauriers' and the 'chaîne des dames' was that the composer of the *Confederation Quadrille* was the piano teacher Zoé Lafontaine (who was soon to be Madame Laurier).

97 Foreman, *A World on Fire*, 724–5.

98 "Manifestation des sympathies de Montréal pour la nation Américaine," *L'Union nationale*, 19 April 1865.

99 C. Lavallée, "Les Victimes de l'inondation," *L'Union nationale*, 18 April 1865. Lavallée had relatives in the town of Sorel who may have been affected by the flooding.

100 The orchestration was possibly made from the vocal score published by Heugel in 1860. It could very well have been one of the works Lavallée directed while with Ellinger.

101 Earlier that year, the Lavallées had moved to 157 Saint-André, between Sainte-Catherine and Mignon (now known as boulevard de Maisonneuve). Smith was living at 381 de la Gauchetière, between German (Hôtel-de-Ville) and Sainte-Élizabeth.

102 *L'Union nationale* did not publish a review of the 27 April concert the next day, but noted only that it had been a magnificent success.

103 See "Vol et Assassinat," *L'Union nationale*, 29 April 1865. Lavallée purportedly said: "One of his assailants had half his face covered by a thick, woollen scarf, and his companion – the one who held him – was a man with a heavy beard wearing a broad-rimmed felt hat." The *Herald* and *L'Ordre* mentioned the mugging only briefly. See "Assault and Robbery," *Montreal Herald*, 2 May 1865, and "Faits divers," *L'Ordre*, 1 May 1865.

104 "Vol et Assassinat," *L'Union nationale*, 29 April 1865.

105  G. Smith, "Les Réflexions Philosophiques d'un Bénéficiaire," *L'Union natio-nale*, 29 April 1865.

106  See [Jules Jehin Prume], *Une Vie d'artiste*, 194, and "Frantz Jehin-Prume," 153–4.

107  "Faits Divers," *L'Ordre*, 31 May 1865.

108  "Faits Divers," *L'Ordre*, 5 June 1865. Lapierre wrote that Prume and Lavallée first met at this time, when Prume invited Lavallée to accompany him in a Vieuxtemps concerto at the first performance. Lapierre wrote that Lavallée surprised Prume by playing the violin part of the concerto for him, but did not perform at the concert. Lapierre seems to have been unaware of the mugging that Lavallée should have been recovering from in May 1865, or that the two did perform together on 1 June and again in the spring of 1873. See Lapierre, *Calixa Lavallée* (1966), 100–1.

109  G. Smith, "Le Concert de M. Jehin Prume," *L'Union nationale*, 3 June 1865. Of Lavallée, Smith wrote: "Mr C. Lavallee has shown to be a true artist, [and] an excellent pianist. His style and playing were highly acclaimed by the brilliant audience that filled Nordheimer's Hall."

110  "Concert de F. Jehin Prume," *L'Union nationale*, 10 June 1865. This account of the concert did not mention that Lavallée was on the program, so evidently he did not perform.

111  C[harles Gustave] Smith, letter to Archbishop Jean-Marie Odin, 10 February 1865 Archbishop of New Orleans (La.) Collection ANO. University of Notre Dame Archives, Notre Dame, Indiana. All four letters are found in Archbishop of New Orleans (La.) Collection (ANO).

112  "Gustave Smith, Professor de Musique," advertisement, *L'Union nationale*, 19 June 1865.

113  Also on the program was the soprano Mme Fleury Urban and cellist Antoine Dessane. See "Testimonial to Fr. Jehin Prume," *New York Herald*, 13 December 1865; and "Concert," *Courrier des États-Unis*, 14 December 1865. The critic of the *Courrier* noted that it was Regnaud's first appearance in New York and predicted a "bel avenir."

114  In 1867, Lanctôt set about creating a Grand Association of working-class French Canadians, but later that year was humiliated in an election defeat to none other than George-Étienne Cartier. In the spring of 1868, he started a new newspaper, *L'Indépendance canadienne*, whose goal was independence from Britain and annexation of Canada to the United States. Finding little support for his ideas, he set off for the US in September 1868.

CHAPTER THREE

1  During the company's stop in Upper Canada, Hamilton's *Daily Spectator* reported that its program "embraced several new and admired songs, a burlesque from the 'Opera de Afrique,' other extravaganzas, and several admired dances by the artistic Frank Kent." *Hamilton Daily Spectator*, 26 March 1866.

2  Frank Dumont, "The Golden Days of Minstrelsy," *New York Clipper*, 19 December 1914.

3 Calixa Lavallée, *Shake Again Galop, an Answer to "Slap Bang" or "Here We Go Again"* (Rochester, NY: Alexander Barnes, 1866). Harry Copeland, "Slap Bang, Here We Are Again, or The Jolly Dogs" (Philadelphia: W.R. Smith, 1866).

4 The topic of the song is a pack of 'dogs' that love to sing and dance. "They always seem so jolly oh! So jolly oh! So jolly oh! / They always seem so jolly oh! Where ever they may be / They dance, they sing, they laugh ha, ha, they laugh ha, ha, they dance they sing, what jolly dogs are we." Rochester historian Blake McKeley has written that "recurrent periods of evangelical and denominational fervor had provided the city of 36,403 with 39 churches in 1850." See McKeley, "When Science was on Trial in Rochester: 1850–1890," 1. Between 1865 and 1881, nineteen new Protestant churches were established. See McKeley, "Rochester's Mid Years; Center of Genesee County Life: 1854–1884," 16.

5 Whatever the reasoning behind the apparent reference to the Shakers, there is no evidence that there was a branch in Rochester. I wish to express my thanks to Starlyn D'Angelo, curator of the Shaker Museum and Library in Old Chatham, New York, for her advice and information on the history of the Shakers.

6 A melody with the same title is found in a number of collections of Irish songs, including *Old Irish Folk Music and Songs* by P.W. Joyce (London: Longmans, Green & Co; Dublin: Hodges, Figgis, & Co, 1909), 105.

7 Only a small proportion of the Irish songs published at the time could be described as nationalistic, and even then, as Williams writes, "the songs of Irish nationalism tended toward vague, overblown romanticism." *'Twas Only an Irishman's Dream*, 109.

8 Duprez usually toured the South in winter to avoid the discomfort and disease that often accompanied the summer heat. Even in the North, the risks were substantial. As the troupe began the trek southward, the *New York Clipper* reported on 25 August that the members were healthy, "notwithstanding rumors of cholera." "Negro Minstrelsy," *New York Clipper*, 25 August 1866, 158.

9 The port city of New Orleans felt the severe effects of the collapse of the rural economy. After steady economic growth through the twenty years preceding the war, rural per capita income in the main cotton-producing states (South Carolina, Georgia, Alabama, Mississippi, and Louisiana) declined from $85 to $38 between 1859 and 1867. See Patrick O'Brien, *The Economic Effects of the American Civil War*, 22–3.

10 See Vandal, *The New Orleans Riot of 1866*.

11 "Academy of Music," advertisement, *Times-Picayune*, 10 October 1865.

12 "St Charles St Opera House," advertisement, *Times-Picayune*, 9 November 1865. "Music for Balls, Soirees, Parades, etc. – Joseph V. Gessner, musician, leader of the original New Orleans Brass Band (formerly of the Washington Artillery)," advertisement, *Times-Picayune*, 9 November 1865.

13 "Negro Minstrelsy," *New York Clipper*, 22 September 1866: 191.

14 "St Charles Theatre," *Times-Picayune*, 10 September 1866.

15 "Negro Minstrelsy," *New York Clipper*, 20 October 1866: 223.

16 *Times-Picayune*, 21 September 1866. The *New York Clipper* reported the early

departure as being due mainly to the "sickly season." "Negro Minstrelsy," *New York Clipper*, 13 October 1866: 215.

17 "Negro Minstrelsy," *New York Clipper*, 6 October 1866: 207. Charles T. Slocum assumed Pond's duties as the company's agent.

18 On 2 March, the *New York Clipper* reported the troupe to "have nearly completed their flying trip through the Eastern country, of twenty-eight nights, it being their second tour this winter through the New England States, and their success has been much greater on their second trip than their first." "Negro Minstrelsy," *New York Clipper*, 2 March 1867: 375.

19 "Le Concert," *Le Journal des Trois-Rivières*, 16 August 1867.

20 See Robbins Landon and Jones, *Haydn*, 301.

21 Warren Richards was the stage name of Richard A. Warren. He may have been the only New Orleans–born member of the New Orleans Minstrels. According to John Smith Kendall, Warren died in New York City on 15 June 1876. See Kendall, "New Orleans' Negro Minstrels," 146.

22 Cockrell, *Demons of Disorder*, 56.

23 Shorey, Duprez & Green's New Orleans and Metropolitan Opera Troupe and Brass Band, Admission card, Brewster, New York, 28 September 1860.

24 See Saxton, "Blackface Minstrelsy" (1975).

25 "Duprez & Benedict's Minstrels," advertisement, *New York Clipper*, 14 September 1867: 183.

26 Ibid.

27 "Negro Minstrelsy," *New York Clipper*, 18 January 1868: 327.

28 "The Minstrels Last Night," *St Paul Daily Pioneer*, 30 April 1869.

29 J.J. McCloskey produced a burlesque of the Ku Klux Klan at Hooley's Minstrel Hall, Brooklyn in April 1867, and the San Francisco Minstrels produced their own in May.

30 See *Massachusetts Vital Statistics: Index to Marriages*, vol. 199, 1866–1870 (Boston: Registry of Vital Records and Statistics), 218.

31 The marriage records provide Lavallée's place of residence simply as "Canada." *Records of the Massachusetts State Archives*. The 1867 edition of the *Lowell Directory* was not published, and the 1866 and 1868 editions have no listing for the family.

32 "Honor to Lavallée: Canada Pays Tribute Today to the Player and Composer," *New York Sun*, 13 July 1933. A William Gentle (and several others with variations of the family name) was a member of the Thirtieth Massachusetts Regiment, which was raised is Lowell in 1861 and was one of those that occupied the city of New Orleans in 1862. https://familysearch.org/pal:/MM9.1.1/F9R L-N3L; www.nps.gov/civilwar/search-soldiers-detail.htm?soldier_id=e2ed80a o-dc7a-df11-bf36-b8ac6f5d926a. (Accessed 10 August 2010)

33 "Original New Orleans Minstrels," advertisement, *Lowell Daily Citizen and News*, 21 December 1867.

34 The marriage records were searched for the author by D.R. Leggat of St Anne's Episcopal Church. Letter dated 27 March 1996.

35 "Negro Minstrelsy," *New York Clipper*, 4 January 1868: 311.

36 "The Street Beggar," a pathetic song with words by Frank Dumont and music

by L.E. Hicks (Indianapolis, IN: H.L. Benham & Co, 1869), was "Respectfully dedicated to Mrs Calixa Lavallée." Its cover featured a young, dark-haired woman standing on a snow-covered sidewalk.

37 *Massachusetts Vital Statistics: Index to Births, vol. 205, 1866–1870* (Boston: Registry of Vital Records and Statistics), 224.

38 In Ontario, the 1867 provincial election resulted in Liberals and Conservatives each winning forty-one seats. They subsequently formed a coalition government with Conservative John Sandfield Macdonald as premier. The Liberals were in power in Nova Scotia. The Confederationalist government remained in power in New Brunswick.

39 *Montreal Directory for 1868–69* (Montreal: John Lovell, 1868), 218, 436, 437. Augustin Lavallée is listed as a "musical instruments repairer." He shared the space at No. 43 with Narcise Beaudry, a jeweller on Côte Saint-Lambert (St Lambert Hill). This street was the bottom two blocks of St Lawrence Street. It ran only from Craig Street (now Saint-Antoine) to Notre Dame until the first decade of the twentieth century, when buildings were demolished to allow traffic through to the river, at which time Côte Saint-Lambert simply became a part of St Lawrence Street (now boulevard Saint-Laurent).

40 In *Música e ópera no Santa Isabel* (pp. 113–4, 125), Santos da Silva locates Petipas in Brazil in 1865. In 1867, she gave a number of concerts in New Orleans, advertising in the local newspapers. Soon after, she settled in Montreal, residing on St George Street with her husband Alfred d'Anglars, a teacher of elocution.

41 "St Patrick's Hall," *Montreal Herald*, 4 September 1868.

42 "Grand Concert," advertisement, *La Minerve*, 16 September 1868.

43 "Le Grand Concert de C. Lavallée," *La Minerve*, 16 September 1868.

44 "Concert de M. Lavallée," *Le Pays*, 15 September 1868.

45 "Canada," *Le Nouveau monde*, 18 September 1868.

46 See Hélène Marcotte, "Benjamin Sulte (baptized Olivier-Benjamin Vadeboncoeur)," *Dictionary of Canadian Biography*.

47 Aristide Filiatreault recalled Maillet's contributions to musical life in "Ludger-L. Maillet: ténor robuste," *La Presse*, 9 August 1913.

48 Newspapers said little about the concert. The *Herald* reported blandly that the concert "gave general satisfaction [to the] large and highly respectable" audience. "City Items," *Montreal Herald*, 17 September 1868.

49 "Arrivée du Lieut.-Gouverneur," *Le Pays*, 17 September 1868.

50 "Le Concert d'hier soir," *La Minerve*, 17 September 1868. "Mr Lavallée should be justly proud of his success last evening as organizer of this musical feast." Petipas claimed to be ill and did not perform. She likely had over-exterted herself, having been a soloist at a performance of Rossini's *Stabat Mater* the night before.

51 "Wanted Immediately, a good first violinist who can arrange well and play Brass to act as Musical Director for Duprez & Benedict's Minstrels. Will give one year's engagement to the right man. Apply, stating lowest terms, to Providence, R. I., until Sept. 25, after that date to Gloucestor, Mass." "Duprez and Benedict," advertisement, *New York Clipper*, 29 August 1868, 168.

52 For a thorough discussion of 'Irish' songs in North America see Williams, *'Twas Only an Irishman's Dream*.

53 "Saint Louis," *Brainard's Musical World*, XIX, no. 8 (August 1882): 125. The song appeared as no. 4683 in the *Musical Bouquet*, published in London in 1874.

54 Library Hall was located at the corner of Randolph and La Salle streets. The *New York Clipper* reported that "Duprez & Benedict's Minstrels were playing in Chicago the past week to poor business, although they give a good show. The position of the hall is pronounced very unfavorable." "Negro Minstrels," *New York Clipper*, 6 June 1868: 70.

55 "Negro Minstrelsy," *New York Clipper*, 28 August 1869: 167. A description and brief history of the building is found in Glazer, *Philadelphia Theatres*.

56 "Negro Minstrelsy," *New York Clipper*, 6 November 1869: 247.

57 Among the other prominent cast members were banjo player Charley Gleason and vocalist 'Sig. Vanderloeff.'

58 "Negro Minstrelsy," *New York Clipper*, 25 Decembre 1869: 303.

59 The *New York Clipper* printed regular updates, noting that minstrelsy was said to be "flourishing in Philadelphia." "Negro Minstrelsy," *New York Clipper*, 29 January 1870: 351. The company's advertisements in Philadelphia newspapers listed him as "Prof. C. Lavallée, Musical Director."

60 Odell, *Annals of the New York Stage*, vol. VII: 217.

61 "City Summary," *New York Clipper*, 5 March 1870: 382. Paine was going through very public divorce proceedings, alleging his wife, who lived in Providence, was adulterous and running a brothel.

62 Odell, *Annals of the New York Stage*, vol. IX: 74.

63 There are numerous sources on Fisk; see Fuller, *Jubilee Jim: The Life of Colonel James Fisk, Jr* (1928); Swanberg, *Jim Fisk: The Career of an Improbable Rascal* (1959); Ackerman, *The Gold Ring: Jim Fisk, Jay Gould and Black Friday, 1869* (1988).

64 "Fifth Avenue Theatre," advertisement, *New York Times*, 18 January 1869. H.L. Bateman had leased Pike's Opera House from Pike in 1868 and moved in his French comic opera company. When Fisk acquired the theatre, he renamed it and cut ticket prices from one dollar to fifty cents, but retained Bateman and his troupe. The *New York Times* reported that "the entire company remains under Mr Bateman's rule, and 'La Pericole' [*sic*] will run its prosperous career to the end. Mr Bingfeld [*sic*] has been appointed manager of the opera, and we venture to say that a better selection could not have been made." "Amusements," *New York Times*, 15 January 1869.

65 Fisk had moved the Opera Bouffe company over to the Fifth Avenue Theatre in April 1869, after closing the Grand Opera House for renovations. The *New York Times* reported that "the attendance overflowed the charming little place, and the beautiful audience was reflected a hundred times in the many mirrors with which the bright place is lined." "Amusements," *New York Times*, 6 April 1869.

66 When the market crashed, victims of scam pursued Fisk and Gould uptown, nearly lynching them, and forcing them to hide out in the Grand Opera House

for the next two weeks. Fisk later had a secret passageway built between the theatre and his home on 23rd Street. See Swanberg, *Jim Fisk*, 158.

67 Just after the September 1869 market collapse, Fisk allowed his contract on the Brooklyn Academy to lapse and leased the Fifth Avenue to Augustin Daly (1838–99). Swanberg (1959, 158) writes that Fisk took a $20,000 loss with the BAM (but confuses the theatre with Manhattan's Academy of Music).

68 "City Summary," *New York Clipper*, 26 March 1870: 406.

69 "City Summary," *New York Clipper*, 12 March 1870: 390.

70 See "Amusements," *New York Times*, 2 January 1870, and "Theatrical Receipts in New York," *Orpheus*, V, no. 12 (June 1870): 153. The San Francisco Minstrels' ticket prices were one dollar for orchestra seats, seventy-five cents in the parquet, fifty cents in the gallery, and six dollars for a private box.

71 "City Summary," *New York Clipper*, 9 April 1870: 11. They added a boy soprano known as Master Fine at about the same time as Dwyer. Wambold returned on 9 May.

72 The song was composed by Frank Campbell with words by Billy Reeves, but was made famous by Howard, whose arrangement was published by White, Smith & Perry (Boston, 1869).

73 "City Summary," *New York Clipper*, 21 May 1870: 54.

74 "City Summary," *New York Clipper*, 1 October 1870: 206.

75 The catalogue of Belgium's Royal Library contains two publications by P. Arnold de Thiers-Neuville: *La laiterie: notions pratiques sur L'art de faire le beurre et de fabriquer les fromages* (Brussels: Stapleaux, 1855); and *Amélioration des principales races bovines de Belgique* (Brussels: Tarlier [1851?]). The Bibliothèque national de France contains another, co-authored by W. Keene: *Du Maïs, de sa culture et des divers emplois dont il est susceptible* (Paris: A. Goin, 1854). Given the dates of these publications, they may have been by the father of Lavallée's librettist.

76 De Thier also published the *Fifth Avenue Polka* (New York: C.H. Ditson, 1870); *The Miller's Bell, a polka* (New York: Benjamin W. Hitchcock, 1873); *Old Father Rhine* (New York: Benjamin W. Hitchcock, 1873); and "Heaven Bless Mama" (Cincinnati: F.W. Helmick, 1875).

77 An article in the *New York Clipper* listed Edwin's leading actors in 1870–71 as "Messrs Stuart Robson, low and eccentric comedian; Edwin F. Thorn, leading; Eugene Eberle, old man; J.H. Chatterton, tenor singer and walking gentleman; Harry Josephs, eccentric comedy; J.W. Colins, general business; Charles T. Parslee Jr, character business and specialty of street boys." Among the leading actresses were Lillie Eldridge, Amelia Harris, Aggie Wood, and Dora Herbert. The article did not mention their specialities. "City Summary," *New York Clipper*, 10 September 1870: 182.

78 Frederick Phillips, *A Bird in the Hand is Worth Two in the Bush* (London: Thomas Hailes Lacy, nd). Douglas William Jerrold, *Black Eyed Susan; or, All in the Downs, a Nautical Melodrama, in Two Acts* (New York: R.H. Elton, 1830). Numerous editions of Jerrold's play were subsequently published in the United States.

79 "City Summary," *New York Clipper*, 5 November 1870: 246.

80 In November and December, Edwin was advertising *Billiards, or, Business Before Pleasure*; *Romeo Jaffier Jenkins*; *Love Among the Roses*; and *Little Jack Sheppard*. On 2 January 1871, Edwin presented the comedy by William Brough, *Kind to a Fault* (1867). Information is taken from the *New York Clipper*, the *New York Times*, and Odell's *Annals of the New York Stage*.

81 The minstrel show manager and historian T. Allston Brown provides a detailed history of Hope Chapel in *A History of the New York Stage: From the First Performance in 1732 to 1901*, vol. 1 (New York: Dodd, Mead and Company, 1903), 288–90. He was living in the theatre building, as was the vocalist Richard Warren, at the time it was destroyed by fire. See "Destructive Fires," *New York Times*, 29 November 1872.

82 "Amusements," *New York Times*, 1 September 1870.

83 Wambold's return made a significant difference, and the company's advertisements featured him and his ballads. In the early months of 1871 the company advertised the "immense success of Wambold's new ballad, 'God Bless the Little Church.'" "San Francisco Minstrels," advertisement, *The Spirit of the Times* 18 February 1871, np.

84 "City Summary," *New York Clipper*, 15 October 1870: 222. The "Railroad Overture" had long been a minstrel show staple. See Winans, "Early Minstrel Show Music," 157; and Mahar, *Behind the Burnt Cork Mask*, 20, 30, and 70.

85 Gardner Quincy Colton used nitrous oxide, or laughing gas, as an anaesthetic when extracting teeth. Colton lectured widely on the use of nitrous oxide and established the Colton Dental Rooms in Philadelphia in 1865. See G.Q. Colton, *Experience in the Use of Nitrous Oxide Gas* (np: np, 1868) and J.J. Colton, *The Physiological Action of Nitrous Oxide Gas, as Shown by Experiments Upon Man and the Lower Animals. Together with Suggestions as to Its Safety, Uses and Abuses* (Philadelphia: S. S. White, 1871). One of their biggest hits of the season was Queen and West's interpretation of Rollin Howard's "Let Me Be." Odell called it "a sort of companion piece to Shoo Fly!" Odell, *Annals of the New York Stage*, vol. IX: 74. On 10 December, the *New York Clipper* reported that "'Let Me Be' continues as attractive as ever," having "held the boards for sixty-two consecutive nights." "City Summary," *New York Clipper*, 10 December 1870: 286.

86 Stanley's reports appeared in the *New York Herald* and the *New York Times* in the summer of 1872, and the same year he published a full account of his discovery in *How I Found Livingstone*.

87 "City Summary," *New York Clipper*, 10 December 1870, 286. In 1870, New York's previously celebrated Ninth Regiment was in financial straits and elected Fisk its "colonel." He filled out the band's ranks with members of the Grand's orchestra, outfitted them in new uniforms, and on 14 April 1870, he led them in a parade down Fifth Avenue on his white stallion.

88 Fisk's production of *Les Brigands* was said to have cost $300,000. "Amusements," *San Francisco Chronicle*, 9 July 1872.

89 "San Francisco Minstrels," *Hartford Courant*, 7 April 1871.

90 "Negro Minstrelsy," *New York Clipper*, 27 May 1871: 63.

91 "Negro Minstrelsy," *New York Clipper*, 10 June 1871: 79.

92  See Morris, *Songs as Sung at Morris Bros', Pell and Trowbridge's Opera House*.
    A floor plan of the 493-seat Morris Brothers' Opera House is found in *The Diagram, Containing Plans of Theatres and Other Places of Amusement in Boston*, 47. The opera house was pulled down in 1872 during construction of Patrick Gilmore's coliseum.

93  See "Negro Minstrelsy," *New York Clipper*, 10 February 1872: 359.

94  "Local Brevities," *Lawrence Sentinel*, 30 March 1872.

95  See "Morris Bros.' Minstrels," advertisement, *Providence Daily Journal*, 10 April 1872.

96  See *Boston City Directory*, 1873: 453.

97  "Hall's Band," advertisement, *Montreal Pilot*, 16 November 1858.

98  See Nicholson, "Patrick Gilmore's Boston Peace Jubilees," 112.

99  "The Fall River Line," advertisement, *New York Times*, 2 July 1873.

100  "The Fall River Line," advertisement, *New York Times*, 22 September–10 November 1869.

101  "Annual Excursion of the Massachusetts Press Association," *Orpheus*, IX, no. 1 (1 July 1873): 6.

102  "Music and the Stage," Boston *Daily Evening Traveller*, 13 December 1872. The fire began in a building at the corner of Summer and Kinston streets on the evening of 9 November 1872. It destroyed much of the area and all of Arch Street. For years after, this part of central Boston was known as the 'burnt district.' See *Illustrated Boston: The Metropolis of New England*, 65.

103  "Musical," *New York Clipper*, 1 January 1873: 312.

104  "Concert Saturday Evening," *Boston Evening Journal*, 23 December 1872.

105  See, Landry, "Laurent-Olivier David." David was elected as a Liberal member of the Legislative Assembly of Quebec in 1886, and in 1903 he was appointed to the Canadian Senate.

106  David, "Enfin! Brilliant Concert." *Le Courier du Canada*, 7 May 1873. Charles Labelle quoted this passage in "Calixa Lavallée," *L'Écho musical*, I, no. 1 (January 1888): 1.

107  Band uniforms were never entirely standard, and during the early years of the war band musicians had often worn elaborate costumes. They were gradually standardized, due especially to the impracticality of carrying extra items on the march. Members of the Fourth may have taken special interest in their uniforms. After Lincoln reviewed the Fourth's brigade in 1861, a member of the Second Rhode Island Regiment reported the Fourth to be quite dapper: "This Regiment wears fine clothes, and the officers sport gold epaulettes and the sergeants woollen ones. It was a curiosity to me as our Regiment has never tried to drew [sic] up very fine. Governor Sprague was present in camp, and the band played on the parade." Rhodes, *All For the Union*, 46. David's 1873 claim that Lavallée had been a lieutenant was repeated by Labelle (1888), Letondal (1915), and others. The obituary in *Werner's Voice Magazine*, XXIII, no. 3 (March 1891): 84, reported that he had risen to the rank of a captain. Lapierre correctly reported that the records show that Lavallée was discharged as a "first class musician," but did not mention that the same war records list him as a private.

108  David, "Calixa Lavallée" (13 March 1873), 131.

109  David, "Calixa Lavallée" (13 March 1873) 131. David continued, "the en-

thusiastic people of these southern countries admired the talent of this young Canadian who was then just eighteen years old." Charles Labelle repeated the story in "Calixa Lavallée," *L'Echo musical*, I, no. 1 (1 January 1888): 1. It has reappeared in many subsequent accounts, including those by Potvin and Kallmann.

110 See Thompson, "Journies of an Immigrant Musician: Jacques Oliveira in Civil War–Era New York and New Orleans."

111 See "Drayton's Parlor Operas," *New York Musical World*, 23, no. 16 (24 December 1859): 2.

112 Havana was the only city in the West Indies that the New Orleans Minstrels performed in after departing from New Orleans in 1863. The day after they left for Cuba, Oliveira performed at a benefit concert at New Orleans's New Opera House. See "Théâtre de l'Opera," advertisement, *L'Abeille de la Nouvelle Orléans*, 27 January 1863.

113 David, "Calixa Lavallée" (13 March 1873) 131. David writes: "he left again, touring the United States, and Mexico, gathering laurels all the way to California."

114 "City Items," *Montreal Herald*, 15 November 1866.

115 "Nos artistes Canadiens aux États Unis, *Le Canada musical*, I, no. 3 (November 1866): 37.

116 Harsh economic conditions and a severe outbreak of yellow fever would force Smith back to Canada in 1869, where he accepted a position at Notre-Dame Cathedral in Ottawa. See Thompson, "Gustave Smith's Louisiana Episode," 7–9.

117 The *New York Clipper* noted: "A violinist, who is A No. 1 with the bow, and can arrange music well, as well as 'blow the trumpet, blow,' is wanted by Manager Duprez to act in the capacity of musical director of Duprez and Benedict's Minstrels." "Negro Minstrelsy," *New York Clipper*, 29 August 1868: 168.

118 In his *Annals of the New York Stage*, George Odell writes of the vocalist Sherwood C. Campbell's "struggle ... to escape from the minstrel stage" and establish himself as an opera singer in the early 1860s. See Odell, *Annals of the New York Stage*, vol. VII: 450. Interestingly, this was the same Campbell whose singing Lavallée had disparaged in a review in *L'Union nationale* in 1864.

119 L.-O. David, "Calixa Lavallée" (13 March 1873).

120 David's wording (see n121) suggests that he may have taken this information from a letter from Lavallée.

121 David, "Calixa Lavallée" (13 March 1873). David writes that, "according to Mr Lavallée himself, his work attracted great enthusiasm among the actors of the Grand Opera House."

122 It is possible that Fisk had agreed to stage *Peacocks in Difficulties*, but no reports about this seem to have been published. In July or early August 1871, Fisk had leased the Grand Theater to John F. Cole and Lewis G. Baker for five years. *Orpheus*, 7, no. 2 (August 1871): 22. They presented a season of dramas in the fall of 1871, opening with Tom Taylor's *Narcisse*. This was followed by *Jasper*, *Oofty Gooft* (performed by the Dutch comedian Gus Phillips); *Eileen Oge*; *Paris, or Days of the Commune*; *The Streets of New York*; A Troop of Mounted Dragoons (was this *Charles O'Malley*?); and *Ticket to Leave Man*. Baker and

Cole retained Henry Tissington as musical director; their business manager was Thomas E. Morris. *Orpheus* VII, no. 2 (August 1871). Having failed to attract audiences, they transferred control of the theatre to Augustin Daly, who opened a production of *La La Rookh* on 8 March 1872.

123 Kowalski, *A Travers l'Amérique*, 68.

124 *Detroit Daily Advertiser and Tribune*, reprinted in "Birchard Hall," *Milwaukee Sentinel*, 28 April 1863.

125 Ibid.

126 In his influential book, *Highbrow / Lowbrow: The Emergence of Cultural Hierarchy in America*, Lawrence Levine argues that a cultural hierarchy emerged only toward the end of the nineteenth century.

127 See Charosh, "'Popular' and 'Classical.'"

128 "Drayton's Parlor Operas," *New York Musical World*, 23, no. 16 (24 December 1859): 2. The same critic acknowledged that Oliveira had used an unfamiliar instrument ("his own having met with some slight accident") and praised him for performing Paganini's *Carnival of Venice* "with exquisite delicacy," even though "it is so easy to exaggerate, and so difficult to keep humor within the bounds of good taste." He performed Artot's *Fantasia on Il Pirata* and *Souvenir de la Sonnambula*, the music of Charles de Bériot, and other standard concert repertoire.

129 Advertisements listed the violinist Oscar Martel among the soloists who were to take part, but he did not perform.

130 "Lavallée," *L'Opinion publique*, 20 March 1873: 141.

131 Ibid. None of the other reviews discussed the cavatina, and no other performances of the piece are known to have taken place.

132 Duprez had actually been in California, after leaving Philadelphia, but I have found no evidence that Lavallée performed there.

133 "Calixa Lavallée," *Montreal Herald*, 14 March 1873, 2.

134 According to their son, Jules, del Vecchio captivated Prume with her interpretation of "Mon Coeur Soupire." See [Jules Jehin Prume et al.], *Jehin-Prume: Une Vie d'Artiste*, 162. The author did not specify whether this was a French translation of Cherubino's arietta ("Voi che sapete che cosa è amor," from Act Two of Mozart's *The Marriage of Figaro*), the romance "Mon cœur soupire des l'amoure" by Martin Pierre Dalvimar (1772–1839), or another work with the same title. Del Vecchio's paternal grandfather, one of Canada's first immigrants from Italy, owned an inn on rue Saint-Paul. The building was passed on to her father, Pierre-Thomas del Vecchio (ca. 1810–ca. 1897) but rented to other businesses. From 1864 to 1879, the *Montreal Directory* lists the family as residing at 64 Saint-Hubert Street. See Henry Leung, "The Del Vecchio House," B. Architecture, McGill University, 1967.

135 The tour opened with Prume in excellent form. The *New York Clipper* reported him to have been "the star of the evening" after the opening concert at New York's Cooper Institute. "City Summary," *New York Clipper*, 13 October 1866: 214. The same note criticized the program for having "too many solos and too few concerted pieces." The other members were Mlle Matilda Plodowski, soprano; Mlle Frida De Gebele, contralto; Sig. Giuseppe Limberti, tenor; Karl Formes, basso; Bernardus Boekelman, pianist; and Prof. S. Behrens,

accompanist. The tour came to an abrupt halt for Prume when his father became seriously ill. He left the company at Havana and travelled to Belgium with del Vecchio. His father died in April 1867, and the couple remained in Europe until summer.

136 Prume's 1869–70 concert tour also featured the soprano Carlotta Patti, pianist Theodore Ritter, basso buffo Giorgio Ronconi, and tenor Theodore Habelmann.

137 The title of the lecture-recital was "A Propos de Vous-Même." See "Lecture and Concert," *Montreal Herald*, 27 May 1873; "F. Jehin Prume's Concert," *Montreal Herald*, 27 May 1873; and "Philharmonic Society," *Montreal Herald*, 28 May 1873. Buies was of Scottish and French-Canadian background. He was educated in Montreal, Dublin, and Paris. In 1933, Raymond Douville published *La vie adventureuse d'Arthur Buies* in the same series as Lapierre's Lavallée biography.

138 "Calixa Lavallée's Concert," *Quebec Daily Mercury*, 10 May 1873.

139 Ibid.

140 "Faits Divers," *Courrier du Canada*, 12 May 1873.

141 Ibid.

142 L.-O. David, "Enfin! Brillant Concert: M. Calixa Lavallée," *Courrier du Canada*, 7 May 1873.

143 In the *Courrier du Canada*, the writer lamented that "only one thing pained us: that audience was select but small." "Faits Divers," *Courrier du Canada*, 12 May 1873. The same column reported that heavy rain had been falling continuously for the previous two days. The *Quebec Daily Mercury* reported that "for the reasons which prevented Prume's Concerts at the St Anne Street Lecture Hall from being largely attended, Lavallée played last evening before a very small audience. The prices of admission were too high, not that the performance was not worth the money, but because people at large are used to the 25 and 50 cents prices and prefer to stay at home rather than pay higher." See *Quebec Daily Mercury*, 10 May 1873.

144 The Montreal advertisements cited Lavallée's "success on the American Continent, and recently in California." To this, the Quebec City advertisements added that he had recently toured Brazil. No records of such travels have yet been located.

145 Lapierre credited Derome with making the financial arrangements, and raising a stipend of $80 a month. See Lapierre, *Calixa Lavallée* (1966), 115.

146 Calixa Lavallée, "The Future of Music in America," *The Folio*, XXX, no. 1 (July 1886): 13.

147 See "Soirée," *Fall River News*, 6 September 1873; "Célébration du 5 septembre," *L'Écho du Canada*, 13 September 1873.

CHAPTER FOUR

1 Victor Hugo wrote in his notebook on 31 December 1870: "We have no longer even horse to eat. *Perhaps* it is dog? *Maybe* it is rat? I am beginning to suffer from pains in the stomach. We are eating the unknown!" *Victor Hugo Central.* http://gavroche.org/vhugo/VHM/vhm-siegeparis.html. (Accessed 15

December 2012) See also, Octave Crémazie, "Journal du siege de Paris," *Lettres et fragments de lettres de Octave Crémazie publiées sous le patronnage [sic] de L'Institut canadien de Québec* (Montreal: Beauchemin, 1886), 178.

2 See Brody, *Paris: The Musical Kaleidoscope*, 101. For a study of antecedents of the musical changes in post-war Paris, see Cooper, *The Rise of Instrumental Music and Concert Series in Paris, 1828–1871.*

3 Among the instrumental ensembles active in the 1870s were the Société Philharmonique and the Concerts Modernes, while the Société de l'Harmonie Sacré began presenting choral concerts in 1873. At the Conservatoire itself, the Société des Concerts du Conservatoire had continued to present concerts since Cherubini created it in 1822. See Frédéric Robert, *La musique française au xixe siècle*, 47–66.

4 Gagnon cites those present as "MM Verreau, Desnoyers, Panneton et Couture, de Montréal; MM Lagacé, Pâquet, Roussel, et moi-même, de Quebec." *Lettres de voyages*, 120.

5 Ibid., 114. In the same paragraph, Gagnon mentions also meeting Lucien Turcotte, a Quebec City law professor, and Amédée Robitaille, a twenty-two-year-old law student and future Liberal member of the Quebec Legislature. He also met Joseph Tassé, a journalist and translator, who would be elected to Parliament as a Conservative in 1878. Couture's biographer, Pierre Quenneville, found no mention of Lavallée in Couture's correspondence. It does seem likely, however, that they were in contact with each other while in Paris. See Quenneville, "Guillaume Couture (1851–1915)," 119.

6 Calixa Lavallée, "Correspondance Privée," *L'Écho du Canada*, 22 November 1873.

7 Calixa Lavallée, "Correspondance privee de 'L'Écho du Canada,'" *L'Écho du Canada*, 31 January 1874.

8 The Conservatoire's archives contain no record of Lavallée's presence, indicating that, like many others, he studied only as an auditor and private student. I wish to express my thanks to Laurence Benoist, archivist at the Conservatoire, and to Florence Clavaud, of the Archives nationales, for examining their respective archives on my behalf.

9 Nichols, *Debussy Remembered*, 7. For further discussion of Debussy's studies with Marmontel, see Lesure, *Claude Debussy, biographie critique*, and Lockspeiser, *Debussy: His Life and Mind.*

10 Cited in Curtiss, *Bizet and His World*, 21.

11 Bellaigue, *Souvenirs de musique et de musiciens*, 33.

12 Marmontel discusses the importance of studying phrasing with a vocal coach under the heading "Des études vocales et leçon d'accompagnement," in *L'Art classique et moderne du piano*, 171–4. See also "L'Art de Phraser," *L'Album musical* [Montreal], III, no. 3 (March 1884): 17–8. Mayer's father-in-law was the famous tenor Manuel García. Her sister-in-law was the legendary mezzo-soprano Maria Malibran (née García). A decade later Marmontel published *Enseignment progressif et rationnel du piano.*

13 Bellaigue, *Souvenirs de musique et de musicians*, 33.

14 Ibid., 40–1.

NOTES TO PAGES 133–7

15 Camille Bellaigue, *L'Année musicale et dramatique*, Octobre 1886–Octobre 1887 (1888): 187.

16 On Lavallée's return to Canada, *Le Canada musical* reported that he had studied with "Marmontel, Boïeldieu, and others"; biographical articles from the 1880s claimed that "he studied under Marmontel, Boïeldieu, Bazin, and others." "Arrivée de Mr. Calixa Lavallée," *Le Canada musical*, II, no. 4 (August 1875): 54; "Calixa Lavallée," *The Folio*, XXVII, no. 2 (February 1885): 61.

17 Bazin, *Cours d'harmonie théorique et pratique*.

18 The libretto of *Le Voyage en Chine* was written by Eugène Marin Labiche and Alfred Delacour.

19 Reprinted as "Un artiste Canadienn," in *L'Écho du Canada*, 4 April 1874.

20 See Devriès and Lesure, *Dictionnaire des éditeurs de musique français vol. 2 de 1820 à 1914*.

21 "New Publications," *Music Trade Review*, III, no. 7 (3 February 1876): 111.

22 "Arrivée de Mr. Calixa Lavallée," *Le Canada musical*, 2, no. 4 (August 1875): 54. The writer described the first two as being "in the bravura style and very exaggerated.

23 "New Publications," *Music Trade Review*, III, no. 7 (18 March 1876): 160.

24 Gertz's roll was for Ampico (no. 5091), Rubenstein's was for the Duo-Art system (no. 6316), and Davis produced one for the Welte system (no. 6205). Herman Avery Wade produced a roll that he titled "The Famous Butterflies," with an arrangement of pieces by Grieg, Thome, Rosenthal, Schutt, Chopin, and Offenbach, as well as Lavallée's *Étude de concert*. See Aeolian Company, New York, "Music for Pianola and Pianola Piano," advertisement, *Bulletin of New Music for the Pianola-Piano, Orchestrelle and Aeolian Grand* (February 1912), 6. There was also an anonymous roll produced in 1904 for Wilcox and White (no. 12128).

25 Bossange was the son of the French-born Montreal bookseller Jean-Hector Bossange (see Fournier, *Les Français au Québec*, 112).

26 *Bossange's Catalogue of Periodicals* shows the firm to have been located at 25 quai Voltaire in Paris in 1869 (on the Left Bank, between the Pont Royal and the Pont du Carrousel). It relocated to the rue du 4 de septembre – which had previously been known as the rue du Dix décembre, and renamed to mark the downfall of Louis-Napoléon. Bossange's Le Havre office was located at 51 quai d'Orléans.

27 Gagnon, *Lettres de voyages*, 118–19.

28 *La leçon de musique* is owned by Boston's Museum of Fine Arts. In an email, Ann Brophy of the Museum writes that one source has suggested that the woman in the painting may have been a singer from Boulogne who was a friend of Mme Manet, but the identity has not been determined with any certainty. Personal communication, 26 July 2005. The musician Louis Lacombe also dedicated a piece of music to Ida Astruc. His song "Un Virtuose de la nuit" appeared in *La Chronique musicale* in 1874 (between pp. 272 and 273).

29 An illustration of the 1877 bust appears as fig. 95 in Sharon Flescher's *Zacharie Astruc* (1978), np.

30 Marcello described the Adagio and Tempo di Minuetto movements from Auguste

Vaucorbeil's String Quartet in D major as containing "few ideas and even less originality, some more or less curious imitations of the style of the old masters and in particular forms of Gluck and Rameau." He noted his preference for Louis Théodore Gouvy's Serenade, which was also in the classical style. See H. Marcello, "Revue des Concerts – Concerts National," *La Chronique musicale*, IV (1874): 31-3.

31 On 20 September 1873, *L'Écho du Canada* reported that Lavallée had been at the newspaper's Fall River offices the day before and mentioned his imminent departure and plan to establish a "national conservatory of music" in Canada on his return. The article concluded: "We wish our friend a happy journey, a speedy return, and above all success in the enterprise that is his mission, to provide our dear Canada with a conservatory of music."

32 Two second prizes in piano were awared to male students: Mr Torrent, another student of Mathias, and Mr Desgranges, a student of Marmontel. In addition to Debussy, certificates of merit were awarded to Mr Falkenberg and Mr Dasautoy (both students of Mathias), and Mr Lemoine (another student of Marmontel). See "Palmarès du Conservatoire de Musique pour l'année 1874," *La Chronique musicale*, V (1874): 154-60. In 1875, Debussy won a first certificate with Chopin's Second Ballade.

33 "Les Concours du Conservatoire," *La Chronique musicale*, V (1874): 145-53.

34 Tragically, Ehrhart died the next year while in Italy. In addition to his first prize, a second grand prize was awarded to a Mr Véronge de la Nux, and an honorable mention to a Mr Wormser, both students of Bazin. See Arthur Pougin, "Le Prix de Rome," *La Chronique musicale*, V (1874): 83-4.

35 Quenneville, "Guillaume Couture."

36 *Musical Courier*, XVI, no. 4 (25 January 1888): 50.

37 "Calixa Lavallée," *Musical Courier*, X, no. 14 (8 April 1885): 212. Lapierre referred to the work as a "Symphonie" in *Calixa Lavallée* (1966), 117. I have found no references to a performance in the leading music periodicals of the time (*La Chronique musicale*, *L'art musical*, and *Le ménestrel*), but they rarely provided the complete programs.

38 Elaine Keillor, ed., *Music for Orchestra II* (1994).

39 Ibid., ix.

40 By the late 1880s, Lavigne was the music director of Sohmer Park, on the Montréal waterfront. In 1891, he brought J.-J. Goulet to Montreal to perform at the park as part of a Belgian orchestra. Goulet himself became music director at the park in 1911. See Cécile Huot, "Sohmer Park."

41 "Concerts populaires," *Le Ménestrel* (1874): 87.

42 "Concert Lavallée," advertisement, *La Minerve*, 7 October 1874.

43 Keillor, *Music for Orchestra II*.

44 "Grand Concert Opératique et Populaire, Vocale et Instrumental au Profit de l'Eminent Artist Canadien." Concert Program. 8 October 1874. Bibliothèque et Archives nationales du Québec. http://collections.banq.qc.ca/bitstream/52327/1940941/1/2740750.pdf. (Accessed 9 June 2010)

45 "Concert Lavallée," advertisement, *La Minerve*, 7 October 1874. "Solo, Chœur avec introduction pour Orchestre composé à Paris, expressément pour ce Concert par M. Calixa Lavallée."

46 Lapierre referred to the librettist simply as "Monsieur Martineau, sulpicien." See Lapierre, *Calixa Lavallée* (1966), 115–16.

47 Flavien Martineau, *Une voix d'outre-tombe*, 203. The text was also contained in the concert program.

48 "Concert Lavallée," *La Minerve*, 9 October 1874. The *Montreal Star* of 9 October simply stated that the concert was "very successful."

49 Given the uniformity of the content of biographical articles published in the 1880s, they may have been based on publicity material supplied by Lavallée. They are discussed in Part Three.

50 Completing the new opera house became more urgent after the Opéra's Salle Le Peletier was destroyed by fire in October 1873.

51 The changing relationship between opera and French identity is examined in Fulcher, *The Nation's Image: French Grand Opera as Politics and Politicised Art*. For a discussion of the symbolism of the Palais Garnier, see pp. 173–80.

52 When on 10 December 1874, the Opéra-Comique opened a new production of Auber's *Domino Noir*; the opening night performance was the opera's 884th. See "Chronologie de l'Année 1874," *La Chronique musicale*, VII (1875): 41.

53 See "Faits Divers," *La Chronique musicale*, V (1874): 141–2.

54 For 1875, the National Assembly provided 800,000 francs for the Opéra; 20,000 fr. for the retirees of the Opéra; 240,000 fr. for the Théâtre-Français; 140,000 fr. for the Opéra-Comique; 100,000 fr. Théâtre-Lyrique; 60,000 fr. for the Odéon; 220,000 fr. for the Conservatoire and provincial facilities; as well a new 4,000 fr. subvention for the Conservatoire de Dijon. See "Faits Divers," *La Chronique musicale*, V (1874): 191.

55 The seventh Société Nationale concert offered a number of other premieres, including two movements of Vincent d'Indy's *Symphonie chevaleresque* (Prière and Allegro), Gabriel Fauré's *Cantique de Jean Racine*, and an Offertoire by César Franck. See "Chronologie de l'Année 1875," *La Chronique musicale*, VIII (1875): 293.

56 See "Concours du Conservatoire," *Revue et Gazette Musicale*, 42 (1875): 237.

57 See *Revue et Gazette Musicale*, 42 (1875): 213–14.

58 *Le Canada musical*, II, no. 5 (September 1875): 77.

59 The dedication in *L'Art moderne du Piano-50 études de salon* was to: "Mon chèr élève Monsieur Calixa Lavallée, Souvenir amical." See "Notes," *Le Canada musical*, II, no. 8 (December 1875): 124. Marmontel listed Lavallée's compositions in *Art classique et moderne du piano*, vol. 2, 68.

60 See "Musical: William Sherwood," *Boston Home Journal*, 14 April 1883; and Calixa Lavallée, "Is it necessary to go abroad to study?" 171. In 1885, *Brainard's* stated that "Lavallée remained in Paris for a number of years, and after leaving the city traveled in Europe." "Biographies of American Musicians: Number Ninety, Calixa Lavallée," *Brainard's Musical World*, XXII (May 1885): 167.

61 Lavallée and the Prumes appear to have been in contact since the couple returned to Canada soon after Lavallée; there they began an important partnership.

62 In 1902, the French jurist Paul Sorin wrote that, "above all it is through the theatre that [the nation's strength] manifests itself abroad. It is by this that

foreigners judge us." "Du Role de l'État en matière d'Art Scénique," PhD, Faculté de Droit de l'"Université de Paris, cited in André Michael Spies, *Opera, State and Society in the Third Republic*, 89.

63 "Port de Québec," *Journal de Québec*, 20 July 1875. The passenger manifest shows the majority of passengers to have been labourers and spinsters, mostly from England but also from Ireland, Scandinavia, and France. For Lavallée, it provides only his name and departure date. It can be found at *Quebec City Passenger Lists Index 1865–1900*. www.collectionscanada.gc.ca/databases/passengers-quebec-1865-1900/001082-119.03-e.php?&interval=20&person_id_nbr=432665&&PHPSESSID=9dtbf9r2485ndp5olr36k7kb42. (Accessed 12 February 2013)

64 In its August 1875 issue, *Le Canada musical* announced the arrival of Calixa Lavallée. "Arrivée de Mr Calixa Lavallée," *Le Canada musical*, 2, no. 4 (August 1875): 54. This periodical had first appeared between September 1866 and August 1867. Another periodical with the same name was published between 1917 and 1930. See Hélène Paul, "*Le Canada musical*," 48–65. In *Le Canada musical* of the 1870s, reviews were often unsigned. Many are likely to have been written by the publisher.

65 Augustin Lavallée had moved the shop several times since 1865, each time to a different location on Côte Saint-Lambert (Nos. 32, 43, 35, and finally to No. 35 1/2). Information on the Lavallées is taken from the *Montreal Directory*.

66 *Montreal Directory, 1875–76*: 33. Cities throughout North America had continued to grow rapidly. The ten largest cities in the United States at the time of the 1870 census were New York (1,478,103), Philadelphia (647,022), St Louis (310,864), Chicago (298,977), Baltimore (267,354), Boston (250,526), Cincinnati (216,239), New Orleans (191,418), San Francisco (149,473), and Buffalo (117,714). Anderton, *Population of the United States*, 45.

67 Bourget had purchased the land in 1854. Upon completion, the new cathedral was designated Saint-Jacques-le-Majeur. In 1955, it was rededicated Cathédrale Marie-Reine-du-Monde (Mary, Queen of the World). See Mgr André M. Cimichella, "Monseigneur Ignace Bourget deuxième évêque de Montréal (1840–1876)," *L'Église de Montréal. Aperçus d'hier et d'aujourd'hui, 1836–1986* (Montreal: Fides, 1986), 69.

68 See Mann.

69 A Monsieur Fortin managed the Palais Musical in 1872, but it subsequently changed names and managers several times. The building was demolished in the early years of the twentieth century, and in 1912 the city erected a new Municipal Court House on the site.

70 In about 1909, the theatre became known as the Académie Théâtre de la Comédie Française. Property developers demolished the building in 1910 to make way for Goodwin's department store (later Eaton's). See Benson and Conolly, *The Oxford Companion to Canadian Theatre*.

71 The Academy's attributes are discussed in "The Academy of Music," *Canadian Illustrated News*, 27 November 1875, 339. The theatres' stage dimensions are listed in *Julius Cahn's Official Theatre Guide*.

72 Gould established the Mendelssohn Choir at the American Presbyterian Church

in 1864. It performed there, at the Mechanics Hall (1876–81), at Queen's Hall (1881–90), and at Windsor Hall (1890–94). See Turbide, "Mendelssohn Choir."

73 "Retour de M. de Madame F. Jehin-Prume," *Le Canada musical*, 2, no. 4 (1 August 1875): 54.

74 Émile Prudent had been a good friend of Antoine Marmontel, who may have introduced Lavallée to his music.

75 "Séance musicale de M. Calixa Lavallée," *Le Canada musical*, 2, no. 6 (October 1875): 86–7. The quintet comprised Augustin Lavallée, B. Shea, A. Maffré, C. Bienvenu, and G. Leclèrc.

76 The concert took place on the first day of the exhibition, which ran from 21 to 25 September. No details about the actual events of the exhibition were contained in the guidebook. *The Provincial Exhibition Annual, A Guide to the Show Grounds, and Hand Book for the City of Ottawa, 1875* (Ottawa: Alex Robertson, 1875).

77 Members of the quintet were Maffré, François Boucher, C. Bienvenu, Alex Wills, and G. Leclerc. Three more musicians (Shea, Stratton, and Augustin Lavallée) joined in the overtures.

78 "Concert," *L'Opinion publique*, 16 September 1875: 442. The 17 October 1875 issue of *Le Ménestrel* (p. 366) noted that "the Canadian newspapers announce the return home of Mr Calixa Lavallée, one of the finest pianists of the New World," and then quoted from *L'Opinion publique*'s review of the 9 September concert.

79 "Séance Musicale de M. Calixa Lavallée," *Le Canada musical*, 2, no. 6 (October 1875): 86.

80 Joseph Marmette, "Chronique de Québec," *L'Opinion publique*, 18 November 1875, 542.

81 Couture, "Chronique musicale," *La Minerve*, 14 December 1875.

82 "Concert de M. Calixa Lavallée," *Le National*, 11 September 1875.

83 "Concert Prume-Lavallée," *Le Canadien*, 10 November 1875.

84 "Concert Prume-Lavallée," *Le Canadien*, 10 November 1875.

85 "Premier Concert Prume-Lavallée à Montréal," *Le Canada musical*, 2, no. 9 (January 1876): 134.

86 Couture, "Chronique musicale," *La Minerve*, 14 December 1875.

87 Ibid.

88 Del Vecchio sang "Le Voyage de l'amour et du temps." Prume played Vieuxtemps's *Appassionata* fantasy, a Bach prelude, a Raff cavatina, and a rondo of his own composition. And Lavallée performed music by Weber and Mendelssohn.

89 "Concert de M. Couture," *Le Canada musical*, 2, no. 9 (January 1876): 135.

90 "Couture's Concert," *Daily Witness*, 29 December 1875.

91 "Le Concert de M. Couture," *Daily Witness*, 29 December 1875. The critic also savaged Mons. Drolet, soloist in the excerpt from Berlioz's *L'Enfance du Christ* and in Couture's *Ave Maria*.

92 "Lessons de Violon," advertisement, *Le Canada musical*, 2, no. 8 (November 1875): 98. Jehin-Prume and Rosita del Vecchio were living at her parents' home on Drolet Street in what is now known as the Plateau-Mont-Royal. (*LovelL's Directory* for 1875–77, 148).

93  Lavallée is listed as the resident of 82 Cathcart Street in the city directory for 1876–77, 1877–78, and 1878–79.

94  See Minute book of the AMQ, Fonds AMQ (P-0379), Bibliothèque et Archives nationales du Québec. Centre Québec.

95  Present at the first meeting were Damis Paul, G.G. Pfeiffer, Albert Rochette, A. Desrochers, and Gustave and Ernest Gagnon. The first resolution passed at that meeting was written: "That it is timely to create, at Quebec City, an association of professional musicians, and that the said association should be called the Academie de musique de Québec." Minute book of the AMQ, Fonds AMQ, ABNQ.

96  Minute book of the AMQ, Fonds AMQ, ABNQ.

97  Letondal became especially active, serving on the examining committees for harmony, organ, piano, violin, solfège, and singing.

98  "Conservatory of Music," *Montreal Star*, 18 April 1876. The English-born musician Charles F. Davies was organist at the Anglican St James the Apostle Church on Sainte-Catherine Street. In 1878, he published the *Church Chant Book* (Montreal: De Zouche). Some time after this, he left Montreal to take up church positions in Windsor and in Detroit. He died in Cleveland, Ohio, in 1922.

99  "Nouvelles," *Le Canada musical*, 2, no. 12 (1 April 1876): 189.

100  For information on Notman, see Triggs, *Notman's Studio*, and Hall, *The World of William Notman*.

101  A description of the building, including the 800-seat hall, is found in *The Hotel Guests' Guide for the City of Montreal*, 59–60.

102  "Prume and Lavallée's Concert," *Montreal Star*, 19 April 1876. Couture later published reviews in the *Star* as William Couture (he had been baptized William Coutu).

103  "Victoria Hall," advertisement, *Quebec Daily Mercury*, 2 January 1874. Frantz Beauvallet's five-act drama *Le Forgeron de Châteaudun* had been given its first performance at the Ambigu-Comique in Paris on 8 January 1871. See also, *Guide to Quebec and the Lower Saint Lawrence* (1882) 109–10. Le Moine, *Quebec, Past and Present*, 411.

104  Little information seems to be available on the size of the Wesleyan Church or its transformation into a lecture hall in 1848 and a concert venue in 1874. Concerning the Music Hall, see Lebel, "La nuit où périt le Music Hall"; and Le Moine, *Quebec, Past and Present*, 412.

105  "Victoria Hall," *Daily Evening Mercury*, 23 May 1876.

106  The sextet included Lavallée's younger brother, Joseph, playing cello. Another cellist, W.D. Campbell, joined Lavallée and Prume in Beethoven's Trio in E-flat major, op. 1, no. 1. "Prume's Second Concert," *Daily Evening Mercury*, 30 May 1876.

107  In recent weeks, *Under the Gaslight* and *Streets of New York* had both been staged to great success. The big hit of the summer at the Academy of Music was *Little Emily*, a sentimental play adapted from Dickens's *David Copperfield*.

108  Guillaume Couture, "Chronique musicale," *La Minerve*, 25 April 1876.

109  See Lefebvre, "Qu'a-t-il manqué à Guillaume Couture?"

110  "Le Concert de M. Couture," *Daily Witness*, 2 June 1876.

111 For the next year, he lived in Paris where he directed the choir at Église Sainte-Clotilde, the church where César Franck was the organist. He may have felt some vindication about the substance of his *Memorare* when it was performed at the 13 January 1877 concert of the Société Nationale de Musique at the Salle Pleyel. See "Concerts et Auditions Musicales," *Revue et Gazette Musical*, 44, no. 4 (1877): 30

112 See "Grand Concert d'Adieu," advertisement, *Le Canada musical*, 3, no. 1 (May 1876): 16.

113 Guillaume Couture, "Concert d'Adieu," *La Minerve*, 6 June 1876.

114 See "Naissance," *Le Canada musical*, 3, no. 3 (July 1876): 46.

115 Joseph François Augustin Lavallée. Baptismal record, Druin Collection. Ancestry.com. (Accessed 16 February 2013)

116 "Chronique musical," *La Minerve*, 21 June 1876.

117 "Séance à l'Académie Commerciale Catholique," *La Minerve*, 28 June 1876.

118 After Lavallée's rendering of the Weber *Konzertstück*, *Le Canada musical*'s correspondent wrote: "What fiery execution. What clarity! What broad, effortless and precise phrasing." "Troisième Concert de Prume et Lavallée," *Le Canada musical*, 3, no. 4 (August 1876): 58.

119 "Nouvelles," *Le Canada musical*, 3, no. 3 (July 1876): 46. Ottawa's *Foyer Domestique* mentioned Lavallée's appointment to the Saint-Jacques post in its September 1876 issue.

120 The *Montreal Star* reported the death on 3 August. *Le Canada musical* reported the death in its September issue: "Déces," *Le Canada musical*, 3, no. 5 (September 1876): 71. The burial record is contained in the Drouin Collection. Ancestry.com. (Accessed 9 September 2010)

121 "Gilmore's Concert Garden," advertisement, *New York Herald*, 10 September 1875. The advertisement noted that *Fantasie* was "composed expressly for, dedicated to and performed by Mr M. Arbuckle."

122 "The Lafayette Statue," *Daily Tribune*, 7 September 1876.

123 See, for example, "La Statue de Lafayette" (*La Minerve*, 9 September 1876), in which the writer mentioned not sharing the enthusiam of some of his compatriots.

124 "Nouvelles," *Le Canada* musical, 3, no. 8 (December 1876): 124. The article also mentions that Lavallée neglected no details, and procured a "magnificent" Hazelton piano from A.J. Boucher (who was the editor of *Le Canada musical*).

125 See "Notes Locales," *La Minerve*, 17 January 1877.

126 Jacquard was listed in Lovell's 1870–71 city directory as "Professor of music, violon-cello, 30 St Antoine." He was also present for the 1871 census, in which he was recorded as a thirty-six-year-old cellist, but left the city some time that year.

127 *Le Canada musical*, 3, no. 9 (January 1877); 139.

128 Ibid. Adrien-François Servais (1807–66) was primarily a composer of cello music.

129 Bishop Fabre announced the formal decision in December 1878 in the form of a letter to the clergy. See Édouard-Charles Fabre, *Lettre circulaire de Mgr L'évêque de Montréal au clergé de son diocèse, MEM Mandement des évêques*

*de Montréal*, IX (28 December 1878), 216–17. See also Marie-Thérèse Lefebvre, "The Role of the Church in the History of Musical Life in Quebec," translated by Beverley Diamond, in *Canadian Music: Issues of Hegemony and
Identity*, Beverley Diamond and Robert Winter, eds. (Toronto: Canadian Scholars Press, 1994), 70–1; and Brian Young, "Édouard-Charles Fabre," *Dictionary of Canadian Biography*. John Finn, a professor at the Catholic Commercial
Academy, replaced Lavallée as choir director at Saint-Jacques. See *Le Canada
musical*, 3, no. 12 (April 1877): 188.

130 Lapierre, *Calixa Lavallée* (1966), 128–30. Lapierre used what could only have
been an imagined dialogue to describe the scene in which Sentenne proposed
the production of *Jeanne d'Arc*.

131 The actress Lia Félix was well received in the title role, but critics dismissed
Gounod's music for *Jeanne d'Arc* as little more than a "bundle of reminiscences." See James Harding, *Gounod* (London: George Allen & Unwin, 1973),
179. See also "Jeanne d'Arc," *L'Illustration*, 13 December 1873.

132 *L'Opinion publique* published a substantial discussion of the work on 4 De-
cember 1873 (see pp. 580–1). See Barbier and Gounod, *Jeanne d'Arc*. Georges
Bizet's piano reduction of the score had been published by Gérard et cie. Jules
Barbier and Charles Gounod, *Jeanne d'Arc, drame en cinq actes* (Paris:
Choudens, 1873)

133 Marmette, "Chronique de Québec," 18 November 1875: 541.

134 See "Grand Concert," *Montreal Star*, 3 March 1877.

135 See "Notes Locales," *Le Nouveau monde*, 3 March 1877. That this ultramontane newspaper reported on the event suggests a form of Church approval of
the production.

136 "'Jeanne d'Arc' at AOM," *Canadian Illustrated News*, 7 April 1877, 214.

137 An 1867 staging of Donizetti's *La Fille du régiment* at the Crystal Palace remained one of the few local productions. See Barrière, "La Société Canadienne-
française," 317–22.

138 See Londré and Watermeier, *History of North American Theater*, 244.

139 "'Jeanne d'Arc' at AOM," *Canadian Illustrated News*, 7 April 1877, 214. The
writer did not specify how many musicians played these "80 instruments" but
assembling an orchestra of more than 50 would have been a formidable task.

140 The full cast list that appeared in the libretto provided only surnames of most
of the performers. See Barbier and Gounod, *Jeanne d'Arc*, 1877. Labelle and
Derome had been married in 1872. See Lefebvre, "'Que sont mes amis devenus
...,'" 166.

141 The Protestant *Daily Witness* was the exception, printing nothing at all about
the production.

142 See "Jeanne d'Arc," *La Minerve*, 15 May 1877.

143 "Before the Footlights," *Canadian Illustrated News*, 26 May 1877: 326.

144 Ibid.

145 See Führer, 19. In Führer's book, the organist leaves Montreal for Chicago.
MacLagan would go to Winnipeg. For information on MacLagan's professional
activities in Winnipeg, see Hartman, "The Golden Age of the Organ in Manitoba: 1875–1919."

146 The Philharmonic Society under MacLagan never attracted strong community

support. After a December 1877 Philharmonic performance, the *Montreal Star* praised the ensemble for its efforts and admonished the audience for being "cold, unsympathetic and very reserved in its applause." "The Philharmonic Concert," *Montreal Star*, 18 December 1877.

147 Also that week, a theatrical troupe managed by Max Strakosch was performing at the Academy of Music, and a variety company performed at the Mechanics' Institute with Henry Prince's band.

148 "Concours de l'Académie de Musique de Québec," *Le National*, 6 June 1877. The results drew criticism from at least one witness, who later published an anonymous letter contesting the AMQ's decisions. "Correspondance," *Le National*, 11 June 1877.

149 "Concours de l'Académie de Musique de Québec," *Le National*, 6 June 1877.

150 See "Concert," *Le National*, 26 June 1877.

151 Thomas Hackett, a member of the Orange Order, was killed during a riot on Victoria Square on 12 July 1877 when Catholics tried to prevent the march from taking place.

152 In November, Lavallée incuded Prume as co-director in the advertisements for *Jeanne d'Arc*, perhaps for its promotional value or perhaps in anticipation of his return to Canada. Advertisments also listed the designer as Garand (*décorateur*), the stage director (*engineer de la scène*) as A.V. Brazeau, the machinist as J.B. Goodman, and the operator of the electrical lights as M.T. Carini. "Jeanne d'Arc," advertisement, *Le National*, 19 November 1877.

153 "Jeanne d'Arc," *La Minerve*, 20 November 1877. Later that winter, Newcomb appeared in the title role of the Troupe Dramatique Français's production of Jules Perrot's *Marie-Jeanne* at the Theatre Royal, so it appears that French was not a problem for her.

154 Theatre Royal," *Le National*, 20 November 1877.

155 "Theatre Royal," *Montreal Star*, 20 November 1877.

156 "Theatre Royal," *Le National*, 26 November 1877.

157 Quenneville, "Guillaume Couture."

158 Other published tributes included *Histoire de Pie IX, Sa Vie et Sa Mort* (Montreal: J.B. Rolland et Fils Libraires, 1878), and *Les annees de Pie IX, de 1846 a 1878: Souvenir* (Montreal: E. Senécal, 1878).

159 "Notes Locales," *La Minerve*, 7 March 1878.

160 "Madame F. Jehin Prume," *La Minerve*, 7 February 1878.

161 See Prume, *Une Vie d'artiste*, 245–6.

162 See Rumilly, *Histoire de la province de Québec*.

163 A brief list of other potential operas Lavallée might have chosen would include Daniel Auber's *Fra Diavolo* (1830) and *Le Domino noir* (1837), Ferdinand Hérold's *Zampa* (1831), Gaetano Donizetti's *La Fille du régiment* (1840), and Ambrose Thomas's *Mignon* (1866). Lavallée may also have considered Gounod's *Faust* (1859), which, although a grand opera, would not have required elaborate sets. It does, however, have three important male roles that Lavallée would have had difficulty casting locally. Gounod's *Roméo et Juliette* (1867) might have been another option, offering a familiar story to the English-speaking population.

164 Kallmann, "Antoine Dessane," *Dictionary of Canadian Biography*.

165  Adam, "La Dame Blanche." The essay was extracted from Adam's *Derniers souvenirs d'un musician* (Paris: Michel Lévy Frères, 1871): 277–94.

166  Scott's popularity with Romantic composers has been most thoroughly explored by Jerome Mitchell in two books on the subject. See *The Walter Scott Operas* and *More Scott Operas*.

167  The humour in Scott's novels is limited mostly to certain characters, such as the English knight, Sir Percie Shafton, in *The Monastery*, and Harry's tutor, Dominie Sampson, in *Guy Mannering*. The tone of both novels is generally serious. There is especially a sense of foreboding in Scott's description of the countryside itself, especially at night. In *Guy Mannering*, lawlessness along the coast is illustrated through the activities of the smugglers, while the gypsies, who are expelled, are treated with some sympathy.

168  In Ottawa, power had shifted between Liberal and Conservative parties, and between two leaders, both born in Scotland: Macdonald and Mackenzie. In Montreal, civic and business leaders were also a factor, and big business was dominated by Scots – people like Sir Hugh Allan, who, among other things, owned the Academy of Music.

169  "Amusements," *The Gazette*, 17 April 1878.

170  Ibid. "All this set to music, suitable to the words and scene – the latter picturesque in itself – and with the addition of the garb of old Scotland and the irrisistable charm of the legend, forms a work in which Mr Lavallée has ample scope to entertain our citizens, and we will be surprised if the result of his labors do not go to make its production an artistic success."

171  See Fiske, *Scotland in Music*, 103.

172  See Mitchell, *The Walter Scott Operas*, 37. Fiske identifies the tune as "'The White Cockade' imperfectly remembered" (*Scotland in Music*, 103). Fiske also identifies the tune with which Dickson greets George Brown in Act I as "The Yellow-Hair'd Laddie," and George Brown's air from Act II, "Viens, gentille dame," as "a crazy version of 'Robin Adair'" (*Scotland in Music*, 103).

173  See Fiske, *Scotland in Music*, 196.

174  The opera was still in the repertoire when commercial recordings of opera selections were first produced at the start of the twentieth century. One of the earliest was a 1904 German-language version of "Viens gentille dame" ("Komm', O Holde Dame") by the Moravian tenor Leo Slezak. A number of selections from the opera were performed and recorded long after the opera slipped from public view. A recording has been preserved of selections from a 1944 French radio broadcast featuring soprano Claudine Collart as Jenny and Louis Arnoult as George, and including a duet and Jenny's ballad "Prenez garde." A 1958 broadcast by the Orchestre Radio-Lyrique, directed by Jules Gressier, featured contralto Solange Michel's singing of "Pauvre Dame Marguerite." Live performances were recorded of "Quel plaisir d'être soldat" by Charles Burles and by Henri Legay, the latter being a performance for Belgian television. Among the recordings made of George's "Viens gentile dame" is one from the 1930s by French tenor David Devriès.

175  Our main source of information on the 1878 production of *La Dame blanche* is a bilingual libretto Lavallée produced for sale at performances. It provides the names of some the technical people involved as well as the cast.

176  The libretto lists only eight cast members. See Scribe and Boiëldieu, *La Dame blanche* (1878).

177  Laurent-Olivier David, "Calixa Lavallée," *La Presse*, 9 November 1912, cited in Lefebvre, "'Que sont mes amis devenus …,'" 165. "One day, when he was choirmaster at St Jacques, Lavallée noticed in the choir the singing of a young man with a striking voice. It was Mr Aristide Filiatreault. The Mass over, Lavallée approached Filiatreault and asked him to his home. Mr Filiatreault did so, and on entering the house, Lavallée told him to have a seat at the piano:
- Come, sing for me what you know best.
Mr Filiatreault sang and sang his best until Lavallée stopped him to say:
- Okay, you sing like a savage.
- You are not saying that I have no voice, Filiatreault said.
- Yes, said Lavallée, [you have] a good voice to shout "fire." But still, one has to learn how to sing, [and] your voice has substance."

178  On 11 March, *La Minerve* reported the first choral rehearsals had taken place and that Lavallée would make a surprise announcement of his guest soloist.

179  See Tinoco Josué, "Correio dos theatros," *O Figaro* no. 74 (May 1877): 591; and Tinoco Josué, "Correio dos theatros," *O Figaro* no. 76 (May 1877): 607. Lacôme's opéra comique was first performed at the Théâtre des Folies Dramatique in Paris on 27 October 1876. The *Diario do Rio de Janeiro* provides more information on Hassani's performances in 1876 and 1877.

180  The engagement of Anna Granger Dow's company at Montreal Academy of Music had begun in December 1877 and continued into the early days of 1878. They presented a number of works, including Balfe's *The Bohemian Girl*, with Granger Dow taking the role of Arline. See *La Minerve*, 19 December 1877; "Our Musical Column," *The Gazette*, 5 January 1878; and "Amusements," *The Gazette*, 5 January 1878.

181  See Scribe and Boiëldieu, *La Dame blanche*, libretto.

182  The introduction to the libretto devotes a paragraph to urging the public to patronize Boisseau & Frère's shop.

183  *The Gazette* listed among the arrivals at the Richelieu Hotel, "Mad Hassani, Vienne, France; Mr Hassani, do." "Hotel Arrivals," *The Gazette*, 12 April 1878.

184  "'La Dame blanche,' or 'The White Lady,'" *The Gazette*, 22 April 1878. The item concluded with what appears to have been a caveat to the otherwise very favourable comments, noting that "The costumes of the Scottish mountaineers are of the kind usually to be found in opera, and everyone is aware of the licence here admitted. In French opera that licence must be extended further, and we may sum up by saying that the whole is picturesque and entertaining."

185  "A Travers la Ville," *Le National*, 24 April 1878.

186  "Amusements," *The Gazette*, 24 April 1878.

187  Guillaume Couture, "Chronique musicale: 'La Dame blanche,'" *La Minerve*, 2 May 1878. The work of set designer Garand was also well received, especially his centrepiece, the Château d'Avenel. See "Causerie Musicale," *La Minerve*, 30 April 1878.

188  Guillaume Couture, "Chronique musicale: 'La Dame blanche,'" *La Minerve*, 2 May 1878.

189 Ibid. The comments also suggest that Lavallée was playing the violin while conducting.

190 *L'Événement* reported the total number of company members making the trip to be sixty-seven. See "La Dame blanche," *L'Événement*, 7 May 1878.

191 "La Dame Blanche," *Daily Telegraph*, 6 May 1878.

192 Marmette called the production a "beautiful success." "L'Art Musical au Canada," *L'Opinion publique*, 23 May 1878, 241.

193 "'La Dame blanche,'" *L'Événement*, 8 May 1878.

194 "Amusements," *The Gazette*, 13 May 1878. The column continued: "Set to music which is pleasing in itself, the opera is admirably acted, and with Mlle Hassani to sustain the principal role, the other parts in able hands, and a capital chorus and orchestra, it may be expected that the nearest approach to grand opera will be reached that we have yet had in Montreal."

195 "Amusements," *The Gazette*, 14 May 1878. (Note: No issues of *The Gazette* were available for May after the 14th.)

196 Guillaume Couture, "Chronique musicale," *La Revue de Montréal*, 3 (1879): 109.

197 Joly defeated the Conservative Joseph-Adolphe Chapleau.

198 In the United States, the founding of private music schools had begun in the 1860s, with the creation of the Cincinnati Conservatory, the New England Conservatory, and others.

199 "Notes locales," *La Minerve*, 1 April 1878.

200 Marmette, "L'Art Musical au Canada," *L'Opinion publique*, 23 May 1878, 242. The comments make one wonder what Marmette knew of Lavallée's career in the United States. It would seem unlikely that Lavallée could have kept it a secret, although there is evidence that he was doing just that and would continue to do so over the rest of his life.

201 "La Dame blanche," *L'Événement*, 8 May 1878.

202 Bibliothèque et Archives nationales du Québec. Fonds du Secrétariat de la Province de Québec, E4. "Établissement d'un conservatoire de musique." Simon Couture cites this letter as: Calixa Lavallée, [et al.] "Petition adressée au lieutenant gouverneur de la province de Québec pour l'établissement d'un conservatoire de musique et de déclamation," Fonds du Secrétariate provincial, M88/5, registre des lettres reçues, 1878, 971. See Couture, "Les Origines du Conservatoire," 138. Couture writes that this letter was also reproduced in *Le Nouvelliste* 44.225 (25 July 1964): 7. An English translation of the letter was published in "O Canada Composer Sought Conservatory," an unidentified newspaper article [ca. 1970] located in the Fonds de la Ville de Québec, Série Conseil, sous-série Conseil et comités; QP1-4/167-9, Dossier "Lavallée, Calixa," Archives de la Ville de Québec.

203 See Calixa Lavallée, "Platon Polichinelle," 22 February 1865; and Legendre, *Albani.*

204 McKinley, *Hockey: A People's History*, 7.

205 The composition is not known to have been published and has perhaps been lost.

206 Lavigne was under contract with the Victoria Rifles and with that military en-

semble used many of his Bande de la Cité, a group that he had led to victory at the 1876 competition in Philadelphia.

207 See "City News," *Montreal Star*, 27 June 1878.

208 "Fanaticism," *Evening Post*, 25 June 1878.

209 *La Minerve*'s editorial ended with: "'you see what is justice to these people: everything for them, nothing for us.'" "Le Jublie Musical," *La Minerve*, 27 June 1878. *The Gazette* focused more on the events of the competition, accusing the judges of "partiality and favouritism." "The Band Festival," *The Gazette*, 26 June 1878.

210 "Montreal Musical Festival," *The Gazette*, 28 June 1878.

211 The reason given for the letter's rejection was that it "was not of the nature to require the publication of notice demanded by the 49th Rule." *Journals of the Legislative Council of the Province of Quebec* v. XII (1878): 29. (See also the *Journals of the Legislative Assembly of the Province of Quebec* v. XI (1877–78).) The 49th Rule outlines the requirements by which private bills were to be accepted for study by the Assembly. See *Parliamentary Procedure: Decisions of the Speakers, Protests, Rules and Regulations of the Legislative Council of the Province of Quebec, with an Index; Decisions of the Speakers, Judges, Rules and Regulations of the Legislative Assembly of the Province of Quebec, with an Index* (Montreal: Imprimerie générale, 1885).

212 "L'Académie de Musique," *L'Événement*, 6 July 1878.

## CHAPTER FIVE

1 "Le Concert d'Adieu," *Journal de Québec*, 13 September 1878.

2 As Britain withdrew its troops in 1871, the federal government established Battery "A" at Kingston and Battery "B" at Quebec City's Citadel.

3 In the 1870s, Quebec City grew by 4.6 per cent (from 59,699 to 62,446); during the same period, Montreal was relatively unaffected by the political changes and its population increased by 35 per cent from 126,314 to 170,745. Census data from Linteau, *Quebec: A History 1867–1929*, 130–8.

4 Gagnon published the piano piece *Stadaconé* in 1858. His *Chansons populaires du Canada* appeared first in 1865–67.

5 See *Cherrier's Directory of Quebec [City], 1879–80*.

6 "M. Calixa Lavallée," advertisement, *L'Événement*, 11 September 1880.

7 The Septuor Haydn became the core of the Orchestre symphonique de Québec, when it was founded in 1902 by Joseph Vézina.

8 Social aspects of Dufferin's term as governor general are well documented by his wife, Hariot Georgina Rowan Hamilton, marchioness of Dufferin and Ava, in *My Canadian Journal*.

9 The Délisles were prominent semi-professional musicians in Quebec City. Clodomire Délisle served as secretary of the Union Musicale, and Octave Délisle was the organist at Saint-Roch Church.

10 "Le Concert d'Adieu," *Journal de Québec*, 13 September 1878.

11 "Farewell Concert," *The Daily Telegraph*, 13 September 1878.

12 *Guía Diplomática de España, Año de 1887*, 426.

13 "La Dame Blanche," *The Daily Telegraph*, 9 May 1878. The *Quebec Mercury* also reported the event in its review, "La Dame Blanche," on 9 May.

14 Compt de Premio-Réal, *Divers Mémoires*, 78.

15 Lavallée, Introduction, *Seize Melodies pour Chant et Piano*, 1.

16 In 1866, George Kastner described the mélodie as "a type of vocal composition of rather arbitrary outline, which by its style and atmosphere falls midway between the French romance, and the German Lied." Kastner, *Parémiologie musicale de la langue française*, 126–7; as quoted in Noske, *French Song From Berlioz to Duparc*, 22–3. See also Katherine Bergeron, *Voice Lessons*, 4–6.

17 Waite, "Campbell, John George."

18 After his term as governor general, the Marquis discussed his experiences in Canada in two books: *Memories of Canada and Scotland* and *Passages of the Past*.

19 "Calixa Lavallée," *The Folio*, XXVII, no. 2 (February 1885): 61.

20 "Faits Divers," *Journal de Québec*, 25 October 1878.

21 See "Notre violoniste Canadien à Paris," *Le Nouveau monde*, 15 May 1878, and "A Travers la Ville," *Le National*, 11 July 1878.

22 Labat, "La Soirée Musicale d'Hier," *Journal de Québec*, 19 November 1878. *The Daily Telegraph* reported that De Sève had been called back on stage a number of times by the audience. It did not mention what he or anyone else performed. Trudel and Laurent performed, as well as Miss Le Vasseur and Miss Daignault.

23 Labat, "La Soirée Musicale d'Hier," *Journal de Québec*, 19 November 1878.

24 "Faits Divers," *Journal de Québec*, 21 December 1878.

25 *Cherrier's Quebec Directory for the Year Ending May 3, 1881* (Quebec City): 204.

26 "Christmas Eve: Midnight Mass," *The Daily Telegraph*, 26 December 1878.

27 See Comte de Premio-Réal, "*Scrap-Book*," 10; and Gale, *Historic Tales of Old Quebec*, 62; *Guide to Quebec and the Lower Saint Lawrence* (1882), 10–12.

28 See Baillairgé, *Vingt ans après*; and Comte de Premio-Réal, "*Scrap-Book*."

29 *Cherrier's Quebec Directory for the Year Ending May 3, 1880*: 34.

30 Fréchette, "À Calixa Lavallée," *Fleurs boréales*, 221.

31 See Fréchette, *Lettres à Basile* and Lemire, *La Vie littéraire au Québec*, vol. 4: 278–89.

32 "A Graphic Account of the St Patrick's Catholic and Literary Institute Concert," *The Daily Telegraph*, 19 March 1879.

33 A few days later, Lavallée sent Lafrance a note telling him that his work had been well received. Lettre à G.-A. Lafrance de Calixa Lavallée. 30 March 1879. P1000.S3.D1091. Bibliothèque et Archives nationales du Québec – Centre régional de Québec.

34 "News Comment," *Ottawa Citizen*, 25 March 1879. For a discussion of the Ottawa soirees hosted by Lorne and Princess Louise, see Wake, *Princess Louise*, 223–33.

35 A week later, the *Ottawa Citizen* reported that Martel had presented the Marquis with a piece he had composed in his honour, *Souvenir d'Écosse*, and also played Vieuxtemps's *Fantasie caprice*, and another composition of his own, referred to as *Air Canadiens*.

36 Calixa Lavallée, letter to unidentified recipient, 26 March 1879. Archives de l'Université Laval (AUL, P209-1/25/10/89 lettre de 26 mars 1879).

37 Ibid. The letter is addressed to "My dear friend." This may have been Joseph Marmette, as the same collection contains another note that Lavallée had sent to Marmette.

38 "News Comments," *Ottawa Citizen*, 31 March 1879.

39 Members of the SSC sang from the choir loft. "St Cecile Society," *The Daily Telegraph*, 14 April 1879. See also *Historique de la Société Sainte-Cécile de Québec*, 22–4.

40 "Paques," *L'Événement*, 14 April 1879. In the letter of 26 March 1879 cited above, Lavallée closed with a request that the recipient (likely Marmette) pass along some information to Joséphine.

41 Records of the Collège de Lévis show that Calixa Jr first attended the school in September 1879. They do not indicate the price of tuition. G.E. Proulx, of the Collège de Lévis, undated letter to the author, [1998].

42 *L'Événement* reported the title of the song but not the composer. Presumably this "Dieu Protège la France" was the "chant héroïque" by Charles Pollet. "Le Concert Lavallée," *L'Événement*, 19 April 1979. Joseph Marmette reported the encore as being "France!" ("Le Concert Lavallée," *Journal de Québec*, 19 April 1879.)

43 The second piece on the program was "Meditation" by Henri Kowalski, sung by Wyse, with organ accompaniment and with obligato violin played by Arthur Lavigne.

44 "Violette" (Quebec City: Arthur Lavigne, 1879).

45 "Faits Divers," *Journal de Québec*, 25 April 1879.

46 Contract between Calixa Lavallée and Reverend Joseph Hennings, 30 April 1879, Archives de l'Église Saint Patrick de Québec, AASPQ Ec232, Bibliothèque et Archives nationales du Québec. Centre régional de Québec.

47 See O'Gallagher, *Saint Patrick's, Quebec*, 34. See also O'Leary, *The History of the Irish Catholics of Quebec*. Saint Patrick's was located on Sainte-Hélène street, which was later renamed for Father McMahon. L'Hôpital Hôtel-Dieu de Québec now uses the church as a research centre. See also Grace, "Apport de l'immigration: l'example des Irlandais," 180–5.

48 "St Patrick's Church," *The Daily Telegraph*, 29 April 1879.

49 Contract between Calixa Lavallée and Reverend Joseph Hennings, 30 April 1879.

50 Ibid.

51 Ibid.

52 "Grand Concert," advertisement, *Le Journal de Québec*, 11 June 1879.

53 See *Historique de la Société Musicale Sainte-Cécile de Québec*, 106. Laurent is listed in the city directory as a partner in Brunet et Laurent, dry goods importers located at 157 Saint-Joseph Street. *Cherrier's Quebec Directory for the Year Ending May 3, 1880* (Quebec City, 1880): 166.

54 See *Le Canada musical*, 6, no. 3 (July 1879): 44. Lapierre reported that the men's chorus sang "God Save the Queen" while the women's chorus sang "Vive la Canadienne," and the orchestra played "Comin' Thro' the Rye." Reviews do not mention this. See Lapierre, *Calixa Lavallée* (1966), 156.

55 "O perfumed breeze" appeared in the "Summer" section of his *Les Perce-neige* collection (pp. 25–6) with a dedication to "Madame D." The general title was one that was used to denote a poem of a serious nature in multiple stanzas of the same type.

56 Legendre, *Les perce-neiges*, 81–2.

57 The Oriflamme ('gold flame') was the sacred banner of the Abbey of St Denis. It reportedly accompanied the French kings in their major battles, beginning with Louis VI's 1121 campaign against the emperor Henry V. It is believed that the banner's last appearance was at the disastrous battle of Maupertuis [near Poitiers] (1356), where the bearer was killed and the flag disappeared. However, some reports suggest a few later appearances. It is sometimes confused with the French king's royal standard (gold fleur-de-lis on blue), which the Oriflamme often accompanied in major campaigns. One of many accounts described the Oriflamme as a crimson silk vexillum with three tails, green fringe, and tassels. http://xenophongroup.com/montjoie/oriflam.htm. (Accessed on 10 March 2011)

58 The international press reported on the marquis and princess's activities. The *Times* reported that the couple was "greatly cheered by the numerous spectators assembled." "Canada," *London Times*, 11 June 1879.

59 "La réception vice-royale," *Le Journal de Québec*, 9 June 1879. Joséphine Lavallée was not listed among the female guests.

60 "A Travers la Ville," *L'Événement*, 11 June 1879.

61 *Le Canada musical* reported the attendance to have been between 1,000 and 1,200, while *L'Événement* wrote that it was 1,500. See *Le Canada musical*, 6, no. 3 (July 1879): 46; and "Visite Vice-Royale," *L'Événement*, 13 June 1879.

62 *The Daily Telegraph* reported attendance to be "fully 1500 people." "The Cantata," *The Daily Telegraph*, 12 June 1879. "Visite Vice-Royale," *L'Événement*, 13 June 1879.

63 *Le Canada musical*, 6, no. 3 (July 1879): 46.

64 Ibid.

65 Marmette, "La Cantate," *Le Journal de Québec*, 13 June 1879.

66 Ibid.

67 "The Cantata," *The Daily Telegraph*, 12 June 1879.

68 "The Cantata," *Daily Telegraph*, 14 June 1879. "Mr Lavallée's genius for construction and combination was powerfully exhibited and deservedly applauded by Her Royal Highness Princess Louis and His Excellency the Marquis of Lorne, who most flatteringly expressed their approval in so many words to Mr Lavallée at the conclusion of the concert." See also "From Quebec," *Evening Post*, 12 June 1879.

69 "La Société Saint-Jean Baptiste," *Journal de Québec*, 26 June 1879.

70 The examinations and meetings were held at the Mechanics' Institute. Other examiners for piano were Gustave and Ernest Gagnon, J.A. Defoy, and Frederick E. Lucy-Barnes, an English musician who had recently settled in Montreal. His wife, Leonora Braham, was the opera singer with Savoy Opera and continued her career in Canada and the US after moving to Montreal. Lucy-Barnes had published a number of songs but his career paled by comparison to his wife's, and he committed suicide in 1880 while she was performing in New York.

71 Guillaume Couture, "Chronique musicale," *La Revue de Montréal*, 3 (1879): 494.

72 A preview referred to the work to be performed as Haydn's Second Mass. See "Grande excursion musicale," *L'Événement*, 23 July 1879.

73 *Reception by the City of Toronto of His Excellency the Governor General of the Dominion of Canada and H.R.H. the Princess Louise* (Toronto: Rolph, Smith, 1879).

74 "Calixa Lavallée," *The Folio*, XXVII, no. 2 (February 1885): 61. "Mr Lavallée used to say afterward, with a sad smile, 'I have received the Princess Louise in the name of the Government of Québec, and "paid the fiddler" myself.'" The article continued, "There was some indignation felt at the time by the most honourable members of Parliament; but Mr Lavallée, who is known for his extreme modesty, begged of them to drop the matter. Such is the reward of loyalty to royalty."

75 See *Sessional Papers* v. 13. *Statement of the Public Accounts of the Province of Quebec for the Fiscal Year Ending 30 June 1879* (Quebec City: Printed by Order of the Legislature, 1880): 69.

76 In 1890, Lavallée wrote of being forced to leave Canada for financial reasons. See Lavallée, "L'Art musical au Canada."

77 *Le Canada musical*, 6, no. 3 (July 1879): 46. "[He] certainly has a right to be proud of this musical work which must mark a new phase in the artistic career of its author."

78 The day of the concert, newspapers reported the arrival of both the piano and Lavallée, and provided the program, which included works by Beethoven, Mendelssohn, and Chopin, as well as Lavallée's own *Le Papillon*. "The Magnificent Grand Piano," *The Gazette*, 29 October 1879. "Notes Locales," *La Minerve*, 29 October 1879.

79 See "Mr Lavallée's Recital," *The Gazette*, 30 October 1879; and "Notes Locales," *La Minerve*, 30 October 1879.

80 After the first of the Quebec City series, *L'Événement*'s unnamed critic noted Lavallée's performance of a composition by Mendelssohn "and many other works, the titles of which we have forgotten. Among them was the *Danse des fées*, of Prudent, one of his favourite pieces and one that the Quebec City public never grows tired of hearing." "Le Concert D'Hier," *L'Événement*, 31 October 1879.

81 Joseph Marmette, "Prume et Lavallée," *Le Journal de Québec*, 31 October 1879. *L'Événement* reported only that the elite of the francophone and anglophone society was present. "Le Concert d'hier," *L'Événement*, 31 October 1879.

82 "All Saints Day," *The Daily Telegraph*, 1 November 1879.

83 See *Le Canada musical*, 6, no. 7 (November 1879): 108.

84 See "Fête de Sainte-Cécile," *L'Événement*, 26 November 1879.

85 The Club Cartier had been formed following the Conservatives' losses in 1874. See *Constitution et reglements du Club Cartier*.

86 "Le Concert du Club Cartier," *Le Courrier de Montréal*, 3 December 1879.

87 "Adresse," *L'Événement*, 13 December 1879.

88 "The Churches," *The Daily Telegraph*, 27 December 1879.

89  Baptismal record, 4 January 1880, Notre-Dame-des-Victoires, Lévis, QC. The McCallums may have provided the Lavallées with accommodations in Lévis. The lawyer William McCallum was living on Saint-Joseph Street in the town.

90  "Exposition scolaire à l'academie des Frères," *Journal de Québec*, 9 January 1880.

91  See "Les Noces d'Or de Mgr. Cazeau," *L'Événement*, 9 January 1880; and *Souvenir du jubilé sacerdotal de Mgr. C. Cazeau, prélat domestique de Sa Sainteté, vicaire-général de L'archidiocèse, célébré à Québec, en janvier 1880*, 73–9.

92  See "Harmonie," advertisement, *L'Événement*, 30 October 1879.

93  "Le Concert Prume Lavallée," *Le Canadien*, 2 March 1880. Joseph Marmette, "Chronique musicale," *Journal de Québec*, 2 March 1880.

94  Lavigne was advertising the song as a new publication in July. "Nuit d'Été," advertisement, *Le Canadien*, 12 July 1880.

95  The obituary in the *Morning Chronicle* referred only to a lung infection brought on by a severe cold. "Death of Mr Patrick Joseph Curran," *Morning Chronicle*, 7 March 1880. Reprinted in Comte de Premio-Réal, "*Scrap-book*," 272.

96  "To-Day's Local Intelligence," *The Daily Telegraph*, 8 March 1880. "Funeral of the Late P.J. Curran, Esq.," *The Post*, 8 March 1880.

97  The funeral cortège in Montreal left from Curran's mother's home on Colborne Street (now the lower end of Peel Street) in Griffintown. "Funeral of the Late P.J. Curran, Esq.," *The Post*, 8 March 1880.

98  Calixa Lavallée, [Notice], *Morning Chronicle*, 10 March 1880.

99  See "A Spencer Wood," *L'Événement*, 11 March 1880.

100  "St Patrick's Night," *Quebec Daily Telegraph*, 18 March 1880. The same night, at the St Patrick's Day concert at Nordheimer's Hall, in Montreal, a Miss Hart also sang Lavallée's "Beautiful Girl of Kildare."

101  "The Mendelssohn Choir," *Montreal Daily Witness*, 7 February 1880.

102  "La Fête de Pâques," *Le Journal de Québec*, 29 March 1880. This Mass is now believed to have been composed by Wenzel Müller (1759–1835).

103  "La Fête de Pâques," *Le Journal de Québec*, 29 March 1880.

104  The program was published in "The Prume-Lavallée Concert," *Quebec Daily Telegraph*, 31 March 1880.

105  "Le Concert Prume Lavallée," *Le Journal de Québec*, 31 March 1880.

106  Potvin and Kallmann examine the evolution of thought on the creation of the song in "O Canada."

107  Lectures included "Agricurture and Colonisation," by S. Lesage, and "The Role of the French in Canada," by Judge Adolphe-Basile Routhier.

108  In later years, Judge Routhier remained active in the legal profession, teaching international law at Université Laval from 1883 and rising to the position of Chief Justice of the Quebec Superior Court in 1904. See Hébert, "Sir Adolphe-Basile Routhier."

109  Octave Crémazie had died in 1879.

110  See "A Spencer Wood," *L'Événement*, 11 March 1880.

111  See Adolphe-Basile Routhier, letter to Thomas Bedford Richardson, 8 January 1907, National Library of Canada. Reprinted by Potvin, in "O Canada." Richardson was the first to produce an English version of "O Canada." A 1980

article in the Ottawa newspaper *Le Droit* elaborated on this account, based on information that Routhier had passed on to his grandson. See Routhier, "Quelques notes historiques sur 'l'O Canada,'" *Le Droit*, 22 July 1980.

112 Ibid.

113 "Chant national," *Le Journal de Québec*, 17 April 1880.

114 Two days later, *Le Canadien* reported that the song had been accepted by Ernest Gagnon, but noted that 5,000 copies would be printed. Whatever the actual print run, only two copies of the first edition are known to be extant. One is in the archives of the Séminaire in Quebec City, and the other is in the Villeneuve Collection of the music library at l'Université de Montréal. The reason for the disappearance of nearly all of these scores is not known, although the actual number printed may have been considerably lower than announced.

115 At the beginning of July 1880, one finds advertisements for both Lavallée's and Lavigeur's "chants nationals" on the same page of *Le Canadien* (see 7 July).

116 "Un Compatriote," letter dated Winsor, Ont., 15 June 1880, "Correspondances," *Le Courrier de Montréal*, 18 June 1880.

117 "The Philharmonic Society's Concert," *The Montreal Daily Witness*, 28 May 1880.

118 "Vente par Encan de Meubles et Effets d'Ameublement au No. 12, rue Sainte-Ursule," *Journal de Québec*, 28 April 1880. The house was owned by François-Xavier Villers. See Fonds de la Ville de Québec, "Lavallée, Calixa," AVQ. Lavallée appears to have arranged to move into 12 Sainte-Ursule early in 1880, as he was listed as the resident of the house in the 1880–81 city directory, which was announced as in-press at the time of the auction. "L'Almanach des adresses de Québec," advertisement, *Journal de Québec*, 1 May 1880.

119 See Chouinard, *Fête Nationale des Canadiens-Français*, 138.

120 "National Anthem: O Canada," Government of Canada, 2014. www.pch.gc.ca/fra/1359402373291/1359402467746#a8. (Accessed 9 November 2014)

121 A literal translation by the author of the first stanza of "O Canada."

122 See Ernest Macmillan, "The Case for 'O Canada,'": 60–3. In 1919, Arthur Letondal downplayed the similarity, finding no problem with the "unconscious influence of the masters," in "Calixa Lavallée," (October 1919), 444. Eugène Lapierre devoted an entire chapter to refuting the connection by comparing the opening three measures with those of eleven other pieces. See Lapierre, *Calixa Lavallée* (1966), 179–93. Lapierre did not compare the music of "O Canada" to that of the "andante sostenuto" theme from Franz Liszt's *Festklänge*.

123 Liszt's music was rarely performed in Canada during this time, but Lavallée may have heard it while in Europe or in the US.

124 Musicians from the Union Musicale and the 9th Battalion band accompanied the large choir; Hardy's Band, of Montreal, and the Bande de Beauport, Quebec, accompanied the plainchant choir. I have found no information on the instruments used.

125 See Chouinard, *Fête nationale des Canadiens-Français* , 140.

126 Wolfgang Amadeus Mozart and Emanuel Schikaneder, *Die Zauberflöte* (New York: Dover, 1985), 113.

127 Lavallée might have opposed the bishop's decree prohibiting women from

singing in churches of the Montreal diocese, but we have no evidence as yet that he harboured ill feelings toward the Church.

128 "Fête de la St Jean Baptiste," *Le Canada musical,* 7, no. 3 (July 1880): 56.

129 In his speech, the governor general apologized for the absence of Princess Louise, who had just left with Prince Leopold for a holiday in the United States.

130 See Chouinard, *Fête nationale des Canadiens-Français,* 200.

131 See "Fête de la St Jean Baptiste," *Le Canada musical,* 7, no. 3 (July 1880): 56.

132 "Le 24 Juin à Québec," *L'Événement,* 25 June 1880. "Les Canadiens Français," *Courrier des États Unis,* 28 June 1880.

133 "St Jean Baptiste," *The Daily Star,* 25 June 1880.

134 Ibid.

135 The inclusion of "O Canada" seems to have been a late change, as the piece did not appear on the program published by Chouinard. Another change was the concluding piece, Adam's *Laudate Dominum,* which replaced the march from Gounod's *La Reine de Saba.* See Chouinard, *Fête Nationale des Canadiens-Français,* 239. See also "La Fête de St-Jean-Baptiste à l'église Saint-Jean," *Journal de Québec,* 28 June 1880.

136 *Le Canada musical,* 7, no. 3 (July 1880): 56.

137 Ibid.

138 "Fête Sainte-Cécile," *L'Événement,* 23 November 1880.

139 "Nouvelles Locales," *Le Canadien,* 7 July 1880.

140 After Lavallée's departure for Quebec City, MacLagan formed the Montreal Operatic Society and staged Sullivan's *H.M.S. Pinafore* in 1879. In 1880, he staged Planquette's *Les Cloches de Cornville* and composed an operetta of his own, *The Queen's Shilling.* He was less successful with the AMQ. On becoming president, he found himself in conflict with other members, most notably his main rival in Montreal, the conductor and organist Frederick Lucy-Barnes. A few months after the twenty-eight-year-old Lucy-Barnes's death, in September, MacLagan left Montreal for Winnipeg.

141 "Quatuor vocal de Québec," *Journal de Québec,* 8 September 1880.

142 Advertisements stated that he would be resuming lessons on 15 September and advised that interested students should visit Lavigne's shop. "M. Calixa Lavallée," advertisement, *Le Canadien,* 8 September 1880. "St Patrick's," *Quebec Saturday Budget,* 18 September 1880.

143 Calixa Lavallée, letter to Joseph Marmette, 22 October 1880, Fonds Maurice Brodeur. Archives de l'Université Laval, Quebec City (AUL, P209-1/25/10/90). Lavallée refers to his friend as Duclos, but in 1880, 924·Asylum Avenue, the address on the letter, was the home of Henry French, owner of the Henry French and Son Flour Mill. The son, Harry French, resided in Boston. See *Geer's Hartford City Directory,* vol. XLIII (July 1880 to July 1881): 73.

144 Calixa Lavallée, letter to Joseph Marmette, 22 October 1880, Fonds Maurice Brodeur. Archives de l'Université Laval, Quebec City (AUL, P209-1/25/10/90).

145 Ibid. Lavallée first refers to the full name, Tachereau Fortier, listed in the Quebec City directory as a clerk with the civil service, living at 51 rue D'Auteuil. See *Cherrier's Quebec Directory, for the Year Ending May 3, 1880* (Quebec City, 1990): 64, 147.

146 Calixa Lavallée, letter to Joseph Marmette, 22 October 1880, Fonds Maurice Brodeur. Archives de l'Université Laval, Quebec City (AUL, P209-1/25/10/90).

147 Marmette, "La Cantate," 13 June 1879.

148 Lavallée, "L'E Muet," 36. The plight of Canadian musicians was raised in an anonymous letter to the editor of the *Montreal Star* in June 1879. The writer, who claimed to be a professional organist, pointed to the irony that "one would naturally suppose that in this City of Churches I could make, at least, a comfortable livelihood." He cited the recent departures of Torrington, Pech, and Warren as evidence of the financial difficulties faced by professional musicians in Montreal. The July 1879 issue of *Le Canada musical* commented on the letter, noting that the writer's claims were "not without basis."

149 "La Cantate," 13 June 1879. After Lavallée left, Adolphe Hamel filled his post at St Patrick's Church.

150 Simon Couture examines these issues in chapter three of his thesis, but focuses on the failure of later attempts to found a conservatory. See Couture, "Les Origines du Conservatoire," 114–35.

151 Linteau, *Quebec: A History 1867–1929*, 225.

152 Lavallée, "L'Art musical au Canada," 71.

153 Guillaume Couture, "Chronique musicale," *La Revue de Montréal*, 3 (1879): 494.

154 Lavallée, "L'E Muet," 36.

155 "Entertainments: the Prume-Lavallee Concert," *Hartford Courant*, 4 December 1880.

156 Ibid. The German violinist August Wilhelmj (1845–1908) was then on a world concert tour that had begun in 1878.

157 Ibid.

158 The *Gazette* mentions this indirectly, writing that del Vecchio had been "cut off in the prime of existence, the full blossom of talent, giving her life for her child, as did poor Parepa Rosa before her." "Madame Prume," *Montreal Gazette*, 12 February 1881. The Scottish soprano Euphronsyne Parepa-Rosa died of complications of childbirth in 1874. Jacques-André Houle discusses the cause of del Vecchio's death in a 1990 article. He discovered that she had given birth only days before she died, but the child did not survive and was buried on 8 February 1881. See Houle, "Frantz Jehin-Prume (1839–1899)." If del Vecchio carried the child to full term, she would have been about seven months pregnant at the time of the Hartford performance.

159 See "A Double Funeral," *The Gazette*, 15 February 1881, and "Feu Madame F. Jehin-Prune," *Le Canada musical*, 7, no. 11 (March 1881): 180–1.

### CHAPTER SIX

1 Lavallée, letter to Joseph Marmette, 22 October 1880.

2 "Wulf Fries," *Boston Musical Herald*, 11, no. 6 (June 1890): 129. Fries joined the faculty of the NEC when it relocated to Boston in the 1860s.

3 Louis Maas was born in Wiesbaden and raised mostly in London. After graduating from King's College at the age of fifteen, he studied with Reinecke and

Paperitz at the Leipzig Conservatorium, and with Liszt during the summers. During the 1881–82 season, he conducted the concerts of Boston's Philharmonic Society. See Jones, *A Handbook of American Music and Musicians*, 89; and "Dr Louis Maas," *Werner's Voice Magazine*, XI, no. 10 (October 1889): 203.

4   *The Folio*, XIX, no. 6 (December 1880): 454.

5   *Boston City Directory* (1881).

6   In 1880, Boston's population was 362,839, New York's had risen to 1,911,698, Philadelphia's to 847,170, and Chicago's to 503,185. See Anderton, *Population of the United States*, 45.

7   In the nineteenth century, the city was at least a temporary home to Ralph Waldo Emerson, Nathaniel Hawthorne, Henry Wadsworth Longfellow, and many other leading figures in American letters. It was a city of scientists, such as Louis Agassiz and Asa Gray, and of researchers and historians, like William Prescott and George Bancroft.

8   Kowalski, *A Travers l'Amérique*, 44.

9   Gottschalk, *Notes of a Pianist*, 157.

10  Ibid., 232, 234.

11  F.O. Jones, ed., *A Handbook of American Music and Musicians*, 19. Among the musical societies established during the 1870s were the Apollo Club (1871) and the Boylston Club (1872).

12  The works most performed by the Handel and Haydn Society (HHS) were Handel's *Messiah* (74 times), Haydn's *Creation* (62), Neukomm's *David* (57), Mendelssohn's *Elijah* (46), and Rossini's *Moses in Egypt* (45). When the Tremont Temple reopened following a major fire, in 1879, the HHS inaugurated the hall with a performance of *Messiah* on 11 October 1880. See Jones, *A Handbook of American Music and Musicians*, 19. Carl Zerrahn directed the HHS's six hundred–member choir throughout the 1880s.

13  The philanthropist Henry L. Higginson established the Boston Symphony Orchestra (BSO), which gave its first performance on 22 October 1881. During its first years, George Henschel conducted the BSO.

14  The Harvard Musical Association's first performance took place at Chickering's music room on 13 November 1844, when it presented Beethoven's Piano Trio in C minor, op. 1, no. 3, Mozart's String Quartet in D minor, K421, and several smaller works, including François Prume's *La Mélancholie*.

15  See William J. Weichlein, *A Checklist of American Music Periodicals, 1850–1900* (Detroit: Information Coordinators, 1970).

16  Henry F. Miller Sr was born in Providence, Rhode Island, and was employed as Brown University organist for several years before relocating to Boston in 1850 to work with the firm of Brown & Allen. For information on Miller and the Miller company, see Jones, *A Handbook of American Music and Musicians*, 99; Dolge, *Pianos and Their Makers*, 337; Ayers, *Contributions to the Art of Music in America*; and Miller catalogues.

17  Miller's sales for 1869 were $148,359, still well behind the top three: Steinway & Sons ($1,205,463), Chickering & Sons ($822,402), and Wm Knabe & Company ($383,511). See "The Piano Trade," *Orpheus*, V, no. 10 (April 1870): 121.

18 Judges at the 1876 Philadelphia Exposition awarded Miller with two medals of honour and two diplomas of merit. See "Henry F. Miller," advertisement, *Music Trade Review*, III, no. 3 (18 December 1876): ix.

19 See Loesser, *Men, Women and Pianos*, 531–6. Miller added Lavallée's name to the firm's advertisements, such as this one that appeared in *The Folio* in October 1881: "Used by more than twenty solo pianists, among them some of the most distinguished artists in the world – Sherwood, Maas, Petersilea, Liebling, Perry, Lavallée etc. – Boston Wareroom 611 Washington Street." "Henry F. Miller Piano Company," advertisement, *The Folio*, XXI, no. 4 (October 1881): 382.

20 In a review of Sherwood's concert in Cleveland, a writer for the *Voice* noted: "The Henry F. Miller Concert Grand Piano used by Mr Sherwood was admired. Its great power and breadth of tone, combined with remarkable purity and sweetness, readily account for the increasing popularity of the piano." *Cleveland Voice*, 25 February 1882; reprinted in Ayars, *Contributions to the Art of Music*, 125.

21 "Music," *Boston Home Journal*, 14 March 1885.

22 *Boston Herald*, 11 March 1885; reprinted in *The Folio*, XXVII, no. 4 (April 1885): 138.

23 The *Globe* simply reported that it had been "many years" since Bishop had been in Boston. See "Stage and Concert Hall," *Boston Globe*, 2 May 1881. In 1873, Bishop travelled from New York to Australia and to Europe via South Africa. When she died of apoplexy in New York on 18 March 1884, an obituary reported Bishop to have sung in twenty languages and to have spoken nine. See "The Late Madame Anna Bishop: The Career of a Most Gifted Singer and a Very Remarkable Woman," *The Voice*, VI, no. 7 (July 1884): 109–10.

24 Gerster was born in Kaschau, Hungary (now Kosice, Slovakia), and studied at the Vienna Conservatory under Madame Marchesi. Her appearances throughout Europe in the mid-1870s attracted the attention of Henry Mapleson, who engaged her for his company's 1878–79 American tour. She made her US debut as Amina in Bellini's *La Sonnambula* on 11 November 1878 at the Academy of Music. From New York, Mapleson's troupe travelled across the country, with Gerster taking much of the credit for its success. Her second tour with Mapleson opened in New York on 18 October 1880, continued throughout the Northeast and Midwest in the early months of 1881, and closed in New York on 9 April 1881. Primary sources of information on Gerster include a thirty-eight-page handwritten curriculum vitae, dated 25 March 1899, in the State Archives, Berlin (Mus. ep E. Gerster, Varia 1). See also Eisenberg, ed., "Etelka Gerster"; Hubbard, *Imperial History and Encyclopedia of Music*; Lahee, *Famous Singers of Today and Yesterday*; and Mapleson, *The Mapleson Memoirs 1848–88*. Cone discusses the Patti-Gerster rivalry in *Adelina Patti Queen of Hearts*, 149–57.

25 "Local Matters: Gerster in Concert," *Baltimore Sun*, 26 May 1881, 4. The Nilsson and Lind performances had taken place some ten and thirty years earlier, respectively.

26 See "Local Matters: Gerster in Concert," *Baltimore Sun*, 26 May 1881: 4; and "The Gerster Concert," *Sunday Item*, 29 May 1881: 6.

27  "Amusements: Madame Etelka Gerster in Concert," *Washington Post*, 25 May
    1881. A Philadelphia critic wrote that "the tone of instrument was superb –
    silvery, clear, brilliant and full." "The Gerster Concert," *Sunday Item*, 29 May
    1881. Perhaps it is only a coincidence, but Miller maintained an office in
    Philadelphia but not in Washington.

28  In June 1881, *The Folio* announced that "Mr Calixa Lavallée, who has made
    a very excellent record as a pianist, within the short time he has been in Boston,
    has accepted a position as teacher at the Petersilea Academy of Music." *The
    Folio*, XX, no. 6 (June 1881): 179.

29  In their 1886 review of Boston conservatories, the *Boston Musical Yearbook*
    noted that the piano was the focus of Petersilea's school: "Students of the pi-
    anoforte are, perhaps, in the ascendancy, owing to the especial labors and
    preparation of Mr. Petersilea in that branch." *Boston Musical Yearbook*, vol.
    III (1885–86): 60. Eben Tourjée established the NEC in Providence, Rhode Is-
    land, in the mid-1860s and moved it to Boston in 1867, where it thrived. In
    1882 the NEC moved from leased rooms in the Music Hall building to the for-
    mer St James Hotel at Franklin Square (Newton and St James Streets.) The site
    allowed it to provide a dormitory for female students, and by 1885, total en-
    rolment exceeded 2,000. See "Music Schools," *Boston Musical Yearbook*, vol.
    III (1885–86): 59. Julius Eichberg created a place for his Boston Conservatory
    by specializing in instruction for string instruments.

30  See F.O. Jones, *A Handbook of American Music and Musicians*; and "Carlyle
    Petersilea," *Musical Courier*, X, no. 15 (15 April 1885): 227.

31  "The Musicians' Convention," *New York Times*, 4 July 1885.

32  "Carlyle Petersilea," *Musical Courier*, X, no. 15 (15 April 1885): 227. The ar-
    ticle continued: Petersilea "possesses the poetic, refined, and highly imaginative
    temperament to render Chopin perfectly, the nobility of soul and the broad in-
    telligence and deep feeling to interpret Beethoven, and superb technic [*sic*] to
    play anything."

33  Petersilea's *System* begins with five-finger studies, proceeding through scales
    and technical studies. It covers basic harmony and concludes with exercises on
    touch and expression. Many of the book's studies are original compositions
    (mostly marches, galops, waltzes, and other popular nineteenth-century dance
    forms) in theme-and-variations form, with each variation introducing a new
    technical exercise. The introduction advised interspersing the studies with
    "compositions of a light and pleasing character; for instance, the Sonatinas of
    Kuhlau and Clementi." Franz Petersilea, *Revised and Enlarged Edition of a
    New and Thorough System for the Piano-Forte*, 5. Carlyle Petersilea discusses
    the method in "The Art of Piano-Playing," *The Folio*, XXIII, no. 6 (June 1883):
    254.

34  Favourable promotion and copious advertising aided the Academy's success.
    *The Folio* reported the school's first semester to have been a "gratifying suc-
    cess" and recommended it "to any one of our friends in search of a thorough,
    practical musical education." See *The Folio*, V, no. 2 (August 1871): 174; and
    *The Folio*, VI, no. 2 (February 1872): 42.

35  *Dexter Smith's Musical, Literary, Dramatic & Art Paper*, IX, no. 2 (January
    1876): 11.

36 Ibid.

37 "Petersilea Academy of Music," advertisement, *The Folio*, XIX, no. 3 (September 1880): 100.

38 *Fall River Line Journal*, III, no. 9 (4 July 1881): 1.

39 Lovell's *Montreal Directory* lists Tremblay as residing at 473 Saint-Denis Street during this time, while Aristide Filiatreault was listed as a music printer at 468 Saint-Denis.

40 In 1881, Tremblay left *Le Courrier de Montréal* to edit another Montreal newspaper, *Le Monde*.

41 For information on the early interest in English-language opera in the US, see Preston, "English Opera Companies, 1841–60," in *Opera on the Road*. William Henry Fry's *Leonora* is generally considered to have been the first grand opera composed in the US. The Seguins gave its premiere on 4 June 1845 in Philadelphia. Among the most successful US composers of comic opera was Julius Eichberg, who produced four operettas in Boston in the 1860s.

42 The *Musical Bulletin* heralded Buck as "one of the most talented and cultured musicians America has produced." Others found the sensational story of the Mormons and polygamy offensive. The full score was never published, and the work received further performances only in Baltimore and Cincinnati. See Crofut, *Deseret, or, A Saint's Affections*; *Musical Bulletin*, I, no. 12 (November 1879): 192; and Knight, "Dudley Buck."

43 See "Musical," *New York Clipper*, 1 October 1881: 455; and "Music – Comic Opera at the Grand," *Chicago Tribune*, 19 February 1882.

44 The *New York Clipper* reported that a benefit for Nelson took place at the Boylston Museum on 27 June 1881. See "Variety Halls," *New York Clipper*, 2 July 1881: 239.

45 See "'The Widow' at the Grand Opera House," *Chicago Tribune*, 24 February 1882.

46 See Voltaire, *Oeuvres Completes*, T. 5.

47 In November 1881, *Boucher and Pratt's Musical Journal* announced that C.D. Hess had purchased the rights to *The Widow*.

48 Hess's Grand Opera Company performed at the Varieties in New Orleans in 1879 with Emma Abbott, Adelaide Randall, and Zelda Seguin leading the cast. Information on Hess's activities has been compiled from the *New York Times* (1869–72, 1880–82), *Orpheus* (1869–80), and the New Orleans Opera Association.

49 See "City Summary," *New York Clipper*, 19 March 1881: 414.

50 See "Musical," *New York Clipper*, 12 March 1881: 403; and "Bijou Opera-House," *New York Times*, 20 March 1881.

51 After New York City, the company performed at Brooklyn's Park Theatre and Philadelphia's Chestnut Street Opera House before moving on to Washington, Baltimore, and cities of the Midwest.

52 The 1 October issue of the *New York Clipper* reported that the New Orleans premiere was to take place on 23 October. *Boucher and Pratt's Musical Journal* announced in October that *The Widow* would soon be premiered in New Orleans, and in November, the same journal reported that Lavallée was returning to Montreal from New Orleans after conducting the premiere. The

November issue of *The Folio* reprinted this report. See "Musical," *New York Clipper*, 1 October 1881: 455; *Boucher and Pratt's Musical Journal*, III, no. 9 (October 1881): 1, and III, no. 10 (November 1881): 1; *The Folio*, XXI, no. 5 (November 1881): 418.

53 Information provided by Jack Belsom of the New Orleans Opera Association. The *New York Clipper* reported that the "attendance increased with each performance" of Audran's operas. See "Musical," *New York Clipper*, 29 October 1881: 523. The company had begun rehearsing Jean Robert Planquette's *The Chimes of Normandy*, which it soon added to its repertoire. See "Musical," *New York Clipper*, 5 November 1881: 544.

54 *L'Album musical* vol. I, Prospectus no. (December 1881): 4. Lapierre repeated the claim that *The Widow* had been first performed in New Orleans. See Lapierre, *Calixa Lavallée* (1966), 213.

55 Both the *Chicago Tribune* of 25 February and the *New York Clipper* of 13 May referred to the 24 February performance as the premiere. In its preview on 24 February, the *Tribune* mentioned that the first performance had twice been put off.

56 "A New Comic Opera at the Grand Opera-House," *Chicago Tribune*, 25 February 1882.

57 Ibid.

58 Ibid.

59 "A New Comic Opera at the Grand Opera-House," *Chicago Tribune*, 25 February 1882.

60 Ibid. *The Folio* reprinted the *Tribune*'s comments, referring to them as "high praise indeed." *The Folio*, XXII, no. 4 (April 1882): 125.

61 "Events of the Past Week," *Chicago Tribune*, 26 February 1882.

62 "Amusements," *St Paul and Minneapolis Pioneer Press*, 9 March 1882. On the day of the premiere, the same newspaper reported that "sales of reserved seats yesterday were sufficient in number to insure a successful engagement financially as well as artistically." "Amusements," *St Paul & Minneapolis Pioneer Press*, 8 March 1882.

63 "Operatic Performances," *Baltimore Sun*, 20 April 1882.

64 Etelka Gerster was then also touring with Strakosch and appeared in *La Sonnambula* on 24 April.

65 "Society Notes," *Washington Star*, 26 April 1882.

66 "'The Widow' at Ford's," *Washington Post*, 26 April 1882.

67 "Hess Acme Opera Company," advertisement, *New York Times*, 1 May 1882.

68 "'The Widow' at the Standard Theatre," *New York Herald*, 9 May 1882.

69 "City Summary," *New York Clipper*, 13 May 1882: 130.

70 "'The Widow' at the Standard Theatre," *New York Herald*, 9 May 1882.

71 "Standard Theatre," *New York Times*, 9 May 1882.

72 Ibid.

73 "City Summary," *New York Clipper*, 13 May 1882: 130.

74 "'The Widow' at the Standard Theatre," *New York Herald*, 9 May 1882.

75 Ibid.

76 "'The Widow' at the Standard," *Music Trade Review*, May 1882, 321.

77   The *Pickwick Theatre Scrapbook* at Missouri Historical Society Archives contains a collection of clippings about *The Widow*'s performances in St Louis.

78   *The Widow* was listed with other works in a preview in the *Daily Picayune* on 26 November, but it was not performed.

79   During the HAOC's engagement in Baltimore, 8–13 October 1883, the company performed *Martha, The Mascot, Chimes of Normandy, The Bohemian Girl, Olivette, Maritana,* and *Fra Diavolo.* Hess had added *Iolanthe* and *Pirates of Penzance* by the time of his company's January 1884 engagement at the St Charles Theater in New Orleans. Hess's acceptance of the Chicago post was reported in "Chicago Correspondence," *The Folio,* XXVI, no. 5 (November 1884): 180.

80   The Young Mens' Christian Union was founded in 1852 by Unitarians who had been excluded from the YMCA. The Boylston Street building was completed in 1876 and is still in use by the YMCU.

81   *The Folio,* XXII, no. 1 (January 1882): 23.

82   "Theatres and Concerts," *Boston Transcript,* 3 December 1881.

83   "Mons. Calixa Lavallee's Concert," *Boston Evening Journal,* 3 December 1881.

84   De Sève continued to perform frequently after accepting a teaching post at the New England Conservatory in the fall of 1881, making his first appearance with the Boston Symphony Orchestra performing Mendelssohn's Concerto in E Minor in February 1882. The following month, the NEC's monthly journal, the *Musical Herald,* remarked that De Sève had "gained a position in the first rank of our resident violinists ... by the facility and expressiveness of his execution." *Musical Herald,* III, no. 4 (April 1882): 92.

85   See "Local News," *Lowell Daily Courier,* 21 January 1882.

86   The *Boston City Directory* lists Lavallée as boarding at 35 Essex St in both 1882 and 1883.

87   See "Music," *Boston Home Journal,* 4 November 1882. These concert series do not appear to have been advertised in newspapers. On 17 December 1881, the *Boston Home Journal* mentioned the closing event in the Bay State Course, thanking Mr Wheeler for "providing at a low price, a first class course, and enabling many, who otherwise would be deprived, to hear renowned artists."

88   *The New York Clipper,* 29 October 1881, 519. In June 1882, *Boucher and Pratt's Musical Journal* reported that he had completed TIQ *(The Indian Question), Settled at Last. Boucher and Pratt's Musical Journal,* IV, no. 5 (June 1882): 16.

89   Sage published at least two other dramatic works: *Destiny, A Drama in a Prologue, Four Acts and an Epilogue,* and an adaptation of Charles Dickens's *A Tale of Two Cities.* TIQ seems to have been Hawley's only published work.

90   See "Musical Matters," *Boston Herald,* 29 January 1882; and "Lavallée's New Opera," *Musical Courier,* VII, no. 6 (8 August 1883): 88.

91   "Lavallée's New Opera," *Musical Courier,* VII, no. 6 (8 August 1883): 88.

92   "Review of New Music," *Musical Courier,* VII, no. 21 (21 November 1883): 304.

93   "Pickwick Theatre," *Spectator,* 18 July 1882.

94   Scheckel, *The Insistence of the Indian,* 8. Scheckel examines the use of Native

American subjects in the arts. See chapter 3, "Domesticating the Drama of Conquest: Pocahontas on the Popular Stage," 41–69. Sitting Bull was the subject of at least one other musical composition at about the same time as *TIQ*, Henry Wienskowitz's *Sitting Bull March*, for piano (New York: S.T. Gordon, 1884).

95 See Finson, *The Voices That Are Gone*, 240–69.

96 See Ingraham, "Assimilation, Integration and Individuation," 227–8. This number is contained in the Beckwith Ensemble CD *À la Claire Fontaine* (Opening Day Records ODR9321).

97 Lavallée, "Musical: The Fiftieth Performance of Pounce & Company." *Boston Home Journal*, 2 June 1883.

98 Ibid.

99 Lavallée, "Musical: Albani," *Boston Home Journal*, 3 March 1883.

100 See Lavallée, "An Utterly Too Too Criticism," *Boston Home Journal*, 7 April 1883; "An 'Off Night,'" *Boston Home Journal*, 10 March 1883; and "William H. Sherwood," *Boston Home Journal*, 14 April 1883.

101 See Lavallée, "Style and Expression," *Annual Report of the Music Teachers' National Association, 1883* (Minneapolis, Minn.: Music Teachers' National Association, 1883): 76–8.

102 Like Lavallée, Bowman later became an important figure in the promotion of American music. At a concert in Minneapolis in 1886, he played two unnamed works in the first part of the program and asked that, during the intermission, members of the audience fill out a ballot, choosing which they believed to be the better work. The two works turned out to be Mendelssohn's Sonata in C minor, and Dudley Buck's Sonata in G minor; of the roughly 400 votes cast, Buck's piece received 70 more than Mendelssohn's. See "A Novelty in Organ Recitals," *Musical Courier*, XIII, no. 23 (8 December 1886): 354.

103 Ouellet writes that local residents reported to him that they believed Lavallée never to have visited. See Ouellet, *Ma paroisse*, 212. The Collège de Lévis supplied Lavallée's student records, which noted that he was registered at the time of his death.

104 See Ouellet, *Ma paroisse*, 212. The reason for Joséphine's move to this village is not known.

105 A report in the *Journal de Québec* attributed Calixa Lavallée Jr's death to an inflammation of the intestines, caused by swimming too soon after eating. See "Suite d'une imprudence," *Journal de Québec*, 15 August 1883.

106 Calixa Lavallée, burial record, 14 August 1883. St-Jean-Chrysostôme, Québec. Druin Collection. Ancestry.com. (Accessed 16 February 2013) The record states that the boy was the child of "Calixa Lavallée, pianist, resident of the United States, and Josephine Gentilly, domiciled in this parish."

## CHAPTER SEVEN

1 "American Composers and Pioneers," *Musical Courier*, XII, no. 12 (24 March 1886): 188.

2 The family lived at 17 Worthington (1884), 20 Delle Ave (1885), 11 Worthington (1886–88), 29 Worthington (1889–90), and finally 4 Brookford (1890–

91). *Boston City Directory*. Developers had constructed the Worthington Street houses during the building boom of the 1870s.

3 Unlike the original words, Elson's quasi-rhyming text contains no references to Saint Peter or to church building. In place of the opening line, "To es Petrus, Tu es Petrus, Tu es Petrus, Alleluia," he writes: "Glory, blessing, praise and honor. The ever-lasting Father."

4 "Musical," *Boston Home Journal*, 19 January 1884.

5 "Calixa Lavallee," *Musical Courier*, X, no. 14 (8 April 1885): 212.

6 The students who took part in the graduates' concert were: Miss Mabelle R. Ward, Miss Maude Turner Moorehouse, Mrs Emma Kiley, Miss Elna May Potter, Miss May J. Day, Miss Maude Nichols, Albert F. Conant, T. Reeves Jones, Miss Tooker, and Mrs Moorehouse. See "Musical: Graduates' Concert," *Boston Home Journal*, 21 June 1884.

7 The *Musical Courier* later published an account of the trip, noting that for two months the entourage had been the guests of Franz Liszt, who had referred to one of Petersilea's students, Milo Benedict, as "the young Rheinberger of America." Liszt was referring to the German organist and composer, Josef Gabriel Rheinberger. *Musical Courier*, X, no. 15 (15 April 1885): 227.

8 Concert audiences in the United States occasionally heard American music in the mid-nineteenth century. William Henry Fry and George F. Bristow were outspoken mid-century advocates of American music, but they did not reach wide audiences. Gottschalk achieved wide popularity in the 1850s and 1860s in part by tailoring his music to popular tastes. No performer-composers emerged to take his place after he left the United States in 1865.

9 "Fighting on Behalf of American Music," *The Folio*, XXII, no. 6 (June 1882): 208. *The Folio* itself was a strong supporter of the cause of American composition. See Johnson, "The 'Folio' of White, Smith and Company."

10 The New York Philharmonic performed 217 different works between 1842 and 1880. Of these, eight were by Americans: five by Bristow and three by Ritter. See Jones, *Handbook of American Music and Musicians*, 111–15.

11 *Musical Courier* VIII, no. 18 (30 April 1884): 284.

12 Cappiani is not known to have published any of her compositions, although she did publish a singing manual, *Practical Hints and Helps for Perfection in Singing* (New York: Leo. Feist, 1908). The Schubert Quartet was founded in 1878 by Johann Beck (1st violin), with Julius Deiss (2nd violin), Charles Reinhart (viola), and Charles Heydler (cello). In 1884–85, William Schramm and J.H. Amme replaced Deiss and Reinhart, respectively. Their concerts took place mostly at Brainard's Parlors and Heard Hall, and featured works by Beethoven, Mendelssohn, and Brahms. In 1890, the group changed its name to the Beck String Quartet. See "Schubert Quartet," *Encyclopedia of Cleveland History*, 2nd ed. (Bloomington: Indiana University Press, 1996).

13 See "Music Teachers' National Association," *The Voice*, VI, no. 8 (August 1884): 127–8.

14 The 1884 meeting saw the election of Dr S.N. Penfield, of New York, as president, and A.A. Stanley, of Providence, as secretary and treasurer. A.R. Parsons (New York), Carlyle Petersilea (Boston), and H.S. Perkins (Chicago) formed the Business Committee, and William Gilchrist (Philadelphia), Dr F.B. Rice

(Oberlin, Ohio), and Dr Florens Ziegfeld (Chicago) comprised the Program Committee.

15 *Cleveland Herald*, 4 July 1884; reprinted in "Calixa Lavallée," *Freund's Music and Drama*, 13, no. 9 (December 1889): 24.

16 "Piano Recital of American Compositions," *The Folio*, XXVI, no. 2 (August 1884): 56. C.B. Cady of Ann Arbor, Michigan, read Whiting's paper.

17 *Musical Courier* VIII, no. 14 (2 April 1884): 212.

18 H.S. Perkins, "MTNA," *The Folio*, XXVI, no. 2 (August 1884): 54.

19 Among the board members were William Sherwood, Louis Maas, and William Mason, for piano; and E.M. Bowman, Frederic Grant Gleason, and William W. Gilchrist for theory.

20 See "American College of Musicians," MTNA *Proceedings*, 1884: np. The ACM's guidelines stated that the first grade "will call for a comprehensive working knowledge of the resources of musical art (choral and orchestral), proficiency in musical history and acoustics, together with special powers as a composer, artist or teacher." The second grade "will call for special powers in the branch followed [such as piano or voice] and a working knowledge of harmony and counterpoint, analysis of musical forms, musical history, principles of acoustics, and the special history of the branch engaged in." The third grade "will call for the special and general preparation needful for those conducting the earlier studies of the musical student. This will involve correct technical knowledge of the branch followed, the principles of teaching, rudiments of harmony and musical forms, and the outlines of musical history."

21 Jules Lavallée, birth certificate, 16 August 1884. Jules Lavallée, death certificate, 31 August 1884. Massachusetts State Archives.

22 "Is It Necessary to Go Abroad to Study?" *The Folio*, XXVI, no. 5 (November 1884): 172.

23 See Holleran, *Boston's "Changeful Times,"* and Warner, *Streetcar Suburbs*.

24 "The French Church," *Boston Herald*, 22 January 1885.

25 "Union Hall," *Boston Evening Journal*, 11 March 1885.

26 "Musical Matters," *Boston Herald*, 11 March 1885.

27 "Music in Boston," *Musical Courier*, X, no. 12 (25 March 1885): 182.

28 "Music," *Boston Home Journal*, 14 March 1885. The review concluded that the success of the performance was "no doubt owing to a superhuman effort on his part, with which the audience was in sympathetic admiration."

29 See the *Boston Herald*, 10 March 1885; reprinted in *The Folio*, XXVII, no. 4 (April 1885): 138, "Music," *Boston Home Journal*, 14 March 1885, and "Music," *Boston Home Journal*, 9 May 1885.

30 See "Calixa Lavallée," *The Folio*, XXVII, no. 2 (February 1885): 61, frontispiece; and "Calixa Lavallée," *Musical Courier*, X, no. 14 (8 April 1885): 212.

31 *Boston Herald*, 10 March 1885; reprinted in *The Folio*, XXVII, no. 4 (April 1885): 138.

32 "Music," *Boston Home Journal*, 9 May 1885. In March, the same newspaper noted: "It has remained for a foreigner not simply to discover the importance of the American musical profession in the respect referred to, but to demon-

strate this importance in a manner at once creditable to his artistic ability, to his tact, and to his exceptional interest in a grossly neglected cause." "Music," *Boston Home Journal*, 14 March 1885.

33 Birth and death records from the Massachusetts State Archives. Ancestry.com. (Accessed 9 March 2009.) Joseph had married some time after the 1881 Census takers had recorded him as a twenty-one-year-old resident of the family home, along with his parents, ages sixty-four and sixty-one, Catherine, twenty-five, Ida, nineteen, Charles, thirty, along with Anna, twenty-six, and her husband Ovide Laliberté, twenty-eight, and their two-year-old son, Alfred.

34 "American College of Musicians," *Werner's Voice Magazine*, VII, no. 7 (July 1885): 113.

35 See "Frederic Archer," obituary, *Appleton's Annual Cyclopedia and Register of Important Events* (New York: D. Appleton & Company, 1901), 406.

36 "Lavallée Defends the M.T.N.A.," *Musical Courier*, XI, no. 4 (29 July 1885): 52.

37 Lavallée remained sensitive to the potential conflict of interest with piano companies. In 1890, in a reply to Edward MacDowell's inquiry about the arrangements made for instruments, Lavallée responded: "When I wrote you it was whether you would accept the invitation to appear as composer and performer at our next meeting. This is all you would have to do at present. Whatever arrangements you make later on with Mr Chickering or any other firm will have to be done by yourself as we have no jurisdiction in the matter and artists are supposed to use the instruments of their choice." Calixa Lavallée, letter to Edward MacDowell, 11 December 1889, MacDowell Collection, Music Division, Library of Congress.

38 Reprinted in "Who Is Petersilea?" *The Folio*, XXV, no. 6 (June 1884): 230.

39 Tourjée referred to the ACM as a "College of Music," which drew a pointed response from the MTNA's president, W.F. Heath. Heath explained that it was an American College of Musicians, not "of Music," and that its "board of examiners for membership do not ask where the applicants get their musical education; and the students of the New England Conservatory will stand as good a chance as any other students, provided they are equally competent." "A Breeze from the West," *The Folio*, XXVIII, no. 3 (September 1885): 98.

40 Thurber paid the rental bill for the Academy of Music, but it was obviously unsuitable for meetings. Even with 400 participants at the opening sessions on 1 July, one commentator pointed out that the building was "much too large and gloomy for a reunion of this sort." "Musicians in Council: Opening Session of the Teachers' Association," *New York Times*, 2 July 1885. For a study of Thurber's contributions to American music, see Rubin, "Jeannette Meyer Thurber."

41 Of the eleven works on the program, only those by Lavallée and Paine are known to have been published.

42 "The Council of Musicians," *New York Times*, 3 July 1885.

43 Ibid.

44 Reprinted in *The Folio*, XXVIII, no. 2 (August 1885): 51.

45 Charles Capen, "Mr Capen on the Music Teachers' National Association," *Musical Courier*, XII, no. 20 (19 May 1886): 320.

46 The members of the program committee were Calixa Lavallée (chair), A.R. Parsons (New York), and F.B. Rice (Oberlin, Ohio). The other officers elected were: A.A. Stanley (Providence), president; Theodore Presser (Philadelphia), secretary and treasurer; Executive Committee: S.B. Whitney (Boston), W.F. Heath (Fort Wayne, Indiana), and Max Leckner (Indianapolis, Indiana). The meeting also saw the passing of a bylaw allowing for the election of vice-presidents from Canada.

47 "MTNA," *Musical Courier*, XI, no. 2 (15 July 1885): 18.

48 See "The Musicians' Convention," *New York Times*, 4 July 1885.

49 Writings on Riel are voluminous. See Thomas, "Riel, Louis."

50 P.U. Vaillant, *Notes Biographiques*, 49. For a thorough account of Bédard's life, see Gendron, "The Life and Times of Pierre Jean-Baptiste Bedard (1842–1884)."

51 Philip T. Silvia Jr examines the conflicts between Fall River's Irish Americans and French Canadians in the period 1870–1885 in "The 'Flint Affair': French-Canadian Struggle for *Survivance*."

52 See Philippe Lemay, *The French-Canadian Textile Worker*; reported by Louis Pare. New Hampshire Federal Writers' Project, 1938–39; *American Life Histories: Manuscripts from the Federal Writers' Project, 1936–1940*, in *American Memory*, Library of Congress. http://memory.loc.gov/. (Accessed 7 September 2008)

53 Start, "A Model New England Village," 711.

54 *L'Indépendant*, 11 December 1885. Reprinted in the *Guide Français de Fall River* (Fall River, 1909).

55 Fréchette's poem appears in the *Nouvelle Lyre Canadienne*, 110–11. A copy of the sheet music for Lavallée's piece is found in the Bibliothèque et Archives nationales du Québec, with the handwritten title "Rallions-nous, Canadiens." The single page had been part of a larger publication, the identity of which has not yet been determined. Hélène Boucher of the Bibliothèque et Archives nationales du Québec, email to the author, 27 October 1998. Ernest Lavigne also completed a setting of the words, which appears not to have been published, and another song, also titled "Rallions-Nous," was composed by Charles-Marie Panneton on words by Benjamin Sulte for the 1874 *Fête nationale* in Montreal. The latter piece was published in *L'Opinion publique* on 2 July 1874.

56 Vanier, *Georges Vanier, Soldier*, 61.

57 Howard Cable's brass quintet arrangement of the *Bridal Rose* (or *Rose nuptial*) has been widely performed. Among the most recent recordings of it are those by the Hannaford Street Silver Band in 1996 and True North Brass in 1998.

58 See Boston City Council, *Proceedings of the Dedication of the Fountain on Eaton Square* (Boston: The Council, 1885).

59 *Musical Courier*, XII, no. 2 (13 January 1886): 21.

60 The Boston Conservatory was located in the Mason and Hamlin building at 154 Tremont.

61 To facilitate production of its expanding line of instruments, Miller moved manufacturing to the nearby town of Wakefield, Massachusetts, in 1884. See Dolge, *Pianos and Their Makers*, 337.

62  Louis Maas, "Calixa Lavallée's Fourth American Concert," *Musical Courier*, XII, no. 11 (17 March 1886): 142.

63  Reviews often mentioned that Lavallée had memorized the works he performed at the 'American concerts.' See, for example, Louis Maas, "Calixa Lavallée's Fourth American Concert," *Musical Courier*, XII, no. 11 (17 March 1886): 142.

64  "Music," *Boston Home Journal*, 1 May 1886.

65  "Music and the Drama," *Daily Evening Traveller*, 27 February 1886.

66  "Music," *Boston Home Journal*, 1 May 1886.

67  The program was printed in "Music in Boston," *Musical Courier*, X, no. 12 (25 March 1885): 182. The other works performed included Wilson G. Smith's *Hommage à Edward Grieg*, Lavallée's "Andalouse," and Arthur Foote's Trio.

68  "Music and the Drama," *Daily Evening Traveller*, 27 February 1886.

69  Louis Maas, "Calixa Lavallée's Fourth American Concert," *Musical Courier*, XII, no. 11 (17 March 1886): 142.

70  "The Music," *Detroit Free Press*, 2 July 1890.

71  "Music and the Stage," *Evening Traveller*, 11 March 1885. "Theatres and Concerts," *Boston Transcript*, 6 May 1885, 1. The *Musical Courier* wrote that "the large size of the audience was encouraging and the appreciation shown was decidedly merited." "Music in Boston," *Musical Courier*, X, no. 12 (25 March 1885): 182.

72  See "Music," *Home Journal*, 14 March 1885.

73  T. Tapper Jr, "American Composers," *The Folio*, XXVII, no. 4 (April 1885): 137.

74  "American Music in Concert," *Daily Globe*, 29 April 1886.

75  *Boston Herald*, 29 April 1886.

76  Under different names, this firm existed for over a century. It was first known as White, Smith & Perry (1867–1874), then White, Smith & Company (1874–ca.1888), and finally White-Smith Music Publishing Company (1889–ca.1980))

77  Antoine Marmontel, *Les Pianistes célèbres* (Paris: Heugel et fils, 1887), 230. Camille Stamaty was a virtuoso and composer who studied with Kalkbrenner and Mendelssohn. He is now best remembered as a pedagogue and the teacher of Gottschalk and Saint-Saëns. See "White, Smith & Company," advertisement, *The Folio*, XXX, no. 2 (August 1886): 61. Lavallée's student, Thomas Tapper Jr, provided the English translation.

78  Lavallée dedicated the 1886 edition to Carlyle Petersilea.

79  Stevens made her Boston debut at Miller Hall on 9 May 1889.

80  Musset called another of his poems from the same period "Andalouse." Hippolyte Monpou and several other composers wrote settings of it. Musset had been popular with musicians since the late 1820s, and *Madame la Marquise*, like many others, was written with music in mind.

81  The translation is by Louis C. Elson (White, Smith & Company, 1886).

82  The comments began: "To the Bolero, not even the most fastidious Spanish musician could object and it is not only admirable in suggesting the piquant and elastic step of the most popular of Spanish dances, but unusual skill has been shown in its vocal adaptation." "Music," *Boston Home Journal*, 14 March 1885.

83 "The Petersilea Concert," *The Folio*, XXIX, no. 6 (June 1886): 278. The soprano Sally Dibblee recorded this song on *Le Souvenir: Canadian Songs for Parlour and Stage*, Centrediscs, CMC-CD 5696, 1996.

84 Hall published at least three volumes of poetry in the 1890s: *Verses* (New York: John W. Lovell, 1890); *Allegretto* (Boston: Robert Brothers, 1893); and *The Age of Fairy Gold* (Boston: Little, Brown, and Company, 1899).

85 Charles Capen, "Mr Capen on the Music Teachers' National Association," *Musical Courier*, XII, no. 20 (19 May 1886): 320.

86 Ibid. A report in the *Boston Transcript* later provided further information on MTNA's budget. It noted that the Association's accounts had risen from a balance of $449.27 at the beginning of the year to roughly $1,200 after the Boston meeting; $600 was to be allocated for the needs of the secretary and treasurer. "The Music Teachers," *Boston Transcript*, 3 July 1886.

87 "The Music Teachers," *Boston Transcript*, 3 July 1886. The interview was published in "Musical Matters," *Boston Herald*, 9 May 1886.

88 Reprinted in "Other People's Opinions," *The Orchestra* [London], (27 March 1886): 616.

89 Calixa Lavallée, "The Future of Music in America," *The Folio*, XXX, no. 1 (July 1886): 13.

90 Sessions were divided between the main hall of Tremont Temple and Meionaon Hall.

91 "The Music Teachers," *Evening Transcript*, 2 July 1886.

92 Ibid.

93 See "Biographies of American Musicians, no. 90, Calixa Lavallée," *Brainard's Musical Journal*, XXII (May 1885): 167.

94 Nineteenth-century writers and composers produced numerous adaptations of the Solomon story. Louis Charles Caigniez had published his *Le Jugement de Solomon*, a "melodrame en trois actes," in 1802. In 1803, it was translated and altered by the American writer William Dunlap and the British writer James Boaden. They both re-titled their adaptations *The Voice of Nature*, "a drama in three acts." Dunlap's was staged at the New York Theatre (New York: David Longworth, 1803), and Boaden's at London's Theatre Royal, Haymarket (London: J. Ridgway, 1803). Thirty years later, Felix-August Duvert published his *Jugement de Solomon, vaudeville en un acte*. It was performed at the Théâtre des Variétés in Paris in 1835 (Paris: Marchant, 1835).

95 "The Music Teachers," *Evening Transcript*, 2 July 1886.

96 "Secretary's Report," MTNA *Proceedings (1886)*, (Minneapolis, 1887), 243.

97 Ibid., 244.

98 Johannes Wolfram, "Ohio Music Teachers' Association versus Music Teachers' National Association," *Musical Courier*, XIII, no. 3 (21 July 1886): 38. Wolfram continued: "It is [Lavallée] to whom the 'National' owes it mainspring of life and attractiveness, for it is he who unfurled the standard of native composers."

99 See "Accident to Mr Lennon," [Boston] *Daily Advertiser*, 10 July 1886; "Obituary: Joseph G. Lennon," [Boston] *Daily Advertiser*, 14 July 1886; and "Death of Mr J.G. Lennon," *Boston Herald*, 14 July 1886.

100 "A Card: Mr Carlyle Petersilea," advertisement, Boston *Daily Journal*, 3 September 1886.

101 "A Card: The Petersilea Academy of Music," advertisement, *Boston Daily Journal*, 3 September 1886.

102 See "Communication from Mr Lavallée," *Musical Courier*, XIII, no. 13 (29 September 1886): 195.

103 See "Lavallée-Gower Correspondence," *Musical Courier*, XIII, no. 23 (8 December 1886): 358. The program committee issued a preliminary report in October 1886 describing new procedures for submitting and selecting works. It lists the types of compositions ("three or four overtures, two or three symphonic movements," etc.) that would be performed at the forthcoming conference. "M.T.N.A.," *Musical Courier*, XIII, no. 14 (6 October 1886): 211.

104 The *Musical Courier* denounced the ACM's opponents and warned against any "filibustering, that could disrupt the business meeting." *Musical Courier*, XIV, no. 23 (8 June 1887): 368.

105 In the spring of 1887, *The Folio* reported that Lavallée had given several more 'American concerts' in the Midwest. The article did not provide any details about these performances. See *The Folio*, XXXI, no. 5 (May 1887): 185.

106 "Soirée-Concert à Fall River," *L'Indépendant*, 15 October 1886.

107 See Club de Raquettes le "Trappeur" de Montréal, Acte d'incorporation, [iii], and Leon Trepanier, "'Le Trappeur.'"

108 See Massicotte, "Raquettes – Clubs – Costume – Chanson."

109 E.Z. Massicotte provided a transcription of a portion of the words but did not indicate if Lavallée's music was ever published. See "Raquette – Clubs – Costume – Chanson." The full text of Tremblay's lyrics are contained in his *Aux chevaliers du noeud coulant*, 281-2.

110 "Les Trappeurs," *Boston Evening Transcript*, 2 February 1887.

111 Protestant-Catholic tensions were rising once again even before the arrival in Montreal of the Irish nationalist William O'Brien, who was campaigning for independence from Britain and denouncing the current governor general, the Marquis of Lansdowne, over evictions from his estates in Ireland.

112 *Musical Courier*, XIV, no. 20 (18 May 1887): 320.

113 See *The Folio*, XXXI, no. 7 (July 1887): frontispiece.

114 In his address, Lavallée focused on the importance of the state organizations and the need for the nominating committee to select their state vice-presidents judiciously. See *Official Report of the Eleventh Annual Meeting of the Music Teachers' National Association, Held at Indianapolis, Ind.* (Minneapolis, MN: MTNA, 1888), np.

115 The intended British delegate, John Gower, withdrew at the last moment for what Lavallée described as "professional duties." The title of his paper appeared on the program as "The Needs of the Musical Profession." See "President's Address," printed in Henry Southwick Perkins, *Historical Handbook of the Music Teachers' National Association, 1876–1893* (Chicago: MTNA, ca. 1893), 67.

116 Programs of the first three concerts featured US works and the fourth comprised only American music. Van der Strucken's regular subscription concerts

featured standard European repertoire. See Bomberger, *A Tidal Wave of Encouragement*, 29–44.

117 Among the works performed in 1887 were Chadwick's *Dedication Ode*, Whiting's cantata *Henry of Navarre*, and the last portion of Ferdinand Dulcken's *Messe Solennelle*.

118 The German-born Leckner had established Indianapolis's Philharmonic Society in the 1860s and from 1873 to 1880 served as director of the city's Maennerchor. See McKinney, "The Performing Arts," in *The Encyclopedia of Indianapolis*, 144; and Mathews, *A Hundred Years of Music in America*, 616.

119 See Clara Brinkerhoff, "Art or Trade?" *American Musician*, reprinted in *Werner's Voice Magazine*, IX, no. 9 (September 1887): 139. The writer of an article in *Church's Musical Visitor* noted that there were sharply divided opinions on the issue. He believed that there was little chance of any piano firm gaining control of the organization, and that "the war now on will be but a war of words." See "The MTNA and the Piano Question," *Church's Musical Visitor*, reprinted in *Werner's Voice Magazine*, IX, no. 8 (August 1887): 129–30.

120 *Musical Courier*, XV, no. 11 (14 September 1887): 162. The *Musical Courier's* notice claimed that the remarks against Lavallée were "started with the aim of damaging an honest and capable, conscientious, and hard-working musician." It reported that Lavallée was the nomination committee's unanimous choice for president in 1887, but that he declined a second term for health reasons. In his place, Lavallée suggested Leckner, and the committee accepted his choice.

121 Leckner was reported to have appointed Lavallée in "Lavallée in London," *Musical Courier*, XVI, no. 2 (11 January 1888): 2. In his history of the early years of the MTNA, Henry Perkins writes that it was Heath, as chairman of the 1887 meeting, who appointed Lavallée as delegate to the meeting in London. See Perkins, *Historical Handbook of the Music Teachers' National Association, 1876–1893*, 67.

122 "Professional Musicians," *Boston Herald*, 30 January 1888.

123 A French translation of the article was published as "Discours prononcé par M. Calixa Lavallée," *L'Écho musical*, I, no. 3 (March 1888): 28.

124 "Conference of the National Society of Professional Musicians," *Musical Times* [London], 1 February 1888.

125 Reprinted in "Musical America," *New York Herald*, 8 January 1888.

126 Lavallée's return aboard the *Umbria* was noted in the *New York Times*, 17 January 1888. See "Lavallée in London," *Musical Courier*, XVI, no. 2 (11 January 1888): 2; *Musical Courier*, XVI, no. 3 (18 January 1888): 37; and "Lavallée's London Letter," *Musical Courier*, XVI, no. 4 (25 January 1888): 60, 62.

127 G.H.W. "Musical Matters," *Boston Traveller*, 16 January 1888.

128 *Musical Courier*, XVI, no. 4 (25 January 1888): 50.

129 See "Feue Madame Lavallée," *La Patrie*, 7 February 1888; "A Travers la Ville," *La Minerve*, 8 February 1888; and "Boston, Mass," *L'Indépendent*, 17 February 1888.

130 "Funerailles imposantes," *La Patrie*, 18 February 1903.

131 "Funeral of Count Premio-Real," *Quebec Daily Mercury*, 20 October 1888; "Les funérailles du compte d'Éspagne," *La Patrie*, 20 October 1888.

132 See Octave Lemieux & Cie, *Catalogue – vente a L'encan.*
133 "Boston, Mass," *L'Indépendent,* 6 April 1888.
134 "Boston, Mass," *L'Independent,* 20 April 1888.
135 Dumont was then residing in New York State. See Roderick C. Macleod, "Gabriel Dumont," *Dictionary of Canadian Biography.*
136 "En avant les braves," *La Patrie,* 18 May 1888.
137 "Calixa Lavallée," *La Patrie,* 18 May 1888.
138 "Brieflets," *Montreal Herald,* 17 May 1888.
139 "Concert at Viger Gardens," *Montreal Herald,* 19 May 1888. The piece may have been Adolphe Schmidt's *Coliseum Grand March* (Boston: Schmidt, 1872), which had been first performed by Gilmore's Band and was often attributed to the bandleader.
140 "The News Around Town," *Montreal Daily Post,* 19 May 1888.
141 "Gabriel Dumont, le heros de Batoche," advertisement, *Le Patrie,* 17 May 1888.
142 The program was printed in "Mechanics' Building, Huntington Av. Grand Charity Festival Decoration Day, Wednesday, May 30," advertisement, *Boston Herald,* 29 May 1888. The House of the Good Shepherd was a convent school and home for "unfortunate women and wayward girls."
143 See "Report Read by Calixa Lavallée at Chicago Conference of the MTNA on July 3," *Musical Courier,* XVII, no. 1 (4 July 1888): 4.
144 See "The Music Teachers' National Association," *The Voice,* X, no. 8 (August 1888): 132. The year's financial report shows total receipts of $6,009.71 and expenses of $5,673.37. See Perkins, "Treasurer's Financial Report," np.
145 See, for example, "The Music Teachers," *Daily Inter-Ocean,* 6 July 1888.
146 Ibid.
147 See "Lavallée's Letter," *Musical Courier,* XVII, no. 6 (8 August 1888): 102.
148 Ibid.
149 "The N.S.P.M. Again!" *Musical Standard,* 35, no. 1256 (25 August 1888): 123. "Latest from the London 'Figaro,'" *Musical Courier,* XVII, no. 11 (12 September 1888): 190.
150 Calixa Lavallée, "Correspondence," *Musical Standard,* 35, no. 1262 (6 October 1888): 216.
151 G.H.W. "Musical Matters," *Boston Traveller,* 8 October 1888.
152 The *Musical Courier* added: "Mr Lavallée was only partly reimbursed, and his total expense and subsequent loss amounted to about $1000 in money spent and lessons lost – all for the benefit of others, for he had nothing to gain." *Musical Courier,* XVII, no. 6 (17 October 1888): 278.
153 The debate in the US continued into November, when the *Musical Courier* reported that Frederic Grant Gleason was to be the representative that year, and: "Mr Lavallée was invited by the English society to contribute a work of his own for the meeting this year, but declined on the grounds that it would be preferable to produce a composition of a native American at first. Mr. Lavallée was also invited as a delegate, but declined for the same reason." "Native American" clearly referred to one who was born in the United States. "The MTNA in England," *Musical Courier,* XVII, no. 22 (28 November 1888): 390.

154 See "M.T.N.A.: Preliminary Report of the Programme Committee," *Brainard's Musical World*, 25, no. 11 (November 1888): 439.

155 "Carney Hospital Festival," *Boston Herald*, 4 September 1888; "The Carney Hospital Festival at Mechanics' Hall," *Boston Daily Journal*, 4 September 1888. Among the participants were the soprano soloists Mrs Jacob Benzing and Mrs A.T. Chelli, baritone Lon F. Brine, and bass Jacob Benzing, as well as Charles Molé and E.N. Lafricain. Jean Missud led the Salem Cadet Band.

156 *Dexter Smith's Musical, Literary, Dramatic, and Art Paper*, I, no. 1 (January 1872): 12.

157 *Dexter Smith's Musical Journal*, IX, no. 4 (April 1876): 104.

158 *Musical Courier*, XVII, no. 25 (19 December 1888): 452.

159 "Ohio Genius," *Cleveland Leader*, 28 June 1889. The *Cleveland Leader* described Lavallée's Suite for Piano and Cello, as the "most notable work" on a program.

160 "Philadelphia Convention," *Werner's Voice Magazine*, XI, no. 9 (September 1889): 189.

161 John Towers, of Manchester, accompanied Chadfield to Philadelphia.

162 See "The Philadelphia Convention," *Werner's Voice Magazine*, XI, no. 9 (September 1889): 189.

163 On 12 July 1889, Van der Stucken led a performance at Trocadero Palace, where he conducted 100 musicians from the Opéra Comique in compositions by Foote, MacDowell, Chadwick, Paine, and others. See Bomberger, *A Tidal Wave of Encouragement*, 45-64.

164 Also on the Program Committee were Wilson G. Smith and Florens Ziegfeld. Albert Ross Parsons was elected president, H.S. Perkins as secretary, and Arthur Foote, Ad. M. Forster, and August Hyllested as the members of the Committee on Examination of American Compositions.

165 The flautist Charles Molé and the violinist Christian Delisle were among the other performers at this event.

166 See "Brilliant Grand Concert," *Lowell Daily Courier*, 1 February 1890; and "Concert," *Lowell Daily Courier*, 3 February 1890. Also performing in Lowell, were Christian Delisle and Lavallée's student Anna Melendy, of Nashua, New Hampshire.

167 Letter to Thibault, published in Lapierre, *Calixa Lavallée* (1966), 267-8.

168 See "Les Canadiennes à l'étranger," *Le Coin de feu, revue mensuelle*, I, no. 2 (February 1893): 33-4.

169 Anna Marie Duval-Thibault, letter to Eugène Lapierre, 5 October 1933. Duval-Thibault Papers, Houghton Library, Harvard University.

170 On a program that included songs by MacDowell, Wilson G. Smith, and James H. Rogers, the soprano Annie S. Wilson sang Lavallée' "Love," which may have been an abbreviated version of "Love Come to Me." Alternatively, it may have been a setting of a different Duval-Thibault poem. A work with this title, dated May 1883, appears in a notebook in her collected papers. Duval-Thibault Papers, Houghton Library, Harvard University. The *Musical Courier* reported that the Detroit soprano Annie Wilson performed the selections "with much delicacy and purity of tone." *Musical Courier*, XXI, no. 2 (9 July 1890): 51.

171 In contrast to the fee of $1,519 paid to the orchestra in Philadelphia, Thomas's orchestra received $4,500. The amount represented an unprecedented expenditure and the event produced a deficit of over $3,000. See "Treasurer's Report," *Proceedings of the* MTNA, 1890.

172 "The Music," *Detroit Free Press*, 3 July 1890. The *Evening News* described the attendance on the first night as "inspiring alike in its proportions and discriminating character." "The Music Teachers," *Detroit Evening News*, 3 July 1890. "The Music," *Detroit Free Press*, 4 July 1890.

173 *Musical Courier*, XXI, no. 1 (2 July 1890): 2.

174 See the *Boston Herald*, 10 March 1885; reprinted in *The Folio*, XXVII, no. 4 (April 1885): 138. See also "Music," *Boston Home Journal*, 14 March 1885: 3. Neither the *Herald* nor the *Home Journal* stated the source of his suffering in their reviews.

175 "The Raconteur," *Musical Courier*, XXI, no. 3 (16 July 1890): 72.

176 Onésime Thibault wrote that during the fall of 1890 Lavallée made numerous visits to Dr Collet. Onésime Thibault, letter to Eugène Lapierre, 1 October 1933. Anna Marie Duval-Thibault Literary Papers, Houghton Library, Harvard University.

177 The note continued: "The physical condition of Mr Calixa Lavallée, of Boston, is such that it has become absolutely impossible for him to pay any further attention to correspondence or appeals for favors unless of the most urgent nature. Mr Lavallée needs rest and his physician has ordered him to abstain from all unnecessary work and excitement." "Personals," *Musical Courier*, XXI, no. 20 (12 November 1890): 481.

178 The death certificate was supplied by the Registry Division of Boston City Hall. See also "Concert Lavallée," *La Minerve*, 24 January 1891; and "Musical Matters," *Montreal Daily Star*, 19 January 1891.

179 "Funeral of Calixa Lavallee," *Boston Herald*, 25 January 1891.

180 See "Lavallée," *L'Indépendant*, 29 January 1891. This was likely the setting of the psalm published by Christoph Willibald von Gluck (Paris: Conservatoire de musique, nd).

181 "Nècrologie," *Le Ménestrel*, 29 March 1891, 104.

182 *Musical Courier*, XXII, no. 4 (28 January 1891): 75.

183 Ibid.

184 "Lavallée," *L'Indépendant*, 29 January 1891.

185 "Au Queen's Hall," *La Minerve*, 24 January 1891.

186 "Musical Matters: The Lavallee Benefit Concert," *Montreal Daily Star*, 26 January 1891.

187 "Calixa Lavallée," *The Folio*, XXVII, no. 2 (February 1885): 61.

188 "Revue Mensuelle," *L'Album musicale*, II, no. 11 (November 1882): 48.

189 The Detroit Conservatory of Music staged two concerts of American works in 1888. The second one was devoted entirely to the music of Edward MacDowell, and the *Free Press* called it "one of the most completely successful concerts yet given in this city." Reprinted in "Detroit," *Brainard's Musical Journal*, XXV, no. 6 (June 1888): 236. For a discussion of the manuscript societies, see Zuck, *A History of Musical Americanisms*, 47–8.

190 "The Manuscript Society," *New York Tribune*, 12 December 1890.
191 The newspaper reported that "Mr Calixa Lavallée inaugurated the movement of giving more prominence to the works of American composers, when he gave the concert devoted exclusively to American compositions, at the meeting of the Music Teachers' National Association, held in Cleveland, Ohio, in 1884." "Incidental Notes," *Boston Home Journal*, 27 March 1886.
192 "Musical Matters," *Boston Herald*, 9 May 1886.
193 Hahn, "President's Address," 13–14. While researching his book on the 'American concerts,' E. Douglas Bomberger "searched for evidence of all-American concerts before 1884 ... [but came] up with virtually nothing." E. Douglas Bomberger, email to the author, 17 November 2000. I wish to express my thanks to Dr Bomberger for his comments.
194 "American Composer at the Music Hall Promenades," *Boston Herald*, 13 June 1894.
195 Carl Fischer acquired Cundy-Bettoney's catalogue in the 1960s but reissued only the *Bridal Rose*. See C.L. Carter, letter to Helmut Kallmann, 22 December 1964, in Lavallée file, Canadian Broadcasting Corporation Music Library, Toronto.
196 "Calixa Lavallée, the Career of an Eminent Musician," *Freund's Music and Drama*, 15, no. 14 (31 January 1891): 1.
197 "Canadian Creative Composers," *Canadian Magazine*, 41, no. 5 (September 1913): 490.
198 Kallmann, A *History of Music in Canada 1534–1914*, 239.
199 "Calixa Lavallée, the Career of an Eminent Musician," *Freund's Music and Drama*, 15, no. 14 (31 January 1891): 1.
200 "Lavallée," *L'Indépendant*, 29 January 1891.
201 See "Calixa Lavallée," *Musical Courier*, X, no. 14 (8 April 1885): 212.
202 Dwight's *Journal of Music* ceased publication in 1881, after twenty-six years espousing the 'good' music of Mozart, Beethoven, and Bach. See Richard Randall Hihn, "Boston, Dwight, and Pianists of Nineteenth-Century America: The European Connection," DMA diss., University of Colorado, 1984.
203 See "Obituaries: Calixa Lavallée," *Werner's Voice Magazine*, XIII, no. 3 (March 1891): 84; and "Was a Gifted Musician," *Boston Globe*, 22 January 1891.
204 Eugene Lapierre wrote that Lavallée used such a code, and that a trunk of manuscripts had been destroyed because they appeared to be only pages of numbers. Although Lapierre did not state his sources, the idea of the "chiffres" may have originated with Duval-Thibault. In a 1933 letter to Lapierre, Duval-Thibault uses the word "chiffre" ('number' or 'code') to describe the format of Lavallée's manuscripts. Lapierre, *Calixa Lavallée* (1966), 195. Anna Marie Duval-Thibault, letter to Eugène Lapierre, 5 October 1933. Anna Marie Duval-Thibault Literary Papers, Houghton Library, Harvard University.
205 *Musical Courier*, XIV, no. 20 (18 May 1887): 320.
206 "Musical Matters," *Montreal Daily Star*, 19 January 1891.
207 *Musical Courier*, XXII, no. 4 (28 January 1891): 75.
208 Alfred De Sève donated $15 to the *Révue-Canada* fund. See "Souscription-Lavallée," *Révue-Canada* (February 1891). Funds collected by the MTNA were

to be sent to H.S. Perkins in Chicago. See "Readers and Singers," *Werner's Voice Magazine*, XIII, no. 2 (February 1891): 56. Pierre Lachance refers to the Fall River benefit in *Documents of Historical Interest to the Catholic Churches of Fall River*, np.

209 National Archives and Records Administration. US, *Civil War Pension Index: General Index to Pension Files, 1861–1934* [database on-line]. Provo, UT: Ancestry.com Operations Inc, 2000.

210 The 1894–95 *Montreal Directory* lists "Lavallée, Mrs J. wid. Calixa. 417 Dorchester." Massicotte discovered and described the 1895 registration in "Dame Calixa Lavallée." The marriage was recorded in Cathédrale Marie-Reine-du-Monde (Montréal), *Registre des mariages*, 1895, p. 170, folio 10.

211 National Archives and Records Administration. US, *Civil War Pension Index: General Index to Pension Files, 1861–1934* [database on-line]. Provo, UT: Ancestry.com Operations Inc, 2000. In *Ma paroise*, Gérard Ouelette (p. 212) writes that Joséphine died in Boston. The Boston Clerk's office has no record of her death in that city, but she may have lived there during the late 1890s.

212 "Un Jeune Canadien est le sujet d'une aventure a Porto-Rico," *Justice de Biddeford*, 15 June 1899.

213 "New Jersey May Have a Duel," *The New York Times*, 14 August 1901; "Rotten Eggs," *Brooklyn Daily Eagle*, 14 August 1901. The young woman was reported to be a Miss Grace Davis and Lavallée's rival was a clerk by the name of George Kanouse. In 1904, newspapers reminded readers of the duel when Kanouse and Davis were married. "New Jersey Man Missing," *New York Times*, 16 April 1902.

214 Thirteen Census of the United States: 1910 – Population. Newark City, Ward 13, New Jersey.

215 *Catalog of Copyright Entries Published by Authority of the Acts of Congress of March 3, 1891, June 30, 1906, and March 4, 1909. Part 3: Musical Compositions* (Washington, DC: Government Printing Office, 1911): 1309.

216 *Registrar's Report*, 27 April 1942. Registration card serial number U-2618. The report described Raoul as 5 feet, 5 inches in height, and 135 lbs, with brown hair and a light complexion. Charles is listed as the contact person. They are both registered as residing at 3432 Forbes Street. Raoul's employer is listed as Morris Klein, 5526 Covode Street.

217 "Musical Matters," *Boston Herald*, 20 April 1890.

### EPILOGUE

1 *Le Papillon* was on the program of a concert of French music in March 1915. "Punahou Will Feature French Compositions," *Honolulu Star-Bulletin* 13 March 1915. Lindley Evans, an Australian pianist, was performing *Le Papillon* in Sydney in 1922. "Say Good-Bye," *Evening News*, 24 August 1922.

2 The exact dates of two of these publications are unknown. Library and Archives of Canada provides the following dates for the three editions: A.J. Boucher, 1880, Edmond Hardy, ca. 1880–1889, and Yon, ca. 1890–99.

3 "Concert at Viger Garden," *Montreal Post*, 19 May 1888. Similarly, the Victo-

ria Rifles Band concluded their concerts with the national songs. See "Dominion Square," *Montreal Post*, 1 June 1888.

4 See Letondal, "Calixa Lavallée et l'Hymne National." During the early years of the twentieth century, "Restons-Français" appears to have been more widely sung than "O Canada." The Montreal publisher Yon included "Restons-Français" in *L'Écrin lyrique* of 1901. *Le Passe-Temps* reprinted the song with piano accompaniment in October 1900, July 1908, May 1928, and again in the special Lavallée issue in August 1933, and with the melody and words only in May 1916, April 1923, and July 1925.

5 *Welcome by the City of Quebec to Their Royal Highnesses the Duke and Duchess of Cornwall and York.*

6 The melody and words of "O Canada" appear on pp. 58–9 of *Chants des Patriotes: Recueil noté de Chansons Patriotiques Canadiennes et Françaises.* The British Library has a copy of the Laurendeau score. Charles Lavallée reissued the Laurendeau arrangement in 1907, and likely performed the solo in concert as he was a leading cornettist of the time.

7 L'Ami, "Chronique musicale," *La Patrie*, 9 January 1904.

8 "Music and the Drama," *Toronto Globe*, 11 February 1907.

9 In reporting on the joint concerts, the Rochester *Democrat and Chronicle* noted that "the French-Canadian hymn 'O Canada' (O Canada terre de nos aieux), which has for several years been authorized by the Dominion government as the Canadian National Anthem, has been in rehearsal for some time past for these concerts. The original words were by the Hon. Judge Routhier and the music by Calixa Lavallee, who lived in Moutreal some years ago." "Music and Musicians," Rochester *Democrat and Chronicle*, 20 January 1907.

10 Mercy E. Powell McCulloch won the competition.

11 Weir's words were first published in 1908 by the Montreal firm Delmar, with the music arranged for solo voice, quartet, or chorus by G.A. Grant-Schaeffer. By the time of Confederation's sixtieth anniversary, in 1927, Weir's text was firmly established as the standard English-language version of the anthem.

12 See *The Virtual Gramophone: Canadian Historical Sound Recordings.* www.collectionscanada.gc.ca/gramophone/index-e.html. (Accessed 7 September 2007)

13 Comte had married Lavallée's niece, Blanche Duquette, in 1900. He wrote for a number of newspapers and other periodicals at that time, including *Le Passe-Temps*, in which he published "Calixa Lavallée: notes biographiques." The same year, a short piece titled "L'Auteur de 'O Canada'" appeared in another Montreal period, *L'Étude musical*, 1, no. 2: 39.

14 See concert programs in the McGill University Archives, Fonds Montreal Orchestra, 1929–43.

15 Lapierre also had the clout and commitment to see it through. Although trained as an organist and journalist, he earned his livelihood primarily as an educator. Throughout much of his career, he was associated with the Conservatoire national de musique (CNM), an institution that functioned as an examining body from 1905 and became affiliated with l'Université de Montreal from 1921. The University appointed Lapierre secretary of the CNM in 1922 and sent him

to Paris to study European music education in 1924. On his return to Montreal in 1928, he became the director of the CNM, taught organ and chant accompaniment, and began to publish articles, mostly on aspects of music in Canada.

16 Ross discusses Desrochers's political ties and manoeuvrings in "Félix Desrochers: General Librarian 1933–1956."

17 See Beckwith, "Father of Romance."

18 The first prize was awarded in 1959 jointly to the vocalists Léopold Simoneau and Pierrette Alarie.

19 On 3 July 1963, CBC broadcast *The Great Song*, a docu-drama on Lavallée's life by Joseph Schull, with Lavallée's music prepared or arranged by Neil Chotem. The show was re-broadcast on 11 July 1967. On 8 July 1966, CBC Radio broadcast an event from the "Winnipeg Pops Concert series" that featured a performance of the *Bridal Rose* overture. And on 10 June 1967, CBC Television broadcast Tom Farley's "The Wandering Minstrel of Vercheres: Calixa Lavallée," which outlined Lavallée's career and achievements. For the CBC/RCA recording of excerpts from *The Widow*, Lavallée's music was arranged by Ovid Avarmaa, and performed by CBC Winnipeg Orchestra and Chorus, conducted by Eric Wild. Also in 1967, the same orchestra and conductor also released a two-disc album with works by a number of nineteenth-century Canadian composers, which included the *Bridal Rose*, overture, and excerpts from *The Widow*.

20 Lefebvre, "L'Histoire du Conservatoire national de musique: 1922–1950," 38. Lapierre dedicated *Calixa Lavallée: musicien national du Canada* to Montpetit.

21 Poirier, "Canadian Musical Style: Illusions and Reality," 249. See Thompson, "Calixa Lavallée," 10–14.

22 Lapierre writes, for example, that Lavallée left Montreal in 1857, two years earlier than had been correctly claimed by L.-O. David and others. He later extended this date back to 1856, when Lavallée would have been just thirteen or fourteen years old. Similarly, he frequently describes events in detail for which there is no record, and for which he could not possibly have proof, for example, the premiere of "O Canada": "Everyone stood, not out of politeness, but electrified by an unstoppable impulse. Never before had French Canadians felt such patriotic exultation flood through their veins. And this surge was given to them by a poor, small village musician through a despised art." Lapierre, *Calixa Lavallée* (1966), 175.

23 Anna Marie Duval-Thibault, letter to Eugène Lapierre, 5 October 1933. Duval-Thibault Papers, Houghton Library, Harvard University. Duval-Thibault writes that Lavallée changed the title of her poem "Violets Blue" to "Sweet Violets" so that it would not be confused with another song that was popular at that time.

24 By the early 1980s, the original headstone had begun to decay. See, Potvin, "L'épopée inachevée. Le monument à Calixa Lavallée."

25 The team capitulated by performing the anthem earlier in the afternoon, hours before the game began. See Jon Margolis, "There Just Isn't Any Such Thing as French Baseball," *Chicago Tribune*, 18 July 1994.

26 See Parks Canada news release, "Plaque unveiled in honor of Calixa Lavallée." Quebec City, 1 July 1995. www.pc.gc.ca/APPS/CP-NR/release_e.asp?id=331& andor1=nr. (Accessed 17 May 2010)

27 See "Tout peut changer!," Comité national des jeunes du Parti Québécois, 9 June 2009. www.cnjpq.org/node?page=53&ist=12. (Accessed 10 November 2010)

28 See Poy, "O Canada! Must Command All of Us"; "Why Margaret Atwood Wants to Change the Lyrics of O Canada," Globe and Mail, 1 October 2013.

29 Charles Labelle, "M. Calixa Lavallée à Londre."

30 "Lavallée," L'Indépendant, 29 January 1891.

31 Lavallée, "l'E Muet," 36.

32 "Calixa Lavallée," Freund's Music and Drama, 13, no. 9 (December 1889): 24.

33 "Calixa Lavallée: Career of an Eminent Musician," Freund's Music and Drama, 15, no. 14 (31 January 1891): 1. In a lengthy excerpt of this article, translated into French, Lapierre omitted the sentence referring to Lavallée's support for annexation. See Lapierre, Calixa Lavallée (1966), 236–8.

34 "Calixa Lavallée," Musical Courier, XXII, no. 4 (28 January 1891): 76. Another obituary reported Lavallée's "constant advocacy of annexation of Canada among his fellow countrymen." See "Recent Deaths – Calixa Lavallée," Boston Transcript, 23 January 1891.

35 In 1891, the Reverend Edouard Hamon published Les Canadiens-Français de la Nouvelle-Angleterre, a briefly influential book in which he advocated annexation of Canada, arguing that the French-Canadian population of New England was large enough and sufficiently isolated to prevent assimilation. See LeBlanc, "The Francophone 'Conquest' of New England." Five years later, the writer Edmond de Nevers proposed a plan similar to that of Hamon. André Sénécal discusses Nevers's book, L'Avenir du peuple canadien-français in "La Thèse messianique et les franco-Américains." See also, Lamonde, Histoire sociale des idées au Québec (1896–1929): 260. For a brief historical survey of attitudes toward annexation, see "Annexation Movement," Canadian Encyclopedia, 1985 ed.

36 "Musical Matters," Boston Herald, 20 April 1890.

37 "Personal Mention," Brooklyn Daily Eagle, 8 July 1887.

38 Onésime Thibault, letter to Eugène Lapierre, 1 October 1933, Anna Marie Duval-Thibault Literary Papers, Houghton Library, Harvard University.

39 Lavallée appears to have been directing his comments at both the politicians who were unwilling to support the arts and the Catholic Church, which shared power with the government and played a large role in the day-to-day lives of the people. Calixa Lavallée, "L'Art musical au Canada," 70.

40 Calixa Lavallée, "Musical: The Fiftieth Performance of Pounce & Company."

41 Calixa Lavallée, "Musical: William H. Sherwood."

42 Bohlman, Music, Nationalism and the Making of the New Europe, 5.

43 Lapierre, Calixa Lavallée (1966), 239.

APPENDIX ONE

1  Kallmann's collection served as the basis for his *Catalogue of Canadian Composers* (Toronto: Canadian Broadcasting Corporation, 1962).

2  The term 'edition' is not easily defined. Publishers often reproduced their competitors' scores, complying with copyright laws by making such basic editorial changes as a few variations in the fingering.

3  The *New York Clipper* reported the English-language title while David referred to the French-language title. Both reported the librettist to be Arnold de Thiers. See L.-O. David, "Galerie National: Calixa Lavallée," *L'Opinion publique*, 13 March 1873: 131, and "City Summary," *New York Clipper*, 10 October 1870: 206.

4  See "Lavallée," *L'Opinion publique*, 20 March 1873: 141.

5  See "City Summary," *New York Clipper*, 10 October 1870: 206.

6  Boston's Bijou Theatre announced plans to produce the work during the 1883–84 season but did not stage it. See "Lavallée's New Opera," *Musical Courier*, VII, no. 6 (8 August 1883): 88.

7  "Galerie national: Calixa Lavallée," *La Presse*, 9 November 1912.

8  *The Folio*, XXIX, no. 5 (May 1886): 238.

9  *Musical Courier*, XVI, no. 4 (25 January 1888): 50.

10  "Paris, le 12 Août, 1874" appears at the top of the manuscript in the BANQ.

11  See Labelle, "Calixa Lavallée."

12  See Jeffrey Robert Anderson, "Calixa Lavallée and His Meditation for Trumpet and Piano," 30.

13  Weir's words are sung in this recording that was made on 24 May 1913 but not released until five or six years later.

14  Newspapers did not report the title of the work. Lapierre referred to it as the "Cantate" and provided the text of the refrain ("Loin du pays, mais pour sa gloire / Aimable ami, chante toujours / et pour assurer ta victoire / Nous te jurons constant secours"). These lines are taken from Martineau's poem "L'Exilé: chant canadien." See Lapierre, *Calixa Lavallée* (1966), 115–16, and Flavien Martineau, *Une voix d'outre-tombe: poesies de M. Martineau, P.S.S* (Montreal: J. Lovell, 1888), 203.

15  See "Biographies of American Musicians, no. 90, Calixa Lavallée," *Brainard's Musical Journal*, XXII (May 1885): 167.

16  "From Mr G.H. Wilson's Year Book for 1887–8," *Musical Courier*, XVII, no. 1 (4 July 1888): 16.

17  Marie Ann Laithe was an amateur or semi-professional contralto in Troy, New York.

18  Marlene Wehrle of Library and Archives Canada, email to the author, 17 March 1998.

19  Advertisements for Lavallée's concert of 26 January 1865 mentioned the recent publication of *L'Oiseau mouche* by Laurent-Laforce. *La Minerve*, 26 January 1865. Boucher acquired all or much of the Laurent, Laforce catalogue in 1865.

20 Guillaume Couture, "Concert d'Adieu," *La Minerve*, 6 June 1876.

21 The title on the White, Smith & Company edition is misspelled as "Movement [*sic*] à la Pavane."

22 A note in the *New York Clipper* reported that the song had been recently composed by Lavallée and Bidaux, and that it was to be performed by Bidaux in the forthcoming tour of Duprez and Green's Minstrels. See "Negro Minstrelsy," *New York Clipper*, 19 September 1863, 182.

23 See "Canada," *Le Nouveau monde*, 18 September 1868.

24 In its review of the 16 January 1877 performance, *La Minerve* cited "E.B. St Aubin" as the author of the work. Emmanuel-Marie de Saint-Albans was a translator at Parliament, and an amateur songwriter. *La Minerve*, 17 January 1877.

25 Only the melodic line and text were published in *Le Passe-Temps* in 1909, and again in 1911.

26 The text was published in E.Z. Mazzicotte, "Raquette – Clubs – Costumes – Chanson – Carnival," *Recherches historique* 28 (1922): 200.

27 Anna Marie Duval-Thibault, letter to Eugène Lapierre, 5 October 1933.

28 "St Patrick's Day," *Repository* (Canton, OH), 16 March 1889.

29 Lapierre, *Calixa Lavallée* (1966), 227.

30 "Obituaries: Calixa Lavallée," *Werner's Voice Magazine*, XIII, no. 3 (March 1891): 84. "Was a Gifted Musician," *Boston Globe*, 22 January 1891.

31 Gustave Comte, "Calixa Lavallée – notes biographiques inédites sur le chantre de la nation," *Le Passe-Temps*, 15, no. 374 (24 July 1909): 315.

32 Arthur Letondal, "Les précurseurs: Calixa Lavallée," *L'Action Française*, III, 10 (October 1919): 442.

# Bibliography

This bibliography is divided into two parts: archival and published resources. Archival resources have been important in researching many aspects of this book. Census data; birth, wedding and baptismal records; and other genealogical sources have been helpful in tracing the Lavallée family and many other individuals. Many archives or historical societies have files on Lavallée containing photocopies of published articles, but only a few have archival materials. There is no single cache of material, but there are scattered remains. These include several letters, a family photograph album, and a deteriorating manuscript of an overture for orchestra.*

Published materials have been the main source of information on Lavallée's activities. Under periodicals, there are listings of city directories, newspapers, and music journals that have been searched, mostly in hard copy. Given the dynamic nature of databases, and Internet-based resources generally, compiling truly complete listings is no longer possible. This is followed by a general listing of books and articles. Digital sources have now made it possible to do much of the research I did at microfilm readers in a fraction of the time, but not everything has been digitized, and many have been done too poorly for the researcher to rely on character recognition. Moreover, much is gained from careful perusal of the daily news of the era we are examining. It is the newspapers and music periodicals that have been the main sources of information of Lavallée's life. I read many of them in McLennan Library at McGill University, at the New York Public Library, and at the Boston Public Library. Many more came to me in the form of inter-library loans. Only long after I began work on this project did newspapers begin to become accessible and searchable in digital form.

### ARCHIVAL SOURCES

Archives de la Ville de Québec. Quebec City.
  Fonds de la Ville de Québec.

---

* In 1933, *La Patrie* reported that Lavallée had left the album with the Quebec City organist Adolphe Hamel, his replacement at St Patrick's Church, and it later became the property of a Chouinard family. See "Souvenir de Calixa Lavallée à Québec," *La Patrie*, 15 July 1933.

Série Conseil, sous-série Conseil et comités; QP1-4/167-9, Dossier "Lavallée, Calixa," Archives de la Ville de Québec.

Archives für Kunst. Berlin.

Mus. ep. G. Gerster, Varia 1.

Eigenhändig gershriebener Lebenslauf, Berlin, 25 März 1899. 19 Blatts (38 beschr.S).

Archives nationales. Paris.

Conservatoire national supérieur de musique et de danse de Paris (AJ37).

Registres d'inscription des élèves admis au Conservatoire.

Archives of the Grand Séminaire de Montréal.

Registre du Grand Séminaire de Montréal. Tome I, 1840–1900.

Bibliothèque et archives Nationale du Québec. Centre Montréal. Département des manuscrits.

Fonds Wilfrid-Pelletier (MSS-020).

Collection of articles concerning Lavallée, sent to Pelletier by Paul-Émile Gosselin.

Fonds Calixa-Lavallée (MSS-150).

Lavallée, Calixa. Letter to unknown recipient. 30 July 1889.

Fonds Joseph-Jean Goulet (MSS-457).·

*Patrie, ouverture*, MSS. Calixa Lavallée.

Bibliothèque et Archives nationales du Québec. Centre régional de Québec.

Fonds Academie de musique du Québec.

Academie de musique du Québec: Minute Book, 1868–80.

Fonds du Secrétariat provincial, M88/5, registre des lettres reçues, 1878, 971.

Lavallée, Calixa et al. "Pétition adressée au lieutenant-gouverneur de la province de Québec pour l'établissement d'un conservatoire de musique et de déclamation." Quebec City, 15 June 1878.

Archives de L'Église Saint-Patrick de Québec.

Contract between Calixa Lavallée and Reverend Joseph Hennings, 30 April 1879 (ASPQ Ec232).

P1000,S3,D1091 Lettre à G.-A. Lafrance de Calixa Lavallée, 20 mars 1879.

Bibliothèque et Archives nationales du Québec. Centre de conservation – Programmes de spectacle.

PRO M 11.41. *Grand concert opératique et populaire, vocal et instrumental au profit de L'éminent artiste canadien M. Calixa Lavallée, Calixa Lavallée: Grande salle de L'Hotel de ville, Montréal, 8 octobre 1874.*

[Quebec (Province)?: s.n.], 1874.

http://collections.banq.qc.ca/ark:/52327/1940941.

Basilique cathédrale Notre-Dame. Ottawa, Ontario.

Notre-Dame Archives, in file Basilique cathédrale Notre-Dame, Doc. Part (Chorale) 1868–1943: I. 4T. 1.

Letter from Gustave Smith to Bishop Guigues, 12 February 1868, New Orleans.

Brown University, Providence, Rhode Island.

John Hay Library, Special Collections.

"Attention Volunteers." Advertising poster, Fourth Rhode Island Regiment.

Providence, RI: Cooke & Danielson, ca. 1861.
Canada. Census records: 1851–1901.
Accessed via Ancestry.com.
Canadian Broadcasting Corporation, Music Library. Toronto, Ontario.
Lavallée file.
Carter, C.L. (Vice President, Sales and Production, Carl Fischer, Inc.). Letter to Helmut Kallmann. 22 December 1962.
Kallmann, Helmut. Letter to Eugène Lapierre. 14 October 1966.
City of Boston, Massachusetts.
Archives and Records Management Division.
Property records: 11 and 29 Worthington Street, 4 Brookford Steet.
City of Boston, Massachusetts. Registry Division.
Death certificates: Jules Lavallée, Calixa Lavallée (son of Joseph Lavallée), Calixa Lavallée.
Birth certificates: Jules Lavallée, Calixa Lavallée (son of Joseph Lavallée).
Collège de Lévis. Lévis, Quebec.
Archives.
Student records of Calixa Lavallée Jr (1879–83).
Conservatoire Royal de Bruxelles. Bibliotheque. Brussels, Belgium.
Liste des Élèves.
Division des archives de l'Université Laval. Quebec City.
Fonds Maurice Brodeur (P209).
Lavallée, Calixa. [Letter to unknown recipient.] 26 March 1879. (AUL, P209-1/25/10/89).
Lavallée, Calixa. Letter to Joseph Marmette. 22 October 1880. (AUL, P209-1/25/10/90).
Fonds Calixa-Lavallée (P354)
Photograph album.
Dubinsky, Ira. Institut canadien Archives. http://collections.ic.gc.ca/icma/fr/index.html (Accessed 10 April 2006).*
Harvard University, Houghton Library. Cambridge, Massachusetts.
Anna Marie Duval-Thibault Literary Papers.
Duval-Thibault, Anna. Letter to Eugène Lapierre. 5 October 1933.
Thibault, Onésime. Letter to Eugène Lapierre. 1 October 1933.
[Mademoiselle] Vertefeuille. Letter to Eugène Lapierre. 1 November 1933.
Notebooks and clipping book.
Theater Collection.
Playbills from New Orleans Minstrels, San Francisco Minstrels, and others.
Library and Archives Canada. Music Division. Ottawa.
Fonds Louis-J.-N. Blanchet MUS 138.
Photographic collection.
Fonds Calixa Lavallée MUS 20 (R14459-0-4-E).
Lavallée, Calixa. Letter to unknown recipient. 30 July 1889.

* The website was taken down at some point after 2006. See Lamonde, Review of Dubinsky, Ira.

Library of Congress, Music Division. Washington, DC.
   Edward and Marian MacDowell Collection, 1861–1960 (ML31.M198).
       Lavallée, Calixa. Letter to Edward MacDowell. 11 December 1889.
Massachusetts Archives, Boston, Massachusetts.
   Vital records (1841–1910).
McCord Museum. Montreal, Quebec.
   Notman Photographic Archives.
McGill University Archives. Montreal, Quebec.
   Fonds Montreal Orchestra, 1929–43. Concert programs.
McGill University Libraries. Montreal, Quebec.
   McLennan Library. Special Collections.
      Theatre programs.
Missouri Historical Society Archives. St Louis.
   Pickwick Theatre Scrapbook.
Music Teachers' National Association. Archives. Cincinnati, Ohio.
   Collection of clippings related to Lavallée.
National Archives at College Park, Maryland. Military records.
   Lavallée, Calixa, military records.
Notre Dame Archives. University of Notre Dame Archives. Notre Dame, Indiana.
   Archdiocese of New Orleans (LA) Collection.
       Letter from Smith, C[harles Gustave] to Archbishop John Mary Odin, C.M.
       of New Orleans. 10 February 1865.
       Letter from Father Dowd of St Patrick's Church in Montreal to Archbishop
       John Mary Odin, C.M. of New Orleans. 31 January 1865.
Quebec Vital and Church Records (Drouin Collection), 1621–1967. (Accessed via
Ancestry.com).
Rhode Island Historical Society. Manuscripts Division. Providence, Rhode Island.
   American Brass Band Records. www.rihs.org/mssinv/Mss256.htm#inventory.
Rhode Island State Archives. Providence, Rhode Island.
   Descriptive Book of the Fourth Rhode Island Volunteers.
       Lavallée, Calixa. Military record.
St Anne's Episcopal Church. Lowell, Massachusetts.
   Lavallée, Calixa, and Josephine Gentilly, marriage record.
Séminaire de Saint-Hyacinthe, Centre d'Archives. Saint-Hyacinthe, Quebec.
   Collection of newspapers clippings about Lavallée.
United States of America. Census records: 1850–1940.
   Including Census of Maryland, 1860.
   Accessed via Ancestry.com.
University of Wisconsin-Madison, The Tams-Witmark Collection.
   Box 20A contains two copies of *The Widow* vocal score belonging to Zelda
   Seguin. Copy 1 is dedicated to her by Lavallée and contains handwritten per-
   formance instructions.

PRINTED PRIMARY AND SECONDARY SOURCES

## City Directories

*The Boston Directory*. Boston: Sampson, Murdock, and Company, 1872–73, 1880–92.

*Boyd's Pictorial Directory of Broadway*. New York: William H. Boyd, 1859.

*Boyd's Rochester Directory*. New York: William H. Boyd, 1866–67.

*Cherrier's Directory of Quebec [City] and Lévis / Almanach des adresses Cherrier de la ville de Quebec*. Quebec City: Cherrier, 1877–81.

*Fall River Directory*. Fall River, MA: Robert Adams, Benjamin Earl & Son, 1882–87.

*Geer's Hartford City Directory*. Hartford, CT: Elihu Geer, 1879–81.

*Lawrence Directory*. Lawrence, MA: W.E. Rice, 1883.

*Lowell City Directory*. Lowell, MA: Joshua Merrill and B.C. Sargeant, 1861–64, 1866–68, 1870.

*Montreal Directory*. Montreal: Lovell and Gibson, and Robert W.S. Mackay, 1842–68; 1875–79, 1891–97.

*New Orleans Directory*. New Orleans: n.p., 1859–60, 1866–67.

*Trow Business Directory of the Buroughs of Manhattan and the Bronx, City of New York*. New York: John F. Trow, 1858–60.

*Trow's New York City Directory*. New York: John F. Trow, 1866–73.

## Newspapers

Albany, NY: *Evening Journal* (1860); Baltimore, MD: *Sun* (1861–65, 1869, 1879, 1881–83); Belleville, ON: *Daily Intelligencer* (1867); Berthier, QC: *La Gazette* (1880); Boston, MA: *Evening Transcript* (1859, 1869, 1871–73, 1881, 1885–86), *Evening Traveller* (1885–91), *Evening Standard* (1886), *Globe* (1872–73, 1881–91), *Herald* (1886–91), *Home Journal* (1880–91), *Evening Journal* (1872, 1881–85); Buffalo, NY: *Daily Courier* (1859, 1871–72); Charleston, SC: *Daily Courier* (1861); Chicago, IL: *Morning Herald* (1881–82), *Tribune* (1882, 1888); Cincinnati, OH: *Daily Times* (1860, 1871), *Inquirer* (1860, 1871); Cleveland, OH: *Leader* (1859, 1863, 1866, 1869, 1871, 1882), *Voice* (1882); Detroit, MI: *Evening News* (1868), *Free Press* (1866, 1868–69, 1890); Fall River, MA: *Daily News* (1885), *L'Écho du Canada* (1873–74), *L'Indépendant* (1885–91); Halifax, NS: *The Evening Express* (1859); Hamilton, ON: *Daily Spectator* (1866); Hartford, CT: *Courant* (1863, 1866, 1871, 1880); Kingston, ON: *Daily News* (1863); Lawrence, MA: *Courier* (1857, 1859), *Sentinel* (1860, 1867, 1868, 1872); London, England: *Times* (1879, 1888); Lowell, MA: *L'Étoile* (1888–91), *Daily Citizen and News* (1867), *Daily Courier* (1880–90), *Weekly Journal* (1867–68); Milwaukee, WI: *Sentinel* (1863, 1867–68, 1882); Minneapolis and St Paul, MI: *Pioneer Press* (1869, 1882); Montreal, QC: *L'Avenir* (1852, 1855–58), *Le Canada* (1879–80), *The Canadian Spectator* (1879–80), *Le Canadien* (1878–80), *Le Courrier* (1879–80), *Daily Transcript and Commercial Advertiser* (1836–65), *Daily Witness* (1878–80), *Le Devoir* (1933, 1942), *The Evening Post* (1879–80), *Gazette* (1855, 1857–1859, 1864–1865, 1873, 1875–

78, 1933), *Herald* (1863–69, 1873), *La Minerve* (1855–60, 1863–69, 1873–78), *Le National* (1875–77), *Le Nouveau Monde* (1868), *L'Ordre* (1864–65), *La Patrie* (1854–58), *La Patrie* (Beaugrand, 1879–91), *Le Pays* (1858–59, 1864–65), *The Pilot* (1859–60), *La Presse* (Blumhart, 1888, 1891, 1903, 1933), *La Presse* (Lanctôt, 1863–64), *La Revue* (1877–80), *Star* (1869, 1873, 1875–78), *True Witness and Catholic Chronicle* (1879–80), *L'Union nationale* (1864–65); New London, CT: *Daily Republican* (1863); New Orleans, LA: *The Bee/L'Abée* (1857–68), *The Courier* (1860), *Delta* (1857–63), *Times-Picayune* (1857–67); New York, NY: *Herald* (1859, 1869–72, 1880–82, 1885), *Times* (1871–72, 1882, 1885); Ottawa, ON: *Citizen* (1875, 1879), *Free Press* (1875), *Gazette* (1879); Philadelphia, PA: *Evening Bulletin* (1881), *Inquirer* (1863, 1869), *Press* (1861), *Sunday Item* (1881), *Sunday Mercury* (1863, 1869); Pittsburgh, PA: *Daily Gazette* (1860, 1866, 1868); *Post* (1860, 1866, 1868); Portland, MA: *Daily Advertiser* (1862–66), *Daily Press* (1872–73); Providence, RI: *Daily Journal* (1859, 1861, 1872, 1886); Quebec City, QC: *Le Courrier du Canada* (1873), *Daily Mercury* (1873), *Daily Telegraph* (1878–79), *L'Événement* (1878–80), *Le Journal de Québec* (1878–80), *Morning Chronicle* (1873); Rio de Janeiro, Brazil: *Diario* (1876–78), *O Figaro* (1876–78); Rochester, NY: *Union Advertiser* (1859–61, 1863, 1872); Saint-Hyacinthe, QC: *Le Courrier* (1853–67, 1879, 1880, 1891); St Louis, MI: *Spectator* (1882), *Times-Democrat* (1871); San Francisco, CA: *Chronicle* (1870–71), *Evening Bulletin* (1869–73); Sorel, QC: *La Gazette* (1867); Springfield, MA: *Daily Republican* (1862, 1863, 1866); Titusville, PA: *Morning Herald* (1871); Toronto, ON: *Daily Telegraph* (1866, 1867), *Globe* (1868, 1891, 1901, 1907); Washington, DC: *Evening Star* (1861, 1882), *Post* (1881–82, 1887); Worchester, MA: *Daily Spy* (1859, 1882).

## Music Journals

*L'Album musical* (Montreal, 1881–84), *Les Beaux-arts* (Montreal, 1863–64), *Boston Musical Times / Musical Times of Boston and New York* (1854, 1860–66, 1869), *Boston Musical Yearbook / Musical Yearbook of the United States* (1883–91), *Boucher and Pratt's Musical Journal* (Montreal, 1881–82), *Brainard's Musical World / Western Musical World* (Cleveland, 1881–88), *Le Canada artistique* (Montreal, 1890), *Le Canada musical* (Montreal, 1866–67, 1875–81), *Dexter Smith's Musical, Literary, Dramatic and Art Paper* (Boston, 1872–78), *L'Echo musical* (Montreal, 1888), *The Etude* (New York, 1883–91), *L'Étude musicale* (Montreal, 1889), *The Folio, A Journal of Music, Art and Literature* (Boston, 1869–72, 1880–91), *Le Ménestrel* (Paris, 1833–1940), *Metronome, A Monthly Review of Music* (Boston, 1871–74), *Musical Bulletin: A Monthly Journal of Musical Events* (Troy, New York and New York City, 1867–73), *Musical Bulletin* (Chicago, 1879–83), *Musical Courier* (New York, 1880–91), *Musical Herald / Boston Musical Herald* (1880–91), *Musical Record* (New York, 1878–91), *Musical Times* (London, England, 1888), *Music Trade Review* (New York, 1875–79), *New York Musical Gazette* (1866–73), *New York Musical Pioneer and Chorister's Budget* (1855; 1861), *Orpheus* (New York and Boston, 1865–80), *Proceedings of the Music Teachers' National Association* (Pittsburgh, 1876–93), *Werner's Voice Magazine / The Voice* (New York, 1879–91).

## Other Serials

*Annuaire de Ville Marie: Origine, Utilité et Progrès des Institutions Catholique de Montréal: Première Année, 1863* (Montreal: Eusèbe Sénécal, 1864); *Canadian Illustrated News* (Montreal, 1875–80); *L'Écho du Cabinet de lecture paroissial* (Montreal, 1859–75); *Fall River Line Journal* (New York and Boston: Fall River Line, 1870–83); *Le Foyer canadien* (Quebec City, 1863–66); *Le Foyer domestique* (Ottawa, 1876–79); *Journals of the Legislative Assembly of the Province of Quebec* (1877–78); *Journals of the Legislative Council of the Province of Quebec* (1878); *Massachusetts Vital Statistics: Index to Births* (Boston: Registry of Vital Records and Statistics, 1867–90); *New England Magazine* (Boston, 1888–91); *New York Clipper* (1859–73, 1881, 1884–85); *L'Opinion publique* (Montreal, 1873–80); *Révue-Canada* (Montreal, 1891); *Sessional Papers, v. 13. Statement of the Public Accounts of the Province of Quebec for the Fiscal Year Ending 30 June 1879* (Quebec City: Printed by Order of the Legislature, 1880); *Wilke's Spirit of the Times* (New York, 1866–72).

## Books and Articles

Abel, Allen. "O Canada Composer Fought for Union." *Winnipeg Free Press*, 15 September 2012. www.winnipegfreepress.com/opinion/westview/o-canada-composer-fought-for-union-side-169880236.html. (Accessed 18 September 2012)

*L'Académie de musique: notes historiques depuis sa fondation.* Quebec City: n.p., 1909.

Achintre, Auguste and J.B. Labelle. *Cantate, La Confédération.* N.p.: n.p., 1868.

Ackerman, Kenneth D. *The Gold Ring: Jim Fisk, Jay Gould and Black Friday, 1869.* New York: Dodd, Mead, ca. 1988.

Adam, Adolphe. "La Dame Blanche." *Le Canada musical*, 2, no. 5 (September 1875): 73–6.

– *Derniers souvenirs d'un musicien.* Paris: Michel Lévy Frères, 1871.

Adams, Charles. *When in the Course of Human Events: Arguing the Cause of Southern Secession.* Lanham, MD: Rowman & Littlefield, 2000.

Adjutant General. *Descriptive Book of the Fourth Rhode Island Regiment Band.* Providence, RI: Fourth Rhode Island Regiment, n.d.

– *Annual Report of the Adjutant General of the State of Rhode Island and Providence Plantations, for the Year 1865.* Providence, RI: E.L. Freeman & Son, 1893.

Aeolian Company, New York. "Music for Pianola and Pianola Piano." Advertisement. *Bulletin of New Music for the Pianola-Piano, Orchestrelle and Aeolian Grand* (February 1912): 6.

Albani, Emma. *Forty Years of Song.* London: Mills & Boon, 1911.

Allen, Geo. H. [George H.] *Forty-Six Months with the Fourth Rhode Island Volunteers in the War of 1861–1865.* Providence: J.A. & R.A. Reid, 1887.

Anderson, Jeffrey Robert. "Calixa Lavallée and His *Méditation* for Trumpet and Piano." DMA thesis, University of Colorado, 1989.

Anderton, Douglas L., Richard E. Barrett, and Donald J. Bogue. *Population of the United States.* 3rd ed. New York: The Free Press, 1997.

Anger, J. Humfrey. *"O Canada": A Patriotic Song: Written to the Melody Composed by Calixta Lavallèe* [sic]. Toronto: n.p., 1908.

*The Annual Volunteer and Service Militia List.* Ottawa: Printed by G.B. Desbarats, 1867.

Argyll, John Douglas, Sutherland Campbell, Duke of. *Memories of Canada and Scotland.* Montreal: Dawson, 1884.

- *Passages from the Past.* London: Hutchinson & Company, 1907.

Atherton, Tony. "'O Canada.'" *Ottawa Citizen*, 1 July 2005, 43 (Special Canada Day wraparound).

Auclair, Élie-J. *Un Éducateur d'il y a Cents Ans, M. Le Curé Charles-Joseph Ducharme, Fondateur du Séminaire de Saint-Thérèse.* Montreal: Arbour et Dupont, 1920.

Audet, Alphonse. "Instruction musicale." *L'Union nationale*, 3 October 1864: 2.

Ayers, Christine Merrick. *Contributions to the Art of Music in America by the Music Industries of Boston 1640 to 1936.* New York: H.W. Wilson, 1937.

Baillairgé, Charles. *Vingt ans après: le Club des 21 en 1879: court biographie de chacun des ses membres.* Quebec City: n.p., ca. 1899.

*Baltzell's Dictionary of Musicians.* Boston: Oliver Ditson, 1911.

Barbier, Jules and Charles Gounod. *Jeanne d'Arc, drame en cinq actes.* Paris: Choudens, 1873.

- *Jeanne d'Arc, opéra lyrique en cinq actes.* Libretto [Montreal]: n.p., 1877.

Barden, Nelson. "Aeolian, Skinner, A History of the Aeolian Company – Music for Musicians." *American Organist*, 24, no. 5 (May, 1990): 254–60.

Baron, John H. *Piano Music from New Orleans, 1851–1898.* New York: Da Capo, 1980.

- "Vieuxtemps (and Ole Bull) in New Orleans." *American Music*, 8, no. 2 (Summer, 1990): 210–26.

Barrière, Mireille. *Calixa Lavallée.* Montreal: Lidec, 1999.

- "Le goupillon, le maillet et la censure du théâtre lyrique à Montréal (1840–1914)." *Les Cahiers des dix*, Numéro 54 (2000), 119–35.

- "Libre opinion – *L'Ô Canada* ne mérite pas son sort." *Le Devoir*, 21 June 2013.

- *L'Opéra français de Montréal: L'etonnante histoire d'un succès ephémere: 1893–1896.* Montreal: Fides, 2002.

- "La Société Canadienne-française et le théâtre lyrique à Montréal entre 1840 et 1913." PhD diss., Université Laval, 1990.

Bazin, François. *Cours d'harmonie théorique et pratique.* 2nd ed. Paris: L. Escudier, 1857.

Bean, Annemarie, James V. Hatch, and Brooks McNamara. *Inside the Minstrel Mask: Readings in Nineteenth-Century Blackface Minstrelsy.* Hanover and London: Wesleyan University Press, 1996.

Beckwith, John. "Father of Romance, Vagabond of Glory: Two Canadian Composers as Stage Heroes." In Robin Elliott and Gordon E. Smith, eds., *Music Traditions, Cultures, and Contexts*, 231–62. Waterloo, ON: Wilfrid Laurier University Press, 2010.

- "Introduction." In Joseph Quesnel, *Lucas et Cécile, comédie mêlée d'ariettes*, ix–xi. Saint-Nicolas, PQ: Doberman-Yppan, 1992.

474

- "Letter from Canada." *Sonneck Society Bulletin*, XVI, no. 2 (1990): 71–2.
Bellaigue, Camille. *L'Année musicale et dramatique, Octobre 1886 – Octobre 1887*. Paris: Delagrave, 1888.
- *Souvenirs de musique et de musiciens*. Paris: Nouvelle Librarie Nationale, 1921.
Benson, Eugene, and L.W. Conolly, eds. *The Oxford Companion to Canadian Theatre*. Toronto: Oxford University Press, 1989.
Beraud, Jean. *350 ans de theatre au Canada français*. Ottawa: Cercle du Livre de France, 1958.
Bergeron, Katherine. *Voice Lessons: French Mélodie in the Belle Epoque*. Oxford: Oxford University Press, 2009.
Bernard, Jean-Paul. *The Rebellions of 1837 and 1838 in Lower Canada*. Translated by Carole Dolan. Ottawa: Canadian Historical Association, 1996.
- *Les Rouges, libéralisme, nationalisme et anticléricalisme au milieu du XIXe siècle*. Montreal: Les Presses de l'Université du Québec, 1971.
Bernard, Kenneth A. *Lincoln and the Music of the Civil War*. Caldwell, ID: Claxton Printers, 1966.
*Billy Morris' Songs as Sung at Morris Bros. Pell and Trowbridge's Opera House*. Boston: G.D. Russell and Company, 1864.
*Bio-Bibliographical Index of Musicians in the United States of America from Colonial Times*. Washington, DC: n.p., 1941.
Blackett, R.J.M. *Divided Hearts: Britain and the American Civil War*. Baton Rouge: Louisiana State University Press, 2001.
Blanchet, L.-J.-N. *Une vie illustrée de Calixa Lavallée*. Montreal: Publications Provinciales, 1951.
Boatner, Mark Mayo. *Civil War Dictionary*. New York: David Makay, 1987.
*Bobby Newcomb's San Francisco Minstrel Songster*. New York: R.M. De Witt [1868].
Body, Albin. *Le Théâtre et la musique à Spa*. Brussels: n.p., 1885.
Bohlman, Philip V. *Music, Nationalism and the Making of the New Europe*. New York and London: Routledge, 2011.
Bolduc, Anicette. "Catalogue collectif des archives musicales au Quebec." *Les Cahiers de L'ARMuQ*, 9 (May 1988).
Bomberger, E. Douglas. *Brainard's Biographies of American Musicians*. Westport, CT: Greenwood Press, 1999.
- *Macdowell*. New York: Oxford University Press, 2013.
- *"A Tidal Wave of Encouragement": American Composers' Concerts in the Gilded Age*. Westport, CT: Praeger, 2002.
Bonefant, Jean Charles. *The French Canadians and the Birth of Confederation*. Ottawa: The Canadian Historical Association, 1996. Bossange, Gustave. *Bossange's Catalogue of Periodicals: Abridged List of the Principal French Papers and Serials with Prices of Subscription for Paris and the United States 1869*. Paris: Gustave Bossange, 1869.
- *Il Canada e L'emigrazione*. Paris: Symonds, 1872.
- *La Nouvelle France, le Canada: appel aux classes nécessiteuses de France*. Paris: G. Bossange, 1872.
- *La Nuova Francia: antica colonia francese: appello alle classi operaie*. Paris: G. Bossange, 1873.

Boston City Council. *Proceedings of the Dedication of the Fountain on Eaton Square.* Boston: The Council, 1885.

*The Boston Manual: Containing Diagrams of Theatres, Complete Street Directory, Hack and Herdic [sic] Fares, Fire Alarm, Lists of Churches and Pastors, Hotels, Banks, Public Buildings, Express Offices, etc. and Other Valuable Information.* Boston: The Manual Company: New England News Company, Agents, 1886.

Bouchard, Gérard. "Le Québec comme collectivité neuve. Le refus de l'américainité dans le discours de la survivance." In Gérard Bouchard and Yvan Lamonde, eds., *Québécois et Américaine. La culture québécoise aux XIXe et XXe siècles,* 15–60. Montreal: Fides, 1995.

Bouchard, Gérard and Yvan Lamonde, eds. *Québécois et Américaine. La culture québécoise aux XIXe et XXe siècles.* Montreal: Fides, 1995.

Bourbonnière, Jules. "Notre musicien national: Calixa Lavallée." *Le Passe-Temps,* Numéro-Souvenir: Calixa Lavallée. 39, no. 864 (August 1933): 20.

[Bourget, Ignace.] *Reglement concernant le chant et la musique dans les églises.* Montreal: L. Perrault, n.d.

Bradley, Ian. *A Selected Bibliography of Musical Canadiana.* Victoria, BC: University of Victoria, 1976.

Brassard, Michèle and Jean Hamelin. "Aristide Filiatreault." *Dictionary of Canadian Biography.* Vol. 14. University of Toronto/Université Laval, 1998. www.biogra phi.ca/en/bio/filiatreault_aristide_14E.html. (Accessed 2 August 2014)

Breton, Raymond. "From Ethnic to Civic Nationalism. English Canada and Quebec." *Ethnic and Racial Studies,* 11, no. 1 (1988): 85–102.

Bridges, Glenn D. "Pioneer Cornetists: Matthew Arbuckle." *The School Musician* (November 1955): 20.

Brinkerhoff, Clara. "Art or Trade?" *American Musician,* reprinted in *Werner's Voice Magazine,* IX, no. 9 (September 1887): 138–9.

Brody, Elaine. *Paris: the Musical Kaleidoscope, 1870–1925.* New York: G. Braziller, 1987.

Brown, T. Allston. *A History of the New York Stage: From the First Performance in 1732 to 1901.* New York: Dodd, Mead and Company, 1903.

Broyles, Michael. *Music of the Highest Class: Elitism and Populism in Antebellum Boston.* New Haven, Yale University Press, 1992.

Buchan, P.H. "'O Canada,' The Story of the Buchan Version." Vancouver, BC: City Archives, 1947.

Buies, Arthur. *Chroniques: Humeurs et caprices.* Quebec City: Electeur, 1873.

– *Petites chroniques pour 1877.* Quebec City: C. Darveau, 1878.

C, L.-S. "Le Premier Stenographe Canadien-Français." *Bulletin des recherches historiques,* 29 (December, 1923): 358–60.

Calderisi, Maria. "Case Study: Illustrated Sheet Music before Confederation." In Yvan Lamonde, Patricia Lockhart Fleming, and Fiona A. Black, eds., *History of the Book in Canada, Volume II, 1840–1918,* 438–9. Toronto: University of Toronto Press, 2005.

– *Music Publishing in the Canadas, 1800–1867 / L'Edition musicale au Canada, 1800–1867.* Ottawa: National Library of Canada, 1981.

*Calixa Lavallée: répertoire d'architecture traditionelle.* Quebec City: Ministère des affaires culturelle, [ca. 1977].

Cameron, Ardis. *Radicals of the Worst Sort: Laboring Women in Lawrence, Massachusetts, 1860–1912.* Urbana: University of Illinois Press, 1993.

*Catalogue des élèves du Séminaire de St Hyacinthe depuis 1818.* Saint Hyacinthe, QC: Des Presses à Pouvoir du "Courrier de Saint-Hyacinthe," 1875.

*Catalogue of Printed Music in the British Library to 1980.* London: K.G. Sauer, 1984.

*Catalogue vente a L'encan par October Lemieux & Cie de la bibliotheque de feu son Excellence le comte de Premio-Réal.* Quebec City: C. Darveau, 1888.

*The Catholic Encyclopedia.* Online edition. 1999. www.newadvent.org/cathen. (Accessed 13 June 2005)

Cazes, Paul de. *Notes sur le Canada.* Paris: Gustave Bossange, 1878.

*Chants des Patriotes: Recueil noté de Chansons Patriotiques Canadiennes et Françaises.* Montreal: J.G. Yon éditeur, 1903.

Charosh, Paul. "'Popular' and 'Classical' in the Mid-Nineteenth Century." *American Music,* 10, no. 2 (Summer 1992): 117–35.

Chartier, Ferrier. "Calixa Lavallée." *L'Action nationale,* 2, no. 1 (September 1933): 60–71.

Chaussé, Gilles. "Les Effets de la Révolution Français sur la montée du nationalisme au Canada Français dans la première moitié du 19e siècle." *History of European Ideas,* 15 (1992): 297–303.

Choquette, C.-P. *1811–1911 Histoire du Séminaire de Saint-Hyacinthe depuis sa formation.* N.p.: Imprimerie des sourds-muets, Tome 1, 1911.

Chouinard, H.J.J.B. [Honoré-Julien-Jean-Baptiste] *Fête nationale des Canadiens-Français célébrée à Québec en 1880.* Quebec City: de L'Imprimerie A. Coté et cie, Éditeurs, 1881.

Cimichella, André M., Mgr. "Monseigneur Ignace Bourget deuxième évêque de Montréal (1840–1876)." In Rolland Litalien, ed., *L'Église de Montréal. Aperçus d'hier et d'aujourd'hui, 1836–1986.* Montreal: Fides, 1986.

Clark, Herbert L. "Famous Cornetists of the Past: Matthew Arbuckle." *Jacob's Band Monthly,* 16 (March 1931): 8–9.

Club de Raquettes Le "Trappeur." *Acte d'incorporation, constitution et reglements du Club de raquettes le "Trappeur."* Montreal: Typographie Joseph Fortier, 1887.

Cockrell, Dale. *Demons of Disorder: Early Blackface Minstrels and Their World.* Cambridge: Cambridge University Press, 1997.

– "Nineteenth-Century Popular Music." In *The Cambridge History of American Music,* 158–85. Cambridge, UK: Cambridge University Press, 1998.

Cole, Donald B. *Immigrant City: Lawrence, Massachusetts, 1845–1921.* Chapel Hill: University of North Carolina Press [1963].

Colman, Francis. "Hapless Lavallée." *Fugue,* 4, no. 7 (March 1980): 41–2.

Colton, G.Q. *Experience in the Use of Nitrous Oxide Gas.* N.p.: n.p., 1868.

Colton, J.J. [John Jay] *The Physiological Action of Nitrous Oxide Gas, as Shown by Experiments Upon Man and the Lower Animals. Together with Suggestions as to Its Safety, Uses and Abuses.* Philadelphia: S.S. White, 1871.

Comte de Premio-Réal. *Divers Mémoires pour servir à L'étude des relations commerciales entre L'Espagne (principalement ses provinces d'outre-mer) et les Provinces confédérées du Canada, 1878–79.* Quebec City: A. Côté et Cie, 1879.

– *'Scrap-Book' contenant divers souvenirs personnel du Canada et des '21.' quelques poésies, etc., etc.* Quebec City: Typographie de C. Darveau, 1880.

– *Seize mélodies pour chant et piano.* Quebec City: Arthur Lavigne, 1879.

Comte, Gustave. "Calixa Lavallée – notes biographiques inédites sur le chantre de la nation." *Le Passe-Temps*, 15, no. 374 (24 July 1909): 315.

– "Le Monument Lavallée, comment on réalisera une idée que 'Le Passe-Temps' a été le premier à lancer." *Le Passe-Temps*, 18, no. 460 (9 November 1912): 437.

– "La première troupe canadienne d'opéra et Calixa Lavallée." *Quinzaine musicale*, 26 December 1931.

Cone, John Frederick. *Adelina Patti: Queen of Hearts.* Aldershot, Eng.: Scholars Press, 1994.

*Constitution et reglements du Club Cartier.* Montreal: n.p., 1874.

Conway, Cecelia. *African Banjo Echoes in Appalachia: A Study of Folk Traditions.* Knoxville: University of Tennessee Press, 1995.

Cook, Ramsay. *Watching Quebec: Selected Essays.* Montreal and Kingston: McGill-Queen's University Press, 2005.

Cooper, Dorith Rachel. "Opera in Montreal and Toronto: A Study of Performance Traditions and Repertoire 1793–1980." PhD diss., University of Toronto, 1983.

Cooper, J.I. "The Social Structure of Montreal in the 1850s." *Historical Papers* (Canadian Historical Association), 1956: 63–73.

Cooper, Jeffrey. *The Rise of Instrumental Music and Concert Series in Paris, 1828–1871.* Ann Arbor, MI: UMI Research Press, 1983.

Courville, Serge, and Robert Garon, eds. *Québec: ville et capitale.* Quebec City: Les Presses de l'Université Laval, 2001.

Couture, Guillaume. "Chronique musicale." *La Revue de Montréal*, 3 (1879): 109–12.

– "Chronique musicale." *La Revue de Montréal*, 3 (1879): 494–6.

Couture, Simon. "Les Origins du Conservatoire de musique du Québec." MMus thesis, Université Laval, 1997.

Cowden, Robert H. *Classical Singers of the Opera and Recital Stages: A Bibliography of Biographical Materials.* Westport, CT: Greenwood, 1994.

Crawford, Richard. *American Musical Landscape.* Berkeley: University of California, 1993.

– *The Civil War Songbook: Complete Original Sheet Music for 37 Songs.* Selected, and with an introduction by Richard Crawford. New York: Dover, 1977.

Croffut, William Augustus. *Deseret, or, A Saint's Affections: An American Opera in Three Acts.* Libretto. New York: n.p., 1880.

Curtis, Benjamin. *Music Makes the Nation: Nationalist Composers and Nation Building in Nineteenth-Century Europe.* Amherst, NY: Cambria Press, 2008.

Curtiss, Mina. *Bizet and His World.* London: Secker & Warburg, 1959.

Dahlhaus, Carl. "Nationalism and Music." In *Between Romanticism and Modernism: Four Studies in the Music of the Later Nineteenth Century.* Translated by Mary Whittall. Berkeley: University of California Press, 1980.

Daniels, D.S. "Again the People Rescue From Oblivion Our 'O Canada' Composer." *Canadian Tribune*, 31 January 1955.

- "Calixa Lavallée." *Sing Out*, 5, no. 2 (April 1955): 9.
David, L.-O. [Laurent-Olivier]. "Calixa Lavallée." In *Gerbes Canadiennes*, 85–98. Montreal: Librarie Beauchemin, 1921.
- *Laurier et son temps*. Montreal: La cie de publications de 'La Patrie,' 1905.
- "Mérédict Lanctôt." *L'Opinion publique*, VIII, no. 34 (23 August 1877): 397–8.
- *Mes contemporains*. Montreal: Eusèbe Senécal et Fils, 1894.
Delisle, Ester. *The Traitor and the Jew: Anti-Semitism and Extreme Right-Wing Nationalism in French Canada From 1929 to 1939*. Translated by Madeline Hébert with Claire Rothman and Käthe Roth. Montreal: Robert Davies, 1993.
Déragon, Chantal. *Étude généalogique d'Isaac Pasquier dit Lavallée jusqu'à nos jours* (1665–2001). Longueuil, QC: Les Éditions Chantal Déragon, 2001.
Desrochers, Félix. "Calixa Lavallée." *Conférence du Club musical et littéraire de Montréal*, 2 (1941–42).
Devriès, Anik and François Lesure. *Dictionnaire des Éditeurs de musique français*. Geneva: Éditions Minkoff, 1988.
*The Diagram: Containing Plans of Theatres and Other Places of Amusement in Boston*. Boston: Jas. A.T. Bird, 1869.
*Dictionnaire biographique des musiciens*. Lachine, QC: Mont-Sainte-Anne, 1922.
*Dictionnaire des littérature de langue française*. Paris: Bordas, 1987.
*Dictionnaire national des contemporains* [Tome cinquieme] Paris: Office Général d'Édition, 1899–1919.
Dimmick, Ruth Crosby. *Our Theatres To-Day and Yesterday*. New York: H.K. Fly, [ca. 1900].
Dolge, Alfred. *Pianos and Their Makers*. Covina, CA: Covina Publishing Company, 1911. New York: Dover, 1972.
Dorgan, Maurice B. *History of Lawrence, Massachusetts, with War Records*. [Lawrence]: The Author, 1924.
Douville, Raymond. *La vie adventureuse d'Arthur Buies*. Montreal: Lèvesques, 1933.
Dubuque, H.A. *Le Guide Canadien-Français [ou Almanach des adresses] de Fall River, et notes historique sur les Canadiens de Fall River*. Fall River, MA: Edmond-F. Lamoureux, Éditeur, 1888.
Dufferin and Ava, Hariot Georgina (Hamilton) Hamilton-Temple-Blackwood, marchioness of. *My Canadian Journal, 1872–8. Extracts from My Letters Home Written While Lord Dufferin was Governor-General*. London: J. Murray, 1891.
Dufresne, Sylvie. "Le Theatre Royal de la rue Côté: 1851–1913." In Raymond Montpetit, Sylvie Dufresne, and Pierre Brouillard, eds., *Groupe de recherche en art populaire, Travaux et conférences, 1975–1979*, 67–171. Montreal: Département d'Histoire de l'Art, Université du Québec à Montréal, 1979.
Dugas, Marcel. *Louis Fréchette, 1839–1908*. Paris: Éditions de la revue mondiale, 1934.
Dumont, Frank. *Lew Benedict's "Far West" Song Book*. Philadelphia: Merrihew, 1871.
*Duprez & Benedict's New Songster*. Philadelphia: Merrihew & Son, ca. 1875.
Duteurte, Benoît. *L'Opérette en France*. Paris: Seuil, 1997.
Edmond, Vivianne. "'Musique et musiciens à Québec: Souvenirs d'un amateur' de Nazaire Le Vasseur (1848–1927)." MMus thesis, Université Laval, 1986.
Eisenberg, Ludwig, ed. "Etelka Gerster." In *Grosses Biographisches Lexikon der Deutschen Buhne im XIX. Jahrhundert*, 321–2. Leipzig: P. List, 1903.

Ellison, Mary. *Support for Secession: Lancashire and the American Civil War*. Chicago: University of Chicago Press, 1972.

Elson, Louis C. *The History of American Music*. Rev. ed. New York: The MacMillan Company, 1915.

Emery, S.L. *A Catholic Stronghold and Its Making, A History of St Peter's Church, Dorchester, Massachusetts*. Boston: Geo. H. Ellis Company, 1910.

*Encyclopedia of Cleveland History*. 2nd ed. Bloomington: Indiana University Press, 1996.

Epton, Nina. *Victoria and Her Daughters*. London: Weidenfeld and Nicholson, 1971.

"Feu Calixa Lavallée." *L'Étoile*, 29 January 1891.

Fields, Warren Carl. "Theodore La Hache and Music in New Orleans, 1846–1869." *American Music*, 8, no. 1 (Fall 1990): 326–50.

Filiatreault, A [Aristide]. "Calixa Lavallée." *Le Canada artistique*, I, no. 4 (April 1890): 65–6.

– "Calixa Lavallée." *Canada-Revue*, 2 (January 1891): 8.

Filteau, Hugette, and Jean Hamelin. "Labelle, Ludger." *Biography Online*. Toronto: University of Toronto Press; Saint-Foy, QC: Les presses de l'Université Laval, 2000. www.biographi.ca. (Accessed 10 June 2011)

Finkel, Ken. "The Rise and Fall of Blackface Minstrelsy in The City of Brotherly Love." *The Philly History Blog*. 5 December 2012. www.phillyhistory.org/blog/index.php/2012/12/the-rise-and-fall-of-blackface-minstrelsy-in-the-city-of-brotherly-love/. (Accessed 11 November 2014)

Finson, Jon W. *The Voices that Are Gone: Themes in Nineteenth-Century American Popular Song*. New York: Oxford University Press, 1994.

Fisher, William Arms. *Notes on Music in Old Boston*. Boston: Oliver Ditson, 1918.

– *One Hundred and Fifty Years of Music Publishing in the US: An Historical Sketch with Special Reference to the Pioneer Publisher Oliver Ditson Company Ltd.* Boston: Oliver Ditson, 1933.

Fiske, Roger. *Scotland in Music: A European Enthusiasm*. Reissue edition. Cambridge: Cambridge University Press, 2008.

Flescher, Sharon. *Zacharie Astruc: Critic, Artist and Japoniste (1833–1907)*. New York: Garland Publishing, 1978.

Foote, Arthur. "A Bostonian Remembers." *Musical Quarterly*, XXIII (1937): 38–9.

Foreman, Amanda. *A World on Fire: Britain's Crucial Role in the American Civil War*. New York: Random House, 2011.

Fournier, Marcel. *Les Français au Québec, 1765–1865: Un Mouvement Migratoire Méconnu*. Montreal: Les Éditions du Septentrion, 1995.

"Frantz Jehin-Prume." *Le Passe-Temps,* V (10 June 1899): 153–4.

Fréchette, Louis-Honoré. *Fleurs boréales; les Oiseaux de neige; Poésies canadiennes*. Paris: E. Rouveyre, 1881.

– *Lettres à Basile a propos des causeries du dimanche de M. A.B. Routhier*. Quebec City: L'Événement, 1872.

Führer, Charlotte. *The Mysteries of Montreal: Memoirs of a Midwife*. Edited by W. Peter Ward. Vancouver: University of British Columbia Press, 1984.

Fulcher, Jane F. *The Nation's Image: French Grand Opera as Politics and Politicised Art*. Cambridge: Cambridge University Press, 1987.

Fuller, Robert Higginson. *Jubilee Jim: The Life of Colonel James Fisk, Jr.* New York: Macmillan, 1928.

Gagnon, Blanche. "Notre Chant National." *La Musique*, 2, no. 18 (June 1920): 103–4.

– "Notre Chant National." *Reminiscences et Actualités.* Quebec City: Librairie Garneau, 1939.

– "Paul Letondal." *La Musique*, 2, no. 15 (March 1920): 43–5.

Gagnon, Ernest. *Chansons populaires du Canada.* Quebec City: Le Foyer canadien, 1865–67.

– *Lettres de voyages.* Quebec City: Délisle, 1876.

Gainsford, John. *Theatrical Thoughts, and Conundrums, Sent to J. Gaisford, on the Occasion of His Benefit at the Theatre Royal.* Montreal: Printed for the Author, By Lovell and Gibson, 1848.

Gale, George. *Historic Tales of Old Quebec.* Quebec City: The Telegraph Printing Company, 1920.

Garofalo, Robert. *A Pictorial History of Civil War Era Musical Instruments and Military Bands.* Charleston, WV: Pictorial Histories, 1985.

Gauthier, Henri. *La Compagnie de Saint-Sulpice au Canada.* Montreal: Séminaire de Saint-Sulpice, 1912.

Gendron, Stéphane. "The Life and Times of Pierre Jean-Baptiste Bedard (1842–1884): A French-Canadian Experience in New England." PhD diss., University of Massachusetts at Boston, 1994.

Gillespie, John. *A Bibliography of Nineteenth-Century American Piano Music, with Location Sources and Composer Biography Index.* Westport, CT: Greenwood Press, 1984.

Gillespie, John, ed. *Nineteenth-Century American Piano Music.* Selected and Introduced by John Gillespie. New York: Dover, 1978.

Glazer, Irvin R. *Philadelphia Theatres, A–Z: A Comprehensive, Descriptive Record of 813 Theatres Constructed since 1724.* Westport, CT: Greenwood Press, 1986.

Gossage, Peter. *Families in Transition: Industry and Population in Nineteenth-Century Saint-Hyacinthe.* Montreal and Kingston: McGill-Queen's University Press, 1999.

Gottschalk, Louis Moreau. *Notes of a Pianist: The Chronicles of a New Orleans Music Legend.* Edited by Jeanne Behrend. Princeton, NJ: Princeton University Press, 2006.

Grace, Robert. "Apport de l'immigration: l'exemple des Irlandais." In Serge Courville and Robert Garon, eds., *Québec: ville et capitale*, 180–5. Quebec City: Les Presses de l'Université Laval, 2001.

Graham, Franklin. *Histrionic Montreal: Annals of the Montreal Stage and Critical Notes of the Plays and Players of a Century.* Montreal: John Lovell & Son, 1902. 2nd ed., New York: B. Blom, [1969].

*Les Graveurs musicales dans L'Illustration: 1843–1899.* Compiled by H. Robert Cohen. Quebec City: Presses de l'Université Laval; New York: Pendragon Press [distribution], 1983.

Greer, Allan. *The Patriots and the People: The Rebellion of 1837 in Rural Lower Canada.* Toronto: University of Toronto Press, 1993.

– *Peasant, Lord, and Merchant: Rural Society in Three Quebec Parishes 1740–1840.* Toronto: University of Toronto Press, 1985.

Grossman, F. Karl. *A History of Music in Cleveland*. Cleveland, OH: Case Western Reserve University, 1972.

*Guía Diplomática de España, Año de 1887*. Madrid: Imprenta y Fundición de M. Tello, 1887.

*Guide to Quebec and the Lower Saint Lawrence. Compiled Expressly for this Season. The Most Complete Guide to Quebec Ever Published*. Quebec City: n.p., 1882.

Hahn, J.B. "President's Address." *M.T.N.A. Proceedings*. Minneapolis, MN: MTNA, 1892.

Hall, Roger. *The World of William Notman: The Nineteenth Century through a Master Lens*. Toronto: McClelland & Stewart, 1993.

Hamel, Réginald. *Louis-Moreau Gottschalk et son temps (1829–1869)*. Montreal: Guérin, 1996.

Hamelin, Jean. "Médéric Lanctôt." *Dictionary of Canadian Biography*. vol. 10. University of Toronto/Université Laval, 1972. www.biographi.ca/en/bio/lanctot_med eric_10E.html. (Accessed 10 June 2011)

Hamelin, Jean, and Pierre Poulin. "Pierre-Joseph-Olivier Chauveau." *Dictionary of Canadian Biography*. vol. 11. University of Toronto/Université Laval, 1982. www.biographi.ca/en/bio/chauveau_pierre_joseph_olivier_11E.html. (Accessed 10 June 2011)

Hamm, Charles. *Yesterdays: Popular Song in America*. New York: W.W. Norton & Company, 1983.

Hamon, Edouard. *Les Canadiens-Français de la Nouvelle-Angleterre*. Quebec City: N.S. Hardy, 1891.

Harding, James. *Gounod*. London: George Allen & Unwin, 1973.

Hartman, James B. "The Golden Age of the Organ in Manitoba: 1875–1919." *Manitoba History*, 29 (Spring 1995). www.mhs.mb.ca/docs/mb_history/29/goldenage oforgans.shtml. (Accessed 24 September 2010)

Harvey, Louis-Georges. *Le Printemps de L'Amérique française: Américanité, anticolonialisme et républicanisme dans le discours politique québécois, 1805–1837*. Montreal: Boréal, 2005.

Hathorn, Ramon. "Sarah Bernhardt and the Bishops of Montreal and Quebec." CCHA, *Historical Studies*, 53 (1986), 97–120.

Hébert, Hélène, Jean-Noël Dion, and Albert Rémillard. *Le Marché de Saint-Hyacinthe et quelques marchés publiques du Québec*. Saint-Hyacinthe: Éditions JML, 1989.

Hébert, Yves. "Sir. Adolphe-Basile Routhier." *Dictionary of Canadian Biography*. vol. 14. University of Toronto/Université Laval, 1998. www.biographi.ca/en/bio /routhier_adolphe_basile_14E.html. (Accessed 10 October 2008)

Henderson, Mary. *The City and the Theatre*. Clifton, NJ: James T. White & Company, [1973].

– *Theater in America: 200 Years of Plays, Players, and Productions*. New York: H.N. Abrams, 1986.

"Henri Gauthier." Advertisement. *Les Beaux-arts*, I, no. 4 (1 July 1863): 32.

"Henry F. Miller." Advertisement. *Music Trade Review*, III, no. 3 (18 December 1876): ix.

Henry F. Miller Firm, Boston. *Henry F. Miller's Catalogue*. Boston: E.E. Rice, printer, ca. 1868.

– *New Illustrated Catalogue Containing Descriptions and Engravings of the Henry F. Miller Piano-Fortes: With a Sketch of the Manufacturer, a Description of His Establishments, and a List of Styles With Engravings, and Numerous Testimonials and Certificates from the Most Distinguished Educators and Musicians*. Boston: Miller Piano Company, 1884.

"Henry F. Miller Piano Company." Advertisement. *The Folio*, XXI, no. 4 (October 1881): 382.

Herz, Henri. *Mes voyages en Amérique*. Paris: A. Fauré, 1866.

Hihn, Richard Randall. "Boston, Dwight, and Pianists of Nineteeth-Century America: The European Connection." DMA diss., University of Colorado at Boulder, 1984.

Hipsher, Edward Ellsworth. *American Opera and Its Composer*. Philiadelphia: Theodor Presser, 1927.

*Histoire du Séminaire de Saint-Hyacinthe (seconde partie)*. Saint-Hyacinthe, QC: Des presses à pouvoir du pouvoir du "Courrier," 1879.

*Historique de La Société musicale Sainte-Cécile de Québec*. Quebec City: La Société musicale Sainte-Cécile de Québec, 1881.

"History of the American Brass Band and Orchestra 1837 to 1920." In *The History of the State of Rhode Island and Providence Plantations: Biographical*. American Historical Society, 1920. http://files.usgwarchives.org/ri/statewide/history/brasband.txt. (Accessed 17 October 2010)

*History of Charles Nestel, Surnamed Commodore Foote; and Joseph Huntler, Surnamed Colonel Small, the Two Smallest Men Living*. New York: Torry Brothers, Printers, 1862.

History of Music Project. *Celebrities in El Dorado, 1850–1906*. New York: AMS Press, [1972].

– *Music in the Gold Rush Era*. New York: AMS Press, [1972].

*History of the State of Rhode Island and Providence Plantations*. Providence: American Historical Society, 1920.

Hitchcock, H. Wiley. *Music in the United States: A Historical Introduction*. Englewood Cliffs, NJ: Prentice Hall, 1969.

Holditch, W. Kenneth, ed. *In Old New Orleans*. Jackson: University of Mississippi Press, 1983.

Holleran, Michael. *Boston's "Changeful Times."* Baltimore, MD: The Johns Hopkins University Press, 1998.

Holliday, Joseph E. "Notes on Samuel N. Pike and his Opera Houses." *Bulletin of the Cincinnati Historical Society*, 2, no. 3 (July 1967): 165–83.

Hopkins, H.W. (Henry Whitmer). *Atlas of the City and Island of Montreal; Including the Counties of Jacques Cartier and Hochelaga*. Montreal: Hopkins, 1879.

*The Hotel Guests' Guide for the City of Montreal*. Montreal: The Railway and Newspaper Advertising Company, 1875.

Houle, Jacques-André. "Frantz Jehin-Prume (1839–99): son apport culturel au milieu québécois." *Les Cahiers de L'ARMuQ*, 12 (April 1990): 48–53.

Howell, Gordon C. "The Development of Music in Canada." PhD diss., University of Rochester, 1959.

Hubbard, W.L. [William Lines], editor. *Imperial History and Encyclopedia of Music*. New York: Irving Squire, ca. 1908.

Huot, Cécile. "Sohmer Park." In *The Canadian Encyclopedia*. Historica Canada, 2006. www.thecanadianencyclopedia.com/en/article/sohmer-park-emc/. (Accessed 10 November 2014)

*Illustrated Boston: The Metropolis of New England*. New York: American Publishing and Engraving Company, 1889.

Ingraham, Mary I. "Assimilation, Integration and Individuation: The Evolution of First Nations Musical Citizenship in Canadian Opera." In Pamela Karantonis and Dylan Robinson, eds., *Opera Indigene: Re/presenting First Nations and Indigenous Cultures*, 211–30. Farnham, Surrey: Ashgate, 2011.

– "Something to Sing About: A Preliminary List of Canadian Staged Dramatic Music since 1867." *Intersections: Canadian Journal of Music / Intersections: revue canadienne de musique*, 28, no. 1 (2007): 14–77.

James, Henry. *The Bostonians*. New York: Dial, 1945.

J.B. "Calixa Lavallée." *Le Monde illustré*, 7, no. 354 (5 February 1891): 655.

*Jean White's Complete Catalogue of Publications for Military Band, Large and Small Orchestra, Violin, 'Cello, Cornet ....* Boston: Jean White, 1891.

[Jehin-Prume, Jules, et al.] *Une Vie d'artiste*. Montreal: R. Constantineau, ca. 1898.

Jenks, Francis H. "Boston Musical Composers." *New England Magazine*, I (January 1890): 475–83.

*The Johnas Chickering Centennial Celebration: A Tribute to the Life and Work of Jonas Chickering*. New York: Cheltenham, 1974.

Johnson, H. Earle. "The 'Folio' of White, Smith and Company." *American Music*, 2, no. 1 (Spring 1984): 88–104.

Jones, F.O., ed. *A Handbook of American Music and Musicians, Containing Biographies of American Musicians*. Canaseraga, NY: F.O. Jones, 1886. Reprint. New York: Da Capo, 1971.

Jones, Preston. "Civil War, Culture War: French Quebec and the American War between the States." *The Catholic Historical Review*, 87, no. 1 (January 2001), 55–70.

*Julius Cahn's Official Theatre Guide Containing Information of the Leading Theatres and Attractions in America*. Vol. 8. New York: Julius Cahn, 1903.

Kallberg, Jeffrey. *"Parisian" Pianists*. New York: Garland, 1993.

Kallmann, Helmut. "The Acceptance of O Canada." *Canadian Composer* (April 1966): 18, 38, 40.

– *Catalogue of Canadian Composers*. Toronto: Canadian Broadcasting Corporation, 1952.

– "Charles Wugk Sabatier." In *The Canadian Encyclopedia*. Historica Canada, 2007. www.thecanadianencyclopedia.ca/en/article/charles-wugk-sabatier-emc/. (Accessed 10 November 2014)

– "Charles-Gustave Smith." *Dictionary of Canadian Biography*. Vol. 12. University of Toronto/Université Laval, 1990. www.biographi.ca/en/bio/smith_charles_gustave_12E.html. (Acessed 10 June 2011)

– *History of Music in Canada, 1534–1918*. Toronto: University of Toronto Press, 1960.

– *Mapping Canada's Music: Selected Writings of Helmut Kallmann*. Edited by John Beckwith and Robin Elliott. Waterloo, ON: Wilfrid Laurier University Press, 2013.

– "Marie-Hippolyte-Antoine Dessane." *Dictionary of Canadian Biography*. Vol. 10. University of Toronto/Université Laval, 1972. www.biographi.ca/en/bio/dessane_marie_hippolyte_antoine_10E.html. (Accessed 10 September 2011).

– "The Mysteries of 'O Canada.'" *Music Canada* (Summer 1980): 18.

Kamien, Roger. *Music: An Appreciation*. 7th ed. New York: McGraw-Hill, 2000.

Kastner, George. *Parémiologie musicale de la langue française*. Paris: G. Brandus et S. Dufour; London: Barther and Lowell, 1866.

Keillor, Elaine. "Marius Barbeau as a Promoter of Folk Music Performance and Composition." In Lynda Jessup, Andrew Nurse, and Gordon E. Smith, eds, *Around and About Marius Barbeau: Modelling Twentieth-Century Culture*, 137–55. Gatineau, QC: Canadian Museum of Civilization, 2008.

– *Music in Canada: Capturing Landscape and Diversity*. Montreal and Kingston: McGill-Queen's University Press, 2008.

Keillor, Elaine, ed. *Music for Orchestra II*. Ottawa: The Canadian Musical Heritage Society, 1994.

Kelly, Stéphane. *La petite loterie: comment la Couronne a obtenu la collaboration du Canada français après 1837*. Montreal: Boréal, 1997.

Kendall, John Smith. *Golden Age of New Orleans Theater*. New York: Greenwood, 1968.

– "New Orleans Negro Minstrels." *Louisiana Historical Quarterly*, 30, no. 1 (January 1947): 128-48.Knight, Ellen. "Dudley Buck." *New Grove Dictionary of Opera*. Oxford Music Online. Oxfordmusiconline.com. (Accessed 8 April 2010)

Koon, Helen Wickham. *Gold Rush Performers*. Jefferson, NC, and London, England: McFarland & Company, 1994.

Kowalski, Henri. *A Travers l'Amerique: impressions d'un musicien*. Paris: E. Lachaud, 1872.

Krehbiel, Henry Edward. *Philharmonic Society of New York*. New York: Novello, Ewer & Company, 1892.

Labelle, Charles. "Calixa Lavallée." *L'Écho musical*, I, no. 1 (January 1888): 1.

– "M. Lavallée à Londres." *L'Écho musical*, I, no. 2 (February 1888): 20.

Lachance, Pierre. *Documents of Historical Interest to the Catholic Churches of Fall River and the "French Canadians" of the City, Excerpted from "The Fall River News."* Fall River, MA: n.p., n.d.

Laflamme, Jean, and Rémi Tourangeau. *L'Église et le théâtre au Québec*. Montreal: Fides, 1979.

Lahee, Henry Charles. *Annals of Music in America*. Chicago: G.L. Howe, 1889.

– *Famous Singers of Today and Yesterday*. Boston: L.C. Page, 1914.

– *The Grand Opera Singers of To-Day; An Account of the Leading Operatic Stars Who Have Sung during Recent Years, Together with a Sketch of the Chief Operatic Enterprises*. Boston: The Page Company, 1922.

Lambton, John George (Lord Durham). *Lord Durham's Report: An Abridgement of Report on the Affairs of British North America*. Edited by G.M. Craig; introductions by G.M. Craig and Janet Ajzenstat; afterword by Guy Laforest. Montreal and Kingston: McGill-Queen's University Press, 2007.

Lamire, Maurice. *La Vie littéraire au Québec, 1870–1894, "Je me souviens."* Vol. 4. Saint Foy, Quebec: Les Presses de l'Université Laval, 1999.

Lamonde, Yvan. *Histoire sociale des idées au Québec (1760–1896)*. Montreal: Fides, 2000.

– *Histoire sociale des idées au Québec (1896–1929)*. Montreal: Fides, 2004.

– Review of Dubinsky, Ira. Institut canadien Archives. *Revue d'histoire de L'Amérique française*, 54, no. 4 (2001): 606–8.

Lamonde, Yvan, and Jonathan Livernois. *Papineau. Erreur sur la personne*. Montreal: Boréal, 2012.

Landry, Jean. "Laurent-Olivier David." *Dictionary of Canadian Biography*. Vol. 15. University of Toronto/Université Laval, 2005. www.biographi.ca/en/bio/david_lau rent_olivier_15E.html. (Accessed 8 September 2009)

Lang, Paul Henry, ed. *One Hundred Years of Music in America*. New York: G. Schirmer, 1961.

Lapierre, Eugène. "Calixa Lavallée, compositeur national, 1842–1891." *Qui?*, 1, no. 2 (September 1949): 33–48.

– *Calixa Lavallée, musicien national du Canada*. Montreal: Editions Albert Lévesque, 1936. 2nd rev. ed., Montreal: Granger Frères Ltée, 1950. 3rd. rev. ed. Montreal: Fides, 1966.

– *Pourquoi la musique*. Montreal: Albert Lévesque, 1933.

– *Un style canadien de musique*. Quebec City: Editions du "Cap diamant," 1942.

Larrick, Geary. "Drumming and Fifing of the Civil War." *NACWPI Journal*, XXXVII, no. 1 (Fall 1988): 8–16.

"The Late Madame Anna Bishop: The Career of a Most Gifted Singer and a Very Remarkable Woman." *The Voice*, VI, no. 7 (July 1884): 109–10.

Lavallée, C[alixa]. "Correspondance." *L'Union nationale*, 21 November 1864.

Lavallée, Calixa. "Advice to Pianoforte Players." *Musical Opinion & Music Trade Review*, 8, no. 90 (1 March 1885): 288–9.

– "L'Art musical au Canada." *Le Canada artistique*, I, no. 4 (April 1890): 70–1.

– "C. Lavallée, Professor de Musique, 90 rue des Allemands." *La Presse*. 10 February 1864.

– "Le Concert de Camille Urso." *L'Union nationale*, 3 December 1864.

– "Correspondence." *The Musical Standard*, 6, no. 1262 (October 1888): 216.

– [A translation of "The Advancement of Music in America."] "Discours pronouncé par M. Calixa Lavallée." *L'Écho musical*, I, no. 3 (March 1888): 28.

– "L'E muet." *Le Canada artistique*, I, no. 2 (February 1890): 35–6.

– "The Future of Music in America." *The Etude*, XXX, no. 1 (July 1886): 13.

– Introduction. *Seize mélodies pour chant et piano*. By the Comte de Premio-Réal. Quebec City: Arthur Lavigne, 1879.

– "Is it Necessary to Go Abroad to Study?" *The Folio*, XXVI, no. 5 (November 1884): 171–2.

– "Louis Maas Concert." *Musical Courier*, XII, no. 11 (17 March 1886): 174.

– "Louis Maas's Chamber Concert." *Musical Courier*, XIV, no. 2 (12 January 1887): 22.

– "Maas's Fourth Chamber Concert." *Musical Courier*, XIV, no. 15 (13 April 1887): 242.

– "MM. Les Rédacteurs." *L'Union nationale*, 19 November, 1864.

– "Musical: Albani." *Boston Home Journal*, 3 March 1883.

- "Musical: The Fiftieth Performance of Pounce & Company." *Boston Home Journal*, 2 June 1883.
- "Musical: An 'Off Night.'" *Boston Home Journal*, 10 March 1883.
- "Musical: An Utterly Too Too Criticism." *Boston Home Journal*, 7 April 1883.
- "Musical: William H. Sherwood." *Boston Home Journal*, 14 April 1883.
- "Musical Matters." *Boston Herald*, 9 May 1886.
- "L'Opéra Anglais." *L'Union nationale*, 30 December 1864.
- "Platon Polichinelle." *L'Union nationale*, 22 February 1865.
- "President's Address." *Official Report of the Music Teachers' National Association, 1887*. Minneapolis, MN: Music Teachers' National Association, 1887, 7–10.
- "Report of Calixa Lavallée, Delegate to London, England." *Annual Report of the Music Teachers' National Association, 1888*. Minneapolis, MN: Music Teachers' National Association, 1888, 15–20.
- "Le Retour de Camille Urso." *L'Union nationale*, 21 December 1864.
- "A Rising Composer." *The Folio*, XXVIII, no. 5 (November 1885): 158.
- "Style and Expression." *Annual Report of the Music Teachers' National Association, 1883*. Minneapolis, MN: Music Teachers' National Association, 1883. 76–8. Reprinted as "Style." *The Musical Standard*, 8, no. 199 (October 1897): 262–3.
- "Les Victims de l'Inondation." *L'Union nationale*. 18 April 1865.
Lavallée, Calixa, and Frantz Jehin-Prume. "Communication." *La Minerve*, 22 May 1877.
Leahy, William Augustine. *The Catholic Churches of Boston and its Vicinity and St John's Seminary, Brighton, Mass: A Folio of Photo-Gravures with Notes and Historical Information*. Boston: McClellan, Hearn and Company, 1892.
Lebel, Jean-Marie. "La nuit où périt le Music Hall." *Cap-aux-Diamants: la revue d'histoire du Québec*, 5, no. 2 (1989): 66. http://id.erudit.org/iderudit/7517ac. (Accessed 8 December 2013)
LeBlanc, Robert G. "The Francophone 'Conquest' of New England: Geopolitical Conceptions and Imperial Ambition of French-Canadian Nationalists in the Nineteenth Century." *American Review of Canadian Studies*, XV, no. 3 (1985): 288–310.
Lefebvre, Marie-Thérèse. "L'histoire du Conservatoire national de musique: 1922–1950." *Les Cahiers de L'ARMuQ*, 3 (1984): 37–51.
- "Marius Barbeau: Une eminence grise dans le milieu musical canadien-français" In Lynda Jessup, Andrew Nurse and Gordon E. Smith, eds., *Around and About Marius Barbeau: Modelling Twentieth-Century Culture*,157–84. Gatineau, QC: Canadian Museum of Civilization, 2008.
- "The Role of the Church in the History of Musical Life in Quebec." Translated by Beverley Diamond. In Beverley Diamond and Robert Winter, eds., *Canadian Music: Issues of Hegemony and Identity*, 65–74. Toronto: Canadian Scholars Press, 1994.
- "Qu'a-t-il manqué à Guillaume Couture? Portrait d'un personnage controversé dans le milieu musical montréalais de la fin du XIXe siècle." *Les Cahiers des dix*, no. 58 (2004): 37–70.
- "'Que sont mes amis devenus ...': le réseau social d'Aristide Filiatreault, musicien et journaliste." *Les Cahiers des dix*, no. 63 (2009): 161–73.

Lefebvre, Marie-Thérèse, and Jean-Pierre Pinson. *Chronologie musicale du Québec, 1535–2004*. Quebec City: Septentrion, 2009.

Legendre, Napoléon. *Albani (Emma Lajeunesse)*. Saint-Jacques, QC: Editions du Pot de fer, 1874.

– *Notre Constitution et nos institutions*. Montreal: J.-A. Plinguet, 1878.

– *Les Perce-Neige. Premières Poésies*. Quebec City: C. Darveau, 1886.

Lemay, Philippe. *The French Canadian Textile Worker*. Reported by Louis Paré. New Hampshire Federal Writers' Project, 1938–39; *American Life Histories: Manuscripts from the Federal Writers' Project, 1936–1940*, in *American Memory*, Library of Congress. http://memory.loc.gov/. (Accessed 19 March 2007)

Lemieux, Rodolph. *Wilfrid Laurier: Conférence Devant Le Club National de Montréal*. Montréal: C. Theoret, 1897.

Le Moine, J.M. [James MacPherson]. *Quebec, Past and Present: A History of Quebec, 1608–1876*. Quebec City: Printed by A. Côté, 1876.

Leonard, William T. *Masquerade in Black*. Metuchen, NJ: Scarecrow Press, 1986.

Lesure, François. *Claude Debussy, biographie critique*. Paris: Klincksieck, 1994.

Letondal, Arthur. "Calixa Lavallée." *L'Action française*, III, no. 10 (October 1919): 434–4.

– "Calixa Lavallée." *La Musique*, 2, no. 14 (February 1920): 26.

– "Un musicien oublié." *Action nationale*, 2, no. 2 (October 1933): 126–35.

Letondal, Paul. *Circulaire: M. P. Letondal agent de la manufacture de pianos Pleyel, Wolff & cie. de Paris, France*. Montreal: n.p., 1878.

Leung, Henry. "The Del Vecchio House." B. Architecture diss. McGill University, 1967.

Le Vasseur, Nazaire. "Musique et Musiciens à Québec: Souvenirs d'un Amateur." *La Musique*, 3, no. 28 (April 1921): 50–3.

– "Musique et Musiciens à Québec: Souvenirs d'un Amateur." *La Musique*, 3, no. 29 (May 1921): 66–9.

– "Musique et Musiciens à Québec: Souvenirs d'un Amateur." *La Musique*, 3, no. 30 (June 1921): 82–3.

Levine, Lawrence. *Highbrow/Lowbrow: The Emergence of a Cultural Hierarchy in America*. Cambridge, MA: Harvard University Press, 1988.

Levy, Alan Howard. *Musical Nationalism: American Composers' Search for Identity*. Westport, CT: Greenwood Press, 1983.

Lewis, Robert. *Manufacturing Montreal: The Making of an Industrial Landscape, 1850 to 1930*. Baltimore, MD: The Johns Hopkins University Press, 2000.

Lingg, Ann M. "Great Opera Houses: New Orleans." *Opera News*, 25, no. 5 (10 December 1960): 22–5.

Linteau, Paul-André. *Histoire de Montréal depuis la Confédération*. Montreal: Boréal, 1992.

Linteau, Paul-André, René Durocher, and Jean-Claude Robert. *Quebec: A History 1867–1929*. Translated by Robert Chodos. Toronto: James Lorimer & Company, 1983.

Lockspeiser, Edward. *Debussy: His Life and Mind*. Volume 1, 1862–1902. Cambridge: Cambridge University Press, 1978.

Loesser, Arthur. *Men, Women and Pianos: A Social History.* New York: Simon and Schuster, 1954. Reprint. New York: Dover, 1990.

Logan, J.D. [John Daniel]. "Canada's First Creative Composer." *Canadian Courier,* 2 (27 January 1912).

– "Canadian Creative Composers." *Canadian Magazine,* 41, no. 5 (September 1913): 486–94.

Londré, Felicia Hardison and Daniel J Watermeier. *The History of North American Theater: The United States, Canada, and Mexico, From Pre-Columbian Times to the Present.* New York: Continuum, 1998.

Longford, Elizabeth. *Darling Loosy: Letters to Princess Louise, 1856–1939.* London: Weidenfeld & Nicolson, 1991.

Lonn, Ella. *Foreigners in the Union Army and Navy.* Baton Rouge: Louisiana State University Press, 1951.

Lord, Francis A., and Arthur Wise. *Bands and Drummer Boys of the Civil War.* New York: T. Yoseloff, 1966. Reprint. New York: Da Capo, 1979.

Lott, Eric. *Love and Theft: Blackface Minstrelsy and the American Working Class.* New York: Oxford University Press, 1993.

– "'The Seeming Counterfeit': Racial Politics and Early Blackface Minstrelsy." *American Quarterly,* 43, no. 2 (June 1991): 223–54.

McAdam, Roger Williams. *The Old Fall River Line, Being an Account of the World Renowned Steamship Line.* Battleboro, VT: Stephen Daye Press, 1937.

McCalla, Douglas. "Canada Corn Act." *The Canadian Encyclopedia.* Historica Canada, 2007. www.thecanadianencyclopedia.com/articles/canada-corn-act. (Accessed 22 November 2011)

Mcgee, Timothy J. *The Music of Canada.* New York: W.W. Norton, 1985.

McWhirter, Christian. *Battle Hymns: The Power and Popularity of Music in the Civil War.* Chapel Hill: University of North Carolina Press, ca. 2012.

Mack, E. *Commodore Foote and the Fairy Queen, Grand March.* N.p.: W.F. Shaw, 1880.

McKeley, Blake. "Rochester's Mid-Years; Center of Genesee County Life: 1854–1884." *Rochester History,* 2, no. 3 (July 1940): 1–24.

– "When Science was on Trial in Rochester: 1850–1890," *Rochester History,* 8, no. 4 (October 1946): 1–24.

McKinley, Michael. *Hockey: A People's History.* Toronto, ON: McClelland & Stewart, 2006.

McKinney, Marianne W. "The Performing Arts." In David J. Bodenhamer and Robert Graham Barrows, eds., *The Encyclopedia of Indianapolis,* 142–52. Indianapolis: Indiana University Press, 1994.

Macleod, Roderick C. "Gabriel Dumont." *Dictionary of Canadian Biography.* Vol. 13. University of Toronto/Université Laval, 1994. www.biographi.ca/en/bio/dumont_gabriel_13E.html. (Accessed 15 May 2014)

MacMillan, Carrie, Lorraine McMullen and Elizabeth Waterston. *Silenced Sextet: Six Nineteenth-Century Canadian Women Novelists.* Montreal and Kingston: McGill-Queen's University Press, 1992.

MacMillan, Ernest. "The Case for 'O Canada.'" *Recorder,* 21, no. 2 (1978): 60–3.

MacNutt, W. Stewart. *Days of Lorne: Impressions of a Governor-General.* Reprint (1955). Westport, CT: Greenwood, 1978.

Madeleine. "The Lesson of Calixa Lavallée." Translated by T. Don Titman, *Musical Review of Canada*, no. 1 (October 1933): 3.

Magnan, Hormidas. "Calixa Lavallée." *Bulletin des recherches historiques*, 33, no. 7 (July 1927): 90, 414.

– "Canada Terre de Nos Aïeus, chant national des Canadien-français." *Bulletin des recherches historiques*, 33, no. 2 (February 1927): 89–92.

– *Cinquantenaire de notre hymne national*. Hormisdas Magnan. Quebec City: n.p., 1929.

– *Origines de nos drapeaux et chants nationaux, armoires, emblèmes, devises*. Quebec City: n.p., 1929.

Mahar, William John. *Behind the Burnt Cork Mask: Early Blackface Minstrelsy and Antebellum American Popular Culture*. Urbana: University of Illinois Press, 1999.

Mann, Susan. *The Dream of Nation: A Social and Intellectual History of Quebec*. 2nd ed. Montreal and Kingston: McGill-Queen's University Press, 2002.

Mapleson, Henry James. *The Mapleson Memoirs: The Career of an Operatic Impressario 1858–1888*. Edited and annotated by Harold Rosenthal. New York: Appleton-Century, 1966.

Marcotte, Hélène. "Benjamin Sulte (baptized Olivier-Benjamin Vadeboncoeur)." *Dictionary of Canadian Biography*. Vol. 15. University of Toronto/Université Laval, 2005. www.biographi.ca/en/bio/sulte_benjamin_15E.html. (Accessed 22 November 2009)

Maretzek, Max. *Revelations of an Opera Manager in Nineteenth-Century America*. New York: Dover, 1968.

Marmontel, Antoine. *L'Art classique et moderne du piano*. Paris: Heugel et cie, 1876.

– *L'Art moderne du Piano – 50 études de salon*. Paris: Heugel et cie., 1875.

– *Enseignment progressif et rationnel du piano*. Paris: Heugel, 1887.

– *Les Pianists célèbres*. 2nd ed. Paris: Heugel et fils, 1887.Martineau, Flavien. *Une Voix d'outre-tombe: poésies de M. Martineau, P.S.S.* Montreal: J. Lovell, 1888.

Mason, William. *Memories of a Musical Life*. New York: Century Company, 1902.

Massicotte, E.-Z. [Édouard-Zotique]. "Dame Calixa Lavallée." *Bulletin des recherches historiques*, 39 (September 1933): 554–5.

– "Mme Calixa Lavallée," *Le Passe-Temps*, Numéro-Souvenir: Calixa Lavallée, 39, no. 864 (August 1933): 42.

– "Raquettes – Clubs – Costume – Chanson." *Bulletin des recherches historiques*, 28 (1922): 196–202.

– "Une société politique secrète à Montréal: Le Club Saint-Jean-Baptiste." *Le Bulletin des recherches historiques*, 21 (1915): 134–8.Mathews, W.S.B. *A Hundred Years of Music in America*. Chicago: G.L. Howe, 1889.

Mattfield, Julius. *A Handbook of American Operatic Premieres, 1731–1962*. Detroit Studies in Music Bibliography No. 5. Detroit: Information Service, 1963.

Mazzola, Sandy. "Bands and Orchestras at the World's Colombian Exposition." *American Music*, IV, no. 4 (Winter 1986): 407–24.

Meadwell, Hudson. "Forms of Cultural Mobilization in Quebec and Brittany, 1870–1914." *Comparative Politics*, 15, no. 4 (1983): 401–17.

Mechanics' Institute of Montreal. *The Mechanics' Institute of Montreal*. Montreal: Mechanics' Institute, 1930.

Mitchell, Jerome. *More Scott Operas: Further Analyses of Operas Based on the Works of Sir Walter Scott*. Lanham, MD: University Press of America, 1996.

– *The Walter Scott Operas: An Analysis of Operas Based on the Works of Sir Walter Scott*. Tuscaloosa: University of Alabama Press, 1977. *The Mollie Darling Songster: Containing the Latest Comic and Popular Copyright Songs of the Popular Authors ... [et al.]: As sung by the San Francisco Minstrels ... [et al.]*. New York: Beadle and Adams, 1871.

Monet, Jacques. "French-Canadian Nationalism and the Challenge of Ultramontanism." *Historical Papers* (Canadian Historical Association, 1966): 41–55.

– *The Last Cannon Shot: A Study of French-Canadian Nationalism 1837–1850*. Toronto: University of Toronto Press, 1969.

Montpetit, Edouard. "L'Art producteur." *Revue trimestrielle canadienne*, 5 (November 1919): 271–81.

Montpetit, Raymond. "Culture et exotisme: les panoramas itinérants et le jardin Guilbault à Montréal au XIXe siècle." *Loisirs et société*, 6, no. 1 (printemps 1983): 71–104.

*Montreal Business Sketches with a Description of the City of Montreal*. Montreal: n.p., 1864.

Morey, Carl. "Frederick Herbert Torrington." *Dictionary of Canadian Biography*. Vol. 14. University of Toronto/Université Laval, 1998. www.biographi.ca/en/bio/torrington_frederick_herbert_14E.html. (Accessed 10 June 2011)

Morin, Léo-Pol. "La Légende de l'art musical canadien et les musiciens de Montréal." *Le Nigog*, 1, no. 1 (January 1918): 13–22.

Mozart, Wolfgang Amadeus and Emanuel Schikaneder. *Die Zauberflöte*. New York: Dover, 1985.

Murfin, James V. *The Gleam of Bayonets: The Battle of Antietam and Robert E. Lee's Maryland Campaign, September 1862*. Baton Rouge: Louisiana State University Press, 1982.

Mussulman, Joseph A. *Music in the Cultured Generation: A Social History of Music in America, 1870–1900*. Evanston, IL: Northwestern University Press, 1971.

Nevers, Edmond de. *L'Avenir du peuple canadien-français*. Paris: Henri Jouve, 1896.

Newsom, Jon. "The American Brass Band Movement." *The Quarterly Journal of the Library of Congress*, 36, no. 2 (Spring 1979): 114–39.

Nichols, Roger. *Debussy Remembered*. Portland, OR: Amadeus Press, 1992.

Nicholson, Jon Seymore. "Patrick Gilmore's Boston Peace Jubilees." DEd diss., University of Michigan, 1971.

Noske, Frits. *French Song from Berlioz to Duparc*. New York: Dover, 1970.

*Nouvelle lyre canadienne: recueil de chansons canadiennes et françaises*. Montreal: Z. Chapeleau, 1890.

*Nouvelle Lyre Canadienne: Recueil de Chansons Canadienne et Françaises*. Nouvelle édition, entièrement refondue et considérablement augmentée. Montreal: Librairie Beauchemin, 1895.

O'Brien, Patrick. *The Economic Effects of the American Civil War*. London: Macmillan Education, 1988.

Octave Lemieux & Cie. *Catalogue – vente a L'encan par October Lemieux & cie de la Bibliotheque de Feu Son Excellence le Comte de Premio-Réal comprenant près de 2,000 volumes*. Quebec City: C. Darveau, 1888.

Odell, George C.D. *Annals of the New York Stage*. New York: Columbia University Press, 1937.

Offenbach, Jacques. *Orpheus in America: Offenbach's Diary of His Journey to the New World*. With Drawings by Alajalov; translated by Lander MacClintock. London: Hamish Hamilton, 1958.

Officer, Lawrence H., and Lawrence B. Smith. 'The Canadian-American Reciprocity Treaty of 1855 to 1866.' *Journal of Economic History*, 28, no. 4 (1968): 598–623.

O'Gallagher, Marianna. *Saint Patrick's, Quebec: The Building of a Church and of a Parish, 1827 to 1933*. Quebec City: Carraig Books, 1981.

O'Leary, James. *The History of the Irish Catholics of Quebec, St Patrick's Church to the Death of Father Patrick McMahon*. Quebec City: Daily Telegraph Printing, 1897.

Olson, Kenneth E. *Music and Musket: Bands and Bandsmen of the American Civil War*. Westport, CT: Greenwood, 1981.

Ottenberg, June C. *Opera Odyssey: Toward a History of Opera in Nineteenth-Century America*. Westport, CT.: Greenwood Press, 1994.

Ouellet, Gérard. *Ma paroisse, Saint-Jean-Port-Joly*. Quebec City: Editions des Piliers, 1946.

Papineau, Louis-Joseph. "Letter from Papineau to George Batchelor, secretary of the Canadian Union Club of New York." *New York Herald*, 26 December 1870.

*Parliamentary Procedure: Decisions of the Speakers, Protests, Rules and Regulations of the Legislative Council of the Province of Quebec, with an Index; Decisions of the Speakers, Judgements, Rules and Regulations of the Legislative Assembly of the Province of Quebec, with an index. 1868–1885*. Collated with the official text, arranged and summarized in an analytical index by Faucher de Saint-Maurice. Montreal: Imprimerie générale, 1885.

Paskman, Daily, and Sigmond Spaeth. *"Gentlemen, Be Seated!" A Parade of the Old-Time Minstrels*. Rev. ed. New York: Clarkson, Potter, 1976.

Pauer, Ernst. *Dictionary of Pianists and Composers for the Piano with Appendix of Manufacurers*. London: Novello, Ewer & Company, 1895.

Paul, Hélène. "*Le Canada musical* (1917–24): miroir d'une ville, reflet de deux continents." *Les Cahiers de L'ARMuQ*, 13 (May 1991): 48–65.

Pelletier, Frédéric. "Le rajeunissement de notre hymne national." *Revue de L'Université d'Ottawa*, 5, no. 11 (January–March 1935): 116–29.

Pelletier, Romain-Octave. "Arrivée de M. Calixa Lavallée." *Le Canada musical*, II, no. 4 (1 August 1875): 54.

*The People's New Songster*. N.p.: Duprez & Green's Minstrels, [1862].

*The Peo[ple's] New Songster, Containing All the New Popular Songs of the Day as Sung by "Duprez & Green's Minstrels."* N.p.: Gustave Bideaux, 1863.

*The People's New Songster, Containing New Popular Songs; Also, the First and Second Night's Programme*. N.p.: Duprez & Green's Minstrels, 1864.

Perkins, Henry Southwick. *Historical Handbook of the Music Teachers' National Association, 1876–1893*. [Chicago?]: MTNA, ca. 1893.

– "Treasurer's Financial Report." *Annual Report of the Music Teachers' National Association, 1888*, n.p. Minneapolis, MN: Music Teachers' National Association, 1889.

Peskin, Allan. "The Civil War: Crucible of Change." *Timeline: A Publication of the Ohio Historical Society*, 3, no. 3 (1986): 12–27.

Petersilea, Carlyle. "The Art of Piano-Playing." *The Folio*, XXIII, no. 6 (June 1883): 254.

– *Letters from the Spirit World*. Chicago: Progressive Thinker Publishing, 1905.

Petersilea, Franz. *A New and Thorough System for the Piano: Including the First Principles of Harmony*. Boston: White & Goulland, 1866.

– *Revised and Enlarged Edition of a New and Thorough System for the Piano-Forte, in 4 Parts*. Boston: White, Smith & Perry, 1872.

Plantinga, Leon. *Romantic Music: A History of Music Style in Nineteenth-Century Europe*. New York: W.W. Norton, 1984.

Plinguet, Joseph A. *Souvenirs sur les commencements de L'Union St. Joseph de Montréal*. Montreal: n.p., 1866.

Poirier, Lucien. "Canadian Musical Style: Illusions and Reality." In Beverley Diamond and Robert Witmer, eds., *Canadian Music: Issues of Hegemony and Identity*, 239–68. Translated by M. Benjamin Waterhouse and Beverley Diamond. Toronto: Canadian Scholars' Press, 1994.

Portes, Jacques. "Le Problème des idéologies du Canada français a la fin du XIXe et au début du Xxe siècle." *Revue d'histoire economique et sociale*, 53, no. 4 (1975): 574–7.

Potvin, Gilles. "Calixa Lavallée." *Dictionary of Canadian Biography*. Vol. 12. University of Toronto/Université Laval, 1990. www.biographi.ca/en/bio/lavallee_cal ixa_12E.html. (Accessed 17 September 2002)

– "Charles Lavallée." In *The Canadian Encyclopedia*. Historica Canada, 1985. www.thecanadianencyclopedia.ca/en/article/charles-lavallee-emc/. (Accessed 11 November 2014)

– "L'épopée inachevée. Le monument à Calixa Lavallée." *Le Devoir*, 23 August 1983.

– "Music in Saint-Hyacinthe." In *The Canadian Encyclopedia*. Historica Canada, 1985. www.thecanadianencyclopedia.ca/en/article/saint-hyacinthe-emc/. (Accessed 11 November 2014)

– "Paul Letondal." In *The Canadian Encyclopedia*. Historica Canada, 1985. www.thecanadianencyclopedia.ca/en/article/paul-letondal-emc/. (Accessed 11 November 2014)Potvin, Gilles, and Helmut Kallmann. "O Canada." In *The Canadian Encyclopedia*. Historica Canada, 1985. www.thecanadianencyclopedia.ca/en/ar ticle/o-canada/. (Accessed 11 November 2014)

Potvin, Gilles, and Susan Spier. "Calixa Lavallée." In *The Canadian Encyclopedia*. Historica Canada, 1985. www.thecanadianencyclopedia.ca/en/article/calixa-la-vallee/. (Accessed 11 November 2014)

Powe, Gregory. "Theatre Royal: Montreal's First Professional Theatre." MA thesis, McGill University, Montreal, 1972.

Poy, Vivienne. "O Canada! Must Command All of Us." *Herizons*, 1 April 2002.

Pratt, Waldo Selden, ed. "Calixa Lavallée." *The New Encyclopedia of Music and Musicians*. New York: Macmillan, 1924.

Preston, Katherine. "American Musical Life before 1900." *Journal of the Society for American Music*, 8, no. 2 (2014): 125–9.

- "Between the Cracks: The Performance of English-Language Opera in Late 19th-Century America." *American Music*, 23, no. 3 (2003): 349–74.
- *Music for Hire: A Study of Professional Musicians in Washington (1877–1900)*. Stuyvesant, NY: Pendragon Press, 1992.
- *Opera on the Road*. Urbana: University of Illinois Press, 1993.
- "To the Opera House? The Trials and Tribulations of Operatic Production in Nineteenth-Century America." *The Opera Quarterly*, 23, no. 1 (2008): 39–65
Quenneville, Pierre. "Guillaume Couture." *Dictionary of Canadian Biography*. Vol. 14. University of Toronto/Université Laval, 1998. www.biographi.ca/en/bio/cou ture_guillaume_1851_1915_14E.html. (Accessed 22 September 2009)
- "Guillaume Couture (1851–1915)." PhD diss., l'Université de Montréal, 1988.
Rauscher, Frank J. *Music on the March, 1862–'65, with the Army of the Potomac 114th Regt. P.V. Collis's Zouaves*. Philadelphia: Press of W.F. Fell and Company, 1892.
*Recueil de Chansons Canadienne et Françaises Divisé en Deux Parties*. Montreal: John Lovell, 1859.
Reid, Philippe. "L'Émergence du nationalisme Canadien-Français: L'Idéologie du *Canadien*." *Récherches Sociographiques*, 21, pts 1–2 (1980): 11–53.
*Relation du voyage de son altesse royale le Prince de Galles en Amerique*. Montreal: Senécal, 1860.
Rhodes, Robert Hunt. *All for the Union, the Civil War Diary and Letters of Elisha Hunt Rhodes*. New York: Orion, 1991.
Rice, Edward Le Roy. *Monarch's of Minstrelsy: From Daddy Rice to Date*. New York: Kenny Publishing, 1911.
Richie, Thomas, and the Comte de Premio-Réal. *"Scrap-book" contenant divers souvenirs personnels du Canada et des "21."* Quebec City: C. Darveau, 1880.
Ritter, Frederic Louis. *Music in America*. New York: C. Scribner's Sons, 1890.
Rivest, Denis. "Patrie de Calixa Lavallée ou ... 'Memoires d'outre-cave.'" *Bulletin de liason de L'ARMuQ*, 10, no. 1 (October 1993): 3.
Robbins Landon, H. C., and David Wyn Jones. *Haydn: His Life and Music*. London: Thames and Hudson, 1988.
Robert, Frédéric. *La musique française au xixe siècle*. 2nd ed. Paris: Les presses universitaires de France, 1970.
Robidoux, Réjean. "Octave Crémazie." *Dictionary of Canadian Biography*. Vol. 10. University of Toronto/Université Laval, 1972. www.biographi.ca/en/bio/crema zie_octave_10E.html. (Accessed 22 September 2009)
Roby, Yves. "Émégrés canadiens-français, franco-américains de la Nouvelle-Angleterre et images de la société américaine." In Gérard Bouchard and Yvan Lamonde, eds., *Québécois et Américaine. La culture québécoise aux XIXe et XXe siècles*, 131–57. Montreal: Fides, 1995.
- *Histoire d'un rêve brisé?: les Canadiens français aux États-Unis*. Sillery, QC: Septentrion, 2007.
Roell, C. H. *The Piano in America: 1890–1940*. Chapel Hill: University of North Carolina Press, 1989.
Root, Deane Leslie. *American Popular Stage Music, 1860–1880*. Ann Arbor, MI: UMI Research Press, 1981.

Ross, Gordon. "Félix Desrochers: General Librarian 1933–1956." *Canadian Parliamentary Review*, 23, no. 3 (2000). www.revparl.ca/english/issue.asp?param=76& art=182. (Accessed 10 January 2005)

Routhier, Adolphe-Basile. "Quelques notes historiques sur 'l'O Canada.'" *Le Droit*, 22 July 1980.

Roy, Léo. "La verité sur Sabatier." *Action nationale*, 57, no. 8 (April 1968): 707–9.

Roy, Pierre-Georges. *L'Église paroissiale de Notre-Dame de la Victoire de Lévis: notes et souvenirs.* Lévis, QC: n.p., 1912.

Rubin, Emanuel. "Jeannette Meyer Thurber." In Ralph P. Locke and Cynthia Barr, eds., *Cultivating Music in America: Women Patrons and Activitists Since 1860*, 134–63. Berkeley and Los Angeles: University of California Press, ca. 1997.

Rumilly, Robert. *Histoire de la province de Québec. Vol. II: Le "Coup d'État."* Montreal: Éditions Bernard Valiquette, 1941.

Rushforth and Donoghue. *Lawrence Mass. Lawrence Up To Date, 1845–1895.* Lawrence, MA.: 1895.

Sage, Will F. *Destiny, A Drama in a Prologue, Four Acts and an Epilogue.* Chicago: West End Advocate Printer, 1878.

– *A Tale of Two Cities.* (Adapted from Charles Dickens.) Chicago: Will F. Sage, 1900.

Salter, Sumner. "Early Encouragement to American Composers." *Musical Quarterly*, 43 (January 1932): 76–105.

Sandwell, Bernard, ed. *Musical Red Book of Montreal.* Montreal: F.A. Veich, 1907.

Santos da Silva, José Amaro. *Música e ópera no Santa Isabel: subsídio para a história e o ensino da da música no Recife.* Recife, Pernambuco, Brazil: Editora Universitária UFPE, 2006.

Sanjek, Russell. *American Popular Music and its Business.* Oxford and New York: Oxford University Press, 1988.

Sauvé, Mathieu-Robert. *Joseph Casavant: Le Facteur d'Orgues Romantique.* Montreal: XYZ éditeur, 1995.

Saxton, Alexander. "Blackface minstrelsy and Jacksonian Ideology." *American Quarterly*, XXVII (March 1975): 3–28.

Scheckel, Susan. *The Insistence of the Indian: Race and Nationalism in Nineteenth-Century American Culture.* Princeton, NJ: Princeton University Press, 1998.

Schonberg, Harold C. *The Great Pianists.* New York: Simon and Schuster, 1963.

– "Keyboard Fantasies." *Opera News* (August 1994): 16–19.

Scribe, Eugène and François-Adrien Boïeldieu. *La Dame blanche, opéra comique en trois actes.* Libretto. Montreal: Ernest Lavigne, 1878.

Sears, Stephen W. *Landscape Turned Red: The Battle of Antietam.* New Haven, CT: Ticknor & Fields, 1983.

Sénécal, André. "La Thèse messianique et les Franco-Américains." *Revue d'histoire de L'Amérique française*, 34, no. 4 (1981): 557–67.

Silvia, Philip T. "The 'Flint Affair': French-Canadian Struggle for Survivance." *Catholic Historical Review*, 65, no. 3 (1979): 414–39.

Silver, A.I. (Arthur Isaac). *The French-Canadian Idea of Confederation, 1864–1900.* 2nd ed. Toronto: University of Toronto Press, 1997.

Slemon, Peter. "Montreal's Musical Life under the Union with an Emphasis on the Terminal Years, 1841–1867." MA thesis, McGill University, Montreal, 1976.

Small, Christopher. *Musicking: The Meanings of Performing and Listening.* Middleton, CT: Wesleyan University Press, 1998.

Smith, Gordon E. "Ernest Gagnon (1834–1915): Musician and Pioneer Folksong Scholar." PhD diss., University of Toronto, 1989.

– "Ernest Gagnon on Nationalism and Canadian Music: Folk and Native Sources." *Canadian Journal for Traditional Music*, 17 (1989).

– "La genèse des Chansons populaires du Canada d'Ernest Gagnon." *Les Cahiers de L'ARMuQ*, 15 (1994): 38–53.

Smith, Gustave. "Du mouvement musical en Canada." *L'Album musical*, I, no. 1 (January 1882): 6.

Southall, Geneva Handy. *Blind Tom, the Black Pianist-Composer, Continually Enslaved.* Lanham, MD: Scarecrow Press, 1999.

*Souvenir du jubilé sacerdotal de Mgr. C. Cazeau, prélat domestique de Sa Sainteté, vicaire-général de L'archidiocèse, célébré à Québec, en janvier 1880.* N.p.: n.p., 1880.

Spies, André Michael. *Opera, State and Society in the Third Republic, 1875–1914.* New York: Peter Lang, 1998.

Spillane, Daniel. *History of the American Pianoforte, Its Technical Development, and the Trade.* New York: D. Spillane, 1890.

Spooner, Henry J. *The Maryland Campaign with the Fourth Rhode Island.* Providence: Snow & Farnham, 1903.

Stamp, Robert M. *Royal Rebels: Princess Louise & the Marquis of Lorne.* Toronto: Dundurn Press, 1988.

Starr, S. Frederick. *Bamboula: The Life and Times of Louis Moreau Gottschalk.* New York: Oxford University Press, 1995.

Start, Edwin. "A Model New England Village." *New England Magazine*, 3 (February 1891): 701–18.

Stewart, George, Jr. *An Account of the Public Dinner to His Excellency the Count of Premio-Real, December 28, 1880.* Quebec City: Morning Chronicle, 1881.

Stouffer, Allen P. "Canadian-American Relations in the Shadow of the Civil War." *The Dalhousie Review*, 57, no. 2 (1977): 332–46.

Strakosch, Moritz [Maurice]. *Souvenirs d'un impresario.* Paris: Ollendorff, 1887.

Stanley, Henry Morton. *How I Found Livingstone: Travels, Adventures, and Discoveries in Central Africa, Including Four Months' Residence with Dr Livingstone.* London: S. Low, Marston, 1872.

Struble, John W. *The History of American Classical Music: MacDowell through Minimalism.* New York: Facts On File, 1995.

Suttoni, Charles R. "Piano and Opera: A Study of the Piano Fantasies Written on Opera Themes in the Romantic Era." PhD diss., New York University, 1973.

Swanberg, W.A. *Jim Fisk: The Career of an Improbable Rascal.* New York: Charles Scribner's Sons, 1959.

Sweeney, Alastair. "Sir George Etienne Cartier." In *The Canadian Encyclopedia.* Historica Canada, 1985. www.thecanadianencyclopedia.ca/en/article/sir-george-etienne-cartier/. (Accessed 11 November 2014)

Sylvain, Philippe. "Charles Wilson." *Dictionary of Canadian Biography.* Vol. 10.

University of Toronto/Université Laval, 1972. www.biographi.ca/en/bio/wilson _charles_10E.html. (Accessed 22 September 2009)

Tanguay, Cyprien. *Dictionnaire généalogique de familles canadiennes*. Vol. 5. Montreal: Eusèbe Senécal et fils, 1888.

Thomas, Lewis H. " Louis Riel (1844–85)." *Dictionary of Canadian Biography*. Vol. 11. University of Toronto/Université Laval, 1982. www.biographi.ca/en/bio/riel_ louis_1844_85_11E.html. (Accessed 12 July 2013)

Thompson, Brian C. "Calixa Lavallée." *Grove Dictionary of American Music*. 2nd ed. New York: Oxford University Press, 2013.

– "Calixa Lavallée (1842–1891): A Critical Biography." PhD diss., The University of Hong Kong, 2001.

– "Grand Tradition: Calixa Lavallée." *Opera Canada*, 38 (Summer, 1997): 8

– "Gustave Smith's Louisiana Episode." *Institute for Canadian Music Newsletter*, 5, no. 1–2 (2007): 8–13.

– "Henry Drayton, English Opera and Anglo-American Relations, 1850–72." *Journal of the Royal Musical Association*, 136, no. 2 (2011): 247–303.

– "Journeys of an Immigrant Violinist: Jacques Oliveira in Civil-War Era New York and New Orleans." *Journal of the Society for American Music*, 6, no. 1 (2012): 51–82.

– "Lavallée Portraits: Images of the 'Musicien National.'" *Institute for Canadian Music Newsletter*, 4, no. 1 (January 2006): 2–7.

Thompson, T[oussaint]. "M. Calixte Lavallée." *L'Union nationale*, 13 January 1865.

Thoreau, Henry D. *A Yankee in Canada*. Boston: Tickner and Fields, 1866. Reprint. Montreal: Harvest House, 1961.

Tischler, Barbara L. *An American Music: The Search for an American Musical Identity*. New York: Oxford University Press, 1986.

Toll, Robert C. *Blacking Up: the Minstrel Show in Nineteenth-Century America*. New York: Oxford University Press, 1974.

Tremblay, Rémi. *Aux chevaliers du noeud coulant*. Saint-Foy, QC: Les Presses de l'Université Laval, 2008.

– *Caprices poétiques et chansons satiriques*. Montreal: A. Filiatreault & cie, 1883.

Trepanier, Leon. "'Le Trappeur,' Le premier de raquetteurs de la partie est de Montréal." *La Patrie*, 12 December 1954.

Triggs, Stanley. *Notman's Studio: the Canadian Picture*. Montreal: McCord Museum of Canadian History, 1992.

Turbide, Nadia. "Mendelssohn Choir of Montreal." In *The Canadian Encyclopedia*. Historica Canada, 1985. www.thecanadianencyclopedia.ca/en/article/men delssohn-choir-of-montreal-emc/. (Accessed 11 November 2014)

Turgeon, J.O. *Biographie de Camille Urso*. Montreal: Imprimé Plinguet & Laplant, 1865.

Turner, Kristen M. "'A Joyous Star-Spangled-Bannerism': Emma Juch, Opera in English Tranlsation, and the American Cultural Landscape in the Gilded Age." *Journal of the Society for American Music*, 8, no. 2 (2014): 219–52.

Ulrich, Homer. *A Centennial History of the Music Teachers' National Association*. Cincinnati: Music Teachers' National Association, 1976.

Vaillant, P.U. *Notes Biographiques sur L'Abbé P-J-B Bédard, le Prête Patriot, Fon-*

*dateur de la Paroisse Notre Dame de Lourdes à Fall River*. Fall River, MA: Typographie Canadienne de P.U. Vaillant, 1886.

Vanauken, Sheldon. *The Glittering Illusion: English Sympathy for the Southern Confederacy*. Washington, DC: Gateway Editions, 1989.

Vandal, Gilles. *The New Orleans Riot of 1866, Anatomy of a Tragedy*. Lafayette, LA: University of Southwestern Louisiana, 1983.

Vaughan Williams, Ralph. *National Music and Other Essays*. London: Clarendon Press, 1996.

Vermeirre, André. *L'Immigration des Belges au Québec*. Sillery, QC: Septentrion, 2001.

"Un violon signé Augustin Lavallée." Radio-Canada.ca, 30 June 2010. www.radio-canada.ca/nouvelles/arts_et_spectacles/2010/06/30/004-violon-bleu.shtml. (Accessed 8 October 2012)

Voltaire. *Oeuvres Completes*. T. 5 Paris: Garnier Frères, 1877.

Voyer, Louise. *Saint-Hyacinthe: de la seigneurie à la ville québecoise*. Montreal: Libre Expression, 1980.

Waite, P.B. "John George Edward Henry Douglas Sutherland Campbell, Marquess of Lorne and 9th Duke of Argyll." *Dictionary of Canadian Biography*. Vol. 14. University of Toronto/Université Laval, 1998. www.biographi.ca/en/bio/campbell_john_george_edward_henry_douglas_sutherland_14E.html. (Accessed 10 June 2011)

Wake, Jehanne. *Princess Louise: Queen Victoria's Unconventional Daughter*. London: Collins, 1988.

Walter, Arnold. *Aspects of Music in Canada*. Toronto: University of Toronto Press: 1969.

Warner, Sam B., Jr. *Streetcar Suburbs: The Process of Growth in Boston, 1870–1900*. Cambridge, MA: Harvard University Press and the M.I.T. Press, 1962.

Weber, Adna Ferrin. *The Growth of Cities in the Nineteenth Century: A Study in Statistics*. Ithaca, NY: 1963.

Weichlein, William J. *A Checklist of American Music Periodicals, 1850–1900*. Detroit: Information Coordinators, 1970.

*Welcome by the City of Quebec to Their Royal Highnesses the Duke and Duchess of Cornwall and York: Complete Official Programme of the Festivities*. Quebec City: n.p., ca. 1901.

White, Harry, and Michael Murphy, eds. *Musical Constructions of Nationalism: Essays on the History and Ideology of European Musical Culture 1800–1945*. Cork, Ireland: University of Cork Press, 2001.

White, William Braid. "The Decline of the American Piano Industry." *The American Mercury*, 28 (February 1933): 210–13.

Williams, W. *The Traveller's and Tourist's Guide through the United States of America, Canada, etc*. Philadelphia: Lippincott, Grambo & Co, 1851.

Williams, William H.A. *'Twas Only an Irishman's Dream: The Image of Ireland and the Irish in American Popular Song Lyrics, 1800–1920*. Urbana and Chicago: University of Illinois Press, 1996.

Willis, Stephen C. "Centenary of Lavallée's Death." *National Library of Canada News*. 23, nos. 7–8 (July/August 1991): 8–9.

Winans, Robert B. "Early Minstrel Show Music, 1843–1852." In Annemarie Bean, James Vernon Hatch, and Brooks McNamara, eds., *Inside the Minstrel Mask: Readings in Nineteenth-Century Blackface Minstrelsy*, 141–62. Hanover, NH: Wesleyan University Press, 1996.

Winks, Robin W. *The Civil War Years: Canada and the United States*. Baltimore, MD: Johns Hopkins University Press, 1960. 4th ed. Montreal and Kingston: McGill-Queen's University Press, 1998.

Wittke, Carl Frederick. *Tambo and Bones: A History of the American Minstrel Stage*. Durham, NC: Duke University Press, 1930. Reprint. New York: Greenwood, 1968.

Young, Brian. "Édouard-Charles Fabre." *Dictionary of Canadian Biography*. Vol. 12. University of Toronto/Université Laval, 1990. www.biographi.ca/en/bio/fabre_edouard_charles_12E.html. (Accessed 10 September 2009)

Zuck, Barbara A. *A History of Musical Americanisms*. Ann Arbor, MI: UMI Research Press, 1980.

# Index

Collet, Pierre A.A., 300, 301
Collier's publishing firm, 312
Collins, Lew, 91, 92
Columbia Mixed Quartet, 312
Comte, Joseph Edmond Gustave, 8, 312–13, 351, 388n30, 462n13, 466n31
Conant, Albert F., 251, 284
Conant, John Willis, 292
Congrès Catholique Canadiens-Français, 217–18, 224–5
Conservatoire de musique du Québec, 314
Contant, Alexis, 161, 167, 302
Cook & Martin, 87
Copeland, George, 302
Copeland, Harry, "Slap Bang, Here We Are Again," 87
Cosmopolitan Hotel and Restaurant, Montreal, 58, 401n10
Courrier·de Montréal, Le, 213
Courrier de Saint-Hyacinthe, Le, 7, 63
Coursol, Charles-Joseph, Judge, 184
Couture, Guillaume, 120–1, 122, 146, 169; on AMQ, 209, 231; in Paris, 128, 136, 137, 141, 427n111; performing, 152, 156, 157–8, 169; writing about Lavallée, 149, 151, 179, 180
Couture, Simon, 316
Couturier, V.L., 161
Craig, James Henry, 4
Crémazie, Octave, xx, 136; "Le Drapeau de Carillon," 17
Crimean War, 11
Crosby's Opera House, Chicago, 109
Crystal Palace, Montreal, 58, 96, 146
culture, high and low, 118–19, 142, 157, 166, 418n126
Cundy, W.H., 273
Cundy-Bettoney, 306
Curran, Patrick Joseph, 119, 198, 199–200, 213, 216, 331, 344
Cuvillier, Augustin, 63

D.L. White's Concert Orchestra, 330
Da Ponte, Lorenzo, 348

Daily Witness (Montreal), 52, 157, 183, 401n6
Danks, E.P., 31
Daoust, Charles, 63
David, L.O., 71, 94; Hommage aux Victimes de 1837–38, 67, 342; political views, xxi, 286, 292; writing on Lavallée, xxii, 7, 15, 113–17, 122, 148, 313, 319
Davies, Dr Charles F., 154, 426n98
Davis, Jefferson, 30, 37
Debussy, Claude, xxii, 128, 130
Defoy, J.A., 158, 209
Délisle, G. Rêve charmant, 188
Denis, Adolphe A., 301, 309
Derome, Caroline, 161, 167
Derome, Léon, 8–9, 70, 158, 300, 308; supporting Lavallée, 15, 122, 165, 388n32
Derome, Marie-Louise, 165
Derome, Mlle, 335
Derome, Rose de Lima (wife of Léon), 9, 158
Derome, Rose de Lima (daughter of Léon), 60, 221, 338, 403n25
Désautels, Mlle, 167
Desbarats, George-Édouard, 69
De Sève, Alfred, 158, 191–2, 213, 251, 264, 285, 301, 351, 447n84
Désiré, Monsieur, 177
Dessane, Antoine, 172, 188, 198
Dessane, Antonia, 188, 191, 213, 227
Dessane, Nancy, 188
Dessaulles, Louis-Antoine, 8, 63
Detroit, Michigan, 99, 118–19, 277–8, 298–300, 335, 347, 408, 426
Detroit Philharmonic Club, 288
Devoir, Le (Montreal), xix–xx
Dewey, Ferdinand, Vagabond Dance, 261
Dibblee, Sally, 327, 346
Dilverd, Thomas, 24, 111
Disraeli, Benjamin, 190
Ditson, Oliver, 252
Dodworth, Emerald Isle, 64
Dodworth's Band, 112